LAW
&
MENTAL
HEALTH
PROFESSIONALS

CALIFORNIA

LAW & MENTAL HEALTH PROFESSIONALS SERIES

Bruce D. Sales and Michael Owen Miller, Series Editors

ARIZONA: Miller and Sales
CALIFORNIA: Caudill and Pope
MASSACHUSETTS: Brant
MINNESOTA: Janus, Mickelsen, and Sanders
NEW JERSEY: Wulach
NEW YORK: Wulach
TEXAS: Shuman

LAW & MENTAL HEALTH PROFESSIONALS

CALIFORNIA

O. Brandt Caudill
Kenneth S. Pope

American Psychological Association
Washington, DC

Special Notice:
The information in this book will *not* eliminate or replace the need for legal counsel, though it can help mental health professionals to become more aware of the complex sets of legal standards to which they are accountable and the laws that govern the diverse areas in which they practice. It can also, as the series editors point out, help them become more intelligent and effective consumers of legal services. However, in no case should a mental health professional "play attorney" (e.g., by giving legal counsel to their patients or themselves). Legal guidance or counsel should always be obtained from a qualified attorney.

The purpose of this book is to present legislation, case law, administrative regulations, and other legal or quasi-legal documents that define, describe, or direct the work of California mental health professionals. To present the material clearly and directly, the original words of the documents, which are in the public domain, are commonly used (without quotations marks, block quotes, and so forth). However, paraphrasing is sometimes used in the interests of clarity, brevity, or relevance.

First printing August 1995
Second printing December 1995
Published by
American Psychological Association
750 First Street, NE
Washington, DC 20002

Copies may be ordered from
APA Order Department
P.O. Box 2710
Hyattsville, MD 20784

In the UK and Europe, copies may be ordered from
American Psychological Association
3 Henrietta Street
Covent Garden, London
WC2E 8LU England

This book was typeset in Palatino by General Graphic Services, York, PA

Text and cover designer: Rubin Krassner, Silver Spring, MD
Printer: Quinn-Woodbine, Inc., Woodbine, NJ
Technical/production editor: Olin J. Nettles

Library of Congress Cataloging-in-Publication Data
Caudill, O. Brandt.
    Law and mental health professionals, California / O. Brandt Caudill, Jr., Kenneth S. Pope.
        p. cm. — (Law & mental health professionals series)
    Includes index.
    ISBN 1-55798-276-7 (acid-free paper)
    1. Mental health personnel—Legal status, laws, etc.—California.
2. Mental health laws—California 3. Forsenic Psychiatry—California. I. Pope, Kenneth S. II. Title. III. Title: Law and mental health professionals. California. IV. Series.
KFC546.P7C38 1995
344.794'044—dc20
[347.940444]   94-40248
                                                                                    CIP

British Library Cataloguing-in-Publication Data
A CIP record is available from the British Library.

Printed in the United States of America

Contents

Editors' Preface

The Need to Know the Law

For years, providers of mental health services (hereinafter mental health professionals, or MHPs) have been directly affected by the law. At one end of the continuum, their practice has been controlled by laws covering such matters as licensure and certification, third-party reimbursement, and professional incorporation. At the other end, they have been courted by the legal system to aid in its administration, providing such services as evaluating the mental status of litigants, providing expert testimony in court, and engaging in therapy with court-referred juveniles and adults. Even when not directly affected, MHPs find themselves indirectly affected by the law because their clients sometimes become involved in legal entanglements that involve mental status issues (e.g., divorce proceedings or termination of parental rights hearings).

Despite this pervasive influence, most professionals do not know about, much less understand, most of the laws that affect their practice, the services they render, and the clients they serve. This state of affairs is particularly troubling for several reasons. First, not knowing about the laws that affect one's practice typically results in the MHP's not gaining the benefits that the law may provide. Consider the law relating to the incorporation of professionals. It confers significant benefit, but only if it is known about and applied. The fact that it has been enacted by the state legislature does not help the MHP, any more than an MHP will be of help to a distressed person who refuses to contact the MHP.

Second, not knowing about the laws that affect the services they render can result in incompetent performance of, and liability for, the MHP either through the civil law (e.g., malpractice law) or through criminal sanctions. A brief example may help underscore this point. When an MHP is asked to evaluate a party to a lawsuit and testify in court, the court (the law's term for the judge) is asking the professional to assess and testify about whether that litigant meets some legal standard. The court is often not concerned with the defendant's mental health per se, although this may be relevant to the MHP's evaluation of the person. Rather, the court wants to know if the person meets the legal standard as it is set down by the law. Not knowing the legal standard means that the MHP is most likely evaluating the person for the wrong goal and providing the court with irrelevant information, at least from the court's point of view. Regretfully, there are too many cases in which this has occurred.

Third, not knowing the law that affects the clients that MHPs serve may significantly diminish their capability for handling their clients' distress. For example, a client who is undergoing a divorce and child custody dispute may have distorted beliefs about what may happen during the legal proceedings. A basic understanding of the controlling law in this area will allow the therapist to be more sensitive in rendering therapy.

The Problem in Accessing Legal Information

Given the need for this information, why have MHPs not systematically sought it out? Part of the reason lies in the concern over their ability to understand legal doctrines. Indeed, this is a legitimate worry, especially if they had to read original legal materials that were not collected, organized, and described with an MHP audience in mind. This is of particular concern because laws are written in terms and phrases of "art" that do not always share the common law definition or usage, whereas some terms and phrases are left ambiguous and undefined or are used differently for different legal topics. Another part of the reason is that the law affecting MHPs and their clients is not readily available—even to lawyers. There are no compendiums that identify the topics that these laws cover or present an analysis of each topic for easy reference.

To compound the difficulty, the law does not treat the different mental health professional disciplines uniformly or always specify the particular disciplines as being covered by it. Nor does the law emanate from a single legal forum. Each state enacts its own rules and regulations, often resulting in wide variations in the way a topic is handled across the United States. Multiply this confusion times the one hundred or so topics that relate to mental health practice. In addition, the law within a state does not come from one legal source. Rather, there are five primary ones: the state constitution; state legislative enactments (statutes); state agency administrative rules and regulations; rules of court promulgated by the state supreme court; and state and federal court cases that apply, interpret, and construe this existing state law. To know about one of these sources without knowing how its pronouncements on a given topic have been modified by these other sources can result in one's making erroneous conclusions about the operation of the law. Finally, mental health practice also comes under the purview of federal law (constitutional and statutory law, administrative rules and regulations, and case law). Federal law authorizes direct payments to MHPs for their services to some clients, sets standards for delivery of services in federal facilities (e.g., Veterans Administration hospitals), and articulates the law that guides cases that are tried in federal courts under federal law.

Purposes of This Series

What is needed, therefore, is a book for each state, the District of Columbia, and the federal jurisdictions that comprehensively and accurately reviews and integrates all of the law that affects MHPs in that jurisdiction (hereinafter state). To ensure currency, regular supplements to these books will also need to be drafted. These materials should be written so that they are completely understandable to MHPs, as well as to lawyers. To accomplish these goals, the editors have tried to identify every legal topic that affects mental health practice, making each one the subject of a chapter. Each chapter, in turn, describes the legal standards that the MHP will be operating under and the relevant legal process that the MHP will be operating within. If a state does not have relevant law on an issue, then a brief explanation of how this law works in other states will be presented while noting the lack of regulation in this area within the state under consideration.

This type of coverage facilitates other purposes of the series. Although each chapter is written in order to state exactly what is the present state of the law and not argue for or against any particular approach, it is hoped that the comprehensiveness of the coverage will encourage MHPs to question the desirability of their states' approach to each topic. Such information and concern should provide the impetus for initiating legislation and litigation on the part of state mental health associations to ensure that the law reflects the scientific knowledge and professional values to the greatest extent possible.

In some measure, states will initially be hampered in this proactivity because they will not know what legal alternatives are available and how desirable each alternative actually is. When a significant number of books in this series is available, however, it will allow for nationally oriented policy studies to identify the variety of legal approaches that are currently in use and to assess the validity of the behavioral assumptions underlying each variant, and ultimately lead to a conclusion as to the relative desirability of alternate approaches.[1] Thus, two other purposes of this book are to foster comprehensive analyses of the laws affecting

---

1. Sales, B. D. (1983). The legal regulation of psychology: Professional and scientific interactions. In C. J. Scheirer & B. L. Hammonds (Eds.), *The master lecture series: Vol. 2. Psychology and law* (pp. 5–36). Washington, DC: American Psychological Association.

MHPs across all states and of the validity of the behavioral assumptions underlying these laws, and to promote political, legislative, and legal action to change laws that are inappropriate and impede the effective delivery of services. Legal change may be required because of gaps in legal regulation, overregulation, and regulation based on invalid behavioral and social assumptions. We hope this process will increase the rationality of future laws in this area and improve the effectiveness and quality of mental health service delivery nationally.

There are three remaining purposes for this series. First, although it will not replace the need for legal counsel, this series will make the MHP an intelligent consumer of legal services. This ability is gaining importance in an era of increasing professionalization and litigiousness. Second, it will ensure that MHPs are aware of the law's mandates when providing expert services (e.g., evaluation and testimony) within the legal system. Although chapters will not address how to clinically assess for the legal standard, provider competency will increase because providers now will be sure of the goals of their service (e.g., the legal standard that they are to assess for), as well as their roles and responsibilities within the legal system as to the particular topic in issue. Third and finally, each book will make clear that the legal standards that MHPs are asked to assess for by the law have typically not been translated into behavioral correlates. Nor are there discussions of tests, scales, and procedures for MHPs to use in assessing for the behavioral correlates of the legal standards in most cases. This series will provide the impetus for such research and writing.

Content and Organization of Volumes

Each book in this series is organized into six sections. Section 1 addresses the legal credentialing of MHPs. Section 2 deals with the different business forms for conducting one's practice. Section 3 then addresses insurance reimbursement and tax deductions that clients can receive for utilizing mental health services. With the business matters covered, the book then turns to the law directly affecting service delivery. Section 4 starts by covering the law that affects the maintenance and privacy of professional information. Section 5 then considers each area of law that may require the services of MHPs. It is subdivided into five parts: families and juveniles, other civil matters, topics that apply similarly in both civil and criminal cases, criminal matters, and voluntary and involuntary receipt of state services by the clients of mental health services. The last section of the book, section 6, discusses the law that limits service delivery and that sets liability for unethical and illegal behavior as a service provider.

Collectively, the chapters in these sections represent all topics pertaining to the law as it affects MHPs in their practices. Two caveats are in order, however. First, the law changes slowly over time. Thus, a supplement service will update all chapters on a regular basis. Second, as MHPs become more involved in the legal system, new opportunities for involvement are likely to arise. To be responsive to these developments, the supplements will also contain additional chapters reflecting these new roles and responsibilities.

Some final points about the content of this book are in order. The exact terms that the law chooses are used in the book even if they are a poor choice from an MHP's point of view. And where terms are defined by the law, that information is presented. The reader will often be frustrated, however, because, as has already been noted, the law does not always define terms or provide detailed guidance. This does not mean that legal words and phrases can be taken lightly. The law sets the rules that MHPs and their clients must operate by; thus, the chapters must be read carefully. This should not be too arduous a task because chapters are relatively short. On the other hand, such brevity will leave some readers frustrated because chapters appear not to go far enough in answering their questions. Note that all of the law is covered. If there is no law, however, there is no coverage. If a question is not answered in the text, it is because California law has not addressed the issue. Relatedly, if an obligation or benefit is created by a professional regulation (i.e., a rule of a professional organization) but is not directly recognized by the law, it is not covered. Thus, for example, professional credentials are not addressed in these volumes.

Bruce D. Sales
Michael Owen Miller
Series Editors

Authors' Preface

The purpose of this book is to provide mental health professionals (MHPs) with an overview of California state law. While certain federal laws and federal cases will be addressed, a comprehensive assessment of the federal law is beyond the scope of this book. California law is based on the state constitution, state statutes, regulations of administrative agencies, the statewide and local rules established by the courts for the handling of cases, and the decisions of appellate courts and the California Supreme Court.

The California Constitution, although it parallels the federal Constitution in many ways, is in some respects much broader. For example, the California Constitution has a specific right of privacy in Article 1, section 1, but the federal Constitution does not. Just as the federal Constitution is the primary source of federal rights, the California Constitution is the primary source of state rights. The California Constitution is cited as follows: Cal. Const. art. I, § 1. The right of privacy is the first section of the first article in the California Constitution.

Statutes are the laws enacted by the California legislature or voted by a majority of the California electorate on ballot propositions at a general election. Although some states do not allow the electorate to directly enact laws, in recent years such ballot propositions have produced significant changes in California law, including victim-oriented criminal provisions and a provision that economic damages must be allocated according to the actual responsibility of a defendant. Prior to enactment, the ballot measures are referred to as propositions. Once a statute has been enacted either by the legislature or by proposition, it will be cited as one of a number of specific codes such as the Family Code, the Welfare and Institutions Code, the Health and Safety Code, the Vehicle Code, or the Business and Professions Code. For example, a provision of the Business and Professions Code would be cited as Bus. & Prof. Code § 4000.

There are two major statutory reporting systems: West Publishing Co.'s system, which is referred to as Annotated California Codes, and Deering's California Code. Both systems also contain annotations that cite to opinions of the attorney general, interpreting the statutes and cases arising under the statutes. Thus, when a question arises as to the application of a particular statutory section or constitutional provision, the reader may obtain additional information by checking the annotation. The annotations should also be checked to determine whether the law has been superseded by a subsequent enactment or held unconstitutional by a court decision. Generally, the reporting systems also provide a brief legislative history.

California has numerous administrative agencies under various state departments. The department that has the most significance for MHPs is the Department of Consumer Affairs because various boards that license MHPs are under that department. However, there are regulations of the Department of Education, the Department of Justice, and other departments that are discussed in this book. State agencies are generally granted rulemaking authority by specific statutes. The agency then enforces its rules through administrative actions against the individuals or entities subject to its rules. As an example, the Psychology Licensing Law delegated power to the Board of Psychology to enact regulations to enforce the law. The Board of Psychology did enact such regulation and now prosecutes administrative cases against psychologists or others subject to the law who violate the regulations. In short, the legislature creates the outline of the law and the administrative agencies fill in the details through regulations.

The regulations of administrative agencies are published by Barclays Law Publishers in a series entitled Official California Code of Regulations. Regulations are cited by the volume number, and then the specific regulation. Thus, a citation to one of the Board of Psychology's regulations would be 16 CCR § 1633. Generally, regulations of the licensing boards governing MHPs are found in Title 16 of the Code of Regulations.

California trial court decisions are not published, and they may not be cited as precedent. While appellate court decisions are published, an appellate court can elect not to certify a particular case for publication, in which event it may not be relied on as a precedent. An appellate court can also elect to certify its decision for partial publication. Typically, this is done where the court believes that part of the opinion addresses some issue of future concern to other litigants or where part of the decision involves particularly sensitive facts that the court feels should not be in the public record.

The California Supreme Court has the power to reverse decisions of Courts of Appeals. In addition, the Supreme Court can decertify a prior publication ordered by an appellate court. Decertification of an appellate decision deprives it of precedential status, so the decision only affects the interests of the parties in the case.

Decisions of trial (lower) courts in California are not reported in any publication. Higher court decisions are published in the official California reporters and by West Publishing Co. The official reporters are California Appellate Reports, for the decisions of the Courts of Appeals, and California Reports, for decisions of the California Supreme Court. Both appellate and Supreme Court decisions appear in California Reporter. At the present time, all three reporting systems are in their fourth series. Thus, a 1994 case would be cited as *Jones v. Jones,* 14 Cal.App.4th 1000, 24 Cal.Rptr.2d 800 (1994), i.e., in volume 14 of the fourth series of California Appellate Reports at page 1000, and at volume 24, page 800 of the California Reporter, second series.

West also publishes a regional reporter system called Pacific Reporter, which combines various appellate court and Supreme Court cases from several western states. This is in its second series; an example of a case citation would be 500 P.2d 279. West also publishes California and Pacific digests, which are compilations of case summaries by topic.

California has six Courts of Appeal:

The First District Court of Appeal includes the counties of Alameda, Contra Costa, Del Norte, Humboldt, Lake, Marin, Napa, San Francisco, San Mateo, Solano, and Sonoma Mendocino.

The Second District Court of Appeal includes the counties of Los Angeles, San Luis Obispo, Santa Barbara, and Ventura.

The Third District Court of Appeal includes the counties of Alpine, Amador, Butte, Calaveras, Coluso, El Dorado, Glenn, Lassen, Modoc, Mono, Nevada, Placer, Plumas, Sacramento, San Joaquin, Shasta, Sierra, Siskiyou, Sutter, Tehama, Trinity, Yolo, and Yuba.

The Fourth District Court of Appeal includes the counties of Imperial, Inyo, Orange, Riverside, San Bernardino, and San Diego.

The Fifth District Court of Appeal includes the counties of Fresno, Kern, Kings, Madera, Mariposa, Merced, Stanislaus, Tulare, and Tuolumne.

The Sixth District Court of Appeal includes the counties of Monterey, San Benito, Santa Clara, and Santa Cruz.

Although an appellate decision from one Court of Appeal is binding on the lower courts in its geographic jurisdiction, it is not binding on trial courts in other jurisdictions within the state, although it does carry significant weight. Generally, a trial court will follow an appellate court's ruling from another jurisdiction if there is no appellate decision on point in its own. Where appellate courts are in conflict, a trial court generally must follow the decision of its own appellate court.

A set of rules governing the handling of matters in court has been established by the California Judicial Council. These rules are referred to as the California Rules of Court and cover matters such as the questioning of jurors, civil and criminal procedure, and experimental programs testing means to expedite the handling of cases. These rules are supplemental to statutory provisions and have the effect of statutes. In addition, the Superior Courts of most counties have a uniform set of local rules of court, which attorneys must comply with. San Francisco, Los Angeles, Orange County, and San Diego have the most extensive local rules. A number of the Courts of Appeals also have local rules governing appeals before them.

Unlike California courts, federal cases are reported at the trial-court level as well as at the appellate level. The trial court for federal cases is the U.S. District Court for a particular district or geographic area. These are reported in the Federal Supplement, abbreviated F. Supp. When a citation is made to such a decision, the year of the decision and the initials for the district court's area are included. Thus, a citation to a case involving the Southern District of California would be 54 F. Supp. 1000 (S.D. Cal. 1994). California has Northern, Southern, Eastern, and Western Districts.

The federal Court of Appeals for California and other western states is the U.S. Court of Appeals for the Ninth Circuit. These cases are reported in the Federal Reporter, which is now in its third series. U.S. Supreme Court decisions are reported in two official reporters and one commonly used unofficial reporter. The official reporters are United States Reports and the Supreme Court Reporter, which are abbreviated U.S. and S. Ct. The unofficial reporter is the Lawyer's Edition of the Supreme Court Reporter, abbreviated L. Ed. The Lawyer's Edition includes annotations and similar cases from around the country.

Federal statutes are contained within the U.S. Code. A citation to Title 26, section 500 of the U.S. Code would be 26 U.S.C. § 500 (1994). There is also an annotated series (U.S.C.A.) with citations to cases and law review articles. Federal administrative agencies such as the Department of Health have also enacted regulations, which are found in the Code of Federal Regulations, C.F.R. A typical citation to the Code of Federal Regulations would be 26 C.F.R. § 500, which stands for section 500 of the regulations under Title 26 of the C.F.R.

This volume also refers to opinions of the California attorney general, which have been compiled in a publication cited as Op. Atty. Gen. These opinions may be relied on by a court in interpreting a statute or regulation but are not dispositive of the issue. Therefore, these opinions may offer some guidance to MHPs but should not be viewed as controlling.

This book is current as of September 1, 1993. Readers should note that particularly with reference to the chapters on licensure and discipline of psychologists and psychiatrists, some new statutory provisions went into effect January 1, 1994, and others on January 1, 1995. In addition, the California Civil Code governed family matters including marriage, child custody, and similar issues until January 1, 1994. However, effective January 1, 1994, the Civil Code provisions were repealed and a comprehensive new statutory code called the Family Code of California went into effect. This is intended to be a restatement and continuation of the prior law. The Family Code applies primarily to those matters discussed in chapters 5A.1 through 5A.23.

Acknowledgments

We are indebted to many people without whose help we could not have completed this project. We would first like to thank Bruce Sales, JD, PhD, and Michael Miller, JD, PhD, the prime movers, who invited us to take on this task, gave generous support, showed superhuman patience during the long course to completion, and were always available for consultation. We also wish to acknowledge our deep appreciation to those who offered their valuable time and considerable expertise to review drafts of the manuscript: Kenneth Austin, PhD, Joe George, JD, PhD, The Honorable Steven Hjelt, Michele Licht, Esq., Daun Martin, PhD, Barry Michaelson, Esq., Thomas O'Conner, Executive Officer of the California Board of Psychology, Marilyn Osborn, PhD, Gary Pohlson, Esq., James Preis, Esq., and Gary Samply, JD. Brandt Caudill would like to acknowledge the invaluable assistance and incredible patience of Von Cutter, his secretary, and the invaluable support of Christine Caudill.

This book would not have been possible without the invaluable dedication, skills, and work of Susan Reynolds, Julia Frank-McNeil, Olin J. Nettles, W. Ralph Eubanks, and Susan Bedford of APA Books; Gary R. VandenBos of Publications and Communications; and Devona Marinich of Marketing Services. We are greatly endebted to them for their care, guidance, and generosity.

Legal
Credentialing

1.0

Licensure and Regulation of Mental Health Professionals

There are many statutes and regulations governing the licensure of mental health professionals (MHPs) in California. As a general matter, to provide mental health treatment an individual must either comply with one of the several licensing laws or fit within an exemption to the license requirements. The laws may have different provisions but generally seek to ensure that only qualified people are admitted to practice, and that individuals who violate the regulations of the boards, state statutes, or the applicable standards of care are subject to professional discipline.

Psychiatrists are licensed by the Medical Board of California under the Medical Practice Act (see chapter 1.1). Psychologists are licensed by the Board of Psychology under the Psychology Licensing Law (see chapter 1.4). The Board of Behavioral Science Examiners licenses educational psychologists (see chapter 1.7); licensed clinical social workers (see chapter 1.6); and marriage, family, and child counselors (see chapter 1.9). On the other hand, credentials for school guidance counselors, school social workers, and school psychologists (see chapter 1.8) are issued by the California Department of Education. Thus, the number of licensing boards and various licensing laws may be somewhat confusing. The chapters in this section of the book address the requirements for each licensure category separately, along with the grounds for denial of licensure and imposition of professional discipline as established by each statute or licensing board.

In addition to the specific licensing laws and regulations governing MHPs, there are general statutes that apply to all licensees of, or applicants to, licensing boards under the Department of Consumer Affairs. These statutes provide a general framework for denial of licensure or imposition of discipline, and create a number of license offenses. These general statutes are discussed in chapter 1.0A.

Chapter 1.0A also discusses the procedure for imposing discipline on licensees of or applicants to the boards under the Department of Consumer Affairs. Further, this subsection discusses special administrative procedures applicable to the Board of Psychology and the Medical Board.

Chapter 1.0B discusses the general statutes applicable to MHPs who are certificate holders of the Commission on Teacher Credentialing of the Department of Education. chapter 1.0B also discusses the special administrative procedures applicable to teacher credentialing for the denial of or imposition of discipline. Specific criteria to obtain credentials are discussed in chapters 1.7 and 1.8.

1.0A

Department of Consumer Affairs

There have been a number of changes in recent years in both the substance and procedure involved in licensing and discipline of licenses; in fact, even the names of the licensing boards have changed. It is important to note that some regulations and statutes referred to in chapters 1.0A and 1.0B went into effect January 1, 1995, or will go into effect July 1995.

All of the licensing boards discussed in this section except for the Commission on Teacher Credentialing are under the Department of Consumer Affairs.[1] The director of the Department of Consumer Affairs has the authority to conduct investigations of the actions of the licensing boards.[2] The director also has the authority to specify guidelines for the licensing boards to use in developing continuing education programs.[3]

At one point, the terms of office of the members of the different boards varied, but the statutes now provide that all board members hold office for a period of four years.[4]

The individual chapters set forth in this section of the book will discuss the regulations and laws applicable to specific boards. There are, however, a set of grounds for denial, suspension, or revocation of license that apply to all licensing boards under the Department of Consumer Affairs.[5] The substance of these grounds has been incorporated in the laws or regulations that specifically apply to psychiatrists (see chapter 1.1); psycholo-

---

1. Bus. & Prof. Code § 101.
2. Bus. & Prof. Code § 116.
3. Bus. & Prof. Code § 166.
4. Bus. & Prof. Code § 130.
5. Bus. & Prof. Code § 480; *Pieri v. Fox*, 96 Cal.App.3d 802 (1979); *Brandt v. Fox*, 90 Cal.App.3d 737 (1979).

gists (see chapter 1.4); marriage, family, and child counselors (see chapter 1.9); licensed clinical social workers (see chapter 1.6); nurses (see chapter 1.2); psychiatric technicians (see chapter 1.3); and licensed educational psychologists (see chapter 1.7). Because these uniform grounds for discipline would apply generally to any licensee of the Department of Consumer Affairs, they are listed here. The specific grounds for discipline of particular licensees are found in chapters 1.1 through 1.9. The general grounds are as follows:

(A) Grounds for Denial of Licensure

Any of the boards under the Department of Consumer Affairs may deny a license to an applicant on any of the following grounds:

1. the applicant has been convicted of a crime that is substantially related to the qualifications, functions, or duties of the business or profession for which the application is made;

2. the applicant has engaged in any act involving dishonesty, fraud, or deceit with the intent to substantially benefit himself or herself or another, or to substantially injure another;

3. the applicant has done any act that if done by a person holding the license, would be grounds for suspension or revocation; or

4. the applicant made a knowingly false statement of fact in an application for the license.[6]

(B) Grounds for Discipline

1. Conviction of a crime if the crime is substantially related to the qualifications, functions, or duties of the business or profession to which the license was issued;[7]

---

6. Bus. & Prof. Code § 480. A conviction for the purpose of this section means a plea or a verdict of guilty, or a conviction following a plea of nolo contendere (no contest). However, no person may be denied a license solely on the basis of a felony conviction if he or she has obtained a certificate of rehabilitation from the superior court. No person who has been convicted of a misdemeanor may be denied licensure if he or she meets all applicable requirements of the criteria of rehabilitation developed by the individual licensing board to evaluate rehabilitation. *Id.* § 480(a)(1) & (b).

7. Under Bus. & Prof. Code § 490, conviction means a plea or verdict of guilty or a conviction following a plea of nolo contendere (no contest).

2. knowingly making a false statement of fact in an application for such a license;[8]

3. making a false statement of material fact or knowingly admitting to stating a material fact in support of another person's application for a license;[9] or

4. securing a license by fraud, deceit, or knowing misrepresentation of fact, or knowingly omitting a material fact.

However, a license can be denied, suspended, or revoked on the ground of a lack of good moral character or any similar ground relating to the applicant's character, reputation, personality, or habits.

(C) License Offenses

In addition to grounds for discipline, there are certain offenses regarding obtaining or displaying licenses that apply to all licensees of the Department of Consumer Affairs. It is a misdemeanor for a licensee to do any of the following:

1. display, cause, or permit to be displayed, or possess a cancelled, revoked, suspended, or fraudulently altered license or a fictitious license;

2. lend his or her license to any other person or knowingly permit the other person to use the license;

3. display or represent a license not issued to him or her as being his or hers;

4. refuse to surrender upon lawful written demand to the license-issuing authority any license, registration, permit, or certificate that has been suspended, revoked, or cancelled;

5. use the license unlawfully in any way;

6. photograph, photostat, duplicate, or in any way reproduce any license in a manner that it could be mistaken for a valid license unless authorized by law;[10] and

7. engage in any conduct that subverts or attempts to subvert any licensing examination, such as removing examination materials from the examination room. This includes communicating with any other examinee during the administration of the licensing examination.[11]

---

8. Bus. & Prof. Code § 490.
9. Bus. & Prof. Code § 499.
10. Bus. & Prof. Code § 119.
11. Bus. & Prof. Code § 123.

It is also an offense, except as otherwise allowed by law, for any person in the healing-arts professions to offer, deliver, receive, or accept any rebate, refund, commission, preference, patronage dividend, discount, or other consideration—whether in the form of money or otherwise—as compensation or inducement for referring patients to another person. However, the payment or receipt of consideration for services other than the referral of patients, if based on a percentage of gross revenue or similar contractual arrangement, is not unlawful as long as the consideration is commensurate with the value of the services furnished.[12]

(D) Refusal to Perform Licensed Activity

Any individual who holds a license from one of the boards under the Department of Consumer Affairs is subject to disciplinary action if he or she refuses to perform the licensed activity, or aids and incites the refusal of another to perform such services, because of an individual's race, color, sex, religion, ancestry, disability, marital status, or national origin.[13]

(E) Award of Costs

The legislature has recently enacted a comprehensive statute allowing any of the boards under the Department of Consumer Affairs to obtain an award of costs as part of an administrative action. The board may request an administrative law judge (ALJ) to direct a license holder found to have committed a violation of the licensing act to pay a sum not to exceed the reasonable cost of investigation and enforcement. However, the finding of the administrative law judge with regard to cost is not reviewable by the licensing board to increase the cost award. The board may reduce or eliminate the cost award but not increase it.

If an order for recovery of costs is made and payment does not occur, the board may enforce the order for repayment in court and may refuse to renew or reinstate the license of any person who has failed to pay costs in accordance with an order. A licensing board, however, has the discretion to conditionally renew or reinstate for a period of one year a licensee who demonstrates financial hardship but agrees to pay the unpaid costs. This

---

12. Bus. & Prof. Code § 658.
13. Bus. & Prof. Code § 125.6.

statute also specifically authorizes the board to seek recovery of costs as part of a stipulated settlement in an administrative case.[14]

(F) Unlicensed Practice

In 1992, the Legislature declared that unlicensed activity in the professions regulated by the Department of Consumer Affairs was a threat to the health, welfare, and safety of the people of California. The Legislature also decreed that there should be a criminal sanction for unlicensed activity to create a strong incentive to obtain a license.[15]

The Legislature therefore decreed that the failure to obtain a license where such a license is required is to be treated as an infraction unless a defendant elects to have the case proceed as a misdemeanor.[16]

(G) Infractions

An infraction is a technical violation of law that is dealt with in summary fashion. The type of infraction most people are familiar with is a traffic violation. An infraction is punishable by a fine of not less than $250 and not more than $1,000. No portion of the minimum fine may be suspended by a court unless the defendant is required to submit proof of a current valid license, registration, or certificate for the profession that was the basis of the conviction.[17]

(H) Administrative Procedure for Boards Other Than the Medical Board and the Board of Psychology

The revocation or suspension of professional licenses is generally governed by the Administrative Procedures Act.[18] This Act specifically applies to all of the agencies mentioned in this section.

---

14. Bus. & Prof. Code § 125.3.
15. Bus. & Prof. Code § 145.
16. Bus. & Prof. Code § 146.
17. *Id.*
18. Gov't Code § 11503.

Until 1993, the procedure, regardless of which licensing board was involved, was generally the same under the Administrative Procedures Act. An accusation would be filed by the attorney general's office, setting forth the charges and the legal basis for the proposed discipline. The licensee was required to file a notice of defense within 15 days, or a default could be entered. A hearing was then scheduled before an independent administrative law judge, provided by the Office of Administrative Hearings, which is an independent state agency.[19] The ALJ would then make a proposed decision, which the licensing board was free to accept, reject, or modify. However, to find that discipline could be imposed, the ALJ was required to find a violation of law or regulation that was established by clear and convincing proof to a reasonable certainty.[20]

If the particular board involved elected to reject the ALJ's proposed decision, then the entire transcript of proceedings would be prepared, and all of the board members who would vote on the case would be required to review the records generated during the proceeding in the transcript and make an independent decision. The only method of appeal was by writ of mandate to the superior court, where the presumption was that the board acted in accordance with its authority, and the burden was on the party challenging the board's decision to show an abuse of discretion.[21] These procedures are still applicable to the MHPs described in this book *except licensees of the Medical Board and the Board of Psychology*. Thus, the procedures described above apply to the Board of Behavioral Science Examiners (see chapters 1.6, 1.7, and 1.9), the Board of Registered Nursing (see chapter 1.2), and the Board of Vocational Nurses and Psychiatric Technicians (see chapters 1.2 and 1.3).

(I) Administrative Procedures for the Board of Psychology and the Medical Board

(I)(1) Investigation

The licensing boards have investigative authority and can obtain records from a patient or a licensee, request a meeting with the licensee, and obtain subpoenas to procure witnesses and documents for hearings. As noted elsewhere in this book, the physi-

---

19. Gov't Code §§ 11503, 11505.
20. *Ettinger v. Board of Medical Quality Assurance*, 135 Cal.App.3d 853 (1982).
21. Civ. Proc. Code § 1094.5.

cian–patient privilege does not apply to investigations or proceedings by the Medical Board, except as incorporated by the Administrative Procedures Act.[22] Members of the Medical Board; the senior assistant attorney general; the Health Quality Enforcement section; and deputies, employees, agents, and representatives of the Medical Board must keep in confidence during the course of investigations the names of any patients whose records are reviewed, and may not disclose or reveal those names, except as is necessary in the course of an investigation, unless and until proceedings are instituted. The authority to examine records of patients in the office of a physician is limited to records of patients who have complained to the Medical Board about that licensee.[23] However, the Medical Board and its investigators and representatives, and members of the attorney general's office, may inquire into any alleged violation of the Medical Practice Act or any other federal or state law, regulation, or rule relevant to the practice of medicine, and may inspect documents relevant to those investigations in accordance with the following procedure:

1. any document relevant to an investigation may be inspected and copies may be obtained when patient consent is given; and

2. any document relevant to the business operations of a licensee, and not involving medical records attributable to identifiable patients, may be inspected and copied where relevant to an investigation of a licensee.

Where documents are inspected or copies received, their acquisition and review must be arranged so as not to unnecessarily disrupt the medical and business operations of the licensee. Where documents are requested from licensees in accordance with the law, the licensee must provide them within 15 days of receipt of the request unless the licensee is unable to provide the documents for good cause. Failure to produce requested documents or copies of the documents after being informed of the deadline constitutes unprofessional conduct.

Searches conducted of the office or medical facility of any licensee must not interfere with the record-keeping format or record preservation of any licensee that is necessary for the lawful care of patients.[24]

Any original documents that are received pursuant to these statutory sections must be returned to the licensee from whom they were obtained within seven calendar days.

---

22. Bus. & Prof. Code § 2225(a).
23. *Id.*
24. Bus. & Prof. Code § 2225(b) to (e).

A licensee who fails or refuses to comply within 15 days with the request for medical records or a court order mandating release of the records to the Medical Board that is accompanied by the patient's written authorization must pay to the Medical Board a civil penalty of $1,000 a day for each day that the documents have not been produced after the 15th day, unless the licensee is unable to provide the documents for good cause.[25]

(I)(2) Interim Suspension

The Medical Board and the Board of Psychology may seek an interim order suspending a license or imposing drug testing, continuing education, supervision, or other license restrictions. The interim orders may be issued by an ALJ of the Medical Quality Hearing Panel only if affidavits in support of the petition show that the licensee has engaged in or is about to engage in acts or omissions constituting a violation of the Medical Practice Act or the Psychology Licensing Law, and the affidavits show that permitting the licensee to continue to engage in practice will endanger the public health, safety, or welfare.[26]

Interim orders of suspension can be issued only after a hearing, unless it appears from facts shown by the affidavit that serious injuries would result to the public before the matter can be heard. The licensee must receive at least 15 days prior notice of the hearing, which must include copies of the affidavits and all other information in support of the order. However, if an interim order is issued without notice, then the administrative law judge issuing the order must cause the licensee to be notified with all supporting documents by a 24-hour delivery service. The notice in that instance shall also include the date of hearing on the order, which is not to be less than 20 days from the date of issuance of the order. Once an interim order has issued, if the statutory criteria are not met, then the order must be dissolved.[27]

At a hearing on the suspension order, the licensee has the right to be represented by counsel, to have a record made of the proceedings (copies of which may be obtained by the licensee upon payment of any reasonable charges), the right to present written evidence in the form of affidavits and documents, and the right to oral argument. It is within the discretion of the ALJ to permit oral testimony at the hearing, and that discretion is intended to be identical to the discretion of a superior court judge to permit testimony at hearings on preliminary injunctions in civil suits.[28] The burden of proof is on the agency seeking an interim

---

25. Bus. & Prof. Code § 2255.5.
26. Gov't Code § 11529.
27. Gov't Code § 11529(b) & (c).
28. Gov't Code § 11529(d).

order, and the standards of proof are equivalent to those for obtaining a preliminary injunction. The interim order is to be granted where the ALJ concludes

1. that there is a reasonable probability that the agency will prevail in the underlying licensing action; and
2. that the likelihood of injury to the public in not issuing the order outweighs the likelihood of injury to the licensee in issuing the order.[29]

When an interim order has issued and an accusation is not filed and served within 15 days of the date from when the parties submitted the matter to the ALJ for decision, the order will be dissolved. Once an accusation is served, then the licensee has, in addition to the rights afforded under the interim hearing provisions, all of the other rights available under the Administrative Procedures Act for hearings on accusations.[30] If the licensee requests a hearing on the accusation, the Board must provide the licensee with a hearing within 30 days of the request unless the licensee stipulates to a later hearing. The decision must be made within 15 days of the date the matter is submitted or the Board must nullify the previously issued interim order, unless good cause can be shown for delay.[31]

Where an interim order is issued, the ALJ must prepare a written decision within 15 days of the hearing, including findings of fact and a conclusion articulating the connection between the evidence produced at the hearing and the decision reached.[32]

Interim orders issued pursuant to the procedures outlined above are subject to judicial review by writ of mandate, however the relief the court may award is limited to a stay of the interim order. Interim orders that are issued and not dissolved may be challenged only administratively, on the hearing on the accusation.[33]

The interim orders provided for are in addition to and not a limitation on the Board's ability to seek injunctive relief.[34]

---

29. Gov't Code § 11529(e). In 1993, the Court of Appeals in the case of *Silva v. Superior Court*, 14 Cal.App.4th 562, held that the prior version of Gov't Code § 11529 was silent as to the standard of proof to be applied in a hearing on an interim order and therefore applied the standard of clear and convincing proof to a reasonable certainty, which the courts had applied to hearings on accusations under *Ettinger v. Board of Medical Quality Assurance*, 135 Cal.App.3d 853 (1982). The legislature then determined to expressly overrule that decision and required the standard of proof to be to the standards for issuance of a preliminary injunction under § 527 1994 statutes.
30. Gov't Code § 11529(f).
31. *Id.*
32. Gov't Code § 11529(g).
33. Gov't Code § 11529(h).
34. Gov't Code § 11529(i).

(I)(3) Discipline of Licensees of or Applicants to the Board of Psychology and the Medical Board

Recent changes to the licensing laws include the creation of a special panel of ALJs to hear cases involving MHPs who are licensees of the Medical Board and the Board of Psychology. This panel is a panel of ALJs under the Office of Administrative Hearings and is referred to as the Medical Quality Hearing Panel.[35] Only the ALJs on this panel may hear cases involving the licensees of and applicants to the Medical Board and the Board of Psychology.

Under the new law, individuals who complain against licensees of or applicants to the Medical Board or the Board of Psychology are to be kept apprised of the actions proposed to be taken against the licensees they have complained about. The complainants are to be given an opportunity to provide a statement to the deputy attorney general assigned to the case. The statements from the complainants are not to be considered by the decisionmakers for the purpose of adjudicating the case, but may be considered after the case is finally adjudicated for the purpose of setting generally applicable policies and standards.[36]

The Division of Medical Quality or the Health Quality Enforcement section of the attorney general's office may establish panels or lists of experts and pay them at prevailing market rates.[37] The Division of Medical Quality may also use volunteer physicians and others in committees or panels to assist the Medical Board or the Board of Psychology in the following types of functions:

1. monitoring licensees who have been disciplined and are subject to terms and conditions of probation or diversion;
2. evaluation and administration of competency examinations;
3. assistance to practitioners with special problems;
4. supervision of licensees with practice restrictions; and
5. advice regarding policy options and preventive strategies.[38]

The proposed decisions and interim orders of the Medical Quality Hearing Panel are to be transmitted to the executive director of the Medical Board or Board of Psychology within 48 hours of filing. The interim orders are all final when filed.[39]

---

35. Bus. & Prof. Code § 2222; Gov't Code § 11371. This panel also hears cases involving non-MHP licensees of Allied Health Boards under the Medical Board.
36. Bus. & Prof. Code § 2330.
37. Bus. and Prof. Code § 2332(a).
38. Bus. & Prof. Code § 2332(b).
39. Bus. & Prof. Code § 2335.

If the decision proposed by the Medical Quality Hearing Panel was not adopted, an order of non-adoption must be issued within 90 calendar days of the date the proposed decision is received by the Medical Board or Board of Psychology. If it is not issued within 90 days, then the decision is final and subject to judicial review. Where members of a panel of the Division of Medical Quality vote by mail, each member must return his or her vote by mail within 30 days from receipt of the proposed decision.[40]

Judicial review in the superior court of a decision revoking, suspending, or restricting a license must take precedence over all other civil actions in the matter of setting the case for hearing or trial. The hearing or trial should be set no later than 180 days from the filing of the action, and a further continuance shall be granted only on a showing of good cause. However, this statutory section was operative only until January 1, 1995, and then will be inoperative until January 1, 1999, when it will again become operative. From January 1, 1995, to January 1, 1999, review of the final decision of an ALJ of the Medical Quality Hearing Panel or a review by the Division of Medical Quality shall be by writ of mandamus directly to a district Court of Appeal (previously such writs of mandamus were directed to superior courts). The Court of Appeal must exercise its independent judgment in review of the proceedings below, and where the court finds that there is relevant evidence that, in the exercise of reasonable diligence, could not have been produced or was improperly excluded at the hearing, it may admit the evidence without remanding the case for further proceedings.[41]

The statutes have also been amended to provide an additional disciplinary option—a letter of reprimand.[42]

Furthermore, the statute setting up the Office of Administrative Hearings, Medical Quality Hearing Panel, provides that there shall be no fewer than five full-time ALJs assigned to the panel, who are required to have medical training. At no time is the panel to constitute more than 25% of the total number of ALJs within the Office of Administrative Hearings. The decisions of the ALJs on the panel, together with any court decisions reviewing those d isions or court decisions relevant to medical quality adjudications, are to be published in a quarterly medical discipline report.

In addition, the ALJs on the panel are to have panels of experts available to them appointed by the Office of Administra-

---

40. Bus. & Prof. Code § 2332(c).
41. Bus. & Prof. Code § 2337.
42. Bus. & Prof. Code § 2233.

tive Hearings with the advice of the Medical Board of California. These panels of experts may be called as witnesses by the ALJS on the panel to testify on the record about any matter relevant to a proceeding and are subject to cross-examination by all parties. The ALJ may award reasonable expert witness fees to any expert, which are to be paid from the contingent fund of the Medical Board of California.[43]

All adjudications except interim suspension orders of licensees of the Medical Board of California and allied health agencies are to be pursuant to the Administrative Procedures Act and conducted by an ALJ from the Medical Quality Hearing Panel.[44]

Because of the extensive nature of the changes, it is possible that there will be subsequent regulations and/or statutory enactments once the effect of the various changes in the law has become apparent.

---

43. Gov't Code § 11371.
44. Gov't Code § 11372.

1.0B

Commission on Teacher Credentialing

MHPs who are employed in the California school system require either licenses from the appropriate board under the Department of Consumer Affairs or certificates issued by the Commission on Teacher Credentialing. The criteria for the issuance of such credentials are discussed in chapters 1.7 and 1.8. The procedure for the imposition of discipline on credential holders is discussed in this subsection. Specific grounds for discipline are discussed in chapters 1.7 and 1.8.

The Commission on Teacher Credentialing is an independent agency created by statute.[1] Of the licensing boards discussed in this section, only the Commission on Teacher Credentialing is not under the Department of Consumer Affairs. However, the Commission on Teacher Credentialing is generally subject to the Administrative Procedures Act in the denial, suspension, or revocation of credentials.[2] This includes the issuance, denial, or revocation of specialist instructional credentials of the type discussed in chapters 1.7 and 1.8.[3]

The Commission is composed of 15 members consisting of the superintendent of public instruction and his or her designee, and 14 members appointed by the governor with the advice and consent of the senate. Six of the appointed members are practicing teachers from public elementary and secondary schools. One member is employed with a services credential, other than an administrative services credential, and one member is a member of a school district governing board. Four members are represen-

---

1. Educ. Code § 44200.
2. Educ. Code § 44246.
3. Educ. Code §§ 44265, 44345, 44346.

tatives of the public who have not been employed in a certified position in a school district and who have not been members of a school district governing board in the preceding five years. One member is a school administrator, and one is a faculty member from a college or university that grants baccalaureate degrees. With the exception of the public members, a member's appointment terminates if he or she is no longer a practicing teacher, holder of a services credential, school administrator, college or university faculty member, or school district governing board member, as the case may be.

Four members are appointed for two-year terms, five members for three-year terms, and five members for four-year terms.[4]

The Commission has delegated its disciplinary authority, in turn, to the Committee on Credentials.[5]

(A) Committee on Credentials

The Commission has delegated to the Committee on Credentials the power to investigate and hear allegations that a service or teaching credential should be revoked or suspended.[6] The Committee on Credentials is composed of seven members with terms not to exceed two years. The members include one full-time certified classroom teacher in public elementary schools, with not less than five years experience. One member is a certified public school administrative employee, and one member is a member of the governing board of any school district. However, the school board member cannot have been employed in a certificated position in the public schools within the preceding five years. Three members are public members who cannot have been employed in certificated positions in the public schools or members of a school district governing board or the county board of education within the preceding five years.[7]

(B) Administrative Procedure

The Committee on Credentials investigates allegations of acts or omissions that would subject an applicant, or holder of a credential, to private admonishment or denial, suspension, or revocation of a credential. The investigation includes investigating the fitness

---

4. Educ. Code § 44210.
5. 5 CCR § 80300 et seq.
6. Educ. Code § 44233.
7. Educ. Code § 44240.

and competence of the applicant or credential holder to perform his or her duties and determining if probable cause exists for private admonition, denial, suspension, or revocation of the credential. Probable cause is established when the weight of the evidence before the Committee on Credentials is sufficient to cause a majority of the Committee to believe the allegations of misconduct or unfitness are true, and that an administrative hearing would result in denial, suspension, or revocation of the credential.[8]

The investigation must begin within 21 days of the allegation being filed with the Committee on Credentials,[9] and must include

1. the extent to which the conduct has adversely affected students or fellow teachers and the probability such adverse effects will continue;

2. the proximity or remoteness in time of the events;

3. the type of certificate involved; and

4. any extenuating or aggravating circumstances.[10]

If the Committee on Credentials determines probable cause exists for discipline, then an administrative hearing is held.[11] The credential applicant or holder must be given 30 days written notice of the specific allegations of misconduct prior to a hearing. The notice must be in ordinary language setting forth the acts or omissions charged and the statute or rules allegedly violated. The credential applicant or holder is entitled to inspect and copy the portion of the investigation on which the allegations are based. The statement of allegations must inform the credential applicant or holder that if the allegations are true, sufficient cause exists for denial, suspension, or revocation of a credential or private admonishment.[12]

The hearing must occur within six months of the charges being filed. All testimony must be under penalty of perjury.[13] The Committee on Credentials makes a recommended decision in writing with a copy to the certificate applicant or holder. If the certificate applicant or holder does not request an administrative hearing within 30 days (or indicates he or she will not seek such a hearing), the Commission may adopt the Committee on Credential's recommendation.[14] However, if a hearing is requested, then

---

8. 5 CCR § 80310.
9. Educ. Code § 44244(b).
10. 5 CCR § 80308.
11. Educ. Code § 44242.
12. Educ. Code § 44244(a).
13. Educ. Code § 44244(b).
14. Educ. Code §§ 44243, 44242.5.

a hearing is held in compliance with the Administrative Procedures Act.

(C) Automatic Suspension

The Commission may automatically suspend or revoke credentials for conviction of sex or narcotics offenses, or upon a determination that an individual is a sexual psychopath. Where proof of
such a crime has been presented to the Commission, the Administrative Procedures Act does not apply.[15]

---

15. Educ. Code §§ 44424, 44265, 44345, 44346.

1.1

Licensure and Regulation of Psychiatrists and Research Psychoanalysts

Psychiatrists are regulated by the general set of statutory laws applicable to the practice of medicine.[1] Among other things, the body of law establishes the Medical Board of California and its functions, establishes licensing requirements and exceptions to licensure, regulates physician conduct, and prescribes sanctions for violations of the statutes. This chapter discusses the requirements for licensure of psychiatrists and the grounds for discipline and also addresses the Impaired Practitioner Division Program. The administrative procedure for imposition of discipline or denial of licensure is set forth in chapter 1.0A, section (I). In addition, chapter 1.0A sets forth additional substantive grounds for discipline or denial of a license.

(A) Medical Board of California

The Medical Board of California (hereafter the Board) is the primary regulatory body governing psychiatrists. Prior to July 1, 1994, the Board was divided into three divisions: Medical Quality, Licensing, and Allied Health Professions. The Division of Allied Health Professions was formerly responsible for the licensing of non-physicians who came within the jurisdiction of the Medical Board. The Board of Psychology was a separate board under the division of Allied Health Professionals.[2] Effective July 1, 1994, the

---

1. *See* Bus. & Prof. Code § 2000 et seq., commonly referred to as the Medical Practice Act (hereafter the Act). The regulations of the Medical Board are referred to as the Medical Practice Regulations. 16 CCR § 1300 et seq.
2. Bus. & Prof. Code § 2006.

statute authorizing the Division of Allied Health Professions became inoperative and was subsumed within the Division of Licensing and the Division of Medical Quality.[3] The Board is composed of 19 members with four-year terms.[4] Members must have been residents of California for the five years preceding appointment. Twelve members must be licensed as physicians and surgeons in California, and seven members must be nonlicensed public members.[5]

Among the responsibilities of the Division of Medical Quality are administration and enforcement of the disciplinary and criminal provisions of the Act and suspending, revoking, or otherwise limiting certificates[6] after disciplinary actions.[7] The Division of Licensing oversees all aspects of licensure, including approval of education programs, development and administration of licensure examinations, issuance of licenses, and administration of the continuing medical education program.[8] Each division may adopt, amend, or repeal regulations within its jurisdiction as necessary to carry out its responsibilities.[9]

(B) Licensure Requirements

All qualified physicians and surgeons are issued a license called a "physician's and surgeon's certificate" that authorizes the holder to use drugs or devices on humans, sever or penetrate human tissue, and use any and all other methods in the treatment of diseases, injuries, deformities, and all other physical and mental

---

3. Bus. & Prof. Code §§ 2003, 2006. *See also* 16 CCR §§ 1365 to 1365.3.
4. Bus. & Prof. Code §§ 2001, 2010. The governor appoints 17 members, and the Senate Rules Committee and the Speaker of the Assembly each appoint one public member.
5. Bus. & Prof. Code § 2007. Members are assigned by the governor to a specific division. Prior to July 1, 1994, the Division of Medical Quality had seven members, the Division of Licensing had seven members, and the Division of Allied Health Professions had five members. Effective July 1, 1994, the Division of Licensing had seven members, three of whom are public members. The Division of Medical Quality had 12 members, four of whom are public members. The Board members assigned to the Division of Allied Health Professions became members of the Division of Medical Quality. Bus. & Prof. Code, §§ 2003, 2006, 2008. The Board is to create a Committee on Allied Health Professions, which will advise the Board and the divisions on issues pertaining to the regulation of allied health professions under the Board's jurisdiction. Effective July 1, 1994, all references to the Division of Allied Health Professions are deemed to refer to the Board. Bus. & Prof. Code, § 2015.
6. Bus. & Prof. Code § 2004.
7. General provisions regarding the Division of Medical Quality are found in Bus. & Prof. Code § 2220, and 16 CCR §§ 1355 to 1356.2.
8. Bus. & Prof. Code § 2005.
9. Bus. & Prof. Code § 2018.

conditions (the terms *certificate* and *license* are used interchangeably in this chapter and in the law).[10] Practicing, attempting to practice, or advertising to practice any mode of treatment without a valid, unrevoked, and unsuspended certificate is a misdemeanor punishable by imprisonment for up to one year.[11] Licenses must be renewed biannually.[12]

To obtain a physician's and surgeon's certificate, an applicant[13] must have

1. completed two years of pre-professional postsecondary education;[14]

2. graduated from an approved medical school[15] that offers an approved curriculum;[16]

3. completed at least one year of postgraduate training in an approved program;[17] and

4. passed a written examination administered by the Division of Licensing.[18]

Special requirements are imposed on foreign applicants or U.S. citizens who attend foreign medical schools.[19] The Division of Licensing also provides for reciprocity in cases where an applicant is licensed in another state.[20]

---

10. Bus. & Prof. Code § 2050 and § 2051. In *CAPP v. Rank,* 51 Cal.3d 1, the California Supreme Court noted that the legislative changes had decreased the distinctions between psychologists and psychiatrists. The Supreme Court concluded that the legislature intended for the practice of psychiatrists and psychologists was similar, with psychiatrists alone being allowed to conduct surgery, prescribe medications, or use electroconvulsive treatment.
11. Bus. & Prof. Code §§ 2052, 2053.
12. Bus. & Prof. Code § 2422.
13. Details regarding making applications are found in 16 CCR §§ 1305 to 1307 and 1351(.5).
14. Bus. & Prof. Code §§ 2088, 2103.
15. Bus. & Prof. Code §§ 2082, 2084, 2103. *See also* 16 CCR §§ 1314, 1315.
16. Bus. & Prof. Code §§ 2085, 2086, 2089 to 2091(.1), and 2103. The Division of Licensing may substitute education and training to remedy deficiencies in an applicant's medical school education and training. Bus. & Prof. Code § 2107.
17. Bus. & Prof. Code §§ 2096, 2103. *See also* 16 CCR § 1321.
18. Bus. & Prof. Code §§ 2103, and 2170 to 2186. *See also* 16 CCR §§ 1328, 1329, 1351. The applicant has the option of taking either (a) Components 1 and 2 of the Federation Licensing Examination (hereafter referred to as FLEX) (produced by the Federation of State Medical Boards), (b) Parts I and II of the Examination of the National Board of Medical Examiners *and* Component 2 of the FLEX, or (c) all of the examination of the Licentiate of the Medical Council of Canada. Successfully taking and passing any one of these three options qualifies an applicant to begin postgraduate training in California hospitals. The Medical Board will administer the FLEX, but an applicant who wants to take the other examinations must personally make the arrangements to do so. 16 CCR § 1328.
19. Bus. & Prof. Code §§ 2100–2122. *See also* 16 CCR §§ 1322 to 1327.
20. Bus. & Prof. Code §§ 2135–2153. *See also* 16 CCR §§ 1334, 1335.

A certificate may be denied to any applicant guilty of unprofessional conduct or any other conduct that could result in revocation or suspension of a license; alternatively, a probationary certificate may be issued to the applicant at the discretion of the Division of Licensing.[21] When an application is denied, the applicant may request a hearing regarding eligibility.[22]

(C) Exceptions to License Requirements

There are a number of exemptions to the requirement for licensure. A California certificate is not required in the following cases:

1. those rendering emergency service;[23]

2. practitioners licensed in other states who consult or lecture in California but do not open an office or treat patients;[24]

3. practitioners licensed in other states who work under the supervision of a California-licensed physician at a state institution or a county general hospital;[25]

4. those engaged in physical fitness testing or guidance programs;[26]

5. postgraduate trainees;[27] and

6. those providing nutritional advice.[28]

(D) Grounds for Discipline

The Division of Medical Quality is charged with taking action against any licensee charged with unprofessional conduct.[29] For the procedure in taking disciplinary actions, see chapter 1.0A.

---

21. Bus. & Prof. Code § 2221. Probationary conditions include practice limited to a supervised environment, restrictions on drug-prescribing privileges, medical or psychiatric treatment, participation in rehabilitation programs, completion of clinical training programs, abstention from the use of alcohol or drugs, and restrictions against engaging in certain types of medical practices.
22. 16 CCR § 1308.
23. Bus. & Prof. Code § 2058.
24. Bus. & Prof. Code §§ 2060, 2072, 2073, 2076.5.
25. Bus. & Prof. Code §§ 2072, 2073; 16 CCR § 1341.
26. Bus. & Prof. Code § 2062.
27. Bus. & Prof. Code § 2065.
28. Bus. & Prof. Code § 2068.
29. Bus. & Prof. Code § 2234.

The Division has the power to investigate

1. complaints from the public or others concerning possible unprofessional conduct, circumstances leading to judgments, and settlements or awards exceeding $30,000 that involve a physician's error, negligence, or omission; and

2. circumstances surrounding cases where there has been a high number of judgments, settlements, or awards against a physician.[30]

Unprofessional conduct includes, but is not limited to,

1. gross negligence;

2. repeated negligent acts;

3. incompetence;

4. acts involving dishonesty or corruption substantially related to the qualifications, functions, or duties of a physician;[31]

5. any conduct that would have warranted denial of a certificate;[32]

6. conviction of any offense substantially related to the qualifications, functions, or duties of a physician;[33]

7. use of any controlled substance, dangerous drug, or alcoholic beverage to the extent that it is dangerous to the licensee or others, or to the extent that it impairs the ability of the licensee

---

30. Bus. & Prof. Code § 2220.
31. An act is substantially related to the qualifications, functions, or duties of a licensee if, to a substantial degree, it evidences a present or potential unfitness of the licensee to perform the functions authorized by the license in a manner consistent with the public health, safety, or welfare. 16 CCR § 1360; Bus. & Prof. Code § 480.
32. Bus. & Prof. Code § 2234.
33. Bus. & Prof. Code §§ 2236, 490. *See also* 16 CCR § 1360. A conviction for a violation of laws or regulations dealing with dangerous drugs or controlled substances constitutes unprofessional conduct. Bus. & Prof. Code § 2237.
When considering suspension or revocation of a license based on the conviction of a crime, the following factors will be considered: (1) the nature and severity of the act(s); (2) the total criminal record; (3) the time elapsed since the commission of the act(s); (4) whether the licensee has complied with any sanctions imposed by law; (5) evidence of any expungement proceedings; and (6) evidence of rehabilitation. 16 CCR § 1360.1.
Further, a conviction in another state can be a basis for discipline. *Marek v. Board of Podiatric Medicine*, 16 Cal.App.4th 1989 (1993).

to safely practice medicine; or more than one misdemeanor or any felony involving these substances;[34]

8. intentional violations of provisions relating to the rights of involuntarily confined inpatients;[35]

9. falsifying any documents related to the practice of medicine;[36]

10. creating or altering any medical record with fraudulent intent;[37]

11. willful and unauthorized violation of professional confidence;[38]

12. false or misleading advertising;[39] or

13. obtaining a certificate or license by fraud or misrepresentation.[40]

The Board is also authorized to investigate and take disciplinary action against licensees who fail to follow infection control guidelines regarding blood-borne infectious diseases[41] and licensees who have had disciplinary action taken against them in another state or by the federal government.[42]

When the Board finds reasonable cause to believe a physician is unable to practice medicine with reasonable skill and safety to his or her patients, it may require the physician to undergo a

---

34. Bus. & Prof. Code §§ 2239, 2240. Section 2240 was repealed effective January 1, 1994, and replaced with § 2280, which provides that no licensee shall practice medicine while under the influence of narcotics or alcohol to such an extent that it impairs his or her ability to practice medicine with safety to the public and his or her patients. A violation of § 2280 is unprofessional conduct and a misdemeanor. It is also unprofessional conduct to furnish these substances to an addict except in emergency or treatment situations. Bus. & Prof. Code §§ 2241, 2241.5. Similarly, prescribing, dispensing, or furnishing dangerous drugs without a prior examination and medical indication is unprofessional conduct. Bus. & Prof. Code § 2242.

35. Bus. & Prof. Code § 2256. See Welf. & Inst. Code §§ 5326.2 to 5326.8.

36. Bus. & Prof. Code § 2261. This has been held to apply where a physician created a phony insurance policy from a bogus insurance company to meet a hospital's requirements of malpractice insurance. Foster v. Board of Medical Quality Assurance, 227 Cal.App.3d 1606 (1991).

37. Bus. & Prof. Code § 2262. In addition to other disciplinary actions for violations of this section, the Board may also impose civil fines of up to $500.

38. Bus. & Prof. Code § 2263.

39. Bus. & Prof. Code §§ 651, 2271, 17500. See also 16 CCR § 1363. False advertising does not require intent to defraud to support discipline. Khan v. Medical Board, 12 Cal.App.4th 1834 (1993).

40. Bus. & Prof. Code §§ 2235, 490.

41. Bus. & Prof. Code § 2221.1.

42. Bus. & Prof. Code § 2305.

professional competency examination.[43] The examination is an oral clinical test of the physician's medical knowledge in the area of his or her specialty or the area of the suspected deficiency. The test is administered by three physician examiners selected by the Board, two of whom must confer a failing grade for the Board to charge the examinee with incompetence under section 2234(d).[44] The Medical Board may also require a licensee or applicant to undergo a psychological evaluation, as discussed in chapter 5B.1.

(E) Penalties

Technically, all violations of the Medical Practice Act are misdemeanors punishable with fines between $200 and $1,200 and/or imprisonment of between 60 and 180 days.[45] Available disciplinary actions include revocation of a certificate, suspension of the right to practice for up to one year, probation,[46] public reprimand, or other actions deemed proper by the Board or the ALJ.[47] A revocation of a physician's certificate requires an affirmative vote by five of the seven members of the Division of Medical Quality.[48] Additionally, the Division of Medical Quality may seek an injunction against a physician when it has reasonable cause to believe that allowing him or her to continue to practice would endanger the public health, safety, or welfare.[49] For a listing of license offenses of a general nature, see chapter 1.0A, section (C).

A physician whose license has been suspended or revoked may petition the Division of Medical Quality for reinstatement or

---

43. Bus. & Prof. Code § 2292(a). Reasonable cause is defined as any of the following: a single act of gross negligence, a pattern of inappropriate prescribing; an act of incompetence causing death or serious bodily injury; or a pattern of substandard care. A hearing may be held to determine if reasonable cause exists, at which the physician has a right to representation of his or her choice. Bus. & Prof. Code § 2292(c).
44. Bus. & Prof. Code §§ 2293(b), (e). A physician who fails the examination may request a hearing to determine if a second examination is warranted.
45. Bus. & Prof. Code §§ 2314, 2315. *See also* chapter 1.0A, sections (C) and (G).
46. Bus. & Prof. Code § 2228 provides for probation, which may include additional training followed by an oral or written examination, submission to a complete diagnostic examination, restriction of the licensee's practice, and community service.
   Physicians who have been placed on probation must cooperate with the Probation Surveillance Compliance Program, which includes submitting to drug tests. 16 CCR § 1363.
47. Bus. & Prof. Code § 2227.
48. Bus. & Prof. Code § 2013(c).
49. Bus. & Prof. Code § 2312.

modification after certain minimum periods have elapsed.[50] However, no petition will be considered while the petitioner is under sentence, including probation or parole, for any criminal offense, nor while there is an accusation or petition to revoke probation pending against the person.[51]

(F) Medical Quality Review Committees

Prior to January 1, 1994, the Division of Medical Quality oversaw 14 medical quality review committees throughout the state.[52] (After January 1, 1994, references to Medical Quality Review Committees are deemed to refer to a panel of the Division of Medical Quality.)[53] Each committee is composed of licensed physicians, licensed nonphysician healing-arts practitioners, and public members.[54] Committee members are appointed by the governor for four-year terms.[55]

Among the duties of the committees were

1. to review the quality of medical care provided by physicians and surgeons;

2. to create physician peer counseling panels where it finds them warranted;

3. to inspect hospitals;

4. to hold disciplinary hearings when grounds are found by the attorney general, make findings, and take disciplinary or other remedial action; and

5. to convene panels to hear petitions for reinstatement or modification of penalties.[56]

---

50. Bus. & Prof. Code § 2307. Generally, three years must pass prior to reinstatement of a license revoked for unprofessional conduct (two years in some cases); two years must pass prior to early termination of probation of three or more years; and one year must pass prior to modification of a condition, or reinstatement of a license revoked for mental or physical illness, or termination of probation of less than three years. *See also* 16 CCR §§ 1359, 1360.2.
51. Bus. & Prof. Code § 2307(c).
52. Bus. & Prof. Code § 2320. The state was divided into 14 districts, each made up of one or more counties. Bus. & Prof. Code § 2322 sets forth those districts. *See also* 16 CCR §§ 1361, 1362.
53. Bus. & Prof. Code § 2332(c).
54. Bus. & Prof. Code § 2323. The exact number and makeup of each committee varies by district, each generally having either 10 or 15 members. The Los Angeles County district is the exception with 40 members.
55. Bus. & Prof. Code § 2324.
56. Bus. & Prof. Code § 2332.

(G) Impaired Physician Program

The Division of Medical Quality also has the duty of establishing diversion evaluation committees that are intended to identify and rehabilitate physicians with impairments due to alcohol or drug abuse or mental or physical illness that affect their competency to practice medicine.[57] Specific duties of the committees include evaluation of physicians who request to participate in the diversion programs,[58] designation of treatment facilities, tailoring of treatment programs for participants, and evaluation of physicians regarding their ability to resume practice.[59]

(H) Application for Admission to the Program

To qualify for the Diversion Program, an applicant must be a licensed physician or otherwise able to practice medicine in California and must meet the following criteria:

1. the applicant must reside in California;
2. the applicant must be found to abuse alcohol or dangerous drugs or to suffer from a mental or physical disability in a manner that may affect his or her ability to practice medicine safely or competently;
3. the applicant must voluntarily request admission to the Impaired Physician Program;
4. the applicant must agree to undergo any medical or psychiatric evaluation ordered by the Diversion Evaluation Committee;
5. the applicant must cooperate with the program in providing authorizations and releases; and
6. the applicant must agree in writing to cooperate with all elements of the treatment program.[60]

---

57. Bus. & Prof. Code §§2340, 2342.
58. *See* generally 16 CCR §§ 1357 to 1357.8.
59. Bus. & Prof. Code § 2352.
60. 16 CCR § 1357.1

(I) Denial of Admission

An applicant for the Diversion Program can be denied admission to the program for any of the following reasons:

1. he or she does not meet the criteria set forth above;
2. he or she has been subject to an adverse disciplinary decision by any state medical licensing authority;
3. complaints have been made that he or she violated the Medical Practice Act;
4. the committee determines that the applicant will not substantially benefit from the program; or
5. the applicant's participation in the program poses too great a risk to public health, safety, or welfare.[61]

(J) Termination From the Program

The Diversion Committee can vote to terminate the physician's participation in the program if he or she has failed to comply with the treatment program or for any of the reasons that would be grounds to deny an application to participate in the program.[62]

(K) Regulation of Research Psychoanalysts

In addition to psychiatrists, the Medical Board also regulates research psychoanalysts. Licenses are not issued. Instead, research psychoanalysts and student psychoanalysts must register with the Division of Licensing of the Medical Board. The Board has established Research Psychoanalyst Regulations.[63]

(K)(1) Definitions

A *research psychoanalyst* is a psychoanalyst who is registered under the regulations with the Division of Licensing.

Student means a person enrolled in a psychoanalytic institution for training in psychoanalysis who is registered with the division.

---

61. 16 CCR § 1357.4.
62. For a case discussing the impaired physician program, *see Kees v. Medical Board of California,* 7 Cal.App.4th 1801 (1992).
63. 16 CCR § 1367; Bus. & Prof. Code § 2018.

Graduate psychoanalyst means a licensed physician, licensed psychologist, licensed clinical social worker, or marriage, family, and child counselor who has had training in psychoanalysis in an amount specified by the Board, or a research psychoanalyst who is a graduate of either a psychoanalytic institute as defined by law or a psychoanalytic institution that the Division of Licensing has deemed to be equivalent to a psychoanalytic institute. The institutes specifically mentioned in the law are the Los Angeles Psychoanalytic Institute, the San Francisco Psychoanalytic Institute, the Southern California Psychoanalytic Institute, and the San Diego Psychoanalytic Institute.[64]

Psychoanalytic institution is defined in the regulations as any institution, institute, department, or program organized to provide training in psychoanalytic theory and technique that meets the criteria established by the Board and that certifies or graduates students in such training.[65]

(K)(2) Registration Not Required

Licensed physicians; licensed psychologists (see chapter 1.4); licensed clinical social workers (see chapter 1.6); marriage, family, and child counselors (see chapter 1.9); and other individuals who are otherwise exempt from the Medical Practice Act are not required to register with the Division of Licensing to engage in practice as a research psychoanalyst.[66]

(K)(3) Application for Registration

The applications for registration must be submitted to the Division and accompanied by such evidence or documents as are necessary to determine the applicant's qualifications and accompanied by a registration fee.[67]

---

64. Bus. & Prof. Code § 2529.
65. 16 CCR § 1367.1. The criteria for an equivalent psychoanalytic institute are set forth in 16 CCR § 1374 and include (1) having a curriculum designed and implemented by a faculty that is predominantly graduate psychoanalysts; (2) ensuring that each student has practical clinical exposure to a wide variety of psychopathologies and training in their differential diagnosis; (3) requiring each research psychoanalyst student to have received a doctoral degree or equivalent prior to admission; (4) requiring each research psychoanalyst prior to admission to have shown achievement in teaching, training, or research with demonstrated aptitude in his or her field of scholarly or scientific endeavor; (5) requiring each student to conduct at least three psychoanalyses under the supervision of three different graduate psychoanalysts, at least one of which must have been taken to termination, except in rare instances where delay may pose an extreme hardship to the student; (6) requiring students to pass a comprehensive examination or writing an approved thesis; and (7) requiring students to take at least 560 hours of specified classroom training.
66. 16 CCR § 1369.
67. 16 CCR § 1367.3.

The Division is required to inform the applicant within 11 days of receipt whether the application is complete and accepted for filing or deficient and, if so, what information is required. Within 71 days after the completion of the application, the Division must advise the applicant of its decision as to whether he or she meets the requirements for registration. For the purpose of this action, completion of the application means that the application form and all required information, documentation, and fees have been filed.[68] When an applicant is from a psychoanalytic institute that claims to be equivalent to an institute specified by law, the applicant must present to the Division all such evidence that the institution complies with the criteria for equivalent psychoanalytic institutes.[69]

The registration fee is $100 for research psychoanalysts and students, except that if the registration will expire one year after its issuance, the fee is $75. The biennial renewal fee is $50.[70]

(K)(4) Supervision of Students

Students may practice psychoanalysis under supervision. The supervisor must be a graduate psychoanalyst who has a minimum of five years of postgraduate clinical experience in psychoanalysis following completion of his or her own psychoanalytic education. The supervisor must provide individual supervision of the student for a minimum of one hour per week per case of patient psychoanalysis for the first year of supervision, and no less than one hour per case each month thereafter. A supervisor can supervise no more students than in the judgment of the training institute he or she can effectively supervise. There must be a minimum of 50 hours of supervision for each case for a total of at least 150 hours of supervision during training.[71]

(K)(5) Grounds for Discipline

The Division may deny, suspend, revoke, or impose probationary conditions on any registrant for unprofessional conduct that is defined to include, but is not limited to, any violation of the

---

68. 16 CCR § 1367.4.
69. 16 CCR § 1375.
70. 16 CCR § 1377. All registrations expire and become invalid at midnight on the last day of February of each even-numbered year if not renewed. The applicant must apply for renewal with a form provided by the Division of Licensing and must provide a verification of continuing student status by the registrar or equivalent office of the psychoanalytical institute attended. 16 CCR §§ 1377.5, 1378.
71. 16 CCR §§ 1372, 1373. This seems to require more supervision than for psychological assistants or marriage, family, and child counselor interns, where the amount of supervision is one hour per week regardless of the number of cases (see chapters 1.7 and 1.10 for comparison).

Research Psychoanalyst Law or any violation of the Research Psychoanalyst Regulations.[72] Because research psychoanalysts are under the authority of the Department of Consumer Affairs, they are also subject to discipline on the following grounds:

1. conviction of a crime if the crime is substantially related to the qualifications, functions, or duties of a research psychoanalyst;[73]
2. knowingly making a false statement of fact in an application for registration;[74]
3. knowingly making a false statement of material fact or knowingly admitting to stating a material fact in support of another person's application;[75] or
4. securing a registration by fraud, deceit, or misrepresentation of fact or knowingly omitting a material fact.

The disciplinary actions in the provision are pursuant to the Administrative Procedures Act, and the same procedures would apply to any other Medical Board licensee as described in chapter 1.0A, section (I).

---

72. Bus. & Prof. Code § 2529; 16 CCR § 1376.
73. Under Bus. & Prof. Code § 490, conviction means a plea or verdict of guilty or a conviction following a plea of nolo contendere (i.e., no contest).
74. Bus. & Prof. Code § 490.
75. Bus. & Prof. Code § 499.

1.2

Licensure and Regulation of Nurses

California does not specifically have a category of nurses referred to as "psychiatric nurses," but instead has registered nurses and licensed vocational nurses. The closest reference to a psychiatric nurse is in the Evidence Code's reference to a registered nurse with a master's degree in mental health nursing as being a psychotherapist for the purposes of the psychotherapist–patient privilege.[1] The administrative procedure for imposition of discipline or denial of licensure is set forth in chapter 1.0A, section (H). In addition, chapter 1.0A sets forth additional substantive grounds for discipline or denial of a license.

(A) Registered Nurses

(A)(1) Definition of Registered Nursing

The practice of registered nursing consists of those functions, including basic health care, which help people cope with difficulties in daily living that are associated with their actual or potential health or illness problems, or the treatment thereof, which require a substantial amount of scientific knowledge and technical skill, and includes all of the following:

1. direct and indirect patient care services that ensure the safety, comfort, personal hygiene, and protection of patients; and the performance of disease prevention and restorative measures;

---

1. Evid. Code § 1010(k). Because their functions are not close to those of psychiatric nurses, this chapter does not discuss special requirements for nurse–midwives. 16 CCR § 1460.

2. direct and indirect patient care services including, but not limited to, the administration of medications and therapeutic agents, necessary to implement a treatment, disease prevention, or a rehabilitative regimen ordered by, and within the scope of licensure of, a physician, dentist, podiatrist, or clinical psychologist;

3. the performance of skin tests, immunization techniques, and the withdrawal of human blood from veins and arteries;

4. observation of signs and symptoms of illness, reactions to treatment, general behavior, or general physical condition, and (a) determination of whether such signs, symptoms, reactions, behavior, or general appearance exhibits abnormal characteristics; and (b) implementation, based on observed abnormalities, of appropriate reporting, or referral, or substandard procedures, or changes in treatment regimen in accordance with standardized procedures, or the initiation of emergency procedures.[2]

(A)(2) Board of Registered Nursing

Registered nurses are governed by the Nursing Practice Act.[3] The Board of Registered Nursing, formerly the Board of Nursing Education and Nurse Registration, is under the jurisdiction of the Department of Consumer Affairs and is responsible for licensing and regulation of registered nurses. The Board is composed of nine members.[4] These members are to be public members. Three members are to be licensed registered nurses who are active in practice, with five years of experience, and who are not engaged as educators or administrators. One member is to be a licensed registered nurse who is active as an educator or administrator in a program to train registered nurses. One member is to be a licensed registered nurse who is an administrator of a nursing service with at least five years of experience. One member also is to be a licensed physician with at least five years of experience.[5] Board members serve for four-year terms.

---

2. Bus. & Prof. Code § 2728. Registered nurses who meet the criteria set forth in this chapter and who possess additional preparation and skills in physical diagnosis, psychosocial assessment, and management of health illness needs may become nurse practitioners. 16 CCR § 1480. However, that specialty is not specifically related to mental health or psychiatric nursing and is not addressed here.
3. Bus. & Prof. Code § 2700.
4. Bus. & Prof. Code § 2701.
5. Bus. & Prof. Code § 2702.

(A)(3) Licensure Requirements

The licensing law sets out the qualifications applicants must meet, the fees that must be paid, and exemptions, to the extent they exist. The law requires that the examination be a written examination of a type designated by the Board.[6]

An applicant must meet the following criteria:

1. be at least 18 years of age;
2. have passed the written examination required by the Board;
3. have filed with the Board a complete transcript indicating successful completion of the courses required for licensure;[7]
4. provide evidence of education equivalent to completion of a high school course of study in the United States or its equivalent;[8] and
5. not be subject to denial of licensure.

Where the Board has a reasonable doubt of the applicant's command of English,[9] the Board may also administer an examination to an applicant to measure the applicant's ability to comprehend English to a degree to permit him or her to discharge duties of a nurse safely.

(A)(4) Interim Permits

The Board of Registered Nursing also grants interim permits, which are not renewable and are in effect to the expiration date or until the results of a written examination are mailed. An interim permit is issued to an applicant whose application for licensure has been approved, if the applicant has completed the education requirements for licensure since the last scheduled examination. However, a person holding an interim permit must practice under the direct supervision of a registered nurse who is required to be present and available on the patient care unit during all the time that the individual is rendering professional services. The interim permittee can only use the following titles: Interim Permittee, Permittee, Nurse Permittee, or Nurse Intern Permittee.

---

6. 16 CCR §§ 1409, 1411.5; Bus. & Prof. Code § 2732.1(b)
7. 16 CCR § 1410(a).
8. Education equivalent to a high school course of study includes any of the following: (1) passing the General Education Development Examination; (2) a degree from any junior college or university accredited by a state agency authorized to accredit such institutions; (3) an evaluation by high school, unified school district, junior college, college, university, or board of education that the Board of Registered Nursing determines establishes an education equivalent to a high school education in the United States; and (4) senior matriculation in any Canadian school that the Board of Registered Nursing determines established an education equivalent to a high school education in the United States. 16 CCR § 1412.
9. 16 CCR § 1413.

The interim permittees are subject to the same disciplinary provisions as applicants and registered nurses.[10] The Board may issue an interim permit to an applicant who is currently licensed in a foreign country and who meets the educational requirements set forth in the law.[11] The Board may also issue temporary licenses for a period of six months upon approval of an application, but the Board may not issue a temporary license more than twice to any individual.[12]

(A)(5) Grounds for Discipline

The Board may refuse to grant licensure or may suspend or revoke a license for any of the following grounds:

1. unprofessional conduct,[13] including:

    (a) incompetence[14] or gross negligence[15] in carrying out usual nursing functions;

    (b) a conviction of practicing medicine without a license;

    (c) nursing-related advertising that violates the law;[16]

2. procuring a certificate by fraud, misrepresentation, or mistake;[17]

3. procuring, aiding or abetting, attempting, agreeing or offering to procure or assist at a criminal abortion;[18]

4. violating or intending to violate, directly or indirectly, or assisting in or abetting the violation of, or conspiring to violate the nursing law;[19]

5. making any false statement in connection with an application for a license;[20]

---

10. 16 CCR § 1414.
11. 16 CCR § 1414.1; Bus. & Prof. Code § 2736.
12. Bus. & Prof. Code § 2733.
13. Bus. & Prof. Code § 2761.
14. *Incompetence* means the lack of, or the failure to exercise, the degree of learning, skill, care, and experience ordinarily possessed and exercised by a competent registered nurse. 16 CCR § 1443. The standards of competency are defined in 16 CCR § 1443.5.
15. *Gross negligence* is defined to include an extreme departure from the standard of care that would have been exercised by a competent registered nurse in similar circumstances. An extreme departure is the repeated failure to provide nursing care as required, or the failure to provide care or to exercise ordinary precaution in a single situation where the nurse knew, or should have known, that the client's life or health could have jeopardized.
16. Bus. & Prof. Code § 2761(a).
17. Bus. & Prof. Code §§ 480, 2761(b).
18. Bus. & Prof. Code § 2761(c).
19. Bus. & Prof. Code § 2761(d).
20. Bus. & Prof. Code § 2761(e).

6. conviction of a felony or any offense substantially related to the qualifications, functions, and duties of a registered nurse;[21]

7. impersonating an applicant or acting as proxy for an applicant in any examination for the issuance of a nursing license;[22]

8. impersonating another licensed practitioner, or permitting or allowing another person to use one's certificate for nursing;[23]

9. aiding or assisting in the violation of the Medical Practice Act;[24]

10. holding oneself out to the public or to another healing-arts practitioner as a nurse practitioner without having met the standards established for nurse practitioners;[25]

11. revocation or suspension of a nursing license in another state or U.S. territory on grounds that would constitute grounds for suspension or revocation of a license in California;[26]

12. except for good cause, failure to protect patients by following infection-control guidelines of the Board and risking transmission of blood-borne infectious diseases from nurse to patient, patient to patient, or patient to nurse;[27] or

13. aiding or assisting, or agreeing to aid or assist any person or persons, whether a licensed physician or not, in the performance of, or arranging for, silicone breast injections.[28]

It is unlawful for anyone to engage in the practice of registered nursing without a license, or to use any title, sign, or device indicating he or she is qualified to practice registered nursing.[29]

---

21. Bus. & Prof. Code §§ 490, 2761(f). A crime is substantially related to the qualifications, functions, or duties of a registered nurse if, to a substantial degree, it evidences present or potential unfitness to perform a registered nurse's duties in a manner consistent with public health, safety, and welfare. Such crimes include child abuse; conviction as a mentally disordered sex offender; assault and/or battery; any crime or act involving the sale, gift, administration, or furnishing of narcotics or dangerous drugs; or violating or conspiring to violate the laws governing nurses. 16 CCR § 1444.
22. Bus. & Prof. Code § 2761(h).
23. Bus. & Prof. Code § 2761(i).
24. Bus. & Prof. Code § 2761(j).
25. Bus. & Prof. Code § 2761(k).
26. Bus. & Prof. Code § 2761(l).
27. Bus. & Prof. Code § 2761(m).
28. Bus. and Prof. Code §§ 2761, 480, 490. In administering discipline, the Board of Registered Nursing's discretion is "virtually unfettered." *Morton v. Board of Registered Nursing*, 235 Cal.App.3d 1560 (1991).
29. Bus. & Prof. Code §§ 2732, 2795.

(A)(6) Exceptions to Licensure

No license is required for any of the following:

1. gratuitous nursing of the sick by friends or family;
2. incidental care of the sick by servants or by housekeepers, as long as they do not practice nursing within the meaning of this chapter;
3. domestic administration of family remedies;
4. nursing services in case of emergency, which includes an epidemic or public disaster; and
5. the performance by anyone of such duties as required in the physical care of a patient and/or carrying out medical orders prescribed by a licensed physician, so long as such person does not try to practice as a professional, registered, graduate, or trained nurse.[30]

Incompetence is defined as the lack of possession of, or the failure to exercise, that degree of learning, skill, care, and experience ordinarily possessed and exercised by a competent registered nurse.[31]

(A)(7) Competency Defined

Unlike some of the other licensing agencies, the Board of Registered Nurses has defined competency. A registered nurse is considered competent when he or she demonstrates the ability to transfer scientific knowledge from social, biological, and physical sciences in

1. formulating a nursing diagnosis through observation of the client's physical condition and behavior, and through interpretation of information obtained from the client and others;
2. formulating a care plan in collaboration with the client that ensures that direct and indirect nursing care services provide for the client's safety, comfort, hygiene, and protection, and for disease prevention and restorative measures;
3. performing skills essential to the kind of nursing action to be taken, explaining the health treatment to the client and family, and teaching the client and family how to care for the client's health needs;
4. delegating tasks to subordinates based on the legal scopes of practice of the subordinates and on the preparation and capability needed in the tasks to be delegated, and effectively supervising nurse care being given by subordinates;

---

30. Bus. & Prof. Code § 2727.
31. 16 CCR § 1443.

5. evaluating the effectiveness of the care plan through observation of the client's physical condition and behavior, signs and symptoms of illness, and reactions to treatment, and through communication with the client and other team members modifying the plan as needed; and

6. acting as the client's advocate, as circumstances require, by initiating actions to improve health care or to change decisions or activities that are against the interest or wishes of the client by giving the client the opportunity to make informed decisions about health care before it is provided.[32]

(A)(8) Investigations and Hearing by the Board

When the Board wants to suspend or revoke a license, it must issue an accusation in compliance with the Administrative Procedures Act, as described in chapter 1.0A, section (H).

Where the Board has reason to believe that a registered nurse is suffering from a mental impairment, the Board can require the registered nurse to submit to a psychological evaluation, as described in chapter 5B.1.

(A)(9) Impaired Practitioner Program

The Board of Registered Nursing has established a diversion program to deal with licensees who are abusing alcohol or drugs or suffering from mental illness.[33] An applicant is eligible for the program if he or she meets the following criteria:

1. is a registered nurse licensed in California;

2. resides in California;

3. is mentally ill or abuses alcohol and/or drugs in a manner that may affect the applicant's ability to safely perform the duties of a registered nurse;

4. voluntarily requests admission to the program;

5. agrees to undergo reasonable medical and/or psychiatric examination necessary for evaluation for participation in the program;

6. cooperates by providing such medical information, disclosure authorizations, and releases of liability as may be requested;

7. agrees in writing to comply with all elements of the Diversion Program;

8. has not had his or her license previously disciplined by the Board for substance abuse or mental illness; and

---

32. 16 CCR § 1443.5; Bus. & Prof. Code § 2761.
33. 16 CCR § 1446.

9. has not been terminated from the Board's Diversion Program or any other diversion program for noncompliance.[34]

The Board has a Diversion Evaluation Committee consisting of three registered nurses, one physician, and one public member, all of whom have expertise in the area of chemical dependency. The Diversion Program director and a nurse or physician consultant interview each applicant and recommend such medical or psychiatric examinations as they deem necessary.[35] The applicant is responsible for all costs incurred in the examinations and rehabilitation aspects of the program. The applicant may be terminated from the program for failure to comply with the terms and conditions.

(A)(10) Penalties

It is unlawful for any person to practice, or offer to practice, nursing without a license, or to use any title, sign, card, or device indicating he or she is qualified to practice nursing without a license.[36] Generally, unlicensed practice is a misdemeanor.[37]

(B) Licensed Vocational Nurses

Licensed vocational nurses are regulated by the Board of Licensed Vocational Nurses and Psychiatric Technicians, which is under the jurisdiction of the Department of Consumer Affairs. The Board is composed of 11 members.[38] The Board members serve 4-year terms.[39] The Board is charged with administering and enforcing licensure discipline in education of licensed vocational nurses.

(B)(1) Licensure Requirements

Applicants for a licensed vocational nurse license must

1. be at least 18 years old;
2. have completed the 12th grade or the equivalent;
3. have completed a course of study at an accredited school or the equivalent;

---

34. 16 CCR § 1447.
35. 16 CCR §§ 1446, 1447.1.
36. Bus. & Prof. Code § 2795.
37. Bus. & Prof. Code § 146.
38. Three of the Board's members are licensed vocational nurses, two are licensed psychiatric technicians, one is a licensed vocational or registered nurse with experience at an accredited school of vocational nurses, and five are unlicensed public members. Bus. & Prof. Code §§ 2841, 2842.
39. Bus. & Prof. Code § 2843.

4. have committed no act that would be grounds for disciplinary action if committed by a licensed vocational nurse;[40]

5. have completed a course in vocational or practical nursing in a school accredited by another state, provided that course is substantially equivalent to that set forth by California law, or complete not less than 51 months of paid general-duty bedside nursing experience in a general acute care facility, including 48 months of medical/surgical, five weeks of obstetrical, and five weeks of pediatric (one of the areas that may substitute for pediatric experience is psychiatric nursing);

6. submit proof of completion of work with at least 54 theory hours of pharmacology.[41] Alternatively, an applicant for licensure may become eligible by completing 36 months of verified full-time paid work experience in a nursing or general acute care facility; 450 hours of theory, which shall include 54 hours in pharmacology and must include the subjects of medical/surgical nursing, obstetrical nursing, although 8 months of the medical/surgical experience may be replaced by a number of specific types of experience, including psychiatric nursing; and

7. complete 175 hours of supervised clinical experience.[42]

(B)(2) Grounds for Discipline

The Board is authorized to carry out disciplinary proceedings and suspend or revoke the licenses of vocational nurses for the following grounds:

1. unprofessional conduct;[43]

2. procuring a license by fraud, misrepresentation, or mistake;[44]

3. giving false information in connection with an application;[45]

4. conviction of any offense substantially related to the qualifications, functions, and duties of a licensed vocational nurse;[46]

5. procuring or assisting in a criminal abortion;[47]

6. mistreating or using excessive force with a patient;[48]

---

40. Bus. & Prof. Code §§ 2866, 480.
41. 16 CCR § 2516; Bus. & Prof. Code § 2873.
42. 16 CCR § 2516.
43. Bus. & Prof. Code § 2878(a).
44. Bus. & Prof. Code § 2878(b).
45. Bus. & Prof. Code § 2878(e).
46. Bus. & Prof. Code § 2878(f).
47. Bus. & Prof. Code § 2878(c).
48. Bus. & Prof. Code § 2878(a)(4).

7. impersonating an applicant or acting as a proxy for an applicant in any examination required for licensure;[49]

8. impersonating another practitioner, misrepresenting professional credentials or licensure status, or permitting another person to use the nurse's license;[50]

9. committing any act involving dishonesty, when related to the duties and functions of a licensed vocational nurse;[51]

10. committing any act punishable as a sexually related crime, if the act is substantially related to the duties and functions of a licensed vocational nurse;[52]

11. except for good cause, a knowing failure to protect patients by failing to follow the Board's infection guidelines, thereby risking transmission of blood-borne infectious disease from nurse to patient, patient to patient, or from patient to licensee;[53] or

12. the denial, suspension, restriction, or other disciplinary action of the individual's license by any other state or by any other California health care professional licensing board, or by any government agency.[54]

Unprofessional conduct includes, but is not limited to, incompetence[55] or gross negligence.[56] Unprofessional conduct includes

1. conviction of practicing medicine without a license;

2. false or misleading advertising;

3. possession of, prescribing, or administering without directions from a licensed physician, a controlled substance or dangerous drug;

4. use of a controlled substance, dangerous drug, or alcohol, to the extent it is injurious to the licensee or to other persons, or impairs the licensee's ability to safely practice the profession;

5. conviction of falsifying prescription records;

---

49. Bus. & Prof. Code § 2878(g).
50. Bus. & Prof. Code § 2878(h).
51. Bus. & Prof. Code § 2878(j).
52. Bus. & Prof. Code § 2878(k).
53. Bus. & Prof. Code § 2878(l).
54. Bus. & Prof. Code § 2878.8.
55. Incompetence is defined as the lack of, and the failure to exercise, that degree of learning, skill, care, and experience ordinarily possessed and exercised by responsible licensed vocational nurses. 16 CCR § 2710.
56. Gross negligence is a substantial departure from the standard of care ordinarily exercised by a competent licensed vocational nurse, and that has, or could have, resulted in harm to the consumer. A conscious disregard or indifference for the health, safety, or welfare of the consumer is gross negligence. 16 CCR § 2579; Bus. & Prof. Code § 2878.

6. failure to report child, elder, or dependent adult abuse;[57] or

7. failure to maintain confidentiality.[58]

(B)(3) Penalties

Violations of the laws governing licensed vocational nurses are misdemeanors punishable by imprisonment up to one year and/or fines up to $1,000. For a list of general license offenses, see chapter 1.0A, section (C).

(B)(4) Procedure for Discipline

The procedure to impose discipline or deny licensure to a licensed vocational nurse is discussed in chapter 1.0A, section (H).

---

57. 16 CCR §§ 2520.1, 2520.2.
58. Bus. & Prof. Code § 2878.

1.3

Licensure and Regulation of Psychiatric Technicians

California does not have a specific license program for psychiatric nurses, as indicated in chapter 1.2. However, the duties of a psychiatric technician are analogous to the duties of psychiatric nurses in other states. This chapter discusses the license requirements for psychiatric technicians and the grounds for discipline or denial of licensure of such individuals. The administrative procedure for imposition of discipline or denial of licensure is set forth in chapter 1.0A, section (H). In addition, chapter 1.0A sets forth additional substantive grounds for discipline or denial of license.

(A) Definition

"Psychiatric technician" is broadly defined as a person who implements procedures or techniques that involve the understanding of cause and effect and are used in the care, treatment, and rehabilitation of mentally ill, emotionally disturbed, or mentally retarded persons, and who has direct responsibility for either administering therapy or for observation and recognition of symptoms.[1]

---

1. Bus. & Prof. Code § 4502.

(B) Board of Vocational Nurse and Psychiatric Technician Examiners

The Board of Vocational Nurse and Psychiatric Technician Examiners is composed of 11 members[2] who serve four-year terms.[3] The Board is charged with administering and enforcing the provisions of the Code dealing with evaluation, licensure, and discipline of psychiatric technicians.[4]

(C) Licensure Requirements[5]

Applicants for a psychiatric technician's license must

1. be at least 18 years old;
2. have completed the 12th grade or the equivalent;
3. have completed a course of study at an accredited school or the equivalent;[6]
4. have committed no act that would be grounds for disciplinary action if committed by a licensed psychiatric technician.[7]
5. Furthermore, subjects of instruction the applicant must have studied include care of the mentally and developmentally disabled, and the course of training must include clinical inpatient experience.[8]

A license may be denied to any applicant who has been convicted of a crime; engaged in any act of fraud, dishonesty, or

---

2. Specifically, the Board is composed of three licensed vocational nurses, two licensed psychiatric technicians, one licensed vocational or registered nurse with experience at an accredited school of vocational nursing, and five unlicensed public members. Bus. & Prof. Code §§ 2841, 2842.
3. Bus. & Prof. Code § 2843.
4. Bus. & Prof. Code § 4503.
5. *See* generally 16 CCR §§ 2565 to 2567.
6. Bus. & Prof. Code § 4511. Equivalent study and training is accomplished by (a) completion of 576 hours of theory and 954 hours of clinical experience, (b) completion of an armed forces course in neuropsychiatric nursing plus one year of related work experience, or (c) completion of 450 hours of theory and 18 months of paid work experience in the area. 16 CCR § 2575.

     Additionally, academic credit will be given for relevant training and experience in health care. Bus. & Prof. Code § 4511.2.

     Accreditation requirements are provided at 16 CCR §§ 2580 to 2589.
7. Bus. & Prof. Code § 4511.
8. Bus. & Prof. Code § 4531.

deceit; or who knowingly made a false statement in the application for license.[9]

A license will be issued to applicants who meet the enumerated requirements and who pass an examination administered by the Board.[10] An interim license may be issued after all requirements are met, pending results from the examination.[11]

Licenses are renewable every two years, and licensees must have completed a minimum of 30 hours of continuing education within the preceding two-year period.[12]

Nursing services may be given by psychiatric technicians or psychiatric technician intern permittees, if adequate medical and nursing supervision is provided by a professional nurse in institutions under the jurisdiction of the State Department of Mental Health, the State Department of Development Services, the State Department of Health Services, or the Department of Corrections. What constitutes adequate medical and nursing supervision for this purpose is to be determined by the directors of the Department of Mental Health, the Department of Health Services, and the Department of Developmental Services. The services to be provided by a psychiatric technician in such circumstances are limited to services he or she is authorized by his or her license to perform. Services rendered by a psychiatric technician intern permittee are limited to those included in his or her basic course of study, performed under the supervision of a licensed psychiatric technician or registered nurse.

The State Department of Mental Health or the Department of Developmental Services may utilize unlicensed graduates of accredited psychiatric technician training programs or psychiatric technician intern permittees to perform skills included in their basic course of study for up to nine months, when supervised by a licensed psychiatric technician or registered nurse.[13]

---

9. Bus. & Prof. Code § 480. The Board may evaluate the rehabilitation of an applicant and assess eligibility based on the following factors: the nature and severity of the act(s); evidence of any subsequent acts that would be grounds for denial of a license; the time elapsed since the act(s); the extent to which the applicant has complied with sanctions imposed by law upon the applicant; and evidence of rehabilitation presented by the applicant. 16 CCR § 2597.

10. Bus. & Prof. Code §§ 4510, 4513. *See also* 16 CCR §§ 2570 to 2572. A license may be issued without an examination to applicants who possess a valid psychiatric technician's license from another state. Bus. & Prof. Code § 4515.

11. Bus. & Prof. Code § 4510.1.

12. Bus. & Prof. Code §§ 4544, 4544.5; 16 CCR § 2592.1. Additional regulations related to continuing education courses are provided in 16 CCR §§ 2592.2 to 2592.7.

13. Bus. & Prof. Code § 2728.

(D) Grounds for Discipline

The Board is authorized to carry out disciplinary proceedings and suspend or revoke the licenses of psychiatric technicians.[14] Grounds for suspension or revocation of license include

1. unprofessional conduct;
2. procuring a license by fraud, misrepresentation, or mistake;
3. giving false information in connection with an application;
4. conviction of any offense substantially related to the qualifications, functions, and duties of a psychiatric technician;[15]
5. procuring or assisting at a criminal abortion; or
6. mistreatment of or using excessive force with a patient.[16]

Unprofessional conduct includes, but is not limited to,

1. incompetence[17] or gross negligence;[18]
2. a conviction of practicing medicine without a license;
3. false or misleading advertising;
4. possession of, prescribing, or administering (without directions from a licensed physician) a controlled substance or dangerous drug;
5. use of a controlled substance, dangerous drug, or alcohol to the extent it is injurious to the licensee or to other persons, or impairs the licensee's ability to safely practice the profession;

---

14. Bus. & Prof. Code § 4520.
15. A crime is substantially related to the qualifications, functions, or duties of a licensed psychiatric technician if to a substantial degree it evidences the present or potential unfitness of the licensee to perform the functions authorized by his or her license in a manner consistent with the public health, safety, or welfare. 16 CCR § 2578.

    When considering suspension or revocation of a license based on the conviction of a crime, the Board may evaluate the rehabilitation of the person and his or her eligibility for a license based on the following: the nature and severity of the act(s); the total criminal record; the time elapsed since the act(s); whether the licensee has complied with sanctions imposed by law; evidence of expungement proceedings; and evidence of rehabilitation submitted by the licensee. 16 CCR § 2579.5.
16. Bus. & Prof. Code § 4521.
17. Incompetence is the lack of, and the failure to exercise, that degree of learning, skill, care, and experience ordinarily possessed and exercised by responsible licensed psychiatric technicians. 16 CCR § 2577.1.
18. Gross negligence is a substantial departure from the standard of care ordinarily exercised by a competent licensed psychiatric technician and which has, or could have, resulted in harm to the consumer. A conscious disregard or indifference for the health, safety, or welfare of the consumer is gross negligence. 16 CCR § 2577.

6. conviction of falsifying prescription records;[19] or

7. failure to report child, elder, or dependent adult abuse.[20]

(E) Penalties

Violation of the laws governing psychiatric technicians are misdemeanors punishable by imprisonment for up to one year and/or fines of up to $1,000.[21] For a list of general license offenses, see chapter 1.0A, section (C).

(F) Procedure for Discipline

The procedure for denying licensure or imposing discipline is set forth in chapter 1.0A, section (H).

---

19. Bus. & Prof. Code § 4521(a).
20. 16 CCR §§ 2577.2 to 2577.4.
21. Bus. & Prof. Code § 4543.

1.4

Licensure and Regulation of Psychologists

While the term *psychologist* might seem clear and self-defining, California has licensed psychologists, licensed educational psychologists, school psychologists, and psychological assistants.

This chapter will address the licensure requirements, scope of practice, and grounds for discipline of licensed psychologists and psychological assistants. The law relating to licensed educational psychologists and school psychologists is discussed in chapter 1.5. The administrative procedure for imposition of discipline or denial of a license is set forth in chapter 1.0A, section (I), along with additional substantive grounds for discipline or denial of a license.

(A) Definition of the Practice of Psychology

The licensure and regulation of psychologists is governed by the Psychology Licensing Law.[1] The practice of psychology is defined as rendering, or offering to render, for a fee to individuals, groups, organizations, or the public, any psychological service involving the application of psychological principles, methods, and procedures of understanding, predicting, and influencing behavior. This includes the principles pertaining to learning, perception, motivation, emotions, and interpersonal relationships; and the methods and procedures of interviewing, counseling, psychotherapy, behavior modification, and hypnosis. The prac-

---

1. Bus. & Prof. Code § 2900 et seq.

tice of psychology also includes constructing, administering, and interpreting tests of mental abilities, aptitudes, interests, attitudes, personality characteristics, emotions, and motivations. The application of such principles and methods includes, but is not limited to, diagnosis, prevention, treatment, and the amelioration of psychological problems, and emotional and mental disorders of individuals and groups. *Psychotherapy* is defined as the use of psychological methods in a professional relationship to assist a person or persons to acquire greater human effectiveness or to modify feelings, conditions, attitudes, and behavior that are emotionally, intellectually, or socially ineffectual or maladjustive.[2]

The law provides that only licensed psychologists may use the terms *psychology, psychological, psychologist, psychological consultation, psychology consultant, psychometry, psychometrics, psychometrist, psychotherapy, psychotherapist,*[3] *psychoanalysis,* and *psychoanalyst.*[4]

In addition, only a psychologist may hold himself or herself out to be trained, experienced, or an expert in the field of psychology.[5]

The practice of psychology does not include prescribing drugs, performing surgery, or administering electroconvulsive therapy, but does include the use of biofeedback instruments that do not pierce or cut the skin to measure physical and mental functioning[6] (although California psychologists are attempting to obtain legislation giving them prescription privileges).

The law provides that communications between psychologists and patients are protected by the psychotherapist–patient privilege.[7]

---

2. Bus. & Prof. Code § 2903.
3. However, other MHPs, including marriage, family, and child counselors; licensed clinical social workers; registered nurses with a master's degree in mental health nursing; licensed educational psychologists; etc. are defined as psychotherapists for the purposes of the psychotherapist–patient privilege. *See* Evid. Code § 1010 and chapter 4.3.
4. This does not preclude research psychoanalysts who are properly registered as described in chapter 1.1 from using the term "research psychoanalyst." As described in chapter 1.1, licensed psychologists are not required to be registered to function as research psychoanalysts.
5. Bus. & Prof. Code § 2902(c).
6. Bus. & Prof. Code §§ 2904, 2903.1. In *California Ass'n of Psychology Providers v. Rank*, 51 Cal.3d 1 (1990), the California Supreme Court concluded, in part, that the legislature had intended by a series of statutory enactments to narrow the gap between psychologists and psychiatrists, and that except for prescribing medication, performing surgery, or administering electroconvulsive therapy, psychologists in a hospital setting should be accorded the same authority as psychiatrists.
7. Bus. & Prof. Code § 2918; Evid. Code § 1919. *See* chapter 4.3 for a detailed discussion of the psychotherapist-patient privilege.

(B) Board of Psychology

The Board of Psychology is established under the Department of Consumer Affairs and is charged with establishing the requirements for the education, licensure, and discipline of psychologists and psychological assistants.[8] The Board of Psychology administers the provisions of the licensing law, and consists of eight members, three of whom are public members.[9] Each member of the Board holds office for a term of four years, and serves until the appointment and qualification of his or her successor, or until one year after the expiration of the term for which he or she was appointed, whichever occurs first. The law precludes any member from serving more than two consecutive terms.[10] In selecting and appointing the members of the Board, except for the public members, the governor is directed to use his or her judgment to select psychologists who represent the varied professional interests of California psychologists, with as wide a representation as possible.[11] The governor appoints one of the public members and five of the psychologists who are members of the Board, and the Senate Rules Committee and the Speaker of the Assembly each appoint one public member.[12]

The members of the Board must be residents of the state, and, except for the public members, each member must be a licensed psychologist. The public members cannot be licensees of the Board of Psychology or any other board under the Division of Allied Health Professions, or chiropractors or osteopaths.[13]

Board members can be removed by the governor for negligence, incompetency, or unprofessional conduct.[14]

The Board holds at least one regular meeting each year and such additional meetings as the chairperson may call, or upon the written request of any two members of the Board.[15]

Among the Board's duties are administering and enforcing the provisions of the licensing law, enacting rules and regulations necessary to effectuate the law, establishing standards of ethical conduct relating to the practice of psychology, and examining and passing upon the qualifications of the applicants for a li-

---

8. Bus. & Prof. Code § 2902.
9. Bus. & Prof. Code § 2920.
10. Bus. & Prof. Code § 2921.
11. Bus. & Prof. Code § 2922.
12. *Id.*
13. Bus. & Prof. Code § 2923.
14. Bus. & Prof. Code § 2924.
15. Bus. & Prof. Code § 2926.

cense.[16] In addition, the Board can order the denial of an application for licensure or revoke or suspend existing licenses.[17]

(C) Licensure Requirements

The statute provides for licensing individuals who meet the criteria specified, who pay the requisite fees, and who pass the examinations specified.[18]

Applicants for licensure must meet the following criteria:

1. cannot be subject to denial of licensure for the grounds set forth in the statute;[19]

2. must possess an earned doctorate degree in psychology, in educational psychology, in education with specialization in counseling psychology or educational psychology, or possess an earned doctorate degree that is deemed by the Board to be equivalent to the degrees specified.[20] The degree or training of the psychologist must be obtained from an accredited or approved university, college, professional school, or other educational institution approved by the Board;[21]

---

16. Bus. & Prof. Code §§ 2928, 2930, 2936, 2931.
17. Bus. & Prof. Code § 2960.
18. Bus. & Prof. Code § 2948.
19. Bus. & Prof. Code §§ 2914(a), 2960.
20. Bus. & Prof. Code § 2914(b); 16 CCR § 1386. Degrees other than those specified in § 2914 are subject to evaluation as an equivalent degree even though the degree uses the term *psychology*. Doctoral degrees earned in programs approved by the American Psychological Association are deemed to be equivalent degrees. A doctor of mental health degree earned in an accredited educational institution is an equivalent degree. Further degrees to be deemed equivalent must meet the criteria of 16 CCR § 1386(d).
21. The law provides that no educational institution shall be denied recognition as an accredited or approved academic institution for the purposes of § 2914(b) solely because its program is not accredited by any professional organization of psychologists (such as the American Psychological Association). Further, there is no requirement that educational institutions register their departments of psychology or doctoral programs in psychology with the Board. Bus. & Prof. Code § 2914(b). Comparable programs are defined as including (1) programs approved by the American Psychological Association; (2) programs that have been in uninterrupted candidacy status by a regional accrediting agency approved by the U.S. Department of Education resulting in accreditation within six years from the date of candidacy; and (3) programs that have had a site visit by representatives of a regional accrediting agency approved by the U.S. Department of Education, representatives of the California Department of Education, or representatives of a similar agency in another state where the results and evaluation of the site visit have been forwarded to the psychology examining committee. Where the programs are located in educational institutions outside the U.S., the program must be approved by the appropriate governmental agency, 16 CCR §§ 1383, 1383.1.

3. must have at least two years of supervised professional practice under the direction of a licensed psychologist or suitable alternative supervision as specified by the Board in its regulations, at least one year of which shall be after being awarded a doctorate in psychology.[22]

4. must take and pass the examination unless exempted by the Board;[23] and

5. those who apply for an initial license or renewal of a license after January 1, 1987 are required to show to the Board's satisfaction that they have completed training in alcohol and chemical substance dependency detection and treatment, child abuse assessment and reporting, and human sexuality.[24]

The Board may appoint commissioners to give all or any part of the examination for licensure. Commissioners need not be members of the Board but must have the same qualifications as a member of the Board. Additionally, the Board may appoint professional commissioners on a short-term basis to examine applicants in areas such as law, ethics, and awareness of community resources.[25]

The statute provides that the Board may examine applicants by written or oral examination, or by both. Currently, absent special circumstances, the examination consists of both an oral and written examination.[26] The applicant must pay the examination fees prescribed at least 30 days prior to the date of the examination.[27]

The Board may examine the applicant's knowledge in whatever theoretical or applied fields of psychology it deems appropriate. It may also examine the candidate's professional skills and

---

22. If the supervising licensed psychologist fails to provide verification to the Board of the experience required within 30 days after being requested to do so by the applicant, the applicant can provide written verification directly to the Board under penalty of perjury, with a copy of the form provided to the supervising psychologist. The applicant shall provide the Board with a declaration under penalty of perjury, stating that the copy of the verified forms has been served on the supervising psychologist. Upon receipt by the Board of the applicant's verification of experience and declaration of service, a rebuttable presumption is created that the professional experience requirements have been met. However, the supervising psychologist shall have 20 days from the date the Board receives the verification to file a rebuttal. Only applicants who have obtained their professional experience in the United States can submit written verification directly to the Board. The Board also is required to establish qualifications for supervising psychologists and to approve them on a case-by-case basis.

23. Bus. & Prof. Code §§ 2914(d), 2941.

24. Bus. & Prof. Code §§ 28, 29, 2914(e); 16 CCR §§ 1387.6, 1387.7, 1382.1.

25. Bus. & Prof. Code § 2947.

26. Bus. & Prof. Code § 2942.

27. Bus. & Prof. Code §§ 2941, 2987.

judgment in the utilization of psychological techniques. Currently, the examination addresses all of these areas.

The written examination utilized by the Board is the Examination for Professional Practice in Psychology, which is a uniform examination prepared by the Association of State and Provincial Psychology Boards.[28] An applicant is required to take and pass the written examination before the oral examination will be given. An applicant is forbidden to remove examination materials from the examination room or to make any notes or record of any nature of questions or answers.[29]

The Board of Psychology notifies applicants of the areas that will be addressed in the oral examination, and the applicants are to be examined in those areas only. A passing grade is 75%, and any applicant scoring below that must be given the reasons in writing for the failure. The Board of Psychology is required to keep an electronic reporting of each oral examination for at least two years following the date of the examination.[30]

An applicant who is unsuccessful on the oral examination may request reconsideration in writing within 60 days following the notification that he or she has failed the examination. If the applicant received a grade of 72.5% or higher, the Board of Psychology shall reconsider the examination. If the applicant received a grade of less than 72.5%, the Board may reconsider the oral examination.

When the examination is reviewed, the review will be conducted by one or more members of the Board of Psychology. Their findings are subject to approval of the Board in its discretion.

The scores on the written examination are not subject to reconsideration.[31]

Any applicant who desires to inspect his or her oral examination rating sheet or the recording of the oral examination can inspect the examination or the tape at the Board's office in Sacramento during regular office hours, upon written request. Applicants are allowed no more than one inspection. At the time of the inspection, no one other than the applicant and a representative of the Board can be present. The applicant is not permitted to make any type of notes or tape recordings at the time of the

---

28. Bus. & Prof. Code § 2943. However, as of November 1993, the Board of Psychology was exploring changing the rules to allow other examinations to be used.
29. 16 CCR § 1388.
30. 16 CCR § 1388.5; Bus. & Prof. Code § 2942.
31. 16 CCR § 1389.

inspection. The Board does not allow any inspection of the written examination.[32]

Applicants for licensure who are graduates from foreign universities, colleges, or professional schools must provide the Board with documents and evidence demonstrating that their formal education meets the requirements of the law. Such applicants must provide the Board with an original diploma or other certificate of graduation with a copy for the Board to retain, a transcript or a comparable document of all coursework completed, a certified translation of all documents that have been submitted in a language other than English, satisfactory evidence of supervised experience comparable to that specified by the Board's regulations, and evidence that a doctoral dissertation was primarily psychological in nature. The Board may elect to require the applicant to file a copy of the dissertation itself, and a statement prepared by the applicant based on the various documents that indicates the chronological sequence of the applicant's study and research. The format of the statement is to be as comparable as possible to a transcript issued by American universities.[33]

(D) Supervised Experience Requirements

The supervised professional experience required by the statute may be accrued only in the following fashion:

1. as a registered psychological assistant;[34]

2. as a registered psychologist;[35]

3. as a psychologist or psychological assistant, or in a student counseling service of an accredited or approved college, junior college, or university, or through a federal, state, county, or municipal government organization that is not primarily involved in the provision of direct health or mental health services. In addition, if the statutory requirements are met, employment by a nonprofit community agency may constitute acceptable experience;[36]

4. experience obtained as a graduate student or psychological intern while pursuing a graduate degree in psychology in an

---

32. 16 CCR § 1390.
33. 16 CCR § 1385.
34. 16 CCR § 1387(a); Bus. & Prof. Code § 2913.
35. 16 CCR § 1387(a); Bus. & Prof. Code § 2909(c).
36. 16 CCR § 1387(a); Bus. & Prof. Code §§ 2909, 2910.

accredited or approved college or university and working in a training program;[37] and

5. experience received in another state or territory of the United States as a psychologist.[38]

For the purpose of the experience requirement, a *qualified primary supervisor* means a psychologist who is engaged in rendering professional services a minimum of one-half time in the same working setting where the person who is being supervised is obtaining experience. The qualified primary supervisor may delegate a portion of the supervision to another licensed psychologist or otherwise qualified individual. The applicant's supervised professional experience, education, and training must be in the same or similar field of psychology.[39]

Two years of satisfactory supervised professional experience are required, one of which must be completed after being awarded a doctoral degree. Where an applicant accumulates all the required experience postdoctorally, the experience must be completed within 60 consecutive months. A year of supervised professional experience consists of not less than 1,500 hours, which must be completed within 30 consecutive months. Applicants may not receive credit for more than 176 hours of supervised professional experience in any one month.[40]

Supervised professional experience may not be accumulated until the applicant has concluded 48 semester/trimester units or 72 quarter units of graduate level coursework in psychology, educational psychology, or their equivalent from an accredited or approved educational institution, or from a program approved by the Board as a comparable program.[41]

A maximum of 12 semester or trimester units, or 18 quarter units of practicum courses may be credited toward the coursework, which is a prerequisite to supervised professional experience. Unit credit awarded for supervised professional experience or dissertations cannot be credited toward the hours that must be accumulated prior to beginning professional supervised experience.[42]

---

37. 16 CCR § 1387(a); Bus. & Prof. Code § 2911.
38. 16 CCR § 1387(a); Bus. & Prof. Code §§ 2912, 2946.
39. 16 CCR § 1387(d). Note that as of July 1, 1994, a qualified primary supervisor must have not less than three years of professional experience following licensure. Also, the supervisor may delegate supervision to a person who meets the requirements of 16 CCR § 1387.3.
40. 16 CCR § 1387(e), (f). Since July 1, 1994, *each year* of supervision must be with a different supervisor.
41. 16 CCR § 1387(g).
42. 16 CCR § 1387(h), (i).

Where an applicant's doctoral degree has been awarded with less than 48 hours of semester/trimester units, or 72 quarter units of coursework in psychology, educational psychology, or courses deemed equivalent by the Board, the applicant may accrue professional experience either from the date all requirements for the doctoral degree have been completed, as verified by the registrar, or after the degree is awarded.[43]

Supervised professional experience must include direct supervision, either individual or group, by a qualified supervisor for a minimum of one hour per week or 10% of the actual time worked per week, whichever is greater. At least one hour per week of supervision is required to be direct, individual, face-to-face supervision between the person supervised and his or her primary supervisor.[44]

The 1,500 hours of supervised professional experience that an applicant may obtain prior to the awarding of a doctoral degree may be obtained either

1. in a training program that is approved by a university, college, or school and that has a training agreement with the educational institution to provide supervised professional experience to a psychological intern; or

2. as a psychological assistant.[45]

The supervised professional experience may consist of work in psychological research for an accredited or approved college or university offering an advanced degree or work in a research organization where psychological research is an important function, if the work for which hourly credit will be granted otherwise complies with the regulations and law.

Prior to January 1, 1989, *suitable alternative supervision* meant supervision by a psychologist licensed or certified in another state or territory of the United States, a diplomate of the American Board of Professional Psychology, or a psychologist who held a doctoral degree in psychology and had a minimum of three years of professional postdoctoral experience. Since January 1, 1988, *suitable alternative supervision* has meant supervision by a psychologist licensed or certified in another state or territory of the United States for a minimum of three years and who possesses a doctoral degree in psychology, in educational psychology, or in education with a field of specialization in counseling psychology or education psychology. Alternatively, supervision can be by a

---

43. 16 CCR § 1387(j).
44. 16 CCR § 1387(l).
45. 16 CCR § 1387(m).

diplomate of the American Board of Professional Psychology whose diploma is in the specialty area to be supervised.[46]

A maximum of 750 hours of supervised professional experience may be earned under a primary supervisor who is not a psychologist but is otherwise licensed, including, but not limited to, Board-eligible or Board-certified psychiatrists, educational psychologists, or clinical social workers.[47]

Supervised professional experience shall be obtained while functioning as a psychologist in an exempt setting, as a psychological assistant, or as otherwise specified, but not while functioning under any other professional license or any other professional capacity. This does not restrict independent practice by a person who holds another professional license (such as a marriage, family, and child counselor, or a licensed clinical social worker) or another professional capacity, but experience gained under the independent practice or license is not counted toward the required hours of supervision to become a psychologist.[48]

Experience obtained under the supervision of a practitioner with whom the applicant has an interpersonal or family relationship or who received monetary payment or other consideration directly from the applicant, is not counted as supervised professional experience.[49]

Applicants are required to take coursework in child abuse assessment and reporting, alcohol and chemical dependency detection and treatment, and human sexuality.[50]

Once an applicant is licensed as a psychologist, he or she may elect to do business as a psychological corporation as discussed more fully in chapter 2.2.

---

46. 16 CCR § 1387(o).
47. 16 CCR § 1387(o)(2). Since July 1, 1994, a new regulation, 16 CCR § 1387.3 prescribes the qualifications of supervisors. Under the new regulation, a supervisor must have at least three years of professional experience following licensure. Further, any person who wants to provide the "alternate supervision" described in § 1387(o)(2) must be a Board-eligible or Board-certified psychiatrist, licensed educational psychologist, licensed clinical social worker, or other licensed MHP. As of January 1, 1995, a person who wants to provide "alternate supervision" must be a Board-certified psychiatrist or a licensed MHP with at least three years of experience following licensure.
48. 16 CCR § 1387(p).
49. 16 CCR § 1387(q), (r).
50. 16 CCR §§ 1387.7, 1387.6, 1382.1.

(E) Exceptions to the Licensing Regulations

There are several general categories of exemption from the provisions of the Psychology Licensing Law. The first is for other professional licensees using hypnotic techniques with certain limitations. Thus, psychiatrists (chapter 1.1); clinical social workers (chapter 1.6); educational psychologists (chapter 1.7); marriage, family, and child counselors (chapter 1.9); psychiatric technicians (chapter 1.3); registered nurses (chapter 1.2); attorneys admitted to the state bar; persons who utilize hypnotic techniques on referral from doctors, dentists, or psychologists; or persons who utilize hypnotic techniques for avocational or vocational self-improvement may do so as long as they do not offer therapy for emotional or mental disorders. Additionally, they cannot use the words *psychological, psychologist, psychology, psychometrist, psychometrics,* or *psychometry,* and cannot imply that they are licensed to practice psychology. Duly ordained members of the recognized clergy or religious practitioners are not precluded from doing work of a psychological nature so long as they do not use the terms *psychological, psychologist, psychology, psychometrist, psychometrics,* or *psychometry.* However, this does not preclude licensed educational psychologists from using the term *psychologist* in their titles.[51]

The next major category of exemption is for those individuals who are performing psychological services solely within a school or other public agency and then offering psychological services to the public for a fee or compensation over and above the salary that they receive for their official duties. This includes individuals who hold valid and current credentials as school psychologists or psychometrists issued by the California Department of Education (see chapter 1.7) and persons employed as psychologists or psychological assistants or employed in a student counseling service by accredited or approved colleges, junior colleges, or universities or federal, state, county, or municipal governmental organizations that are not primarily involved in the provision of direct health or mental health services. Without a license, these individuals may consult or disseminate their research findings and scientific information to other accredited or approved academic institutions or government agencies.

In addition, individuals who meet the educational requirements for psychologists and who have one year or more of professional experience of the type approved by the Board can

---

51. Bus. & Prof. Code § 2908.

provide psychological services if employed by a nonprofit community agency that receives a minimum of 25% of its financial support from a federal, state, county, or municipal government organization, for the purpose of training and providing the services. Any such individuals must be registered by the agency with the Board at the time of employment, and are exempt from the licensing law for a period of two years from the date of registration.[52]

Salaried employees of accredited or approved academic institutions, public schools, or governmental agencies can engage in activities of a psychological nature so long as they perform those activities as part of the duties for which they are hired, perform the duties solely within the jurisdiction of their organization, do not offer their services to the public for a fee, and do not use terms such as *psychology, psychological, psychologist, psychometrist, psychometrics,* or *psychometry.*[53]

The licensing law does not preclude graduate students or psychological interns from engaging in psychological activities as part of a training program so long as the activities constitute a part of a supervised course of study and they are clearly identified by terms such as *psychological intern* or *psychological trainee,* or another term indicating the training status and level of training. The term *psychological intern* is reserved for persons enrolled in a doctoral program of psychology or social psychology at an accredited or approved college or university.[54]

Additionally, the licensing law does not restrict a person who is licensed or certified as a psychologist in another state or territory from offering psychological services in California for a period not to exceed 30 days in any calendar year.[55]

(F) Grounds for Discipline

The Board of Psychology can deny an application for license, issue a license with terms and conditions, order the suspension or revocation of a license, or impose probationary conditions upon a license for any of the following reasons:

---

52. Bus. & Prof. Code § 2909(d).
53. Bus. & Prof. Code § 2910.
54. Bus. & Prof. Code § 2911.
55. Bus. & Prof. Code § 2912.

1. conviction of a crime substantially related to the qualifications, functions, or duties of a psychologist or psychological assistant;[56]

2. use of any controlled substance or dangerous drug, or any alcoholic beverage to any extent or in a manner dangerous to himself or herself, any other person, or the public, or to the extent that such substance use impairs his or her ability to perform the work of a psychologist with safety to the public;[57]

3. fraudulently or negligently misrepresenting the type or status of the license or registration that the person actually holds. A licensee is also precluded from misrepresenting or permitting the misrepresentation of his or her personal qualifications, affiliations, or purposes, or those of any institution, organization, product, or services with which he or she is associated;[58]

4. impersonating another person who holds a psychology license or allowing one's own license or registration to be used by another person;[59]

5. using fraud or deception in applying for a license or registration, or in passing the examinations required;[60]

6. accepting commissions or rebates or other forms of remuneration for referring professionals to other professionals;[61]

7. violating the provisions of the statute governing unlawful advertising;[62]

8. the willful or unauthorized breach of confidentiality by communicating information received in professional confidence;[63]

9. violating any rule of professional conduct promulgated by the Board;[64]

10. gross negligence in the practice of his or her profession;[65]

---

56. Bus. & Prof. Code § 2960(a). Under § 2963, a plea or verdict of guilty or a conviction following a plea of nolo contendere made to a charge substantially related to the qualifications, functions, and duties of a psychologist or psychological assistant is deemed to be a conviction for the purpose of this section.
57. Bus. & Prof. Code § 2960(b).
58. Bus. & Prof. Code § 2960(c); 16 CCR § 1396.2.
59. Bus. & Prof. Code § 2960(d).
60. Bus. & Prof. Code § 2960(e).
61. Bus. & Prof. Code § 2960(f).
62. Bus. & Prof. Code § 2960(g).
63. Bus. & Prof. Code § 2960(h).
64. Bus. & Prof. Code § 2960(1).
65. Bus. & Prof. Code § 2960(j). Gross negligence is defined as an extreme departure from the standard of care. *Franz v. Board of Medical Quality Assurance*, 31 Cal.3d 124, 181 Cal.Rptr. 732 (1982). Simple negligence will not support discipline unless it falls under another category.

11. violating any provisions of the law or the regulations adopted under the law;[66]

12. aiding or abetting any other person to engage in the unlawful practice of psychology;[67]

13. suspension, revocation, or imposition of probationary conditions by another state, where the person also holds a license or registration from California, and where the act for which the disciplinary action was imposed would constitute a violation of California law;[68]

14. the commission of any dishonest, corrupt, or fraudulent act, or any act of sexual abuse or sexual relations with a patient, or sexual misconduct that is substantially related to the qualifications, functions, or duties of a psychologist or psychological assistant;[69]

15. functioning outside his or her field of competency as established by his or her education, training, and experience;[70]

16. willful failure to submit verification of supervised experience to the Board on behalf of an applicant for licensure;[71]

17. a licensee either alone or in conjunction with a partnership or group using any fictitious, false, or assumed name, or any name other than his or her own, or as the name of a professional corporation in any public communication, advertisement, or announcement without obtaining a fictitious name permit;[72]

18. knowingly undertaking any activity in which the temporary or more enduring personal problems in the psychologist's personality may result in inferior professional services or harm to a patient or client;[73] and

19. failure to comply with the reporting requirements of the child abuse reporting law.[74]

---

66. Bus. & Prof. Code § 2960(k).
67. Bus. & Prof. Code § 2960(l).
68. Bus. & Prof. Code § 2960(m).
69. Bus. & Prof. Code §§ 2960(n), 726, 729; see Cooper v. Board of Medical Examiners, 49 Cal.App.3d 931, 123 Cal.Rptr. 563 (1975), and Dresser v. Board of Medical Quality Assurance, 130 Cal.App.3d 506 (1982), where psychologists' licenses were revoked for sexual activity with patients. Effective January 1, 1995, Bus. & Prof. Code § 2960.1 mandates revocation of license when an Administrative Law Judge (ALJ) finds that a licensee has had sex with a patient or with a former patient, where the professional relationship was terminated for the purpose of engaging in sex.
70. Bus. & Prof. Code § 2960(o); 16 CCR § 1396.
71. Bus. & Prof. Code § 2960(p).
72. Bus. & Prof. Code §§ 2960(q), 2920.5.
73. 16 CCR § 1396.1.
74. 16 CCR § 1397.1; Penal Code § 111166.

Although no specific statutory section exists defining dual relationships, when the Board finds that a dual relationship existed to a patient's detriment, a license may be suspended or revoked. However, the Board has experienced great difficulty in drafting an enforceable regulation concerning dual relationships, and instead has elected to proceed under either the definition contained in Principle 6 of the American Psychological Association's Ethical Principles or the theory that it is a type of gross negligence.[75]

In addition, the Board of Psychology can require a licensee or applicant to submit to a psychological evaluation to ascertain if his or her mental status is a risk to patients or the public, or to determine if the licensee is an impaired practitioner.[76] (See chapter 5B.1.)

(G) Penalties

A violation of the Psychology Licensing Law is a misdemeanor punishable by imprisonment in the county jail, not exceeding six months, or a fine not exceeding $2,000.[77] For a list of general license offenses see chapter 1.0A, section (C).

(H) Procedure for Discipline

The procedure for denial of licensure or imposition of discipline is the same as for psychiatrists, as discussed in chapter 1.0A, section (I).

---

75. *See* Jeffrey Younggren and Darlene Skorka, *The Nontherapeutic Psychotherapy Relationship*, 16 Law & Psychol. Rev. 13, 24-25 (1992).
76. Bus. & Prof. Code § 820.
77. Bus. & Prof. Code § 2970.

1.5

Subdoctoral and Unlicensed Psychologists

While some states allow individuals with master's degrees in psychology to practice independently as psychologists, in California individuals without doctoral degrees are allowed to practice psychology only to the extent that they fit within an express exemption to the Psychology Licensing Law. The majority of subdoctoral individuals practicing under the Psychology Law are psychological assistants. This chapter discusses the requirements for psychological assistants and psychologists exempt from licensure. The administrative procedure for imposition of discipline or denial of registration or licensure to psychological assistants is set forth in chapter 1.0A, section (I). In addition, chapter 1.0A sets forth additional substantive grounds for discipline or denial of a license.

(A) Psychologists Exempted From Licensure

(A)(1) Other Licensed MHPs

Only a licensed psychologist can use any title that includes the words *psychologist, psychology, psychological, psychological consultation, psychology consultant, psychometry, psychometrics, psychotherapy, psychotherapist, psychoanalysis,* and *psychoanalyst.*[1] There is a blanket exemption providing that the Psychology Licensing Law shall not be construed to prevent qualified licensed professionals, such as physicians; clinical social workers; educational

---

1. Bus. & Prof. Code § 2902(c).

psychologists; marriage, family, and child counselors; optometrists; psychiatric technicians; registered nurses; attorneys admitted to the bar; or individuals from using hypnotic techniques on referral from doctors, dentists, psychologists, or individuals using hypnotic techniques that offer avocational or vocational self-improvement and do not offer therapy of emotional or mental disorders. In addition, duly ordained members of the recognized clergy or duly ordained religious practitioners are not precluded from doing work of a psychological nature consistent with the laws governing their respective professions, so long as they do not hold themselves out by any title or description of services that implies that they are psychologists or licensed to practice psychology. However, licensed educational psychologists can use the word *psychologist* in referring to themselves as licensed educational psychologists.[2]

(A)(2) Public Employees/Nonprofit Agencies

Another category of exemptions concerns public employees. Public employees can perform psychological activities and use titles that would otherwise be prohibited, provided they are performing the services in question as part of the duties for which they were employed, they are performing those services solely within the confines of or under the jurisdiction of the organization by which they are employed, and they do not offer psychological services to the public for a fee over and above the salary they receive for performance of their official duties. Public employees who are specifically recognized to come within this exemption are as follows:

1. persons who hold valid and current credentials as school psychologists issued by the California Department of Education (*see* chapter 1.7);

2. persons who hold valid and current credentials as psychometrists issued by the California Department of Education (see chapter 1.7);

3. persons employed as psychologists or psychological assistants, or student counseling services by accredited or approved colleges, junior colleges, or universities; federal, state, county, or municipal government organizations that are not primarily involved in the provision of direct health or mental health services. However, without being licensed, these individuals can consult or disseminate their research findings and scientific information to other academic institutions or govern-

---

2. Bus. & Prof. Code § 2908.

mental agencies. These individuals may also offer lectures to the public for a fee without being licensed; and

4. individuals who possess an earned doctoral degree in psychology or in educational psychology, or in education with a field of specialization in counseling psychology or educational psychology (see chapter 1.7) or who possess an earned doctorate degree deemed equivalent by the Board to one from an accredited or approved university, college, or professional school. In addition, such persons must have one or more years of professional experience of a type that the Board determines will competently and safely permit the person to engage in the activities for which a license is required, if such individuals are employed by nonprofit community agencies that receive a minimum of 25% of their financial support from federal, state, county, or municipal governmental agencies for the purpose of training and providing services. However, these individuals shall be registered by the agency with the Board at the time of their employment, and shall be exempt from the licensing requirement for a maximum period of two years from the date of the registration.[3]

(A)(3) Individuals Employed by Academic Institutions

The law does not prevent or restrict activities of a psychological nature by persons who are salaried employees of accredited or approved academic institutions, public schools, or governmental agencies, so long as the following conditions are met:

1. they are performing the psychological activities as part of the duties for which they were hired;

2. the activities are performed solely within the jurisdiction or confines of the organization in question;

3. they do not use any title that incorporates the words *psychology, psychological, psychologist, psychometry, psychometrist,* or *psychoanalyst;*

4. they do not offer their services to the public for a fee; and

5. they do not provide direct health or mental health services.[4]

An additional exemption exists for graduate students or psychological interns pursuing a course of study leading to a graduate degree in psychology in an accredited or approved college or university who are working in a training program, provided that their services are part of a supervised course of study and the individuals are designated by a title, such as *psychological intern* or

---

3. Bus. & Prof. Code § 2909(a) to (e).
4. Bus. & Prof. Code § 2910.

psychological trainee, which clearly indicates their training status. The term *psychological intern* is reserved for individuals enrolled in a doctoral program in psychology or social psychology at an accredited or approved college or university.[5]

The Psychology Licensing Law also exempts psychologists who are licensed or certified in another state or territory of the United States or in a foreign country, only to the extent that they do not practice for more than 30 days in California in any calendar year.[6]

Only individuals who have a license or fall under the specified exemptions are allowed by law to call themselves psychologists or to use any of the other terms identified above that connote psychology practice. For many individuals the most significant limitation is the inability to use the term *psychotherapist*. The Board of Psychology will investigate and pursue claims of unauthorized practice.

(B) Rights and Responsibilities of Subdoctoral and Licensed Psychologists

Generally, anyone who falls within the categories specified as being exempt is still held to the standards of confidentiality that a licensed psychologist is held to. Psychological assistants, for example, are included within the psychotherapist-patient privilege and can be subject to civil suit and Board of Psychology discipline for failure to keep confidentiality. In addition, while no case has expressly so held, the Board of Psychology has generally taken the position that the standard of care does not vary between psychologists and psychological assistants, except that the psychologist can be held to a higher and broader standard because of the supervisorial duties imposed by law. However, a psychological assistant or exempt psychologist still is required to provide services within the standard of care, and to comply with the Board of Psychology's regulations, which include not functioning outside his or her field of competency,[7] not misrepresenting his or

---

5. Bus. & Prof. Code § 2911.
6. Bus. & Prof. Code § 2912.
7. 16 CCR § 1396. In *People v. Stanley*, 36 Cal.2d 253 (1984), a criminal defendant contended that it was improper to allow a psychological assistant to testify as to Rape Trauma Syndrome because she was not qualified. The Supreme Court disagreed. The court stated that while a psychological assistant's qualifications were not overwhelming, her six years of clinical experience did qualify her as an expert.

her qualifications or affiliations, not allowing his or her temporary or more enduring personal problems to result in inferior
professional services or harm to a patient or client,[8] and avoiding
sexual misconduct. In addition, a psychological assistant is required to identify his or her status to patients or clients (e.g., "I am
Dr. A.B., a registered psychological assistant to Dr. C.D.") when
engaging in any psychological activity.[9]

(B)(1) Definition of Psychological Assistant

To qualify as a psychological assistant, an individual must be
employed by a licensed psychologist, a licensed physician who is
board certified in psychiatry by the American Board of Psychiatry
and Neurology, by a clinic that provides mental health services,
or by a psychological corporation, a licensed psychology clinic, or
a medical corporation performing limited psychological functions.[10] The psychological assistant must have completed a master's degree in psychology or in education, with a field of specialization in psychology or in counseling psychology. In the alternative, the psychological assistant must have been admitted to a
doctorate degree program in psychology or in education, with a
field of specialization in psychology or in counseling psychology
after having satisfactorily completed three or more years of postgraduate education in psychology and having passed preliminary
doctoral examinations. An individual may also qualify as a psychological assistant with a doctoral degree from a California accredited or approved university, college, or professional school in
the United States or Canada.[11]

(B)(2) Limited Scope of Psychological Assistants

A psychological assistant is entitled to engage in only limited
psychological services and must be at all times under the immediate supervision of the licensed psychologist or the Board-certified
psychiatrist. The supervisor is responsible for ensuring that the
extent, kind, and quality of the psychological services the assistant provides are consistent with the assistant's training and
experience. In addition, the supervisor is responsible for the
psychological assistant's compliance with the regulations of the
Board of Psychology.[12]

No licensed psychologist can employ or supervise more than
three psychological assistants at any given time unless given specific authorization by the Board. In addition, no Board-certified

---

8. 16 CCR §§ 1396.2, 1396.1.
9. 16 CCR § 1396.4.
10. Bus. & Prof. Code § 2913.
11. Bus. & Prof. Code § 2913(b); 16 CCR § 1391.6.
12. Bus. & Prof. Code § 2913(c).

psychiatrist can employ or supervise more than one psychological assistant at any time. Clinics, psychological corporations, and medical corporations may not employ more than 10 psychological assistants at one time. No contract clinic may employ or supervise more than one psychological assistant for each designated full-time staff psychiatrist who is qualified and supervises psychological assistants. A psychological assistant is not allowed to provide psychological services to the public for money except as an employee of a licensed psychologist, licensed psychiatrist, contract clinic, psychological corporation, or medical corporation.[13]

The Board of Psychology regulations require the supervisor to be present on the premises at least 50% of the time professional services are being rendered by the psychological assistant. In addition, the supervisor is required to provide a minimum of one hour per week of individual, face-to-face supervision to the psychological assistant unless more supervision is required by regulation or by the nature of the limited functions performed by the psychological assistant.[14] A supervisor is required to inform each patient in writing prior to the rendering of services by the psychological assistant that the assistant is unlicensed and under the direction and supervision of the supervisor as an employee.[15] The supervisor of the psychological assistant is required to make a report before January 1 of each year, on a specific form put out by the Board, showing the nature of the limited psychological functions performed by the assistant and the total number of hours of supervision that year.[16] (See chapter 1.7 for a detailed discussion of the 1994 changes to the law regarding the qualifications and duties of supervisors.)

The supervisor or employer of a psychological assistant is precluded from charging a fee for supervision of the psychological assistant. In addition, a psychological assistant is precluded from having a proprietary interest (i.e., an ownership interest, such as being a partner or shareholder in a corporation) in the business of the supervisor. Additionally, the psychological assistant cannot rent, lease, or sublease office space from the supervisor.[17]

---

13. Bus. & Prof. Code § 2913(d).
14. 16 CCR § 1391.5.
15. 16 CCR § 1391.6(b).
16. 16 CCR § 1391.10.
17. 16 CCR § 1391.8.

(C) Grounds for Discipline

The grounds for discipline of a psychological assistant are the same as those discussed in chapter 1.4 for psychologists.

(D) Procedure for Discipline

The procedure for denial of licensure or disciplining a psychological assistant is discussed in chapter 1.0A, section (I).

1.6

Licensure and Regulation of Social Workers

This chapter addresses the requirement for social workers to become licensed and the grounds for which licenses may be denied, suspended, or revoked. The requirements for functioning as an associate clinical social worker are also discussed. Unlicensed social workers can function in a school setting, as addressed in chapter 1.8. The administrative procedure for imposition of discipline or denial of licensure is set forth in chapter 1.0A, section (H). In addition, chapter 1.0A sets forth additional substantive grounds for discipline or denial of a license.

(A) Definitions

There are two types of social work: clinical and nonclinical. The social worker licensing law defines clinical social work as follows:

1. *The practice of clinical social work* is defined as a service in which a special knowledge of social resources, human capabilities, and the part that unconscious motivation plays in determining behavior is directed at helping people to achieve more adequate, satisfying, and productive social adjustments. The application of social work principles and methods includes, but is not restricted to, counseling and using applied psychotherapy of a nonmedical nature with individuals, families, or groups; providing information and referral services; providing or arranging for the provision of social services; explaining or interpreting the psychosocial aspects in the situations of individuals, families, or groups; helping communities to organize,

provide, or impose social or health services; or doing research related to social work.

2. *Psychotherapy* is defined as the use of psychosocial methods within a professional relationship to assist the person or persons to achieve a better psychosocial adaptation to acquire greater human realization of psychosocial potential and adaptation, to modify internal and external conditions that affect individuals, groups, or communities in behavior, emotions, and thinking in respect to their intrapersonal and interpersonal processes.[1]

As described in chapter 1.1, licensed clinical social workers can function as research psychoanalysts without registering with the Medical Board.

(B) Board of Behavioral Science Examiners

Initially, the Board regulating social workers was called the Board of Social Work Examiners of the State of California, then the Social Worker and Marriage Counselor Qualifications Board of the State of California. However, currently the Board of Behavioral Science Examiners licenses social workers; marriage, family, and child counselors (chapter 1.9); and educational psychologists (chapter 1.7).

This Board is a division of the Department of Consumer Affairs and has 11 members.[2] Of the 11 members of the Board, two are state licensed clinical social workers; one is a licensed educational psychologist; two are marriage, family, and child counselors; and six are public members. Except for the six public members, each member of the Board must hold at least a master's degree from an accredited college or university and have at least two years of experience in his or her profession.[3] The members of the Board are appointed for a term of four years. The governor appoints four of the public members and all five licensed members with the advice and consent of the senate. The Senate Rules Committee and the Speaker of the Assembly each appoint one public member.[4]

Among the Board's duties are the following:

---

1. Bus. & Prof. Code § 4996.9.
2. Bus. & Prof. Code §§ 4990.2, 4990.1.
3. Bus. & Prof. Code § 4990.3.
4. Bus. & Prof. Code § 4990.5.

1. to enforce the provisions of the statute;
2. to examine and evaluate the qualifications of all applicants for licensure as a clinical social worker or for registration as an associate clinical social worker;
3. to adopt rules and regulations as may be necessary for the enforcement of the law and to prescribe the qualifications for licensure;[5] and
4. to take disciplinary action including the suspension or revocation of a license of a licensee or registrant who is guilty of unprofessional conduct.[6]

(C) License Requirements

To be licensed as a clinical social worker, an applicant must be at least 21 years of age, and must have received a master's degree from an accredited school of social work, had two years of post master's degree experience, completed adequate instruction and training in the subject of alcoholism and other chemical substance dependency, and not committed any crimes or acts that would constitute grounds for denial of licensure.[7]

(D) Associate Clinical Social Workers

To be registered as an associate clinical social worker, an individual must possess a master's degree from an accredited school or department of social work and must not have committed any crimes or acts constituting grounds for denial of licensure.[8] As part of the licensing process, the applicant must take and pass the oral and written examinations. If the applicant qualifies for licensure and successfully passes the examinations, the Board shall issue a license.[9]

The associate clinical social worker status is designed for individuals who wish to be credited with experience toward licensure requirements. It is analogous to the psychological assistant position discussed in chapters 1.4 and 1.6. As with the psychological assistants, an associate clinical social worker cannot

---

5. Bus. & Prof. Code § 4990.14.
6. Bus. & Prof. Code § 4992.3.
7. Bus. & Prof. Code § 4996.2.
8. Bus. & Prof. Code § 4996.18.
9. Bus. & Prof. Code § 4996.1.

provide social work services to the public for a fee except as an employee of a licensed supervisor.[10]

Supervisor is defined to mean responsibility for and control of the quality of social work services being provided, and is not equivalent to consultation. The supervisee shall have at least one hour per week of direct supervision for each week of experience claimed. At least half the hours of required supervision shall be individual supervision, which means that the supervisor and supervisee meet alone during the session, as distinct from group supervision. The remaining hours may be group supervision, which means one supervisor meeting with a group of no more than eight supervisees at a time.[11] A registrant employed in a private practice setting cannot pay his employer for supervision and shall be compensated fairly by the employer. The registrant in private practice can only be paid by his or her employer, and cannot receive any remuneration directly from patients. The registrant cannot have any proprietary interest in the employer's business, and cannot perform services at any place except where the employer regularly conducts business.[12] A registrant employed in a setting other than private practice can receive supervision by a person not employed by his or her employer when the supervisor has signed a written contract with the registrant's employer to accept the supervisory responsibility.[13]

An associate clinical social worker is required to inform each client or patient prior to performing any professional services that he or she is unlicensed and is under the supervision of a licensed professional. Any experience obtained under the supervision of a spouse or relative by blood or marriage shall not be credited toward the required hours of supervised experience. By the same token, any experience that is obtained under the supervision of a supervisor with whom the applicant has a personal relationship that undermines the authority or effectiveness of the supervision shall not be credited toward the required hours of supervised experience.[14]

---

10. Bus. & Prof. Code § 4996.18.
11. Bus. & Prof. Code § 4996.20(b).
12. Bus. & Prof. Code § 4996.20(c).
13. Bus. & Prof. Code § 4996.20(d).
14. Bus. & Prof. Code § 4996.18(f), (g).

(E) Exceptions to Licensing

(E)(1) Other Licensed MHPs

The statute does not preclude qualified professionals in other licensure categories from doing work of a psychosocial nature that would otherwise be done by licensed clinical social workers. However, when such professionals provide psychosocial services, they cannot hold themselves out to the public with any title or description that includes the words *psychosocial* or *clinical social worker* and cannot state or imply that they are licensed to practice clinical social work. Other professionals who may engage in work of a psychosocial nature are

1. physicians or surgeons;
2. licensed psychologists;
3. members of the State Bar of California;
4. licensed marriage, family, and child counselors; and
5. priests, rabbis, or ministers of any religious denomination.[15]

(E)(2) Public Employees/Nonprofit Agencies

In addition, the statute does not restrict or prevent activities of a psychosocial nature on the part of certain categories of individuals employed by governmental agencies or organizations, so long as the duties for which they are employed are performed under the jurisdiction of the organization by which they are employed. However, such individuals cannot offer clinical social work services to the public for a fee over and above the salary they receive for the performance of their official duties. These individuals include persons

1. employed by the U.S. Department of Health and Human Services;
2. employed in family or child services agencies;
3. employed in proprietary or nonproprietary private psychiatric clinics;
4. employed in accredited colleges, junior colleges, or universities;
5. employed in federal, state, county, or municipal government organizations or nonprofit organizations engaged in research, education, and services where the services are defined by a board composed of community representatives and professionals; and

---

15. Bus. & Prof. Code § 4996.13.

6. utilizing hypnotic techniques by referral from individuals licensed to practice medicine, dentistry, or psychology, or persons utilizing hypnotic techniques for avocational or vocational self-improvement and who do not offer therapy for emotional or mental disorders.[16]

(E)(3) Individuals Employed by Academic Institutions

In addition, the statute does not restrict or prevent work of a psychosocial nature on the part of individuals employed by accredited academic institutions, public schools, government agencies, or nonprofit institutions engaged in training of graduate students, or social work interns pursuing a course of study leading to a master's degree in social work from an accredited college or university or working in a recognized training program. However, these activities or services must constitute a part of a supervised course of study, and the individuals in such a program must be designated as social work interns or some other title indicating the training status appropriate to their level of training. The term *social work intern* is reserved for persons enrolled in a master's or doctoral training program in social work at an accredited school or department of social work.[17] Clinical social work services can be offered by individuals from other states in California, if the services are performed no more than five days in any calendar month. If an individual meets the requirements for licensure and resides in a state or territory of the United States or a foreign country that does not grant a certification or a license to clinical social workers, he or she may offer clinical social work services in California for a period not to exceed 30 days in any calendar year, without being licensed here.[18]

(F) Grounds for Discipline

The Board can refuse to issue a registration to an associate clinical social worker, or a license to an applicant, or may suspend or revoke the registration or license of any associate clinical social worker or licensed clinical social worker if the Board determines the individual has been guilty of unprofessional conduct. Unprofessional conduct is defined to include, but is not limited to,

1. the conviction of a crime substantially related to the qualifications, functions, or duties of a licensee or a registrant. A plea

---

16. Bus. & Prof. Code § 4996.14.
17. Bus. & Prof. Code § 4996.15.
18. Bus. & Prof. Code § 4996.16.

or verdict of guilty, or a conviction following a plea of nolo contendere, is considered to be a conviction within this provision of the statute;

2. securing a license or registration by fraud, deceit, or misrepresentation on any application for licensure or registration submitted to the Board, whether the individual subject to discipline is the applicant or is supporting an application;

3. self-administering any controlled substance or dangerous drugs or any alcoholic beverage, to the extent or in a manner as to be dangerous or injurious to the applicant or licensee, any other person, or to the public or to the extent that such substance use impairs the ability of the person applying for or holding a license or registration to conduct with safety to the public the practice authorized by the registration or license. In addition, the conviction of more than one misdemeanor or any felony involving the use, consumption, or self-administration of controlled substances, dangerous drugs, or alcoholic beverages as specified is grounds for discipline. Further, the Board shall deny the application for registration or license and shall revoke the license or registration of any person who uses or offers to use drugs in the course of providing clinical social work (this does not apply to licensed physicians);

4. gross negligence or incompetence in the performance of clinical social work;

5. violating, attempting to violate, or conspiring to violate the statute or any regulation adopted by the Board;

6. misrepresenting the type or status of license or registration the individual holds, or otherwise misrepresenting or permitting the misrepresentation of his or her education, professional qualifications, or professional affiliations;

7. impersonating another registrant or applicant or allowing another person to use his or her license or registration;

8. aiding and abetting any unlicensed or unregistered person to engage in conduct for which a license or registration is required;

9. intentionally or recklessly causing physical or emotional harm to any client;

10. committing any dishonest, corrupt, or fraudulent act substantially related to the qualifications, functions, or duties of a licensee or registrant;

11. engaging in sexual relations with a client, soliciting sexual relations with a client, committing an act of sexual abuse or sexual misconduct with the client, or committing an act

punishable as a sexually related crime if that act or solicitation is substantially related to the qualifications, functions, or duties of a clinical social worker;

12. performing or holding oneself out as being able to perform any professional services beyond the scope of the individual's license or allowing any registered associate clinical social worker or intern under supervision to perform professional services beyond the scope of their competency;

13. failing to maintain confidentiality except as otherwise required or permitted by law[19] of all information received from a client in confidence during a course of treatment and all information about the client obtained from tests;

14. failing to disclose to the client prior to the commencement of treatment the fee that will be charged for professional services or the basis for the fee;

15. paying, accepting, or soliciting any consideration, compensation, or remuneration, with a monitor or otherwise, for the referral of professional clients. Collaboration among two or more licensees in a case is allowable, but no fee can be charged for the collaboration except where it has been disclosed to the client;

16. advertising in any manner that is false, misleading, or deceptive;

17. reproducing or describing in public or in any publication subject to general public distribution any psychological tests or other assessment device, the value of which depends in whole or in part on the naivete of the subject in ways that might invalidate the test; and

18. any conduct in the supervision of any registered associate clinical social worker that violates the statute or any of the rules or regulations adopted by the Board.[20]

In addition, by regulation the Board has required that all licensed clinical social workers include their license or registration number in any professional advertisements unless such advertisement carries the full name of the licensee or corporation as filed with the Board and the designation of the type of license

---

19. *Compare Belmont v. California State Personnel Board*, 36 Cal.App.3d 518 (1976), where unlicensed social workers were held to be outside the psychotherapist–patient privilege, with *Luhdorff v. Superior Court*, 166 Cal.App.3d 485 (1985), where an unlicensed social worker was held to be within the privilege under Evid. Code § 1012.

20. Bus. & Prof. Code § 4992.3. Effective January 1, 1995, Bus. & Prof. Code § 4992.33 mandates revocation of license where an ALJ finds that a licensee engaged in sexual conduct with a patient or with a former patient, where the relationship was terminated to engage in sex.

held, e.g., *licensed clinical social worker*.[21] As a practical matter, it is in the interest of the licensee or registered intern to list the license number in any professional advertising to avoid a potential problem.

(G) Procedure for Discipline

The procedure for imposing discipline on licensed clinical social workers is the same as for marriage, family, and child counselors and licensed educational psychologists, as described in chapter 1.0A, section (H).

(H) Penalties

A violation of the Social Work Licensing Law is a misdemeanor punishable by imprisonment in the county jail, not to exceed a period of six months, or by a fine not to exceed $1,000, or both. For a list of general license offenses, see chapter 1.0A, section (C).

---

21. 16 CCR § 1811.

1.7

Licensure, Credentialing, and Regulation of Psychologists in the Schools

While licensed psychologists (see chapter 1.4) can function in the school system, such services are more typically provided by licensed educational psychologists and credentialed school psychologists.

Licensed educational psychologists and credentialed school psychologists generally address issues regarding the learning process or provide psychological services in a school setting. This chapter discusses the requirements for licensure of educational psychologists and credentialing of school psychologists, as well as grounds for revocation or suspension of such credentials or licenses. The administrative procedure for imposition of discipline or denial of licensure of educational psychologists is discussed in chapter 1.0A, section (H). In addition, chapter 1.0A sets forth additional substantive grounds for discipline or denial of licensure of educational psychologists. The administrative procedure for imposition of discipline or denial of credentialing of school psychologists is set forth in chapter 1.0B.

(A) Functions of an Educational Psychologist

The functions that a licensed educational psychologist can perform include the following:

1. educational evaluation, diagnosis, and limited test interpretation. The test interpretation is limited to the assessment of academic ability, learning patterns, achievement, motivation,

and personality factors directly related to academic learning programs;

2. counseling services for children or adults to remedy academic learning problems; and

3. educational consultation, research, and direct educational services.[1]

(B) Board of Behavioral Science Examiners

Educational psychologists are licensed by the Board of Behavioral Science Examiners, which also licenses marriage, family, and child counselors (chapter 1.9) and clinical social workers (chapter 1.6)

This Board is a division of the Department of Consumer Affairs and has 11 members.[2] Of the 11 members of the Board, two members are state-licensed clinical social workers; one is a licensed educational psychologist; two are marriage, family, and child counselors; and six are public members. Except for the six public members, each member of the Board must hold at least a master's degree from an accredited college or university and have at least two years of experience in his or her profession.[3] The members of the Board are appointed for a term of four years. The Governor appoints four of the public members and the five licensed members with the advice and consent of the senate. The Senate Rules Committee and the Speaker of the Assembly each appoint one public member.[4]

(C) Qualifications for Licensure

To obtain a license as an educational psychologist, an individual must possess at least a master's degree in psychology, educational psychology, school psychology, or counseling and guidance, or a degree that the Board, through its regulations, deems

---

1. Bus. & Prof. Code § 4986.10.
2. Bus. & Prof. Code §§ 4990.2, 4990.1.
3. Bus. & Prof. Code § 4990.3.
4. Bus. & Prof. Code § 4990.5.

equivalent and that is obtained from educational institutions approved by the Board.[5]

The applicant must meet the following criteria:

1. be at least 18 years of age;

2. not have committed any acts or crimes constituting grounds for denial of licensure;

3. have successfully completed 60 semester hours of postgraduate work devoted to pupil personnel services or have experience that the Board deems equivalent;[6] and

4. furnish proof of three years of full-time experience as a credentialed school psychologist in the public schools or experience that the Board deems equivalent.[7] If the applicant can provide proof of one year's internship working full-time as a school psychologist intern in the public schools in an acccredited internship program, one year's experience shall be credited;

5. furnish written statements from two sponsors who have personal knowledge of his or her professional competence. These statements must include a description of the applicant's functioning and an evaluation of his or her professional competence. The individuals who provide the statements as sponsors must also be qualified to be licensed educational psychologists;

6. be examined by the Board with respect to the professional functions to be performed as a licensed educational psychologist; and

---

5. Bus. & Prof. Code § 4986.20(a). Degrees deemed equivalent include a master's degree or its equivalent from a college or university accredited by the Western Association of Schools and Colleges, Northwest Association of Secondary and Higher Schools, Middle States Association of Colleges and Secondary Schools, New England Association of Colleges and Secondary Schools, North Central Association of Colleges and Secondary Schools, or Southern Association of Colleges and Schools. 16 CCR § 1854.

6. Equivalent experience includes teaching an approved course in pupil personnel services at an accredited institution if the applicant has taught the course for at least two semesters, the course has not been submitted by the applicant for credit as a postgraduate course, and the course is not a practicum or fieldwork course. 16 CCR § 1855.

7. Regarding experience equivalent to three years as a school psychologist: no more than one year of experience will be granted for any 12-month period; part-time experience may be accumulated if it is obtained within six calendar years; and parochial or private school experience may be deemed equivalent at the Board's discretion. If alternative experience is allowed, the applicant's sponsors must verify the experience in a written statement that includes information regarding the applicant's skill in administering tests, interpreting tests to other parties, classifying subjects for special programs, recognizing and diagnosing learning problems, recommending solutions, recognizing and ameliorating behavior problems, interpreting standardized group test scores, and using therapeutic techniques. 16 CCR § 1857.

7. have at least one year of supervised professional experience in an accredited school psychology program or under the direction of a licensed psychologist, or alternative experience that the Board determines to be suitable.[8]

If these criteria are met and the fees required by the Board are paid, a license shall be issued as an educational psychologist.[9]

(D) Grounds for Discipline

The Board may refuse to issue a license or may suspend or revoke the license of any licensed educational psychologist who is found guilty of unprofessional conduct that has endangered, or is likely to endanger, the health, welfare, or safety of the public.[10] Unprofessional conduct includes, but is not limited to,

1. conviction of any crime substantially related to the qualifications, functions, and duties of an educational psychologist.[11] When a licensed educational psychologist has been convicted of a crime, the record of the conviction is deemed to be conclusive evidence of the conviction;[12]

2. securing a license by fraud or deceit;[13]

3. using any narcotic or hypnotic drug or alcoholic beverage to an extent or in a manner that is dangerous to the licensee or to any other person or to the public, and to the extent that such substance abuse impairs his or her ability to perform his or

---

8. Bus. & Prof. Code § 4986.20(a) to (h). Experience equivalent to one year of supervised professional experience includes a minimum of 720 hours under professional supervision in the following: utilization of all instruments within the prescribed course of study at the institution attended with a wide variety of subjects, administration of other tests used by school psychologists, consultation with teachers regarding children in special education programs, referral to and use of community agencies, and oral and written communication of results. Additionally, the supervisor must consult with the intern weekly and have a valid credential in school psychology and a minimum of two years of experience. Finally, there must be a general supervisor who coordinates intern placement and meets with the local supervisor and/or the intern at least three times during the internship. The general supervisor must be either a credentialed school psychologist, a licensed psychologist, a licensed educational psychologist, or a state or accredited training institution designated supervisor of school psychology trainees. 16 CCR § 1857.
9. Bus. & Prof. Code § 4986.40.
10. Bus. & Prof. Code § 4986.70.
11. A substantial relationship exists if the crime evidences a present or potential unfitness of the licensee to perform the functions authorized by the license in a manner consistent with the public health, safety, or welfare. 16 CCR § 1812.
12. Bus. & Prof. Code § 4986.70(a).
13. Bus. & Prof. Code § 4986.70(b).

her work as a licensed educational psychologist with safety to the public;[14]

4. improper advertising;[15]

5. violating or conspiring to violate the terms of the statute on the licensure of educational psychologists;[16]

6. committing any dishonest or fraudulent act as a licensed educational psychologist resulting in a substantial injury to another;[17]

7. soliciting or having sexual relations with a client or committing an act of sexual abuse or misconduct, if the act or solicitation is substantially related to the qualifications, functions, or duties of an educational psychologist;[18]

8. failing to maintain confidentiality of all information received from a client during the course of therapy, except as required or permitted by law;[19]

9. failing to comply with the child abuse reporting requirements;[20]

10. misrepresenting qualifications or the type or status of license;[21]

11. intentionally or recklessly causing physical or emotional harm to a client;[22]

12. failing to disclose to a client the fee to be charged prior to commencement of treatment;[23]

13. holding oneself out as able to perform services beyond one's area of competence or allowing someone under one's supervision to do so;[24]

---

14. Bus. & Prof. Code § 4986.70(c).
15. Bus. & Prof. Code § 4986.70(d); 16 CCR § 1858. Licensed educational psychologists who advertise must include their license number unless the advertisement contains the licensee's name as registered with the Board and the type of license issued. 16 CCR § 1811.
16. Bus. & Prof. Code § 4986.70(e).
17. Bus. & Prof. Code § 4986.70(f). Note that this specific subsection is somewhat more vague, and perhaps broader, than for licensed psychologists and marriage, family, and child counselors, whose licensing laws require the dishonest or fraudulent act to be related to the qualifications, functions, or duties of the position and generally refers to the injury in terms of the patient, not "another." See Bus. & Prof. Code §§ 2960(n), 4982(j). Cf. 16 CCR § 1858(e), which states the conduct must be substantially related to the qualifications, functions, or duties of a licensee.
18. 16 CCR § 1858(k).
19. Penal Code § 11166; 16 CCR § 1858(o).
20. 16 CCR § 1858(h).
21. 16 CCR § 1858(a), (g).
22. 16 CCR § 1858(d).
23. 16 CCR § 1858(l).
24. 16 CCR § 1858(i), (j).

14. when employed by another person or agency, encouraging the client to use one's private practice for further counseling without the approval of the employer;[25]

15. impersonating a licensee or allowing another to use one's license;[26] or

16. reproducing or describing in public, or in publications distributed to the general public, any psychological test or assessment device that depends in whole or part on the naivete of the test subject, in a manner that might invalidate the test.[27]

When a license or registration has been denied, the Board will evaluate the rehabilitation of the applicant and the applicant's present eligibility for a license or registration based on the following criteria:

1. the nature and severity of the acts or crimes that were grounds for denial;

2. evidence of subsequent acts that would also be grounds for denial;

3. the time elapsed since the commission of the acts or crimes;

4. the extent of compliance with the terms of probation, parole, restitution, or other sanctions; and

5. evidence of rehabilitation submitted by the applicant.[28]

Where a license has been suspended or revoked, in addition to the preceding factors, the Board will consider

1. evidence of expungement proceedings;[29]

2. if a false statement was made in the application for licensure, evidence that the statement was unintentional, inadvertent, or immaterial; and

3. efforts made by the applicant to either correct a false statement made in an application or to conceal the truth regarding facts required to be disclosed.[30]

(E) Penalties

A violation of the provisions of the statute on licensed educational psychologists is technically a misdemeanor.[31] When any person

---

25. 16 CCR § 1858(f).
26. 16 CCR § 1858(b).
27. 16 CCR § 1858(n).
28. 16 CCR § 1813.
29. *See* Penal Code § 1203.4.
30. 16 CCR § 1814.
31. Bus. & Prof. Code § 4986.81.

has engaged in or is about to engage in acts or practices that constitute or will constitute a violation of the provisions of this statute, the attorney general or the district attorney of the county in which the acts take place, or are about to take place, can petition the superior court for an injunction or other appropriate order restraining such conduct.[32] Further, the Board may adopt, amend, or repeal rules of professional conduct in order to establish and maintain a high standard of integrity and dignity, provided that the rules of the Board are not inconsistent with section 4986.70.[33]

(F) Credentialed School Psychologists

The qualifications for a school psychologist are a valid certificate issued by the appropriate agency and a services credential with a specialization in health. A services credential with a specialization in health is issued by the Commission on Teacher Credentialing. Any school district can employ psychologists with these qualifications.[34]

Individuals who are credentialed as school psychologists are not allowed to offer services to the public for a fee, but may provide those services only within the context of the educational system.

The minimum requirements for a services credential with a specialization in health are

1. five years of college or university education or five years of approved professional preparation;

2. the possession of a valid license certificate of registration appropriate to the designated health service, which has been issued by the appropriate California licensing agency (for marriage, family, and child counselors; social workers; and educational psychologists, this would be the Board of Behavioral Science Examiners; for psychologists, this would be the Board of Psychology); and

3. such additional requirements as may be required by the Commission.

A services credential with a specialization in health authorizes the holder to perform health services as approved by the Commission at all grade levels.[35]

---

32. Bus. & Prof. Code § 4986.90.
33. Bus. & Prof. Code § 4987.
34. Educ. Code § 44874.
35. Educ. Code § 44267.

Other requirements for the issuance of certificates are

1. taking the oath to support the Constitution and the laws of the United States and the state of California;[36]

2. knowledge of the Constitution of the United States from a college level course;[37]

3. when required by the Commission, producing a certificate from a licensed physician attesting that the individual is free from contagious and communicable or disabling diseases that would make it unfitting for the applicant to instruct or associate with children;[38]

4. good moral character and producing reasonable evidence of such moral character; and

5. no determination of being a sexual psychopath, conviction of any sex offense, or conviction of any offense involving controlled substances, unless a certificate of rehabilitation has been obtained and probation has been terminated. However, as to an individual who has been convicted of a controlled substance offense, the Commission must also determine that the person has been rehabilitated for at least five years or has received a certificate of rehabilitation and pardon.[39]

Credentials are valid until revoked, suspended, or expired by law.[40]

(G) Grounds for Discipline

The credentials can be revoked pursuant to a hearing before the Commission for immoral or unprofessional conduct, persistent defiance of and refusal to obey the laws regulating the duties of persons serving in the school system, or for any cause that would have warranted the denial of an application.[41]

However, the California Supreme Court has expressly held that to deny a certificate on the grounds of immoral or unprofessional conduct, there must be some nexus between the conduct and the teacher's duties. Where the sole cause was a teacher's private homosexual activity, a court found a lack of nexus and ruled that discipline could not be imposed.[42]

---

36. Educ. Code § 44334.
37. Educ. Code § 44335.
38. Educ. Code § 44336.
39. Educ. Code § 44436.
40. Educ. Code § 44435.
41. Educ. Code § 44421.
42. *Morrison v. State Board of Education*, 1 Cal.3d 214 (1969).

A license can be revoked as described in chapter 1.0B for conviction of a crime;[43] conviction of a sex or narcotics offense;[44] under the prior sexual psychopath law, being determined to be a sexual psychopath;[45] or immoral and unprofessional conduct or disobedience.[46]

(H) Procedure for Discipline

The procedure on disciplining credentialed school psychologists is discussed in chapter 1.0B.

---

43. Educ. Code § 44424.
44. Educ. Code § 44425.
45. Educ. Code § 44426.
46. Educ. Code § 44427.

Credentialing and Regulation of School Counselors and Social Workers

The California Department of Education and the Commission on Teacher Credentialing (see chapter 1.0B) set the criteria for the hiring and continued employment of various professionals in the school system. Other than the licensed educational and school psychologists discussed in chapter 1.7, social workers and school guidance counselors generally provide mental health-related services in the school system. This chapter discusses the criteria for credentialing school, social, and guidance counselors, and the grounds for discipline. The administrative procedure for the imposition of discipline or denial of a credential is set forth in chapter 1.0B.

(A) Types of Credentials

The Commission on Teacher Credentialing issues only two types of credentials: a teaching credential and a services credential.[1] There are, in turn, four categories of credentials based on time and status:

1. an internship credential, which is valid for two years;

2. a preliminary credential, pending completion of the fifth year of study, which is for five years;

3. a life credential, which is valid for the life of the holder; and

4. an emergency credential, which is valid for one year.[2]

---

1. Educ. Code § 44250.
2. Educ. Code § 44251.

The credential most applicable to social workers and school guidance counselors is either a service credential with specialization in pupil personnel services or a service credential with specialization in health.

(B) Services Credential With Specialization in Pupil Personnel Services

The minimum requirements for a services credential with a specialization in pupil personnel services are a bachelor's degree or a higher degree, except in professional education, from an approved institution, and a fifth year of study. An additional requirement would be any specialized professional preparation that the Commission may establish, including supervised field experience and direct classroom contact. The services credential with a specialization in pupil personnel services authorizes the holder to perform, at all grade levels, services approved by the Commission as designated on the credential, which may include, but are not limited to, school counseling, school psychology, child welfare, attendance services, and school social work.[3]

(C) Services Credential With Specialization in Health

The minimum requirements for a services credential with a specialization in health are

1. five years of college or university education or five years of approved professional preparation; and

2. the possession of a valid license certificate of registration appropriate to the designated health service, which has been issued by the appropriate California licensing agency (for marriage, family, and child counselors; social workers; and educational psychologists, this would be the Board of Behavioral Science Examiners; for psychologists, this would be the Board of Psychology); and

3. such additional requirements as may be required by the Commission.

---

3. Educ. Code § 44266.

A services credential with a specialization in health authorizes the holder to perform at all grade levels health services as approved by the Commission, but not services such as audiometrist, occupational therapist, or physical therapist.[4]

Additionally, there are special health credentials for school nurses.[5]

(D) Additional General Requirements

Other requirements for the issuance of certificates are

1. taking the oath to support the Constitution and laws of the United States and the state of California.[6] (Although in the past that requirement has been subject to constitutional attack);[7]

2. knowledge of the Constitution of the United States from a college level course;[8]

3. when required by the Commission, producing a certificate from a licensed physician attesting that the individual is free from contagious and communicable or disabling diseases that would make it unfitting for the applicant to instruct or associate with children;[9]

4. good moral character and producing reasonable evidence of such moral character; and

5. not having been determined to be a sexual psychopath, convicted of any sex offense, or convicted of any offense involving controlled substances, unless a certificate of rehabilitation has been obtained and probation has been terminated. However, as to an individual who has been convicted of a controlled substance offense, the Commission must also determine that the person has been rehabilitated for at least five years or has received a certificate of rehabilitation and pardon.[10]

One lawsuit contended that the state was liable for the molestation of students by teachers where a teaching credential was not denied and an applicant had been convicted of a sex offense.

---

4. Educ. Code § 44267.
5. Educ. Code § 44267.5.
6. Educ. Code § 44334.
7. *MacKay v. Rafferty*, 321 F.2d 1177 (D.C. 1970), aff'd, 400 U.S. 954.
8. Educ. Code § 44335.
9. Educ. Code § 44336.
10. *Id.*

However, the suit was unsuccessful because the court concluded the statute was not intended to create a basis for civil suits.[11]

Credentials are valid until revoked, suspended, or expired by law.[12]

(E) Grounds for Discipline

The credentials can be revoked pursuant to a hearing before the Commission for immoral or unprofessional conduct, persistent defiance of and refusal to obey the laws regulating the duties of persons serving in the school system, or for any cause that would have warranted the denial of an application.[13]

However, the California Supreme Court has expressly held that to deny a certificate on the grounds of immoral or unprofessional conduct, there must be some nexus between the conduct and the teacher's duties. Where the sole cause was a teacher's private homosexual activity, a court found a lack of nexus and held that discipline could not be imposed.[14]

A credential or certificate can be revoked for conviction of a crime,[15] conviction of a sex or narcotics offense[16] under the prior sexual psychopath law, being determined to be a sexual psychopath,[17] or immoral and unprofessional conduct or disobedience.[18]

(F) Procedure for Discipline

The procedure for imposing discipline on an MHP with a credential or certificate from the Department of Education is discussed in chapter 1.0B.

---

11. *State v. Superior Court*, 8 Cal.App.4th 954 (1992).
12. Educ. Code § 44435.
13. Educ. Code § 44421.
14. *Morrison v. State Board of Education*, 1 Cal.3d 214 (1969).
15. Educ. Code § 44424.
16. Educ. Code § 44425.
17. Educ. Code § 44426.
18. Educ. Code § 44427.

1.9

Licensure and Regulation of Marriage, Family, and Child Counselors

This chapter discusses the requirements for licensure of marriage, family, and child counselors (MFCCs) and MFCC interns under the Marriage, Family, and Child Counseling Law,[1] as well as grounds for denial of license and imposition of discipline on MFCCs. The administrative procedure for imposition of discipline or denial of licensure is set forth in chapter 1.0A, section (H). In addition, chapter 1.0A sets forth additional substantive grounds for discipline or denial of a license.

(A) Definition of MFCC Practice

The practice of marriage, family, and child counseling is defined as performing services with individuals, couples, or groups where interpersonal relationships are examined for the purpose of achieving more adequate, satisfying, and productive marriage and family adjustments. This includes relationship and premarital counseling. The application of marriage, family, and child counseling principles and methods includes, but is not limited to, the use of applied psychotherapeutic techniques to enable individuals to mature and grow within marriage in the family and providing explanations and interpretations of the psychosexual and psychosocial aspects of relationships.[2]

A person is engaging in the practice of marriage, family, and child counseling by performing or offering to perform or holding himself or herself out as able to perform such services for remu-

---

1. Bus. & Prof. Code § 4980 et seq.
2. Bus. & Prof. Code § 4980.02.

neration in any form, including donations.[3] No person may for remuneration engage in the practice of marriage, family, and child counseling unless he or she holds a valid license as an MFCC, or unless he or she is specifically exempt from the licensure requirement. Nor may any person advertise himself or herself as performing the services of a marriage, family, child, domestic, or marital consultant or in any way use similar titles to imply that he or she performs marriage, family, and child counseling services without a license. Persons licensed under the Psychology Licensing Law and the Social Work Act may engage in the practice of marriage, family, and child counseling and may advertise that they practice marriage, family, and child counseling, but may not advertise that they hold an MFCC license.[4] As discussed in chapter 1.1, MFCCs can function as research psychoanalysts without registering with the Medical Board.

Although MFCCs can use applied psychotherapeutic techniques and are psychotherapists for the purpose of the psychotherapist-patient privilege under the Evidence Code, they cannot use terms such as *psychotherapist*, *psychological consultation*, and *psychotherapy* in holding themselves out to the public.[5] MFCCs can diagnose and treat mental disorders and construct, administer, and interpret psychological tests, within the scope of their licenses.[6]

(B) Board of Behavioral Science Examiners

The Board of Behavioral Science Examiners administers the provisions of the licensing law[7] and consists of 11 members, six of

---

3. Bus. & Prof. Code § 4980.10. This statute does not constrict, limit, or withdraw the Medical Practice Act, the Social Work Licensing Law, the Nursing Practice Law, or the Psychology Licensing Law. The statute does not apply to any priest, rabbi, or minister of the gospel of any religious denomination when performing counseling services that are part of his or her pastoral or professional duties, or to any person who is admitted to practice law in the state of California or who is licensed to practice medicine when providing counseling services as part of his or her professional practice. In addition, the law does not apply to an employee of a governmental entity or of a school, college, university, or of an institution that is both nonprofit and charitable, if his or her practice is performed solely under the supervision of the school or organization by which he or she is employed and if he or she performs such functions as part of his or her employment. Bus. & Prof. Code § 4980.01.
4. Bus. & Prof. Code § 4980(b).
5. Bus. & Prof. Code § 2902; 49 Op. Atty. Gen. 104 (1967).
6. 58 Op. Atty. Gen. 186 (1975); 66 Op. Atty. Gen. 278 (1984).
7. Bus. & Prof. Code § 4980.07.

whom are public members.[8] Each member of the Board holds office for a term of four years.[9] Two members of the Board shall be licensed clinical social workers, one member shall be a licensed educational psychologist, and two members shall be licensed MFCCs. Each nonpublic member of the Board must hold at least a master's degree from an accredited college or university and shall have at least two years of experience in his or her profession.[10] The governor appoints four of the public members and five of the licensees who are members of the Board with the advice and consent of the senate. The Senate Rules Committee and the Speaker of the Assembly each appoint one public member.[11]

Among the Board's duties are administering and enforcing the provisions of the licensing law, enacting regulations to effectuate the law, establishing standards of ethical conduct for MFCCs, and examining and passing upon the qualifications of the applicants for licenses.[12] In addition, the Board can order the denial of an application for licensure or registration, or revoke or suspend existing licenses or registrations.[13]

(C) Licensure Requirements

The individuals who are seeking to become MFCCs must meet the statutory criteria, pay the requisite fees, and pass the specified examination. Applicants for licensure must meet the following criteria:

1. be at least 18 years old;[14]

2. possess a doctorate degree or master's degree in marriage, family, and child counseling; marital and family therapy; psychology; clinical psychology; counseling psychology; or counseling with an emphasis on marriage, family, and child counseling; or social work with an emphasis on clinical social work. The degree must be obtained from a school, university, or college accredited by the Western Association of Schools and Colleges, Northwest Association of Secondary and Higher Schools, or an essentially equivalent accrediting agency as

---

8. Bus. & Prof. Code §§ 4990.1, 4990.3.
9. Bus. & Prof. Code § 4990.5.
10. Bus. & Prof. Code § 4990.3.
11. Bus. & Prof. Code § 4990.5.
12. Bus. & Prof. Code §§ 4980.34, 4980.35, 4980.60, 4982.
13. Bus. & Prof. Code § 4982.25.
14. Bus. & Prof. Code § 4980.40(e).

determined by the Board or as approved by the Council for Private Post Secondary and Vocational Education;[15]

3. have at least two years of professional experience in interpersonal relationships; marriage, family, and child counseling; and psychotherapy under the supervision of a licensed MFCC, licensed clinical social worker, licensed psychologist, or licensed physician certified in psychiatry by the American Board of Psychiatry and Neurology. As of January 1, 1994, experience cannot be obtained under the supervision of an individual who has also provided therapeutic services to the supervisee. Where the supervisorial relationship began on or before December 31, 1988, and remains in continuous effect thereafter, the supervisor may be a licensed physician who has completed a residency in psychiatry;[16]

4. take and pass an oral and written examination unless exempted by the Board;[17]

5. complete the course work specified by the Board, including course work in contemporary professional ethics and the statutory, regulatory, and case law that delineates the scope of practice, ethical standards, psychotherapist-patient privilege, confidentiality, dangerousness of patient to self and others, human sexuality, alcoholism or chemical substance dependency, and child abuse assessment and reporting;[18] and

---

15. Bus. & Prof. Code § 4980.40(a). Accrediting agencies equivalent to the Western Association of Schools and Colleges include the Middle States Association of Colleges and Secondary Schools, New England Association of Schools and Colleges, North Central Association of Colleges and Secondary Schools, and Southern Association of Colleges and Schools. In addition, the Credentials Evaluation Service of the International Education Research Foundation, Inc., when it evaluates foreign degrees as being equivalent to the degrees required by the licensing law and where those foreign degree programs meet the educational requirements for equivalent degrees and specific course content and educational requirements set forth by the statute. Further, the state of California, Department of Education, Bureau of School Approvals, is deemed an equivalent accrediting agency with respect to its functions under the Education Code when applied to a master's degree or doctoral program that meets the requirements for an equivalent degree and the specific course content and educational requirements of the statute. 16 CCR § 1832.

16. Bus. & Prof. Code § 4980.40(f).

17. Bus. & Prof. Code §§ 4980.40(g), 4980.50.

18. Bus. & Prof. Code §§ 4980.40(d), 4980.41; 16 CCR §§ 1807, 1807.2, 1810.

6. not have committed acts or crimes constituting grounds for denial of licensure.[19]

The statute provides that the Board shall examine the applicant with regard to his or her knowledge and professional skills and his or her judgment in the use of appropriate techniques and methods.[20] The application and all required supporting documents must be filed with the Board no later than 60 days before the scheduled written examination, and the fees must be paid before the exam is administered.[21] The applicant who fails the written or oral examination may retake the examination within one year of the date and the failure without further application, upon payment of the required examination fees. Thereafter, the applicant shall not be eligible for further examination unless a new application is filed that meets all requirements of the law and unless all required fees are paid.[22] An applicant who is unsuccessful on the exam may request reconsideration in writing within 30 days following the date of mailing of the notification that he or she has failed the exam. The Board shall retain all written examinations for at least one year following the date of the examination and shall keep an accurate record of all oral examinations for at least one year following the date of the examination.[23]

In order to qualify as a doctorate or master's degree program, for purposes of the licensing law, the program shall contain no less than 48 semester units or 72 quarter units of instruction, including no less than 12 semester units or 18 quarter units of course work in marriage, family, and child counseling and marital and family systems approaches to treatment. The coursework must include

1. salient theories of a variety of psychotherapeutic orientations that are directly related to marriage, family, and child counseling and marital and family systems approaches to treatment;

---

19. Bus. & Prof. Code § 4980.50; However, where an applicant has passed the written examination but is the subject of a complaint or is under Board investigation for acts or conduct that, if proven to be true, would constitute grounds for the Board to deny licensure, the Board shall permit the applicant to take the oral examination but may withhold the results of the examination or notify the applicant that a license will not be granted until the investigation is complete. In addition, the Board may deny any applicant who has previously failed the written or oral examination permission to retake either examination pending the completion of an investigation of complaints against the applicant. *Id.*
20. Bus. & Prof. Code § 4980.50.
21. Bus. & Prof. Code § 4984.7; 16 CCR § 1805.
22. 16 CCR § 1833.3; Bus. & Prof. Code § 4984.7(g), (h).
23. Bus. & Prof. Code § 4980.50.

2. theories of marriage and family therapy and how they can be used to intervene therapeutically with couples, families, adults, children, and groups;

3. developmental issues and life events from infancy to old age and their effect upon individuals, couples, and family relationships. This may include course work focusing on specific family life events such as childbirth, child rearing, adolescence, marriage, divorce, etc., and the psychotherapeutic, psychological, and health implications of them; and

4. a variety of approaches to the treatment of children.[24]

In addition to the 12 semester or 18 quarter units of course work specified above, for a doctorate or master's degree to qualify, the program must contain not less than six semester units or nine quarter units of a supervised practicum in applied psychotherapeutic techniques, and assessment, diagnosis, prognosis and treatment of premarital, couple, family, and child relationships, including dysfunctions, healthy functioning, health promotion, and illness prevention in a supervised clinical placement that provides supervised fieldwork experience within the scope of an MFCC license. Supervised practicum hours shall be evaluated, accepted, and credited as hours of trainee experience by the Board. Beginning January 1, 1995, the practicum must include a minimum of 150 hours of face-to-face experience counseling individuals, couples, and groups. In addition, the practicum hours shall be considered as part of the 48-semester-unit or 72-quarter-unit requirement for licensure.[25] The degree program must also include the following:

1. provide an integrated course of study that trains students generally in the diagnosis, assessment, prognosis, and treatment of mental disorders;

2. prepare students to be familiar with the broad range of matters that may arise within marriage and family relationships;

3. train students specifically in the application of marriage and family relationship counseling principles and methods;

4. encourage students to develop personal qualities that are intimately related to the counseling situation, such as integrity,

---

24. Bus. & Prof. Code § 4980.40(a).
25. Bus. & Prof. Code § 4980.40(b). Educational institutions are encouraged by the state to include the practicum experience in low-income and multicultural mental health centers. Further, as an alternative to the qualifications set forth above, the Board shall accept as equivalent degrees, master's or doctorate degrees granted by educational institutions, provided that these degree programs are approved by the Commission on Accreditation for Marriage and Family Therapy Education.

sensitivity, flexibility, insight, compassion, and personal presence;

5. teach students a variety of effective psychotherapeutic techniques and modalities that may be utilized to improve, restore, or maintain healthy individual, couple, and family relationships;

6. permit an emphasis or specialization that may address any one or more of the unique and complex array of human problems, symptoms, and needs of Californians served by MFCCs; and

7. prepare students to be familiar with cross-cultural morals and values, including familiarity with a wide range of racial and ethnic backgrounds among California's population.[26]

(D) Supervised Professional Experience

The supervised professional experience required by the statute shall consist of 3,000 hours obtained over a period of not less than 104 weeks. Not less than 1,500 hours of experience shall be gained subsequent to the granting of the applicant's master's or doctorate degree. For applicants enrolled in a qualifying degree program after January 1, 1995, no more than 750 hours of counseling and direct supervision contact can be obtained prior to the granting of a master's or doctorate degree. However, this limitation does not apply to professional enrichment activities. Professional enrichment activities may include group, marital, or conjoint family or individual psychotherapy received by an applicant. This psychotherapy may include up to 100 hours taken subsequent to enrollment and commencing a qualified degree program, or as an intern, and each of those hours shall be triple-counted toward the professional experience requirement. The psychotherapy must be from a licensed MFCC, licensed clinical social worker, licensed psychologist, licensed physician certified in psychiatry by the American Board of Psychiatry and Neurology, or a licensed physician who has completed a residency in psychiatry. Except for personal psychotherapy hours earned after enrollment and commencement of classes in a qualifying degree program, no hours of experience may be obtained prior to becoming a trainee. All the supervised experience shall be gained within the six years immediately preceding the date the application for licensure is filed, except that up to 500 hours of clinical experience

---

26. Bus. & Prof. Code § 4980.37.

gained in the supervised practicum required as part of the applicant's education shall be exempt from the six-year requirement.[27]

(E) Trainees and Interns

The experience may be gained as a trainee or as an MFCC intern. Effective January 1, 1994, a *trainee* is defined as an unlicensed person currently enrolled in a master's or doctorate degree program designed to qualify the person for licensure as an MFCC and who has completed no less than 12 semester units or 18 quarter units of course work in any qualifying degree program. An *intern* is defined as an unlicensed person who has earned a master's or doctorate degree qualifying him or her for licensure and who is registered with the Board.[28] A trainee may gain supervised experience in a governmental entity, school, college, university, nonprofit or charitable corporation, or a licensed health facility, if the experience is gained by the trainee solely as a part of the position for which he or she is employed. An MFCC intern may gain experience in the same setting as a trainee may, or when the intern is employed in a private practice owned by a licensed MFCC, a licensed psychologist, a licensed clinical social worker, a licensed physician and surgeon, or a professional corporation of any of those licensed professionals. An intern or trainee may gain hours of experience as a volunteer, but the supervision requirements still apply. Employment of an intern in a private practice setting cannot commence until the applicant has been registered as an intern with the Board. When an intern is employed in a private practice setting, the intern should be under the direct supervision of a licensed MFCC, a licensed clinical social worker, a licensed psychologist, or a licensed physician certified in psychiatry by the American Board of Psychiatry and Neurology.[29]

Interns are required to register with the Board in order to be credited for postdegree hours of experience gained toward licensure, regardless of the setting where the hours are gained. All postdegree hours of experience are to be gained as a registered intern; however, postdegree hours of experience can be credited toward licensure where the applicant applies for the intern registration within 90 days of the granting of the qualifying master's or doctorate degree, and the registration is thereafter granted by the

---

27. Bus. & Prof. Code § 4980.43(a), (d)(2).
28. Bus. & Prof. Code § 4980.03.
29. Bus. & Prof. Code § 4980.43(b), (c).

Board.[30] Since January 1, 1994, trainees may perform services for a governmental entity, school, college, university, nonprofit or charitable operation, or a licensed health facility, and that work may constitute experience for the license requirements if the experience is gained by the trainee solely as part of the position for which he or she is employed. The trainee may work in such settings provided that he or she is designated by the title *trainee* and the activities constitute part of the trainee's supervised course of study. A trainee may gain hours of experience outside the required practicum. As of January 1, 1995, all hours of experience gained by a trainee must be coordinated between the trainee's school and the site where the hours are being accrued. The school must approve each site and have a written agreement detailing each party's responsibilities, including the methods by which supervision will be provided. The agreement must provide for regular progress reports and evaluations of the trainee's perform- ance at the site. If an applicant for licensure has gained hours of experience while enrolled in a school other than the one con- firming the other degree, it is the applicant's responsibility to provide to the Board satisfactory evidence that the hours of trainee experience were gained in conformance with the law.[31]

Trainees and interns are not allowed to receive any remuner- ation from patients or clients and can be paid only by their employer. The interns are precluded from paying their employers for supervision, but are required to be paid fairly.[32]

Trainees and interns are allowed to perform services only at the place where their employer regularly conducts business and are precluded from having a proprietary interest in the bus- iness.[33] Interns and trainees are required to receive at least one hour of individual supervision per week for a minimum of 52 weeks. A trainee must also receive one hour of direct supervision contact for every five hours of client contact in each setting in which exposure is gained. An intern must also receive at least one hour of direct supervision contact for every 10 hours of client contact in each setting in which experience is gained. The 5:1 and 10:1 ratios just referred to apply to all hours gained after January 1, 1995. One hour of direct supervision contact means one hour of face-to-face contact in a group of not more than eight people. Any experience obtained under the supervision of a spouse or relative by blood or marriage will not be credited toward the required hours of experience. Any experience obtained under the supervi- sion of a supervisor with whom the applicant has a personal

---

30. Bus. & Prof. Code § 4980.43(d), (e).
31. Bus. & Prof. Code § 4980.42.
32. Bus. & Prof. Code § 4980.43(c), (f).
33. Bus. & Prof. Code § 4980.43(g).

relationship that undermines the authority or effectiveness of the supervisor will not be credited toward the hours of experience.[34] No intern or trainee will be given credit for more than 40 hours of experience in a given week. No more than 500 hours of experience will be credited for providing group therapy or counseling. Up to 500 hours of experience will be credited for administering and evaluating psychological tests of counselees, writing clinical reports, and writing progress and/or process notes. However, for any person who enrolled in a qualifying degree program on or after January 1, 1990, no more than 250 hours of experience will be credited for such work. Additionally, no more that 250 hours of experience will be credited for actual time spent counseling or crisis counseling on the telephone for individuals who enrolled in a qualifying degree program on or after January 1, 1990. Not less than 500 hours of experience can be gained in diagnosing and treating couples, families, and/or children for any person who enrolled in a qualifying degree program on or after January 1, 1990.[35]

Where interns are employed in private practice and are supervised by someone other than the employer, the supervisor must be employed by and practice at the same site as the intern's employer. In a setting that is not a private practice, the authorized supervisor may be employed by the employer on either a paid or voluntary basis; however, if the employment is on a voluntary basis, there must be a written agreement between the supervisor and the organization prior to the commencement of supervision wherein the supervisor agrees to ensure that the extent, kind, and quality of counseling performed by the person being supervised is consistent with that person's training, education, and experience, and is appropriate in extent, kind, and quality.[36]

Trainees are not allowed to perform services in a private practice. Trainees and interns may perform services only as employees and not as independent contractors. Trainees and interns cannot have a proprietary interest in their employer's business.[37] Additionally, since January 1, 1991, each trainee and intern has

---

34. Bus. & Prof. Code §§ 4980.40(f), 4980.43(c); 16 CCR § 1833(b). *Supervision* is defined as the review, evaluation, and assessment of assigned experience on an individual or group basis. Individual supervision means a 1:1 ratio of supervisor to applicant, while group supervision means a group of no more than eight persons is receiving supervision from one supervisor. The Board has specified that during each week in which experience is claimed, an applicant shall have at least one hour of individual supervision or two hours of group supervision for each work setting. No more than three hours of supervision, whether individual or group, shall be credited during any single week. 16 CCR § 1833(b) & (b)(1).
35. 16 CCR § 1833(a)(3) to (6).
36. 16 CCR § 1833(b)(4), (d)(1).
37. Bus. & Prof. Code § 4980.43(j).

been required to maintain a log of all hours of experience gained toward licensure. The log must be in a form specified by the Board, and must be signed by the supervisor on a weekly basis. The Board shall have the right to require an applicant to submit all or any portion of the log as the Board deems necessary to verify hours of experience.[38]

(F) Criteria for Supervisors

The Board has also established criteria for supervisors, interns, and trainees. Each supervisor is required to sign under penalty of perjury a statement entitled "Responsibility Statement for Supervisors for the MFCC License." This statement affirms that the supervisor meets and will comply with certain criteria, including the following:

1. the supervisor is licensed in California, is either an MFCC, a licensed clinical social worker, a psychologist, or a physician who is certified in psychiatry by the American Board of Psychiatry and Neurology or for supervisorial relationships in effect on or before December 31, 1988. The supervisor is a licensed physician who has completed a residency in psychiatry. If the supervisor is not licensed as an MFCC, he or she shall also affirm that he or she has sufficient experience, training, and/or education in marriage, family, and child counseling to competently practice marriage, family, and child counseling in California. Further, the supervisor must keep informed of the developments in marriage, family, and child counseling;[39]

2. the supervisor must have and maintain a current license in good standing. The supervisor must notify the intern or trainee of any disciplinary action, including suspension or probation, which could affect the supervisor's ability or right to supervise;[40]

3. the supervisor must have practiced psychotherapy for at least two years within the five-year period immediately preceding any supervision and must have averaged at least five patient/client contact hours per week;[41]

4. the supervisor affirms that he or she has sufficient experience, training, and/or education in the area of clinical supervision to competently supervise trainees or interns, and that he or she

---

38. 16 CCR § 1833(d)(2) and (3), (e).
39. 16 CCR § 1833.1(a)(1); Bus. & Prof. Code § 4980.40(f).
40. 16 CCR § 1833.1(a)(2).
41. 16 CCR § 1833.1(a)(3).

knows or understands the laws and regulations pertaining both as to supervision of trainees and interns and as to the experience required for licensure as an MFCC;[42]

5. the supervisor affirms that he or she will take reasonable steps to ensure that a trainee or intern properly assesses and examines the patient or client, implements an appropriate treatment plan, and is acting within the scope of an MFCC license and his or her competence. The supervisor shall monitor the quality of counseling or psychotherapy performed by the intern or trainee by direct observation, audio or video recording, via progress and process notes or records, or by any other means deemed appropriate by the supervisor. The supervisor shall inform the intern or trainee prior to the commencement of supervision of the methods by which the supervisor will monitor the quality of counseling or psychotherapy being performed;[43]

6. the supervisor shall provide at least one hour of individual supervision or two hours of group supervision in each week wherein a qualifying experience is gained by the intern or trainee. Individual supervision means a 1:1 ratio of supervisor to intern or trainee, and group supervision means supervision of a group of no more than eight persons by one supervisor;[44]

7. the supervisor agrees not to provide supervision to a trainee unless the trainee is employed in a governmental entity, school, college, university, nonprofit or charitable corporation, or licensed health facility. The supervisor agrees not to provide supervision to an intern unless the intern is employed in a governmental entity, school, college, university, nonprofit or charitable corporation, licensed health facility, or private practice.[45]

The statement that the supervisor is required to sign shall be given to the intern or trainee prior to the commencement of counseling or supervision, and the intern or trainee shall file the statement with the Board within 30 days of commencing employment. The supervisor shall give at least one week's written notice to an intern or a trainee of the supervisor's intent not to certify any further hours of experience. A supervisor who has not provided such a written notice shall sign for hours of experience obtained in good faith where such supervisor actually provided the required supervision.[46]

---

42. 16 CCR § 1833.1(a)(4), (5).
43. 16 CCR § 1833.1(a)(6).
44. 16 CCR §§ 1833.1(a)(7), 1833(b).
45. 16 CCR § 1833.1(a)(8), (9).
46. 16 CCR § 1833.1(b), (c).

The Board has also specified criteria for the acceptance of supervised experience gained outside of California.[47]

Interns are required to have at least a master's degree and to be registered with the Board prior to performing any duties, and to file for renewal of registration annually for a maximum of five years. They may keep their intern status for a total of six years. Interns must inform each client or patient prior to performing any professional services that he or she is unlicensed and under the supervision of their supervisor, specifying the status of the supervisor. Under certain circumstances, the Board may extend the six-year period of time.[48] Within 30 days of the commencement or termination of employment in any allowable work setting, a registered intern must notify the Board in writing of the beginning or termination of employment. The notice shall include the name of the registered intern, the full name and address of the employer, the type of work setting where the intern is gaining hours of experience, and the date employment commenced or terminated. A failure to notify the Board within 30 days of the commencement or termination of employment may lead the Board to not accept hours of experience gained during that period prior to notification. This applies to gaining hours of experience as an employee or as a volunteer.[49]

Before January 1, 1994, trainees were required to register with the Board, but that requirement has been repealed. Before January

---

47. 16 CCR § 1833.2. For supervised experience gained outside California on or after January 1, 1991, the supervisor must have been licensed or certified by the state in which the supervision occurred and possessed a current license not under suspension or probation. The supervisor must have been licensed or certified by that state for at least two years prior to acting as a supervisor as either a psychologist, clinical social worker, physician certified in psychiatry by the American Board of Psychiatry and Neurology, or as an MFCC or similarly titled marriage and family practitioner. Where the state in which the experience was gained does not license or certify MFCCs or similarly titled marriage and family practitioners, experience may be obtained under the supervision of a person who at the time of the supervision held a clinical membership in the American Association of Marriage and Family Therapists for at least two years and must have maintained such membership throughout the period of supervision. The Board may also allow any person to be examined who has met the education and experience for licensure while residing outside of California, whose education has been outside California, but has experience within California. Such a person must have gained a minimum of 250 hours of supervised experience and direct counseling within California while registered as an intern with the Board, and must have completed a two-semester or three-quarter-unit course in California Law and Professional Ethics for MFCCs. In addition, he or she must have completed a minimum of seven contact hours of training or course work in child abuse assessment and reporting, 10 contact hours of training or course work in sexuality, and 15 contact hours of course work in alcoholism or chemical substance dependency. Bus. & Prof. Code § 4980.90.
48. Bus. & Prof. Code § 4980.44.
49. Bus. & Prof. Code § 4980.45(b).

1, 1994, interns and trainees were required to notify the Board within 30 days of the commencement or termination of employment in any allowable work setting. A failure to notify the Board within 30 days could lead to the hours of experience not being accepted. Effective January 1, 1994, this requirement was repealed and can be waived by the Board for notifications received before January 1, 1994. *Employment* means the gaining of hours of experience in an allowable work setting as an employee or a volunteer. Trainees are also required to inform each client or patient prior to performing a professional service that he or she is unlicensed and under supervision, as well as the status of the supervisor.[50]

Effective January 1, 1994, educational institutions preparing individuals for licensure as MFCCs are required to encourage, and to consider requiring, their students to undergo individual, marital, or conjoint family or group counseling or psychotherapy as appropriate. Each supervisor is required to consider, advise, and encourage his or her interns and trainees to undertake individual, marital, or conjoint family or group counseling or psychotherapy as appropriate.[51]

(G) Exceptions to Licensing Regulations

The licensing act does not preclude individuals licensed under the Medical Practice Act, the Social Work Licensing Law, the Nursing Practice Act, or the Psychology Licensing Law from providing marriage, family, and child counseling services so long as they do not advertise themselves as MFCCs. The statute does not preclude priests, rabbis, and ministers of the gospel from performing counseling services as part of their pastoral or professional duties. Individuals admitted to practice law in California who provide counseling services as part of their professional practice are also not required to have a license. The statute does not apply to employees of governmental entities, schools, colleges, universities, or of any institution both nonprofit and charitable if his or her practice is performed solely under the supervision of the entity, school, or organization by which he or she is employed, and if he or she performs such functions as the part of the position for which he or she is employed.[52] In addition, within the parameters set forth above, trainees and interns do not need a

---

50. Bus. & Prof. Code § 4980.48.
51. Bus. & Prof. Code § 4980.43(1).
52. Bus. & Prof. Code § 4980.01.

license to provide services so long as they comply with the requirements of laws and regulations.

(H) Grounds for Disciplinary Action

The Board can deny an application for registration or a license, or order the suspension or revocation of a license or registration if a licensee, registrant, or applicant is found guilty of unprofessional conduct. Unprofessional conduct includes, but is not limited to, the following:

1. the conviction of a crime substantially related to the qualifications, functions, or duties of a licensee or registrant;[53]

2. securing a license by fraud, deceit, or misrepresentation on any application for licensure or registration whether the acts are engaged in by the applicant for the license or registration, or by a licensee in support of any application;[54]

3. self-administering any controlled substance or dangerous drug or any alcoholic beverage to any extent or in a manner dangerous or injurious to the applicant or licensee, or registrant, or to any other person or to the public, or to the extent that such use impairs the ability of such person applying for or holding a registration or license to conduct with safety to the public the practice authorized by the registration or license; or the conviction of more than one misdemeanor or any felony regarding the use, consumption, or self-administration of any of the controlled substances, dangerous drugs, alcoholic beverages, or any combination thereof; further, the Board shall deny an application for a registration or license or revoke the license or registration of any person other than a licensed physician or surgeon who uses or offers to use drugs in the course of performing marriage, family, and child counseling services;[55]

---

53. Bus. & Prof. Code § 4982(a). A plea or verdict of guilty or conviction following a plea of nolo contendere made to a charge substantially related to the qualifications, functions, or duties of a licensee or registrant shall be deemed to be a conviction for the purposes of this section. A record of convictions shall be conclusive evidence only of the fact that the conviction occurred, and the Board may inquire into the circumstances surrounding the commission of the crime in order to fix the degree of discipline or to determine if the conviction is substantially related to the qualifications, functions, or duties of a licensee or registrant.
54. Bus. & Prof. Code § 4982(b).
55. Bus. & Prof. Code § 4982(c).

4. gross negligence or incompetence in the performance of marriage, family, and child counseling;[56]

5. violating, attempting to violate, or conspiring to violate any of the provisions of the law or any regulation adopted by the Board;[57]

6. misrepresenting the type or status of a license or registration held by the individual or otherwise misrepresenting or permitting misrepresentation of his or her education, professional qualifications, or professional affiliations to any person or entity;[58]

7. impersonating another by any licensee, registrant, or applicant for a license or registration, or any licensee allowing any other person to use his or her license or registration;[59]

8. aiding or abetting any unlicensed or unregistered person to engage in conduct for which a license or registration is required;[60]

9. intentionally or recklessly causing physical or emotional harm to any client;[61]

10. committing any dishonest, corrupt, or fraudulent acts substantially related to the qualifications, functions, or duties of a licensee or registrant;[62]

11. engaging in sexual relations with a client, soliciting sexual relations with a client, committing an act of sexual abuse or sexual misconduct with a client, or committing an act punishable as a sexually related crime, if that act or solicitation is substantially related to the qualifications, functions, or duties of an MFCC;[63]

12. performing or holding oneself out as being able to perform, or offering to perform, or permitting any registered trainee or registered intern under the individual's supervision to perform any professional services beyond the scope of the license or beyond the level of competency as established by his or her education, training, or experience;[64]

---

56. Bus. & Prof. Code § 4982(d); *see Franz v. Board of Medical Quality Assurance,* 31 Cal.3d 124 (1982).
57. Bus. & Prof. Code § 4982(e).
58. Bus. & Prof. Code § 4982(f).
59. Bus. & Prof. Code § 4982(g).
60. Bus. & Prof. Code § 4982(h).
61. Bus. & Prof. Code § 4982(i).
62. Bus. & Prof. Code § 4982(j).
63. Bus. & Prof. Code §§ 4982(k), 720, 726, 729. Effective January 1, 1995, Bus. & Prof. Code § 4982.26 mandates revocation of license where an ALJ finds that a licensee had sex with a patient or with a former patient, where the professional relationship was terminated for the purpose of engaging in sex.
64. Bus. & Prof. Code § 4982(l); 16 CCR § 1845(a), (b).

13. failing to maintain confidentiality, except as otherwise required or permitted by law, of all information that has been obtained or received from a client in confidence during the course of treatment, and all information about the client obtained from tests or other means;[65]

14. prior to the commencement of treatment, failing to disclose to the client or prospective client the fee to be charged for the professional services or the basis upon which the fee will be computed;[66]

15. paying, accepting, or soliciting any consideration, compensation, or remuneration, whether monetary or otherwise, for the referral of professional clients; all consideration, compensation, or remuneration shall be in relation to professional counseling services actually provided by the licensee, while nothing prevents collaboration among two or more licensees in a case or cases, but no fee shall be charged for that collaboration except where disclosure of the fee has been made prior to the commencement of treatment to the client;[67]

16. advertising in any manner that is false or misleading or deceptive;[68]

17. reproducing, or describing in public or in any publication subject to general public distribution, any psychological tests or other assessment device, the value of which depends in whole or in part on the naivete of the subject in ways that might invalidate the test or device;[69]

18. any conduct while supervising a registered intern or registered trainee by any licensee that violates the rules or regulations adopted by the Board;[70]

19. performing or holding oneself out as being able to perform professional services beyond the scope of one's competence as established by one's education, training, or experience;[71]

20. permitting a registered trainee or registered intern under one's supervision or control to perform or hold himself or herself out as competent to perform professional services beyond the trainee or intern's level of education, training, or experience;[72] and

21. failing to comply with child abuse reporting requirements.[73]

---

65. Bus. & Prof. Code § 4982(m).
66. Bus. & Prof. Code § 4982(n).
67. Bus. & Prof. Code § 4982(o).
68. Bus. & Prof. Code § 4982(p).
69. Bus. & Prof. Code § 4982(q).
70. Bus. & Prof. Code § 4982(r).
71. Bus. & Prof. Code § 4982(s); 16 CCR § 1845(a).
72. Bus. & Prof. Code § 4982(t); 16 CCR § 1845(b).
73. 16 CCR § 1845(c); Penal Code § 11166.

In addition, the Board may place a license or registration on probation under the following circumstances:

1. in lieu of, or in addition to, any order of the Board suspending or revoking a license or registration;

2. upon the issuance of a license to an individual who has been found guilty of unprofessional conduct but has otherwise completed all education, training, and experience required for licensure;

3. as a condition upon the reissuance or reinstatement of any license that has been suspended or revoked.

The Board is authorized to adopt regulations establishing a monitoring program to ensure compliance with the terms of probation and has in fact established such a program.[74] The Board has also established criteria for rehabilitation for the denial of licensure suspensions and revocations, which allows the Board to consider the nature and severity of the acts involved; subsequent acts; the time since the commission of the acts; compliance with terms of probation, parole, and restitution; and evidence as to whether any false statements were made, together with proof of rehabilitation.[75]

(I) Administrative Procedure

The procedures regarding discovery and conduct of administrative hearings to revoke or suspend the license of an MFCC are governed by the Administrative Procedures Act, as discussed in chapter 1.0A. Where the Board believes an MFCC is suffering from a mental impairment, the Board can require the MFCC to submit to a psychological evaluation, as described in chapter 5B.1.

---

74. Bus. & Prof. Code § 4982.2.
75. 16 CCR §§1813, 1814.

1.10

Licensure and Regulation of Hypnotists

Hypnotism as a technique is recognized in California, but its use may create evidentiary problems in criminal cases. While the term *hypnotist* may seem clear, California does not have such a statutory definition. Because hypnotists are not licensed, there are no set criteria to hold oneself out as a hypnotist. Since there is no state license for hypnotists, the certification of an individual by a private organization as a hypnotist may be misinterpreted as a form of licensure. The law does address situations where hypnosis is used to treat medical or psychological conditions.

(A) Authorization for Use of Hypnosis

The Psychology Licensing Law states that it does not preclude qualified members of certain professional groups from practicing hypnosis upon referral from individuals licensed to practice medicine, dentistry, or psychology, where the individuals using the hypnotic techniques are doing so for avocational, vocational, or self-improvement purposes and not for therapy for emotional or mental disorders. The categories of professionals who can provide hypnotic techniques upon referral from individuals licensed to practice medicine, dentistry, or psychology include physicians; licensed clinical social workers; licensed educational psychologists; marriage, family, and child counselors; optometrists; psychiatric technicians; registered nurses; and attorneys licensed to practice before the California state bar.[1] Anyone who is not licensed by the state of California in one of the specified capacities, and who treats an emotional or mental disorder through hypnotherapy violates the law.

(B) Hypnosis by MFCCs

While there are no general requirements for hypnotic training, there are specific criteria governing the use of hypnosis by marriage, family, and child counselors (MFCCs). These regulations require an MFCC licensee to submit proof of education and experience to the Board of Behavioral Science Examiners and receive a notification from the Board that they had met the criteria prior to using hypnosis in their counseling.

The MFCC must complete 40 hours of approved hypnosis education in courses approved by the Board of Behavioral Science Examiners, in which no less than 10 hours must be in a clinical setting. For the purposes of these regulations, a *clinical setting* is a setting where there is direct observation of the patient by the licensee gaining either the education or experience. The licensee is required to submit proof to the Board of successful completion of the required number of education hours, by means of a certificate, transcript, or similar document. In addition, providers of hypnosis education must apply for approval to offer the hypnosis education on forms provided by the Board, and the courses must be taught by approved course instructors. The courses will not be approved for more than one year. The Board must approve any change in course content. Courses in hypnosis education that are taken outside the state of California may be considered comparable by the Board, and may be accepted. For an instructor to be approved as a hypnosis education course instructor, he or she must be knowledgeable, able, current, and skillful in the subject matter of the course. This standard can be met by two of the following three criteria:

1. completion of specialized training in hypnosis;
2. experience in teaching hypnosis within a two-year period preceding the date of application for approval of the hypnosis education course; and
3. six months of experience working with hypnosis over a three-year period that precedes the application for approval.

---

1. Bus. & Prof. Code § 2908.

Experience must be in a clinical setting under the supervision of a physician, dentist, licensed psychologist, or a licensed MFCC who has held a certificate in hypnosis issued by the Board for at least six months. The licensee must receive at least 30 hours of experience in an individual setting or in a setting where there are no more than nine additional individuals under supervision. The supervisor must indicate that the experience demonstrates that the licensee has the competency and ability to use hypnosis without further supervision while performing the duties of an MFCC.[2]

(C) Hypnosis by Other MHPs

While other licensees may not be subject to regulations as specific as for MFCCs, any licensee can be disciplined for practicing beyond the scope of his or her competency. Therefore, any licensee must have an adequate background in hypnosis to be able to use the technique.

MHPs using hypnosis must also be aware that if statutorily mandated precautions are not taken, a patient's testimony may be excluded in a criminal case. This is discussed more fully in chapter 5D.12.

In one case, an osteopath's license was revoked for putting patients into hypnotic trances and speaking in an offensive sexual manner to them.[3]

---

2. 16 CCR § 1834.6.
3. *Shea v. Board of Medical Examiners*, 81 Cal.App.3d 564 (1978).

1.11

Licensure and Regulation of Polygraph Examiners

California did have a statute licensing polygraph examiners, which was repealed effective January 1, 1990. Thus, at present there is no licensure requirement for these practitioners.[1]

---

1. Bus. & Prof. Code §§ 9300 to 9321 were enacted by 1983 statutes Chapter 1107, and were repealed by 1987 California statutes, Chapter 121D, page 140.

1.12

Sunset Law Agencies

A sunset law requires the legislature to review and assess whether various components of state government, specifically administrative agencies, should continue to exist. The law sets certain dates by which the agency's authority to act will terminate unless the legislature expressly authorizes its continuation. By the same token, regulations and statutes will have no force or validity past the agency's termination date. California does not have a general sunset provision applying to the agencies relevant to this book, except the licensing of polygraph examiners (see chapter 1.11), although such provisions exist with reference to other agencies in the state.

In 1994, the Legislature created the Joint Legislative Sunset Review Committee, which is charged with evaluating all of the licensing boards under the Department of Consumer Affairs and determining whether there is a continuing need for each board's existence.[1] The committee is to report to the Legislature on its findings and recommendations. Among the factors the committee is to consider is whether the boards perform their duties efficiently and effectively, the impact of the boards' regulations on competition and business growth, and whether the boards are protecting the public or the regulated industry.[2]

1. Bus. & Prof. Code § 473.
2. Bus. & Prof. Code § 473.4.

Forms of Business Practice

2.1

Sole Proprietorship

Generally, the most common form of private practice is a sole proprietorship, where the MHP is the only owner, with or without professional employees. While there are generally no rules or regulations applicable to the formation of sole proprietorships (other than the regulations governing licensure), as there are with partnerships and professional corporations, there is a specific requirement that no fictitious name may be used for a business practice unless it has been approved by the appropriate licensing agency, and a fee paid.[1] Thus, before MHPs can hold themselves out under a fictitious name, they must obtain the approval of their licensing board. In addition, a Fictitious Name Statement must be filed with the appropriate county clerk.

A sole proprietorship is the simplest form of practice, but problems may arise if the MHP has no MHP employees, should emergency clinical situations occur. Therefore, if an MHP intends to practice as a sole proprietor, prudence suggests having a competent and readily available MHP as a backup to provide care to patients in the event of an emergency or unavailability of the MHP who is the business owner. On the other hand, sole proprietorship offers the greatest flexibility in practice and avoids problems that arise from conflicting interests of multiple owners.

---

1. For example, Bus. & Prof. Code § 2930.5 (psychologists); § 4980.46 (MFCCs).

2.2

Professional Corporations

MHPs in private practice who are not sole proprietors operate either as a partnership (see chapter 2.3) or as a professional corporation. A professional corporation is different from a general corporation in a number of respects, as discussed below. The professional corporation may offer tax, insurance, and other benefits associated with regular corporations. However, the law provides a professional corporation with much more limited protection against liability than it provides to regular corporations. Physicians; psychologists; marriage, family, and child counselors; licensed clinical social workers; and registered nurses may incorporate under their respective licensing laws.[1]

(A) Benefits of Incorporation

There are three main benefits to incorporation:

1. tax benefits,
2. spreading or sharing of professional liability, and
3. general business aspects.

A discussion of the benefits available under professional corporations is so complex as to require a separate volume. Briefly, however, tax-qualified retirement plans are available to corporate employees and officers as long as the requirements of the Corporations Code, the Internal Revenue Code, and the Employee

---

1. Corp. Code § 202.

Retirement Income Security Act of 1974 (ERISA) are met.[2] The nonretirement benefits of a professional corporation include the availability of medical plans that, if properly structured, can provide a nontaxable benefit to the MHP and deductions for the professional corporation of premiums on group life insurance for employees of the corporation, a dependent care assistance program, and a group legal services plan.

The sharing of liability will be discussed more fully below, but it is qualified in scope.

(B) Corporation Formation and Operation Procedures

The California legislature authorized certain professions to practice in corporate form under the Moscone-Knox Professional Corporation Act of 1968. No professional can practice in corporate form unless the statutes explicitly authorize such incorporation. Currently, the statutes expressly authorize physicians, certified physicians' assistants, chiropractors, clinical social workers, MFCCs, and psychologists to incorporate. The statutes provide that the principal stockholders in the corporation must be professionals licensed in the specific discipline in which the corporation is practicing.[3] However, all of the shareholders, directors, officers, agents, and professional employees of the corporation must be licensed or certified members of that particular profession.[4] The general California Corporations Code applies to the formation of professional corporations. Various requirements exist, such as the preparation of articles and bylaws, filing initial articles with the secretary of state, designating an agent for service of process, transferring existing contracts to the new entity, holding meetings of the board of directors, preparing corporate books and minutes, and submitting the applications for certificates of registration to the appropriate professional licensing board.[5]

---

2. The provisions of ERISA and the Internal Revenue Code that govern professional corporations have been amended by numerous tax acts over the last several years, so any MHP considering a professional corporation must consult with a competent tax attorney or accountant to ascertain whether the current tax benefits warrant incorporation.
3. Under certain circumstances, 50% of the stockholders may be of different professional licensees so long as those licensees are also licensees allowed to incorporate professionally. 16 CCR 1397.35.
4. Bus. & Prof. Code § 2408; 16 CCR § 1343; Corp. Code §§ 13401, 13401.8.
5. Bus. & Prof. Code §§ 200 to 213, 110, 13401.

Where there is no contrary provision specified in the Moscone–Knox Professional Corporation law, the general California Corporations Code provisions take precedence.[6]

A professional corporation generally uses various employees who must work under the supervision of licensed or certified corporate personnel. These individuals may not hold themselves out as being authorized to engage in the independent practice of the profession for which the corporation is licensed. Thus, the professional corporation law does not expand any of the requirements of licensing laws or the criteria that the licensing boards use in evaluating any individuals' fitness to practice. In addition, unlicensed employees cannot be accurately described as independent contractors.

(C) Liability Issues

A critical distinction between a general corporation and a professional corporation is that the shareholders of a professional corporation remain liable to claims of malpractice under certain conditions. Generally, professionals operating a professional corporation may limit their personal liability for the malpractice of their business associates.[7] However, this rule is subject to a number of exceptions. First, the assets of the professional corporation are subject to all corporate obligations, including malpractice claims. The personal assets of the individual employee performing the work in question are subject to any malpractice obligations arising from that work or service.[8] Additionally, the personal assets of any employee supervising the work are subject to any malpractice obligations arising from it.[9]

The law requires attorneys, chiropractors, dentists, optometrists, and osteopaths to personally guarantee the malpractice obligations of their professional corporations within certain prescribed limits.[10] While no such requirement presently exists as to doctors, psychologists, MFCCs, and Licensed Clinical Social Workers, it is possible that such a requirement may be extended to those corporations in the future. While attorneys are unconditionally required to personally guarantee their malpractice obligations, chiropractors, dentists, optometrists, and osteopaths may avoid the personal guarantee by providing malpractice insurance within specified limits, in which case they have no per-

---

6. Corp. Code § 13403.
7. Bus. & Prof. Code § 6160.
8. Civ. Code § 2343(3).
9. *Id.*
10. Bus. & Prof. Code § 6171; 16 CCR §§ 367.8, 1059, 1547, 1671.

sonal liability within the insurance policy limits (except for intentional torts). In the absence of the malpractice insurance, the professionals are jointly and severally liable for the malpractice liability. Again, this may be extended at some point in the future to the other professionals listed above.

The professional corporation must meet the criteria and ethical standards set by the licensing board that licenses or certifies its shareholders. The corporation cannot engage in any acts that are prohibited to professionals practicing in noncorporate form. If any shareholder of the professional corporation becomes legally disqualified, either temporarily or permanently, to render the professional services that the particular professional corporation is or was rendering, the corporation must acquire all of the shares of the disqualified shareholder within 90 days following the date of disqualification or suffer suspension or revocation of the certificate of registration of the corporation by the governmental agency that regulates the profession in which the corporation is engaged.[11]

Similarly, when a shareholder dies, the corporation must transfer the shares within six months. Where a transfer is required, shares can be transferred only to a licensed person or to the corporation itself, and any transfer in violation of the restriction is void.[12]

Shares of capital stock in the professional corporation that are issued to a nonlicensed person are void. Shareholders of professional corporations are precluded from entering voting trusts, proxies, or other arrangements vesting another person who is not licensed with the authority to exercise the voting power of any or all of those shares.[13]

(D) Termination of a Professional Corporation

A professional corporation continues until such time as it is either voluntarily or involuntarily dissolved, pursuant to the law governing the dissolution of general corporations.

---

11. Corp. Code §§ 13401(d), 13401.5, 13407.
12. Corp. Code § 13407.
13. Corp. Code § 13406.

2.3

Partnerships

A partnership is an association of two or more persons to carry on a business for profit as co-owners.[1] Partners agree to combine their resources and to share responsibility for each other's acts. There are two kinds of partnerships: limited and general. In a general partnership, each of the partners is a co-owner, and although their percentage interest in the business may be different, their substantive responsibilities and liabilities are not. In a limited partnership, there are one or more general partners and a number of partners whose financial commitment is limited and whose liability is therefore accordingly limited. MHPs are generally not allowed to have limited partnerships because of the restrictions on liability of the limited partners. Thus, as used herein, the term *partnership* will mean a general partnership. This chapter discusses formation and dissolution of partnerships, and the types of partnership interests, including oral and apparent partnerships, as well as the rights and duties between partners. Also discussed are the economic structure of the partnership and how capital accounts, income, and profits may be divided.

(A) Partnership Interests and Classes

Partners can agree to various arrangements involving the rights and shares of ownership. The three major aspects of a partnership interest are

---

1. Corp. Code § 15006.

1. income or profit,
2. equity ownership, and
3. voting rights.

In structuring a partnership, professionals can set up different classes of partners who have varying equity interests, voting rights, and entitlement to income. The use of different classes of partners is most common in law partnerships and usually entails a two-tier partnership structure in which a person becomes a junior partner with an entitlement to income and profits and some voting rights but no equity ownership. There is typically a period of time before the junior partner can acquire an equity ownership and become a general partner. It is rare to see different classes of ownership in MHP partnerships, but there is no rule or regulation prohibiting it. However, the regulations may limit partners from different disciplines. For example, the regulations for physicians provide that no partnership agreement can allow for fees to be combined or shared between a physician and a podiatrist or any other nonphysician.[2]

(B) Formation of the Partnership

The formation of a partnership is relatively simple in that it is created by two people agreeing orally or in writing to become partners and act as co-owners of a business. Generally, a corporation is required to assert its business purpose in the articles of incorporation and bylaws. Since a partnership may be formed orally, no such declaration is technically necessary. It is, however, sound practice to have a written partnership agreement that clearly explains the purpose of the business and what services are required of or anticipated from each partner. A written agreement can help avoid potential problems such as when a professional in a professional partnership may own additional business entities and wishes to allocate his or her time between those entities and the professional partnership and to keep the income completely separate.

(C) Oral/Apparent Partnership

Problems can arise for MHPs as businesspersons from what are alleged to be oral partnership agreements. In essence, if individu-

---

2. 16 CCR § 1349.

als are held out to the public in a manner that creates the impression that there is a partnership, then the purported partners may be estopped from denying that such an agreement exists, even if it was never their intent to have such an agreement.[3]

One factor in estopping partners from denying existence of a partnership may be the absence of a written partnership agreement. This problem mandates the existence of a written partnership agreement clearly delineating the respective duties, obligations, and compensation of the partners and equally mandates clarity of the status of individuals associated with the MHPs' business. However, a written agreement will not bar claims by individuals who are not aware of its existence. A written agreement can be important evidence of how the partners intended to hold themselves out to the public. The most common situation in which a patient or creditor can believe that a partnership exists where none was intended is where a group of MHPs share a suite of offices and advertise under a common name such as "Eating Disorder Clinic," yet each individual is a sole practitioner.

Technically, the fact that common expenses such as leasing, secretarial, and advertising expenses are shared is not necessarily indicative that a partnership exists. Any sharing of profits, however, is generally interpreted as a sign that a partnership exists.

In these circumstances, each MHP must be extremely cautious to clarify with his or her patients that the grouping of professionals is simply an association and not a partnership. Marketing under a common name carries the risk that the individual sole proprietors will be deemed to be a partnership insofar as the public is concerned.

The Medical Board requires a fictitious name permit to be filed with it and approval obtained before any fictitious name can be used.[4] The Board of Psychology had a similar requirement that was recently rescinded.[5]

(D) Capital Accounts

When a partnership agreement is prepared, it addresses generally the money, assets, or other resources committed to a partnership by each individual partner. This establishes what is known as a *capital account* representing the partners' ownership interest in the firm. Adjustments to this account are made periodi-

---

3. Corp. Code §§ 15007, 15016. *Estopped* or *estoppel* means that a party is precluded from taking an action or position, usually on equitable grounds.
4. 16 CCR § 1344.
5. Bus. & Prof. Code § 2405.

cally to reflect additional contributions of money or assets and to deduct monies withdrawn by the partners. When the partnership is formed, the partners can agree that contributions of different natures are to be treated as equal. For example, one partner may contribute $30,000 in cash; another contributes a client base; and yet another partner contributes various unpaid services.

(E) Structuring Partnership Income and Profits

Generally, a partner's ownership interest in the business is expressed in the partner's capital account and his or her share of income and profits. A partner's percentage interest of income and profits can vary so that the partnership can accommodate the cash flow and tax needs of the individual partners. For example, one partner can receive a guaranteed monthly salary of $3,000 and a 30% share of the net profits while another partner can agree to take $2,000 a month and receive 40% of the profits. Ultimately, however, this creates tax ramifications that are beyond the scope of this volume, but generally, the Internal Revenue Service has a policy of looking to the substance of partnership transactions rather than the label used by the partners. This means that the structuring of the ownership interest and transactions between the partners and the partnership must be carefully monitored to ensure compliance with IRS requirements. This is particularly important when, for example, the partnership leases office space from another partnership that includes some of the members of the professional partnership.

(F) Rights and Duties Between Partners

Corporate shareholders generally have no obligation or duties to each other aside from being responsible for the amount of money that their shares represent. Partners, however, maintain a much different relationship. Because partners share economic benefits and potential liability, each partner has a fiduciary obligation to the others requiring each to avoid putting his or her personal interests ahead of the partnership in such a fashion as to disadvantage the other partners. The partners have equal rights in the management and conduct of the business. Generally, however, this right is modified in the partnership agreement to leave the daily management issues to one particular partner who is designated as *managing partner*. Each partner has the right to inspect the partnership books,[6] to receive all financial and other information that may affect the partnership, and to demand an accounting wherein all of the partnership income and expenditures are documented. Partners are required to report all business-related income to the partnership and cannot unilaterally decide that a particular payment is not partnership income.

As a matter of law, each partner is the agent of the other for acts performed in the scope of the partnership business.[7] Therefore, each partner can bind every other partner so long as the acts are within the scope of the partner's authority. Partners cannot unilaterally assign partnership property in trust for creditors, nor can they unilaterally sell partnership assets.[8] Partners are not allowed to acknowledge liability in litigation against the partnership without their partners' consent.[9] Because of the effect on capital accounts, no equity partner generally is allowed to lend or advance money to the partnership without the written consent of the other partners because to do so could increase that partner's interest. Partners are required to execute all the written documents necessary to carry on the partnership business. Partners are precluded from selling, leasing, trading, exchanging, conveying, or disposing of the property of the partnership without the consent of the other partners. They are also precluded from becoming a surety guarantor or endorser for any person or firm in the name of the partnership without consent of the other partners.

Generally, partnership agreements provide that a partner cannot mortgage, hypothecate (encumber), or assign his or her share of the partnership profits or capital. It is a common practice for partnership agreements to contain a dollar limitation (e.g., $2,500) on the amount that an individual partner can obligate the partnership without consent of the other partners.

Generally, the partnership agreement provides that partners shall not engage in any other occupation or activity to which they devote a substantial amount of their time without the consent of the other partners.

Any wrongful act, error, omission, or malpractice committed by a partner acting in the scope of the partnership business subjects the other partners to liability to the same extent.[10]

Thus, if an MHP is negligent in the treatment of a patient, then all the partners who are in the partnership at the time those

---

6. Corp. Code §§ 15019 to 15022.
7. Corp. Code § 15009(1), (2).
8. Corp. Code § 15009(3)(a).
9. Corp. Code § 15009(3)(d).
10. Corp. Code § 15013.

acts occurred are equally liable, whether or not they are still with the partnership. On the other hand, an act that is clearly outside the scope of the partnership business, such as the sexual assault of a neighbor, does not subject the individual partners to liability under most circumstances.

In short, while the partners are unconditionally liable for the professional errors and omissions of their partners in the scope of the business, they are not responsible for the acts of the partner outside the scope of the business. Partners are jointly and severally liable:[11] a plaintiff can choose to proceed against all of the partners or only one of the partners and collect the entire amount from any one or more partners. In fact, in some instances it is in the best interests of the plaintiff to sue the partners who did not engage in the questioned activity because they may remain in the jurisdiction while the wrongdoer has fled or is incarcerated or may not be entitled to insurance coverage because of the intentional nature of the acts at issue in the litigation. Because any partner's acts can lead to liability of the other partners, MHPs must be cautious to adequately investigate the background, training, and licensure status of potential partners.

(G) Dissolution of a Partnership

A partnership can be dissolved by agreement of the partners, operation of law, or by the terms of a written partnership agreement. Generally, a written partnership agreement cannot be dissolved by a subsequent oral agreement but has to be dissolved pursuant to a dissolution agreement, or by operation of law.[12] Dissolution can occur in the following situations:

1. when the terms of the partnership agreement state either a date certain or an event that will trigger dissolution. Most partnerships specify a particular term, and if that term is not extended, the arrival of the termination date acts as a termination of the partnership;[13]

2. when no definite term is specified, the partnership can dissolve when any partner decides that he or she wishes to dissolve the partnership;

3. when the agreement provides that partners can be expelled (e.g., for engaging in criminal activity), the agreement gener-

---

11. Corp. Code § 15015.
12. Corp. Code §§ 15029 to 15033.
13. Corp. Code § 15031.

ally also requires certain payments to be made to the expelled partners to compensate them for their partnership interest;

4. when the occurrence of any event makes it unlawful for the partnership business to continue, such as one or more partners losing their license to practice their profession;

5. when the death of any partner (although this can be modified by the partnership agreement to provide that the partnership will continue and that special insurance will be used to pay out the appropriate partnership interest to the deceased partner's estate);

6. when a physical or mental disability precludes a partner from continuing in the business;

7. when a partner is guilty of conduct that prejudices the carrying on of the business, such as causing the loss of a major client;

8. when a partner breaches the agreement in such a fashion that it is impractical to carry on the business with that partner;

9. when the business can be carried on only at a loss; and

10. when a dissolution would be equitable.

The dissolution of the partnership terminates the authority of the partners and their respective liability to each other, except to the extent necessary to conclude all business, including the dissolution of the partnership. However, all liabilities and debts that accrued before the date of dissolution are the responsibility of all partners. Further, to ensure that there is no misperception as to the continued liability of the partnership, a dissolution agreement is necessary.

At dissolution of the partnership, the partners are entitled to receive the amount equal to their capital account once the other liabilities of the business have been satisfied. If there is not a sufficient amount for each partner to take a full repayment of capital, then the amounts are paid on a pro rata basis.

Finally, a partnership agreement also typically addresses the extent to which a partner's share may be transferred or impaired by a divorce action. In addition, provisions are made to allow the partnership the option to buy out the interest of a partner who wishes to withdraw so that the withdrawal does not force termination of the partnership.

2.4

Health Maintenance Organizations

A health maintenance organization (HMO) provides a health care plan in which members receive health care services in return for prepaid fees, usually in the form of fixed periodic payments. The HMO also contracts with health care providers, often on a salaried basis, to furnish the health care services. Mental health professionals may be employed by HMOs directly or may be providers who contract with the HMO. This chapter discusses the regulation and licensing of HMOs, the extent to which HMOs are required to provide mental health services, and the issue of provider malpractice liability.

(A) Regulation

In California, regulation of HMOs falls under the Knox–Keene Health Care Service Plan Act of 1975.[1] A health care service plan under the act is any entity that arranges for the provision of health care services to its members in return for a prepaid or periodic charge.[2]

---

1. Health & Safety Code §§ 1340 to 1399.64. HMOs are also regulated by Federal law under the Health Maintenance Organization Act of 1973 (*see* 42 U.S.C. § 300e *et seq.*)
2. This also includes plans that reimburse or pay for health care services.

(B) Licensing

Health care service plans must be licensed by the Commissioner of Corporations.[3] Among the requirements for licensure are:

1. all facilities utilized by the plan must be licensed by the Department of Health Services; and

2. all personnel employed by, or under contract to the plan must be licensed by their respective state license boards; and

3. the plan must provide basic health care services.[4] These services include physician services, hospital inpatient and ambulatory care services, diagnostic laboratory services, home health services, preventive health services, and emergency services.[5]

(C) Mental Health Services

While not included as basic services, HMOs must provide up to 20 outpatient visits per year as necessary for short-term evaluative or crisis intervention mental health services.[6] Health care service plans may, but are not required to, include coverage for more extensive mental health services.[7] An example of the more extensive mental health services is community residential treatment services as alternatives to inpatient care.[8]

---

3. Health & Safety Code § 1349. Plans operated by insurers must also be licensed by the insurance commissioner unless exempted. HMOs differ from insurers in that the insurers have indemnity contracts as a significant financial proportion of their business. However, at least one court has intimated that a health care provider sponsoring a prepaid health care plan stands in the same quasi-fiduciary capacity as respects plan beneficiaries as an insurer does. *California Physicians Service v. Superior Court* 9 Cal.App.4th 1321 (1992). A fiduciary or quasi-fiduciary status could lead to the imposition of duty the health plan does not anticipate. Further, Employee Assistance Plans may be exempt from the Knox–Keene requirements under Health & Safety Code § 1349.2.
4. Health & Safety Code § 1367.
5. Health & Safety Code § 1345(b).
6. Health & Safety Code § 1373(h)(1–7); 42 CFR p. 151. Federal law also requires short-term (not to exceed 20 visits) outpatient evaluative and crisis intervention mental health services as an element of basic health services. 42 U.S.C. § 300e-1(1)(D).
7. Health & Safety Code § 1373(h)(1). A plan that offers outpatient mental health services in some contracts must inform prospective group contractholders as to the availability of these services. *See Weisman v. Blue Shield of California*, 163 Cal.App.3d 61 (1984) (medical doctor receiving psychoanalysis sued Blue Shield for cutting the number of sessions and having unqualified peer review).
8. Health & Safety Code § 1373(h)(7).

Where more extensive mental health services are covered, a member may select any licensed psychologist, or, upon referral by a licensed physician and surgeon, any licensed marriage, family, and child counselor; licensed clinical social worker; or registered nurse with a masters degree in psychiatric mental health nursing with two years of experience.[9] However, a health care service plan may restrict a member's choice to providers affiliated with, or under contract to, the plan to which the member belongs.[10]

A health care service plan contract written or issued for delivery outside of California that provides mental health benefits to California residents may not prohibit the selection of California licensed psychologists; marriage, family, and child counselors; clinical social workers; or registered nurses with master's degrees in psychiatric mental health nursing to provide services in California that are within the scope of the contract.[11]

Health care service plans must pay for services rendered in state hospitals so long as the services would have been otherwise covered.[12] However, a plan does not have to pay in excess of what such services would have cost if performed at a contracting hospital.

No health care plan can deny a claim for hospital, medical, or surgical services for the sole reason that the person while served was confined in a city or county jail, if the person is otherwise entitled to reimbursement under the contract.

(D) Providers Liability

Contracts between health care providers and health care service plans must be in writing.[13] The contracts must contain a clause stating that, should the plan fail to pay for services provided, individual members are not liable directly to the provider.[14] Providers and their agents are precluded by law from attempting to collect from, or maintaining any action for collection against, individual members for payment of covered services provided,

---

9. Health & Safety Code § 1373(h)(2).
10. Health & Safety Code § 1373(h)(5).
11. Health & Safety Code §§ 1373.7, 1373.8. The legislative intent behind these sections is for the mutual benefit of residents covered under the contract and California licensees qualified to render their services. However, the statute does not specifically require that the mental health professional be affiliated with the plan.
12. Health & Safety Code § 1374.12.
13. Health & Safety Code § 1379(a).
14. *Id.*

regardless of whether or not a contract exists between the plan and the provider.[15]

The extent to which HMOs are subject to malpractice liability is an open question at this time,[16] although various professional articles have discussed potential vicarious liability for negligence of member physicians, liability for negligent selection and control of physicians, and intentional acts.[17]

---

15. Health & Safety Code § 1379(b)&(c).
16. Health & Safety Code § 1374.11.
17. David Oakley and Eileen Kelley, *Liability for Malpractice of Member Physicians: The Case of IPA Model HMOs,* 23 Tort and Insurance Law Journal 624 (1988).

2.5

Preferred Provider Organizations

Preferred provider organizations (PPOs) may be health care service plans and may be governed by the Knox–Keene Health Care Service Plan Act of 1975.[1] There are two basic types of PPOs. The provider-based PPO is established by a hospital or by health care providers and provides contracts for health care services. Purchaser-based PPOs are third-party payers who provide contracts for health care services and who assemble a base of providers, contracting with them for their services.[2] PPOs typically reimburse providers at fixed, negotiated rates. Mental health professionals may apply to be providers for PPOs. Generally, providers are required to submit written applications and sign written contracts agreeing to abide by terms and conditions.

The proliferation of HMOs and their contractual relationship with PPOs have had the effect of diminishing the available patient base for MHPs who are not members of PPOs. However, PPOs offer a source of patient referrals that MHPs may not otherwise be able to obtain. Thus, not joining a PPO may negatively impact on an MHP's practice.

---

1. *See* Health & Safety Code §§ 1340 to 1399.64. The Knox–Keene Act is also discussed in chapter 2.4.
2. *See Preferred Provider Organizations and Provider Contracting: New Analyses Under the Sherman Act,* 37 Hastings Law Journal 377 (1985).

2.6

Independent Practice Associations

Independent practice associations (IPAs) are groups where individual providers contract to deliver services to HMO members who prepay premiums. An IPA may also take a corporate form and act as an intermediary between MHPs under contract to the IPA and the HMO. IPA providers are paid on a fee-for-service basis according to a negotiated fee schedule. IPA providers typically maintain private practices and treat both group and individual patients. IPAs generally do not own facilities; patients are seen in providers' private offices and are sent to private clinics and hospitals. Mental health professionals may be involved in IPAs as providers who contract through the IPA with an HMO. As HMOs proliferate, it is increasingly important for MHPs to be able to participate in IPAs, or they face a diminished patient base.

(A) Regulation

Because the definition of a health care service plan encompasses any plan that provides health care services to members in return for prepaid charges,[1] IPAs are also governed by the Knox–Keene Health Care Service Plan Act of 1975.[2] Thus, IPAs are subject to regulation by the California Department of Corporations.

---

1. The complete definition is "any person who undertakes to arrange for the provision of health care services to subscribers or enrollees, or to pay for or to reimburse any part of the cost for such services, in return for a prepaid or periodic charge paid by or on behalf of such subscribers or enrollees." Health & Safety Code § 1345(f).
2. *See* Health & Safety Code §§ 1340 to 1399.64. Interestingly, Section 1373 refers to "all health care service plans and individual practice associations." This would imply there is a distinction; however, neither this, nor any other section, treats the two differently.

2.7

Hospital, Administrative, and Staff Privileges

Psychologists and psychiatrists can obtain hospital staff privileges. This chapter discusses rules governing the granting or denial of staff privileges, as well as statutorily mandated reports arising from the restriction, suspension, revocation, or denial of staff privileges.

(A) Agency and Administrative Positions

There are no statutory qualifications for the position of Director of Mental Health who oversees the State Department of Mental Health.[1] Each state hospital has three officers: a clinical director, a hospital administrator, and a hospital director.[2] Of these, only the clinical director is required to be a licensed practitioner.[3]

Each program at a state hospital has a program director appointed by the Director of Mental Health.[4] Program directors may be licensed psychiatrists, psychologists, psychiatric technicians, or clinical social workers.[5]

---

1. Welf. & Inst. Code § 4301.
2. Welf. & Inst. Code § 4300.
3. Welf. & Inst. Code § 4308. The clinical director must be a licensed physician who is a qualified specialist in a branch of medicine that includes diseases affecting the brain and nervous system.
4. Welf. & Inst. Code § 4301.
5. Welf. & Inst. Code § 4308. If the program director is not a licensed physician, a licensed physician must be available to assume responsibility for all acts requiring performance by a licensed physician. However, program directors of medical surgical units must be licensed physicians. *Id.*

(B) Hospital Staff Privileges

Hospitals with five or more physicians on the staff are required to create rules that

1. formally establish a medical staff and provide for annual or biennial appointments;
2. restrict the staff to competent licensed practitioners;
3. provide periodic review of clinical work; and
4. specify procedures for maintaining accurate and adequate medical records.[6]

Prior to granting staff privileges to any psychiatrist or psychologist, all licensed hospitals and health care service plans must request a report from the Medical Board regarding the filing of any reports concerning the practitioner.[7]

(C) Denial of Staff Privileges

When an application for staff privileges is denied, or privileges are terminated, restricted, or revoked for medical disciplinary reasons, the chief of staff must file a report with the state licensing agency having jurisdiction over the licensee (either a psychiatrist or psychologist).[8] *Medical disciplinary cause or reason* means the aspect of a licensee's competence or professional conduct that is reasonably likely to be detrimental to patient safety or the delivery of patient care.[9] The report must identify the licensee and describe the relevant facts and circumstances of the disciplinary cause or reason. The licensee must be provided with a copy of the report. Hospital records regarding the applications for staff privileges and the grant, denial, suspension, or revocation of such privileges are immune from discovery in a civil litigation.[10]

---

6. Bus. & Prof. Code § 2282. Failure to establish such rules constitutes unprofessional conduct. *Id.* Hospitals with fewer than five physicians are required only to restrict the staff to competent, licensed practitioners and maintain accurate and adequate records. *Id.* § 2283.
7. *See* Bus. & Prof. Code § 805 and the discussion *infra*.
8. *Id.* Such a report is referred to as an 805 Report.
9. Bus. & Prof. Code § 805(a)(6).
10. The California Supreme Court reaffirmed the immunity under Evid. Code § 1157 in *Alexander v. Superior Court*, 5 Cal.4th 1218 (1993). *Elam v. College Park Hospital*, 132 Cal.App.3d 332 (1982); *Henry Mayo Newhall Memorial Hospital v. Superior Court*, 81 Cal.App.3d 626 (1978); *West Covina Hospital v. Superior Court*, 153 Cal.App.3d 134 (1984).

The board of directors of local hospital districts must provide for appellate review of actions, decisions, or recommendations of the board regarding staff privileges.[11] A health facility[12] may establish terms and conditions for the appointment of mental health professionals to their staff.[13]

(D) Staff Privileges for Psychologists

If a hospital offers services that both psychologists and physicians may perform, the services may be performed by either without discrimination. Psychologists can be given primary responsibility for the admission, diagnosis, treatment, and discharge of their patients.[14]

(E) Staff Privileges for Psychiatrists: Exceptions

In a recent case, the California Supreme Court held that the legislature intended to allow psychologists and psychiatrists to provide the same services, except for three areas that were reserved to psychiatrists:

1. the prescription, administration and monitoring of medication;

2. the use of electroconvulsive therapy; and

3. the use of psychosurgery.

(F) Guidelines for Psychologists

The California Psychological Association's Committee on Hospital Practice has prepared guidelines for psychologists regarding hospital practice issues such as medication, electroconvulsive therapy, use of restraints, seclusion, etc. These guidelines are

---

11. Health & Safety Code § 32150.
12. A "health facility" includes all facilities operated for the diagnosis, care, prevention, and treatment of human illness, whether physical or mental.
13. *California Ass'n of Psychology Providers v. Rank*, 51 Cal.3d 1 (1990).
14. Health & Safety Code § 1316.5. Hospitals may require staff members to have insurance, and an attempt to evade that requirement through creation of a phony insurance policy subjected one physician to discipline in *Foster v. Board of Medical Quality Assurance*, 227 Cal.App.3d 1606 (1991).

patterned after an Inpatient Psychiatric Quality Screen developed by the Health Care Financing Administration. However, these guidelines do not have the force of law, nor are they binding on non-psychologists.[15]

---

15. California Psychological Association, *Hospital Practice Guidelines* (1992).

2.8

Zoning for Community Homes

Zoning is the process by which state and local government identify what types of activities and buildings may occur in a given geographic area. Typically, zoning regulations focus on consistency in having areas designated as residential, business, or mixed. Zoning ordinances have been used on occasion to try and exclude businesses deemed objectionable, such as adult theaters or bars.[1] MHPs may become involved in zoning cases as persons whose businesses are affected by zoning regulations or as witnesses on the effect of zoning things. This chapter addresses attempts to restrict community homes through zoning.[2]

(A) Legality of Prohibition of Community Homes

Historically, residential neighborhoods have been reluctant to accept community homes for people who are mentally disabled. A common reaction has been the enactment of zoning ordinances prohibiting such community homes in areas zoned for single-family residential use. The U.S. Supreme Court held that such

---

1. *See Paris Adult Theater I v. Slaten,* 413 U.S. 49 (1973), and discussion in chapter 5D.24 herein.
2. For licensing issues, see the California Community Care Facilities Act. Health & Safety Code § 1500 et seq.

zoning is not precluded, as long as the zoning ordinance bears a rational relationship to legitimate state interests.[3] However, addressing the facts of the case before it, the Court held that requiring a special use permit for a proposed group home showed an irrational prejudice against people who are mentally retarded.[4]

To counteract such prejudice and its effects on people who are mentally disabled, California has established policies encouraging residential living facilities for mentally and physically handicapped persons. For instance, the Legislature declared that mentally and physically handicapped persons are entitled to live in normal residential surroundings and should not be excluded therefrom because of their disability.[5] The Legislature also stated an intention to "establish a system of residential treatment programs in every county" as an alternative to institutional care, based on the concept of residential, community-based treatment.[6] According to the Legislature, there is an "urgent need to establish a coordinated and comprehensive statewide service system of quality community care for the mentally ill, developmentally and physically disabled, and children and adults who require care or services by a facility or organization issued a license or special permit."[7]

In furtherance of these policies, state-authorized licensed or certified group homes[8] that provide 24-hour care and serve six or fewer mentally disordered or otherwise handicapped persons or dependent and neglected children are deemed residential uses for

---

3. *City of Cleburne v. Cleburne Living Center, Inc.*, 473 U.S. 432 (1985). In applying the rational basis test, the Court refused to find mental retardation a quasi-suspect class. The rational basis standard is the easiest standard for the government to meet, and government actions are typically upheld unless a clear abuse of discretion is found.
4. *Id.* As used in this book, the terms *mentally disabled, mentally retarded,* and *mentally handicapped* are interchangeable and reflect the differing usage in different statutes.
5. Welf. & Inst. Code § 5115. Similarly, the State Department of Developmental Services and State Department of Mental Health are directed to institute a joint program to encourage the establishment of sufficient numbers and types of living arrangements, in communities as well as state hospitals, to meet the needs of persons served by those departments. *Id.* § 4510.
6. Welf. & Inst. Code § 5450. The remainder of this chapter of the Code lays out the related provisions regarding the community residential treatment system.
7. Health & Safety Code § 1501.
8. Also included are family care homes and foster homes.

zoning purposes.[9] These homes are permitted in all residential zones, including zones for single-family dwellings.[10]

(B) Policy Against Discrimination

California law prohibits cities and counties from discriminating "in the enactment, enforcement, or administration of any zoning laws, ordinances, or rules and regulations between the use of property for the treatment of general hospital or nursing home patients and the use of property for the psychiatric care and treatment of patients, both inpatient and outpatient."[11] For instance, in a zone where rest homes and convalescent homes are conditionally permitted, a city may not prevent a facility for mental patients.[12]

A city or county may deny a residential care facility's request for a license if another residential care facility is within 300 feet of the proposed location.[13] Foster family homes and residential care facilities for the elderly should not be considered when making this determination.[14]

---

9. Welf. & Inst. Code §§ 5115, 5116. This clear legislative intent preempts the field of zoning such that all municipal regulations must yield to these policies and regulations.
10. Welf. & Inst. Code § 5116. *See also* Health & Safety Code § 1566.3 for the same rule. Section 1566.3 additionally states that residents and operators of such facilities "shall be considered a family for the purposes of any law or zoning ordinance which relates to the residential use of property." These provisions do not affect private contractual rights such as deed restrictions precluding such facilities. *Seaton v. Clifford* 24 Cal.App.3d 46, 100 Cal.Rptr. 779 (1972).
11. Welf. & Inst. Code § 5120.
12. *City of Torrance v. Transactional Living Centers for Los Angeles, Inc.* 30 Cal.3d 516, 179 Cal.Rptr. 907 (1982).
13. Health & Safety Code § 1520.5. This section also directs the director of mental health to deny applications for licenses if similar overcrowding would result.
14. Health & Safety Code § 1520.5(f).

Insurance Reimbursement and Deductions for Services

3.1

Insurance Reimbursement for Services

There are a variety of insurance carriers and plans available in California, all of which generally provide for reimbursement for services provided by psychiatrists and other medical doctors. However, individual insurance companies and individual policies may seek to exclude certain categories of mental health professionals from their reimbursement provisions. California law provides that insurance carriers licensed in California must provide coverage for certain mental health professionals. These are referred to as freedom-of-choice laws. This chapter addresses the circumstances under which insurance carriers are required to cover MHP services and the extent to which insurance carriers may receive medical information to make reimbursement decisions.

(A) Types of Insurance Affected

California law specifies that if a health care service plan contract, policy of disability insurance, self-insured employee, welfare benefit, or hospital service plan contract is licensed in California and provides coverage solely for California residents (even if it was written or issued for delivery outside of California) and has benefits within the scope of practice of a licensed clinical social worker, licensed registered nurse, or a marriage, family, and child counselor, the plan cannot prohibit the selection of such licensees to perform services in California, even where the licensees are not licensed in the state where the contract or policy is written or issued for delivery.[1]

Some plans, however, may require a physician referral or may not reimburse for services provided by psychologists, psychological assistants, or marriage, family, and child counselor interns.

(B) Required Coverage of Psychiatric Services

A health care service plan, or specialized health care service plan, may provide coverage for professional mental health services or for the exclusion of such services. If the terms and conditions include coverage for services provided in a general acute hospital or acute psychiatric hospital and do not restrict or modify the choice of providers, the coverage shall extend to care provided by a psychiatric health facility licensed by the state department of health services, or one that has obtained a waiver of licensure by the state department of mental health.

A health care service plan that offers outpatient mental health services, but does not cover such services in all of its group contracts, is required to communicate to prospective group contract holders regarding the availability of outpatient coverage for the treatment of mental or nervous disorders.[2]

A disability insurance policy may provide for payment of medical and professional mental health services on a reimbursement basis or may exclude such services.[3]

As of January 1, 1990, all health care service plans that cover hospital, medical, or surgical expenses are required to offer treatment of substance abuse.[4]

(C) Prohibiting Denial of Reimbursements for Psychological Services

California requires that any health plan that provides coverage for professional mental health services cannot prohibit a member

---

1. Health & Safety Code § 1373.8; Ins. Code §§ 10176.7, 10177.8, 11512.8.
2. Health & Safety Code § 1373(h)(1).
3. Ins. Code § 10176.
4. Health & Safety Code § 1367.2.

from selecting any licensed psychologist or, upon referral by a physician, any licensed marriage, family, and child counselor, licensed clinical social worker or registered nurse, who possesses a masters degree in psychiatric/mental health nursing and two years of supervised experience in psychiatric/mental health nursing.[5] However, all health care service plans and individual practice associations that offer mental health benefits are required to make reasonable efforts to make available to the members the services of licensed psychologists. The failure of a plan or association to comply with this requirement is not deemed to constitute a misdemeanor.[6]

Health care service plan coverage for professional mental health services may include community residential treatment services that either are alternatives to inpatient care and are directly affiliated with the plan or to which enrollees are referred by providers affiliated with the plan.[7]

A disability insurance policy that provides for the inclusion or exclusion of professional mental health services cannot prohibit the insured from selecting a licensed psychologist to perform services covered by the terms of the policy. Nor can the policy prohibit the insured upon referral by a physician from selecting a licensed clinical social worker, marriage, family, and child counselor, or registered nurse with a masters degree in psychiatric/mental health nursing and two years of supervised practice in psychiatric/mental health nursing.[8]

A self-insured employer welfare benefit plan that includes California residents (but which may be written or issued for delivery outside of California) where benefits are provided within the scope of licensed clinical social workers, registered nurses with a masters degree in psychiatric/mental health nursing, and MFCCs shall not prohibit persons covered by the plan from selecting those licensees.[9]

In recent years there has been a controversy over whether some of these plans would come within the scope of ERISA and are pre-empted. However, if a company that is involved in an ERISA plan chooses to underwrite the risk through insurance, then state freedom-of-choice plans would not be pre-empted.[10]

Under California law, the inclusion of psychological services is not mandatory at this time, although where such services are provided, freedom-of-choice is mandated.

5. Health & Safety Code § 1373(h)(1)(2)
6. Health & Safety Code § 1373(h)(5).
7. Health & Safety Code § 1373(h)(7).
8. Ins. Code §§ 10176, 10176.7, 10177.
9. Ins. Code § 10177.8.
10. *Metropolitan Life Ins. Co. v. Massachusetts*, 105 U.S. 2380 (1985).

(D) Disclosure by Psychotherapists to Insurance Companies

Under the confidentiality of Medical Information Act, as discussed more fully in chapter 4.2, the disclosure of information to insurance companies is permissible under certain circumstances, primarily where it is necessary to determine responsibility for payment, to allow determinations regarding coverage, or to allow quality or peer review.[11] However, such information cannot be disclosed beyond the purposes for which it is sought. The information to be disclosed is to be limited to the information necessary for the insurance carrier to ascertain the responsibility for payment. Furthermore, persons or entities who are engaged in the business of furnishing administrative services to programs that provide payment for health care services cannot knowingly use or disclose, or permit its employees or agents to use or disclose, medical information possessed in connection with performing administrative functions for such a program, except as reasonably necessary in connection with the administration or maintenance of the program or as required by law.[12] California also has an Insurance Information and Privacy Protection Act, which carriers are required to comply with, and which accords some protection to personal and medical information.[13]

Generally carriers have reviewers whose task is to determine whether services are usual, customary, and reasonable and carriers decline to pay all other services. The law does allow disclosure to such individuals, with respect to medical necessity, level of care, quality of care, and justification of charges.[14]

(E) Civil Suits Over Denials

Patients can bring suits against insurance carriers for failure to pay for mental health treatment. In one case, the patient was a medical doctor who sued over Blue Shield's failure to pay for all of his psychoanalytic treatment. The patient alleged that Blue Shield had unqualified persons reviewing claims and that it failed to pay in a timely fashion. He recovered $25,000.[15]

The California Supreme Court has refused to find that retrospective review of medical or mental health services by an insur-

---

11. Civ. Code § 56.10.
12. Civ. Code § 56.26.
13. Ins. Code §§ 791 to 791.26.
14. Civ. Code § 56.10(c)(4).
15. *Weisman v. Blue Shield of California,* 163 Cal.App.3d 61 (1984).

ance carrier frustrates the insured's goal of attaining peace of mind through insurance. The court has agreed that an insurance carrier can refuse to pay for services that were not "medically necessary." The *medically necessary* standard is an objective one and is not intended to delegate the treatment decision to the carrier by the doctor.[16] However, a carrier cannot use a *medically necessary* standard that is significantly at variance with the standard used by the medical community.[17]

In a recent case, a patient had been admitted to the hospital for major depression, drug dependency, and anorexia. The treating physician determined he needed three to four weeks of inpatient hospitalization. After ten days, his insurance company refused to pay for any further hospital care. He was discharged solely for lack of funds and committed suicide within three weeks. The defendants, in the case brought by his survivors and estate, included a company hired to perform general utilization review for the insurer, which claimed that only the physicians could be liable for the discharge decision. The court rejected this argument, holding that claims could be asserted against both the company performing the utilization review and the insurers for the denial of benefits.[18]

(F) Retaliation Proscribed

The Legislature has expressly provided that a physician cannot be punished by a payor for appealing a payor's decision to deny payment for medical care the physician believes impairs his or her ability to provide medically appropriate care to the patient.[19]

---

16. *Sarchett v. Blue Shield of California*, 43 Cal.3d 1 (1987).
17. *See Hughes v. Blue Cross of Northern California*, 215 Cal.App.3d 832 (1989), where a young man was hospitalized after he had taken an overdose of aspirin and stabbed himself with a screwdriver a number of times. The consultant for Blue Cross recommended significantly less treatment than the other physicians involved in the patient's care. The consultant conceded at trial he generally spent 12 minutes evaluating each claim and that his opinion of what was "medically necessary" might be more restrictive than the medical community's standard. The Court of Appeals upheld an award against Blue Cross.
18. *Wilson v. Blue Cross of Southern California*, 222 Cal.App.3d 660 (1990).
19. Bus. & Prof. Code § 2056.

3.2

Mental Health Benefits in State Insurance Plans

Unlike some states, California does not mandate that health insurance provided for California government employees include mental health benefits.

3.3

Tax Deductions for Services

Under both federal and California law, in certain circumstances, mental health services may be tax deductible. This chapter discusses the extent to which services provided by MHPs are deductible and the extent to which MHPs can deduct continuing education and their personal therapy costs as business expenses.

(A) Medical Deduction

Mental health services are a medical deduction.

The Internal Revenue Code allows a deduction for medical expenses that exceed a certain percentage of tax-adjusted gross income. There is a similar deduction under California law.

Under federal law, deductions for services of psychiatrists and psychologists are both expressly recognized.[1] The services of other mental health professionals, collectively referred to as "psychotherapists" under federal law, may be deductible even if such individuals are not licensed or certified by the applicable state.[2] Psychotherapy is deductible as a medical expense for a child with psychiatric problems who is sent to a private school specializing in learning disability.[3]

---

1. Rev. Rul. 1953-143, 1953-2 C.B. 129.
2. Rev. Rul. 1963-91, C.B. 54.
3. *Greisdorf v. Commissioner*, 54 T.C. 1684 (1970).

(B) Medical Deduction Denied

A deduction was denied, where a psychiatrist recommended that a mentally ill child be sent to a particular school without resources to provide psychological services and no psychiatrist or psychologist on staff.[4] Deductions were also denied where a psychiatric patient contended that shopping sprees and home remodeling were therapeutic for her.[5]

(C) Legal Fees

Legal fees related to psychiatric care may be deductible as a medical expense when involuntary confinement is necessary and legal proceedings had to be initiated to effectuate it.[6] However, a deduction was denied for legal fees incurred in obtaining a divorce on the advice of a psychiatrist.[7] Further, spiritual counseling[8] and Church of Scientology auditing or processing are not deductible.[9]

(D) Mental Health Services as a Business Deduction

Under federal law, health services may be deductible as a business expense to the extent that they are ordinary and necessary expenses involved in the carrying on of a trade or business. This may be particularly true if the business is a small closely held one and the services are provided to key employees. However, if the medical or mental health services are not clearly identified as such, and are instead being taken as a business deduction without specifying their nature, either the Franchise Tax Board or the Internal Revenue Service may raise questions. The use of mental health services to assist employees and key personnel appears to be becoming more accepted.

---

4. *Kaufman v. Commissioner*, 76-1 T.C. 9182.
5. *Rabb v. Commissioner*, 31 T.C.M. (CCH) 476 (1972).
6. *Gerstacker v. Commissioner*, 414 F.2d 448 (6th Cir. 1969); *Smith v. Commissioner*, 44 T.C.M. (CCH) 672 (1982).
7. *Jacobs v. Commissioner*, 62 T.C. 813 (1974).
8. *Miller v. Commissioner*, 40 T.C.M. (CCH) 243 (1980).
9. *Brown v. Commissioner*, 523 F.2d 365 (8th Cir. 1975).

(E) Mental Health Services Received by MHPs

As with other professionals, MHPs are not allowed to deduct the cost of the education necessary to begin their careers. In essence, any education that is a prerequisite to becoming licensed or practicing as an MHP is not deductible as any type of business expense.[10] By the same token, the cost of review courses to obtain licensure are not deductible, nor are expenses associated with an internship or psychological assistantship. The rule is that any expense incurred to attain the basic entrance to a field or profession is not deductible. Once an MHP has begun employment as a professional, subsequent education may be deducted if certain criteria are met. Generally, the criteria are that the courses must be actually related to the business in question, must help the professional maintain or meet minimum requirements of the job or performance, and must involve improving or maintaining the individual skills or must be required by law.[11]

A specific example in the IRS regulations allows a psychiatrist to deduct the cost of a program of study at an accredited psychoanalytic institute because the study maintains or improves existing skills but doesn't qualify him or her for a new business.

However, cases diverge on whether the personal analysis required to become a psychoanalyst is deductible. In one case the psychoanalysis was deductible because the psychoanalyst suffered from an anxiety reaction, even though it had a secondary advantage of qualifying him as a psychoanalyst.[12] In contrast, two psychiatrists who had completed their psychiatric training could not deduct the cost of required personal analysis as medical expenses.[13]

(F) Continuing Education

Thus, continuing education courses are deductible, particularly when required by the licensing authority. However, MHPs should be aware that the IRS will on occasion closely scrutinize seminars in resort areas that appear to have minimal professional training involved. Further, educational expenses that lead to a new business are not deductible. To the extent that psychother-

---

10. Treas. Reg. § 1.62-5(a)(2).
11. *Internal Revenue Service Regulations* § 1.62-5(a).
12. *Starrett v. Commissioner*, 41 T.C. 877 (1964).
13. *Namrow v. Commissioner*, 288 F.2d 648 (4th Cir. 1961); Rev. Rul. 1956-263 1956-1 C.B. 135; *cf. Voight v. Commissioner*, 74 T.C. 82 (1980).

apy is a necessary part of an MHP's practice, there is some authority allowing it to be deducted if a professional has begun his or her practice.[14]

---

14. *Voight v. Commissioner,* 74 T.C. 82 (1980); *Porter v. Commissioner,* 52 T.C.M. 615 (CCH) (1986).

Privacy of Professional Information

4.1

Ownership, Maintenance, and Access to Records

The issues surrounding ownership, maintenance, and access to patient records that are maintained by MHPs is an area where MHPs vary greatly in their individual practices and procedures. Since many of these practices may be in violation of the law, this chapter focuses on technical requirements regarding maintenance and access to records.

(A) Statutory History

Prior to the enactment of the Confidentiality of Medical Information Act (as discussed in chapter 4.2), the maintenance and disclosure of medical and mental health records were primarily governed by the regulations of the licensing boards and the Health and Safety Code.[1] With the enactment of the Confidentiality of Medical Information Act, the confidentiality and disclosure requirements have become more explicit.

(B) Requirement to Keep and Obtain Records

Over and above the requirements discussed above, the case law suggests a duty to not only maintain notes but to obtain notes from other prior mental health professionals early in treatment. In a failure to warn case, the Ninth Circuit Court of Appeals held

---

1. Health & Safety Code §§ 1795 to 1795.26

that the Veterans Administration Hospital had an obligation to obtain, review, and if necessary communicate information from prior psychiatric records to avoid a possible risk of violence by a patient.[2] Mental health professionals who elect not to take notes are doing so at their peril because in a civil suit or an action before the licensing board, the absence of notes will be considered a deviation from the required standard of care.

(C) Alcohol and Drug Abuse Records

Alcohol and drug abuse records are confidential under both California law and federal law to the extent that the institution provides services within the scope of federal law.[3]

Where a mental health provider provides care to a minor for a drug or alcohol problem, the treatment plan must include the minor's parents, if appropriate, as determined by the health care provider. The health care provider rendering the treatment or counseling must state in the minor's treatment record whether and when an attempt was made to contact the parents or legal guardian and the results of the attempt to contact. If no such contact is attempted the record must state why, in the health care provider's opinion, it would not be appropriate to contact the parents. This section expressly applies to physicians and surgeons, registered nurses, psychologists, clinical social workers, and marriage, family, and child counselors (see chapter 5A.21).[4]

(D) Maintenance of Records

In addition to the requirements imposed by California laws and regulations, the Board of Behavioral Science Examiners and the Board of Psychology have relied on the ethical principles promulgated by the American Psychological Association and have applied them to both psychologists and marriage, family, and child counselors, even though the individual licensees may not be members of the American Psychological Association. The American Psychological Association has established record-keeping guidelines that govern the content and retention of records.[5] In addition, the *Specialty Guidelines for Clinical Psychologists* contain

---

2. *Jablonski ex rel. Pahls v. United States*, 712 F.2d 391 (9th Cir. 1983).
3. Welf. & Inst. Code § 5330.
4. Civ. Code § 34.10; Family Code § 6929. Interestingly enough, originally the Health & Safety Code definition of *health care provider* did not include psychologists. Health & Safety Code § 1795.10; however, this was amended in 1994, to be effective January 1, 1995.
5. "Record keeping guidelines." (1993). *American Psychologist, 89,* 984–986.

an express requirement that records be kept setting forth various minimal information about each patient.[6] While no express regulation of the Medical Board, Board of Psychology, or Board of Behavioral Science Examiners expressly requires note-taking or recordkeeping, the Boards have found the failure to take notes or keep records to be gross negligence and a significant departure from the standard of care.[7] Furthermore, psychiatrists are required to keep records on the prescriptions of certain dangerous drugs.

The degree to which records of supervision sessions must be maintained has not been addressed, although, for example, the supervisor of a psychological assistant is required to inform each client or patient in writing prior to the services that the assistant is unlicensed and under the direction and supervision of the supervisor.[8] In the absence of other definitions, the criteria set forth in the *Specialty Guidelines* for clinical psychologists should be followed.

As to records created by a marriage, family, and child counselor, social worker, or other health care provider (and psychologists, as of January 1, 1995), the law requires the records to be preserved for a minimum of seven years following the discharge of the patient except that the records of unemancipated minors should be kept one year after the minor has reached the age of 18, but in no event less than seven years.[9]

The law provides that any person injured as a result of a licensee's abandonment of health records can bring an action for damages suffered as a result of the loss of the records.[10]

Abandonment is defined to mean leaving patients treated by the licensee without access to medical information to which they are entitled.

Patients and their representatives have a right of access to complete information regarding their condition and care.[11] The law expressly includes mental health records, which are defined as records relating to the evaluation or treatment of a mental disorder, and alcohol and drug abuse records.[12]

The term *patient records* is defined to mean any form or medium maintained by, or in the custody or control of, a health care provider relating to the health history, diagnosis, or condition of a

---

6. American Psychological Association, *Specialty Guidelines for the Delivery of Services by Clinical Psychologists* (1981), as amended June 2, 1989) § 2.3.3.
7. Bus. & Prof. Code § 4982, 2960(j).
8. 16 CCR § 1391.6.
9. Health & Safety Code § 1795.
10. Health & Safety Code § 1795.25. (Again, this does not include psychologists.)
11. Health & Safety Code § 1795.
12. Health & Safety Code § 1795.10(b).

patient relating to treatment provided or proposed to be provided to the patient. This does not include any information given to the health care provider by a person other than the patient or another health care provider, and where disclosure is required, material received from another person may be removed prior to copying. *Patient records* also does not include information contained in an aggregate form, such as indexes or registers.[13]

(E) Access to Records

Any adult patient may get his or her records upon providing the health care provider with a written request for the records and payment of reasonable clerical costs, which are defined by statute. Minor patients who are authorized by law to consent to medical treatment can also obtain their records upon written request and payment of costs. However, a patient who is a minor has a more limited right of access: The minor can inspect only patient records pertaining to health care of a type that the minor is lawfully authorized to consent to. In addition, a special edition of the law states that where a minor's representative has requested access to patient records, and the health care provider determines that disclosure would have a detrimental effect on the provider's professional relationship with the minor patient, or on the minor's physical safety or psychological well-being, disclosure can be withheld. The decision of the health care provider as to whether or not the records are available for inspection under that statutory section will not lead to any form of liability unless the decision is found to have been in bad faith.

When a health care provider determines there is a substantial risk of significant adverse or detrimental consequences to a patient as a result of receiving a copy of mental health records that have been requested, the provider can decline to permit inspection and provide copies subject to four conditions:

1. the health care provider must make a written record to be included with the requested mental health records, which contains the date of the request and explains the reason for the refusal to permit inspection or copying. This must include a description of the specific adverse or detrimental consequences to the patient that the provider anticipates would occur if inspection or copying were permitted;

---

13. Health & Safety Code § 1795.10(d).

2. the health care provider must permit inspection or copying of the mental health records to a licensed physician, surgeon, or psychologist designated by the patient;

3. the health care provider must inform the patient of his or her refusal to permit access or copying and inform the patient of the right to permit inspection by or provide copies to licensed physicians, surgeons, psychologists, or licensed clinical social workers, to be designated by the patient; and

4. the health care provider shall indicate in the health records of the patient whether the patient makes a request to have a physician, surgeon, or psychologist review the records.[14]

Any patient who is denied inspection or copying of the records other than in compliance with the above statutory sections can bring an action for damages against the health care provider and can obtain an award of costs and attorney fees if he or she prevails.[15] The health care provider has the option of preparing a summary of the records for inspection and copying by the patient instead of providing copies of the actual records. The summary record must be made available to the patient within 10 working days of the date of the patient's request for records. If more time is needed because the record is of extraordinary length or because the patient was discharged from the licensed health facility within the preceding ten days, the health care provider can notify the patient of the fact that the summary will be delayed, but in no case can the summary be provided more than 30 days after the patient's request. In preparing the summary, the health care provider is not obligated to include information not in the original records. It is also permissible for the health care provider to confer with the patient to clarify the patient's purpose for obtaining the records. If the patient is requesting information only about certain injuries, illnesses, or episodes, the health care provider is not required to prepare a summary that addresses issues other than those identified by the patient. Where a summary is prepared for each injury, illness, or episode, the information to be provided shall include:

1. the chief complaint or complaints, including any pertinent history about them;

2. any findings from consultations or referrals with other health care providers;

3. any diagnosis;

4. the treatment plan and any medications prescribed;

---

14. Health & Safety Code § 1795.14.
15. Health & Safety Code § 1795.16.

5. the progress of treatment;

6. the prognosis, including any significant continuing problems or conditions;

7. pertinent reports of diagnostic procedures and tests and all discharge summaries;

8. any objective findings from the most recent physical examination, including blood pressure, weight, and actual values from routine statutory tests; and

9. the summary shall contain a list of all current medications prescribed, including dosage and any sensitivities or allergies to medications the patient has.

In preparing the summary, the health care provider can charge no more than a reasonable fee based on the actual preparation time and cost. It was the California legislature's intent to have the summaries made available at the lowest possible cost to the patient.[16]

Where copies of the records are provided instead of summaries, the health care provider is entitled to charge a fee for the cost of copying that does not exceed 25 cents per page, or 50 cents per page if the records are copied from microfilm, together with any additional reasonable clerical costs incurred in making the records available. When copies are provided, the copies must be transmitted within 15 days after receiving the written request.[17]

---

16. Health & Safety Code § 1795.20.
17. Health & Safety Code § 1795.12(b).

4.2

Confidential Relations and Communications

Generally, there is no confidentiality except as provided by law. Often MHPs make the erroneous assumption that matters can be deemed confidential simply by agreeing to hold them confidential. In reality, California does not recognize matters as confidential unless they are expressly given confidentiality by a statute or by the California Constitution.

This chapter will discuss the statutory and constitutional basis for confidentiality and circumstances under which disclosure can be made, as well as the consequences of unauthorized disclosure.

(A) Confidentiality Under the Constitution

The confidentiality between mental health professionals and patients initially derives from the California Supreme Court's decision articulating the psychotherapist–patient privilege.[1] Subsequently, the California Constitution was amended to include Article I, section 1, which contains an express right of privacy:

> All people are by nature free and independent and have inalienable rights. Among these are enjoying and defending life and liberty, acquiring, possessing, and protecting property, and pursuing and obtaining safety, happiness, and privacy.

---

1. *In re Lifshutz*, 2 Cal.3d 415 (1970).

The California legislature then enacted a comprehensive law entitled the Confidentiality of Medical Information Act.[2] In addition, the various licensing statutes address confidentiality as to each licensee. The constitutional provisions and Confidentiality Act cut across all licensure lines and are the primary source of confidentiality at the present time. Therefore, these different statutes will be addressed with a reference to the individual statutory provisions left to the chapter on privilege. Further, where there are drug or alcohol programs funded by federal law, a separate confidentiality entitlement and provisions may exist.[3]

The right of privacy in California has been held to provide protection beyond that afforded by the federal Constitution.[4] The right of privacy has been specifically held to apply to communications between a patient and physicians, psychologists, and psychiatrists.[5] The cases have held that the constitutional right of privacy overrides any statutory enactment. Thus, where a licensed clinical social worker disclosed information about a patient in a declaration in a civil suit, the immunity that it is accorded to witnesses in civil proceedings for statements they make was held to be superseded by the constitutional right.[6]

The legislature has reflected the interest in protecting the confidentiality and privacy of medical and psychological information through the Confidentiality of Medical Information Act.[7] This act sets specific criteria under which medical information can be released and requires a written authorization to release any medical or psychological information.[8] Further, a recipient of medical information pursuant to an authorization provided under the code may not further disclose that medical information except in accordance with a new authorization or as specifically required and permitted by law.[9] However, unless the patient expressly makes a written request to the contrary, the statute does not prevent a provider of health care upon inquiry from releasing information about the patient's name, address, age, and sex; the general description and the reason for the treatment; the general nature of the injury; the general condition of the patient; or other information that is not defined as medical information.[10]

---

2. Civ. Code § 56.
3. 42 U.S.C. § 2900 et seq.
4. *People v. Teresinski*, 30 Cal.3d 822 (1982); *American Academy of Pediatrics v. Van de Kamp*, 214 Cal.App.3d 831 (1989).
5. *Estate of Urbaniak v. Newton*, 226 Cal.App.3d 543 (1991); *Urbaniak v. Newton*, 19 Cal.App.4th 1937 (1993); *Cutter v. Brownbridge*, 183 Cal.App.3d 830 (1986); *Davis v. Superior Court*, 7 Cal. App.4th 1008 (1992).
6. *Cutter v. Brownbridge, supra* note 5.
7. Civ. Code § 56; *Heller v. Norcal Mutual Ins. Co.*, 8 Cal.4th 30 (1994).
8. Civ. Code § 56.11.
9. Civ. Code § 56.13.
10. Civ. Code § 56.16.

As defined in the statute, *medical information* means any individually identifiable information in possession of or derived from a provider of health care regarding a patient's medical history, medical or physical condition, or treatment.[11]

Under the statute, the case law, and the Constitution, medical and mental health professionals are required to keep patient records confidential and not disclose information unless they receive a written authorization or certain court orders including subpoenas. Under the Confidentiality of Medical Information Act, a provider of health care can disclose medical information if disclosure is compelled by any of the following:

1. a court order;

2. a board, commission, or administrative agency for purposes of adjudication pursuant to its lawful authority;

3. by a party to a proceeding before a court or administrative agency pursuant to a subpoena duces tecum, notice to appear, or any provision authorizing discovery in a proceeding before a court or administrative agency;

4. by board, commission, or administrative agency pursuant to an investigative subpoena;

5. by an arbitrator or arbitration panel when arbitration is lawfully requested by either party pursuant to subpoena duces tecum authorized by the Code of Civil Procedure or any other provision authorizing discovery in a proceeding before an arbitrator or arbitration panel;

6. by a search warrant lawfully issued to a governmental law enforcement agency; and

7. when otherwise specified by law.

Further, a provider of health care may disclose medical information to the following persons or entities:

1. to providers of health care or other health care professionals or facilities for purposes of diagnosis or treatment of the patient. This includes, in an emergency situation, the communication of patient information by radio transmission between emergency medical personnel at the scene of an emergency, and emergency medical personnel at a health facility;

2. to an insurer, employer, health care service plan, hospital service plan, employee benefit plan, governmental authority, or any other person or entity responsible for paying for health

---

11. Civ. Code § 56.05(b). Under *Inabnit v. Berkeson*, Cal.App.3d 1230 (1988), compliance with the statute and Civ. Proc. Code § 19855.3 gives the professional a complete defense in a suit for breach of confidentiality.

care services rendered to the patient, to the extent necessary to allow responsibility for payment to be determined and payment to be made. If the patient is, by reason of a comatose or other disabling medical condition, unable to consent to the disclosure of medical information and no other arrangements have been made to pay for the health care services, the information may be disclosed to a governmental authority to the extent necessary to determine the patient's eligibility for, and to obtain payment under, a governmental program. The information may also be disclosed to another provider as necessary to assist the other provider in obtaining payment for health care services rendered by that provider to the patient;

3. to any person or entity that provides billing, claims management, medical data processing, or other administrative services for providers. However, no information so disclosed can be further disclosed in any that would be violative of the statute;

4. to organized committees and agents of professional societies or of the medical staff of hospitals, or to licensed health care service plans to professional standards review organizations, to utilization and quality control peer review organizations as established under federal law, or to persons or organizations insuring, responsible for, or defending professional liability that a provider may incur if the committees, agents, plans, organizations or persons are engaged in reviewing the competence or qualifications of health care professionals or in reviewing health care services with respect to medical necessity, level of care, quality of care, or justification of charges;

5. the information in the possession of any provider of health care may be reviewed by any private or public body responsible for licensing or accrediting the provider of health care. However, no patient-identifying medical information may be removed from the premises except as expressly permitted or required by law;

6. the information may be disclosed to the county coroner in the course of an investigation;

7. the information may be disclosed to public agencies, clinical investigators, health care research organizations, and accredited public or private non-profit educational or health care institutions for bona fide research purposes, but not in any way that would allow identification of the patient;

8. to a provider of health care that has created medical information as a result of employment-related health care services to an employee, conducted at the specific prior written request

and expense of the employer, may disclose to the employee's employer that part of the information that (a) is relevant in a lawsuit, arbitration, grievance, or other claim or challenge to which the employer and the employee are parties and in which the patient has placed in issue his or her medical history, mental or physical condition, or treatment, provided that it may only be used or disclosed in connection with that proceeding; or (b) describes the functional limitations of the patient that may entitle the patient to leave from work for medical reasons or limit the patient's fitness to perform his or her present employment;

9. unless the provider is notified in writing of an agreement by the sponsor, insurer, or administrator to the contrary, the information may be disclosed to a sponsor, insurer, or administrator of a group or individual insured or uninsured plan or policy that the patient seeks coverage by or benefits from, if the information was created by the provider of health care as a result of services conducted at the specific prior written request and expense of the sponsor, insurer, or administrator for the purpose of evaluating the application for coverage or benefits;

10. the information may be disclosed to a group practice pre-payment health care service plan by providers that contract with the plan and may be transferred among providers that contract with the plan for the purpose of administering the plan, but medical information may not otherwise be disclosed by the health care service plan;

11. the information may be disclosed to an insurance institution, agent, or support organization if the institution, agent, or support organization has complied with certain requirements under the Insurance Code; and

12. the information relevant to the patient's condition and care may be disclosed to a probate court investigator engaged in determining the need for an initial conservatorship or contin-uation of an existing conservatorship if the patient is unable to give informed consent, or to a probate court investigator, probation officer, or domestic relations investigator engaged in determining the need for an initial guardianship or contin-uation of an existing guardianship.[12]

Information may also be disclosed to a certain extent to comply with reporting provisions of the Business and Professions

---

12. Civ. Code § 56.10.

Code governing settlements involving mental health professionals.[13]

There are some additional specific disclosures authorized by
special statutory sections.[14]

Disclosures are also authorized in circumstances where the
patient makes an express threat of harm against a readily identifiable third party[15] for reporting child abuse[16] or elder abuse.[17]

(B) Liability for Violations

Where information is disclosed in contravention of the constitutional and statutory provisions, a plaintiff can recover compensatory damages.[18] In addition, the Confidentiality of Medical Information Act allows the recovery of punitive damages not to exceed
$3,000, attorney fees not to exceed $1,000, and the cost of litigation.[19] Further, any violation of the provisions of the Confidentiality of Medical Information Act that results in economic loss or
personal injury to a patient is punishable as a misdemeanor.[20]

There is also a more general invasion of privacy statute,
which applies to intentionally eavesdropping or recording a confidential communication without the consent of all parties to the
communication.[21] For such a violation, the person whose rights
have been violated may obtain damages in the amount of $3,000
or three times the amount of actual damages, if any.[22]

Additionally, unauthorized disclosure of confidential information may result in discipline by a licensing agency.

---

13. Civ. Code § 56.105.
14. Civ. Code § 56.3.
15. Civ. Code § 43.92.
16. Penal Code § 11166.
17. Welf. & Inst. Code § 15601.
18. *Cutter v. Brownbridge, supra* note 5.
19. Civ. Code § 4456.35.
20. Civ. Code § 56.36
21. Penal Code §§ 632, 637.2.
22. Penal Code § 637; *Friddle v. Epstein,* 16 Cal.App.4th 1649 (1993).

4.3

Privileged Communications

A privileged communication is a communication that the holder of the privilege must authorize disclosure of and testimony about. Privileges are generally established by statutes or case law. This chapter discusses the criteria for a communication to be privileged, limitations of the privilege, and how the privilege may be waived.

The circumstances under which the privilege can be claimed (or must be claimed), limitations on the privilege, and the circumstances that constitute waiver of the privilege are discussed separately for psychologists, marriage, family, and child counselors, psychiatrists, and licensed clinical social workers. MHPs must also be aware of potential liability for making an unauthorized disclosure of privileged information.

(A) Origin of the Privilege

In California, the psychotherapist–patient privilege was first articulated by the Supreme Court and then was codified by statute. The California Constitution also contains an express section on the right of privacy, which has been held to include the psychotherapist–patient privilege.[1]

---

1. *In re Lifschutz*, 2 Cal.3d 415; Evid. Code §§ 1012 to 1015; Cal. Const. art. I, § 1.

(B) Purpose of the Privilege

The purpose of the privilege is to encourage clients or patients to discuss all of the problems that they are experiencing in a candid manner, and not to withhold information out of a concern that it might prove embarrassing. While the privilege applies to protect the client from unauthorized disclosures by the mental health professional, it does not protect the client from a subpoena for records that complies with certain statutory provisions, or from court orders requiring an MHP to testify.[2]

(C) Criteria for Privileged Communications

Contrary to popular belief, merely asserting that a communication is privileged will not cloak it with confidentiality unless it falls within the criteria for the psychotherapist–patient privilege or some other statutory exception to disclosure. MHPs must be aware of the requirements and limitations of the law not only so that they can advise their clients of its limitations, but also so that they will not be misled into inadvertent and improper disclosure due to ignorance of the precise parameters of the law.[3] In addition to the other privileges discussed below, counselors of sexual assault and domestic violence victims may have a limited privilege to withhold information unless a court determines that disclosure of the information is necessary in a criminal proceeding.[4]

(D) Psychologists

(D)(1) Privilege for Psychologists

The Evidence Code section on confidentiality is incorporated into the psychology licensing law.[5] It is analogous, but not identical, to the attorney–client privilege and the priest–penitent privilege. The Evidence Code's definition of a psychotherapist specifically includes psychologists, but the law sets forth a series of specific requirements for the privilege to apply. The first, and perhaps the most obvious, is that the communication must be from a patient

---

2. *Inabnit v. Berkson*, 199 Cal.App.3d 1230 (1988).
3. *Cutter v. Brownbridge*, 183 Cal.App.3d 836 (1983); *People v. Stritzinger*, 34 Cal.3d 505 (1983).
4. Evid. Code §§ 1035 to 1037.7.
5. Bus. & Prof. Code § 2918; Evid. Code § 1010.

to a person who qualifies as a psychotherapist. The privilege exists only as to communications with professionals specified in the Evidence Code.

(D)(2) Definitions

The term *psychotherapist* is defined to include the following:

1. a person who is authorized, or reasonably believed by the patient to be authorized, to practice medicine, who devotes, or whom the patient reasonably believes devotes, a substantial portion of his or her time to the practice of psychiatry;

2. a licensed psychologist;

3. a licensed clinical social worker when he or she is engaged in applied psychotherapy of a nonmedical nature;

4. a credentialed school psychologist;

5. a licensed marriage, family, and child counselor; and

6. a registered psychologist assistant; a registered marriage, family, and child counselor intern; and a registered associate clinical social worker (all of whom must be under supervision);

7. a person exempt from the psychology licensing law[6] who is under the supervision of a licensed psychologist or board-certified psychiatrist;

8. a psychological intern[7] who is under the supervision of a licensed psychologist or board-certified psychiatrist;

9. a trainee[8] who is fulfilling his or her supervised practicum[9] and is supervised by a licensed psychologist, board-certified psychiatrist, licensed clinical social worker, or licensed marriage, family, and child counselor; and

10. a licensed educational psychologist.[10]

An individual who does not fit within the specific statutory definition of a psychotherapist cannot claim the psychotherapist–patient privilege.[11] The privilege does apply to professional cor-

---

6. Under § 2909(d) of the Bus. & Prof. Code.
7. As defined in § 2911 of the Bus. & Prof. Code.
8. As defined in § 4980.03(c) of the Bus. & Prof. Code.
9. As defined in § 4980.40(b) of the Bus. & Prof. Code.
10. Evid. Code § 1010.5.
11. For example, psychiatric social workers who aren't licensed. *Belmont v. California State Personnel Board,* 36 Cal.App.3d 518 (1976); unsupervised student interns or psychology students, *People v. Gomez,* 34 Cal.App.3d 874 (1982). However, in *Luhdorff v. Superior Court,* 166 Cal.App.3d 485 (1985), the privilege was extended to a nonlicensed social worker who was working under the supervision of a psychologist on the theory he was a person to whom the disclosure of information was necessary in the patient's interests, under Evid. Code § 1012.

porations of psychiatrists, psychologists, marriage, family, and child counselors, and/or licensed clinical social workers.

The law defines a *patient* as one who consults a psychotherapist or submits to an examination by the psychotherapist for the purpose of securing a diagnosis or for preventative, palliative, or curative treatment of his or her mental or emotional condition. A person who submits to an examination of his or her mental or emotional condition for the purpose of scientific research on mental or emotional problems is also considered to be a patient for the purposes of this provision.[12] Once it is established that the therapist is one statutorily recognized to have a privileged relationship, and the person making the communication qualifies as a patient, the communication must be a confidential communication within the meaning of the statute.

The statute defines *confidential communication* as information transmitted between a patient and a psychotherapist in the course of that relationship and in confidence by means that, so far as the patient is aware, disclose the information to no third parties other than those who are present to further the interests of the patient or to whom disclosure is reasonably necessary to achieve the purpose for which the psychotherapist is consulted.

Confidential communication includes information learned in an examination of the patient, any diagnosis made, and any advice given by the psychotherapist in the course of that relationship.[13] The statute expressly recognizes that disclosure may be necessary for the purposes of treatment or in the best interests of the patient, including disclosure to individuals who are not licensed psychotherapists, such as unlicensed social workers, secretaries, and other professionals with whom the patient has a separate privilege, such as the patient's physician or attorney, and participants in group therapy.[14]

The California Supreme Court in a recent case stated that the privilege can cover information that was never confidential, but which was communicated to the therapist in confidence, as well as information that had lost its confidential status. The court stated that the privilege may survive even the broadest disclosure

---

12. Evid. Code § 1011.
13. Evid. Code § 1012; *Mavroudis v. Superior Court*, 102 Cal.App.3d 594 (1980).
14. In *Farell L. v. Superior Court*, 203 Cal.App.3d 521 (1988), the Court of Appeals held that a crime victim's communications with other patients in group therapy were privileged and that she could not be cross-examined on the communications. The court concluded that the other group therapy participants were persons who were present to further the patient's interests within the meaning of Evid. Code § 1012. *See also Luhdorff v. Superior Court*, 166 Cal.App.3d 485 (1985); *Huelter v. Superior Court*, 87 Cal.App.3d 544 (1978).

of the most secret information, particularly if the patient is unaware of the disclosure (such as eavesdropping).[15]

The statute provides that the patient has a privilege to refuse to disclose, and to prevent another person from disclosing, confidential communications between the patient and the therapist. To do so, the privilege must be claimed by someone who is recognized to be a holder of the privilege, or someone who is authorized to claim the privilege by the holder of the privilege, or by the psychotherapist, except that the psychotherapist may not claim the privilege if there is no holder in existence or if he or she is otherwise instructed by a person authorized to permit disclosure.[16] Disclosure may also be authorized where the patient has waived the privilege, such as where the patient has put his or her emotional condition at issue in litigation.

There are a number of similarities between the psychotherapist–patient privilege, the attorney–client privilege, and the priest–penitent privilege. There are also some differences, particularly with reference to individuals who are not formally licensed, such as psychological assistants, interns, etc.

(D)(3) Assertion and Waiver of the Privilege

Typically, California courts will not take at face value the assertion that a privilege exists. Instead, the court must be presented with some form of evidence indicating that all of the statutory criteria are met and that there has been no waiver. Where there is an issue as to whether the privilege exists, the court may take evidence at an *in camera* hearing to determine whether or not the privilege applies. The public is not allowed to be present at an *in camera* hearing, which usually takes place in the judge's chambers without a court reporter transcribing the proceedings. If the court determines that the privilege applies, no disclosure will be permitted unless an exception exists. On the other hand, if the court determines that a privilege does not apply or has been waived, then the information can be disclosed.

(D)(4) Limitations on the Scope of the Privilege

The privilege extends only to those communications for which the client has a reasonable expectation of confidentiality, and where the client is seeking some form of psychological services. An open question is whether the privilege applies where the putative patient is actually seeking to establish a psychotherapeutic relation-

---

15. *Menendez v. Superior Court*, 3 Cal.4th 435, 447-48 (1992).
16. Evid. Code §§ 1014 to 1015.

ship for the purpose of creating a psychiatric defense, as opposed to actually receiving psychological care.[17]

The privilege is limited by the following exceptions:

1. there is no privilege where litigation is pending and the mental or emotional condition of the patient has been tendered as an issue by the patient, a party claiming through the patient, a party claiming as a beneficiary of the patient on a contract to which the patient was a party, or the patient's heirs in an action for the injury or death of the patient;[18]

2. there is no privilege if the psychotherapist is appointed by order of the court to examine the patient, except where the psychotherapist is appointed by order of the court upon request of the lawyer for a criminal defendant to assist the lawyer in determining whether the defendant should enter or withdraw a plea based on insanity, or present a defense based on his mental condition;[19]

3. there is no privilege if the services of the psychotherapist were sought or obtained to enable or aid someone to plan or commit a crime or a tort, or to escape detection or apprehension after the commission of the crime or tort;[20]

4. there is no privilege as to communications relevant to an issue between parties to litigation, all of whose claims derive from a deceased patient, without regard to whether the claims arise technically from a will or whether the patient has died without a will;[21]

5. there is no privilege as to communications relevant to an issue of a breach by the therapist or by the patient of a duty arising out of the psychotherapist–patient relationship (such as where the patient alleges that the therapist committed malpractice);[22]

6. there is no privilege as to a communication relevant to an issue concerning the intention of the patient with respect to a

---

17. In the criminal case of *Menendez v. Superior Court*, 3 Cal.4th 435 (1992), two brothers who were accused of killing their parents sought to assert the psychotherapist–patient privilege as to communications with their therapist, Dr. Jerome Oziel. The brothers allegedly threatened to kill Dr. Oziel. The California Supreme Court held that the dangerous patient exception under § 1024 applied to certain of the conversations because the exception required only a reasonable cause for the therapist to believe that the patient was dangerous and disclosure was necessary. The Court concluded that the exception does apply when the person the patient is a danger to is the therapist. *Id.* at 451.
18. Evid. Code § 1016. *People v. Mickle*, 54 Cal.3d 140 (1991).
19. Evid. Code § 1017.
20. Evid. Code § 1018.
21. Evid. Code § 1019.
22. Evid. Code § 1020.

deed of conveyance, will, or other writing affecting an interest in property, or where there is an issue as to the validity of such an instrument executed by a now-deceased patient;[23]

7. there is no privilege for proceedings initiated at the request of a criminal defendant to determine to his or her sanity;[24]

8. there is no privilege if the psychotherapist has a reasonable belief that the patient is a danger to himself, or to the person or property of another, and the disclosure of the communication is necessary to prevent the threatened danger (in fact, in such circumstances disclosure may be mandated);[25]

9. there is no privilege in any action brought by or on behalf of the patient to establish his or her competency;[26]

10. there is no privilege as to any information that the psychotherapist or the patient is required to report to a public employee, or information required to be recorded in a public office if the report or record is open for public inspection;[27]

11. there is no privilege where the psychologist or psychotherapist is mandated to make a report of child or elder abuse, although this exception is to be read restrictively.[28] However, reports of child abuse and elder abuse are themselves confidential and cannot be disclosed except as specified by statute; thus the exception to the psychotherapist–patient privilege is somewhat offset by the confidentiality accorded the reports;[29] and

12. there is no privilege where the patient is a child under age 16, and the psychotherapist has reasonable cause to believe the patient has been the victim of a crime and believes that disclosure is in the best interest of the child.[30]

---

23. Evid. Code §§ 1021 to 1022.
24. Evid. Code § 1023.
25. Evid. Code § 1024. However, the duty to warn and the nonexistence of the privilege apply only where the risk of harm is to people other than the patient. The risk of self-inflicted harm is not covered by § 1024. *Bellah v. Greenson*, 81 Cal.App.3d 614 (1978); *Luhdorff v. Superior Court*, 166 Cal.App.3d 488 (1985). Where the threatening statements are disclosed to the prospective victim, the statements are no longer confidential and the therapist can therefore testify about the substance of the warning and the statements in therapy which led to the warning being made. *People v. Wharton*, 53 Cal.3d 522 (1991); *People v. Clark*, 50 Cal.3d 583 (1990). Civ. Code § 43.92.
26. Evid. Code § 1025.
27. Evid. Code § 1026.
28. Penal Code § 11166; Welf. & Inst. Code §§ 15630 to 15631. *People v. Stritzinger*, 34 Cal.3d 503 (1983).
29. Penal Code § 11167.5; Welf. & Inst. Code § 15633.5.
30. Evid. Code § 1027.

Another potential exception is in child custody evaluations where the local court rules for the family law department specify that there is no privilege between the court-appointed evaluator and the individuals evaluated, although sometimes the stipulations specify that the evaluator cannot be called as a witness.[31]

(E) Marriage, Family and Child Counselors

(E)(1) Privilege for Marriage Counselors

The statute licensing marriage, family, and child counselors does not contain an express confidentiality provision, although reference is made to requiring such counselors to take coursework in the psychotherapist–patient privilege and confidentiality,[32] and a breach of confidentiality is grounds for discipline.[33] However, marriage, family, and child counselors are defined as psychotherapists within the meaning of the Evidence Code provisions on the psychotherapist–patient privilege, although paradoxically marriage, family, and child counselors and other non-psychologists are precluded from using the term *psychotherapist* to describe themselves.[34]

The Board of Behavioral Science Examiners can issue investigative subpoenas and subpoenas to compel the attendance of witnesses at administrative hearings.[35] However where the subpoena seeks the production of records of patients who have not complained about the licensee, the production of the records must be justified by good cause or a showing of waiver on the part of the patient.[36] The Board must demonstrate that the records it seeks are relevant and material to the Board's inquiry.[37]

(E)(2) Assertion and Waiver of the Privilege

There is no distinction between psychologists and marriage, family, and child counselors in terms of the breadth of the psychotherapist–patient privilege. As with psychologists, the mere assertion of the privilege will not suffice; proof must be offered that

---

31. *Los Angeles Superior Court Family Law Department Manual* § XI-C; *Gootee v. Lightner,* 224 Cal.App.3d 587 (1990).
32. Bus. & Prof. Code § 4980.41.
33. Bus. & Prof. Code § 4982.
34. Bus. & Prof. Code § 2902(c).
35. Gov't Code §§ 11181, 11510; *Board of Medical Quality Assurance v. Gherardini,* 93 Cal.App.3d 669 (1979).
36. *Wood v. Superior Court,* 166 Cal.App.3d 1138 (1985).
37. Bus. & Prof. Code § 4980.41.

the relationship exists and meets the criteria set forth in the Evidence Code to have the materials be deemed privileged.

(E)(3) Limitations on the Scope of the Privilege

There is no distinction between the limitations on the privilege as applied to psychologists and as applied to marriage, family, and child counselors.

(F) Psychiatrists

(F)(1) Privilege for Psychiatrists

Originally, psychiatrists were covered only by the general physician–patient privilege, while licensed psychologists were covered by the psychotherapist–patient privilege, which was then in the Business and Professions Code, but not in the Evidence Code. In 1965, the legislature created the psychotherapist–patient privilege as set forth in Evidence Code (sections 1010 et seq.). The new privilege covered both psychologists and psychiatrists and was intended to be broader than the physician–patient privilege. At the time the new law was enacted, the physician–patient privilege did not apply in criminal proceedings, civil actions arising out of the patient's criminal conduct, or certain administrative proceedings. The psychotherapist–patient privilege did apply in criminal, civil, and administrative proceedings.[38]

The physician–patient privilege provides that the patient has a privilege to refuse to disclose, and to prevent another from disclosing, a confidential communication between the patient and the physician. The privilege must be claimed by a holder of the privilege, or a person authorized by the holder to claim the privilege, or by the physician. However, the physician cannot claim the privilege if there is no holder, or if he or she is otherwise instructed by an authorized person to permit disclosure. The physician–patient relationship and privilege exists with a medical or podiatry corporation.[39]

(F)(2) Definitions

A *confidential communication* for the purpose of the privilege means information, transmitted between the patient and the physician in the course of the relationship and in confidence, by a means that, so far as the patient is aware, discloses the information to no third parties. A communication to third parties is not a

---

38. Comment, Senate Committee on the Judiciary, 1965 Stat., ch. 299, § 1014.
39. Evid. Code § 994.

disclosure where the third parties are present to further the interest of the patient in the consultation, or where communication to the third parties is reasonably necessary for the transmission of the information or to accomplish the purpose for which the physician is consulted. (Disclosure has the connotation of the patient voluntarily revealing information to a third party with no intent that it be kept confidential.) Information includes the diagnosis and the advice given by the physician in the course of the relationship.[40] A *holder of the privilege* is defined to mean:

1. the patient when he or she has no guardian or conservator;
2. a guardian or conservator when the patient has one; and
3. the personal representative of the patient when he or she is dead.[41]

A *physician* is defined to mean a person authorized, or who the patient reasonably believes to be authorized, to practice medicine in any state or nation.[42] A *patient* is a person who consults a physician or submits to an examination by a physician for the purpose of securing a diagnosis, or preventive, palliative, or curative treatment of his or her physical or emotional condition.[43]

(F)(3) Assumption and Waiver of the Privilege

As with the other professionals, the mere assertion of the privilege will not be accepted by the court absent proof that the relationship existed. Instead, the court will determine whether the privilege exists, usually with an *in camera* examination if there is any question. The court must determine that the communication was a confidential communication between patient and physician, that the patient or physician believed that the communication was necessary as part of the treatment, and that the person asserting the privileges is a holder of the privilege as defined by statute. These requirements are generally the same as the psychotherapist–patient privilege.

(F)(4) Limitations on the Scope of the Privilege

The physician–patient privilege will not apply in the following circumstances:

1. in any criminal proceeding;[44]

---

40. Evid. Code § 992.
41. Evid. Code § 993.
42. Evid. Code § 990.
43. Evid. Code § 991.
44. Evid. Code § 998.

2. in any action to recover damages based on the criminal conduct of the patient;[45]

3. when there is a breach by the physician or the patient of a duty arising from the physician–patient relationship;[46]

4. in litigation where an issue concerning the patient's mental or emotional condition is tendered by the patient, or any party claiming through the patient, or any party claiming as a beneficiary of the patient through a contract to which the patient is a party;[47]

5. as to a communication relevant to an issue between parties, all of whom claim through a deceased patient;[48]

6. in a proceeding to commit the patient or otherwise place him or her, or his or her property, under the control of another because of his or her mental or physical condition;[49]

7. in a proceeding brought upon on behalf of the patient to establish his or her competence;[50]

8. as to information that the physician or patient is required to report to a public employee, or as to information required to be recorded in a public office, if such a report or record is open to public inspection;[51]

9. in a proceeding brought by a public entity to determine whether a right, authority, license, or privilege (including the right or privilege to be employed by the public entity or to hold a public office) should be revoked, suspended, terminated, limited, or conditioned;[52] and

10. if the services of the physician were sought or obtained to enable anyone to commit a crime or tort, or to escape detection or apprehension after the commission of a crime or tort.[53]

---

45. Evid. Code § 999.
46. Evid. Code § 1001.
47. Evid. Code § 996.
48. Evid. Code § 1000.
49. Evid. Code § 1004.
50. Evid. Code § 1005.
51. Evid. Code § 1006.
52. Evid. Code § 1007. However, in hearings governed by the Administrative Procedure Act, the Act specifically provides that the physician–patient privilege applies. *Board of Medical Quality Assurance v. Gherardini*, 93 Cal.App.3d 669 (1979); Bus. & Prof. Code § 2225.
53. Evid. Code § 997.

(G) Social Workers

(G)(1) Privilege for Social Workers

Communications between licensed clinical social workers and their clients are within the scope of the psychotherapist–patient privileges set forth in the Evidence Code.[54] However, communications between unlicensed social workers and their patients may not be privileged unless the social worker falls within an exemption or is supervised by a person who meets the statutory criteria.[55] As with marriage, family, and child counselors, while there is no explicit incorporation of the psychotherapist–patient privilege in the social work statute, a violation of confidentiality is grounds for discipline.[56]

(G)(2) Liability for Breach of Confidentiality

If a psychiatrist, a psychologist, a marriage, family, and child counselor or a licensed clinical social worker breaches a patient or client's confidentiality, the MHP may be subject to civil suit and professional discipline. As noted above, regulations of each of the licensing boards make the breach of confidentiality grounds for discipline and possible loss of licensure. In addition, there is the possibility of civil litigation over the breach of confidentiality. If the disclosure takes place in the context of litigation, the mental health professional may be protected by California statute, which provides that no claims can be asserted against witnesses in judicial proceedings because of their testimony.[57] However, at least one court has interpreted the constitutional right of privacy and the psychotherapist–patient privilege as overriding the immunity provided by the general statute immunizing witnesses for their testimony and communications.[58] In that particular situation, a licensed clinical social worker provided a declaration to one spouse for use against the other spouse in litigation. The court was careful to point out that there had been no indication of a waiver of the privilege by the party seeking to assert confidentiality. The court also noted that its decision did not undercut any other legal defenses available to the therapist.

---

54. At the present time, a privileged communication between a licensed clinical social worker and a client is no different from one between a psychologist and a patient. There is, however, the anomaly that social workers, as with marriage, family, and child counselors, cannot legally refer to themselves as psychotherapists. Bus. & Prof. Code § 2902(b).
55. *Belmont v. California State Personnel Board*, 36 Cal.App.3d 518 (1976); *Luhdorff v. Superior Court*, 166 Cal.App.3d 874 (1985).
56. Bus. & Prof. Code § 4992.3(m).
57. Civ. Code § 47.
58. *Cutter v. Brownbridge*, 183 Cal.App.3d 836 (1983).

Since this decision was decided prior to a trilogy of California Supreme Court cases that gave a broad and sweeping effect to the immunity accorded witnesses under the Civil Code,[59] it is not clear to what extent this decision will be followed in the future. In addition, to the extent the MHP is acting as an evaluator or mediation for litigation purposes, he or she may be entitled to quasi-judicial immunity from suit.[60]

Finally, case law also indicates that where a subpoena for records is sent that includes a notice to consumer, telling the patient that his or her records are being subpoenaed, the failure on the part of the patient to object to disclosure of the records allows the MHP not only to disclose the records, but to testify in the proceeding; the patient cannot subsequently bring suit over the testimony.[61]

A recent case held that the notice to consumer is constitutionally required even where not specifically required by statute. In that case, the Court of Appeals found that subpoenas for patient records issued in an administrative hearing, under the Government Code, must include notice to the consumer.[62]

---

59. *Silberg v. Anderson*, 5 Cal.3d 205 (1990); *Pacific Gas & Elec. Co. v. Bear Stearns*, 50 Cal.3d 1118 (1990); *Kimmell v. Goland*, 51 Cal.3d 202 (1990).
60. *Howard v. Drapkin*, 222 Cal.App.3d 848 (1990).
61. *Inabnit v. Berkson*, 199 Cal.App.3d 1230 (1988); Civ. Code § 56.10; Civ. Proc. Code § 1985.3.
62. *Sehlmeyer v. Department of General Services*, 17 Cal.App.4th 1072 (1993).

4.4

Search, Seizure, and Subpoena of Records

The question of the extent to which an MHP's office may be searched and records seized can arise where the target of a criminal or administrative investigation is either the MHP or the patient. Generally, the demand for information will be in the form of a subpoena. Searches and subpoenas may constitute exceptions to confidentiality or privilege, however the mere seizure of records does not mean that they will be admitted at trial. Instead, a court may evaluate whether the records should be admitted on an *in camera* basis and then determine whether to allow disclosure. In an *in camera* hearing, the matter is presented to the judge in chambers, without public access, and generally a court reporter is not present.

(A) Search and Seizure

The question in this area concerns the seizure of items for which an individual has an expectation of privacy. The search and seizure can take place in either a criminal or an administrative context. For a criminal search of records in the possession of a psychotherapist (or a lawyer, physician, or a member of the clergy) at the time the warrant is issued, the court shall appoint a Special Master who will accompany the person serving the warrant. When the warrant is served, the Special Master will inform the person served of the specific items being sought and that he or she has the opportunity to provide the requested documents.

If in the judgment of the Special Master the person fails to produce the requested items, the Special Master conducts a search for the items in the area specified in the warrant. If the person served claims that certain items should not be disclosed, those items are sealed by the Special Master and taken to the Superior Court for a hearing. At the hearing, the person served can raise any issues of privilege. The hearing must be within three days of the service of the warrant unless an expedited hearing is not feasible, in which case the hearing will be at the earliest possible time. The court is required to provide sufficient time for the person served to obtain counsel, make a motion, and present evidence.[1]

(B) Subpoena

A subpoena is an order of the court compelling a witness to appear at a specified location on a specified date and time and provide either, or both, testimony and records at trial or in deposition. A subpoena that calls for documentary evidence such as therapy notes, billing records, and patient journals is typically referred to as a *subpoena duces tecum*. Such subpoenas generally call for documentary evidence in any form, including books, papers, audiotapes, videotapes, and computer-generated information.[2]

In most civil actions, subpoenas are served by process servers, or they can be served by the marshall's office. Witnesses who are subpoenaed are entitled to receive a check for one day's attendance and travel, which is generally less than $50. The only time that expert fees are required to be tendered is when an expert retained for the purpose of litigation is subpoenaed for a deposition. If the fee is not paid, the expert does not have to appear. A percipient treating MHP may be entitled to be paid his or her normal hourly fee for the time spent testifying, but only to the extent that the deposition calls for the exercise of the professional's expertise.[3] A percipient witness is one who observed or is involved with events as they developed, as opposed to an expert who is hired after the events occur to render opinions based on what transpired. While percipient witnesses are generally lay people, an MHP who treats a party to litigation for injuries sustained would also be a percipient witness to the injuries and aftermath of the injuries. Technically, it is possible for a deposition of a percipient treating MHP to be limited to factual issues so that no expert fee must be paid. In such a situation, the questions would be limited to what the patient said or did, what the

---

1. Penal Code § 1524.
2. Evid. Code § 250.
3. Civ. Proc. Code § 2025.

therapist said or did, and what the fees were. If questions are asked calling for an expert's opinion, such as what caused the condition observed, or what the prognosis is, then the fee must be paid.

A witness can be compelled to attend and testify at a court hearing, at a deposition, or at an administrative hearing. If the subpoena requires the production of documentary evidence, and it would be unreasonable or oppressive, a motion to quash or modify the subpoena can be made by the person to whom the subpoena is directed or the person whose records are being subpoenaed.

The fact that a subpoena is issued does not mean that the privilege that exists between an MHP and patient is breached, unless the subpoena is accompanied by a notice or a release, called a notice to consumer. (The term "consumer" is used because the notice requirement exists as to several types of records, including financial records.) If a subpoena is served with such a notice and the patient does not timely object or act as specified in the statute to protect his or her legal rights to confidentiality, the records can be produced and the MHP can testify, because the patient's failure to act is deemed to be a consent to disclosure.[4] If a subpoena is served without a notice to consumer and if it is not from the legal counsel for the patient, the MHP should assert the privilege until an express release or waiver is established.[5] In some instances, the court may determine that the privilege is waived as a matter of law, i.e., by the patient tendering his or her mental condition as an issue. As noted above, the failure to assert confidentiality where it is appropriate may result in potential civil liability and possible professional discipline. Where a subpoena has been served, even if it is of questionable validity, the failure to appear at the time and place specified may result in contempt proceedings until there is an agreement to testify. In fact, the California Supreme Court case establishing the psychotherapist–patient privilege arose in a circumstance where the therapist went to jail rather than disclose the records, even though the patient himself had not expressed an objection to disclosure.[6]

Subpoenas can also be issued by state agencies investigating claims of misconduct, or to procure the attendance of witnesses and production of documents at administrative hearings.[7] When the agency is trying to obtain records of a patient who has not complained against a licensee, the agency must give the patient some notice of the subpoena. The scope of the subpoena can be

4. Civ. Code § 56.10; *Inabnit v. Berkson,* 199 Cal.App.3d 1230 (1988).
5. Evid. Code § 1015.
6. *In re Lifshutz,* 2 Cal.3d 415 (1976).
7. Gov't Code § 11510.

tailored to limit the production to those records that are relevant and necessary.[8]

---

8. *Wood v. Superior Court*, 166 Cal.App.3d 1138 (1985); *Board of Medical Quality Assurance v. Gherardini*, 93 Cal.App.3d 669 (1979); *Board of Medical Quality Assurance v. Hazel Hawkins Memorial Hospital*, 135 Cal.App.3d 561 (1982); *Sehlmeyer v. Department of General Services*, 17 Cal.App.4th 1072 (1993); Gov't Code § 11510.

4.5

Freedom of Information and Open Public Hearings

California has a very strong policy favoring disclosure of information collected by government agencies to the individuals to whom the information relates and to public hearings on administrative matters. These laws will generally be most important to MHPs when they are the subject of an administrative action to impose discipline, as discussed in chapter 1.0, or when they are the subject of information collected by the government.

(A) Regulation

Under the Information Practices Act of 1977, individuals are entitled to review the records maintained on them by governmental agencies, unless an exception applies.[1] The Office of Information Practices in the Executive Office of the State Personnel Board is mandated to assist individuals to identify which records contain information about them and to help them secure access to the data.[2] The Office of Information Practice also investigates complaints about violations of the statute.[3] The conditions under which agencies may disclose personal or confidential information to third parties is limited.[4] Individuals are entitled to inquire and

---

1. Civ. Code § 1798 et seq.; a major exception to the disclosure is if the agency determines that releasing the information would seriously interfere with efforts to apprehend criminals, prevent a crime, or endanger the life of an informant. Civ. Code § 1798.40.
2. Civ. Code § 1798.5.
3. Civ. Code § 1798.6.
4. Civ. Code § 1798.24.

to be notified as to whether an agency is maintaining records on them, and may inspect and obtain copies of the records.

Individuals can request that an agency amend its records.[5] Civil actions can be brought when the agency refuses to comply with a request to inspect records or fails to maintain records with the accuracy, relevancy, recovery, timeliness, and completeness that is necessary to assure fairness, or if the agency fails to comply with the statute or rules in a way that has an adverse effect on the individual.[6] The plaintiff can seek injunctions, civil damages, and attorney fees.[7] If an individual's records are improperly disclosed, a civil action for invasion of privacy can be brought in which a prevailing plaintiff can get general damages, attorney fees, and a minimum of $2,500 in punitive damages.[8] In addition, state employees who intentionally violate the act are subject to discipline, including termination.[9] Obtaining records of personal or confidential information from an agency under false pretenses is a misdemeanor, punishable by a fine of up to $5,000 and one year in jail. However, the Information Practice Act does not abridge or limit the rights of litigants in civil or administrative proceedings.[10]

(B) California Public Records Act

In addition, the California Public Records Act requires that most records kept by government agencies be open to public inspection,[11] and that most proceedings before public agencies be open to the public.[12] The California Supreme Court recently upheld the right of access to records under the Public Records Act in two cases. In one case, the court held that while the Federal Freedom of Information Act and the Public Records Act should be given similar interpretations, the federal criteria are not to be grafted onto California's law by lower court decisions.[13]

---

5. Civ. Code §§ 1798.32 to 1798.37.
6. Civ. Code § 1798.45 to 1798.53.
7. Civ. Code § 1798.53.
8. Civ. Code § 1798.55.
9. Civ. Code § 1798.56.
10. Civ. Code § 1798.71.
11. Gov't Code § 6250 to 6265; *Williams v. Superior Court,* 5 Cal.4th 337 (1993); *Roberts v. City of Palmdale,* 5 Cal.4th 365 (1993).
12. Gov't Code §§ 11120 to 11132; § 54950 et seq.
13. *Williams v. Superior Court, supra* note 11.

(C) Exceptions to California Public Records Act

Unless an exception applies under the California Public Records Act,[14] records classified as public records are open to inspection at all times during the office hours of state and local agencies, and can be inspected by anyone.[15] Public records include any writing, including videotape, audiotape, films, and computer data, that contains information relative to the conduct of the public's business, and is prepared, owned, used, or retained by any state or local agency, including the Governor's Office.[16] The exemptions to the Public Records Act are too numerous to list, but examples include the following:

1. preliminary drafts, notes, or interagency or intra-agency memoranda that the public agency doesn't retain in the ordinary course of business, provided the public interest in withholding the records clearly outweighs the interest in disclosure;

2. personnel, medical, or similar files, the disclosure of which would be an unwarranted invasion of privacy; and

3. law enforcement investigative files (extensively discussed in a recent Supreme Court case).[17]

The public may be excluded, under certain circumstances, when the agency goes into executive session. While license revocation hearings before the state licensing agencies are open to the public, the actual voting of the Board members on the decision to accept or reject the administrative law judge's proposed decision is not open to the public. Closed sessions are permissible where the agency is considering the appointment, employment, dismissal, or complaints against a public employee. (However, the employee must be given written notice of his or her right to elect to have a public hearing.[18]) Agencies involved in administering professional or business licensing examinations can hold closed sessions to prepare, approve, grade, or administer the examinations.[19] By the same token, advisory bodies of agencies involved in licensing of professionals or businesses may conduct closed

---

14. Gov't Code §§ 6254 to 6254.25, 11125.5, 11126 (closed hearings to consider the appointment, employment, dismissal of, or complaint against, a public employee); §§ 11126.3 to 11126.5, 54986.9, 54956.5 to 54956.95.
15. Gov't Code § 6253.
16. Gov't Code § 6252.
17. Gov't Code §§ 6254, 6254.1 to 6254.25; *Williams v. Superior Court, supra* note 11.
18. Civ. Code § 11126(a).
19. Civ. Code § 11126(b).

sessions to discuss matters that would lead to an unwarranted invasion of privacy of an applicant or licensee if discussed at an open hearing, if such a session is held *before* any civil, criminal, or administrative disciplinary action is filed by the agency.[20] There are numerous other exceptions.

---

20. Civ. Code § 11126(c).

Practice Related to the Law

Families and Juveniles

5A.1

Competency to Marry

MHPs may be involved in premarital and marital counseling. Such counseling may be particularly important for underage individuals. This chapter discusses the criteria that should be met for marriage.

(A) Definition of Marriage

Marriage is defined as a personal relationship arising out of a civil contract between a man and a woman.[1] The consent of parties capable of making that contract is necessary, but consent alone will not constitute a marriage. A license must be issued and the marriage solemnized as authorized by law. After a marriage is licensed, solemnized, and authenticated, a certificate of registry of the marriage is returned to the couple. However, noncompliance with this requirement by individuals other than the parties to the marriage does not invalidate the marriage.[2]

(B) Conditions for Marriage

The statute expressly mentions consent, which presupposes having the capacity to consent. The law provides that any unmarried

---

1. Fam. Code § 300. While some municipalities may have enacted ordinances recognizing same-sex marriages, these marriages are not legal under the Civil Code.
2. Fam. Code § 306; the technicalities regarding the issuance of licenses for marriage are discussed in *id.*, §§ 350-360.

male or female 18 years or older is capable of consenting to and consummating a marriage. The Supreme Court may grant permission to persons under 18 to marry after a proper showing of the written consent of:

1. the parents of each person who is under age; or
2. one of the parents or the guardian of each such person.

As part of an order to allow an underage person to marry, the court may require the parties to participate in premarital counseling concerning the social, economic, and personal responsibilities incidental to marriage. Mental health professionals may counsel an underage person about these responsibilities. The parties to the prospective marriage may not be compelled to confer with counselors provided by religious organizations of any denomination. In determining whether to require premarital counseling, the court shall consider, among other factors, the ability of the parties to pay for the counseling.[3]

---

3. Fam. Code §§ 301, 302.

5A.2

Guardianship for Adults

MHPs may be involved in guardianship or conservatorship proceedings in providing psychotherapy to, or evaluation of, a proposed ward. MHPs may also be selected as guardians or guardians *ad litem*. Because the term *guardian* no longer applies to adults, except as guardians *ad litem*, this chapter addresses the role of a guardian *ad litem*. Guardians for adults are now referred to as conservators. (*See* chapter 5A.3.)

California formerly made a distinction between guardians and conservators of adults. However, in 1991, the legislature enacted transitional provisions that provide that whenever the term *guardian* is used with reference to an adult or a married minor, the term means *conservator* of the adult—of the person, in the case of a married minor.[1] The legislature provided that where an adult had nominated a person to serve as guardian if a future guardian was needed, this nomination would be of a conservator. Thus, a person functioning as a guardian for an adult is actually referred to as a *conservator* and is appointed as discussed in chapter 5A.3.

(A) Guardian Ad Litem

The term *guardian ad litem* means a guardian for the purpose of litigation. A guardian *ad litem* is not a party to the proceeding, but is representative of a party. The guardian *ad litem's* role is greater than that of an attorney because of his or her power to make

---

1. Prob. Code § 1490.

decisions about the litigation and about settlement.[2] A guardian *ad litem* cannot compromise a fundamental right of the ward, however, such as the right to trial by jury, without good cause—for example, an offsetting benefit to the ward.[3]

A guardian *ad litem* can be appointed for insane spouses in dissolution proceedings,[4] and for unborn children.[5]

(B) Appointment of a Guardian Ad Litem

A guardian *ad litem* can be appointed for a minor (*see* chapter 5A.11), an insane or incompetent person, or a conservatee if a judge of the court in which the litigation is pending deems it expedient, and even if a guardian or conservator exists.[6] A guardian *ad litem* for an adult who is insane or incompetent can be appointed upon the application of a relative or friend of the person, by any party to the litigation, or by the court on its own motion.[7] A guardian *ad litem* can also be appointed for a judge who is in administrative proceedings to be censured, removed, retired, or admonished, and has been adjudged insane or incompetent, or if it appears he or she is not competent.[8]

---

2. *Civ. Proc. Code* §§ 372, 373.5.
3. *Delos Santos v. Superior Court,* 27 Cal.3d 677 (1980).
4. Fam. Code § 2332.
5. *Civ. Proc. Code* § 373.5.
6. *Civ. Proc. Code* § 372.
7. *Civ. Proc. Code* § 373(c).
8. Cal. Ct. C.P.R. 910(d).

5A.3

Conservatorship for Adults

A conservatorship can be of an estate, a person, or both. Conservatorship of an estate generally occurs when an individual is found by the court to lack the legal capacity to enter into financial transactions, and this lack of legal capacity creates a risk that his or her estate will be adversely impacted or dissipated.[1] MHPs may become involved in the conservatorship proceedings when asked to evaluate the proposed conservatee and to express professional opinions about his or her ability to manage finances. Additionally, MHPs may provide psychotherapy services for the conservatee. This chapter addresses the requirements for establishment and termination of conservatorships.

(A) Application for Conservatorship

A conservator may be appointed when it is established to the satisfaction of the court that there is a need for one because the proposed conservatee is substantially unable to manage his or her own financial resources.[2] However, isolated instances of negligence or improvidence do not establish substantial inability to manage financial resources for the purposes of this statute. There

---

1. Prob. Code § 1872. Temporary conservatorships set up to protect the person and estate can be established pending a hearing on a permanent conservatorship. *Conservatorship of Gray,* 12 Cal.App.3d 513 (1970). A person who is nominated as a guardian of an adult is deemed to be a conservator. Prob. Code § 1488.
2. Prob. Code §§ 1800.3, 1801.

must be some proof of a more consistent inability to manage finances or of consistent acts of negligence or improvidence.[3]

An action to appoint a conservator can be brought by the proposed conservatee. When the proposed conservatee voluntarily seeks the establishment of the conservatorship, the standard of proof is lesser: The proposed conservatee must establish to the satisfaction of the court merely that good cause exists for the appointment.[4] He or she may nominate, in a written application to the court, a particular individual, and the court shall appoint the nominee as conservator unless the court finds that the appointment of the nominee is not in the best interests of the proposed conservatee.[5]

Actions for conservatorship can also be brought without the conservatee's consent. An involuntary conservatorship proceeding is initiated by a verified petition filed in superior court indicating the conservatee's age, residence, heirs, spouse, and children (if any), the nature of the disabling condition or problem, and the location of all significant assets. Notice of the proceeding must be given to any interested person. *Interested person* is defined by statute to include the conservatee's heirs, children, spouses, creditors, beneficiaries, and any other persons having a property right and/or claim against a trust estate or the estate of a decedent that might be affected by the conservatorship proceeding. Additionally, an *interested person* includes any person having priority for appointment as a personal representative, and a fiduciary representing an interested person.[6]

(B) The Conservatorship Hearing

A person who is the subject of an involuntary conservatorship is entitled to many of the same procedural protections as a criminal defendant. For example, a proposed involuntary conservatee has the right to a trial by jury, the right to present evidence, and the right to counsel appointed by the court.[7]

The court can appoint a conservator if it determines that the conservatee lacks the capacity to enter into financial transactions

---

3. Prob. Code § 1801.
4. Prob. Code § 1802.
5. Prob. Code § 1810.
6. Prob. Code § 48.
7. *Conservatorship of Tedesco,* 22 Cal.App.4th 662 (1993).

affecting the estate.[8] This proceeding is heard by the court without a jury, and expert testimony from MHPs is provided either in declaration form or by live testimony. The court may appoint legal counsel to represent the conservatee's interests during the conservatorship proceedings. In addition, a guardian *ad litem* (see chapter 5A.2) may be appointed for the conservatee throughout the course of the hearings, to make decisions on behalf of the conservatee.[9]

(C) Authority and Responsibilities of the Conservator

Under a conservatorship of the estate, a conservatee retains only minimal rights to control property. The conservatee can control his or her salary, make a will (assuming the testamentary capacity exists), and enter into transactions to obtain the necessities of life for him or herself and the spouse or children.[10] Generally, transactions between third parties and a conservatee after the appointment of a conservator are unenforceable against the estate. Thus, anyone who chooses to enter into a contractual or other business relationship with a conservatee generally does so at their own peril. An MHP entering into a contract to provide therapy, for example, runs the risk of not being paid.

A conservator has the authority to maintain and defend legal actions for the benefit of the conservatee and can settle claims and actions either for the benefit of or against the estate.[11] Generally, the court requires the conservator to post a bond that is approximately the value of the estate.[12] When the proposed conservatee nominates the conservator, the court can reduce the bond or waive it entirely; however, the courts generally require some bond.[13]

---

8. Prob. Code § 1872. The appointment of a conservator of the estate is an adjudication that the conservatee lacks the legal capacity to enter into any transaction that would bind the estate, including making gifts. This applies to both temporary and permanent conservatorships. *O'Brien v. Dudenhopper,* 16 Cal.App.4th 327 (1993).
9. Prob. Code § 1821.
10. Prob. Code § 1871. To guide conservators, the California Judicial Council has promulgated Form 6C348, entitled "Duties of Conservator," which summarizes the duties of the conservator and the rights of the conservatee. In addition, the Judicial Council has made available a *Handbook for Conservators.*
11. Prob. Code §§ 2462, 2500.
12. Prob. Code § 2320.
13. Prob. Code § 2321.

Once the conservator has been appointed, he or she must file an inventory and appraisal of the estate within 90 days of appointment and must submit an annual accounting to the court for the first year and every two years thereafter.[14] The parties who have been served with notice of the conservatorship may challenge the appraisals and petition the court about the assets within the estate.[15]

The conservator has the power to buy and sell property; borrow and lend money; lease estate property; adjust, settle, or resolve claims; hire attorneys and accountants to do work for the estate; grant or take options; create easements or servitudes; obtain partitions; and become involved in reorganizations, mergers, or dissolutions that may affect estate property.[16] Court approval is not required for the conservator to exercise these powers.[17] However, if the conservator seeks to bring an action for partition of real property, or to settle property interest claims or personal injury claims, prior court approval is required.[18]

(D) Termination of the Conservatorship

Generally, a conservatorship continues until it is either terminated by order of the court or by the death of the conservatee.[19] An order of the court is usually based on an application made by or on behalf of the conservatee to have the proceeding terminated. If the conservatorship is terminated, the estate is returned to the control of the former conservatee.

If the conservator resigns or dies, or is removed by the court, another successor may be appointed in the same manner as specified above.

---

14. Prob. Code §§ 2610, 2620.
15. Prob. Code §§ 2614, 2616
16. Prob. Code § 2591.
17. Prob. Code § 2450.
18. Prob. Code §§ 2463, 2501, 2504.
19. Prob. Code § 1860.

5A.4

Annulment

Where parties are validly married and seek to terminate that relationship, a divorce can be obtained. However, an annulment is where parties seek to have a marriage declared void and to treat it as if it had never occurred. MHPs may be involved in annulment proceedings in assessing the parties' capacity to consent to marriage or in providing therapy to them in the course of the process. The distinctions may be important in several respects, not the least of which is that in some religions there is special significance to a marriage being annulled as opposed to being dissolved by divorce.

(A) Void Marriages

The law describes two categories of marriages as void and illegal from inception. The first category is incestuous marriage which is defined as one between parents and children, ancestors and descendants, brothers and sisters, uncles and nieces, or aunts and nephews.[1] The second category of void marriage is bigamy: a subsequent marriage by a person who is already married—(unless the former marriage has been dissolved or annulled before the subsequent marriage, or the spouse is absent and is not known to be living for the five preceding years marriage, or is reputed or believed to be dead). If a second marriage has taken place under the belief that the spouse was dead, the subsequent

---

1. Civ. Code § 4400; Fam. Code § 2200. Technically, anyone who knowingly solemnizes any marriage forbidden by law is subject to a fine of $100 to $1,000 and/or several months in jail under Penal Code § 359.

marriage is valid until a proceeding is brought to have it determined to be null because the spouse is actually alive.[2]

(B) Grounds for Annulment

Marriages may be annulled in the following circumstances:

1. the party who commences the proceeding, or on whose behalf the proceeding is commenced, was without the capacity to consent to the marriage, unless after attaining the age of consent, the party freely cohabited with the spouse;

2. the husband or wife of either party was living and the marriage was then in force, but the husband or wife was absent, or not known to the party commencing the proceeding to be alive for the five years preceding the subsequent marriage, for which the judgment of nullity is sought, or the spouse was generally reputed or believed to be dead;

3. either party was of unsound mind, unless such party, after coming to reason, freely cohabited with the other as husband and wife (clearly, MHPs might be involved in testifying to a party's mental condition here);

4. the consent of either party was obtained by fraud, unless such party afterward, with full knowledge of the facts constituting the fraud, cohabited with the other as husband and wife;

5. the consent of either party was obtained by force, unless such party afterward freely cohabited with the other as husband and wife; and

6. either party was at the time of the marriage physically incapable of entering into the marriage state, and such incapacity continues and appears to be incurable.[3]

The effect of a judgment of annulment is to restore the parties to the status of unmarried persons. However, the judgment is conclusive only as to the parties to the proceedings and those claiming under them.[4]

Whenever a determination is made that a marriage was either void or voidable, and the court finds that either or both parties believed in good faith that the marriage was valid, the court shall declare the party or parties to have the status of putative spouses and shall declare the division of community property or quasi-community property as if the marriage had not been void or

---

2. Civ. Code §§ 401, 4425(b); Fam. Code §§ 2200, 2210.
3. Civ. Code § 4425.
4. Civ. Code § 4429, 4451; Fam. Code §§ 2210, 2212.

voidable. This property is referred to as *quasi-marital property*. The court can reserve jurisdiction to make the property division subsequent to the judgment. The property that is divided is liable for the debts of the parties to the same extent as if the property had been community or quasi-community property.[5] In a proceeding to annul a marriage, the custody of children follows the same standards as that of valid marriages.[6]

The court may make orders for the support of a party to a marriage deemed annulled, may award attorney fees and costs under certain circumstances, and, upon request, may order restored the birth name or former name of the wife.[7]

---

5. Civ. Code § 4452; Fam. Code § 2251.
6. Civ. Code §§ 4454, 4600; Fam. Code § 2253.
7. Civ. Code §§ 4455, 4456, 4457; Fam. Code § 2255.

5A.5

Dissolution of Marriage

Marriages are dissolved only by the death of one of the parties, a judgment of dissolution (divorce), or a judgment of nullity. California has a "no fault" divorce law that does not require a party to prove anything other than irreconcilable differences. Thus, most litigation centers around the division of property, child support, child maintenance, and child custody (*see* chapter 5A.6). MHPs often are involved in child custody assessments and providing psychotherapy to those who are going through the divorce process. Therapy may be provided to individuals, couples, or families, and may be ordered by the court as part of an attempt to avoid a divorce. Generally, when child custody is at issue, many California courts require some form of psychiatric or psychological assessment of all parties to the marriage, and this may include any individuals who might be having extended contact with the children. California also has a statutory policy of encouraging mediation to try to avoid divorce. MHPs can serve as mediators and in that capacity they have quasi-judicial immunity from lawsuits by disgruntled parties to the mediation.[1]

(A) Divorce Procedure

A proceeding for dissolution of a marriage or for separation is commenced by filing in superior court a petition for either dissolution or a legal separation. A copy of the petition, together with a

---

1. *Howard v. Drapkin*, 222 Cal.App.3d 843 (1990). In the author's experience, participating as a witness or making an evaluation in a custody case leads to a disproportionate number of complaints against MHPs to professional associations and licensing boards, and civil suits. See, e.g., *Gootee v. Lightner*, 226 Cal.App.3d 587 (1990); *Roe v. Superior Court*, 229 Cal.App.3d 832 (1991).

copy of the summons, must be served on the spouse in the same fashion as civil actions are generally served.[2] The petition is required to state the grounds upon which the divorce or legal separation is sought. The spouse who does not initiate the action is required to file an answer or other response prior to a formal hearing.

The court must file a judgment and a statement of decision, as in other civil cases. If the court determines that the requested dissolution should be denied, judgment denying dissolution will be entered. If the court determines that dissolution ought to be granted, a judgment will be entered declaring that the parties are entitled to have their marriage dissolved, and making provisions for allocation of property, child support, and maintenance.[3] The court may retain jurisdiction to modify its orders regarding support and maintenance.

The decision that a marriage shall be dissolved is not deemed final until six months have expired from the date of service of a copy of the summons and petition, or from the date of appearance of the responding spouse, whichever occurs first. However, the court may extend the six-month period if good cause is shown. The decree dissolving the marriage shall specify the date on which the decree becomes effective for the purpose of terminating the marriage. If an appeal is taken from the judgment or a motion for new trial is made, the dissolution of the marriage does not become final until the motion or appeal has been decided.[4]

(B) Grounds for Divorce

The law specifies the grounds for divorce to be irreconcilable differences that have caused the irremedial breakdown of a marriage or incurable insanity.[5] *Irreconcilable differences* are defined as those grounds determined by the court to be substantial reasons for not continuing the marriage and that make it appear the marriage should be dissolved.[6] Dissolution on the grounds of incurable insanity can occur only upon proof, including competent medical or psychological testimony, that the spouse who is allegedly insane was insane at the time the petition was filed, and remains incurably insane. However, no decree granted on the ground of insanity relieves a spouse from any obligation imposed by law for the support of the spouse who is insane, and the court may make such other orders for support or require a bond to be

---

2. Civ. Code § 4503.
3. Civ. Code §§ 4512, 4514.
4. Civ. Code § 4514.
5. Civ. Code § 4506; Fam. Code § 2310.
6. Civ. Code § 4507; Fam. Code § 2311.

posted if circumstances require. If a general guardian exists, or a guardian has been appointed for the allegedly insane spouse, then the pleadings have to be served upon both the insane spouse and the guardian. The guardian shall take such steps as necessary to defend and protect the interests of the spouse.[7]

(C) Summary Dissolution

California also has a summary-disposition procedure, which can be used to dissolve a marriage in which: (a) irreconcilable differences have caused the irremedial breakdown of the marriage; (b) there are no children born before or during the marriage (or adopted by the parties during the marriage); and (c) the marriage has lasted not more than five years. This procedure can be used only where neither party has an interest in real property. There is an exception for the lease of a residence occupied by either party if the lease does not include an option to purchase and if it terminates within one year of the date of the filing of the petition. There also must be no unpaid obligations in excess of $4,000 incurred by either or both of the parties after the date of their marriage, excluding any debt with respect to an automobile.

In addition, the total fair market value of community property assets, excluding encumbrances and automobiles, and including the value of any deferred compensation or retirement plans, must be less than $25,000, and neither party must have separate assets or property in excess of $25,000.

To use the summary procedure, the parties must have executed an agreement setting forth the division of assets and the assumption of liabilities, and must have executed any documents or other evidence of transfer necessary to effectuate the agreement. The parties must waive rights to spousal support and waive their rights to appeal.

The court provides a summary–dissolution brochure. Both parties must read the brochure before electing to proceed.[8]

If all these conditions are met, a joint petition is filed with the court. The petition, signed under oath by husband and wife, states that every condition is met and provides the mailing address of both spouses. The joint petition must also state whether the wife wants to have her maiden or former name restored. The court may dissolve the marriage within six months of the date of filing.[9]

---

7. Civ. Code § 4510; Fam. Code § 2311.
8. Civ. Code § 4450; Fam. Code § 2400.
9. Civ. Code § 4453; Fam. Code § 2403-2404.

5A.6

Child Custody After Marital Dissolution

There are several ways in which child custody determinations can arise, such as when a marriage is annulled, a legal separation occurs, a divorce decree is entered, or a prior divorce decree is modified. MHPs are typically involved in the evaluation of the spouses to provide the court with information on which a custody determination can be based. Generally, one MHP is appointed to evaluate all sides, but each side may provide additional testimony from its own independently retained MHPs.

Most courts have a family law department and the local rules of court address whether psychiatric and/or psychological evaluation is required as a matter of course.[1]

(A) Criteria to Establish Court Jurisdiction

Unless all relevant parties continue to reside in the same jurisdiction, there may be some question as to which court has the proper jurisdiction to determine custody rights. Jurisdiction is provided under the Uniform Child Custody Jurisdiction Act. The act was adopted to avoid jurisdictional conflicts and competition between the courts of the various states and to ensure that a custody decree is rendered in the state that can best decide the interests of the

---

1. *See, e.g., Los Angeles Superior Court Family Law Department Manual*, § XI "Psychiatric Evaluation Services," where provisions are made for such examinations. Los Angeles Superior Court also maintains a panel of MHPs from which the court can select an evaluator.

child.[2] A secondary purpose of the Uniform Child Custody Jurisdiction Act was to deter abductions and other unilateral removals of children undertaken to obtain custody awards, and to avoid relitigating custody decisions in different states.

A California court has jurisdiction under the statute if either of the following conditions are met:

1. California is the home state of the child at the time of commencement of the proceeding, or was the child's home state within six months before commencement of the proceeding and the child is absent from the state because of his or her removal or retention by a person claiming custody or for other reasons, and a parent or person acting as a parent continues to live in California; or

2. it is in the best interests of the child that a California court assume jurisdiction because:

    (a) the child and his or her parents, or the child of one contestant, have a significant connection with California and there is available in the state substantial evidence concerning the child's present or future care, protection, training, and personal relationships;

    (b) the child is physically present in California and (1) the child has been abandoned, or (2) it is necessary in an emergency to protect the child because he or she has been subjected to or threatened with mistreatment or abuse, or is otherwise neglected or dependent (which includes a child who has a parent who is the victim of domestic violence); or

    (c) it appears that no other state than California would have jurisdiction under the criteria set forth above, or another state has declined to exercise jurisdiction on the ground that California is the more appropriate forum to determine custody of the child, and it is in the best interests of the child that a California court assume jurisdiction.

Except as provided in the specific situations above, the physical presence of a child in California of one of the parties seeking custody or visitation rights is not sufficient in and of itself to confer jurisdiction on a California court to make a child custody determination. The physical presence of the child, while desirable, is not a prerequisite to jurisdiction to determine custody.

In fact, the court may decline to exercise jurisdiction where a child has been wrongfully brought into California from another state or improperly removed from the custodial parent or in

---

2. Civ. Code § 5150; Fam. Code § 3400 et seq.

violation of another state's custody decree. However, the California court shall not consider as a factor against a petitioner the removal of a child from the person with legal custody if there is evidence that the taking or retention of the child was a result of domestic violence against the petitioner.[3]

(B) Legal Standards In Custody Determination

It is the public policy of California to ensure that minor children have frequent and continuing contact with both parents after the parents have separated or dissolved the marriage, and to encourage parents to share the rights and responsibilities of child rearing, except where that contact would not be in the best interests of the child.[4] In awarding custody, the order of preference according to the best interests of the child is as follows:

1. to both parents jointly or to either parent (if the court makes an order for custody to either parent, the court shall consider, among other factors, which parent is more likely to allow the child or children frequent and continuing contact with the non-custodial parent, and the court shall not prefer a parent as custodian based on the parent's sex);

2. if to neither parent, to the person or persons in whose home the child has been living in a wholesome and stable environment; and finally

3. to any other person or persons deemed by the court to be suitable and able to provide adequate and proper care and guidance to the child.

Before the court makes any order awarding custody to a person or persons other than a parent, without the consent of the parents, it must make a finding that an award of custody to a parent would be detrimental to the child and that the award to a non-parent is necessary to serve the best interests of the child. However, the allegations that parental custody would be detrimental to the child, other than as a statement of ultimate fact, are not to appear in the pleadings filed with the court. Further, the

---

3. Civ. Code § 5152 (*see, e..g., Lough v. Superior Court*, 8 Cal.App.4th 136) (1992); Fam. Code § 3403; Civ. Code § 5157.
4. Civ. Code § 4600; Fam. Code § 3040. In fact, the right to custody of one's children is seen as a fundamental constitutional right, so state interference must be clearly warranted. *In re Robert P.*, 61 Cal.App.3d 310 (1976).

court in its discretion may exclude the public from a hearing on the issue of parental fitness.

There is a presumption, affecting the burden of proof, that joint custody is in the best interests of a minor child, subject to the court making a determination of what the best interests of the child are. In making a determination as to what the best interest of the child are, the court shall consider the following:

1. the health, safety, and welfare of the child;

2. any history of abuse by one parent against the child or against another parent. As a prerequisite to considering allegations of abuse, the court may require substantial independent corroboration, including but not limited to written reports by law enforcement agencies, child protective services or other social welfare agencies, courts, and medical facilities or other public agencies or private nonprofit organizations providing services to victims of sexual assault or domestic violence; and

3. the nature and amount of contact with both parents.[5]

In any proceeding where custody or visitation is at issue, the court may require both the child and the parents of the child to participate in outpatient counseling with a licensed MHP for not more than six months, if the court finds that the dispute between the parents or between the parent and the child poses a substantial danger to the best interests of the child, and that counseling is in the best interest of the minor child. Under both the Civil Code and the new Family Code, the purpose of the counseling is to facilitate communication between the parties regarding their minor child's best interest, to reduce conflict regarding visitation or custody, and to improve the quality of parenting skills of each parent. The court shall fix the cost and order the entire cost of services to be borne by the parties in proportion as the court deems reasonable.[6] However, family reunification services shall not be ordered as part of child custody or visitation rights proceedings.[7]

No parent shall be awarded custody of or unsupervised visitation with any child if he or she has been convicted of child abuse, unless the court finds there is no significant risk to the child.[8] MHPs may be involved in conducting assessments and rendering professional opinions about the presence or absence of such risk.

---

5. Civ. Code §§ 4600.5, 4608; Fam. Code § 3022.
6. Civ. Code § 4608.1; Fam. Code § 3190.
7. Civ. Code § 4608; Wel. & Inst. Code § 16507. It appears there is no equivalent proscription in the new Family Code.
8. Civ. Code § 4610; Penal Code §§ 273A, 273D, 647.6.

If a court determines that an accusation of child abuse or neglect made during a child custody proceeding was false, and the person making the accusation knew it to be false at the time the accusation was made, the court may impose reasonable monetary sanctions not to exceed $1,000 plus reasonable attorney fees.[9]

(C) Mental Health Evaluation

As noted above, the court may order mental health counseling for parents and minors in connection with child custody. Local rules of court may require this as part of typical custody proceedings. The court is not limited to any specific category of MHP and can designate any licensed MHP. Further, the court has the authority to appoint independent experts to advise it as to such matters as the court deems necessary.[10] There have been a number of cases where MHPs engaged in the evaluation of individuals for custody purposes have been sued for bias or incompetence. Most of these claims have been summarily dismissed by the courts based on various litigation privileges and public policy.[11]

Generally, the duty of an MHP conducting such an examination is to provide his or her best opinion to the court, taking into account the best interests of the child. Thus, the fact that one parent might be dissatisfied with an opinion does not give rise to a cause of action under California law. As one court put it:

> Freedom of access to the courts and encouragement of witnesses to testify truthfully will be harmed if neutral experts must fear retaliatory lawsuits from litigants whose disagreement with an expert's opinions perforce convinces them the expert must have been negligent in forming such opinions.[12]

The ruling quoted above concluded that the party has an opportunity to attack the opinion of the expert in cross-examination and that that is the extent of the remedy that exists. Further, an independent evaluator does not owe a duty of care that can be the basis of a civil suit by the party being evaluated, if the evaluation is in conjunction with the court proceeding.[13] However, the state license boards and professional association ethics committees are not precluded from disciplining MHPs for such evaluations when grounds to do so exist.

---

9. Civ. Code § 4611.
10. Evid. Code § 730 et seq.
11. *Gootee v. Lightner*, 224 Cal.App.3d 587 (1990); *Silberg v. Anderson*, 50 Cal.3d 205 (1990).
12. *Gootee, supra* note 11 at 593.
13. *Id.*

(D) Confidentiality and Privileged Communications

While, as a general rule, information received by MHPs in a consultation or examination is confidential, this is not true where the evaluation is for the purposes of a custody evaluation.[14] However, when an MHP has treated the custody litigants in private therapy that was not for the purpose of a court evaluation, a written waiver of the psychotherapist–patient privilege must be obtained before testifying. One licensed clinical social worker was sued for providing a declaration to one spouse's counsel during the course of an action, and it was held that such a cause was valid because the privilege had not been waived by the evaluated spouse.[15] As a practical matter, despite the breadth of the privileges and case law protecting MHPs from suit for rendering their opinions in custody and dissolution matters, such suits are filed with distressing regularity as an apparent tactic to call into question an MHP's testimony in the underlying action. MHPs engaged in custody evaluations must be aware that frivolous suits are an ever increasing risk of that particular type of practice.

---

14. *Id.; Howard v. Drapkin*, 222 Cal.App.3d 843 (1990); Evid. Code § 1016 (patient-litigant exception); Evid. Code § 1017 (no privilege if evaluated pursuant to court order).
15. *Cutter v. Brownbridge*, 183 Cal.App.3d 386 (1986).

5A.7

Reporting of Elder Abuse

While the obligation to report abused children has been a part of California law since the 1960s, the requirement to make reports about elder and dependent adults who may be abused or neglected was first enacted in 1982.[1] California has a comprehensive statute called the Elder Abuse and Dependent Adult Civil Protection Act, which specifically declares that infirm elderly persons and dependent adults are a disadvantaged class. Although some states require reporting of abuse of elder or dependent adults in an institutional setting only, the obligation in California is as broad as the duty to report child abuse. In short, any MHP who becomes aware of elder abuse in his or her professional practice may have a duty to report it. Further, family members have been prosecuted for failing to properly care for elder or dependent adults.

(A) Institutionalized Elderly Persons

(A)(1) Definitions

A *dependent adult* is defined to mean any person between the ages of 18 and 64 who has physical or mental limitations that restrict his or her ability to carry out normal activities or to protect his or her rights, including, but not limited to, persons who have physical or developmental disabilities or whose physical or mental abilities have diminished because of age. This includes individu-

---

1. Welf. & Inst. Code § 15600.

als who are inpatients at a 24-hour health facility. *Elder* means any person who is 65 years or older.

Physical abuse means assault with or without a deadly weapon, battery, unreasonable physical restraint, prolonged or continual deprivation of food or water, and sexual assault.

Abuse also means the use of a physical or chemical restraint or psychotropic medication under the following circumstances:

1. for punishment;
2. for a period significantly beyond which the restraint or medication was authorized pursuant to a doctor's instructions; and
3. for any purpose not consistent with being authorized by a physician.

Neglect is defined as the negligent failure of any person having the care or custody of an elder or dependent adult to exercise the degree of care that a reasonable person in a like position would exercise. Note, *neglect* includes, but is not limited to, the following:

1. failure to assist in personal hygiene or in providing food or clothing;
2. failure to provide medical care for physical and mental health needs. However no person shall be deemed neglected or abused solely because he or she voluntarily relies on treatment by spiritual means through prayer in lieu of medical treatment;
3. failure to protect from health and safety standards; and
4. failure to prevent malnutrition.

Abandonment means the desertion or willful forsaking of an elder or dependent adult by anyone having care or custody of that person under circumstances in which a reasonable person would continue to provide care or custody.

Fiduciary abuse means a situation in which a person who has the care or custody of, or who stands in a position of trust to, an elder or dependent adult takes, secretes, or appropriates their money or property for any use or purpose not in the due or lawful execution of his or her fiduciary duty.

Abuse of an elder or dependent adult means physical abuse, neglect, intimidation, cruel punishment, fiduciary abuse, abandonment, isolation, or other treatment with resulting physical harm or mental suffering, or the deprivation by a care custodian of goods or services that were necessary to avoid physical harm or mental suffering.

Isolation means acts intentionally committed for the purpose of preventing, and that do in fact serve to prevent, an elder or dependent adult from receiving his or her mail or telephone calls.

Isolation also means falsely telling a caller or prospective visitor that an elder or dependent adult is not present, does not wish to talk with them, or does not wish to meet with them, where the express wish of the elder or dependent is to have such contact, and the false statements are made for the purpose of preventing the elder or dependent from having contact with family, friends, or concerned persons. *Isolation* also includes false imprisonment and physical restraint for the purpose of preventing contact with visitors. Various acts that are deemed to constitute isolation are subject to a rebuttable presumption that they do not constitute isolation for the purposes of the statute if they are performed pursuant to the instructions of a licensed doctor who is caring for the adult and gives the instructions as part of medical care. Further, the acts specified do not constitute isolation if they are performed in response to a reasonable perceived threat of danger to property or physical safety.

A care custodian for the purpose of the statute means an administrator or an employee excepting persons who do not work directly with elders or dependent adults as part of their official duties in any of the following public or private facilities:

1. 24-hour facilities as defined in the Health & Safety Code;
2. clinics;
3. home health care agencies;
4. adult day care agencies;
5. secondary schools that serve 18- to 22-year-old dependent adults and postsecondary educational institutions that serve dependent adults or elders;
6. sheltered workshops;
7. camps;
8. community care facilities and residential care facilities as defined in the Health & Safety Code;
9. respite care facilities;
10. foster homes;
11. regional centers for persons with developmental disabilities;
12. state department of social services and state department of health services licensing divisions;
13. county welfare departments;
14. offices of patients rights advocates;
15. office of long-term care ombudsman in a hospital setting;
16. offices of public conservators and public guardians; and

17. any other protective or public assistance agency that provides heath services or social services to elderly or dependent adults.[2]

(B) Who Must Report

The duty to report is imposed on any elder or dependent adult care custodian, health practitioner, or employee of a county adult protective services agency or local law enforcement agency, who in the course of his or her professional capacity or within the scope of his or her employment either has observed an incident that reasonably appears to be physical abuse, has observed an injury that clearly indicates that physical abuse has occurred, or is told by an elder or dependent adult that he or she has experienced behavior constituting physical abuse. Where any care custodian, health practitioner, or employee of an adult protective services agency or law enforcement agency has knowledge of or reasonably suspects that other types of elder or dependent abuse have been inflicted upon an elder or dependent adult, or that the elder's emotional well-being is endangered in any other way, they must report it either to a long-term care ombudsmen coordinator (when the abuse is alleged to have occurred in a long-term care facility) or to the county adult protective services agency (when the abuse occurs anywhere else).[3]

Any person who knows or reasonably suspects that an elder or dependent adult has been the victim of abuse may report the abuse to a long-term care ombudsman coordinator (when the abuse is alleged to have occurred in a long-term care facility) or to the county adult protective services agency (when the abuse is alleged to have occurred anywhere else). *Reasonable suspicion* means that it is objectively reasonable for a person to entertain such a suspicion based upon facts that could cause a reasonable person in a like position to suspect abuse.[4]

(C) When to Make a Report

A report must be made immediately, or as soon as possible, by telephone and in writing within two working days of when the reporter knows of or suspects the physical abuse.[5]

---

2. Welf. & Inst. Code § 15610.
3. Welf. & Inst. Code § 15630.
4. Welf. & Inst. Code § 15631.
5. Welf. & Inst. Code § 15630.

(D) Making a Report

The report is made to a long-term care ombudsman coordinator or to a local law enforcement agency when the physical abuse is alleged to have occurred in a long-term care facility, and is made to the county adult protective services agency or to a local law enforcement agency when the abuse is alleged to have occurred anywhere else.[6] The report should contain the following information (unless it is unavailable):

1. the name, address, telephone number, and occupation of the person reporting;
2. the name and address of the victim;
3. the date, time, and place of the incident;
4. other details, including the reporter's observations and beliefs concerning the incident;
5. any statement relating to the incident made by the victim;
6. the name of any individuals believed to have knowledge of the incident; and
7. the name of any individuals believed to be responsible for the incident and their connection to the victim.

When two or more persons who are required to report a known or suspected physical abuse, the telephone report shall be made by a member of the team, selected by mutual agreement, and a single report shall be made and signed by that person. Any member of the team who has knowledge that the person designated to report has failed to do so shall make the report.[7]

(E) Immunity From Liability

The reporting duties under this statute belong to the individual, and no supervisor or administrator is allowed to impede or inhibit the reporting duties, and no person making such a report shall be subject to any employment sanction for making such a report. Internal procedures to facilitate reporting, ensure confidentiality, and apprise supervisors and administrators of the reports may be established provided they are not inconsistent with the statute.[8]

---

6. Welf. & Inst. Code § 15630(a)(1).
7. Welf. & Inst. Code § 15630(a)(2) & (b).
8. Welf. & Inst. Code § 15630(e).

Any care custodian, health practitioner, or employee of an adult protective service agency or local law enforcement agency who reports a known or suspected instance of elder or dependent adult abuse is given immunity from civil or criminal liability whether any report is required or authorized by the article. However, any other person reporting a known or suspected instance of elder or dependent abuse is given conditional immunity unless it can be proven that a false report was made and that the person knew that the report was false. Further, any care custodian, health practitioner, or employee in an adult protection services agency or law enforcement agency who, pursuant to a request from an adult protective services agency or a law enforcement agency, provides the agency with access to the victim of a known or suspected instance of elder or dependent adult abuse is not subject to civil or criminal liability as a result of providing that access.[9]

The California legislature has recognized that, as with child abuse reporting, even though immunity is provided, the immunity does not eliminate the possibility that civil actions may be brought against persons required to make reports of abuse. Therefore, as with child abuse reporting cases, the legislature has provided that where a reporter who would be immune from suit is sued and prevails on a motion to have the case dismissed before trial or at trial, the State Board of Control may pay attorney fees of up to $50,000 that the reporter has incurred in his or her defense.[10]

(F) Confidentiality and Privilege

The reports are confidential by law and may be disclosed only under extremely limited circumstances.[11] However, the physician–patient privilege and the psychotherapist–patient privilege do not apply to the specific information required to be reported by this law. It is somewhat less clear the extent to which an attorney is required to report, but when an attorney reports without violating his or her oath and duties, no attorney–client privilege would apply to such information.[12]

---

9. Welf. & Inst. Code § 15634(a) & (b).
10. Welf. & Inst. Code § 15634(c).
11. Welf. & Inst. Code § 15633.5.
12. Welf. & Inst. Code § 15637.

(G) Failure to Report

Any person who fails to report an incident of elder or dependent adult abuse is guilty of a misdemeanor and can be punished by imprisonment in the county jail for a period not exceeding six months, by a fine of not exceeding $1,000, or by both.[13]

While there are no cases specifically on point in this regard, it must be presumed that, as with child abuse reporting, if a report should have been made and is not made, someone can sue for damages suffered that might have been avoided had a timely report been made.[14]

(H) Civil Actions

In 1991, the legislature enacted some specific provisions governing civil actions alleging elder and dependent adult abuse. The statutes provide that when it is proven by clear and convincing evidence that a defendant is liable for physical abuse, neglect, or fiduciary abuse of an elder or dependent adult, and the defendant has been found guilty of recklessness, oppression, fraud, or malice in the commission of the abuse, then in addition to all other remedies the court shall award to the plaintiff reasonable attorney fees and costs, including any reasonable fees for the services of the conservator dealing with the litigation. In addition, certain limitations imposed by the Probate Code on damages recoverable in actions of this type would not apply, but the damages cannot exceed $250,000 for non-economic damages.[15]

The legislature also provided that the department of the Superior Court having jurisdiction over probate conservatorships shall have concurrent jurisdiction over civil actions involving claims of elder and dependent adult abuse if a conservator has been appointed for the plaintiff prior to the initiation of the action. The court has the discretion to transfer the matter to the general civil calendar of the Superior Court if it determines that is appropriate. The court does not lose jurisdiction upon the death of an elder or dependent adult. The right to maintain an action is transferred to the personal representative of the decedent upon

---

13. Welf. & Inst. Code § 15634.
14. *Landeros v. Flood,* 17 Cal.3d 399 (1976).
15. Welf. & Inst. Code §§ 15657, 15657.1. In *ARA Living Centers-Pacific Inc. v. Superior Court,* 18 Cal.App.4th 1556 (1993), the appellate court gave retroactive effect to the attorney fees provisions of the statute, but held that the award of damages for an elder's pain and suffering could be asserted only for injuries inflicted after the statute was amended.

petition, or, if none exists, to the person or persons entitled to succeed to the decedent's estate.[16]

(I) Criminal Liability for Elder Abuse

Under the Penal Code, the infliction of abuse, pain, or mental suffering on an elder or dependent adult is a crime.[17] The law also imposes liability on persons having the care or custody of an elder or dependent adult for endangering them or allowing them to be injured. Three appellate cases have dealt with elder abuse.[18] A 1993 case expressly upheld the constitutionality of the statute and the conviction of a woman for failing to take care of her dependent father.[19] In that case, the father was under the care of the defendant's brothers whom she knew to be poor housekeepers, and she was also aware that her brothers failed to obtain necessary medical care for her father for months. The Court of Appeals concluded that the daughter had a duty to care for the father, relying in part on statutes imposing a duty of support on parents and children of people in need who are unable to work.[20] The California Supreme Court reversed the Appellate Court and held that criminal liability for failure to protect an elder or dependent adult from abuse was limited to those individuals who had a legal duty to prevent the abuse. Although caretakers had such a duty, a daughter who did not reside with or care for the victim did not.

In another case, the California Medical Association argued that this statute improperly allowed health care providers to be criminally prosecuted for professional negligence.[21] However, the Court of Appeals held that the legislature did not intend to exclude health care providers from criminal liability under the act. In fact, the court noted that medical practitioners, who are often in charge of the care and custody of a dependent adult, would seem to be one of the prime target groups the statute was aimed at. The court further stated that the fact that health care providers were required to report elder abuse did not relieve them from criminal liability for engaging in such acts themselves.[22]

---

16. Welf. & Inst. Code § 15657.3.
17. Penal Code § 368.
18. *People v. Superior Court*, 205 Cal.App.3d 51 (1988); *People v. McKelvey*, 230 Cal App.3d 399 (1991); *People v. Heitzman*, 18 Cal.App.4th 1400 (1993), reversed 9 Cal.4th 189 (1994).
19. *People v. Heitzman, supra* note 19.
20. Civ. Code § 206.
21. *People v. Superior Court, supra* note 19.
22. *Id.* at 61.

5A.8

Reporting of Child Abuse

MHPs in California are required to report all known or suspected instances of child abuse. This chapter discusses the circumstances in which a report is required, who must report, and when the report must be made, as well as the consequences of failing to make a required report and the immunities available for making a report.

(A) Definitions

A *health practitioner* for the purposes of the child abuse reporting act is defined as a physician and surgeon; psychiatrist; psychologist; dentist; resident; intern; podiatrist; chiropractor; licensed nurse; dental hygienist; optometrist; a marriage, family and child counselor; any emergency medical technician I or II; paramedic; psychological assistant; marriage, family, and child counselor trainee; unlicensed marriage, family and child counselor intern; state or county public health employee who treats a minor for a venereal disease or any other condition; a coroner; medical examiner or any other person who performs an autopsy; or a religious practitioner who diagnoses, examines or treats children.[1]

Reasonable suspicion means that it is objectively reasonable for a person, based upon facts that would cause a reasonable person in a like position, to suspect child abuse. The Department of Social Services has paraphrased this definition as "if you suspect, re-

---

1. Penal Code § 11165.8.

port." However the pregnancy of a minor, by itself, does not constitute the basis of reasonable suspicion of sexual abuse.[2]

A *child* is a person under the age of 18.[3]

Child abuse is defined as a physical injury inflicted by other than accidental means on a child by another person. *Child abuse* includes the sexual abuse of a child or any act or omission that would constitute willful cruelty or unjustifiable punishment or unlawful corporal punishment or injury. *Child abuse* also means the neglect of a child or abuse in out-of-home care. Child abuse does not mean a mutual fight between minors. Child abuse does not include an injury caused by reasonable and necessary force used by a peace officer to quell a disturbance threatening physical injury to person or damage to property, for purposes of self defense, to obtain possession of weapons or other dangerous objects within the control of the child, or to apprehend an escapee.[4]

Sexual abuse means sexual assault or sexual exploitation, including rape, rape in concert, incest, sodomy, lewd or lascivious acts upon a child under 14, oral copulation, or penetration of a genital or anal opening by a foreign object.

Sexual exploitation is broadly defined to reach any act which involves a minor in obscene sexual acts or prostitution, including depicting a minor in sexual conduct in videos, films, slides and/ or live shows.[5]

(B) Who Must Report

The law requires any child care custodian, health practitioner, or employee of a child protective agency who has knowledge of or observes a child in his or her professional capacity, or within the scope of his or her employment, whom he or she knows or reasonably suspects has been the victim of child abuse, to report the known or suspected instance of child abuse to a child protective agency. If two or more persons who are required to report are present and jointly have knowledge of a known or suspected instance of child abuse, and if there is an agreement among them, the telephone report may be made by a member of the team

---

2. Penal Code § 11166(a).
3. Penal Code § 11165.
4. Penal Code § 11165.6. Child abuse does not include, and reporting is not required of voluntary sexual acts between minors, *Planned Parenthood Affiliates of California v. Van de Kamp*, 181 Cal.App.3d 245 (1986); *People v. Stockton Pregnancy Control Medical Clinic Inc.*, 203 Cal.3d 225 (1988). Reporting is required of consensual sex acts between a minor and an adult.
5. Penal Code § 11165.1. This also may constitute pornography (*see* chapter 5D.24).

selected by mutual agreement and a single written report may be made and signed by that person.

A commercial film and photographic print processor who has knowledge of or observes film, photograph, videotape, negatives, or slides depicting a child under the age of 14 engaged in an act of sexual conduct is required to report the abuse to a law enforcement agency.

Any other person who has knowledge of or observes a child whom he or she knows or reasonably suspects has been a victim of child abuse may report the known or suspected instance of child abuse to a child protective agency.[6]

(C) When to Make a Report

Once a MHP knows or reasonably suspects that a child has been the victim of abuse, he or she must report the incident immediately, or as soon as practically possible by telephone, and then prepare a written report within 36 hours. When an MHP has knowledge of or reasonably suspects that mental suffering has been inflicted on a child, or a child's emotional well-being is endangered in any other way, the MHP *may* report such known or suspected instances of child abuse to a child protective agency, but it is not required.[7]

The statute does not impose on MHPs any duty to investigate child abuse—only to report it.[8]

(D) Immunity From Liability

Because reporting is mandatory, MHPs who report a known or suspected instance of child abuse are immune from any civil or criminal liability for a report that is either required or authorized by the law. Any other person reporting a known or suspected

---

6. Penal Code § 11166.
7. Penal Code § 11166(b); The California Department of Social Services Office of Child Abuse Prevention has prepared a handbook to assist mandated reporters: State of California Department of Social Services Office, Adult and Family Services Division, Family and Children's Services Branch, Office of Child Abuse Prevention Publication No. 132, *The California Abuse and Neglect Reporting Law—Issues and Answers for Health Practitioners*.
8. *People v. Younghanz*, 156 Cal.App.3d 811 (1984). In fact, the recent case of *James W. v. Superior Court*, 17 Cal.App.4th 246 (1993), suggested that when therapists go from reporting to investigating abuse, they are beyond their area of competence and not immune from suit.

instance of child abuse cannot be sued civilly or be subject to criminal liability unless it is proven that a false report was made and the person knew that the report was false, or that the report was made with reckless disregard for the truth.

When the California legislature was considering the type of immunity to be given to health professionals making required reports, it concluded that to allow such claims to be asserted against health professionals would defeat the statutory purpose, because, in virtually every instance a report was made, someone would assert that the reporter knew or should have known that the report was false. Thus, the immunity in the statute is unqualified as to MHPs and other mandatory reporters, and qualified as to non-mandatory reporters.

Despite their immunity, suits are still filed against MHPs alleging that child abuse reports were made where no abuse actually occurred or that the MHP made the report due to bias or incompetence.[9] Because health professionals might be required to defend themselves in litigation to establish the existence and scope of the immunity, the legislature has provided that where a mandatory reporter, including an MHP, is sued for making a report and prevails on either a demurrer or a motion for summary judgment, the reporter may be reimbursed reasonable attorney fees from the State Board of Control, not to exceed $50,000.[10]

A *demurrer* is a response to a complaint that asserts that, assuming all facts plead in the complaint to be true, there is a key legal deficiency or a complete legal defense.[11] The immunity provided would be a complete defense to an action. A *summary judgment motion* is a motion supported by declarations that the facts are essentially not in dispute and that the only issues remaining are legal issues for the court to resolve. If the court agrees that no factual issues exist, the judge may decide the case without a trial.[12]

The immunity applies only if the report of child abuse is made to the authorities identified in the statute. For example, a recent federal case held that the immunity did not protect a California psychologist from a civil suit for defamation over a report of child abuse made to authorities in Texas, where no report was made in California.[13]

---

9. Penal Code § 11172; *Storch v. Silverman*, Cal.App.3d 671 (1986); *Krikorian v. Barry*, 196 Cal.App.3d 1211 (1987); *Ferraro v. Chadwick*, 221 Cal.App.3d 86 (1990); *Thomas v. Chadwick*, 224 Cal.App.3d 813 (1990); *McMartin v. Children's Institute Int'l*, 212 Cal.App.3d 1393 (1989), *cert. denied*, 494 U.S. 1057 (1990).
10. Penal Code § 11172(c).
11. Civ. Proc. Code § 430.10.
12. Civ. Proc. Code § 437c.
13. *Searcy v. Auerbach*, 980 F.2d 609 (9th Cir. 1993).

A recent state case held that the immunity did not extend to treating therapists who were not involved in reporting or evaluating child abuse.[14] In that case, the court concluded that if the allegations were true, the therapist had lost her objectivity and took on an investigatory or prosecutorial role, and may have led the child to falsely accuse her father.

(E) Confidentiality and Privilege

Although MHPs are generally required to keep communications from clients confidential, the child abuse reporting law constitutes an express exception to confidentiality.[15] However, the California Supreme Court has interpreted the waiver of confidentiality imposed by the child abuse reporting law to be limited in scope. When an MHP made an initial report of child abuse, the confidentiality was waived; however, when a deputy sheriff subsequently called the MHP and sought additional details, confidentiality was not waived, and a subsequent criminal conviction was reversed.[16]

Even though reporting may lead to criminal prosecution, an MHP is not required to give a patient warnings against self incrimination.[17] The mandatory reports required by the law are themselves confidential and may be disclosed only to specifically authorized persons or agencies—generally those involved in investigations of child abuse and multidisciplinary teams involved in the prevention, identification, and treatment of child abuse.[18]

The law defines three categories of reports: unfounded, unsubstantiated, and substantiated. A *substantiated report* is a report that is determined by a child protective agency investigator, based upon credible evidence, to constitute child abuse or neglect. An *unfounded report* is one where it is determined by a child protective agency investigator that the charges are false, or inherently improbable, involve an accidental injury, or do not otherwise constitute child abuse. An *unsubstantiated report* is one that is determined by a child protective agency investigator not to be unfounded, but the findings are inconclusive and there is insuffi-

---

14. *James W. v. Superior Court*, 17 Cal.App.4th 246 (1993).
15. Penal Code § 11171(b); *Roe v. Superior Court*, 229 Cal.App.3d 832 (1991). The child abuse reporting statute takes precedence over conflicting statutes providing for confidentiality. 58 Ops. Atty. Gen. 824 (Welf. & Inst. Code § 5328); *People v. Stockton Pregnancy Control Medical Clinic Inc.*, 203 Cal.3d 225 (1988). Civ. Code § 56.11 on minor's confidentiality).
16. *People v. Stritzinger*, 34 Cal.3d 505 (1983).
17. *People v. Battaglia*, 156 Cal.App.3d 1058 (1984).
18. Penal Code § 11167.5; Welf. & Inst. Code § 830.

cient evidence to determine whether the child abuse occurred.[19] Reports determined to be unfounded are not kept in the database.

(F) Failure to Report

Failure to report a known or suspected instance of child abuse can subject an MHP to criminal charges, civil suit, and professional discipline.[20]

---

19. Penal Code § 11165.9.
20. Penal Code § 11172(e); *Landeros v. Flood*, 17 Cal.3d 399 (1976); *People v. Stockton Pregnancy Control Medical Clinic Inc.*, *supra* note 15; *People v. Bernstein*, 197 Cal.App.3d Supp 34 (1987).

5A.9

Abused and Neglected Children

California law provides a structured framework for the protection of abused, neglected, and abandoned children as dependents of the juvenile court, and also provides services for their families. The law also focuses on trying to keep families together without imperiling children. The legislation establishes a standard of proof of clear and convincing evidence before removing children from their parents, requires the status of the case to be reviewed every six months, and requires reunification services and permanency planning hearings for children who could not be returned to a parent within 18 months.[1] At a permanency planning hearing, a Juvenile Court may select one of three possible permanent plans: adoption, guardianship, or long-term foster care.

When abuse and neglect have been alleged, the law allows for children to be temporarily removed from their parents pending a hearing. Then there is an interim investigation and a hearing at which the court makes dispositional findings. Review hearings are held every six months.[2]

At any of these stages, MHPs may be involved in providing evidence.

(A) Definitions:

Under California law, a minor who may be adjudged to be a dependent child of the court is one who has been subjected to any of the following circumstances:

---

1. Penal Code §§ 361 to 366.25; *Cynthia D. v. Superior Court*, 5 Cal.4th 242 (1993).
2. *Cynthia D. v. Superior Court*, *supra* note 1; Welf. & Inst. Code §§ 366, 395.

1. The minor has suffered, or there is a substantial risk that the minor will suffer, serious physical harm inflicted non-accidentally by the minor's parents or guardian. The court may find there is a substantial risk of serious future injury based on the manner in which a less serious injury was inflicted, or a history of repeated injuries on the minor or the minor's siblings or both. *Serious physical harm* as used here does not include reasonable and age-appropriate spanking to the buttocks where there is no evidence of serious injury.

2. The minor has suffered or there is a substantial risk that the minor will suffer serious physical harm or illness as a result of the failure or inability of his or her parent or guardian to adequately supervise or protect the minor; or the willful or negligent failure of the minor's parent or guardian to adequately supervise or protect the minor from the conduct of a person with whom the minor has been left; or by the willful or negligent failure of the parent or guardian to provide the minor with adequate food, clothing, shelter, or medical treatment; or by the inability of the parent or guardian to provide regular care for the minor due to the parent or guardian's mental illness, developmental disability, or substance abuse. However, when a minor comes within the court's jurisdiction on the basis of a parent or guardian's willful failure to provide medical treatment, based on the parent's decision to provide spiritual treatment through prayer, the court must give deference to the parent or guardian's medical treatment, non-treatment, or spiritual treatment through prayer and in accordance with the tenets and practices of a recognized church or religious denomination, and not assume jurisdiction unless necessary to protect the minor from serious physical harm or injury.

3. The minor is suffering serious emotional damage or is at substantial risk of suffering serious emotional damage evidenced by severe anxiety, depression, withdrawal, or untoward aggressive behavior toward self or others as a result of the conduct of the parent or guardian, or where the minor has no parent or guardian capable of providing appropriate care.

4. The minor has been sexually abused or there is a substantial risk the minor will be sexually abused by his or her parent or guardian or member of their household, or the parent or guardian has failed adequately to protect the minor from sexual abuse when the parent or guardian knew or reasonably should have known the minor was in danger of sexual abuse.

5. The minor is under the age of five and has suffered severe physical abuse by a parent or by any person known to the parent. *Severe physical abuse* means any of the following:

    (a) any single act of abuse that causes physical trauma, that if left untreated would cause permanent physical disfigurement, permanent physical disability, or death;

    (b) any single act of sexual abuse that causes significant bleeding, deep bruising, or significant external or internal swelling, or;

    (c) more than one act of physical abuse, each of which causes bleeding, deep bruising, significant external or internal swelling, bone fracture, or unconsciousness; or

    (d) the willful prolonged failure to provide adequate food.

6. The minor's parent or guardian has been convicted of causing the death of another child through abuse or neglect.

7. The minor has been left without any provision for support because the minor's parent has been incarcerated or institutionalized and cannot arrange for the minor's care, or a relative or other person with whom the child resides is unwilling or unable to provide care or support, and the whereabouts of the parents are unknown.

8. The minor has been freed for adoption by one or both parents for twelve months by either relinquishment or termination of parental rights, or an adoption petition has not been granted.

9. The minor has been subjected to an act or acts of cruelty by the parent or guardian or a member of their household.

10. The minor's sibling has been abused and neglected as defined above, and there is a substantial risk the minor will be abused or neglected.

The California legislature has expressed its intent to provide maximum protection for children who are currently being physically sexually or emotionally abused, neglected, or exploited, and to protect children who are at risk of harm. The protection is to focus on preservation of the family whenever possible.[3]

At least one case has held that where a child is born with dangerous drugs in its body, there is a presumption that the child meets these serious physical harm requirements to support a determination of dependency.[4]

---

3. Welf. & Inst. Code § 300.
4. *In re Monique T.*, 2 Cal.App.4th 1372 (1992); *In re Steven W.*, 221 Cal.App.3d 629 (1990).

(B) Temporary Custody

The law specifically allows for any peace officer to take a minor into temporary custody without a warrant when the officer has reasonable cause for believing that the minor meets any of the criteria set forth above and has an immediate need for medical care, or is in immediate danger of physical or sexual abuse, or the physical environment or the fact the child is left unattended poses an immediate threat to the child's health or safety. In cases where the child has been left unattended, a peace officer must first attempt to contact the child's parent or guardian to determine if the parent or guardian is able to assume custody of the child. If the child's parent or guardian cannot be contacted, the peace officer must notify a social worker in the County Welfare Department to assume custody of the child. The peace officer may also take temporary custody of a minor who is in a hospital when release of the minor to the parent poses an immediate danger to the child's health or safety or where the minor is found in any street or public place suffering from any sickness or injury that requires care and medical treatment, hospitalization, or other remedial care.[5]

This code section also allows a peace officer to take a minor into temporary custody for violating orders of the Juvenile Court. Suits have been brought against an investigator and a social worker who took a child into custody under the statutory authority. In one case, the investigator then returned the child to the custody of the father who allegedly sexually abused her, but the court found that the investigator had immunity.[6]

A social worker in the County Welfare Department acting within the scope of his or her regular duties may receive and maintain, pending investigation, temporary custody of a minor who has been delivered to him or her by a peace officer pursuant to the temporary custody authority. A social worker also has the power to take into temporary custody a minor who has been declared to be a dependent child by the juvenile court or whom the social worker has reasonable cause to believe has suffered or is at risk of serious physical harm or illness as a result of the failure or inability of the parent or guardian to adequately supervise and protect. The social worker can also take a minor into custody where the minor has been left without any provision for support, or the social worker has reasonable cause to believe that

---

5. Welf. & Inst. Code § 305.
6. *Hall ex rel. M.K. v. Harder*, 716 F. Supp. 1323 (E.D. Cal. 1989); *Jenkins v. County of Orange*, 212 Cal.App.3d 278 (1989); *Alicia T. v. County of Los Angeles*, 222 Cal.App.3d 869 (1990).

the minor has an immediate need for medical care, or is in immediate danger of physical or sexual abuse, or that the physical environment poses an immediate threat to the minor's health and safety. Courts have given social workers and investigators immunity for the decision to remove the child from the parents.

Before taking a minor into temporary custody, a social worker must consider whether there are any reasonable services available that, if provided to the parent, guardian, or caretaker, would eliminate the need to remove the minor from custody. The social worker must also consider whether referral to public assistance programs would eliminate the need for temporary custody of the minor. If such services are available, they must be utilized.[7]

A peace officer or social worker who takes a minor into temporary custody must immediately inform the parent, guardian, or responsible relative through the most efficient means available that the minor has been taken into protective custody and that a written statement is available that explains the parent or guardian's procedural rights and the preliminary stages of the dependency investigation and hearing.[8] The officer is required to provide a written statement specifying the conditions under which the minor will be released, any hearings that will be required, the right to counsel, the right not to incriminate oneself, and the rights of appeal by the minor and his or her parents, guardians, or responsible relatives.

The peace officer also has the option of taking a minor into temporary custody, or taking the minor to a community service program for abused or neglected children, which provides shelter, care, or counseling. In this situation, the receiving organization is obligated to notify the minor's parent or guardian.[9]

When a parent or guardian is given notice of the minor being taken into temporary custody, the court may issue an order that the parent not be notified of the exact whereabouts of the minor if to do so would endanger the child or his or her foster family, or there is a likelihood that the parent or guardian would flee with the child. If it is impossible or impractical to obtain such an order authorizing nondisclosure before a detention hearing, and if the peace officer or social worker has a reasonable belief that the minor or his or her foster family would be endangered by the disclosure of the minor's exact whereabouts, the peace officer or social worker may refuse to disclose where the minor is being held.[10]

---

7. Welf. & Inst. Code § 306.
8. Welf. & Inst. Code § 307.4.
9. Welf. & Inst. Code § 307.5.
10. Welf. & Inst. Code § 308.

A minor who has been taken into temporary custody has the right to make within an hour at least two telephone calls. One to a parent or guardian, and one to an attorney at public expense. Any officer or employee who deprives a minor of the right to make these calls is guilty of a misdemeanor.[11]

(C) Investigation by the Probation Officer

Once a minor has been taken into temporary custody, the probation officer immediately begins an investigation of the circumstances of the minor and the facts surrounding the minor's being taken into custody. The probation officer is required to attempt to keep the minor with the family through services, and must release the minor to the custody of the parent or guardian unless one of the following conditions applies:

1. the minor has no parent, guardian, or reasonable relative, or those individuals are not willing to provide care;

2. the minor must be detained for his or her own protection, and there's no reasonable means by which the minor can be protected in his or her home or the home of a relative;

3. there is substantial evidence that a parent, guardian, or custodian is likely to flee the jurisdiction;

4. the minor has left the place in which he or she was placed by the juvenile court; or

5. the minor is under the care of a physician, hospital, clinic, or other medical facility and cannot be immediately moved and is therefore deemed to be taken into custody by a probation officer.[12]

In one case, a child was taken into temporary custody following her mother's mental breakdown and institutionalization on an involuntary basis. The child was released to the custody of the father, and the mother then filed suit unsuccessfully challenging the decision.[13]

---

11. Welf. & Inst. Code § 308.
12. Welf. & Inst. Code § 309.
13. *In re Phoenix V.*, 218 Cal.App.3d 787 (1990).

(D) Adjudication of Child Abuse or Neglect

California law provides a series of hearings on the issue of child abuse and neglect. When a petition has been filed to declare a child a dependent of the court, a detention hearing must be held by the juvenile court no later than the next judicial day. At the hearing, the parents are entitled to court-appointed counsel if they cannot afford counsel. At the hearing, the Department of Social Services bears the burden of making a *prima facie* showing that the minor is an abused and neglected child and that there's need for detention under the specific situation. The Juvenile Court must make findings regarding whether reasonable efforts were made to prevent or eliminate the need to remove the minor from his or her home, and, if the minor is detained, must order services to be provided as soon as possible to reunify the minor and his or her family.[14]

The court sets a hearing on a dependency petition, referred to as a jurisdictional hearing, since at this hearing the court determines whether it should hear the case, based on the allegations of the minor. The jurisdictional finding must be made by a preponderance of the evidence.[15]

If the court finds jurisdiction, it conducts a disposition hearing. At this hearing the court considers whether the child may remain with the parents or whether the child must be removed from the parents. The standard of proof for removal is clear and convincing evidence.[16]

In such proceedings, the child is appointed an independent legal counsel whose duty is to represent the best interests of the child. If the child is removed from the parents' custody, the court makes orders regarding reunification services, and must inform the parents that their parental rights may be terminated if they do not reunify within 12 months.[17]

In all cases in which a petition is filed alleging neglect or abuse of a child, or in which a prosecution is initiated under the Penal Code because of neglect or abuse, the probation officer or social worker who files a petition is deemed to be the guardian *ad litem* to represent the interests of the minor unless the court

---

14. *Cynthia D. v. Superior Court*, 5 Cal.4th 242 (1993); Welf. & Inst. Code §§ 315, 319.
15. *Cynthia D. v. Superior Court*, *supra* note 14; Welf. & Inst. Code § 355; Cal. Ct. C.P.R. 1450.
16. *Cynthia D. v. Superior Court*, *supra* note 14; Welf. & Inst. Code § 1361; Cal. Ct. C.P.R. 1456(c).
17. *Cynthia D. v. Superior Court*, *supra* note 14; Cal. Ct. C.P.R. 1456(e); Welf. & Inst. Code § 361.5.

appoints another adult as a guardian *ad litem.* However, the guardian *ad litem* may not be the attorney responsible for presenting evidence alleging child abuse or neglect in judicial proceedings.[18]

Following a determination that a child is a dependent child, six-month review hearings are held at which there is a statutory presumption that the child will be returned to parental custody unless the court finds by a preponderance of the evidence that the return of the child would create a substantial risk or detriment to the physical safety or well-being of the minor.[19] At the six-month review hearings the Department of Social Services, not the parent, has the burden of proof.

If the child is not returned at the six-month review, a hearing is held at 12 months, referred to as a permanency planning hearing, where the court considers evidence and makes determinations as to how to proceed. At 18 months, there is a review hearing followed by hearings at six-month intervals after the establishment of a permanent plan.[20]

In the hearings to determine whether a child has been abused and neglected and what position would be appropriate, the testimony of MHPs is often essential.

(E) Dispositional Alternatives

Once the court determines that a child has been abused or neglected, the court has several alternative dispositions. The statutory preference is for the court to return the child to the custody of the parents unless there is a substantial risk of emotional and physical harm to the minor.

The Supreme Court has noted that there is a difference in the standards of proof for the termination of parental rights hearing and the dispositional hearing. The standard of proof in a proceeding to terminate parental rights is clear and convincing evidence.[21] However, dispositional hearings have a lower standard of proof: preponderance of the evidence. As the Supreme Court has noted, by the time a case gets to a dispositional hearing, the purpose is not to accumulate further evidence of parental unfitness and danger to the child, but to begin the task of finding the child a permanent alternative family placement.[22]

---

18. Welf. & Inst. Code § 326.
19. Welf. & Inst. Code § 366. *Cynthia D. v. Superior Court, supra* note 14; Cal. Ct. C.P.R. 1460.
20. Welf. & Inst. Code §§ 366.2 to 366.3; Cal. Ct. C.P.R. 1462, 1465.
21. *In Re Angelia P.*, 28 Cal.3d 908 (1981).
22. *Cynthia D. v. Superior Court*, 5 Cal. 4th 242 (1993).

By the time the proceedings get to the point of a dispositional hearing, there have been multiple specific findings of parental unfitness. Except for a temporary period, the grounds for the initial removal of the child had to be established under clear and convincing evidence standards. Further, there must have been a series of hearings dealing with reunification efforts, which presumably are unsuccessful, and where the court in each hearing considered whether the child should be returned to the parents. Only after the state has repeatedly established that the child's return to the custody of the parent would be detrimental is a dispositional hearing held.[23]

Once a parent's conduct has been found to grievously endanger the child, the parent is no longer in the same position as a parent whose neglect or abuse has not been clearly established. Further, the interest of parent and child have diverged, and the child's interest must be given more weight.

The dispositional hearing stage contemplates termination of parental rights only when there is clear and convincing evidence that the child is likely to be adopted.[24]

In upholding California's system, the California Supreme Court contrasted the California scheme with the New York scheme found deficient by the U.S. Supreme Court in 1982. The California Supreme Court concluded that California's dependency statutes provide parents a more level playing field because of the requirements that counsel be appointed for parents unable to afford one whenever a petitioning agency recommended out-of-home care, and that counsel for the parents give access to records relevant to the case that are maintained by state or local public agencies, by hospitals or other medical or non-medical practitioners, or by child care custodians. The California Supreme Court also pointed to the requirement that the petitioning agency not only produce clear and convincing evidence that initial removal of the child was necessary, but also that the agency make reasonable efforts to prevent or eliminate the need for removal. Finally, the California Supreme Court pointed with approval to the fact that once the child is removed, there is a statutory presumption that he or she will be returned, with the burden on the state to persuade the court otherwise.[25]

Following hearings on the dependency of the child, the court may either

1. find the minor to be a person meeting the statutory criteria, but not declare the minor to be a dependent child of the court,

23. *Id.*; Welf. & Inst. Code § 366.26.
24. Welf. & Inst. Code § 366.26; *Cynthia D. v. Superior Court, supra* note 22.
25. *Cynthia D. v. Superior Court, supra* note 22; *Santosky v. Kramer*, 455 U.S. 745 (1982).

order services be provided to keep the family together, and place the minor and the minor's parent or guardian under the supervision of a probation officer for a period of time;[26] or

2. determine the minor to be a dependent child of the court.[27]

Once the court has determined that the minor is a dependent child of the court, it may either

1. limit the control to be exercised over the child by any parent or guardian and limit the parent's power to make decisions governing the child, including educational decisions, but only as necessary to protect the child;[28] or

2. remove the child from the physical custody of his or her parents if the statutory criteria are met.

When the court removes the child from the parent's custody, the court may direct that the child be under the supervision of a probation officer, who may place the child in any of the following settings:

1. the home of a relative, including a non-custodial parent;

2. a foster home in which the child has been placed before an interruption in foster care;

3. a licensed community care facility;

4. with a foster family agency, to be placed with a suitable licensed foster family or a certified family home; or

5. a home or facility in accordance with the Federal Indian Child Welfare Act.

In order to facilitate reunification of the family if the minor is taken from physical custody and is not placed with relatives, the minor must be placed in foster care in the county of residence of the parents or guardians, if possible.[29]

The court may also order a parent with whom the minor was not residing when the abuse occurred to assume custody of the minor.[30]

Ultimately, however, if at the end of an 18-month period, the child cannot be safely returned to the care and custody of a parent or guardian without court supervision, the court may explore terminating parents' rights and allowing the child to be adopted.[32]

---

26. Welf. & Inst. Code § 360(a).
27. Welf. & Inst. Code § 360(c).
28. Welf. & Inst. Code § 361(a).
29. Welf. & Inst. Code § 361.2.
30. Welf. & Inst. Code.
31. Welf. & Inst. Code. § 361.5.

5A.10

Termination of Parental Rights

A parent's interest in the continued custody, care, and relationship with his or her children is a fundamental civil and constitutional right. By the same token, children have a fundamental interest in belonging to a family and being protected from abuse and neglect.[1] The laws regarding dependence, adoption, and foster care try to strike a balance between these interests by terminating of parental rights only as a last resort. MHPs may be involved in proceedings to terminate parental rights, as evaluators of the parents and children, or responding to an evaluation previously done.

(A) Nature of Parental Rights

Parental rights can be terminated either voluntarily or involuntarily. Involuntary termination generally arises if a minor is placed under the custody of the Department of Social Services or in a foster home following the parents' conviction of child abuse or neglect. The abuse of parental authority can lead to a civil action brought by the minor, or by a relative of the third degree of the minor, or by the county supervisors in the county where the minor resides. When abuse of parental authority is established, the minor may be freed from the parents' dominion, although the duty of support and education will be enforced.[2] Additionally, a minor may bring an action to be declared an emancipated minor free of parental control under terms described below.

---

1. *In re Marilyn H.*, 5 Cal.4th 295 (1993); *Stanley v. Illinois*, 405 U.S. 645 (1972).
2. Civ. Code § 203.

The most common termination of parental rights, however, is through the adoption process, discussed in detail in chapter 5A.14. The involuntary termination of parental rights is not readily allowed by the courts because parental rights are a fundamental right.[3] However, a minor may be declared a dependent of the court under certain circumstances, as discussed below, and following a hearing that could result in termination of the parental rights.[4]

During a proceeding to declare a minor free from the custody and control of his or her parents, the court may appoint legal counsel on behalf of the minor. If a minor cannot afford legal counsel, the court can appoint counsel at public expense. If a parent appears without counsel and is unable to afford counsel, the court is required to appoint counsel unless the right to counsel is knowingly and intelligently waived. However, the same attorney cannot represent both the minor and his or her parent. The public defender may be appointed as counsel for either the parent or the minor.[5] The standard of proof is clear and convincing evidence.[6]

(B) Dependent Child of the Court

A minor may be adjudged to be a dependent child of the court if any of the following circumstances is found to exist:

1. The minor has suffered serious physical harm inflicted non-accidentally by the minor's parent or guardian, or there is a substantial risk that the minor will suffer such harm. The court may find a substantial risk of serious future injury based on the manner in which a less serious injury was inflicted, a history of repeated infliction of injuries on the minor or the minor's siblings, or a combination of these and other actions by the parent or guardian. Serious physical harm does not include reasonable and age-appropriate spanking of the buttocks when there is no serious physical injury.

2. The minor has suffered, or there is a substantial risk that the minor will suffer, serious physical harm or illness due to the failure and ability of the minor's parent or guardian to adequately supervise or protect the minor or to protect the minor

---

3. *In re Robert P.*, 61 Cal.App.3d 310 (1976); *Cynthia D. v. Superior Court*, 5 Cal.4th 242 (1993).
4. Welf. & Inst. Code § 300.
5. Civ. Code §§ 237, 237.5; Fam. Code §§ 7804, 7860 to 7864.
6. Welf. & Inst. Code § 361; *Cynthia D. v. Superior Court, supra* note 3.

from the conduct of the custodian with whom the minor has been left. An alternative ground is the willful and negligent failure of the parent or guardian to provide the minor with adequate food, clothing, shelter, or medical treatment, or the inability of the parent or guardian to provide regular care for the minor due to the parent or guardian's mental illness, developmental disability, or substance abuse. However, when the parent or guardian's failure to provide adequate medical treatment involves a specific decision to provide spiritual treatment through prayer, the court is required to give deference to the parent's or guardian's medical treatment, non-treatment, or spiritual treatment through prayer in accordance with the tenets and practices of a recognized church or religious denomination, and shall not assume jurisdiction unless necessary to protect the minor from suffering serious physical harm or illness.

3. The minor is suffering emotional damage, or is at substantial risk of suffering serious emotional damage, evidenced by severe anxiety, depression, withdrawal, or untoward aggressive behavior towards self or others as a result of the conduct of the parent or guardian. However, a minor will not be declared a dependent under these circumstances if the failure to provide adequate mental health treatment is based on a sincerely held religious belief and if a less intrusive judicial intervention is available. (This particular category of dependency clearly would call for testimony by MHPs as to the various mental conditions listed above.)[7]

4. The minor has been sexually abused, or there is a substantial risk that the minor will be sexually abused by the minor's parents, guardian, or a member of the minor's household, or the parent or guardian has failed adequately to protect the minor from sexual abuse that the parent or guardian knew or should have known the minor was in danger of experiencing.

5. A minor under the age of five has suffered severe physical abuse by a parent if the parent knew or reasonably should have known of the abuse. Severe physical abuse is defined as any single act of abuse that causes physical trauma of sufficient severity that if it is left untreated it would cause permanent physical disfigurement, permanent physical disability,

---

7. Under this section, intervention arises where there is parental fault in causing the emotional harm, either through omission or commission, or where there is no parental fault but the parents are unable to prove adequate mental health treatment. Three facts must be shown to prove parental fault: (1) the offending conduct was *by a parent*, (2) the conduct caused the harm, and (3) serious emotional harm, or the risk of such harm, to the child.

or death; any single act of sexual abuse that causes significant bleeding, deep bruising, or significant external or internal swelling; or more than one act of physical abuse, each of which causes bleeding, deep bruising, significant external or internal swelling, bone fracture, or unconsciousness. Additionally, severe physical abuse may include the willful or prolonged failure to provide adequate food. A pre-condition to the minor being removed from the physical custody of the minor's parents or guardian on the basis of severe physical abuse is an allegation of severe physical abuse made by a probation officer pursuant to another statutory section.

6. The minor's parent or guardian has been convicted of causing the death of another minor through abuse or neglect.

7. The minor has been left without any provision for support, or the minor's parent or guardian has been incarcerated or institutionalized, or cannot arrange for the minor's care. Alternatively, if a relative or other adult custodian of the minor has been unwilling or unable to provide care or support for the minor, and the whereabouts of the parents is unknown, the minor may be declared a dependent under this section.

8. The minor has been freed for adoption from one or both parents for 12 months by either relinquishment or termination of parental rights, or an adoption petition has not been granted.

9. The minor has been subjected to an act or acts of cruelty by the parent or guardian or a member of his or her household, or the parent or guardian has failed to adequately protect the minor from acts of cruelty when the parent or guardian knew or reasonably should have known the minor was in danger of being subjected to such acts.

10. The minor's sibling has been abused or neglected and there is a substantial risk that the minor will be abused or neglected. The court must consider the circumstances of the abuse or neglect of the sibling, the age and gender of each child, the nature of the abuse and neglect of the sibling, the mental condition of the parent or guardian, and any other factors the court considers probative in determining whether there is a substantial risk to the minor.

The protection to be provided to the minor is to focus on the preservation of the family whenever possible. It is not the intent of the law to disrupt the family unnecessarily or intrude inappropriately in the family life, or to prohibit reasonable methods of parental discipline. Further, a physical disability, such as blindness or deafness, cannot be the focus of the court's determination that a parent's disability prevents him or her from exercising care and control of a minor.[8] Further, the court must guard against acting with a class or lifestyle bias.[9]

The Department of Social Services, a county welfare department, a licensed private or public adoption agency, a county adoption department, or a county probation department may initiate an action to declare a minor free from the custody and control of his or her parents. The action can be instituted by the county counsel or district attorney upon the request of the state or county agencies specified. The petition seeking the termination of parental rights must be verified, and if at the time of the filing of the petition, the minor is in the custody of the petitioner, department, or agency, the petitioner may continue to have custody of the minor pending the hearing, unless the court makes other orders that it believes will best serve and protect the welfare of the minor.[10]

Additionally, any interested person may petition the Superior Court for an order declaring the minor free from the custody and control of either or both parents. Upon the filing of the petition, the clerk of the court is to notify the juvenile probation officer, the court investigator, or the county department designated by the board of supervisors to investigate the circumstances alleged to bring the minor within the scope of the statutory section regarding freedom from parental custody and control.

A written report shall be made to the court by the probation officer, court investigator, or county department. The report must state that the person making the report explained to the minor the nature of the legal action to end parental custody and control. The report must include a statement of the minor's feelings and thoughts concerning the action, the minor's attitude toward his or her parents, and particularly whether the minor would prefer living with them. The report must include a statement that the minor was informed of his or her right to attend the hearing on the petition, and the minor's feeling concerning the hearing. If the age or the physical, emotional, or other condition of the minor precludes meaningful responses to the explanation, inquiries, and information required by law, a description of the minor's condition shall be included in the court report.

The court shall receive the report into evidence and shall read and consider the contents in rendering judgment.[11]

---

8. Welf. & Inst. Code § 300. Note that the failure to provide necessary clothing, food, shelter, and medical care for a child may be a misdemeanor under Penal Code § 270.
9. *In re Cheryl E.*, 161 Cal.App.3d 587 (1984).
10. Civ. Code § 232.9; Fam. Code §§ 212, 7840.
11. Civ. Code § 233; Fam. Code § 7851.

(C) Declaring a Minor Free of Parental Control

The minor may be declared to be free of parental custody and control when any of the following conditions is met:

1. The minor has been left by his or her parents in the care and custody of another for a period of six months, or by one parent in the care and custody of the other parent for a period of one year, without any provision for the minor's support and without communication from the parent or parents, with the intent on the part of the parents to abandon the minor. The failure to provide support or to communicate shall be presumptive evidence of the intent to abandon. If the parents have made only token efforts to support or communicate with the minor, the court may declare the minor abandoned by the parent or parents. In those cases where the minor has been left without provision for the minor's protection and the whereabouts of the parents are unknown, a petition may be filed 120 days following the discovery of the minor. However, the petition may not be heard until the 180th day after the discovery of the minor.

2. The minor has been neglected or cruelly treated by either or both parents, the minor has been a dependent minor of the juvenile court, and the parents have been deprived of the minor's custody for one year prior to the filing of a petition.

3. The parents of the minor suffer a disability because of the habitual use of alcohol or any controlled substance, or the parents are morally depraved, if the minor has been a dependent minor of the juvenile court and the parents have been deprived of the minor's custody continuously for one year immediately prior to the filing of the petition. Disability means any physical or mental incapacity that renders the parents unable adequately to care for and control the minor;

4. The parents are convicted of a felony and the facts of the crime prove the unfitness of the parent to have future custody and control of the minor.

5. The parent or parents have been declared by a court of competent jurisdiction to be developmentally disabled or mentally ill, and the director of mental health or the director of developmental services and the superintendent of the hospital, if any, in which the parents are inmates or patients, certify that the parents would not be capable of supporting or controlling the minor in the proper manner.

6. The minor's parents are mentally disabled and likely to remain so in the foreseeable future. Mentally disabled means suffering any mental incapacity or disorder that renders the parents unable to adequately care for and control the minor. To support a finding under this section requires the evidence of any two experts, each of whom shall be psychiatrists certified by the American Board of Psychiatry and Neurology, or licensed psychologists with doctoral degrees in psychology and at least five years of post-graduate experience in diagnosis and treatment of mental disorders. If the parent or parents reside in another state or foreign country, the expert testimony can be provided by affidavit by a physician and surgeon of that state or foreign country who has been certified by a medical organization or society to practice psychiatric or neurological medicine, or by a psychologist who is licensed in that state or that country. If the rights of any parent are sought to be terminated pursuant to this particular section and the parent has no attorney, the court shall appoint an attorney for the parent, if the parent requests one.

7. The minor has been in an out-of-home placement under the supervision of the Juvenile Court, the county welfare department, or other public or private licensed minor-placing agency for a one-year period, and the court finds that the return of the minor to the minor's parents would be detrimental to the minor, and if the parent or parents have failed during that period and are likely to fail in the future to maintain an adequate parental relationship with the minor, which includes providing a home and care and control for the minor.

8. A minor has found to be a dependent minor of the juvenile court, and the Juvenile Court has determined that reunification services shall not be provided to the minor's parents or guardian.[12]

At all such termination proceedings, the court is required to consider the wishes of the minor and to act in the best interests of the minor. The testimony of the minor may be taken in chambers and outside the presence of the parents if the parents are represented by counsel and counsel is present and if any of the following circumstances exists:

1. the court determines that testimony in chambers is necessary to ensure truthful testimony;

---

12. The legislature has emphasized the necessity to provide reunification services and to help the parents overcome the problems that led to the removal of the minor. *In re Marilyn H. supra*, note 1; Welf. & Inst. Code § 361.5.

2. the minor is likely to be intimidated by a formal courtroom setting; or

3. the minor is afraid to testify in front of his or her parents.[13]

If the court allows testimony to be taken in chambers, the parent or parents may elect to have the court reporter read back the testimony or have the testimony summarized by counsel. By the same criteria, testimony may be taken outside the presence of the guardian or guardians.

To support a finding that a minor is free of parental custody and control, the standard of proof is clear and convincing evidence.[14] It is the policy of California that judicial proceedings to declare a minor free from parental custody and control should be determined as expeditiously as possible and shall have precedence over other civil matters set for trial.[15]

(D) Adoption Termination

The termination of parental rights arises when a birth mother voluntarily surrenders a minor to an adoption agency. At the time that a minor is adopted, the birth parents are relieved of all parental duties and responsibility for the minor and also have no rights over the minor.[16]

There are two general types of adoption: through a state agency and independent adoption. This topic is discussed more fully in chapter 5A.14. If a minor is 12 years or older, California law provides that he or she must approve the adoption.[17]

Generally, the voluntary surrender of a minor to an adoption agency is referred to as relinquishment. The birth father or mother may relinquish a minor to the Department of Social Services or any licensed adoption agency by way of a written statement signed before two subscribing witnesses and acknowledged before an authorized official of the Department of Social Services or the licensed adoption agency. The written relinquishment statement when acknowledged by the official is *prima facie* evidence of the right of the birth parent to the sole custody of the minor and the corresponding sole right to relinquish custody. A birth parent who is a minor has the same right of relinquishment as an adult: The relinquishment cannot be revoked by reason of the birth parent's age.

---

13. Fam. Code §§ 7891, 7892.
14. Civ. Code § 232; Fam. Code §§ 7800 to 7821.
15. Civ. Code § 232.3.
16. Civ. Code § 221.76; Fam. Code § 8617.
17. Civ. Code § 221.13; Fam. Code § 8701.

If the birth father or mother resides outside of California and the minor is being cared for and is placed for adoption by the Department of Social Services or by a licensed adoption agency, the birth father or mother may relinquish the minor by written statement signed before a notary on a form prescribed by the Department of Social Services. The form must be signed by an authorized official of the Department of Social Services or the licensed adoption agency. The form signifies the willingness of the Department of Social Services or the adoption agency to accept the relinquishment.

When a certified copy of the relinquishment document is filed with the Department of Social Services, the relinquishment is final and can be rescinded only by the mutual consent of the Department of Social Services, or the licensed adoption agency to which the minor was relinquished, and the parent or parents relinquishing the minor.

The birth parent may name in the relinquishment the person or persons with whom the birth parent intends the placement of the minor to be made. If specific individuals are named as receiving the placement in the relinquishment and the minor is not placed with those individuals, or is removed from the home prior to the granting of the adoption, the Department of Social Services and licensed adoption agency must give a notice within 72 hours of the decision not to place the minor for adoption with the specified individual, or to remove the minor from the home of the specified individual. If a notice is sent as described above, three things can happen:

1. if the birth parent requests that of the relinquishment be rescinded, the Department of Social Services, or the licensed adoption agency, must rescind the relinquishment;

2. if the birth parent does not request rescision of the relinquishment, the Department of Social Services or licensed adoption agency can select adoptive parents for the minor; or

3. if the birth parent and the Department of Social Services or adoption agency wish to identify a different person or persons during the 30-day period with whom the minor is intended to be placed, the initial relinquishment shall be rescinded and a relinquishment identifying the newly designated individuals shall be completed.

The filing of a relinquishment with the department terminates all parental rights and responsibilities, except as to the rights described above referencing the 30-day period when the original individual for whom placement was intended is not allowed to receive the minor.[18]

Either on or before the time the relinquishment is signed, the birth parent signing the relinquishment shall be advised orally and in writing by the Department of Social Services, or the licensed adoption agency, that he or she may at any time in the future request all information about the status of the minor's adoption, except for personal identifying information about the adoptive family. This information includes, but is not limited to

1. whether the minor has been placed for adoption;
2. the approximate date that an adoption was concluded; and
3. if the adoption was not completed or is vacated for any reason, whether adoptive placement of the minor is again being considered.[19]

The Department of Social Services is required to give the birth parents a written statement that communicates in a clear and concise manner the following information:

1. that it is in the best interests of the minor that the birth parent keep the Department of Social Services, or licensed adoption agency, informed of any health problems the parent develops that could affect the minor;
2. that the birth parent keep his or her address current with the Department of Social Services, or adoption agency, in order to permit a response to inquiries concerning medical or social history;
3. that under certain circumstances the minor may obtain disclosure of the name and address of the birth parent, so the birth parent must indicate whether or not he or she wishes his or her name or address to be disclosed; and
4. that the birth parent may change his or her decision as to whether or not his or her name and address can be disclosed by sending a notarized letter to the Department of Social Services, or licensed adoption agency, to that effect.

The relinquishment will be filed in the Office of the County Clerk in the county where the adoption takes place. The file is not open to inspection by anyone other than the parties to the adoption proceedings, their attorneys, and the Department of Social Services, except on an order of a judge of the Superior Court.[20]

---

18. Civ. Code § 222.10; Fam. Code § 8700.
19. Civ. Code § 222.13; Fam. Code § 8701.
20. Civ. Code § 222.15; Fam. Code § 8702.

When parental rights are terminated, the licensed adoption agency responsible for the placement of the minor, or the Department of Social Services, sends a written notice to the birth parents encouraging them to keep the agency advised of their current address to permit a response to any inquiry concerning medical or social history made on behalf of the minor.[21]

When a minor has been relinquished or parental rights have been terminated, the Department of Social Services, or licensed adoption agency, is responsible for the care of the minor and is entitled to exclusive custody and control of the minor until an order of adoption has been granted. Prior to the granting of the order of adoption, a temporary placement may be terminated at the discretion of the Department of Social Services or adoption agency. In the event of termination of the replacement for temporary care or for adoption, the minor shall be returned promptly to the physical custody of the agency.

Only the prospective adoptive parents with whom the minor has been placed for adoption by the Department of Social Services, or a licensed adoption agency, may file a petition to adopt a minor who has been relinquished or declared free from custody and control of either or both birth parents. Once a petition for adoption has been filed, the minor may not be removed from the custody of his or her prospective adoptive parents except with the approval of the court upon motion by the Department of Social Services, or a licensed adoption agency, after notice to the prospective adoptive parents, supported by affidavits stating the grounds for which removal is sought.

The Superior Court may order the adoption even if the Department of Social Services, or a licensed adoption agency, refuses to consent, if the court finds the refusal to consent is not in the best interests of the minor. However, if a minor has been in foster care for a period of more than four months and has substantial emotional ties to the foster parents or parent, and the minor's removal from foster care would be seriously detrimental to his or her well-being, the foster parents may request to be considered to adopt the minor. The foster parent shall be considered along with all other prospective adoptive families. The Department of Social Services or the adoption agency must take into consideration any relevant factors that it deems necessary in determining which adoptive parent is in the best interests of the minor.

---

21. Civ. Code § 222.18, Fam. Code § 8703.

There is a rebuttable presumption that the decision of the Department of Social Services, or licensed adoption agency, as to the adoptive parent is in the best interests of the minor.[22]

When the minor is in the custody of a public agency, or licensed adoption agency, and the individuals whose consent for adoption is required by law are deceased, an action may be brought by the Department of Social Services, or licensed adoption agency, with notice to all relatives up to the third degree of an order granting custody and control to the department or licensed adoption agency.[23]

A minor cannot be placed for adoption unless a written medical report on the minor's medical background and, if available, the medical background of the minor's biological parents has been submitted to the prospective adoptive parents and they have acknowledged receipt of it. The medical report shall include all diagnostic information, including current medical reports on the minor, psychological evaluations, and scholastic information, as well as all known information regarding the minor's developmental history and family line.[24]

(E) Independent Adoptions

While in some states, parents may not contract to terminate their parental rights, the California Supreme Court has determined that such contracts are valid. The legislature has enacted rules proscribing attorneys from representing both the prospective adoptive parents and birth parents of a minor in negotiations and proceedings concerning adoption, unless written consent is obtained from them that contains various specific provisions.[25] When independent adoption is pursued, the selection of the prospective adoptive parents must be personally made by the birth parent or parents and cannot be delegated to an agent. The selection of the prospective adoptive parents must be based on the personal knowledge of the birth parents.[26] The process of independent adoption is discussed in chapter 5A.14.

---

22. Civ. Code § 222.2; Fam. Code § 8704. A rebuttal presumption means the court will presume a certain fact is true, but on contradictory evidence can elect to disregard the presumption.
23. Civ Code § 222.22; Fam. Code § 8705.
24. Civ. Code § 222.26.
25. Civ. Code § 224.10; Fam. Code § 8800.
26. Civ Code § 224.2; Fam. Code § 8801.

(F) Surrender Termination

A licensed adoption agency with whom a minor been entrusted due to a voluntary surrender of parental rights may institute an action in Superior Court seeking termination of the parental rights and transfer of the custody to the agency.[27]

---

27. Civ. Code § 222.2; Fam. Code § 8704.

5A.11

Guardianship for Minors

A guardian is an adult who is appointed to represent the interests of a minor (who is called a *ward*), due to the minor's age, mental condition, or both. The term *guardian* (except guardians *ad litem*) is now reserved for minors, and the person performing analogous functions for an adult is referred to as a *conservator*.[1] MHPs may become involved in providing psychotherapy to or assessing the minor at the guardian's request. In addition, MHPs may be requested to provide information in the guardianship proceedings as to the ward's mental condition, the relationship between the ward and the proposed guardian, and/or the necessity for a guardian. MHPs may provide such testimony either to a court investigator or in testimony. This chapter addresses the requirements and procedures governing the appointment of a guardian.

(A) Appointment of Guardian

A guardian may be appointed for a minor in a number of different circumstances, including where a lawsuit is pending and some individual needs to be designated to make the appropriate decisions about the conduct of the litigation. This type of guardian is referred to as a guardian *ad litem* and his or her authority is generally limited to acting for a party involved in litigation.

A guardian may be appointed for the person or estate, or both, of a minor. The test is what is in the best interest of the

---

1. Prob. Code §§ 1490, 1488. The Juvenile Court has prepared a manual, written in lay terms, describing guardianship—Form JV-350.

proposed ward, taking into account the guardian's ability to manage and preserve the estate.[2]

Because of the change in law regarding use of the term *guardian* for an adult, transitional provisions of the law indicate that where a parent or other person before January 1, 1981, appointed a person to serve as guardian of the person or estate, or both, of a minor, or as a guardian of the property a minor would receive from that parent, the appointment is deemed to be a nomination of a guardian under the code sections set forth below. The transitional provisions apply whether or not the appointment of the person as a guardian is made in a will or deed, so long as the person that signed the document had, at the time, sufficient capacity to form an intelligent preference.[3]

A nomination of a guardian may be made in a petition for the appointment of a guardian. A parent may nominate a guardian of the person or estate, or both, of a minor child in two cases: (1) when the other parent nominates, or consents in writing to the nomination of, the same guardian for the same child, or (2) when, at the time the petition for appointment of a guardian is filed, the other parent is dead or lacks legal capacity to consent to the nomination, or the consent of the other parent would not be required for adoption of the child.[4]

A parent or any other person may also nominate a guardian for property that a minor is to receive by virtue of a gift, deed, trust, will, succession, insurance, or any other benefits of any kind.[5]

A relative or another person on behalf of a minor, or the minor if he or she is twelve years of age or older, may file a petition seeking the appointment of a guardian. The petition must request that a guardian of the person or estate, or both, be appointed. The petition must specify the name and address of the proposed guardian, the name and date of birth of the proposed ward, and that the appointment is necessary. So far as is known to the petitioner, the names and addresses of all of the following individuals must be included:

1. the parents of the proposed ward;
2. the person having legal custody or care of the proposed ward;
3. the relatives of the proposed ward within the second degree of kinship;

---

2. Prob. Code § 1514.
3. Prob. Code § 1489.
4. Prob. Code § 1500.
5. Prob. Code § 1501.

4. in the case of guardianship of the estate, the spouse of the proposed ward, if any; and

5. any person nominated as guardian by the parents.[6]

If the proposed ward is a patient and/or on leave of absence from a state institution under the jurisdiction of the Department of Mental Health or the Department of Developmental Services, the petition shall also state that fact and name the institution.

The petition must further state, so far as is known by the petitioner, whether or not the proposed ward is receiving or is entitled to receive any benefits from the Veterans Administration, and the amount of such benefits.

If the petitioner has knowledge of any pending adoption, juvenile court, marriage dissolution, domestic relations, custody, or other similar proceeding affecting the proposed ward, those proceedings must be disclosed in the petition.

If the petitioners have accepted or intend to accept physical care or custody of a child with intent to adopt, the petition must state that whether or not an adoption petition has been filed.

In the event that the ward also becomes the subject of an adoption decision, the court will consolidate the guardianship and adoption petitions for the hearing.[7] When a petition is brought to appoint a non-relative of the ward as a guardian, the petition must contain the following information as well:

1. a statement by the proposed guardian that the guardian will properly submit any required information relating to the investigation of him or her for guardianship;

2. a disclosure of any petition for adoption by the proposed guardian of the minor; and

3. a statement of whether or not the proposed guardian is licensed as a foster family home.[8]

These additional requirements for non-relative guardianships do not apply in the following circumstances:

1. the petition is for guardianship of the estate exclusively;

2. the director of the Department of Developmental Services is appointed guardian;

3. the director of the department designated by the county board of supervisors to provide social services is appointed guardian;

4. the public guardian is appointed guardian; or

---

6. Prob. Code § 1510.
7. Prob. Code
8. Prob. Code § 1541, 1543.

5. the guardianship results from a permanent placement for a dependent child, pursuant to the Welfare and Institutions Code section on dependent children.[9]

The filing of a petition leads to a hearing, where testimony may be given.

(B) The Guardianship Hearing

Before any hearing can be held, at least 15 days' notice must be given to interested parties. The statute specifies the individuals upon whom notice must be given, who generally include the ward, the person with legal custody of the ward, the parents, and any person nominated as a guardian.[10] Unless a court otherwise requires, notice is not required to be given to parents or relatives of a ward who has been relinquished to an adoption agency or has been judicially declared free from a parent's custody or control.[11]

Unless the court waives the requirement, a court investigator, probation officer, or domestic relations investigator must make an investigation and file with the court a report concerning the proposed guardianship. Investigations where the proposed guardian is a relative are to be made by a court investigator. Investigations where the proposed guardian is a non-relative are to be made by the county agency designated to investigate potential dependency cases. The report must include, but is not necessarily limited to, the following factors:

1. a social history of the guardian;
2. the social history of the proposed ward, including, to the extent feasible, an assessment of any identified developmental, emotional, psychological, or educational needs of the proposed ward, and the capability of the petitioner to meet those needs;
3. the relationship of the proposed ward to the guardian, including the duration and character of the relationship. The circumstances of how the guardian acquired physical custody of the ward are to be discussed. The report also must address the ward's attitude concerning the proposed guardianship, unless that attitude is affected by the ward's developmental, physical, or emotional condition; and

---

9. Prob. Code § 1540.
10. Prob. Code § 1511.
11. Prob. Code

4. the anticipated duration of the guardianship and the plans of both natural parents and proposed guardians for a stable and permanent home for the child. This particular requirement may be waived when the proposed guardians are relatives.[12]

The court is to read and consider the report prior to ruling on the petition for guardianship. The person who prepared the report may be called and examined by any party to the proceedings.[13]

If any party to the proposed guardianship alleges that the minor's parents are unfit, as defined in the statutes governing dependent children, the case is referred to the county agency designated to investigate such potential dependencies, and the guardianship proceedings cannot be completed until a full investigation has been completed.[14]

The reports required by the statute are confidential and can be made available only to individuals who have been served in the proceeding or their attorneys.[15]

For the purpose of making the report, the investigator has access to the proposed ward's school records, probation records, and public and private social services records, and to an oral or written summary of the proposed ward's medical records and psychological records, which is to be prepared by any physician, psychologist, or psychiatrist who made or who is maintaining those records. The physician, psychologist, or psychiatrist must be available to clarify information regarding these records to the investigator.[16]

The reporting requirements do not apply to guardianships that result from a permanency plan for dependent children pursuant to the Welfare and Institutions Code.[17]

After having considered all the information, the court appoints a guardian and specifies whether he or she is a guardian of the estate, the person, or both. In so doing, the court is to be guided by what appears to be the best interest of the proposed ward, taking into account the proposed guardian's ability to manage and preserve the estate, as well as the proposed guardian's concern for and interest in the welfare of the ward. If the ward is of sufficient age to form an intelligent preference as to the person to be appointed as a guardian, the court gives consideration to that preference in determining the person to be

---

12. Prob. Code § 1513(a).
13. Prob. Code § 1513(b).
14. Prob. Code § 1513(c).
15. Prob. Code § 1513(b).
16. Prob. Code § 1513(e).
17. Prob. Code § 1513(f).

appointed.[18] No guardian may be appointed for a minor who is married or whose marriage has been dissolved (except where the marriage has been declared null).[19] However, a conservator of the person may be appointed for a minor who is married or whose marriage has been dissolved (see chapter 5A.3).[20]

Certain statutory obligations are common to both guardianship and conservatorship. The relationship of guardian and ward, and conservator and conservatee are both fiduciary relationships.[21] Further, both guardians and conservators are subject to regulation and control of the court.[22]

The court has the power to appoint two or more joint guardians for a minor.[23] When the guardian has been nominated by the parents, the guardian has the same authority with respect to the person of a ward as a parent having legal custody of a child. The guardian can exercise such authority without notice, hearing, or court authorization, instructions, approval, or confirmation in the same manner as if such authority were exercised by a parent having legal custody of a child, except to the extent the court determines otherwise. A guardian of the estate has the various powers over the estate but must exercise them using ordinary care and diligence.[24] If the guardian breaches a fiduciary duty with regard to the estate, he or she may be charged with any loss in value or any profit made as a result of the breach of duty.[25]

A guardian may be appointed pursuant to a parental nomination for a guardian of specific property, not compromising the entire estate. A guardian who is so appointed has the same duties as a guardian of the estate, but only as to the nominated property. These duties include the responsibility of providing an inventory and accounting regarding disposal of the property that is entrusted to the guardian.[26]

A guardian or a conservator has care, custody, and control of the education of the ward. Among the powers a guardian has is the same right as a parent having legal custody of a child to give consent to medical treatment to be performed upon the ward or to require the ward to receive medical treatment. However, if the ward is 14 years of age or older, no surgery may be performed upon the ward without the consent of both the ward and the guardian, or a court order authorizing the treatment. In an emer-

18. Prob. Code § 1514.
19. Prob. Code § 1515.
20. Prob. Code § 1800.3.
21. Prob. Code § 2101.
22. Prob. Code § 2102.
23. Prob. Code § 2105.
24. Prob. Code § 2401.
25. Prob. Code § 2401.3.
26. Prob. Code § 2109.

gency in which the ward faces loss of life or serious bodily injury if the surgery is not performed, such consent is not necessary. The guardian's consent is not necessary for any situation where the ward alone may consent to treatment.[27]

A ward may not be involuntarily placed in a mental health treatment facility against his or her will. Instead, the procedures outlined in chapter 5A.19 on the civil commitment of minors apply.[28]

When a ward requires medical treatment for a medical condition that cannot be performed without consent, and the ward is unable to give informed consent, the guardian may petition the court for an order authorizing such treatment.[29]

(C) Guardian of the Estate

Guardians of the estate also have specified powers over the property entrusted to them that are too numerous to mention here but include the power to contract; the power to operate a business; to sell (publicly or privately) personal property; to borrow money; to lend money; to pay, collect, compromise, arbitrate, or otherwise adjust claims or debts; and to employ professionals, including attorneys, accountants, and investment counselors.[30]

Guardians are required to make periodic accounting and reports, including an account on termination.[31]

The guardian's compensation is set by court order pursuant to a petition.[32]

Guardians may be removed, primarily for the failure to use ordinary care and diligence in the management of the estate, for failure to file inventories or accounts as required by the court, and for conviction of felonies, gross immorality, and so on.[33]

(D) Guardianship Termination

A guardianship of a person or estate, or both, terminates when the ward obtains the age of majority or dies. Additionally, a guard-

---

27. Prob. Code § 2353.
28. Prob. Code § 2356.
29. Prob. Code § 2357.
30. Prob. Code § 2591.
31. Prob. Code § 2620 et seq.
32. Prob. Code § 2640 et seq.
33. Prob. Code § 2650.

ianship of a person will terminate upon the adoption or marriage of the ward.[34]

Upon petition of the guardian, a parent, or the ward of the court, the court may order the guardianship terminated if the court determines that it is no longer necessary for the ward to have a guardian, or that it is in the ward's best interest to terminate the guardianship.[35]

A guardian *ad litem* may be appointed for a minor plaintiff upon application of the minor if he or she is 14 years or older. If the minor plaintiff is younger than 14, the application must be made by a relative or friend. A guardian *ad litem* may be appointed for a defendant minor who is 14 or older if he or she applies to the court within 10 days of the service of the summons on him or her. If the minor defendant is not yet 14, or if the minor neglects to apply for a guardian *ad litem*, one can be appointed on application by the minor's relative or friend, by any party, or by the court on its own motion.[36] For a description of the powers of a guardian *ad litem*, see chapter 5A.2.

---

34. Prob. Code § 1600.
35. Prob. Code § 1601.
36. Civ. Proc. Code § 373.

5A.12

Conservatorship for Minors

While minors are the only individuals at the present time who have guardians (except guardians *ad litem*), the procedures to establish a conservatorship for a minor are governed by the same statutory provisions as those for adults. See chapter 5A.3. However, conservatorships for minors are limited to conservatorships of the person of minors who are married or whose marriage has been dissolved.[1] Otherwise, the relationship is a guardianship, as described in chapter 5A.11.

---

1. Prob. Code § 1800.3.

5A.13

Foster Care

The foster care system provides for the placement of children who had been adjudged dependent or wards of the court in a home environment but without establishing the relationship of parent and child between the foster parents and the child. In recent years, the law has shifted and foster care is less favored as an alternative than reunification of the family or formal adoption.[1] Foster homes, however, are still an important part of the juvenile dependency system. MHPs may be involved in assessing children for placement in foster homes or in treating them while they are there. Under California law foster homes must be licensed and regularly reviewed.

(A) Definitions

A *foster family home* is defined as any residential facility providing 24-hour care for six or fewer foster children, which is owned, leased, or rented and is the residence of the foster parents in whose care the children have been placed.[2]

A *foster family agency* is any individual or organization engaged in the recruiting, certifying, and training of, and providing professional support to, foster parents, or in finding homes and other places for placement of children for temporary or permanent care who require that level of care as an alternative to a

---

1. *Cynthia D. v. Superior Court*, 5 Cal.4th 242 (1993).
2. Health & Safety Code § 1502(a)(5).

group home. Private foster family agencies are required to be organized and operated on a nonprofit basis.[3]

A *small family home* is any residential facility providing 24-hour care for six or fewer foster children who have mental disorders or developmental or physical disabilities and will require special care and supervision as a result of their disabilities.[4]

As used in the Health & Safety Code, a *license* is a basic permit to operate a community care facility that is not transferable.[5]

Therapeutic day services facility is a facility that provides non-medical care, counseling, educational, and vocational support or social rehabilitation services on less than a 24-hour basis to persons under 18 who would otherwise be placed in foster care or who are returning from foster care.[6]

(B) Licensing Requirements

The Department of Social Services provides for the licensure of foster care homes under the Community Care Facilities Act.[7] This law asserts that it is the state's policy to make proper placement of every child in residential care facilities, when placement is in the best interests of the child, with particular focus on the individual child's needs.[8] Pursuant to the statute, children with varying designations and varying needs may be placed in the same licensed foster family home or with a foster family agency for subsequent placement in a certified home. Children with developmental disabilities, mental disorders, or physical disabilities may be placed in licensed foster family homes or certified family homes, provided that an appraisal is made of the child's needs, and the ability of the receiving home to meet those needs, by the placement agency and the licensee, or in the case of certified family homes, the placement agency and the foster family agency.[9]

There are two levels of possible authorization for foster homes. The first is a home that has an independent license, and the second is a home that has been certified by a foster family agency that has a license.

A foster family agency is precluded from certifying a family home that is already licensed by the Department of Social Services

---

3. Health & Safety Code § 1501(a)(4).
4. Health & Safety Code § 1502(a)(6).
5. Health & Safety Code § 1503.
6. Health & Safety Code § 1502(a)(3).
7. Health & Safety Code § 1500 et seq.
8. Health & Safety Code § 1501.1.
9. Health & Safety Code

or a county. Further, the department, or a county, is not allowed to license a family home that is certified by a foster family agency. In either circumstance, the pre-existing license or certificate is forfeited by obtaining the second license.[10] To obtain a license for a foster home or permit to provide specialized services, an individual must establish to the satisfaction of the department the following facts:

1. that the applicant has the ability to comply with the rules and regulations promulgated by the department;

2. that the applicant is of reputable and responsible character. This requires in part a criminal record clearance, employment history, and character references. If the applicant is a business entity and not an individual, similar evidence must be submitted regarding the members or shareholders of the business;

3. that the applicant has sufficient financial resources to maintain the standards of service required by the regulations;

4. that any prior or present service by the applicant as an administrator or general partner, corporate officer, or director or person who held a beneficial ownership of 10% or more in any other community care facility or licensed facility has been disclosed;

5. that any revocation or other disciplinary action taken against a license the applicant held or holds has been disclosed;

6. that the applicant has submitted a signed statement that he or she has read and understood the community care facility licensure statute and regulations that pertain to the applicant's category of licensure; and

7. any other information which may be required by the department.

The failure of the applicant to cooperate with the licensing agency in completing an application shall result in a denial.[11]

There are detailed statutory requirements for the criminal record investigation and prior employment history investigation to be done before a license is issued.[12] As with other licensees, the department has established criteria for temporary and permanent loss of licensure.[13] As with other licensees, administrative hearings are held before the Office of Administrative Hearings. A suspension, revocation, or denial of license may be based on any of the following circumstances:

---

10. Health & Safety Code § 1506.6.
11. Health & Safety Code § 1520.
12. Health & Safety Code § 1522, 1522.05, 1522.07.
13. Health & Safety Code § 1550 to 1551.5.

1. a violation by the licensee of the rules and regulations established by the department;

2. aiding, abetting, or permitting a violation of the law or the rules and regulations;

3. conduct inimical to the health, morals, welfare, or safety of either an individual receiving services from the facility or the public;

4. the conviction of a licensee (or certain categories of employees) of a crime; or

5. a licensee of any facility knowingly allowing any child to have illegal drugs or alcohol.[14]

The law also provides proceedings for obtaining temporary suspensions.[15]

(C) Placement of Children in Foster Homes

As the Supreme Court has noted, the preference for foster homes has decreased somewhat in favor of adoption and family reunification.[16] Despite this fact, placement of children in foster homes is still an option for a court evaluating whether a child is a dependent child and must be removed from parental custody. When a minor is being considered for placement in a foster home, he or she has the right to make a brief statement to the court regarding the decision on placement. The court is entitled to disregard any preferences expressed by the minor, but the court may also consider it. The minor's right to make such a statement is not limited to the initial placement but applies to any continued proceedings regarding additional placements or return to parental custody.[17] Under the Family Code, there are a series of priorities for foster care placement that require placement in the following order:

1. Before any child may be placed in long-term foster care, each relative whose name has been submitted as a possible caretaker, either by the child or by other persons, must be evaluated as an appropriate placement resource.

---

14. Health & Safety Code § 1550.
15. Health & Safety Code § 1550.5.
16. *Cynthia D. v. Superior Court*, 5 Cal.4th 242 (1993).
17. Welf. & Inst. Code § 399; Fam. Code § 7954.

2. If a relative is not available, or if placement with relatives is not in the child's best interest, placement must be made with a foster parent with the same racial or ethnic identification as the child. If the child has a mixed racial or ethnic background, placement must be made with a family of the racial or ethnic group with which the child has the most significant contacts; and

3. When neither of the first two options can be made, the child must be placed with a family of a different racial background or ethnic identification that has evidence of sensitivity to the child's race, ethnicity, and culture. The religious background of the child shall also be considered in determining an appropriate placement.[18]

Nothing in the law precludes simultaneous searches for a relative and for a foster family.

Every public and private agency is required to maintain records showing that a diligent search has been made for families that meet the criteria of racial and ethnic background set forth above.[19]

These requirements do not apply when the foster care setting is intended not to exceed 30 days.[20]

Under California's adoption law, foster parents cannot be precluded from seeking to adopt foster children that are placed in their care.[21]

The law also allows for counties to institute a program of advocates for pupils who are in foster care, to assist them through the educational system. One of the purposes of the advocates is to educate foster parents on how to enroll the pupil in school and what educational services are available. However, this program is not available in any school district that has a foster youth services program.[22]

The court may direct that a foster parent or relative with whom a child is placed must participate in a program of counseling or education, including a parent education or parenting program.[23]

A person providing residential foster care to a child may give the same legal consent for that child as a parent, except for the following: (a) marriage; (b) entry into the armed forces; (c) medical and dental treatment, except that consent may be given for

---

18. Fam. Code § 7950.
19. Fam. Code §§ 7951, 7952.
20. Fam. Code § 7952.
21. Fam. Code § 870.4.
22. Welf. & Inst. Code §§ 400 to 404.
23. Welf. & Inst. Code § 362(c).

ordinary medical and dental treatment including, but not limited to, immunizations, physical examinations, and x-rays; and (4) if the child has been voluntarily placed by the parents, those items that are agreed to in writing by the parents prior to the placement.[24]

Licensed community care facilities are periodically inspected and evaluated for quality of care by the Department of Social Services. Any duly authorized officer, employer, or agent of the department may on presentation of proper identification enter and inspect a facility providing personal care, supervision, and services at any time, with or without advance notice. However, foster family homes considered private residences are not subject to such inspection without advance notice. Inspection visits to foster family homes must be made during normal business hours unless the serious nature of a complaint requires otherwise. Unannounced visits do not constitute the annual evaluation visit required by law.[25] The law requires an annual evaluation of each foster home and as often as necessary to ensure the quality of care being provided. Following the evaluation, the home must be given written notice of all deficiencies. If there is a finding of non-compliance with rules and regulations, the department may require a foster family agency to revoke the certification of a family home and other action as the department deems necessary for the protection of a child with the home.[26]

(D) Placement Review

The status of every child in foster care is to be reviewed periodically as determined by the court, but no less frequently than once every six months from the date of the original disposition hearing, until the permanent placement has been completed. The court will determine the continuing necessity for a determination of appropriateness of the placement, the extent of compliance with the case plan, and the extent of progress that has been made towards alleviating or mitigating the causes necessitating placement in foster care, and shall project a likely date by which the child may be returned to the home or placed for adoption or legal guardianship. Each supplemental report that is filed must include, but is not limited to, a factual discussion of the following topics:

---

24. Health & Safety Code § 1530.6.
25. Health & Safety Code § 1533.
26. Health & Safety Code § 1534.

1. whether the county welfare department or probation officers considered child protective services as a possible solution to the problem at hand and offered those services to qualified parents;
2. what plan, if any, for return of the child is recommended to the court by the county welfare department and probation officer;
3. whether the child appears to be eligible to be considered for further court action to free that child from parental custody or control; and
4. what actions, if any, have been taken by the parents to correct the problems that caused the child to be made a dependent child.[27]

Foster family homes and foster family agencies having physical custody of a minor are required to be given notice of all review hearings. The foster parent may file with the court a report containing his or her recommendation concerning the disposition of the minor, which shall be considered by the court.[28] The court is required to consider returning the child to the parents or guardians unless by a preponderance of the evidence the court finds that return of the child will create a substantial risk of detriment to the physical or emotional well-being of the minor. The burden of establishing that is on the probation department. The failure of the parent or guardian to participate regularly in any court-ordered treatment programs is *prima facie* evidence that return of the child would be detrimental. The court must consider the efforts demonstrated by the parent or guardian, and the extent to which the parent or guardian cooperated with and availed himself or herself of services provided.[29]

As the California Supreme Court has indicated, there is a series of hearings at six-month intervals, the third of which may lead to termination of parental rights. At each hearing, the court considers whether return to the parents is appropriate, and that option is given priority. Thus, a foster care agency will have three opportunities to provide information about the child's care and what would constitute a placement in the child's best interests.

At the stage where the parental rights have been terminated, a foster parent may apply to adopt the child as part of the normal adoption process.

---

27. Welf. & Inst. Code § 366.1; *Cynthia D. v. Superior Court*, 5 Cal.4th 242 (1993).
28. Welf. & Inst. Code § 366.2.
29. Welf. & Inst. Code §§ 366.2, 366.21.

5A.14

Adoption

California allows the adoption of children and requires certain criteria to be met before individuals will be allowed to adopt children. The adoption process strives to protect the rights of the child, the biological parents, and the adoptive parents as much as possible. Adoption may be either voluntary, through relinquishment of parental rights, or involuntary through a proceeding terminating parental rights. MHPs may be involved in the adoption process as experts providing testimony regarding the qualifications of a particular set of adoptive parents or the mental status of a child who is subject to adoption.

(A) Adoption Requirements

(A)(1) Birth Parents

As discussed in detail in chapter 5A.10, California allows the termination of parental rights through voluntary relinquishment of the child to an adoption agency.[1] The rights of birth parents are discussed extensively in chapter 5A.10.

(A)(2) Adoptive Parents

Under California law, an adoptive parent means a person who has petitioned the court, and obtained an order or final decree, for the adoption of a particular child.[2] An agency adoption is the adoption of a child where the Department of Social Services or an agency licensed by the department is a party to or joins in the

---

1. Civ. Code § 221.76; Fam. Code § 8617.
2. Civ. Code § 220.20; Fam. Code § 8503.

petition for adoption.[3] A *full-service adoption agency* is a licensed entity engaged in the business of providing adoption services that does all of the following:

1. assumes the care, custody, and control of a child through parental relinquishment to the agency or in voluntary termination of parental rights;
2. assesses the birth parents, prospective adoptive parents, or child;
3. places children for adoption; and
4. supervises adoptive placements.

Such agencies are required to be organized and operated on a nonprofit basis.[4] An *independent adoption* means the adoption of a child where neither the Department of Social Services nor an adoption agency licensed by the department is a party.

A *non-custodial adoption agency* is licensed and provides the following services:

1. assesses the prospective adoptive parents; and
2. matches children freed for adoption with assessed and approved prospective applicants.

In an independent adoption, the selection of the prospective adoptive parents is made personally by the birth parent, not delegated to an agent.[5] The selection must be based on the birth parents' personal knowledge of the prospective adoptive parent or parents.

When a child has been relinquished to the Department of Social Services or a licensed adoption agency, or the child has been declared free from parental custody and control and referred to the department, no petition for adoption can be filed except by prospective adoptive parents with whom the child has been placed by the department or the agency.

Even when an adoption is an independent one, the law requires that the Department of Social Services, or delegated county adoption agency, investigate the proposed adoption and submit to the court a full report of the facts disclosed by the inquiry and make a specific recommendation regarding whether the adoption should be allowed. When the investigation discloses a serious question concerning the suitability of the petitioners, the report must be filed immediately.[6]

---

3. Civ. Code § 220.20(b); Fam. Code §§ 8506, 8700 et seq.
4. Civ. Code § 220.10(h); Fam. Code § 8521.
5. Civ. Code § 224.20; Fam. Code § 8801.
6. Fam. Code § 8807.

As part of the investigation, either the department or delegated county adoption agency must interview the petitioners and all persons whose consent is required for the adoption as soon as possible after the filing of the adoption petition. Because of this requirement, when a petition for an independent adoption is filed, petitioners must file with the district office of the Department of Social Services, or delegated county adoption agency, a copy of the petition and the names, addresses, and telephone numbers of all parties to be interviewed.[7]

The agency adoption process also involves evaluations of the adoptive parents. The department or licensed adoption agency is required to conduct an investigation of each prospective adoptive parent, including submitting their fingerprints for a criminal check. The criminal record, if any, must be taken into consideration when evaluating the prospective adoptive parent, and an assessment of the effects of any criminal history on the ability of the adoptive parent to provide adequate care and guidance to the child must be included in the report to the court.[8]

When a child is considered for adoption, the law requires that an attempt be made to match the racial, ethnic, and religious background of the child if at all possible.[9]

Before the court will allow an agency adoption to be consummated, the prospective adoptive parents and the child must both appear before the court for a court examination. The examination of each person must be conducted separately but within the physical presence of every other person (as contrasted with the termination of parental rights). The court requires the prospective adoptive parents to execute and acknowledge an agreement in writing that the child will be treated as their lawful child in all respects. If the court is satisfied that the interests of the child will be promoted by the adoption, the court may make and enter an order of adoption.[10]

If a child is over the age of 12, his or her consent is necessary for an adoption.[11]

(A)(3) Adoptive Child

An evaluation must be made of the adoptive child before the child is placed for adoption. The written report must be prepared on the child's medical background addressing all known diagnostic information, including medical reports, psychological evaluation,

---

7. Fam. Code § 8808.
8. Fam. Code § 8712.
9. Fam. Code §§ 8708, 8709, 8710.
10. Fam. Code §§ 8718, 8612, 8613.
11. Fam. Code § 8602.

and scholastic information, together with all information that is known about the child's developmental history and family life.[12]

A licensed adoption agency is required to cooperate with the department in developing a plan to discreetly transmit to prospective adoptive parents pertinent medical information about the child's background and prospective needs.

(B) Petition for Adoption

A petition for adoption can be filed as either part of an independent adoption or an agency adoption. However, no petition may be filed to adopt a child relinquished to the Department of Social Services, or licensed adoption agency, concerning a child declared free from the custody and control of his or her parents and referred to the department or adoption agency for placement, except by the prospective adoptive parents with whom the child has been placed for adoption by the department or licensed adoption agency. Once the adoption petition has been filed, the department or licensed agency can remove the child from the prospective adoptive parents only with the approval of the court upon a motion with notice.[13]

The Family Code provides that the adoption petition, relinquishment or consent, agreement, order, report to the court from an investigating agency, and any power of attorney or deposition filed regarding an adoption petition are not open to inspection by anyone other than the parties to the proceedings, their attorneys, and the Department of Social Services, except upon the written authorization of a judge of the superior court. In turn, a judge may not authorize anyone to inspect these records except in exceptional circumstances and for good cause. Upon a written request by any party to the proceedings and an order of the court where documents are allowed to be disclosed, they will not be disclosed unless the name of the child's birth parents and any information tending to identify the birth parents is deleted.

Upon the request of the adoptive parents or the child, a court may issue a certificate of adoption that states the date and place, the child's birth name, the names of the adoptive parents and the name that the child has taken. Unless the child is adopted by a stepparent, the certificate shall not state the name of the child's birth parents.[14] However, the Department of Social Services and a licensed adoption agency may furnish information related to an

---

12. Fam. Code § 8706.
13. Fam. Code § 8704.
14. Fam. Code § 9200.

adoption petition to the juvenile court, county welfare department, public welfare agency, or private welfare agency licensed by the department, if it is believed that the child's welfare will be promoted thereby.[15]

The medical reports provided by the law may be produced to the adoptive child when the child turns 18 or when he or she presents a certified copy of his or her marriage certificate. The report may also be produced to an adoptive parent. If access to the report is denied, a petition may be filed with the court seeking review of the reasonableness of the denial. However, the names and addresses of any persons mentioned in the report must be removed.[16]

If an adult is adopted as a child, and his or her birth parents have each filed a written consent with the department or a licensed adoption agency, contact may be arranged between the birth parents and the child. However, neither the department nor a licensed adoption agency may solicit the execution of written consents of this type.[17]

Additionally, the law provides procedures whereby an adopted child may obtain information regarding biological siblings.[18] Further, the law allows the release of letters, photographs, or items of personal property to an adoptee, birth parent, or adoptive parent upon written request and under certain circumstances.[19]

Finally, stepparent adoptions are allowed by petition, following an investigation by the county welfare department or probation officer.[20] For a stepparent adoption, a home study is prepared, which means a physical investigation of the premises where the child is residing.[21]

(C) Approved Agency Adoption

Adoption agencies must be licensed to engage in the business of adoption services. Licenses are granted by the Department of Social Services, and agencies may be licensed as full-service adoption agencies[22] or as noncustodial adoption agencies.[23] The county may delegate a particular adoption agency to provide the

---

15. Fam. Code § 9201.
16. Fam. Code § 9202.
17. Fam. Code § 9204.
18. Fam. Code § 9205.
19. Fam. Code § 9206.
20. Fam. Code § 9001.
21. *Id.*
22. Fam. Code § 8521.
23. Fam. Code § 8533.

services required by law, and that agency is then referred to as the delegated county adoption agency.[24]

As noted above, proceedings on adoptions are not open to the public, nor are the records open to the public in general. The court may hold proceedings regarding adoption in closed court, despite the requirement that most court hearings be open to the public.[25]

The court will proceed with the adoption if it concludes that it is in the best interests of the child, and may proceed despite an objection by the department or the agency.

(D) Independent Adoption

California does allow independent adoptions, but the legislature has expressed concern that the lawyering involved in such adoptions may be deficient when conflicts of interest deprive the clients of undivided loyalty and effort. Therefore, the legislature has declared that in an independent adoption proceeding, whether or not written consent is obtained, multiple representation by an attorney should be avoided whenever a birth parent displays the slightest reason for the attorney to believe a controversy may arise. In such circumstances, it is the duty of the attorney to withdraw promptly from the case, advise the parties to obtain independent counsel, refrain from taking positions in opposition to any of those former clients, and maintain an impartial, fair, and open attitude toward new attorneys that may enter the case.

It is unethical for an attorney to undertake the representation of both the prospective adoptive parents and the birth parents of the child in any negotiations or proceedings in connection with an adoption, unless written consent is obtained from both parties. Consent must be filed with the court and must include the following specifics:

1. a notice to the birth parents of their right to have an independent attorney advise them, and that the prospective parents may be required to pay reasonable attorney fees up to $500 for that representation;

2. a notice to the birth parents that they may waive their right to an independent attorney and may be represented by the attorney representing the prospective adoptive parents;

3. a waiver by the birth parents of representation by an independent attorney; and

---

24. Fam. Code § 8515.
25. Fam. Code § 7643.

4. an agreement that the attorney representing the prospective adoptive parents shall represent the birth parents.[26]

In an independent adoption, the selection of the prospective adoptive parents is made by the child's birth parents and may not be delegated.[27]

The petition in an independent adoption must be filed in the county in which the petitioner resides. The court clerk then must notify the Department of Social Services in Sacramento of the pendency of the proceeding. The petition must contain an allegation that the petitioners will file promptly with the Department of Social Services, or adoption agency the information required. If the child is the subject of a guardianship petition, the adoption petition must so state and must include the information regarding the guardianship.[28]

An independent adoption is predicated on the consent of the birth parents; if the birth parent refuses to give the required consent or withdraws the consent, the court will hold a hearing to order the child restored to the care and custody of the birth parents.[29]

If the Department of Social Services or the adoption agency recommends denial of a petition, or if the petitioner is asked to withdraw the petition and the court agrees with the recommendation that the child be removed from the home of the petitioners, the court must commit the child to the care of the Department of Social Services, or the designated county adoption agency, to arrange adoptive placement or make a suitable plan.[30] In an independent adoption, the Department of Social Services, or adoption agency, is required to accept the consent of the birth parents to adoption and, before filing a report with the court, ascertain whether the child is properly subject to adoption and whether the proposed home is suitable for the child.[31] If the Department of Social Services, or adoption agency, fails without good cause to conduct interviews of the petitioners and the persons whose consent is required for an independent adoption, within 45 working days of the filing of the petition, the petitioners on 10 days' written notice may request the court in which the petition has been filed to permit the signing of the consent by any person whose consent is required in the presence of the court.[32]

---

26. Fam. Code § 8800.
27. Id.
28. Fam. Code § 8802.
29. Fam. Code § 8804.
30. Fam. Code § 8805.
31. Fam. Code §§ 8806 to 8808.
32. Fam. Code § 8809.

For an independent adoption, the petitioner must pay a fee of $500 to the Department of Social Services, or adoption agency, before the favorable report is filed. The revenues from these fees are to be used only for funding the state program for independent adoptions.[33]

If the finding of the department investigation is that the home of the petitioners is not suitable for the child or that the required consents are not available, and the department or the adoption agency recommends that the petitions be denied, the clerk of the court upon receipt of the report shall submit it to the court for review.[34]

(E) Adoption Subsidies

California does not have a program of adoption subsidies of the type available in other states.

(F) Surrogacy

The California Supreme Court recently upheld the legality of contracts for surrogate children. The court also concluded that the child of a surrogacy agreement's natural mother is the genetic mother, and therefore that the husband and wife are the natural parents. The court expressly stated that surrogacy contracts did not violate state or federal constitutional provisions or public policy.[35] The court reasoned that gestational surrogacy differed in crucial respects from adoption and so is not subject to adoption statutes, including the proscription against payment for the consent to adopt a child.[36] The court also concluded that under a surrogacy contract, the payments to the surrogate mother were meant to compensate her for her services in gestating the fetus and undergoing labor, rather than for giving up parental rights to her child. The court rejected the contention that surrogacy contracts exploit poor women.

---

33. Fam. Code § 8810.
34. Fam. Code § 8822.
35. *Johnson v. Calvert*, 5 Cal.4th 84 (1993).
36. *Id.* at 96–97; Penal Code § 273.

5A.15

Delinquency

California has a comprehensive statutory scheme for dealing with complaints involving activities of juveniles that would be criminal if committed by an adult. In many instances the statutes juveniles are charged with violating, the forum in which their conduct is evaluated, and the available penalties are substantially different from those for an adult offender.

Originally juvenile proceedings were described as being primarily for the protection and benefit of minors.[1] However, in 1984, the focus shifted to the protection of society from minors, as a result of the increased incidence of minors being involved in violent crimes.[2] MHPs may become involved in assessing or treating delinquent juveniles and in testifying in delinquency proceedings.

(A) Definitions

As used in this chapter, a *juvenile* is a person who is under the age of 18.

Under California's juvenile justice system a peace officer can take a juvenile into temporary custody for violating a federal or state law or a local ordinance.[3]

However, when a juvenile is arrested and detained on suspicion of having committed a crime, he or she is not formally

---

1. *In re Ricardo M.*, 52 Cal.App.3d 744 (1975).
2. *In re Javier A.*, 159 Cal.App.3d 913 (1984).
3. Welf. & Inst. Code §§ 602 to 607; *Alfredo A. v. Superior Court*, 5 Cal.4th 1 (1993).

charged with the crime in the same way that adults are. Instead, a determination is made as to whether to commence wardship proceedings through a petition filed by the prosecuting attorney.[4] The announced purpose of the Juvenile Court law is to protect the safety of the public and the minor and to strengthen the minor's family ties whenever possible—removing the minor from the custody of the parents only when necessary for the minor's welfare or for the safety and protection of the public.[5] If a minor is removed from parental custody, reunification becomes a primary goal.[6] When a minor is under the jurisdiction of the juvenile court due to delinquent conduct, it is the intent of the law that he or she receive care, treatment, and guidance, but still be held accountable for his or her behavior.

Included within the meaning of *guidance* is punishment. Punishment under the juvenile court law includes payment of a fine by the minor; compulsory community service by the minor; limitations on the minor's liberty as a condition of probation; commitment to a local detention or treatment facility such as a juvenile hall, a camp, or a ranch; or commitment of the minor to the California Youth Authority. (The California Youth Authority is equivalent to a prison for adults.)[7]

Although a Juvenile Court proceeding may involve conduct that is criminal in nature and although evidence is presented in the manner of a criminal trial, an order to determine a minor to be a ward of the juvenile court is not a conviction for any purpose, and no proceeding in Juvenile Court is deemed a criminal proceeding. Juveniles are not entitled to trial by jury.[8]

(B) Petition to Declare a Minor Delinquent

The law provides that when a minor violates the law by committing a crime other than violation of curfew, he or she is within the exclusive jurisdiction of Juvenile Court, and no other court has jurisdiction to conduct a preliminary examination or try the

---

4. Welf. & Inst. Code §§ 609, 650; *Alfredo A. v. Superior Court, supra* note 3.
5. Welf. & Inst. Code § 202.
6. *Id.*
7. *Id.*
8. *Id.* § 203; *In re Mitchell P.*, 22 Cal.3d 946 (1978) *cert. denied*, 444 U.S. *sub nom Ponting v. California* 845 (1979). For a case discussing at length the history of the right to jury trial in general and deploring the unavailability of the right to minors, *see Matter of Javier Cabral A.*, 159 Cal.App.3d 913 (1984).

case, unless a determination has been made that the minor should be tried as an adult.[9]

A petition can be filed seeking to declare a minor a ward of the court in any of the following situations:

1. when a minor has persistently and habitually refused to obey the reasonable and proper orders of his or her parents or guardians;
2. when a minor is beyond the control of parents or guardians; or
3. if a school attendance review board determines that the available public and private services are insufficient or inappropriate to correct the habitual truancy of a minor.[10]

When the grounds for the wardship are that the minor is a truant or out of control, the action may be commenced by a petition filed by the minor's probation officer, or the district attorney after consultation with the probation officer. When a petition is filed because the minor has committed an act that would be a crime for an adult, the action is commenced by the filing of a petition by the prosecuting attorney.[11] When a complaint is made to a probation officer or district attorney that the minor meets the criteria for being out of control or truant, an investigation is commenced that may lead to the probation officer recommending alternatives to a wardship proceeding, including specific programs of supervision for the minor for a period not to exceed six months.[12]

When a minor is charged with an act that would constitute a crime if committed by an adult, he or she is entitled to legal counsel.[13] If the minor cannot afford counsel, counsel will be appointed unless there is an intelligent waiver of the right to counsel. If the minor's parent or guardian does not furnish counsel but has the ability to pay for counsel, the court shall appoint counsel at the expense of the parent or guardian.

A minor has the rights of non-self incrimination, confrontation by witnesses, and cross-examination of witnesses.[14] A minor has generally the same defenses available to him or her as does an adult, except that hearings involving minors do not have juries and are closed to the public. No person other than the minor; a parent, guardian, or relative of the minor; or witness will be permitted to be present in any such hearings.[15]

---

9. Welf. & Inst. Code §§ 602, 603.
10. Welf. & Inst. Code §§ 601, 601.1, 601.3, 650.
11. Welf. & Inst. Code § 650.
12. Welf. & Inst. Code §§ 653, 654.
13. Welf. & Inst. Code §§ 679, 700.
14. Welf. & Inst. Code § 702.5.
15. Welf. & Inst. Code § 675.

However, prosecuting witnesses are entitled to have two family members present for their support, and a judge may admit those individuals deemed to have a direct and legitimate purpose before the court. Members of the public can be admitted on the same grounds as in an adult criminal proceeding when a minor is charged with any one of approximately 24 crimes, most involving violence, such as murder, arson, rape, etc.[16]

(C) Detention Hearing

A minor can be taken into temporary custody by a peace officer without a warrant where a peace officer reasonably believes the minor is a person qualifying for a wardship petition on the ground of having committed a crime or being a truant, or if the minor is a ward of the juvenile court where the peace officer has reasonable cause to believe that the minor has violated an order of the juvenile court or has escaped from commitment ordered by the court. Additionally the peace officer may take the minor into temporary custody if he or she is found in any street or public place suffering from any sickness or injury that requires medical treatment, hospitalization, or remedial care. When the minor is being taken into custody and the officer believes that he or she has committed a crime or has violated an order of the Juvenile Court, the officer is required to advise the minor that anything he or she says can be used against him or her, the right to remain silent, the right to have counsel, and the right to have appointed counsel (the *Miranda* warning).[17]

An officer that has taken a minor into temporary custody may release the minor, or deliver the minor to a public or private agency that has an agreement to provide shelter, care, counseling, or diversion for such minors. The officer can obtain the minor's written execution of a promise to appear and immediately release the minor. Or the officer can choose to take the minor without unnecessary delay before the probation officer in the county in which the minor was taken into custody or in which the minor resides, and turn custody over to the probation officer. In no case can the peace officer delay the delivery of the minor to the probation officer for more than 24 hours if the minor has been taken into custody without a warrant on the belief that the minor has committed a misdemeanor crime.[18] If the officer determines that the minor should be brought to the attention of the Juvenile

---

16. Welf. & Inst. Code § 676.
17. Welf. & Inst. Code § 625.
18. Welf. & Inst. Code § 626.

Court, he or she can prepare a written notice to the minor to appear before the county probation officer and deliver the notice to the minor, parent, or guardian with a written notice or promise that either or both will appear at a set time before the probation officer.

When an officer takes a minor before a probation officer or the juvenile hall or any other place of confinement, he or she is required to notify the minor's parent or guardian or responsible relative that the minor is in custody and where he or she is being held.

After the minor has been taken to a place of confinement, except where it is physically impossible, he or she is allowed within three hours to make at least two telephone calls, one to a parent or guardian and one to an attorney.

When a minor is delivered to a probation officer and taken into temporary custody, the probation officer is required to immediately investigate the circumstances of the minor and the facts surrounding his or her being taken into custody. The probation officer shall immediately release the minor into the custody of a parent, guardian, or responsible relative unless one of the following conditions exists:

1. the minor is in need of proper and effective parental control but has no parent, guardian, or responsible relative, or no such person is willing to assume and exercise such control;

2. the minor is destitute or has not been provided with the necessities of life;

3. the minor's home is an unfit place by reason of neglect, cruelty, depravity, or physical abuse;

4. continued detention of the minor is a matter of immediate and urgent necessity for the protection of either the minor or the personal property of another;

5. the minor is likely to flee the jurisdiction of the court;

6. the minor has violated an order of the juvenile court; or

7. the minor is physically dangerous to the public because of a mental deficiency disorder, or abnormality.[19]

The probation officer also has several options if he or she believes that 24 hours of secured detention is not necessary in order to protect the minor or the personal property of another.[20] When the probation officer determines that a minor should be retained in custody, he or she must immediately proceed with

---

19. Welf. & Inst. Code § 628.
20. Welf. & Inst. Code § 628.1.

filing a petition with the clerk of the Juvenile Court, who will set a detention hearing.

A minor must be released within 48 hours after being taken into custody unless within that period of time a petition to declare the minor a ward is filed with the juvenile court or a criminal complaint against the minor is filed in a court of competent jurisdiction. An exception is where the minor willfully represents his or her age as over 18.

If a minor has been held in custody for more than 24 hours by the probation officer and is subsequently released without a petition being filed, the probation officer must prepare a written explanation as to why the minor was held in custody for more than 24 hours; this report must be prepared within 72 hours after the minor's release from custody and filed with the court.[21]

When a minor has been taken into custody, a hearing must be held as soon as possible, but in any event before the end of the next judicial day after a petition to declare the minor a ward has been filed. The hearing must be before a judge or referee of the Juvenile Court who will determine whether the minor shall be further detained. An exception to the next judicial day requirement is if the minor has been taken into custody without a warrant on the belief that he or she has committed a misdemeanor that does not involve violence, threat of violence, or the possession or use of weapons, and if the minor is not currently on probation or parole; in these cases, the hearing can take place as soon as possible but no later than 48 hours after the minor is taken into custody after a petition declaring the minor a ward has been filed. If the minor is not brought before the court within 24 hours, that decision must be subjected to written review and approval by a probation officer who is a supervisor as soon as possible after it is known that the minor will not be brought before the judge or referee within 24 hours.

The hearing under this law to determine whether a minor shall be further detained is referred to as a detention hearing. If a minor is not brought before a judge or referee of the Juvenile Court within this statutorily prescribed period, the minor must be released from custody.[22]

---

21. Welf. & Inst. Code § 631.
22. Welf. & Inst. Code § 632; *Alfredo A. v. Superior Court*, 5 Cal.4th 1 (1993)

(D) Dispositional Hearing

The jurisdictional hearing has the function of determining guilt or innocence, although those terms are not used. The dispositional hearing determines punishment to be meted out.

Once a petition has been filed, the clerk of the juvenile court shall set a jurisdictional hearing within 30 days, except that if the minor is detained in custody at the time of filing the petition, the hearing must be within 15 days of the order of the court directing detention.

At the detention hearing or at any time thereafter, a minor may with the consent of his or her counsel admit the allegations of a petition and waive the jurisdictional hearing to determine whether he or she comes within the authority of the Juvenile Court.

The role of the judge in juvenile proceedings is first to ascertain the jurisdiction of the Juvenile Court, and then to hear all information relative to the present condition and future welfare of the minor. The hearings are to be conducted in an informal and nonadversarial atmosphere with a view to obtaining the maximum cooperation of the minor and all persons interested in his or her welfare, with such provisions as the court may choose to make regarding the disposition and care of the minor. However, when there is a contested issue of fact or law, the proceedings are more adversarial.[23]

At the dispositional hearing, the court shall first consider the question of whether the minor comes within various statutory provisions granting exclusive authority to the Juvenile Court. Two legal standards of proof and levels of evidence are involved in dispositional hearings. The admission of evidence is governed by the rules of evidence, the Evidence Code, and prior judicial decisions. When the petition contends that the minor is a person who is engaged in a crime, there must be proof beyond a reasonable doubt supported by evidence that is admissible in a criminal trial that the minor committed the crime.[24] When it is contended that the minor is either beyond parental control or a truant or a dependent child needing the court's protection, proof is established by a preponderance of the evidence, with evidence of the type that is admissible at civil trials.[25]

If it was believed that the minor had made admissions or confessed, but at the hearing the minor denies such confessions or admissions, the court may continue the hearing to allow the

---

23. Welf. & Inst. Code § 680.
24. Welf. & Inst. Code §§ 602, 701.
25. Welf. & Inst. Code §§ 701, 300, 601, 121.

prosecution to subpoena witnesses to prove the factual allegations. If the minor does not have legal counsel at the hearing, the court must deem that all objections that could have been made to the evidence were in fact made.[26]

At the hearing, if the court concludes after the presentation of evidence in support of the petition that the minor does not meet the statutory criteria for a person who has committed a crime, or is a truant or beyond parental control, the court shall order that the petition be dismissed and the minor discharged from any detention. However, if a motion to that effect is not granted at the close of the presentation of the evidence in support of the petition, the minor proceeds to offer evidence.[27] After hearing all of the evidence, the court makes a finding as to whether or not the minor qualifies under one of the above statutory criteria for dependent child, truant/beyond parental control, or criminal. If none of the criteria are met, the petition is dismissed and the minor is discharged. If the court finds that any of the criteria are met, it makes its findings and order accordingly, and then proceeds to hear evidence on the proper disposition of the minor. The court may continue the hearing to receive a social study by the probation officer, to refer the minor to a juvenile justice community resource program, or to receive other evidence. If the minor is not being detained the court may continue the hearing for not more than 30 days. If the minor is being detained, the continuance cannot exceed 10 judicial days. If the minor is not detained, there may be an additional continuance of up to 15 days.

If the court finds that the minor has committed an offense that if committed by an adult would be punishable as either a felony or as a misdemeanor, the court shall make a declaration as to whether the offense is a misdemeanor or a felony.[28] If the court determines that the minor has committed an offense that would be a crime for an adult, or is a truant or beyond parental control and a petition for commitment of the minor to the California Youth Authority has been filed, the court may, if it concludes it is in the best interests of the minor, require that the minor be subject to observation and diagnosis at a treatment center of the California Youth Authority. In such instances, the court may continue the hearing and order the minor temporarily placed at a diagnostic center for a period not to exceed 90 days. The director of the California Youth Authority within 90 days must have the minor observed and examined, and forward a report and recommendation to the court regarding the minor's future care, supervision,

---

26. Welf. & Inst. Code § 701.
27. Welf. & Inst. Code § 701.1.
28. Welf. & Inst. Code § 702.

and treatment.[29] After considering the evidence, including any diagnostic report and any social study of the minor, the court may make a disposition.[30] As discussed in chapter 5A.18, under certain circumstances a minor accused of committing an offense that would be a crime if committed by an adult may be deemed unfit for juvenile court and transferred for trial as an adult.[31]

After considering the various evidence regarding the minor's disposition, the court has a number of options. If the court finds that the minor is a person who is truant or beyond parental control, or has committed a crime, it may order the minor to be a ward of the court. If the court finds that a minor is such a person by reason of commission of certain offenses, it may, without determining that the minor is a ward of the court, place the minor on probation or under the supervision of a probation officer for a period not to exceed six months. The court has a series of options in terms of what conditions it can impose as part of probation. If the offense involved unlawful possession, use, or furnishing of a controlled substance, the minor's probation must include certain specific conditions. If the minor fails to comply with the conditions of probation, the court may determine the minor to be a ward of the court.[32]

(E) Minor Determined to Be a Ward of the Court

In any case where a minor is determined to be a ward of the court or a dependent child, the court may limit the control over the ward by any parent or guardian. While generally a dependent child cannot be taken from the physical custody of a parent or guardian, a ward of the court can be removed if the court finds any of the following:

1. that the parent or guardian is incapable of providing, or has failed or neglected to provide, proper maintenance, training, and education for the ward;
2. that the ward has been tried on probation and has failed to reform; or
3. that the ward's welfare requires that custody be removed from the parent or guardian.

---

29. Welf. & Inst. Code § 704.
30. Welf. & Inst. Code § 706.
31. Welf. & Inst. Code § 707.
32. Welf. & Inst. Code § 725.

In any case in which the ward is removed from the physical custody of the parent or guardian as a result of a determination that the ward has committed an offense that would be a crime if committed by an adult, the court's order must specify that the ward will not be held in physical confinement for a period in excess of the maximum term of imprisonment that could be imposed upon an adult convicted of the same offense.[33] Physical confinement means confinement in a juvenile hall, ranch, camp, forestry camp, juvenile home, or any institution operated by the California Youth Authority.

If a minor is adjudged to be a ward of the court, the court may make any and all reasonable orders for the care, supervision, custody, conduct, maintenance, and support of the minor, including medical treatment.[34] Where the minor has been adjudged a ward of the court based on certain specified offenses, the minor is not eligible to be placed on probation without supervision of a probation officer.[35] However, except in those specified instances the care, custody and control of the minor is ordered by the court under the supervision of a probation officer. The probation officer may place the minor in several settings:

1. a relative's home;

2. a licensed community care facility; or

3. with a foster family agency.[36]

As part of the court's various orders, it can order mental health counseling and other treatment services.[37] The court can also order restitution and impose fines under certain circumstances.[38]

The court cannot commit to the California Youth Authority a ward that is under the age of 11 or who is suffering from any contagious, infectious, or other disease that would endanger the lives or health of other inmates.[39] In addition, the court cannot commit a ward to the California Youth Authority unless it is fully

---

33. Welf. & Inst. Code § 726.
34. Welf. & Inst. Code § 727.
35. Welf. & Inst. Code §§ 727, 707; Penal Code § 459; Health & Safety Code § 11350.
36. Welf. & Inst. Code § 727.
37. Welf. & Inst. Code § 727. An order requiring a father to participate in psychological counseling and to release treating information to the Department of Social Services was upheld in the case of *In re Lumonica H.*, 220 Cal.App.3d 634 (1990). The father there contended that his right against self-incrimination was potentially violated by the order. However, the court held that any admissions he made could not be used against him in subsequent criminal proceedings for child abuse.
38. Welf. & Inst. Code §§ 728, 730.5, 731.
39. Welf. & Inst. Code § 733.

satisfied that the ward will benefit from the services available at the youth authority.[40]

(F) Disclosure of Mental Health Information

The records of proceedings involving juveniles are generally confidential. The petition filed in a juvenile court proceeding, the reports of the probation officer, and any other documents filed in the case are made available to the probation officer and can only be reviewed by court personnel, the district attorney, city attorney authorized to prosecute criminal or juvenile cases under state law, the minor who is the subject of the proceedings, or his parents, guardian or attorneys, and such other individuals as specifically designated by the court.

In addition, child protective agencies may gain access to some of the information if affidavits are filed stating that the information is necessary and relevant to a criminal investigation and proceeding brought to declare a minor a dependent child or ward of the juvenile court.[41] There is, however, an express exception to the confidentiality of juvenile court records in cases involving serious acts of violence. Even so, it is the legislative intent that even in cases involving serious acts of violence, the dissemination of Juvenile Court records be as limited as possible consistent with the need to work with a minor in an appropriate fashion and to protect other students or school staff who may be at risk.

However, when a minor is enrolled in a public school from kindergarten through grade twelve and is found by a court of competent jurisdiction to have used, sold, or possessed narcotics, his or her court records shall be provided within seven days to the superintendent of the school district where the minor attends school. That information should then be expeditiously transmitted to a teacher, counselor, or minister with direct supervisorial or disciplinarian responsibility over the minor, who the superintendent believes needs the information to work with the student in an appropriate fashion to avoid being needlessly vulnerable or to protect other persons from being vulnerable. The information is not to be further disseminated, and an intentional violation of that confidentiality is a misdemeanor punishable by a fine not to exceed $500.[42]

---

40. Welf. & Inst. Code § 734. For a case where commitment to the California Youth Authority was upheld, *see In re Tyrone O.*, 209 Cal.App.3d 145 (1989).
41. Welf. & Inst. Code § 827.
42. Welf. & Inst. Code § 807.

In one case, the court held that there is no duty to give *Miranda* warnings to juveniles in drug counseling because they are not interrogation sessions. That case involved a juvenile who volunteered that he had committed arson. The court agreed that that communication was not entitled to confidentiality because of the risk the juvenile posed to his co-residents at the facility and at future placements.[43]

(G) Diversion and Juvenile-Family Crisis

While California law stresses the importance of reconciliation of families in custody disputes and in the context of dependent children, there is not a *per se* diversion program as exists in some states.

---

43. *In re Kevin F.*, 213 Cal.App.3d 178 (1989).

5A.16

Competency of Juveniles to Stand Trial

There are two separate judicial systems for dealing with individuals charged with crimes. Adults are generally prosecuted under criminal statutes in Superior Court (although pretrial procedures may take place in Municipal Court). Juveniles who are accused of acts that would be crimes if committed by adults are subject to the juvenile justice system, which uses different procedures and substantive law. chapter 5A.18 addresses the criteria for determining if a juvenile should be tried as an adult or tried in Juvenile Court. This chapter addresses the competency of juveniles to be tried in juvenile court proceedings. MHPs may be called to evaluate and testify as to the mental competency of juveniles.

(A) Constitutional Protections

Juveniles have many of the procedural and constitutional protections granted to adult criminal defendants, such as rights against self-incrimination. Because the state has a continuing paternal interest in the protection of minors, however, the constitutional protections may not be as strong as those for adults.[1] The fact that juveniles are not entitled to a jury trial, for example, has been upheld as not unconstitutional.[2]

---

1. *People v. Haynes,* 160 Cal.App.3d 1122 (1984).
2. *Matter of Javier Cabral A.,* 159 Cal.App.3d 913 (1984); *In re Hector R.,* 152 Cal.App.3d 1146 (1984).

(B) Appreciation of the Wrongfulness of Conduct

One protection that applies equally to adults and juveniles is that an individual must appreciate the wrongfulness of his or her conduct before he or she can be deemed to be a ward of the court.[3]

A determination that a juvenile appreciates the wrongfulness of his or her conduct is a finding of a sufficient mental capacity to support a proceeding.[4] When necessary, Juvenile Court can initiate proceedings to determine the mental competency of a juvenile, and can suspend those proceedings to refer the juvenile for evaluation.[5]

Juveniles 14 years of age and older are capable of committing crimes as a matter of law unless they suffer from some statutory disability.[6] But if a juvenile does not appreciate the wrongfulness of his or her act and is under the age of 14, Juvenile Court has no jurisdiction (that is, no authority to hear the case) and the juvenile is presumed to be incapable of committing a crime.[7] Thus, for minors under 14, mental capacity is key for determining which court system will hear the case.[8]

For a discussion of the law governing the mental competency of adults to stand trial, *see* chapter 5D.5. For a discussion of a juvenile's use of insanity as a defense, *see* chapter 5A.17.

---

3. *In re Billy Y.*, 220 Cal.App.3d 127 (1990); *In re Michael B.*, 149 Cal.App.3d 1073 (1983) (reversing a nine-year-old's conviction for involuntary manslaughter because the prosecution failed to prove that he made a knowing, intelligent, and voluntary waiver of his rights against self-incrimination. Another ground for reversal was the failure to establish that the minor appreciated the criminal nature of his acts.).

4. *In re Nirran W.*, 207 Cal.App.3d 1157 (1989).

5. Welf. & Inst. Code § 602; Penal Code § 4011.6; *In re Mary T.*, 176 Cal.App.3d 38 (1985).

6. *In re Tony C.*, 21 Cal.3d 888 (1978); Penal Code § 26.

7. *In re Mary T., supra* note 5.

8. *Shortridge v. Municipal Court*, 151 Cal.App.3d 611 (1984).

5A.17

Nonresponsibility Defense

A juvenile charged with a crime has the right to assert that he or she should not be held legally responsible for acts that otherwise would be crimes. MHPs may be involved in assessments and testifying as to the mental condition of minors in Juvenile Court proceedings. If a non-responsibility defense succeeds, MHPs may also be involved in the treatment of juveniles determined to be insane.

(A) Invoking the Right to Assert Nonresponsibility as a Defense

Juveniles are accorded some, but not all, of the constitutional protection enjoyed by adults accused of crimes. Juveniles are entitled, for example, to notice of the charges against them, and the rights to counsel, against self incrimination, and confrontation and cross-examination of witnesses.[1]

Juveniles have the same rights as adults to invoke defenses, such as insanity, to allegations that they engaged in a criminal activity. For example, when a 14-year-old was found to be mentally retarded and immature, the court held that his incriminatory statement was improperly admitted into evidence in a juvenile court proceeding.[2]

If a juvenile's insanity defense is successful, it will preclude the court from proceeding with the wardship because it lacks

---

1. *In re Gault*, 387 U.S. 1 (1967).
2. *In re P.*, 7 Cal.3d 801 (1972); *In re Ramon M.*, 22 Cal.3d 419 (1978).

jurisdiction.[3] Proof of a juvenile's insanity deprives the court of jurisdiction.[4] The juvenile is then committed to a state hospital for care and treatment as described in chapter 5A.19.[5]

(B) Procedure for Invoking Nonresponsibility Defense

A minor may respond to a petition charging him or her with acts that would be a crime if committed by an adult by entering a plea of not guilty by reason of insanity. Where a minor enters such a plea and enters a general denial of the facts alleged in the petition, the court first holds with a hearing on the charges as if no insanity plea has been made. If the factual allegations of the petition are sustained, or if the minor denies the factual allegations of the petition only by reason of insanity, then a hearing is held to determine on whether the minor was insane at the time the offense was committed.[6]

If the court finds that the minor was insane at the time the offense was committed (and has not regained sanity), the court shall direct the minor be confined in a state hospital for the care of the mentally disordered, or in any other appropriate public or private mental health facility. As an alternative, the court may order the minor to participate in outpatient treatment.

If the factual allegations of the petition specify any act that would be a felony and are found to be true, the court shall direct the minor to be confined in a state hospital or other public or private mental health facility approved by the community program director (formerly, the county mental health director). The confinement shall be for a minimum of 180 days before the minor can be released to outpatient treatment. Before the court orders a minor to be confined in a state hospital or other facility, or to undergo outpatient treatment, the court must order the community program director or his or her designee to evaluate the minor. The evaluation is submitted to the court within 15 days of the order with a written recommendation as to whether the minor should be committed or required to undergo outpatient treatment. If it appears to the court that the minor has fully recovered sanity, the minor is to be remanded to the custody of the probation department until his or her sanity has been finally determined.

---

3. *In re Vicky H.*, 99 Cal.App.3d 484 (1979).
4. *In re M.G.S.*, 267 Cal.App.2d 329 (1968).
5. Welf. & Inst. Code § 702.3.
6. Welf. & Inst. Code § 702.3(a).

(C) Test for Insanity

The test for juvenile insanity is the same as that for adults, as discussed in chapter 5D.9.

(D) Release from Commitment

Where a minor has been committed to a state hospital or other facility, or ordered to undergo outpatient treatment, he or she cannot be released from confinement or from outpatient treatment unless the court has a hearing of the type required for adults who have been found insane (*see* chapters 5D.5 and 5D.8) and a determination is made that the minor's sanity has been restored.[7]

(E) Length of Commitment

A minor cannot be committed pursuant to this procedure for a period longer than age 25. However, if at the conclusion of the commitment, the minor represents a substantial danger of physical harm to others by reason of a mental disease, defect, or disorder, the commitment may be extended in accordance with the circumstances for extending the commitment of adults (*see* chapter 5D.9).[8] Although adults may be provided with a jury trial in such proceedings, minors may not.[9]

---

7. Welf. & Inst. Code § 702.3(b); Penal Code § 1026.2.
8. Welf. and Inst. Code §§ 607, 702.3(c).
9. Welf. & Inst. Code § 702.3(f).

5A.18

Transfer of Juveniles to Stand Trial as Adults

The Juvenile Court has the primary jurisdiction over juvenile offenders. However, the court has the power to transfer a juvenile to the regular criminal courts for trial as an adult. This is generally done when it appears that the more lenient approach of the juvenile system would not benefit the offender, or when the crime was particularly violent or heinous. MHPs may play an important role in the evaluation of juveniles for fitness to be tried as adults and may offer evidence critical to that determination at a hearing as to a juvenile's mental status or prior attempts at rehabilitation.

(A) Juveniles Tried as Adults

Despite the emphasis on treating juveniles differently than adults, the law recognizes that certain juveniles are so hardened or vicious that they should be tried as adults.

Generally, the more unsuccessful history a juvenile has of rehabilitation and the higher the level of criminal sophistication, the more appropriate is trial as an adult. Some crimes are so brutal that the juvenile is tried as an adult because if the juvenile were committed to the California Youth Authority, he or she would be required to be dismissed at the age of 21.

(B) Initiation of Transfer to an Adult Court

When a juvenile was 16 years of age or older when the acts at issue occurred, and the acts include certain designated violent crimes,[1] the district attorney can petition to have him or her tried as an adult. A juvenile may also waive his or her right to be treated as a juvenile and thereby be treated as an adult, including the right to trial by jury.[2]

(C) Fitness Hearing

When the juvenile has been accused of any one of 24 specific crimes the court has a probation officer conduct a study on the behavioral patterns and social history of the minor with regard to unfitness to be tried as a juvenile. However, following the submission of the report and any other relevant evidence, the juvenile is presumed to be unfit and a proper subject for transfer to adult court, unless the juvenile court concludes that there are extenuating or mitigating circumstances, or that the juvenile would be amenable to the care, treatment, and training program available through Juvenile Court. The 24 crimes that trigger the presumption that the juvenile is not fit for trial as a juvenile mostly involve violence.[3] When the probation department does not submit the required social study report, a determination that a minor is unfit for treatment is void.[4] The social study report to determine whether a juvenile is a fit subject for transfer to adult court is similar to that for a dispositional hearing, but does not need to address the alternative facilities potentially available to rehabilitate the juvenile. In short, the report for the fitness hearing is for a more limited purpose and would not be acceptable as a social study for the purposes of a dispositional hearing.[5]

---

1. These crimes include but are not limited to murder; arson of an inhabited building; rape, sodomy, or oral copulation by force or threat; lewd acts on children; kidnapping for ransom, robbery, or with bodily harm; assualt with force or firearms; carjacking with a deadly weapon; torture; aggravated mayhem; escape with force or violence from a juvenile hall, home, ranch or camp; and manufacturing or selling 1/2 ounce or more of controlled susbtances. Welf. & Inst. Code § 707; *People v. King*, 5 Cal.4th 59 (1993).
2. *In re Rodney F.*, 203 Cal.App.3d 177 (1988).
3. Welf. & Inst. Code § 707(b) & (c); Cal.Juv.Ct.R.Crim.P. 1483. These crimes are listed in note 1, *supra*.
4. *Raul P. v. Superior Court*, 153 Cal.App.3d 294 (1984).
5. *In re Devin J.*, 155 Cal.App.3d 1096 (1984).

The hearing on whether a juvenile should be tried as an adult is based on the probation officer's report on the behavioral patterns and social history of the juvenile, together with any other relevant evidence that the petitioner or the juvenile may wish to submit.

(D) Test for Determining Suitability for Transfer

In determining whether a juvenile is suitable for trial as an adult, Juvenile Court considers the following factors:

1. the degree of criminal sophistication exhibited by the juvenile;
2. whether the juvenile can be rehabilitated prior to the expiration of Juvenile Court's jurisdiction (age 21), although a minor who is committed to the Youth Authority or to a mental institution may actually be held until age 25;
3. the juvenile's prior delinquent history;
4. the success of previous attempts by the court to rehabilitate the juvenile; and
5. the circumstances and gravity of the offense alleged to have been committed.[6]

The court's determination that a juvenile is not fit to be in the juvenile system may be based on any one or a combination of the five factors set forth above. The court must recite its conclusions as to these factors.

When a court's findings of fact are insufficient to contradict the presumption that a minor charged with murder is unfit for Juvenile Court, the court's decision can be reversed.[7] In this regard, the presumption that a minor charged with certain felonies is unfit for Juvenile Court reverses the traditional burden of proof.[8]

---

6. Welf. & Inst. Code §§ 607, 707.
7. *People v. Superior Court*, 213 Cal.App.3d 54 (1989).
8. *Ramona R. v. Superior Court*, 37 Cal.3d 802 (1985).

(E) When a Minor Is Declared Unfit for Juvenile Court

Once a minor has been declared not a fit subject for Juvenile Court, the district attorney or another appropriate prosecuting officer may file an accusatory pleading against the juvenile in a court of criminal jurisdiction, and from that point the case proceeds as a typical criminal case. The Juvenile Court may order that the minor be transferred to the custody of the sheriff if the judge finds that the presence of the minor in a juvenile hall would endanger the safety of the public or other inmates. However, minors who have been declared not fit, if they are detained, can remain in the juvenile hall pending final disposition by the criminal court or until they obtain the age of 18, whichever occurs first.

When a minor is found to be not a fit subject for the Juvenile Court, at the conclusion of a fitness hearing, he or she shall be entitled to be released on bail or on his or her own recognizance on the same circumstances, terms, and conditions as an adult alleged to have committed the same offense.[9]

(F) When a Minor Is Declared Fit for Juvenile Court

If, after a fitness hearing, the court finds that a minor *is* fit to be tried as a juvenile, it proceeds to a jurisdictional hearing, as described in chapter 5A.18.[10]

---

9. Welf. & Inst. Code § 707.1; Cal.Juv.Ct.R.Crim.P. 1483(e).
10. Welf. & Inst. Code 1483(e)(2).

5A.19

Voluntary Admission and Civil Commitment of Minors

California provides specific statutes for the civil commitment of minors that contain procedural safeguards to protect against commitment of minors who are not mentally ill. MHPs can be involved in assessing minors for involuntary hospitalization, treating minors while hospitalized, and/or assessing minors after a period of hospitalization to determine if continued hospitalization is appropriate.

(A) Statutory History

The involuntary commitment of minors involves two statutes: The Lanterman–Petris–Short Act,[1] which also governs the involuntary commitment of adults (*see* chapter 5E.4), and the Children's Civil Commitment and Mental Health Act of 1988.[2] Generally, the Children's Civil Commitment and Mental Health Act applies only to the initial 72 hours of mental health evaluation and treatment, but it takes precedence over any conflicting provisions of the Lanterman–Petris–Short Act.[3] When a person is involuntarily hospitalized contrary to the provisions of these two statutes, a cause of action for false imprisonment might lie.[4]

---

1. Welf. & Inst. Code § 5000 et seq.
2. Welf. & Inst. Code §§ 5585 to 5585.25.
3. Welf. & Inst. Code § 5585.2.
4. *See Brimmer v. California chapter 1 Medical Inc.*, 180 Cal.App.3d 678 (1986), where an adult was unsuccessfully hospitalized after a suicide attempt and was put on a 72-hour hold. She subsequently sued for false imprisonment but was unsuccessful.

(B) Criteria for Involuntary Hospitalization

The criteria for involuntary hospitalization as to minors and adults are somewhat different. Both adults and minors can be involuntarily committed when they are a danger to others or to themselves, or are gravely disabled.[5] However, the definition of *gravely disabled* is somewhat different for adults and minors.

For a minor, the term *gravely disabled* means the inability to use the elements of life that are essential to health, safety, and development, including food, clothing, and shelter, even though the minor may have been provided those necessities by others. For the purposes of this definition, mental retardation, epilepsy, other developmental disabilities, alcoholism, drug abuse, or repeated antisocial behavior do not in themselves constitute a mental disorder.[6]

(C) Test for Involuntary Hospitalization

A minor may be involuntarily hospitalized where he or she, as a result of a mental disorder, is a danger to himself or herself or others, or is gravely disabled, and an authorization for voluntary treatment is not available.

(D) Procedure for Involuntary Hospitalization

A peace officer, member of the attending staff of an evaluation facility designated by the county, members of a mobil crisis team, or another professional person designated by the county may, upon probable cause, take or cause the minor to be taken into custody. This person may place him or her in a facility designated by the county and approved by the Department of Mental Health as a facility for 72-hour treatment and evaluation of minors. The facility must make every effort to notify the minor's parents or legal guardian as soon as possible after the minor is detained.

---

5. Welf. & Inst. Code § 5150.
6. Welf. & Inst. Code § 5585.25.

The officer, staff member, or professional person who begins this process must give the facility a statement in writing stating the probable cause that existed, and his or her belief that the minor met the statutory criteria. If the probable cause is based on the statement of another person, the person may be liable in a civil action for intentionally giving a statement that he or she knows to be false.[7]

Once a minor has been detained under this statute, he or she must receive a clinical evaluation from a multidisciplinary team of his or her medical, psychological, developmental, educational, social, financial, and legal conditions to the extent they may appear to be a problem. The evaluation must include a psychosocial evaluation of family, living environment, or both. The evaluation services must be provided by properly qualified professionals with training, supervised experience, or both in diagnosis and treatment of minors. The law requires every effort to be made to involve the minor's parent or legal guardian in the clinical evaluation.[8] If in the opinion of the professional person conducting the evaluation, the minor will require additional mental health treatment, a treatment plan must be written and must identify the least restrictive placement alternative in which the minor can receive the treatment. The minor's legal guardian, parents, or caretaker must be consulted and informed as to the basic recommendations for treatment and placement. Every effort must be made to obtain the consent of the minor's parent or legal guardian prior to treatment and placement. However, the fact that a parent or legal guardian's consent cannot be obtained does not preclude involuntary treatment of a minor who is gravely disabled or a danger to himself or others, in accordance with the provisions of Lanterman–Petris–Short Act.[9]

As with adults, minors must be placed in a facility approved by the Department of Mental Health as a facility for 72-hour evaluation and treatment, however, the counties are required to ensure that minors under the age of 16 are not held with adults who are receiving psychiatric treatment under the Lanterman–Petris–Short Act.[10]

When a minor who has been hospitalized under these procedures is being evaluated for release from treatment, an aftercare plan must be developed that includes educational training aids necessary to the minor's well-being.[11]

---

7. Welf. & Inst. Code § 5585.5; *Cunha v. Superior Court*, 2 Cal.3d 352 at 356 (1970).
8. Welf. & Inst. Code § 5585.52.
9. Welf. & Inst. Code § 5585.53.
10. Welf. & Inst. Code § 5585.55.
11. Welf. & Inst. Code § 5585.57.

It should also be noted that legally emancipated minors who require voluntary treatment are considered adults and do not come under this statute.[12]

(E) Independent Clinical Review

Once a minor has been admitted, the facility is required to inform the minor in writing of the availability of an independent clinical review of his or her further inpatient treatment. This notice must be witnessed and signed by an appropriate representative of the facility.

Within one working day, the facility must notify the patient-rights advocate in the hospital of the admission of the minor. In addition, the minor must be provided with a booklet by the Department of Mental Health outlining the specific rights of minors in mental health facilities, which includes the phone number of the local patient-rights advocate.[13]

If a minor does request an independent clinical review of his or her continued inpatient treatment, the patient-rights advocate must be notified of the request as soon as practical, but not later than one working day. The advocate's role is to provide information and assistance to the minor regarding the right to an independent clinical review. The independent review may be requested up to 10 days after admission.[14]

The independent clinical review must be conducted by a licensed psychiatrist with training and experience in treating adolescent psychiatric patients, who is a neutral party to the review, having no direct financial relationship with the treating clinician, nor a personal or financial relationship with the patient or the patient's parents or guardians. However, nothing prevents a psychiatrist affiliated with a health maintenance organization from providing the independent clinical review where the admitting, treating, and reviewing psychiatrists are also affiliated with the health maintenance organization that predominantly serves members of a prepaid health-care service plan.[15]

The psychiatrist conducting the independent clinical review must consider all reasonably available clinical information that is relevant to establishing whether the minor meets the admission criteria. The psychiatrist must privately interview the minor and must consult the treating clinician to review alternative treatment

---

12. Welf. & Inst. Code § 5585.59.
13. Welf. & Inst. Code § 6002.15(c).
14. Welf. & Inst. Code § 6002.20.
15. Welf. & Inst. Code § 6002.25.

options that may be suitable. If the minor has received medication while an inpatient, the psychiatrist conducting the review must be informed of that fact and of the probable effects of the medication. The psychiatrist must also be informed of the proposed treatment plan, whether the minor has had any previous independent clinical review at any facility, and the results of that review.[16]

(F) Standard of Clinical Review

The standard by which a psychiatrist determines whether confinement is necessary includes the following factors:

1. whether the minor continues to have a mental disorder;
2. whether further inpatient treatment is reasonably likely to be beneficial to the minor's mental disorder; and
3. whether the placement in the facility represents the least restrictive, most appropriate available setting, within the constraints of reasonably available services, facilities, and resources with which to treat the minor.[17]

(G) Timing of Clinical Review

The clinical review must take place within five days of the minor's request for review.[18]

(H) Conduct of Clinical Review

The clinical review is to be conducted at the facility the minor is in, at a location compatible with and least disruptive of the treatment being provided to the minor. The review must be located in a way to ensure privacy.[19] The minor has the right to be present at the review, to be assisted by the patient advocate, and to question persons who recommend inpatient treatment. If the minor is unwilling to attend, the review proceeds with the advocate representing the minor.[20] The review may be closed to anyone other than the minor, his or her parents or legal guardian, a representative of the facility, the minor's advocate, the psychia-

---

16. Welf. & Inst. Code § 6002.30(a) & (b).
17. Welf. & Inst. Code § 6002.30(c).
18. Welf. & Inst. Code § 6002.30(d).
19. Welf. & Inst. Code § 6002.30(f).
20. Welf. & Inst. Code § 6002.30.

trist conducting the review, and the persons presenting information in favor of or in opposition to the inpatient treatment. The psychiatrist has discretion to limit the number of participants and the time they have to speak.[21] Legal representation is not allowed in the review process.[22]

The psychiatrist is responsible for creating a record of the proceeding.[23]

(I) Decision After Review

The decision of the reviewing psychiatrist is binding. If the psychiatrist determines that further inpatient treatment is reasonably likely to be beneficial, and that placement in the facility represents the least restrictive, most appropriate setting, then the continued inpatient treatment is authorized.[24]

The psychiatrist's determination that admission criteria have been met terminates when the minor is discharged from the facility.[25]

If the reviewing psychiatrist determines that further inpatient treatment in the facility is not reasonably likely to be beneficial or does not represent the least restrictive, most appropriate available treatment setting, then the minor must be released the same day to a custodial parent or guardian.[26]

Except when the minor makes an express threat against a readily ascertainable third party, and no warning as required by law is given, the reviewing psychiatrist, treating MHP, and the facility are immune from civil or criminal liability for any conduct of the released minor, the minor's parent or guardian, or any other person entitled to custody of the minor.[27]

(J) Judicial Review

The statutory procedures do not preclude a minor who is involuntarily committed from pursuing his or her release by a writ of a habeas corpus in Superior Court.

---

21. Welf. & Inst. Code § 6002.30(l).
22. Welf. & Inst. Code § 6002.30(i).
23. Welf. & Inst. Code § 6002.35(a).
24. Welf. & Inst. Code § 6002.35(b).
25. Welf. & Inst. Code § 6002.35(c).
26. Welf. & Inst. Code § 6002.35(d).
27. Welf. & Inst. Code § 6002.35(d); Civ. Code § 43.92.

(K) Voluntary Admission of Minors 14 Years or Older

A minor who has been declared to be within the jurisdiction of Juvenile Court may, with the advice of counsel, make voluntary application for inpatient or outpatient mental health services.[28] The court may authorize the minor to make such an application if the court determines from the evidence before it that the minor suffers from a mental disorder that may reasonably be expected to be cured or ameliorated by a course of treatment offered by the hospital or facility in which the minor wishes to be placed, and if there is no other hospital, program, or facility that might better serve the minor's medical needs.[29] If the minor is accepted as a voluntary patient, the Juvenile Court may issue an order to the minor and to the person in charge of the hospital facility or program, that if the minor leaves or demands to leave prior to the time that he or she is discharged by the superintendent or person in charge, he or she will be returned to Juvenile Court for a further dispositional hearing pursuant to the law.[30]

Minors who are not subject to the jurisdiction of Juvenile Court who are between the ages of 14 and 18 may be voluntarily admitted pursuant to procedures that inpatient psychiatric facilities are required to have. In essence, a minor who is not legally emancipated, not detained involuntarily, not voluntarily committed pursuant to the sections discussed above, and not a dependent of Juvenile Court can be voluntarily admitted when the minor's admitting diagnosis is either: (1) a mental disorder only (resistance to treatment may be a product of mental disorder but is not in itself enough to imply the presence of a mental disorder or constitute evidence that the minor meets the admission criteria), or (2) a mental disorder and a substance abuse disorder.[31]

Prior to accepting a written authorization for treatment, the facility must ensure that its representative has given a full explanation of the treatment philosophy, including where applicable the use of seclusion, restraint, and medication, and the degree of involvement of family members in the minor's treatment to the parent, guardian, or other person entitled to the minor's custody. This explanation must be given both orally and in writing, and must be documented in the minor's treatment record.

---

28. Welf. & Inst. Code §§ 6552, 5003.
29. Welf. & Inst. Code § 6552.
30. *Id.*
31. Welf. & Inst. Code § 6002.10.

As part of the admission process, the professional person responsible for the minor's admission must confirm in writing that the minor meets the admission criteria set forth above.[32]

---

32. Welf. & Inst. Code § 6002.159(a) & (b).

5A.20

Education for Handicapped Children

The U.S. Congress required states to provide for education for individuals with exceptional needs in the Individuals with Disabilities Education Act.[1] California's legislature in turn has enacted statutes designed to comply with the federal law to ensure that individuals with exceptional needs can participate in free and appropriate public education.[2] It was the intention of the California legislature that the state statutory scheme not provide broader rights than those imposed under the federal law.

MHPs may become involved with the laws relating to handicapped children (now referred to as *individuals with exceptional needs*) as members of teams that design specialized educational programs for them, including programs to deal with any emotional problems they may have. MHPs may also be involved in their evaluation or treatment or in behavioral intervention.

(A) Definitions

The educational system uses a number of very specialized terms in this area. Only those that are relevant to a basic understanding of the system and to MHPs are defined here.

1. *Individuals with exceptional needs* were formerly referred to as handicapped individuals. The law was changed because of the perception that the term *handicapped* was in some respects

---

1. 20 U.S.C. § 56031.
2. Educ. Code § 56000 et seq.

derogatory. Individuals must meet the following criteria to be considered as having exceptional needs:

(a) the individual has an impairment that requires instruction, services, or both, which cannot be provided with modification under regular school programs;

(b) the individual is between the ages of three and 18 and has been identified by a special education local plan or county offices as requiring intensive special education and services; and

(c) the individual is between 19 and 21 and was enrolled in or eligible for a program under the special education program prior to his or her 19th birthday but has not yet completed his or her prescribed course of study or has not met statutory proficiency standards. An individual who has not yet met statutory proficiency standards may be allowed to continue in special education until age 22.

Pupils whose educational needs are due primarily to unfamiliarity with the English language, temporary physical disabilities, social maladjustments, or environmental, cultural, or economic factors are not *individuals with exceptional needs*.[3]

2. *Special education* means a specially designed course of instruction at no cost to the parent to meet the unique needs of individuals with exceptional needs whose educational needs cannot be met with a modification of a regular instruction program. Special education also provides related services that may be needed to assist these individuals to benefit from the specially designed instruction. The intent of special education is to promote maximum interaction between children or youth with disabilities and children or youth who are not disabled in a manner that is appropriate for the needs of both. There is a full continuum of program options to meet the educational and service requirements of individuals with exceptional needs in the least restrictive environment.[4]

3. *Severely disabled* means individuals with exceptional needs who require intensive instruction, training, and programs for people with the following profound difficulties:

(a) autism, which is defined to include the following:[5]

---

3. Educ. Code § 56026(e); 5 CCR § 3030.
4. Educ. Code § 56031. While this chapter deals with special education for handicapped children, programs are available for handicapped adults, *see e.g.,* Educ. Code § 44345 on Community College Programs. These programs generally focus on physical handicaps and involve MHPs to a much lesser extent.
5. 5 CCR § 3030(g).

(1) an inability to use oral speech for appropriate conversation;

(2) a history of extreme withdrawal or relating to people inappropriately and continued impairment in social interaction from infancy through early childhood;

(3) an obsession to maintain sameness;

(4) an extreme preoccupation with objects or inappropriate use of objects, or both;

(5) extreme resistance to controls;

(6) peculiar motor mannerisms and motility patterns; and

(7) self-stimulating, ritualistic behavior.

(b) blindness;

(c) deafness;

(d) severe orthopedic impairment;

(e) serious emotional disturbances;[6]

(f) severe mental retardation; and

(g) those individuals who would have been ineligible for enrollment in a developmental center for handicapped students under prior law.[7]

4. An *Individualized Education Program* (IEP hereafter) is a report prepared by a team of professionals, referred to as the IEP team. The IEP contains the following information:

(a) the present levels of the pupil's educational performance;

(b) the annual goals for the pupil, including short-term instructional objectives;

(c) the specific special educational instruction and related services;

(d) the extent to which the pupil will be able to participate in regular educational programs;

(e) the projected date for initiation and the anticipated duration of programs and services;

---

6. A serious emotional disturbance means exhibiting one or more of the following characteristics over a long period of time and to a marked degree that adversely affects educational performance: (1) an inability to learn that cannot be explained by intellectual, sensory, or health factors; (2) an inability to build or maintain satisfactory interpersonal relationships with peers and teachers; (3) inappropriate types of behaviors or feelings under normal circumstances exhibited in several situations; (4) a general pervasive mood of unhappiness or depression; and (5) a tendency to develop physical symptoms or fears associated with personal or school problems. 5 CCR § 3030(c) .

7. Educ. Code § 56030.5.

(f) appropriate objective criteria, evaluation procedures, and schedules for determining, at least annually, whether the short-term instructional objectives are being met.[8]

The IEP can also include the following:

(g) prevocational career education for pupils in kindergarten and grades one through six;

(h) vocational education, career education, or work experience education, or any combination of the three, in preparation for employment, including independent living skills training for pupils in grades seven through twelve;

(i) any alternative means and modes necessary for the pupil to complete the district's prescribed course of study and meet the proficiency standards for graduation;

(j) for students whose primary language is other than English, linguistically appropriate goals, objectives, programs, and services;

(k) extended school-year services when needed;

(l) provision for the transition into regular class programs if the pupil is to be transferred from special classes or non-public, non-sectarian schools into regular classes for any part of the school day; and

(m) for pupils with low incidence disabilities, special education services, materials, and equipment.[9]

5. The IEP team includes the following members:

(a) a representative designated by the school administration who may be an administrator, program specialist, or other specialist knowledgeable of program options appropriate for the pupil, but who cannot be the pupil's teacher;

(b) the pupil's present teacher, or if the pupil does not presently have a teacher, the teacher who has the most recent and complete knowledge of the pupil and has observed the pupil's educational performance; and

(c) one or both of the pupil's parents or a representative selected by the parents for both.

Where appropriate, the team may also include the following:

(d) the individual with exceptional needs;

(e) other individuals whose knowledge or expertise is necessary for the development of the IEP; and

---

8. Educ. Code § 56345.
9. Id.

(f) if the individual with the exceptional needs has been assessed, a person who has conducted the assessment of the pupil, or a person who is knowledgeable about the assessment and is qualified to interpret the results.[10]

6. *Low incidence disabilities* means a severe handicapping condition with an expected incidence rate of less than one percent of the total state-wide enrollment in kindergarten through grade twelve. A *severe handicapping condition* means hearing impairments, vision impairments, and severe orthopedic impairments, or any combination of those conditions.[11]

7. *Positive behavioral interventions* may be developed by an IEP team as part of a behavioral intervention plan. Such plans are based on a functional analysis assessment conducted under the supervision of a person who has documented training in behavior analysis, with an emphasis on positive behavioral interventions. The behavioral interventions may include the following:

(a) altering the identified antecedent event to prevent the occurrence of the behavior;

(b) teaching the individual alternative behaviors that produce the same consequences as the inappropriate behaviors (e.g., teaching the individual to make requests or protests using socially acceptable behavior);

(c) teaching the individual adaptive behavior such as choice-making, self-management, relaxation techniques, and general skill development, which ameliorate the negative conditions that promote the display of inappropriate behavior; and

(d) manipulating the consequences for the display of targeted inappropriate behaviors and alternative acceptable behaviors, so that it is the alternative behaviors that more effectively produce the desired outcome.[12]

(B) IEP Team

The parents have the right to present information to the IEP team in person or through a representative, and have the right to participate in meetings relating to eligibility for special education services.[13]

---

10. Educ. Code § 56341(d).
11. Educ. Code § 56026.5; 5 CCR §§ 3030, 3031.
12. 5 CCR § 3052(a) & (b).
13. Educ. Code § 56341.

The IEP team meets whenever the pupil has received an initial formal assessment or any subsequent assessment. The team also meets whenever the pupil demonstrates a lack of anticipated progress or upon request of the parent or teacher. The team must meet at least annually to review the pupil's progress via an IEP, to review the appropriateness of the placements, and to make any necessary revisions. [14]

All referrals for special-education–related services lead to an assessment and initial assessment plan. [15] The assessments are required to be administered by qualified personnel who are competent in both the oral or sign–language skills and written skills of the individual's primary language or mode of communication, and who have a knowledge and understanding of the cultural and ethnic background of the person. [16]

(C) Referral and Special Education Evaluation

The Board of Education is required to adopt rules and regulations to effectuate the full education program. Among these standards are size and scope standards for use by districts, special-education local plan areas, and county offices. The Board of Education is also to adopt uniform rules and regulations relating to parental due-process rights. [17] The statutory scheme requires each district to develop a local plan that involves special and regular teachers selected by peers and parents. [18]

The special-education process requires the establishment of various plans and has resulted in a number of hearings that have lead to the enactment of an Alternate Dispute Resolution pilot program. This pilot program is intended to provide an omnibus person who shall receive issues or grievances submitted by parents, individuals, public agencies, or organizations, and bring the issues to the attention of the public education agency, or provide advice regarding available resources and options and propose a solution and systematic change. The program is also intended to allow a district, special-education local plan area, or county office to use a mediator to provide a structured process that allows parents, pupils, and public education agencies a voluntary

---

14. Educ. Code § 56343.
15. 5 CCR §§ 3021; 3022.
16. 5 CCR § 3023.
17. Educ. Code § 56100.
18. Educ. Code § 56171.

method to reach a settlement of their differences.[19] In developing the local plans, school districts are required to actively involve special and regular teachers selected by their peers and parents selected by their peers.[20] Community advisory committees are also established and composed of parents of individuals with exceptional needs enrolled in public and private schools, parents of other pupils enrolled in schools, pupils and adults with disabilities, regular and special education teachers and other school personnel, representatives of other public and private agencies, and persons concerned with the needs of individuals with exceptional needs.[21]

Each district's special-education local plan area or county offices are required to provide for the identification and assessment of an individual's exceptional needs and the planning of a structural program to meet these assessed needs. Identification procedures include systemic methods of utilizing referrals of pupils from teachers, parents, agencies, or appropriate professional persons, and other members of the public. These procedures are coordinated with school site procedures for the referral of pupils with needs that cannot be met with modification of the regular instructional program.[22]

(D) Placement in a Special Education Program

Once an initial evaluation has been conducted, a meeting is held to determine to what extent the pupil is eligible for special education, and to ascertain what category of impairment the pupil has. Whenever an assessment of the development or revision of an IEP is to be conducted, the pupil's parents shall be given a written notice of the proposed assessment plan within 15 days of the referral for assessment. Certain other time periods may apply, depending on the time of the school year. Attached to the assessment plan is a copy of a notice to the parent of the rights they have with regard to the assessment plan. Further, a written explanation of all procedural safeguards under the federal Individuals with Disabilities Education Act and under California law must be included in the notice to parents of their rights. This notice must include information on the procedures for requesting an informal meeting, a prehearing mediation conference, a medi-

19. Educ. Code § 56138.
20. Educ. Code § 56171.
21. Educ. Code § 56192.
22. Educ. Code § 56302.

ation conference, or a due-process hearing. The timelines for completing each process, whether the process is optional, and the type of representatives that can participate must also be disclosed.

The proposed assessment plan given to parents must meet the following requirements:

1. in a language easily understood by the general public;
2. provided in the primary language of the parent or other mode of communication used by the parent, unless to do so is not clearly feasible;
3. explain the types of assessments to be conducted; and
4. state that no IEP will result from the assessment without the consent of the parent.

No assessment shall be conducted unless the written consent of the parent is obtained prior to the assessment, except where the public education agency prevails in a due-process hearing relating to such an assessment.[23]

Individuals with exceptional needs who are placed in a public hospital, state-licensed children's hospital, psychiatric hospital, proprietary hospital, or a health facility for medical purposes are still the educational responsibility of the school district, special-education local plan area, or county office in which the hospital or facility is located.[24]

The testing assessment materials must be selected and administered so as not to be racially, culturally, or sexually discriminatory. The tests and assessment materials must also be provided and administered in the pupil's primary language or mode of communication unless that is not feasible. The tests and other assessment materials must have been validated for the specific purpose for which they are used, and must be administered by trained personnel in conformance with the instructions provided by the producer of such test materials. However, individually administered tests of intellectual or emotional functioning must be administered by a psychometrist or credentialed school psychologist (see chapter 1.7) where available. The test and assessment materials must include those tailored to assess specific areas of educational need, not just tests designed to produce a single general-intelligence quotient. The test must be selected and administered to best ensure that when a test is administered to a pupil with impaired sensory, manual, or speaking skills, the test

---

23. Educ. Code § 65321.
24. Educ. Code § 56167.

results accurately reflect the pupil's aptitude and achievement level.

The pupil is to be assessed in all areas related to suspected disability, including, where appropriate, health and development; vision; hearing; motor abilities; language function; general ability; academic performance; self-help, orientation, and mobility skills; career and vocational abilities and interests; and social and emotional status. Where appropriate, a developmental history is obtained.[25] Any psychological assessment of pupils must be conducted by an credentialed school psychologist (*see* chapter 1.7) who is trained and prepared to assess cultural and ethnic factors appropriate to the pupil being assessed. Any health assessment must be conducted by a credentialed school nurse or physician who is trained and prepared to assess cultural and ethnic factors appropriate to the student being assessed.[26]

The IEP team prepares a written report that includes, but is not limited to the following:

1. whether the pupil may need special education and related services;
2. the basis for making that determination;
3. the relevant behavior of the pupil noted during observation in an appropriate setting;
4. the relationship of that observed behavior to the pupil's academic and social functioning;
5. the educationally relevant health, developmental, and medical findings, if any;
6. for pupils with learning disabilities, whether there is such a discrepancy between achievement and ability that it cannot be corrected without special education and related services;
7. a determination of the effects of environmental, cultural, or economic disadvantages wherever appropriate; and
8. the need for specialized services, materials, and equipment for pupils with low incidence disabilities.[27]

Parents of a pupil will be given written notice that he or she may obtain a copy of the findings of the assessment. The notice shall include a statement that an IEP team conference will be scheduled, including the parent and his or her representatives, to discuss the assessment, the educational recommendations, and the reasons for the recommendations. The notice must also say the parent has a right to obtain at public expense an independent

---

25. Educ. Code § 56320.
26. Educ. Code § 56324.
27. Educ. Code § 56327.

educational assessment of the pupil from qualified specialists if a parent disagrees with an assessment.

Once the meeting has taken place, after a determination is made as to the assessment of the student, the program options include

1. individual and group consulting of the pupil and/or parents;
2. consultation with pupils, parents, teachers, and others regarding the effect of family and social factors on the pupil's learning and development;
3. developing a network of community resources for the pupil and family;[28] and
4. designated instruction and services to be provided by the regular class teacher, the special class teacher, or a resource specialty. The services may include but are not limited to
   (a) language and speech development and remediation;[29]
   (b) audiological services;[30]
   (c) orientation and mobility instruction;[31]
   (d) instruction in the home or hospital;[32]
   (e) adapted physical education;[33]
   (f) physical and occupational therapy;[34]
   (g) vision services and therapy;[35]
   (h) specialized driver-training instruction;[36]
   (i) counseling and guidance;[37]
   (j) psychological services other than assessment and development of IEP (providing a credentialed or licensed psychologist or other qualified person to the pupil and/or parents);[38]
   (k) parental counseling and training;[39]
   (l) health and nurse services;[40]
   (m) social worker services;[41]

---

28. 5 CCR § 3051.13.
29. 5 CCR § 3051.1.
30. 5 CCR § 3051.2.
31. 5 CCR § 3051.3.
32. 5 CCR § 3051.4.
33. 5 CCR § 3051.5.
34. 5 CCR § 3051.6
35. 5 CCR §§ 3051.7, 3051.75.
36. 5 CCR § 3051.8.
37. 5 CCR § 3051.9.
38. 5 CCR § 3051.10.
39. 5 CCR § 3051.11.
40. 5 CCR § 3051.12.
41. 5 CCR § 3051.13.

(n) specially designed vocational education and career development;[42]

(o) recreational services;[43] and

(p) specialized services for individuals with low incidence disabilities, such as readers, transcribers, and vision and hearing services.[44]

5. as needed, the continuum may include special classes and centers that enroll pupils with similar and more intensive education needs. The classes and centers enroll pupils when the nature or severity of the disability precludes their participation in the regular school program for the majority of the schoolday. The intent, however, is that this shall occur only when the nature and severity of the handicap is such that education and regular classes with the use of supplementary aids and services will not be adequate;[45]

6. nonpublic and nonsectarian schools are to be maintained and continued as an alternative special education service. These schools are developed pursuant to written contracts with the school district. The institutions must be evaluated and certified before they can be so used;[46] and

7. state special schools, which are to be used only when an IEP team recommends so, based upon a finding that no appropriate placement is available in the local area. Referrals for further assessment and referrals to the California School for the Deaf and Blind or the Diagnostic School for Neurologically Handicapped Children do not constitute such placements;[47]

Resource specialists are assigned to regular classroom teachers for the majority of the schoolday to provide instruction and services for the pupil.[48]

Under certain circumstances, early education for individuals with exceptional needs may be provided, as well as home-based education.[49]

Once the initial placement has occurred, parents and pupils may initiate a series of hearings to contest the assessment.

---

42. 5 CCR § 3051.14.
43. 5 CCR § 3051.15.
44. 5 CCR § 3051.16.
45. Educ. Code §§ 56361, 56364.
46. Educ. Code §§ 56361, 56366.
47. Educ. Code §§ 56367, 56361.
48. Educ. Code §§ 56361, 56362.
49. Educ. Code §§ 56425 to 56430.

(E) Parental Rights/Due Process

As noted above, before an assessment begins the parents must receive written notice and give written consent. The notices to the parents about the assessment must be in language understood by the parents and must state the right to attend the meetings that affect the student's qualification for special education. As noted above, the assessments must be conducted by individuals who are conscious of ethnic, cultural, and sexual bias so as to most accurately reflect the child's needs. The parents have the opportunity to request independent assessment by qualified specialists at the public expense; however, if the request occurs after a due-process hearing, it is at the parent's expense.[50]

A due-process hearing can be requested by a written request filed with the school's superintendent and provided to the other party. Within three days following the receipt by the agency of a copy of such a request, the agency shall advise the parent of free or low-cost legal services and other relevant services available within the geographic area. Within 45 days after receipt of the written hearing request, the hearing must be commenced, including any mediation, and a final administrative decision must be rendered unless a continuance has been granted.[51] The public education agency and the parents may meet informally to try to resolve the issues regarding identification, assessment, or educational placement of the child. Such informal meetings are conducted by the district superintendent, county superintendent, or director of the public education agency, or their designee.[52] When a superintendent receives a written request by a parent for a hearing, he or she must notify the parties of a proposed date for a mediation conference with notice, which also includes all rights regarding procedural safeguards, including the right to waive a mediation conference. At that point, the superintendent must also inform the public education agency of his or her responsibility to advise the parent of free or low-cost legal services or the relevant services in the area.[53]

The mediation conference is intended to be an intervening informal process conducted in a nonadversarial atmosphere before an administrative due-process hearing. The conference generally must be completed within 15 days of receipt of the request for the due-process hearing.

---

50. Educ. Code § 56329.
51. Educ. Code § 56502.
52. *Id.*
53. *Id.*

Before the mediation, a parent has the right to examine and receive copies of any documents contained in the pupil's file maintained by the public education agency. Based on the mediation conference, the issues may be resolved; however, such a resolution cannot conflict with state or federal law and must be to the satisfaction of both parties. If resolved, a written resolution is mailed to both sides within 10 days, and a copy is filed with the advisory commission on special education. If the mediation conference fails to resolve the issues, a state-level hearing is held. If the mediation conference is unsuccessful, the mediator shall list all unresolved issues, which shall be reviewed and approved by the parties initiating the hearing. The list of issues then becomes the basis for the state level hearing.[54]

The due-process hearing is required in part by the federal law.[55] The hearing can be initiated whether it is a proposal to initiate or a refusal to initiate or change the identification, assessment, or educational placement of the child. In addition, such a hearing may be requested when the parent refuses to consent to the assessment of the child.[56] At a due-process hearing the parent has the right to (a) examine pupil records, (b) have the pupil who is the subject of the hearing present at the hearing, and (c) have the hearing opened to the public.[57]

The hearing must be conducted by a person knowledgeable in administrative hearings under contract with the Department of Education. The parents and school representatives to the hearing have the right to be accompanied and advised by counsel and by individuals with special knowledge or training relating to the problems of handicapped children. Both sides have the right to present evidence, cross-examine, compel the attendance of witnesses, and submit written and oral arguments. A written or electronic verbatim record of the hearing is made. The hearing officer submits written findings of fact and a decision. No evidence can be introduced that has not been disclosed five days prior to the hearing. If the decision of the hearing is adverse, either party can exercise a right to appeal to a Superior Court, however, an appeal does not automatically stay the final administrative determination.[58]

The due-process rights of pupil and parent include the following rights:

---

54. Educ. Code § 56503.
55. Educ. Code §§ 56500.1, 56500.2; 20 U.S.C. § 1400 et. seq.
56. Educ. Code § 56501.
57. Educ. Code; *Nevada County Office of Education v. Superintendent of Public Instruction,* 149 Cal.App.3d 767 (1983).
58. Educ. Code § 56505.

1. to be accompanied and advised by counsel and by individuals with special knowledge or training relating to children or youths with disabilities;
2. to present evidence and oral and written arguments;
3. to confront, cross-examine, and compel the attendance of witnesses;
4. to a written or electronic verbatim record of the hearing;
5. to written findings of fact and decisions;
6. to be informed at least 10 days prior to the hearing of the issues to be decided. Upon request of a parent who does not have an attorney, the hearing agency shall provide a mediator to assist the parent in formulating issues and proposing a resolution; and
7. to prohibit introduction of any evidence not disclosed at least five days before the hearing.[59]

The public education agency is not entitled to use an attorney for the actual presentation of its written argument, oral argument, or evidence unless certain criteria are met, such as notifying the parent in advance that the agency will use an attorney. In addition, the agency must provide to the parent a listing of attorneys knowledgeable in mediation conferences, IEP meetings, and state hearings. Under certain circumstances, the agency may be required to pay for the parent's attorney.[60]

---

59. Educ. Code § 56507.
60. Educ. Code § 56505.

5A.21

Services for Minors— Consent and Confidentiality

This chapter discusses the extent to which a minor can obtain mental health services and/or treatment for narcotics addiction without his or her parents' consent, and the extent to which a minor's therapy with an MHP is considered confidential against a request for disclosure by the parents. This chapter also addresses the issue of the extent of a minor's privacy rights beyond confidentiality.

(A) Definition of Mental Health Treatment or Counseling

For the purposes of the Family Code, mental health treatment or counseling services are defined to mean mental health treatment, on an outpatient basis, by any of the following providers:

1. a governmental agency;
2. a person or agency under contract to a governmental agency to provide such services;
3. an agency that receives funding from community united funds;
4. a runaway house or crisis resolution center; or
5. a professional person.

A professional person is defined to mean a marriage, family, and child counselor; licensed educational psychologist; credentialed school psychologist; clinical psychologist; the chief administrator of a governmental agency providing mental health treatment or counseling; or a person designated as an MHP in the regulations.[1]

Because psychiatrists and psychiatric nurses are also covered by laws governing medical care, this chapter discusses the provision of such care to minors. *Medical care* is defined as x-ray examination, anesthetic, medical, or surgical diagnosis or treatment and hospital care under general or special supervision, and upon the advice of, or to be rendered by, a physician.[2]

(B) Consent by a Minor to Medical Services

When a minor is 16 or older, the consent of a parent or guardian is necessary to permit medical care, but if the minor has no parent or guardian available to give consent, a minor may apply to a court for consent.[3]

In addition, a minor may consent to medical care if the following criteria are met:

1. the minor is 15 years of age or older;
2. the minor is living separate and apart from his or her parents or guardian (with or without the parents or guardian's consent); and
3. the minor is managing his or her own financial affairs, regardless of the source of his or her income.

However, where medical or mental health services are provided to minors without their parents' or guardian's consent, the parents (or guardian) are not liable for the services provided. With or without the consent of the minor patient, a physician is allowed by law to advise the minor's parents or guardian of the treatment that has been given or is needed if the physician has a reason to know, on the basis of information provided by the minor, the whereabouts of the parent or guardian.[4]

---

1. Fam. Code § 6924.
2. Fam. Code § 6902.
3. *Id.*
4. Fam. Code § 6922.

(C) Consent to Mental Heath Services

A minor who is 12 or older may consent to mental health treatment or counseling on an out-patient basis if the following criteria are met:

1. the minor is mature enough, in the opinion of the attending professional person, to participate intelligently in the outpatient services; and

2. the minor would present a danger of serious physical or mental harm to self or others without the mental health treatment or counseling; or

3. the minor is alleged to be a victim of incest or child abuse.[5]

However, a minor cannot receive electroconvulsive therapy, psychosurgery, or psychotropic drugs without the consent of the minor's parents or guardian.

A minor may also consent to medical care related to the prevention or treatment of pregnancy but cannot be sterilized without his or her parent or guardian's consent. A minor cannot receive an abortion without the consent of the parent or guardian, except as provided in the Therapeutic Abortion Act (*see* chapter 5A.22).[6] MHPs who are counseling or treating pregnant minors should be aware of the consent requirement.

A minor who is 12 or older, and who has alleged to have been sexually assaulted or raped, may consent to medical care relating to the diagnosis or treatment of the condition and the collection of medical evidence.[7] An MHP treating a sexually abused minor should be aware of the extent to which the minor can consent to both medical and psychological care.

(D) Treatment for Narcotic Addiction

A minor who is 12 years of age or older may consent to medical care and counseling relating to the diagnosis and treatment of a drug or alcohol-related problem. The treatment plan must include the involvement of the minor's parent or guardian, if determined by the professional person or treatment facility to be appropriate. The professional person must state in the minor's treatment record whether and when attempts were made to contact the parent or guardian, and whether the attempts were successful. The pro-

---

5. Fam. Code § 6924(b).
6. Fam. Code § 6925.
7. Fam. Code §§ 6927, 6928.

fessional person must also state why, in his or her opinion, it would be appropriate or inappropriate to contact the parent or guardian.[8]

(E) Privacy Rights for MHP Services

A minor has rights to privacy and confidentiality that are substantially similar to those of adults. However, the fact that an individual is a minor may allow those rights to be subordinated to a compelling state interest or a particular law.[9]

A professional person, as defined above, who is providing mental health treatment or counseling to a minor, is required to attempt to contact the minor's parent or guardian to involve them in the minor's treatment, unless, in the professional person's opinion, it would be inappropriate.[10] The professional person is required to note in the client's records when and where he or she attempted to contact the parent or guardian, and must state his or her opinion as to whether it would be appropriate to contact the parent or guardian.[11] The statute contemplates, but does not specify, that the professional person will advise the parent or guardian that the minor is receiving mental health treatment and request them to participate in the treatment. In fact, the parent or guardian is only liable for the mental health treatment to the extent that the services are rendered with the parent or guardian's participation.[12]

A professional person providing medical treatment to a minor who has been a victim of a sexual assault is also required to contact a minor's parent or guardian unless the parent or guardian is believed to have committed the assault. As with mental health services, the professional person is required to note in the records the date and time of the attempt to contact the parent or guardian and whether the attempt was successful or unsuccessful.[13]

The Evidence Code provides that where a minor has been provided mental health treatment under these sections, the MHP can invoke the psychotherapist–patient privilege on behalf of the minor. This would allow the MHP to refuse to disclose informa-

---

8. Fam. Code § 6929.
9. *American Academy of Pediatrics v. Van de Kamp*, 214 Cal.App.3d 831 (1989), which upheld a preliminary injunction against a portion of the Therapeutic Abortion Act, requiring unemancipated minors to have parental consent for abortion. *See* chapter 5A.22.
10. Fam. Code § 6924(c).
11. *Id.*
12. Fam. Code § 6924(e).
13. Fam. Code § 6928.

tion to third parties and to not testify about the minor's communications. However, if a report is required under the Child Abuse Reporting Act, such a report would still have to be made as discussed in chapter 5A.8. Additionally, the psychotherapist–patient privilege does not apply when the minor is under 16 and the MHP has reasonable cause to believe that the minor has been the victim of a crime and that the disclosure of the communication is in the minor's best interest.[14]

Where a parent does participate in treatment, but only for the purposes of the child, no psychotherapist–patient relationship arises between the parent and the therapist.[15] In one case a child was the subject of a juvenile dependency hearing based on his alleged molestation by his father. The father sought to call the child's psychotherapist as a witness in the dependency proceedings. He asserted that, as a parent, he was entitled to obtain information about the child's confidential communications to the therapist. The court considered the various statutes, including the right of a parent to have access to a child's records and concluded that no statute gave a parent the right to demand disclosure of the confidential communications made by a minor to a psychotherapist. Instead, the court noted that the parents' entitlement to information depended on the facts of the case and that, except in very special circumstances, parents should be denied access to the records and testimony of a child's psychotherapist.[16]

---

14. Evid. Code § 1027; *People v. Stritzinger*, 34 Cal.3d 505 (1983).
15. *Schwarz v. Regents of the University of California*, 226 Cal.App.3d 149 (1990).
16. *In Re Daniel C.H.*, 220 Cal.App.3d 814 (1990).

5A.22

Consent for Abortion

MHPs who are treating adults should be aware of the circumstances in which their patients may obtain abortions. In addition, MHPs who provide mental health services to sexually active minors (including MHPs working in the schools) should be aware of the circumstances under which minors may consent to an abortion. The extent to which minors can consent to other medical or mental health services is discussed in chapter 5A.21. This chapter discusses the circumstances under which abortions may be performed on adults or minors, exceptions to the parental consent requirement for unemancipated minors, and penalties for illegal abortions.

(A) Therapeutic Abortion Act

Generally, adults can consent to abortions so long as the statutory criteria are met. While parental consent can be required for performing an abortion on an unemancipated minor, the U.S. Supreme Court has ruled that it is Constitutionally impermissible for a state to give parents a right to disapprove an emancipated minor's consent for an abortion.[1]

However, California enacted a statute that requires unemancipated minors to obtain parental or guardian consent for an abortion.[2] A minor may petition the court, however, for an order allowing an abortion. Under California's general abortion

---

1. *Planned Parenthood of Central Missouri v. Danforth*, 428 U.S. 52 (1976).
2. Health & Safety Code § 25958.

statute, the Therapeutic Abortion Act,[3] a doctor is allowed to perform an abortion or assist in an abortion only if the following conditions are met:

1. the abortion takes place in a hospital accredited by the Joint Commission on Accreditation of Hospitals;
2. the abortion is approved in advance by a committee of medical staff of the hospital, consisting of no more than three licensed physicians who unanimously consent; and
3. the committee finds that either there is a substantial risk that continuance of the pregnancy would gravely impair the physical and mental health of the mother, or the pregnancy resulted from rape or incest.

The statutory requirements for therapeutic abortion must be comprehensible to a patient and where they are vague, the physician has standing to assert the patient's rights.[4] As with any other medical procedure, an abortion that is not competently performed may lead to a successful malpractice action.[5]

(B) Authorization for an Abortion Based on Rape or Incest

Upon receipt of an application for an abortion on the grounds that the pregnancy resulted from rape or incest, the hospital's committee of the medical staff must immediately notify the district attorney in the county in which the alleged rape or incest occurred. The committee must send the district attorney the applicant's affidavit attesting to the alleged rape or incest.

If the district attorney informs the committee that there is probable cause to believe a rape or incest occurred, the committee may approve the abortion.[6] If the committee does not receive a reply from the district attorney within five days of the notice, the committee may approve the abortion.

If the district attorney advises the committee that there is not probable cause to believe a rape or incest occurred, the abortion shall not be approved unless the person who applied for the

---

3. Health & Safety Code § 25950.
4. *See People v. Barksdale*, 8 Cal.3d 320 (1972), in which a physician was charged with performing an abortion without complying with the requirements of the Therapeutic Abortion Act. The California Supreme Court upheld the dismissal of the charges and found parts of the act to violate due-process rights.
5. *Stills v. Gratton*, 55 Cal.App.3d 698 (1976).
6. Health & Safety Code § 25952.

abortion successfully petitions the Superior Court for the locality in which the rape or incest allegedly occurred. If such a petition is filed, the district attorney must file an affidavit with the court stating the reasons for concluding that no rape or incest occurred. Evidence or witnesses may be offered. If the court finds by a preponderance of the evidence that the pregnancy resulted from a rape or incest, the court shall issue an order to that effect. The committee may then approve the abortion. The court may hold hearings on the petition *in chambers* and without a formal record.

(C) Medical Personnel Not Required to Perform Abortion

Under California law, no employer can require a physician, registered nurse, licensed vocational nurse, or any other person employed by, or with staff privileges at, a hospital to participate in an abortion if that person has filed a written statement indicating a moral, ethical, or religious basis for refusal to participate in the abortion, nor can such a person be subject to discipline or penalty for refusing to participate in an abortion.[7]

(D) Exception to Consent Requirement

Except in a medical emergency requiring immediate medical action, no abortion shall be performed upon an unemancipated minor unless she has first given written consent to the abortion and has obtained the written consent of one of her parents or legal guardian. If one or both of the minor's parents or guardian refuse to consent to the abortion, or if the minor elects not to seek the consent of one or both of the parents, the minor may file a petition with the Juvenile Court. The court shall assist the minor, or the person designated by the minor, in preparing a petition and notices required. The court shall ensure that the minor's identity is kept confidential and shall upon request appoint counsel to represent the minor. A hearing must occur within three days of the filing of the petition. At the hearing, the court shall consider the evidence and determine either:

---

7. Health & Safety Code § 25955.

1. that the minor is sufficiently mature and informed to make the decision on her own and that the minor has consented to the abortion, in which case the court shall grant the petition; or
2. that the minor is not sufficiently mature and informed to make a decision whether the abortion would be in her best interest.

If the court finds that the abortion would be in the minor's best interest, the court shall grant the petition without the consent of, or notice to, the parents or guardian. Judgment is required to be entered within one court day of the submission of the matter.[8]

(E) Penalty for Illegal Abortion

It is a misdemeanor punishable by up to 30 days in jail and $1,000 fine for any person to knowingly perform an abortion on an unmarried or unemancipated minor without complying with the requirements of the law.[9]

---

8. The U.S. Supreme Court has accepted parental notice requirements in other states. *Hodgson v. Minnesota*, 497 U.S. 417 (1990); *Ohio v. Akron Center for Reproductive Health*, 497 U.S. 502 (1990).
9. Health & Safety Code § 25958; *American Academy of Pediatrics v. Van de Kamp*, 214 Cal.App.3d 831 (1989).

5A.23

Evaluation and Treatment of Children at the Request of a Noncustodial Parent

MHPs may be requested to evaluate or treat a child by a parent who does not have physical custody of the child. MHPs should be aware in responding to such requests of the extent to which they should be complied with, and the related issue of the extent to which a noncustodial parent can obtain information on a child's therapy from the therapist.

(A) Noncustodial Parent's Rights in General

A noncustodial parent may request mental health services for a child, or ask an MHP to state opinions regarding the child's mental condition, in a custody proceeding. If a parent does not have joint custody, there generally is no basis for the noncustodial parent to intrude upon the control that the court has entrusted to the other party. However, given the presumptions favoring joint custody, both parties often have joint legal custody, but one party has primary physical custody. Generally, the parent with primary physical custody can select what medical or mental health care a child receives, and the other parent can contest this decision in court. If a parent has neither physical nor legal custody, the MHP's provision of services to the minor could put him or her at risk of some type of litigation by the other parent.[1]

---

1. Fam. Code § 30225 (former Civil Code § 4600.5).

(B) Providing Information to Noncustodial Parent

Generally, a parent has no entitlement to breach the child's psychotherapist–patient privilege.[2]

In one case, a psychotherapist was treating a child whose parents were getting a divorce. The parents had joint legal and physical custody, but the father then agreed to let the mother have sole physical custody based on the therapist's recommendation. The father met with the therapist several times for the purpose of his son's treatment. The wife then abducted the son and moved him to Europe. The father filed suit against the therapist and others for conniving with the wife in the abduction, but the Court of Appeals held that the therapist owed a duty only to the child, not to the parent.[3] Thus, even when a parent technically had joint legal custody, no claim could be asserted against the therapist.

Given the emphasis on confidentiality in California law and a minor's statutory confidentiality rights (*see* chapter 5A.21), an MHP would be at risk if he or she provides information to a noncustodial parent except insofar as specifically authorized by statute.

---

2. *In re Daniel C. H.*, 220 Cal.App.3d 814 (1990), where a child was allegedly sexually abused by the father and in the custody of his mother, and the court refused to let the child's psychotherapist testify. This case strongly articulates the child's right of confidentiality. *Bellah v. Greenson*, 81 Cal.App.3d 614 (1987).
3. *Schwarz v. Regents of the University of California*, 226 Cal.App.3d 149 (1990).

5A.24

Duty to Report Injuries From Criminal Conduct

A new statute that may require some MHPs to make reports to law enforcement officials where the MHP knows or reasonably suspects a patient has been the victim of certain specified crimes—generally crimes of violence or sexual abuse. Because the duties imposed by this law are intended to be as broad in scope as the Child Abuse Reporting Act (*see* chapter 5A.8), it is important for MHPs to be aware of the reporting law and how it applies to them. This chapter also discusses the extent to which the required reports are an exception to the psychotherapist–patient and physician–patient privileges (*see* chapter 4.2), as well as the statutory immunity from suit given to MHPs who make reports.

(A) Duty to Report

California law requires certain designated health practitioners employed in a health facility, clinic, physician's office, or local or state public health department who in their professional capacity provide medical services for a physical condition to a patient who has suffered from any wound or injury inflicted by means of a knife, gun, or other deadly weapon to report such wounds or injuries to specified law enforcement officers. Recently this statute was amended to also require reporting of wounds or physical injuries resulting from assault or abusive conduct as defined in the statute.[1] Under the new law, any health practitioner em-

---

1. Penal Code § 11160. The law originally did not limit the reporting duty to health practitioners providing medical services for a physical condition. The statute was amended in 1994, effective January 1, 1995, to use the language "medical services for a physical condition." Unfortunately, the term "medical services" is still not defined, and is ambiguous.

ployed in a health facility, clinic, physician's office, or local or state public health department must make a report by telephone immediately or as soon as practically possible, and a written report within two working days, if a reporting situation exists.[2]

(B) Definitions

Health practitioner has the same meaning as in the Child Abuse Reporting Act: physicians and surgeons, psychiatrists, psychologists, dentists, residents, interns, registered nurses, MFCCs, psychological assistants, MFCC trainees, and religious practitioners who diagnose, examine, or treat children.[3]

The term *reasonably suspects* means that it is objectively reasonable for a person to entertain a certain suspicion, based upon facts that could cause suspicion in a reasonable person in a like position, drawing when appropriate, on his or her training and experience.[4]

The term *assaultive or abusive conduct* includes 24 types of conduct, including assaults with weapons ranging from stun guns to machine guns and knives, torture, murder, and manslaughter. The following acts are of particular importance to MHPs:

1. sexual battery;
2. incest;
3. spousal rape;
4. procuring any female to have sex with another man in violation of the law;
5. child abuse or endangerment;
6. spousal abuse;
7. lewd and lascivious acts with a child;
8. elder abuse; and
9. sodomy, oral copulation, or genital or anal penetration with a foreign object.

For the purposes of this statute, the term *injury* does not include any psychological or physical condition brought about solely through self-administration of a narcotic or a dangerous drug.[5]

---

2. Penal Code § 11160(b)(1-2).
3. Penal Code §§ 11165.8, 11162.5(a).
4. Penal Code § 11162.5(d).
5. Penal Code § 11160(c).

(C) Reporting Requirements

Reporting is required whenever any health practitioner employed in one of the settings specified knows or reasonably suspects a patient is suffering from either:

1. a wound or other injury inflicted by his or her own act or inflicted by another, or the injury is by a knife, firearm, or other deadly weapon; or

2. a wound or other physical injury where the injury is a result of assault or abusive conduct.[6]

Thus, as currently phrased, the reporting obligation would include a situation where an individual who is mentally disturbed inflicts a wound on himself or herself by means of a knife, firearm, or other deadly weapon.

Where a report is required under the Child Abuse and Neglect Reporting Act (*see* chapter 5A.8) or the Elder Abuse and Dependent Adult Civil Protection Act (*see* chapter 5A.7), no report would be required under the new law.

As with the Child Abuse Reporting Act, when two or more people are required to report and jointly have knowledge of a known or suspected instance of violence, they can agree to have one person make the report.[7]

The report is required to include, but is not limited to, the name of the injured person, if known, the injured person's whereabouts, the character and extent of the person's injuries, and the identity of any person the injured person alleges inflicted the wounds or injuries, or who engaged in assault or abusive conduct upon the injured person.[8]

A physician or surgeon who is treating a person coming within the scope of this act must make a report to a local law enforcement agency and include a copy of that report in the medical records. It is recommended that the medical records also include any comments by the injured person regarding past domestic violence or the name of any person suspected of inflicting a wound, injury, or engaging in assault or abusive conduct. A map of the injured person's body showing and identifying injuries and bruises when treated should be filled out and included in the medical records.[9]

---

6. Penal Code § 11160(a)(1-2).
7. Penal Code § 11160(e).
8. Penal Code § 11160(b)(4).
9. Penal Code § 11161.

(D) Immunity From Suit

When a report is made pursuant to the statute, a health practitioner has immunity from civil and criminal liability.[10] A health practitioner may provide access to a victim of a known or suspected instance of abuse upon request from an adult protective services agency or local law enforcement and is immune from civil or criminal liability as a result of allowing such access.[11]

In the event a health care provider is sued for making a report pursuant to the statute, even though immunity exists, he or she may be able to recover the costs of reasonable attorney fees from the Board of Control, as in similar situations under the Child Abuse Reporting Act (*see* chapter 5A.8). If the court dismisses such an action against a health practitioner upon a demurrer or motion for summary judgment, the Board of Control may pay the practitioner up to $50,000 for legal fees.[12]

(E) Privileges Inapplicable

In any court proceeding or administrative hearing, neither the physician–patient privilege nor the psychotherapist–patient privilege applies to the information required to be reported by this article. However, the reports are required to be kept confidential by the health facility, clinic, or physician's office that submitted the report and by law enforcement agencies, and can only be disclosed by local law enforcement agencies to those involved in the investigation of the report or in enforcement of a criminal law implicated by the report. In no case shall the person suspected or accused of inflicting the wound or injury or engaging in assault or abusive conduct or that person's attorney be allowed access to or informed of the injured person's whereabouts.[13]

It is not clear to what extent this statute may lead to litigation against health care providers, but if the Child Abuse Reporting statute is a fair example, several cases will probably be brought to test the parameters of the immunity.

---

10. Penal Code § 11161.9(a).
11. Penal Code § 11161.9(c).
12. Penal Code § 11163.
13. Penal Code § 11163.2.

(F) Penalties

A failure to report such injuries is a misdemeanor punishable by six months in jail and a fine not to exceed $1,000.[14]

---

14. Penal Code § 11162.

Other Civil Matters

5B.1

Mental Status of Licensed/Certified Professionals

As discussed in chapter 1.0, an MHP may be required to undergo physical and/or psychological examinations if his or her licensing agency believes that the MHP is impaired or unable to practice safely due to mental or physical illness or substance abuse. In this situation, MHPs are requested to evaluate other professionals to determine if they are impaired. This chapter discusses the circumstances in which such evaluations may be ordered, what actions the licensing agency can take when an impairment is found, and the conditions for reinstatement. Also discussed are legal challenges to such evaluations, and the evaluation and discipline of impaired attorneys.

(A) Evaluation of Licensees

(A)(1) Test for Ordering an Evaluation

When any person holding a license, certificate, or permit from a licensing agency under either the Department of Consumer Affairs or the mental health sections of the Business and Professions Code may be unable to practice his or her profession safely because of impairment due to mental or physical illness or chemical dependency, the licensing agency may order the individual to be examined by one or more physicians, surgeons, or psychologists designated by the agency.[1]

The requirements of the Business and Professions Code apply to MHPs and interns, registered nurses, licensed vocational

---

1. Bus. & Prof. Code § 820.

nurses, psychiatric technicians, doctors, podiatrists, dentists, chiropractors, and physical therapists. Failure to comply with an order compelling an examination constitutes grounds for the suspension or revocation of that individual's license or certificate.[2]

(A)(2) Discipline of Impaired Licensee

If a licensing board determines on the basis of an evaluation, that the individual's ability to practice his or her profession safely is impaired because of mental illness or physical illness or chemical dependency, the licensing board can take any of several steps, including

1. revoking the certificate or license;
2. suspending the right to practice;
3. placing the individual on probation; and
4. taking such other action as the agency in its discretion deems proper.

(*See* chapter 1.0(A) for the administrative procedure to revoke or suspend the licenses of individuals licensed by the Department of Consumer Affairs.)

(A)(3) Reinstatement of Licensee Previously Found to Be Impaired

Once a certificate or license has been suspended or revoked, it cannot be reinstated until the agency has received competent evidence of the absence of, or the control of the condition that caused the disciplinary action. In addition, in deciding to reinstate an individual whose license has been suspended or revoked, the agency must act with due regard for the public health and safety. The agency may impose terms and conditions to be complied with by the licensee after reinstatement, including, but not limited, to the following:

1. requiring the individual to obtain additional professional training and pass an examination upon the completion of the training;
2. requiring the individual to pass an oral, written, practical, or clinical examination, or any combination thereof, to demonstrate his or her present fitness to engage in the profession;
3. requiring the individual to submit to a complete diagnostic examination by one or more physicians and surgeons or psychologists appointed by the agency. If the agency requires the

---

2. Bus. & Prof. Code § 821; *Kees v. Board of Medical Quality Assurance*; 7 Cal.App.4th 1801 (1992); *Miller v. Board of Medical Quality Assurance*, 193 Cal.App.3d 1371 (1987).

individual to submit to such an examination, the agency shall receive and consider any other report of a complete diagnostic examination given by a physician or surgeon or psychologist of the licensee's choice;

4. requiring the licensee to undergo continuing treatment; and

5. restricting or limiting the extent, scope, or type of practice of the licensee.[3]

(A)(4) Closed Hearing on Impaired Licensees

Despite the general requirement that meetings of licensing agencies be public, a licensing agency may convene in closed session to consider any evidence relating to a licensee's mental or physical illness. However, the licensing agency may convene in closed session only to the extent it is necessary to protect the licensee's privacy.[4]

(A)(5) Confidentiality of Evaluation

If an evaluation is performed and it is determined that there is insufficient evidence to bring an action against the licensee, all agency records of the proceedings, including the order for examination, investigative reports, if any, and the report of the physicians or psychologists are to be kept confidential and are not subject to discovery or subpoena. If there are no further proceedings conducted to determine the licensee's fitness for a period of five years from the date of the agency's determination to proceed with an evaluation, the agency must purge and destroy all records pertaining to the proceedings. If new proceedings are instituted during the five-year period against the licensee, the records, including the report of physicians or psychologists, may be used in the proceedings and would then be available to the licensee under the discovery sections of the Government Code (*see* chapter 1.0).[5]

(A)(6) Legal Challenges to Evaluations

The authority of the agencies to conduct such evaluations has been challenged unsuccessfully as an unconstitutional violation of due process.[6]

---

3. Bus. & Prof. Code §§ 822, 823.
4. Bus. & Prof. Code § 827.
5. Bus. & Prof. Code § 828.
6. In *Smith v. Board of Medical Quality Assurance*, 202 Cal.App.3d 327-28 (1988), and *Alexander D. v. State Board of Dental Examiners*, 231 Cal.App.3d 92 (1991), the government's interest in protecting the public from unsafe or incompetent practitioners was held to be a compelling one that justified allowing such evaluations without full due-process protection.

At least one court has held that while repetitive mental examinations are permissible if there is a showing of good cause, in the absence of a showing of good cause, a licensee does not have to undergo a second psychiatric examination because a second examination would constitute an invasion of privacy.[7] In that case, the court construed Section 820 as allowing a mental examination only if such an examination is the least intrusive means of determining a licensee's mental condition. The court therefore concluded that the evaluation provision was not an unconstitutional invasion of privacy.

Participation in a diversion program for impaired practitioners does not preclude disciplinary action.[8]

(B) Mental or Physical Disease or Defect of Credentialed School Personnel

The Committee on Credentials of the Commission on Teacher Credentialing cannot initiate an administrative hearing solely on the ground that an applicant or licensee is suffering from a contagious and communicable disease, or other disease or defect of mind or body, unless probable cause[9] appears from the evidence that either

1. the condition of the applicant or licensee constitutes a health hazard to students or persons with whom the individual must associate in carrying out his or her duties, or

2. because of the disease or defect, the applicant or licensee is unable to perform his or her duties.[10]

Any denial, suspension, or revocation of a credential for physical or mental disease or defect is limited to the period of actual disability, and the credential is restored upon presentation of satisfactory evidence that the disability no longer exists.[11]

---

7. *Kees v. Board of Medical Quality Assurance,* 7 Cal.App.4th 1801, 1814-15 (1992); it should be clear, however, that the court there supported the initial psychiatric exam although it felt that it was overbroad.
8. *Id.* at 1809-11; *B. W. v. Board of Medical Quality Assurance,* 169 Cal.App.3d 219 (1985); Bus. & Prof. Code § 2340 et seq.; 16 CCR § 1357.
9. Probable cause is established when the weight of the evidence before the committee is sufficient to cause a majority of the committee to believe that the allegations of misconduct or unfitness are true and that an administrative hearing would result in denial, suspension, or revocation of the credential in issue. 5 CCR § 80310.
10. 5 CCR § 80309(a).
11. 5 CCR § 80309(b).

(B)(1) Psychiatric Examination

The Committee may require an applicant or licensee to submit to an examination by a designated licensed psychiatrist if it appears from the evidence the applicant or licensee has been under psychiatric treatment, within the prior year, as a condition of probation imposed by a court for acts that would constitute grounds for discipline. Such an examination may also be required when the applicant or licensee has committed acts or omissions that would constitute grounds for disciplinary action, but for the reasonably probable existence of some mental defect or disability.

The psychiatrist is required to prepare a written report that states his or her opinion as to whether the applicant or licensee is able to perform his or her duties, and if not, the probable duration and severity of the disability. The psychiatrist's fee for the examination is paid by the Commission.

An applicant or licensee's refusal to submit to a psychiatric examination within 30 days of service of a request for such an examination is ground for revocation or suspension of a credential. (This is an exception to the general requirement that proof of illness must be established before the Committee can revoke a credential.)[12]

(C) Evaluation and Discipline of Impaired Attorneys

The discipline of attorneys in California is governed by the Supreme Court, and a special tribunal called the State Bar Court hears attorney discipline cases.[13]

(C)(1) Test for Evaluation

If an attorney is believed to be subject to some type of mental or emotional disability that would prevent him or her from competently functioning, the State Bar can direct an examination to occur by an MHP.

(C)(2) Discipline of Impaired Attorney

When an attorney requires involuntary commitment or when he or she has been determined to be insane or mentally incompetent, or when a guardian or conservator has been appointed based on

---

12. 5 CCR § 80309(c).
13. Cal. Ct. R. 900 et seq.

his or her mental state, the attorney's bar membership is changed to inactive, which means that he or she cannot practice law.[14]

An attorney may also be involuntarily changed to inactive status after a hearing where the State Bar Court finds he or she is unable, or habitually fails, to perform his or her duties competently or is unable to practice law without substantial threat of harm to the public, based on mental infirmity, illness, or habitual use of intoxicants or drugs.[15]

(C)(3) Reinstatement of Impaired Attorney

If the attorney returns to mental competency or can demonstrate that he or she is no longer a threat to the public, he or she may be restored as an active member.[16]

---

14. Bus. & Prof. Code §§ 6007, 6006; *Newton v. State Bar*, 33 Cal.3d 480 (1983); *Conway v. State Bar*, 47 Cal.3d 1107 (1989).
15. Bus. & Prof. Code §§ 6007, 6006; *Newton v. State Bar*, 33 Cal.3d 480 (1983); *Conway v. State Bar*, 47 Cal.3d 1107 (1989).
16. *Hyland v. State Bar*, 59 Cal.2d 765 (1963).

5B.2

Workers Compensation Benefits

Workers compensation benefits are recoverable for employment-related accidents, injuries, or diseases acquired in the course of employment, if the accident, injury, or disease is proven to have occurred as a result of the work environment.

The premise behind workers compensation is that it is in the best interests of all concerned to give workers the certainty of swift compensation in return for lower payments for the injuries suffered in work-related injuries. This trade-off requires an employee to forgo the right to pursue a civil suit for a larger recovery (but a less certain result). The benefit to the employer is immunity from civil suits, which generally lead to higher awards to injured employees.[1]

Unlike some other states California does allow recovery for stress-related injuries and psychiatric injuries suffered on the job. At the end of 1994, the issue of false or inflated stress claims is under legislative consideration because of alleged abuses in the system. In 1992 and 1993, a series of new code sections went into effect that were intended by the legislature to address widespread fraud in the workers compensation system. Included were criminal and civil sanctions directed against those medical or mental health professionals who provide false or inflated reports of workers compensation injuries.

(A) The Role of MHPs

Generally, MHPs become involved in the workers compensation system through rendering opinions as to the degree of impair-

---

1. *Cole v. Fair Oaks Fire Protection Dist.*, 43 Cal.3d 148 (1987).

ment and/or emotional distress suffered by an individual in an alleged work-related incident. MHPs may be retained by employers who try to show that the injuries are pre-existing or not as severe as alleged. Typically, there is an agreed-upon examiner or evaluator who prepares a report, which is made available to both sides. Both sides are then able to introduce reports contradicting or disputing the examiner's findings.

Only psychiatrists and psychologists can provide mental health services without a medical referral to workers compensation applicants. A marriage, family, and child counselor (MFCC), licensed clinical social worker (LCSW), or others who wish to provide mental health services to applicants must be aware that they can do so only pursuant to a referral by a physician, without the consent of the employer, if those services are to be compensated as part of the workers compensation award.[2]

This does not preclude an MFCC or LCSW from providing mental health services without a referral, which are compensated if the employer agrees in advance. In essence, the employer's advance agreement eliminates the requirement of a physician referral. The mere assertion by an applicant's attorney to an MFCC or LCSW that the fees will be covered is not sufficient to make the employer responsible for payment Also, these professionals can provide services the employer compensates if the employer agrees in advance. Thus, before becoming involved in a workers compensation case, an MHP who wants to be paid through that system must make clear that his or her services are of the type authorized to be paid under the system.

The California Supreme Court has taken a broad view that virtually any work-related injury or complaint, with the exception of sexual discrimination, should remain within the workers compensation system. For example, in a case where an employee was involved in labor negotiations and alleged that management deliberately inflicted emotional distress on him that led to a paralyzing stroke, the Supreme Court held that workers compensation was the employee's exclusive remedy.[3]

(B) Right of Privacy in Evaluations

While generally there is no right of privacy in workers compensation evaluations because they are for the purpose of litigation,

---

2. Labor Code § 3209.3 authorizes psychologists; § 3209.8 sets forth the law regarding MFCCs and LSCWs.
3. *Cole v. Fair Oaks Fire Protection Dist.*, supra note 1. This includes causes of action for intentional or negligent infliction of emotional distress. *Shoemaker v. Myers*, 52 Cal.3d 1 (1990); *Livitsanos v. Superior Court*, 2 Cal.4th 744 (1992).

MHPs should be aware that in one case the appellate court determined that the applicant's right of privacy had been violated by an evaluator's disclosure to an insurance carrier that the applicant had AIDS. In that situation, the worker was undergoing a physical examination and some blood was spilled in the examining room. The applicant advised the nursing staff that he had been diagnosed with AIDS but wished that fact to remain confidential. When the information was communicated to the insurance carrier for the employer, the patient filed suit. The patient died of AIDS before trial, but the appellate court allowed his estate to maintain the action in the name of the patient. This case appears to establish the principle that a right of privacy may attach to information of a confidential nature that is communicated in an evaluation but is not related to the injury under evaluation.[4]

(C) Workers Compensation Liens

In many instances, MHPs are requested to take liens to secure payment from the ultimate workers compensation award instead of receiving payment for services as rendered. If there is an inadequate amount of money to cover all of the existing liens and other commitments, the MHP may be required to accept only a pro rata share of his or her fees. Further, taking a lien can allow an opposing party to raise ethical issues and charges of bias because the MHP then has a financial interest in the outcome of the case. However, no statute forbids an MHP from taking such a lien.

(D) Qualified Medical Evaluators

Qualified medical evaluators may be appointed by an agency called the Industrial Medical Council. The council consists of nine medical doctors, at least one of whom should be a psychiatrist, at least one specialist in occupational medicine, two osteopaths, two chiropractors, and one psychologist, who must be licensed.[5] The nine medical doctors and the osteopaths of the council represent medical specialties concerned with the treatment of industrial injury and disease. The governor appoints four medical doctors, two osteopaths, and one chiropractor to the council. The Senate Committee on Rules appoints two medical doctors—a psychiatrist and a chiropractor. The speaker of the assembly appoints an

---

4. *Estate of Urbaniak v. Newton*, 226 Cal.App.3d 1128 (1991).
5. Labor Code § 139.

occupational medicine specialist and a psychologist. The speaker of the assembly and the Senate Committee on Rules alternate in appointing the remaining medical doctor.

The term of the office of the members of the council is four years, and the members hold office until the appointment of successors. Any interim vacancies are filled by the original appointing authority for the unexpired term.[6]

Members who are medical doctors are appointed after consultation with their state and local professional associations.[7] The psychologists must be board certified in clinical psychology or hold a doctoral degree in psychology from an accredited university or professional school, and must have not less than five years of postdoctoral experience in the diagnosis and treatment of mental and emotional disorders. The psychiatrists must be board certified in their specialty.[8] Members of the council, within the scope of their respective professional training, engage in the following activities:

1. maintain liaisons with the medical, osteopathic, chiropractic, and psychological professions;
2. counsel and assist the administrative director and perform other duties as the administrative director may request;
3. assist in recruiting professionals for the medical bureau of the division;
4. assist in developing guidelines for the determination of disputed questions of clinical fact, including guidelines for the range of time normally required to perform an initial comprehensive medical–legal evaluation, or any other evaluation, as well as the content of those procedures;
5. suggest standards for improving care furnished to employees;
6. undertake continuing studies of developments in the field of rehabilitation, and continuously inform treating physicians of these developments;
7. recommend reasonable levels of fees for professionals performing services under these statutory schemes; and
8. monitor and measure changes in the cost and frequency of the most common medical services.[9]

Additionally, the Council is supposed to appoint an advisory committee on psychiatric injuries, with psychologists and psychi-

---

6. Labor Code § 139(b).
7. Labor Code § 139(c).
8. Labor Code § 139(d)(1).
9. Labor Code § 139(e).

atrists as members, and is to consider the advisory committee's recommendations concerning psychiatric injuries.

The Industrial Medical Council appoints qualified medical evaluators in each of the respective specialties to provide for the evaluation of medical issues in workers compensation cases. The evaluations produced are referred to as *medical–legal evaluations*. The appointments are for four-year terms. Although the statute uses the term *physician* regarding medical evaluators, the language specifically allows the appointment of psychologists who meet the criteria. The requirements to be appointed as a qualified medical evaluator, as far as psychologists and psychiatrists are concerned, are as follows:

1. The evaluator must devote at least 20% of his or her total practice time to providing medical treatment, or has served as an agreed medical evaluator on eight or more occasions in the 12 months before applying to be a qualified medical evaluator, and

2. he or she must be either board certified or qualified for board certification, within a time period specified by the council, in his or her specialty by an appropriate board recognized by the council. Additionally, psychologists must meet one of the following requirements:

   (a) board certification in clinical psychology by a board recognized by the council;

   (b) hold a doctoral degree in psychology from a university or professional school recognized by the council with not less than five years of postdoctoral experience in the diagnosis and treatment of emotional and mental disorders; or

   (c) have not less than five years of postdoctoral experience in the diagnosis and treatment of emotional and mental disorders and have served as an agreed medical evaluator on eight or more occasions before January 1, 1990. Alternatively, an evaluator can be qualified if he or she has served as an agreed medical evaluator on eight or more occasions before January 1, 1979.[10] However, no individual whose full-time practice is limited to forensic evaluation disability is to be appointed as a qualified medical evaluator.[11]

If the evaluator requests to be reappointed, and the basic criteria for appointment are met, he or she shall be reappointed if the following conditions are met:

---

10. Labor Code § 139.2.
11. Labor Code § 139.2(c). The Business & Professions Code provides that only individuals who are accepted as qualified by the Industrial Medical Council may refer to themselves as *qualified medical evaluators*.

1. the evaluator has completed formal evaluations within a reasonable time after assignment;

2. the evaluator has not had more than 30% of his or her evaluations of unrepresented employees rejected by a workers compensation judge at a contested hearing during the most recent four-year period during which the evaluator served as an evaluator. If the judge does not rely on the qualified medical evaluator, the judge is required to make a specific finding to that effect and shall give notice to the evaluator;

3. the evaluator has completed within the previous 24 months at least eight hours in continuing education and disability evaluation approved by the Industrial Medical Council; and

4. the evaluator has not been terminated or suspended during his or her most recent term as a qualified evaluator.

If the evaluator does not meet any of these four criteria, the Industrial Medical Council uses its discretion to reappoint or deny reappointment.

Generally an evaluator cannot be terminated during a term unless the licensing authority has suspended, revoked, or terminated his or her license to practice in California. However, evaluators may be suspended or terminated if a hearing determines that they engaged in any of the following:

1. paying rebates or referral fees;

2. violating the proscription against persons other than the evaluator who signs medical legal report examining the injured employee or participating in the non-clerical preparation of the report (except for a nurse performing functions routinely performed by a nurse). This means that the evaluator is responsible for taking a complete history, reviewing, and summarizing the medical records, and composing and drafting the conclusions of the report;[12]

3. failing to follow the medical procedures established by the council in 10 or more formal medical evaluations during a 12 month period;

4. failing to comply with the time-frame standards established by the council on 10 or more occasions during a 12-month period; or

5. failing to meet the criteria for evaluators set forth above.[13]

In the event that an evaluator is terminated or suspended based on finding a violation as described above, the council may,

---

12. Labor Code §§ 139.2, 4628.
13. Labor Code § 139.2(k).

in its discretion, place the evaluator on probation. It must, however, report to the appropriate licensing board the name of any qualified evaluator who is disciplined.

Qualified medical evaluators are required to pay a fee as determined by the Industrial Medical Council for appointment or reappointment.

(E) The Medical–Legal Evaluation Report

The medical–legal evaluation report must include the date the evaluation was conducted and the location, together with a statement that the evaluator signing the report actually performed the evaluation. The report must state whether the evaluation was in compliance with the guidelines established by the Industrial Medical Council, naming and listing the qualifications of each person who performed any services in connection with the report, other than clerical work, including diagnostic studies. If the report indicates that the evaluation was not in compliance with the guidelines, the report shall explain in detail any variance and the reasons therefore.

No amount may be charged in excess of the direct charges for the evaluator's professional services and reasonable costs of laboratory examinations, diagnostic studies, and other medical tests, and the reasonable costs of clerical work necessary to produce the report. Direct charges for the evaluator's professional services shall include reasonable overhead expenses.

A failure to comply with the provisions of the law makes the report inadmissible as evidence and eliminates any liability for payment of the expenses incurred in connection with the report. A knowing failure to comply with the law may subject an evaluator to a civil penalty of up to $1,000 for each violation. The civil penalties can be assessed by a workers compensation judge or the Appeals Board. An evaluator who has been assessed a civil penalty may be terminated, suspended, or placed on probation as a qualified medical evaluator. A knowing failure to comply with the requirements of law can also subject the physician to contempt proceedings before the Appeals Board.

When any person bills for medical–legal evaluation, diagnostic procedures, or diagnostic services performed by persons who are not employed by the reporting evaluator or a medical corporation owned by the reporting evaluator, the physician shall specify the amount paid, or to be paid, for the evaluations, procedures, and services.

The reports are required to contain the following declaration by the evaluator signing the report: "I declare under penalty of perjury that the information contained in this report and its attachments, if any, is true and correct to the best of my knowledge and belief except as to information that I have indicated I received from others. As to that information, I declare under penalty of perjury that the information accurately describes the information provided to me and, except as noted herein, that I believe it to be true."

The declaration must be dated and signed by the evaluator and indicate the county in which it was executed.

(F) Mental Stress/Disorder

A psychiatric injury is compensable if a mental disorder causes disability or the need for medical treatment, and if it is diagnosed pursuant to the latest edition of the American Psychiatric Association's Diagnostic and Statistical Manual of Mental Disorders. To establish that a psychiatric injury is compensable, an employee must demonstrate by a preponderance of the evidence that actual events of employment were responsible for at least 10% of the total causation from the sources contributing to the psychiatric injury. However, claims for psychiatric injury cannot be asserted unless the employee has been employed for at least six months. The six-month limitation does not apply if the injury is caused by a sudden and extraordinary employment condition as distinguished from regular and routine employment events, such as discipline, work evaluation, transfer, layoff, demotion, or termination.[14]

As noted above, California expressly recognizes stress as a job-related disability coming under the workers compensation system, although the frequency and magnitude of these claims is still in controversy. The test is used for determining whether emotional distress or mental illness is compensable:

1. at the time of the injury, both the employer and the employee are subject to the compensation provisions of the law;

2. at the time of the injury, the employee is performing service incidental to his or her employment and is acting within the course of his or her employment;

---

14. Labor Code § 3208.3. *See, e.g., Rubalcava v. WCAB*, 220 Cal.App.3d 901 (1990), where the major issue was the extent of psychiatric injury due to amputation of an employee's fingers.

3. the injury is proximately caused by the employment, either with or without negligence;[15] and

4. the injury is disabling, not just upsetting.[16]

The California Supreme Court has held that an employee can state a cause of action against an employer where the employer fraudulently conceals from the employee, the employee's doctors, and the state that the employee was suffering from a work-related disease, thereby preventing treatment and inducing the employee to continue working under hazardous conditions.[17]

The California Supreme Court has also ruled that when an employee asserts that an employer caused him or her emotional distress, and the conduct attributed to the employer consists of actions which are a normal part of the employment relationship, such as demotions, criticism of work practices, and negotiation of grievances, the claim for emotional distress comes within the exclusive provisions of the Labor Code, and a separate suit cannot be brought.[18]

---

15. Labor Code § 3600.
16. In *Livitsanos v. Superior Court*, 2 Cal.4th744 (1992), the California Supreme Court held that it was possible to have work-related stress or psychiatric injury that was upsetting, but not disabling. The court concluded that only disabling injuries were compensable.
17. *Johns-Manville Products Corp. v. Superior Court*, 27 Cal.3d 465 (1980). The Supreme Court in *Cole v. Fair Oaks Fire Protection District*, 43 Cal.3d 148 (1987) commented that the workers compensation system balances the advantage to the employer of immunity from liability from lawsuits against the employee's entitlement to swift and certain compensation. Although the employee obtains swifter compensation, he or she surrenders the right to a potentially larger recovery.
18. *Cole v. Fair Oaks Fire Protection Dist.*, 43 Cal.3d 148, 160 (1987). *But see Argawal v. Johnson*, 25 Cal.3d 932 (1979), allowing a civil suit based on an employer's racially demeaning remarks.

5B.3

Vocational Disability Determinations

California has various services that are available for physically or mentally impaired individuals who are eligible for rehabilitation services and who desire to seek employment.[1] An individual who is eligible for vocational rehabilitation services may be provided with psychological and social services assistance in skill training, family consultation, and hospitalization if necessary. These services are generally provided by MHPs, who also may be involved in assessing individuals to determine if they are eligible for such services.

(A) Eligibility Requirements

Individuals are eligible for vocational rehabilitation services if they are handicapped, blind, deaf, or developmentally disabled.[2]

(B) Definitions

Handicapped means under a physical or mental disability that constitutes a substantial handicap for employment, but of such a nature that vocational rehabilitation services may render him or her able to engage in gainful employment.[3]

Disadvantaged means handicapped or disadvantaged by reason of youth, advanced age, low educational attainments, ethnic

---

1. Welf. & Inst. Code § 19100.
2. Welf. & Inst. Code §§ 19151, 19153, 19200, 19350.
3. Welf. & Inst. Code § 19151.

or cultural factors, a prison or delinquency record, or any other condition that constitutes a barrier to employment. In addition, members of an individual's family may be included in the provision of services to a disadvantaged individual, if necessary.

In addition to physical restoration services, an individual can be offered therapeutic treatment necessary to correct or substantially modify physical or mental conditions that are either stable or slowly progressive and constitute a substantial barrier to employment.[4]

(C) Evaluation and Rehabilitation

A determination of an individual's eligibility for vocational rehabilitation is based on an examination conducted either by a physician, if the problem is of a physical nature, or an MHP, if the problem is due to a mental condition or illness. The examination should assess and document the following factors:

1. the disabling condition and a diagnosis of it;
2. the functioning capacities of the individual; and
3. the individual's general health status.

A licensed clinical psychologist is allowed to evaluate an individual whose disability is due to

1. mental or emotional disorder;
2. alcohol or drug abuse;
3. mental retardation; or
4. a specific learning disability.[5]

For mental retardation, the examination must be a valid test of intelligence that includes assessments of the individual's social, functional, and educational progress and achievements. In assessing specific learning disabilities, the examination is to include valid tests of intelligence, based on an individual's ability to process information through analysis and synthesis. The examination of general learning disabilities is to include examination of the areas of achievement, reading, spelling, math, language, visual, perceptual, and auditory performance.[6] These examinations must be done before an individual is placed in extended evaluation or is determined to be eligible for vocational rehabilitation.[7]

---

4. *Id.* §19150.
5. 9 CCR § 7077.
6. 9 CCR.
7. Welf. & Inst. Code § 19326.

The statute requires a preliminary diagnostic study to determine whether an individual is disadvantaged and has an employment handicap, and therefore needs services. The diagnostic study consists of an evaluation of pertinent medical, psychological, vocational, educational, cultural, social, and environmental factors that bear on the individual's handicap to employment and rehabilitation potential. This includes, to the degree needed, an evaluation of the individual's personality, intelligence level, and educational achievements, work experience, vocational aptitudes and interests, personal and social adjustments, employment opportunities, and other pertinent data.[8]

(D) Psychological and Psychiatric Services

Psychiatric and psychological services can include evaluation, testing, and treatment. Psychiatric counseling, however, is only to be provided by psychiatrists licensed by the Medical Board, psychologists licensed by the Board of Psychology, or by other MHPs as allowed within the scope of their licenses and upon special certification by the chief medical consultant to the Department of Rehabilitation. Only individuals who are licensed by the Board of Behavioral Science Examiners as LCSWs, or MFCCs can qualify as other MHPs for the purpose of this statute.[9]

Psychological testing is only to be done by licensed psychiatrists, licensed psychologists, vocational psychologists, or educational psychologists who have been certified.[10] A vocational psychologist is a psychologist licensed by the Board of Psychology who is functioning as a consultant where there is no local psychiatric consultant to the Department.

Psychological services can be provided to an eligible client to correct or substantially modify his or her condition to try to produce a physical and mental condition that is stable or shows progress and that would allow him or her to prepare for suitable employment.[11]

---

8. *Id.*
9. 9 CCR §§ 7160.5, 7295.7.
10. 9 CCR §§ 7160.5, 7029.3, 7295.7.
11. 9 CCR § 7160.

(E) Rehabilitation

Habilitation services are community-based services purchased or provided for adults with developmental disabilities, including supportive employment or competitive employment, with the purpose of preparing and maintaining the individual's highest level of vocational functioning or preparing the individual for referral to other vocational services.[12]

Among the services available for individuals who qualify for vocational disability are residential rehabilitation facilities for the mentally retarded. These facilities are intended to serve mentally retarded individuals who do not need intensive medical and psychiatric care but require a protective living environment. The goal of these facilities is to develop mentally retarded individuals to the maximum level of physical, psychological, social, and vocational functioning of which they are capable.[13] A program called Independent Living Rehabilitation Service provides services for severally disabled individuals in accordance with federal law.[14]

---

12. Welf. & Inst. Code § 19450.
13. *Id.*
14. Welf. & Inst. Code § 19750.

5B.4

Emotional Distress as a Basis for Civil Liability

Emotional distress is a term used by the law to refer to what is commonly called pain and suffering or mental distress. California recognizes as independent torts the negligent and intentional infliction of emotional distress. While historically some jurisdictions have required a plaintiff to allege a physical injury together with emotional distress, California does not require any physical injury—an action brought solely for emotional distress may succeed. Because of the sensitive nature of the relationship between MHPs and their patients, emotional-distress claims can be made against MHPs quite readily. In addition, when emotional distress is part of a larger claim, an MHP will be requested to evaluate the plaintiff.

(A) Intentional Infliction of Emotional Distress

To establish a claim for intentional infliction of emotional distress, a plaintiff must show that the defendant engaged in extreme and outrageous conduct with the intention of causing, or in reckless disregard of causing, emotional distress, which proximately caused substantial and severe emotional distress. The plaintiff must prove that the defendant acted either intentionally to produce the distress or engaged in acts recklessly when there was a high probability that emotional distress would flow from the acts. The amount of outrageousness has been defined as conduct that is so extreme as to go beyond all bounds of decency and to be regarded as intolerable in a civilized society,[1] such as child molestation. As with any other tort, the defendant's action must have been the direct cause of the emotional distress, and the emotional distress must be severe and substantial.

Claims of intentional infliction of emotional distress can be decided by the court on a motion determining whether the conduct described in the complaint meets the legal standard of outrageousness. The target of the intentional action, which is an essential component of a claim of this type, does not have to be the plaintiff, but can be a close relative or companion of the plaintiff.[2]

(B) Negligent Infliction of Emotional Distress

California recognizes negligent infliction of emotional distress when the defendant's negligence has directly and proximately caused the plaintiff substantial emotional distress. For example, a mother was able to bring a claim for negligent infliction of emotional distress against a psychotherapist for molesting her child, who was a patient, even though the mother did not observe the abuse because the mother was herself a patient and therefore a direct victim of the therapist's acts. The mother's role in taking the child to therapy was also a factor.[3]

A hospital was held directly liable to a man for negligently advising his wife that she had a venereal disease when in fact she did not. When the woman communicated the erroneous diagnosis to her husband, their marital relationship was destroyed. Subsequently, when it was determined that the diagnosis was incorrect, the husband brought an action against the hospital for negligent infliction of emotional distress. The court held that it was reasonably foreseeable that a negligent diagnosis of a venereal disease would cause emotional distress to a married couple. This case articulated the principle that a person who is not physically present may be a direct victim by virtue of his or her relationship with either the allegedly negligent party or another victim of negligence.[4]

---

1. *State Rubbish Ass'n. v. Siliznoff*, 38 Cal.2d 330 (1952); *Alcorn v. Anbro Engineering Inc.*, 2 Cal.3d 493 (1970); *Cerventez v. J.C. Penney Co.*, 24 Cal.3d 1579 (1979).
2. However, when an employee is suing an employer, generally, intentional infliction of emotional distress is barred by the exclusive remedy of the workers compensation law. *Shoemaker v. Myers*, 52 Cal.3d 1 (1990).
3. *Marlene F. v. Affiliated Psychiatric Clinics*, 43 Cal.3d 583 (1989).
4. *Molien v. Kaiser Foundation Hospital*, 27 Cal.3d 916 (1980).

An unresolved issue is the extent to which a bystander may recover for negligent infliction of emotional distress on a family member. Recently, the California Supreme Court has clarified this to indicate that under circumstances where there is a familial relationship between the bystander and the person injured, and the bystander witnesses the conduct or the damage, the bystander may recover.[5]

(C) Emotional Distress as an Element of Damages

Emotional distress may be an element of damages in a variety of circumstances, with the general exception of breach of contract actions. The creation or exacerbation of psychological problems that are causally connected to a defendant's actions may be a proper basis for a jury verdict on damages, even if there is no underlying physical injury. Emotional distress claims are not allowed as part of a wrongful death action, nor are they allowed to be asserted by children against parents.[6]

Further, there are some torts where emotional distress is the single largest component of damage, such as slander and invasion of privacy. No special method of proof of emotional distress is necessary to maintain damages of that type.

---

5. *Thing v. LaChusa*, 48 Cal.3d 644 (1989).
6. *Holliday v. Jones*, 215 Cal.3d 102 (1989).

5B.5

The Insanity of Wrongdoers and Civil Liability

Diverse circumstances can give rise to the question of whether a party to litigation, or a defendant in a criminal action, is sane. Perhaps the most common circumstance is when the defense asserts that the accused was insane[1] or mentally impaired at the time that the acts in issue were committed. In a civil suit, a person may contend that he or she was not able to form the requisite intent for certain tortious acts because of his or her mental condition. Whenever an insurance company asserts that certain claims are not covered because the acts were intentional in nature, the mental status of the insured becomes a factor. In such instances, MHPs may be asked to conduct an evaluation and render an opinion about issues such as mental status or competence when the event or injuries occurred, possible future restoration to mental competency, and/or appropriate penalties.

(A) The Liability of an Insane Person

Under California law, a person of unsound mind, of whatever degree, is still civilly liable for any wrongs done by him or her, but is not liable for punitive damages unless at the time the acts were committed, he or she was capable of knowing that the acts were

---

1. *Mental illness* is a medical diagnosis that is not sufficient to establish that a person is insane for the purposes of criminal law, and it is not for doctors to formulate the legal definition of insanity. *People v. Huddleston*, 275 Cal.App.2d 859 (1969). A criminal defendant must establish that the illness made him or her insane under the McNaughten test. *People v. Kelly*, 1 Cal.4th 495 (1992).

wrongful.[2] When an individual has a condition that is controllable by medication, failure to take the medication may be a form of reckless disregard of the consequences to others that would subject the person to punitive damages.[3]

(B) Insanity and Liability Defense

For public policy reasons, California provides that no one can be insured against the consequences of intentional acts.[4] The theory is that the availability of insurance for intentional misconduct would encourage such misconduct. In 1978, the California Supreme Court decided a case involving a Dr. Lovelace who shot and killed his employer, Dr. Clemmer. Dr. Lovelace was tried and convicted of second-degree murder. He pleaded not guilty by reason of insanity, but subsequently withdrew this plea. He was then sued civilly by Dr. Clemmer's heirs, who obtained a judgment against him for wrongful death. Dr. Lovelace's insurance carrier, however, refused to pay the judgment because the killing was a willful act. Dr. Clemmer's heirs argued that Dr. Lovelace lacked the requisite mental capacity and intent. The Supreme Court interpreted *intentional* and *willful* within the meaning of the Insurance Code exclusion to mean a preconceived design to inflict injury, and therefore it concluded that Dr. Clemmer's conduct was not intentional because of his mental state.[5] Other cases have held that where the insured had mental or emotional disorders, the acts were not intentional and therefore not compensable by insurance.[6] Recent cases, however, tried to draw a line where the defendant/insured is accused of child molestation. The current policy seems to be that acts of child molestation are intentional and willful as a matter of law and therefore excluded from

---

2. Civ. Code § 41.
3. *See Taylor v. Superior Court*, 24 Cal.3d 890 (1979), which held that malice could be found where an alcoholic with prior drunk-driving convictions was driving while intoxicated.
4. Ins. Code § 533.
5. *Clemmer v. Hartford Insurance Co.*, 22 Cal.3d 865 (1978).
6. *Congregation of Rodef Sholom of Marin v. American Motorists Insurance Co.*, 91 Cal.App.3d 690 (1979), finding that an arsonist could not be deemed to act intentionally if he suffered from a mental disease or defect that deprived him of the capacity of intent to set the fire and cause the damage or the capacity to govern his misconduct in accordance with reason.

insurance coverage unless the insured presents credible evidence that he or she did not intend to harm the victim.[7]

(C) Procedural Rights of Insane Persons

Generally, the major protection for an insane or incompetent person is the assignment of a guardian or a guardian *ad litem* if there is no guardian or conservator (*see* chapters 5A.2 and 5A.3).[8] The guardian *ad litem* has the power to represent the individual in the litigation and to settle the claim, to enter judgment for or against the individual, and to satisfy any judgment or order.[9]

Guardians *ad litem* do not have control over other aspects of an individual's life. While the guardian *ad litem* is typically an attorney, he or she may also be a lay individual who arranges for legal counsel. The determination as to whether a guardian *ad litem* is warranted is made on a case-by-case basis, given the facts concerning the individual.

---

7. *See State Farm Casualty Co. v. Estate of Jenner*, 856 F.2d 1359 (9th Cir. 1938), where a federal appeals court held that a defendant and insured who offered expert testimony that he was a pedophile and as such never intended to harm his victims had stated a basis to get around the intentional exclusion in insurance. However, it is also clear that there must be more than just the self serving statements of the defendant.
8. Civ. Proc. Code § 372.
9. *Id.*; Cal. Ct. R. 41.

5B.6

Competency to Contract

There are many forms of contracts that an MHP may enter into, including buying or selling real property, contracts to procure services, contracts to provide services and contracts to receive medical care. It is essential to the validity of a contract that the parties are capable of contracting, have given their consent, the contract has a lawful object, and there is a sufficient cause or consideration to support the contract.[1] The issue of competency arises when there is a question as to whether the parties are capable of contracting and capable of giving their consent. There are two different concepts involved—legal capacity and mental competency. An example of a contract where the party does not have the legal capacity to contract but is mentally competent is in the case of a minor. As a general matter, minors can have valid contracts for certain necessities, which are discussed more fully in chapter 5A.21. Generally, the issue of competency arises only when one party is seeking to oppose enforcement of the contract. MHPs may become involved in such a matter on either side of the case, to evaluate the mental condition of the party seeking to escape performance.

(A) Legal Test of Competency to Contract

There are two possibilities that arise when it appears that a person was not mentally competent to enter into a contract. If the person

---

1. Civ. Code § 1550.

was without any understanding or has been judicially determined to be insane, the contract is void and of no effect. However, if the person had mental problems but was not wholly unable to understand the terms of the contract, the contract is voidable, meaning that it could be voided but was not automatically voided. Such a contract would be binding on both parties until such time as it was rescinded or until a court of law made a determination that it was void.[2] Generally, the lack of competency of one party to a contract can only be raised by the purportedly incompetent party, not by the other side. In determining whether a contract should be found to be void, the knowledge of the party whose competency is not at issue is generally not pertinent.

The law has been interpreted to require a lack of capacity to understand the particular events or transaction at issue.[3] It is obvious that one basis for establishing that a person is entirely without understanding is through the opinion of experts in mental health, but such opinions, while admissible, do not foreclose the issue.[4] The conduct of the party whose competency is in question may also be a basis for determining whether there was a lack of competency to contract.[5]

Once an individual has been judicially determined to be incompetent, he or she can make no contract or conveyance (a transfer of real property), delegate any legal power he or she holds, or waive any of his or her rights until he or she has been restored to their mental capacity.[6]

Where a conservator of the person has been appointed, there is a presumption of incompetency. However, under the Probate Code, a conservatee may still be able to enter into a limited number and type of contracts (*see* chapter 5A.3). Generally, a conservatee can enter into contracts for necessary items.

---

2. Civ. Code §§ 38 to 40. *Smalley v. Baker*, 262 Cal.App.2d 824 (1968).
3. In *Mills v. Kopf*, 216 Cal.App.23 780 (1963), a psychiatrist testified that a patient was not competent to transact ordinary business because of an agitated depression to a psychotic degree. This was offset by testimony of family members that she was grief- stricken, forgetful, and despondent, but not bereft of her senses. The appeals court upheld the trial court's refusal to accept the psychiatrist's testimony over conflicting evidence, and found that the patient was competent to transact business.
4. *Id.*
5. *Hughes v. Grande*, 78 Cal.App.2d 555 (1947).
6. Civ. Code § 40.

Competency to Sign a Will

MHPs may become involved in disputes over a person's will, either where the person making the will (referred to as the "testator") was a patient of the MHP, or where the MHP is asked to testify as an expert in litigation, by a party either supporting or challenging the will. The key question is whether the decedent was competent to make a legally effective will. This chapter discusses the general nature of wills and the requirements for a valid will, as well as the tests used by courts to determine if a person is competent or incompetent to make a will (referred to as *testamentary capacity*). MHPs may also be asked to testify as to whether a particular individual exercised undue influence over the person making the will.

(A) Transferring Property on Death

There are two methods by which property can pass upon the death of a person: through specific directions given in a will, or by statute when no will exists. The individual making the will is referred to as a *testator*. The person who is charged with carrying out the directions of the will is referred to as an *executor* or *personal representative*. When no will is left, the property passes through a statutory scheme referred to as intestate succession, which is beyond the scope of this book to explain in detail, but which is based on marital or familial relation to the dead person.

(B) Testator's State of Mind

To have an effective will, the testator must be of sound mind. If it is subsequently determined that the testator did not have the mental capacity to make a will or was subject to undue influence, then the will may be set aside. Typically, these issues arise when family members who would normally be the object of the testator's request are left out and other individuals receive the bulk of the estate. MHPs may be involved in disputes over the mental capacity of a testator, either as the treating therapist of the testator, or as an expert retained to address the testator's mental competency once the facts and circumstances of the will are made known. Because the will does not become operative until the testator dies, unless the testator communicates the contents of the will, disputes over the beneficiaries and distributions do not arise until after the testator's death.

There are some practical problems for an MHP attempting to render an opinion about the testator's state of mind at the time the will was executed based solely on documents reviewed after the fact or on the testimony of third-party witnesses. Thus, the MHP's opinion is more likely to be accepted as valid when he or she actually treated or examined the testator, either at the time of his or her bequest or at the time of death.

(C) Tests of Testamentary Capacity

Under the California Probate Code, any person who is 18 years or older and who is of sound mind may make a will.[1] The key question is whether the testator had the requisite mental capacity to be able to understand the nature of his or her acts, to know the property that he or she had, the persons to whom bequests would normally be made, and how their interests would be affected by the will. Sometimes the people who would be the natural objects of bequests are referred to as the *objects of the testator's bounty*.[2] Under the Probate Code, a person is not mentally competent to make a will, if at the time the will is made, either of two conditions apply:

1. the testator does not have sufficient mental capacity to be able to
   (a) understand the nature of the testamentary act;

---

1. Prob. Code § 6100.
2. *Estate of Smith*, 200 Cal. 152 (1926).

(b) understand and recollect the nature and situation of his or her property; or

(c) remember and understand his or her living relations, spouse, parents, and those whose interests are affected by the will;

or

2. he or she suffers from a mental disorder with symptoms including delusions or hallucinations, which result in the person's devising his or her property in a way that he or she would not have done but for the delusions or hallucinations.[3]

Isolated acts or isolated behavior does not equal lack of mental capacity.[4] By the same token, if the testator was in a period of lucidity at the time the will was executed and not suffering from hallucinations or delusions, then testamentary capacity will probably be found. The key question is the mental state of the testator *at the time of the execution of the will.* Evidence of a mental disorder before or after the execution of the will is pertinent insofar as it supports conclusions regarding the testator's state of mind at the time of execution, but it is not dispositive.[5] A history of substance abuse by itself is not sufficient to support a lack of testamentary capacity.[6] Old age, feebleness, forgetfulness, filthy personal habits, personal eccentricities, failure to recognize old friends or relatives, physical disability, absentmindedness, and mental confusion were held not to constitute grounds for finding that a testator lacked testamentary capacity.[7] In fact, the courts have recognized that an individual can have an extremely debilitating physical disease and be under potent medication but still retain the requisite mental capacity.[8]

The fact that a testator committed suicide may be relevant to a determination of mental condition at the time that the will was executed, but is not dispositive. The longer the period of time between the execution of the will and the suicide, the less likely

---

3. Prob. Code § 6100.5.
4. *Estate of Wright*, 7 Cal.2d 348 (1936).
5. *See Estate of Clegg*, 87 Cal.App.3d 594 (1978), where Mrs. Clegg was diagnosed before executing the will as having senile dementia, a progressive disease. The will was set aside in part because her doctor testified he did not believe she knew the nature of the will or her property, and did not know who her living relatives were.
6. *Estate of Garvey*, 38 Cal.App.2d 449 (1940); *Estate of Arnold*, 16 Cal.2d 573 (1940).
7. *Estate of Selb*, 84 Cal.App.2d 46, 49 (1948).
8. *Estate of Mann*, 184 Cal.App.3d 593 (1986). This principle can be particularly important in situations such as those involving AIDS patients who are suffering from debilitating physical conditions but retain sufficient rationality to make valid wills. No such case has been reported, to the author's knowledge, as of yet.

the suicide will be deemed to be indicative of a mental disorder at the time the will was executed.[9]

(D) Proving Testamentary Incapacity

Once the testator has died, the will is submitted to probate. At that point, a party who objects to the will must present evidence that the testator lacked the requisite mental capacity. The determination of mental capacity is a factual one, which is made by a jury and rarely disturbed on appeal.[10]

(E) Undue Influence

A related ground for attacking provisions in a will is to accuse one of the persons benefiting from the will of exercising undue influence or fraud on the testator. Undue influence is defined in general as the use of a confidential relationship for the purpose of taking unfair advantage of someone, taking advantage of another's weakness of mind, or taking grossly aggressive and unfair advantage of another's necessities or distress.[11] Undue influence can be asserted in a number of different circumstances outside the will situation. The test of proving undue influence is whether the person accused of exercising the influence exerted a pressure that overpowered the testator's mind and suppressed his or her volition or free will at the time the will was executed.

For a will to be set aside, generally a confidential relationship must be established. With respect to gifts or conveyances during life, the susceptibility of the testator to imposition, extreme age, or infirmity, together with some evidence of circumstances suggesting coercion, will shift the burden of proof to the person benefiting from the gift. That person then must show affirmatively that the transaction was fair and free from influence.[12] Where a patient provides a bequest to an MHP in a will, the issue of undue influence by the MHP may arise.

The testimony of MHPs obviously can be important in determining whether in a particular situation undue influence occurred. Here again, the question of whether undue influence occurred is one for the jury to determine, however, it is not proper for a jury to invalidate a will on the ground of undue influence

---

9. *Estate of Collins*, 150 Cal.App.2d 702 (1957).
10. *Estate of Fritschi*, 60 Cal.2d 367 (1963).
11. *Civil Code*, § 1575.
12. *O'Neil v. Spillane*, 45 Cal.App.3d 147, 155 (1975).

just because the jury has its own belief as to how the testator should have disposed of his or her property.[13]

In both undue influence and lack of testamentary capacity situations, a part of the will may be stricken and a part may be upheld to the extent it is based on the testator's free will.[14]

---

13. *Estate of Fritschi*, 60 Cal.23 367, 373 (1963).
14. *Estate of Molera*, 23 Cal.App.3d 993 (1972).

5B.8

Competency to Vote

A sufficient mental impairment can disqualify an individual from voting in elections. MHPs may be involved in evaluating an individual whose competency to vote is at issue.

(A) Definition of Mental Incompetency

For the purposes of being eligible to vote, a person is deemed mentally incompetent and disqualified from voting if the court finds that he or she is not capable of completing an affidavit of voter registration and any of the following conditions apply:

1. a conservator of the person, or of the person and estate, has been appointed;

2. the person has been found not competent to stand trial and a trial or judgment has been suspended; or

3. the person has pleaded not guilty by reason of insanity and has been found not guilty for that reason and is deemed to be gravely disabled.

If any of the competency proceedings under the authority of the Welfare and Institutions Code is heard by a jury, the jury must unanimously find that the person is not capable of completing an affidavit of voter registration before the person can be disqualified from voting.[1]

---

1. Elec. Code § 707.5

(B) Eligibility to Vote

To be eligible to vote in a state election, an individual must register to vote and must not be mentally incompetent.[2] A person is deemed mentally incompetent if, during the course of various proceedings, the court finds the person to be not capable of completing an affidavit of voter registration *and*

1. a conservator for the person or the person's estate has been appointed (*see* chapter 5A.2),[3] or

2. the person has been found not competent to stand trial or has been found not guilty by reason of insanity and is deemed to be gravely disabled (*see* chapters 5D.5 and 5D.14).

However, the disqualification may be temporary and may be reinstated upon the termination of a conservatorship or the restoration of an individual to mental health.[4]

When a conservatorship has been established (*see* chapter 5A.3), the court investigator should during the periodic review of the conservatorship review the conservatee's capability to complete an affidavit of voter registration. If the investigator determines the conservatee is capable of completing the affidavit, the court holds a hearing to determine if the person is in fact capable of completing the affidavit. If the court finds that the person is capable of completing the affidavit, the person's right to register to vote shall be restored, and the court shall notify the county clerk.

If a person has not previously been found incapable of completing such an affidavit but the investigator determines the person is no longer capable of completing such an affidavit, the court shall hold a hearing to determine if the person is capable of completing the affidavit. If the court determines that the person is not able to complete the affidavit, the court notifies the person to be disqualified from voting, and the county clerk.

A disqualification may be contested by the conservatee.[5]

Any person who has pleaded and has been found not guilty by reason of insanity, or who has been found incompetent to stand trial, or who has been convicted of a felony and judicially determined to be a mentally disordered sex offender, or who has been convicted of a felony and is being treated for matters related to that offense at a state hospital shall be disqualified from voting

---

2. Elec. Code §§ 707.5, 707.6.
3. Welf. & Inst. Code §§ 5352.5, 5008; Penal Code §§ 1370, 1026; Prob. Code § 1400.
4. Prob. Code § 1865.
5. Elec. Code § 707.75.

during the time the person is involuntarily confined, pursuant to a court order, in a public or private facility. The court shall notify the county clerk of the commitment to a treatment facility. The person's rights are restored upon his or her release.[6]

---

6. Elec. Code § 707.8.

5B.9

Competency to Obtain a Driver's License

An MHP may be involved in providing evidence regarding the mental competency of an applicant for a driver's license. Licenses may be denied for several reasons, including some mental disorders or disabilities, and substance abuse.

(A) DMV Had Discretion to Deny Licenses

In California, the Department of Motor Vehicles controls the issuance of driver's licenses. The department may deny a driver's license on certain discretionary grounds,[1] and is required to deny a license on certain mandatory grounds.[2] Among the grounds for discretionary refusal of a driver's license is when an individual is rendered incapable of safely operating a motor vehicle because of alcoholism, excessive and chronic use of alcoholic beverages, or addiction to, or habitual use of, any drug.

(B) Denial of License Due to Drug Use

A person who is addicted to narcotic drugs may be denied a driver's license unless that person is participating in a methadone

1. Veh. Code § 12806.
2. Veh. Code § 12805.

maintenance program under the specified statutory scheme. If the person is participating in the methadone maintenance program, he or she may be issued a probationary license subject to reasonable terms and conditions if the drug usage does not affect the person's ability to exercise reasonable and ordinary control in operating a motor vehicle.

(C) Test for Denial of Licensure Due to Mental Disorder

Licenses may also be denied on a discretionary basis to any individual

> who has a disorder characterized by lapses of consciousness or who has experienced, within the last three years, either a lapse of consciousness or an episode of marked confusion caused by any condition which may bring about recurrent lapses, or who has any physical or mental disability, disease, or disorder which could affect the safe operation of a motor vehicle unless the department has medical information which indicates the person may safely operate a motor vehicle.

In making a determination as to whether an individual suffers from lapses of consciousness or mental disability, disease, or disorder, the department can rely on any relevant information available to it, including testimony by MHPs.[3] The denial of driver's licenses to individuals who suffer from epilepsy has been held to be a legitimate exercise of the state's police power.[4]

(D) Licenses Revoked in Other Jurisdictions

Under certain circumstances, the department must refuse to issue a driver's license to an individual who has been subject to license revocation or suspension in another jurisdiction.[5]

---

3. Veh. Code § 12806. While the Department of Motor Vehicles has discretion to issue or not issue a license, it is not liable for the issuance of a license to an individual who has problems with the use of alcohol and then gets into an accident. *Johnson v. Mead*, 191 Cal.App.3d 156 (1987).
4. *People v. O'Neil*, 62 Cal.2d 748 (1965).
5. Veh. Code § 12805.

(E) Grounds for Licensure in Spite of Mental Defects

The department is not required to refuse to issue a license for an applicant's physical or mental defect which in the opinion of the department does not affect the applicant's ability to exercise reasonable and ordinary control in operating a motor vehicle.[6] However, the DMV must consider each applicant on a case-by-case basis and allow the applicant to show whether the medical condition has been compensated for.[7]

---

6. Veh. Code § 12806.
7. In *Smith v. Department of Motor Vehicles*, 163 Cal.App.3d 321 (1984), the DMV was ordered to reinstate the license of a truck driver who suffered from diabetic retinopathy in both eyes and was blind in one eye, although under federal regulations, he would have been disqualified from driving a truck.

5B.10

Product Liability

Product liability is the overall legal theory covering several specific doctrines about defective products. This theory recognizes that a consumer may not have access to information necessary to establish the factual chain in the production of a particular product. Therefore, as a matter of public policy the burden of proof may be shifted. An MHP may be called to testify about the foreseeability of a risk and/or the adequacy of a warning.

(A) Nature of Product Liability

If a product is defective, the manufacturer may be sued for negligence, breach of contract, breach of express warranty, breach of implied warranty of fitness for use, and strict liability.[1] An action based on strict liability holds liable a manufacturer or seller of products if (1) it places the product on the market either knowing it is defective or without adequately inspecting for defects, and (2) a defective or dangerous condition of the product causes personal injuries, death, or property damage to foreseeable users, consumers, or even mere bystanders.[2] However, the California Supreme Court has held that strict liability theories cannot be asserted against providers of services, and that professionals who sell their services for the guidance of others in their financial

---

1. *Breach of express warranty* relates to explicit representations as to how a product will perform or how safe it is. *Breach of implied warranty* means that the product is sold with an implicit representation that it is either safe or fit for the specific use attributed to it.
2. *Greenman v. Yuba Power Products, Inc.*, 59 Cal.2d 57 (1963); *La Jolla Village Homeowners Ass'n v. Superior Court*, 212 Cal.App.3d 1131 (1989).

and personal affairs are not liable in the absence of negligence (i.e., conduct falling below the applicable standard of care) or intentional misconduct.[3]

The cases discussing the failure to extend strict liability to professionals have generally arisen in a construction context involving design professionals, although a number of cases have arisen as a result of blood transfusions, which is treated as a provision of a professional service.[4]

Thus, while strict liability and breach of implied warranty theories could not be asserted against MHPs in malpractice litigation, MHPs may be involved in testifying about whether the warnings are adequate to apprise an average consumer of the product's risks.

(B) Elements of a Product Liability Claim

The purpose of the strict liability doctrine is to ensure that the cost of injuries resulting from defective products are borne by the manufacturers that put the products in the stream of commerce, rather than by the injured persons who are generally powerless to ascertain that the defect exists and protect themselves from it.[5] Because the strict liability in tort doctrine involves a public policy decision about assigning responsibility for reducing hazards, the elements of a cause of action include whether the allocation of risk distribution in a particular case supports or works against public policy.

The elements of a cause of action for strict liability include the following:

1. That the product was used by the consumer in a manner that was reasonably foreseeable and/or intended by the manufacturer.[6]

2. That the product was in fact defective and that this condition existed at the time that it left the defendant's control.[7]

---

3. *Gagne v. Bertran*, 43 Cal.2d 41 (1954).
4. *See, e.g., Swett v. Gribaldo Jones & Assocs.*, 40 Cal.App.3d 573 (1974). While blood banks cannot be sued on strict liability or breach of implied warranty theories, they can be sued on general negligence theories. *Osborn v. Irwin Memorial Blood Bank*, 5 Cal.App.4th 234 (1992).
5. *Greenman v. Yuba Power Products, Inc.*, *supra* note 2.
6. *Id.*; *Kriegler v. Eichler Homes Inc.*, 269 Cal.App.2d 224 (1969); *Del Mar Beach Club Owners Ass'n v. Imperial Contracting Co.*, 123 Cal.App.3d 398 (1981).
7. *Erickson v. Sears Roebuck & Co.*, 240 Cal.App.2d 793 (1966).

3. That the defendant knew or should have known that the ultimate consumer would use the product without inspecting it, or that an inspection was not possible.

4. That the product actually caused or contributed to the injuries or damages suffered by the consumer.

The defect in question may involve either manufacturing or design.[8] However, the item must have been placed in commerce; a product that is never placed in commerce is not subject to a strict liability action.[9]

Additionally, a plaintiff cannot sue under a strict liability if the product that he or she received has not yet malfunctioned, even if it is claimed that the product *may* malfunction in the future.[10] While there have been a number of cases brought by plaintiffs seeking to recover damages for nondefective heart valves because they had been recalled by the manufacturer, no appellate court has found a basis for such a recovery.

A product may be defectively designed when it has failed to perform as a reasonable, ordinary consumer would expect when using the product in the intended or reasonably foreseeable manner, or where the risk of danger from the product as designed outweighs its utility.[11] MHPs may be called upon to give expert testimony about "reasonable expectations" concerning the product.[12] To establish a design defect, the plaintiff must meet only one of these two criteria. At that point, the burden of proof shifts to the defendant to show that the product as designed had benefits that outweighed the alleged risks.[13]

Strict liability also can apply where the defect is alleged to be a failure to warn the consumer of the product's risks.[14] Again, MHPs may be involved in testifying about whether particular warnings are adequate.

---

8. *Cronin v. J.B. Olson Corp.*, 8 Cal.3d 121 (1972). The law requires a manufacturer to foresee some degree of misuse and abuse of the product and to take reasonable precautions to minimize the harm.
9. *Thibos v. Pacific Gas and Electric Co.*, 186 Cal.App.3d 337 (1986).
10. *Khan v. Shiley, Inc.*, 217 Cal.App.3d 838 (1990). In that case, the plaintiff had a heart valve implanted. Later, some of the heart valves started to malfunction; however, at the time of the suit the plaintiff's valve had not malfunctioned. The court held that while the plaintiff could sue for fraudulent misrepresentations, he could not sue on product liability theories because the product had not malfunctioned—the suit was premature.
11. *Grimshaw v. Ford Motor Co.*, 119 Cal.App.3d 757 (1981); *Barker v. Lull Engineering*, 20 Cal.3d 413 (1978).
12. *Roseburg v. Minnesota Mining & Manufacturing Co.*, 181 Cal.App.3d 726 (1986) (breast implants).
13. *Barker v. Lull Engineering Co.*, supra note 11.
14. *Anderson v. Owens-Corning Fiberglass Co.*, 53 Cal.3d 987 (1991); *Prevatt v. Pennwalt*, 192 Cal.App.3d 438 (1987).

Strict liability applies only to cases in which harm is associated with a *foreseeable* use of the product. There is no duty to warn of an unforeseeable use[15] or where the plaintiff's injury is an idiosyncratic allergic reaction.[16] However, drug manufacturers' liability for inherently unsafe drugs has created some difficulties in the case law. In a landmark case, the California Supreme Court held that manufacturers of DES could be sued based on their share of the market, although they could not be held strictly liable for defects in the drug. The Court indicated that the manufacturers could be held liable for failure to warn of potential side effects.[17] Because of the difficulty for consumers in trying to establish that the DES they received was from a particular manufacturer, particularly given the lapse of time, the Court concluded that liability could be based on the market share of DES sales that each manufacturer had.

(C) Defenses to Product Liability Claim

There are a number of defenses to product liability claims, including the statute of limitations. In addition to the statute of limitations, California allows the defense of comparative negligence.[18] This concept essentially means that a plaintiff's negligence can be assessed to reduce any award by the percentage attributable to the plaintiff's own conduct. When there are several parties, each party is supposed to be held liable only for its own percentage of fault. The California Supreme Court expressly extended the comparative fault doctrine to strict liability cases.[19]

California also recognizes the defense of assumption of the risk. There are three types of assumption of the risk:

1. Express assumption of the risk, such as a signed release or waiver that identifies the risk being assumed, commonly found in sporting activities;
2. Reasonable implied assumption of the risk; and

---

15. *Dosier v. Wilcox-Crittendon Co.*, 45 Cal.App.3d 74 (1975). However, no warning is needed for a risk that is common knowledge or generally recognized. *Holmes v. J.C. Penny Co.*, 133 Cal.App.3d 216 (1982).
16. *Carmichael v. Reitz*, 17 Cal.App.3d 958 (1971).
17. *Sindell v. Abbott Labs.*, 26 Cal.3d 588 (1980); *Brown v. Superior Court*, 44 Cal.3d 1049 (1988).
18. *Li v. Yellow Cab Co.*, 13 Cal.3d 804 (1975); *American Motorcycle Association v. Superior Court*, 20 Cal.3d 578 (1978).
19. *Daley v. General Motors Corp.*, 20 Cal.3d 725 (1978); *Safeway Stores Inc. v. Nest-Kart*, 21 Cal.3d 322 (1978).

3. Unreasonable implied assumption of the risk.

Following the adoption of comparative negligence, it was believed for a time that the assumption of the risk doctrine had for all intents and purposes been abolished. Later, assumption of the risk was categorized as reasonable and unreasonable, with reasonable assumption of the risk being assertable as an affirmative defense. Then in 1992, the California Supreme Court replaced these categories with primary and secondary assumption of risk. *Primary assumption* of the risk is where there is a legal conclusion that there is no duty on the part of the defendant to protect the plaintiff from a particular risk. This is a complete defense to a claim.[20] *Secondary assumption* of the risk is where the plaintiff has a duty of care but knowingly encounters a risk of injury caused by the defendant's breach of the duty. Here, the plaintiff's conduct is deemed equivalent to comparative negligence, so this defense is not an absolute bar to a recovery.

An example of a primary assumption of the risk that would constitute a complete bar is a fire-fighter suffering injury while fighting a blaze. The party who negligently started the fire had no legal duty to protect the firefighter from the very danger that he or she is employed to confront.[21]

Another defense to a product liability claim is that the product was used in an unforeseeable manner that caused an injury that would not have resulted had the product been used in a foreseeable manner.[22] Another affirmative defense is alteration of the product after it left the defendant's control.[23] However, a plaintiff's unreasonable use of a product will not be a complete defense if the product was in fact defective and contributed to the injury.[24]

If a product has a defective design, the defenses include

1. that the design met the standards established by custom and practice of the industry;

---

20. *Ford v. Gouin,* 3 Cal.4th 339 (1992); *Knight v. Jewett,* 3 Cal.4th 296 (1992); *Donohue v. San Francisco Housing Authority,* 16 Cal.App.4th 658 (1993).
21. *Knight v. Jewett, supra* note 20, at 309-10; *see Donohue v. San Francisco Housing Authorities, supra* note 20, where a firefighter was injured falling on slick stairs in a building owned by the San Francisco Housing Authority because of the Housing Authority's failure to install non-slip adhesive treads, but the court concluded that this was a secondary assumption of the risk case requiring allocation of comparative fault, not a complete defense.
22. *Dosier v. Wilcox-Crittendon Co.,* 45 Cal.App.3d 74 (1975). The question of foreseeability is one of fact for a jury, and in *Bigbee v. Pacific Tel. & Tel. Co.,* 34 Cal.3d 49 (1983), the Supreme Court held that it was foreseeable that a drunk driver could drive off the road, onto a sidewalk, and strike a telephone booth in which the plaintiff was making a phone call.
23. *Williams v. Beechnut Nutrition Corp.,* 185 Cal.App.3d 135 (1986).
24. *Daley v. General Motors Co.,* 20 Cal.3d 725 (1978).

2. that there was no practical and feasible alternative design;

3. that the product's characteristics were known to the public, and that an ordinary consumer would recognize the risk; and

4. that the product was unavoidably unsafe and was accompanied by an adequate warning.

Thus, MHPs may be involved in testifying in product liability cases.

5B.11

Unfair Competition

The legal doctrines that have evolved in the area of unfair competition are based on the notion that a business competitor should not be able to gain an advantage through false advertising, theft of trade secrets, or mislabeling products. A typical case alleging unfair competition would claim that a person's or company's services were marketed in a deceptive manner to lead the public to believe that they were actually the services of another or endorsed by another. For example, a group of psychologists unrelated to the American Psychological Association could market their services using the APA acronym, leading consumers to believe that the services were provided by the American Psychological Association. MHPs may be involved in such actions as plaintiffs, defendants, or witnesses to testify as to the effects on the public of the competitive practices in question.

(A) Types of Unfair Competition

California law recognizes two types of unfair competition: statutory and common law. Since the available remedies differ depending on which theory is pursued, it is important for MHPs to be aware of the distinctions.

(B) Legal Test of Unfair Competition

In 1992, the California Supreme Court discussed the differences between the two types of unfair competition and concluded that common law unfair competition was generally the act of passing off one person's goods or services as those of another. The Court, explained that this was a remedy against the wrongful exploitation of trade names and common law trademarks that were not otherwise entitled to legal protection.[1] The statutory definition of unfair competition is found in the Unfair Business Practices Act.[2] Under this statute, unfair competition means any unlawful, unfair, or fraudulent business practice, and any unfair, deceptive, untrue, or misleading advertising.[3] In a prior decision, the Court interpreted the statutory definition as meaning anything that can properly be called a business practice and is still forbidden by law.[4]

The Court indicated that the state statute was intended to expand legal remedies against deceptive business practices and was patterned after the federal law that established the Federal Trade Commission.[5]

At common law, to establish the tort of unfair competition a plaintiff had to establish a competitive injury. The Unfair Business Practices Act, however, was intended to make it easier to prove such a claim; therefore, the tort elements are not needed—only a showing that the members of the public are likely to be deceived.[6]

As a trade-off, however, the remedies under the Unfair Business Practices Act are primarily equitable in nature, meaning that compensatory damages are not generally awarded. Instead, the court may order a defendant to restore any money or property that has been acquired by means of unfair competition, and it may enter orders enjoining any person from performing, or proposing to perform, an act of unfair competition.[7] Thus under the statutory unfair competition claim, specific proof of each element—deception, reliance, and injury—is not necessary to establish liability.[8]

(C) Trademark Confusion

Trademarks are words, names, letters, and pictures used by a specific entity to designate goods and services. To be a trademark,

---

1. *Bank of the West v. Superior Court*, 2 Cal.4th 1254, 1263 (1992).
2. Bus. & Prof. Code § 17200 et seq.
3. Bus. & Prof. Code § 17200; *Bank of the West v. Superior Court, supra* note 1.
4. *Barquis v. Merchants Collection Ass'n*, 7 Cal.3d 94 (1972).
5. *Bank of the West v. Superior Court, supra* note 1, at 1263-64.
6. *Id.* at 1266-67
7. *Id.* at 1267; Bus. & Prof. Code § 17203.
8. *Bank of the West v. Superior Court*, 2 Cal.4th 1254 (1992); *Committee on Children's Television Inc. v. General Foods Corp.*, 35 Cal.3d 197 (1983).

a name must not be common or generic, and typically must be attached in some fashion to the product. Federal law provides a comprehensive scheme for the registration of trademarks. California also has a trademark law, which[9] distinguishes between a *tradename*, which involves the business and goodwill of an enterprise, and a *trademark*, which attaches to specific goods and services.[10] As defined in the California statute, a trademark means any word, name, symbol, or device, or any combination thereof, that is adopted and used by a person to identify goods made or sold by him or her and to distinguish them from goods made or sold by others.[11] A service mark means a mark used in the sale or advertising of services for the same purposes.[12]

A tradename is defined by statute as a word, name, symbol, device, or any combination thereof, used by a person to identify his or her business, vocation, or occupation, and to distinguish it from the business, vocation, or occupation of others.[13]

While most disputes over trademarks, service marks, or tradenames concern allegedly similar products where the person with the registered name or mark is attempting to stop the usage of it by others, MHPs need also to be aware that in the sale of a business the trademark may or may not be sold. In one case, a business and its goodwill were sold and the purchasers were surprised to discover that it did not include the tradename because it was not specifically included in the sale.[14]

Once a trademark is registered with the Secretary of State, a certificate of registration is issued, which is *prima facie* evidence of ownership of that mark and is valid for a period of ten years from the date of registration. The registration may be renewed for an additional ten years six months before the expiration of the first term. The mark can be renewed for successive periods of ten years in a similar manner.[15]

Any person who procures a registration by making false or fraudulent statements, orally or in writing, is liable for all damages sustained as a consequence of that filing.[16] The owner of a registered mark is entitled to file suit for damages and for various types of injunctions forbidding its use without the registrant's consent.[17]

---

9. Bus. & Prof. Code § 14200.
10. *Golden Door, Inc. v. Odishe*, 437 F.Supp. 956 (1980), *aff'd*, 646 F.2d 347 (1980).
11. Bus. & Prof. Code § 14207.
12. Bus. & Prof. Code § 14206.
13. Bus. & Prof. Code § 14208.
14. *Balesteri v. Holler*, 87 Cal.App.3d 717 (1978); *Golden Door, Inc. v. Odishe supra* note 10.
15. Bus. & Prof. Code §§ 14240, 14241, 14250.
16. Bus. & Prof. Code § 14300.
17. Bus. & Prof. Code §§ 14320, 14330, 14340.

By the same token, any person who has first adopted and used a tradename, whether within or outside of California, is its original owner and may restrain use of the tradename by others.[18]

The proper filing of a Fictitious Business Name Statement establishes a rebuttable presumption that the registrant has the exclusive right to use a tradename as a fictitious business name as long as the registrant is the first to file a statement using the fictitious business name in that county and is actually engaged in the trade or business using the fictitious name.[19]

The issue of prior confusion arises when a company sells a product that is substantially the same as a product that has been granted protection under the trademark law. The concerns include the fact that if the similar product is of inferior quality it may lead to injury of the first company's business reputation by consumers dissatisfied with the second company's goods. In addition, where confusion exists, there is a potential for dilution of the distinctive quality of a registered trademark or tradename.[20] An example of potential dilution is when the Academy of Motion Picture Arts and Sciences, which awards the Oscars, brought an action against a company that was using a statuette similar to the Oscar. The court found that even though the motion picture academy could not establish any economic damages, there was a potential for dilution of the significance of the Oscar and its effect in the movie industry.[21] In that case, as in most other cases, the issue was the likelihood of confusion in the mind of the public, an issue about which MHPs may testify.

18. Bus. & Prof. Code §§ 14400 to 14402.
19. Bus. & Prof. Code § 14411. A presumption is an assumption of fact the law requires to be made from another fact or facts found, or otherwise established, but it is not evidence. Evid. Code § 600. A presumption can be conclusive or rebuttable. Rebuttable presumptions affect either the burden of producing evidence or the burden of proof. *Id.* § 601. A fact or group of facts that is *prima facie* evidence of another fact establishes a rebuttable presumption. *Id.* § 602.
20. Bus. & Prof. Code § 14330.
21. *Academy of Motion Pictures Arts & Sciences v. Creative House Promotions, Inc.,* 944 F.2d 1446 (9th Cir., 1991).

5B.12

Employment Discrimination

MHPs can be involved in employment discrimination actions in at least three ways: as plaintiffs alleging they were the victims of discrimination; as defendants accused of discrimination; and as experts testifying as to the effects of discrimination on the individual plaintiffs.

This chapter discusses what types of employment discrimination are prohibited and the penalties for such discrimination.

(A) Prohibited Discrimination

Both California and federal law prohibit discrimination on the basis of race, sex, age, religious beliefs, and other grounds. California has enacted two separate statutes to address these issues: the California Fair Employment and Housing Act (FEHA)[1] and the Unruh Civil Rights Act.[2]

Under the FEHA, employers are not allowed to discriminate on the basis of race, religious creed, color, national origin, ancestry, physical disability, mental disability, medical condition, marital status, sex, or age.[3] *Mental disability* is defined as any mental or psychological disorder, such as mental retardation, organic brain syndrome, emotional and mental illness, learning disability, but does not include mental disabilities excluded from

---

1. Gov't Code § 12900; *Robinson v. Fair Employment & Housing Comm'n* 2 Cal.4th 226 (1992).
2. Civ. Code §§ 51 to 53.
3. Gov't Code §§ 12920 to 12995.

coverage under the federal Americans With Disabilities Act.[4] Discrimination on any of these grounds is a prohibited employment practice.[5] As employers, MHPs must be aware of discrimination issues, particularly those involving discrimination on the basis of mental disabilities.

In addition, one case has suggested that using the original Minnesota Multiphasic Personality Inventory[6] (i.e., rather than the MMPI-2 or MMPI-A) as a screening device for employment may run afoul of California law because certain questions on the original MMPI deal with sexual orientation or religious beliefs about which employers are no longer allowed to ask.[7]

(B) Application of the Fair Employment and Housing Act

The FEHA applies to employers who regularly employ five or more persons, but it does not include a nonprofit religious association or corporation.[8] By contrast, under the Federal Civil Rights Act, Title VII, an employer is a person who has 15 or more employees for each working day in each of 20 or more calendar weeks.[9] In a 1992 case, the California Supreme Court concluded that the reference to five or more persons did not mean five full-time employees—that the FEHA included part-time employees in a professional-practice setting. The court noted that, unlike some other states, California did not elect to exempt small businesses from the pregnancy leave provisions of the anti-discrimination law.[10] Thus, MHPs need to be fully aware that they too may be subject to the FEHA.

---

4. Gov't Code § 12926(i). The Americans With Disabilities Act is found at 42 U.S.C. § 12211.
5. Gov't Code §§ 12940 to 12948.
6. For annotated listing of state and federal case law involving the MMPI, see Pope, K.S., Butcher, J.N., & Seelen, J. (1993). The MMPI, MMPI-2, & MMPI-A in court: A practical guide for expert witnesses and attorneys. Washington, DC: American Psychological Association.
7. Soroka v. Dayton Hudson Corp., 235 Cal.App.3d 654 (1991), appeal dismissed as moot, 93 Daily Journal DAR 14,329. This type of dismissal essentially removes the earlier decision as a precedent: i.e., it cannot be cited or relied on as a precedent.
8. Gov't Code § 12926(c); Robinson v. Fair Employment & Housing Comm'n, 2 Cal.4th 226 (1992).
9. 42 U.S.C. § 2000E(b); Robinson v. Fair Employment & Housing Comm'n, supra note 7.
10. Id. at 242.

(C) Authority of the Fair Employment and Housing Commission

The FEHA is enforced by the Fair Employment and Housing Commission (FEHC), which commission can order unlawful or discriminatory practices to cease, or payment of back wages, but not compensatory or punitive damages.[11]

(D) Application of the Unruh Civil Rights Act

Generally, the government brings actions enforcing the FEHA, and private individuals bring actions under the Unruh Civil Rights Act, which may in turn refer to the sections of the FEHA establishing various practices to be illegal.[12] The Unruh Act proclaims:

> All persons within the jurisdiction of this state are free and equal, and no matter what their sex, race, color, religion, ancestry, national origin, or disability are entitled to the full and equal accommodations, advantages, facilities, privileges, or services in all business establishments of every kind whatsoever.[13]

The Unruh Act also provides that a violation of any right of any individual under the American with Disabilities Act constitutes a violation of the Unruh Act.[14]

(E) Penalties for Illegal Discrimination

If a violation of the Unruh Act is found, a jury may award up to a maximum of three times the actual damages, but in no case less than $250.[15] However, where the right to be free from violence is violated, a person who violates the law can be subject to actual damages, punitive damages, a civil penalty of $25,000, and attorney fees.[16]

In addition to private actions, actions may be brought by the attorney general, a district attorney, or a city attorney.[17]

---

11. *Peralta Community College Dist. v. Fair Employment & Housing Comm'n*, 5 Cal.3d 40 (1990); *Robinson v. Fair Employment & Housing Comm'n, supra* note 7.
12. *Gayer v. Polk Gulch, Inc.*, 231 Cal.App.3d 515 (1991).
13. Civ. Code § 51.
14. *Id.*
15. Civ. Code § 52.
16. Civ. Code § 52(b).
17. Civ. Code §§ 52, 52.1.

Civil/Criminal Matters

Jury Selection

The selection of individuals from a panel of prospective jurors to constitute a trial jury is an art, not a science. While the procedures are clearly defined, determining who will constitute a favorable juror is a task that involves many subjective factors. MHPs may be involved in the jury selection process in a number of different ways, such as formulating questions to ask potential jurors, evaluating juror responses, and so forth.

(A) Types of Juries

There are three kinds of juries in California: grand juries, trial juries, and juries of inquest.[1] The term *juror* as it is most commonly used refers to an individual sitting on a trial jury. A *jury of inquest* is a body of citizens called before a sheriff, coroner, or other ministerial officer to inquire into particular facts, usually where it appears a homicide may have occurred.[2] A *grand jury* is a special body convened to determine whether cause exists to charge individuals with crimes.[3] A trial jury actually hears civil and criminal trials and renders verdicts on the facts.

(B) Creation of Jury List

People are selected for jury service at random from sources that provide a representative cross-section of the population in the

---

1. Civ. Proc. Code § 193.
2. Civ. Proc. Code § 194(f).
3. Penal Code § 888. A grand jury is composed of 23 jurors in a county with a population of oscr 4 million, and 19 jurors in other counties.

area that the court serves. The sources from which juror names are drawn may include customer mailing lists, telephone directories, utility company lists, lists of registered voters, and the Department of Motor Vehicles' list of licensed drivers and identification card holders.[4] These sources lead to the creation of a master juror list, which is used to send juror questionnaires. The juror questionnaires are used to create a qualified juror list from which prospective jurors are summoned.[5] Certain counties have slightly different venires (panels) because their population is small.[6]

(C) Juror Qualifications

The qualifications for being a juror are set by law, while the qualities that make a good juror for a particular party are subjective in nature and vary from case to case.

All U.S. citizens are eligible and qualified to be prospective trial jurors unless

1. they are less than 18 years old;
2. they are not domiciled in the state of California;
3. they are not residents of the jurisdiction in which they are summoned to serve;
4. they have been convicted of malfeasance in office or a felony and their civil rights have not been restored;
5. they do not have sufficient knowledge of the English language;
6. they are already serving as grand jurors or trial jurors in any court of the state; and
7. they are the subject of conservatorships.[7]

No eligible person is exempt from service as a trial juror by reason of occupation, race, color, religion, sex, national origin or economic status. Loss of sight or hearing or another disability that impedes a person's ability to communicate or impairs the person's mobility is not by itself a ground for disqualification. An eligible person may be excused from jury service only for undue hardship upon themselves or upon the public.[8] Some of the common grounds for excusing jurors based on hardship is if the employer will not pay the juror for the time at court, creating an

---

4. Civ. Proc. Code § 197. Trial jurors for criminal and civil actions are formed in the same manner. Penal Code § 1046.
5. Civ. Proc. Code § 98.
6. Civ. Proc. Code §§ 199, 199.5, 200.
7. Civ. Proc. Code § 203.
8. Civ. Proc. Code § 204.

extreme financial burden; the prospective juror must travel an excessive distance or has no readily available means of public or private transportation; the prospective juror has a physical or mental disability or impairment not affecting his or her competency to act as a juror but that would expose him or her to undue risk of mental or physical harm; the prospective juror's services are immediately needed for protection of the public health and safety (e.g., police or sheriffs), and it is not feasible to make alternative arrangements to relieve the person of those responsibilities during the period of service; or the prospective juror has a personal obligation to provide actual and necessary care to another, including sick, aged or infirm dependents or a child who requires the prospective juror's personal care and attention, and no comparable substitute care is available or economically practical.[9]

(D) Criminal Trials

(D)(1) When a Jury is Allowed

Both the California Constitution and the U.S. Constitution guarantee a criminal defendant a right to a jury trial. The right does not apply, however, to most motor vehicle violations, except driving under the influence of drugs or narcotics.[10] Upon the request of the criminal defendant, the court, in its discretion, may allow a trial to proceed without a jury. Generally, nonjury trials are requested where the facts are so extreme as to bias excessively a jury against a defendant.

(D)(2) Jury Size

Juries in criminal cases consist of 12 persons but at least 2 additional jurors chosen as substitutes so that if a voting juror becomes ill during the trial, it can proceed with a substitute. While the substitute jurors are required to take the same oath and listen to the evidence, they do not become voting jurors unless they replace another juror.

(D)(3) Unanimity Requirement

In criminal cases, a jury must reach a unanimous verdict.

(D)(4) Change of Venue

Venue is the location of the court in which the action will be heard. Both criminal and civil defendants may request that the location

---

9. Judicial Administration Standards § 4.5(d).
10. Penal Code § 1042.5.

of the trial be moved to another county within the state for good cause. Before ordering a change of venue in a criminal case, the court should consider attempting to impanel a jury that could be fair and impartial. If a change of venue is ordered, the court may consider whether to move the jury rather than move the pending action. When a criminal action's venue is changed, the county in which the action originated should reimburse the county receiving the case for any ordinary expenditure and any extraordinary but reasonable and necessary expenditure.[11]

The most common reason for a change of venue is the likelihood that media coverage will prevent a fair or impartial trial in that county. MHPs may be called upon to conduct surveys of residents of a particular county to ascertain the level of general knowledge about a particular case and the extent to which the public has already predetermined guilt or innocence based on media reports or widespread hostility toward particular parties or groups. Such surveys may then be made part of the motion to change venue. However, the mere fact that a trial engenders extensive publicity does not mean that venue will be changed.[12]

Other alternatives to change of venue are delaying the trial and conducting more intensive examination of potential jurors. All that is required is for the jurors to state that they can set aside the knowledge derived from media reports and other sources and make a decision based only on information received at trial. Of course, a mere verbal assurance does not mean that he or she can or will actually do so.[13]

(D)(5) Voir Dire

Voir dire is the term used to describe the process whereby the judge and attorneys ask questions of jurors to determine whether any of them should be excused because of bias or other reasons. Each side is allowed a certain number of peremptory challenges—which do not have to be explained and for which no justification is necessary—to the jury members. The number of challenges available depends on the number of parties. If there are only two parties, each party is entitled to six peremptory challenges. If there are more than two parties, the court divides them into two or more sides, according to their mutual interests; each side is entitled to a total of eight peremptory challenges.[14]

---

11. Penal Code §§ 1036.7, 1037; Judicial Administration Standards §§ 4 to 4.2.
12. A practical problem can arise when a case is so well known that it would be notorious in any county, such as the prosecution of Los Angeles police officers for beating Rodney King.
13. *People v. Carter*, 56 Cal.2d 549 (1961).
14. Penal Code § 601.

The parties are not limited in the number of challenges they may make for cause.[15] *Cause* generally means that the juror is unable to be impartial or does not meet the qualifications to be a juror. Among the more common grounds for challenges for cause are inability to understand English sufficiently to follow the proceedings, bias, prejudice, a personal relationship with a party or attorney, or direct knowledge of the subject matter from a personal relationship. The purpose of voir dire is to allow the attorneys to evaluate which jurors they wish to peremptorily exclude and to determine the extent to which cause exists to disqualify any others. When a prospective juror is challenged for cause, however, the court does not automatically grant the challenge and may in rare cases try the challenge to the juror.[16] Generally, the court also addresses the jurors to explore various questions that will be universal to all jurors.[17] At the conclusion of the court's inquiry, the court permits counsel to ask additional questions. The scope and the length of voir dire is left to the discretion of the trial court.[18]

Among the typical voir dire questions are whether the jurors are acquainted with the parties, counsel, witnesses, issues, location of the incident, and so forth. The court often inquires into the prospective jurors' general attitudes toward the legal system.

MHPs may be involved as jury selection consultants, assisting the attorneys in formulating questions for jurors and observing the potential jurors. MHPs may help attorneys prepare profiles of the characteristics a desirable juror would have for a particular case.

(E) Civil Trials

(E)(1) Where a Jury is Allowed

In California the right to a jury trial in civil actions is a constitutional right under Article I, Section 16. The actions in which a right of a jury trial is allowed are specified by statute.[19] However, the right to a jury trial exists only as to issues of fact and not as to issues of law, which are determined by the court.[20] Further, jury trials are not allowed in cases where the primary relief is equitable in nature and in certain proceedings of a unique nature, such as probate and divorce. In determining whether the right to a jury

---

15. Penal Code § 602.
16. Penal Code § 603.
17. *See* §§ 8 and 8.5 of *Judicial Administration Standards;* Rules of Court, Appendix Division 1, Section A(c)-(d). Cal. Ct. R. 228.
18. Cal. Ct. R. 228.
19. Civ. Proc. Code § 592.
20. Civ. Proc. Code §§ 90, 591, 592, 589.

exists, the court looks to the essence of the action, not the form in which the parties style it.[21]

Some typical equitable actions that do not involve the right to a jury trial include foreclosure of liens and mortgages, specific performance on a contract, an action for an injunction, a constructive trust, and a declaration of rights. Some proceedings where there is no statutory right to a jury trial include the dissolution of a corporation, a proceeding to require a state officer or agency to perform in a certain way (*mandamus*), and habeas corpus proceedings.[22] Of course, the right to a jury may be waived, either expressly or by failure to comply with court rules and procedures.[23]

(E)(2) Jury Size

A civil jury consists of 12 people or any lesser number agreed upon by the parties in open court. In municipal or justice court, a jury may consist of eight persons or fewer if agreed upon by the parties.[24] Alternate jurors usually are impaneled for the same reasons as in a criminal case.

(E)(3) Unanimity Requirement

Unlike criminal verdicts, there is no requirement that a civil verdict be rendered by unanimous vote. Instead, under the California Constitution, three-fourths of the jury (normally, nine) must agree to render a verdict.[25]

(E)(4) Change of Venue

As with a criminal case, the venue may be changed on the motion of a party with good cause shown.[26] Civil cases may also be moved to another venue because of prejudicial publicity, MHPs may play a role in providing evidence to support the change of venue.

(E)(5) Voir Dire

Procedures governing voir dire in civil suits and criminal trials are essentially the same. However, jury selection in a complex civil case can often be somewhat cumbersome when there are multiple parties.

---

21. *People v. One 1941 Chevrolet Coupe*, 37 Cal.2d 283 (1951).
22. *O'Brien v. Superior Court*, 61 Cal.App.3d 62 (1976), allowing habeas corpus suits to contest involuntary commitment, contempt proceedings, and child support.
23. Civ. Proc. Code § 631.
24. California Constitution, art. I, § 16.
25. Civ. Proc. Code § 613.
26. However, a party to a civil proceeding, unlike a party in a criminal trial, may offer to stipulate to a change of venue. If the opponent does not agree and venue is ultimately changed, the party that refused to change the venue may be sanctioned. Civ. Proc. Code §§ 397, 396b.

Expert Witnesses

Witnesses are generally divided into two categories: lay and expert. A *percipient witness* is a witness who has knowledge of the facts that the litigation concerns, either from direct observation or personal involvement as the events unfolded. As such, both lay people and experts can be percipient witnesses. Usually the term *expert witness* connotes an expert retained for the litigation who has some specialized knowledge, skill, experience, training, or education that allows him or her to testify to matters that are outside the general knowledge of a jury or judge.[1] There are important differences between the nature of testimony that is allowed from lay and expert witnesses. For example, opinion testimony is generally not allowable from lay witnesses,[2] whereas expert witnesses are allowed to testify to opinions and to take the opinions of others into account in formulating their opinions.[3] The decision whether to allow expert testimony is left to the discretion of the trial judge and generally will not be disturbed absent an abuse of discretion. Generally, the court must determine that the expert has some specialized training or knowledge that would shed light on an area that is beyond the expertise of the trier of fact.[4] MHPs are frequently called to testify as expert

---

1. Evid. Code § 720.
2. A lay witness can testify to an opinion that is rationally based on the perception of the witness and helpful to understanding his or her testimony. Evid. Code § 800. For example, a spouse can testify as to his or her spouse being intoxicated, *People v. Garcia*, 27 Cal.App.3d 639 (1972), and a property owner can testify as to the value of his or her property, *Hansford v. Lassar*, 53 Cal.App.3d 364 (1975).
3. Evid. Code §§ 801, 804.
4. *Pfingsten v. Westenhaver*, 30 Cal.2d 12 (1952); *Miller v. Los Angeles Flood District*, 8 Cal.3d 689 (1973).

witnesses in a number of different areas, especially the standard of care for MHPs, the effects of particular events on an individual's emotional condition, custody cases, competency determinations, and whether a defendant was sane or insane at the time of alleged criminal acts.

(A) Qualifying as an Expert Witness

To be qualified as an expert witness, an individual must be found to have specialized knowledge, experience, training, or education.

As a general matter, by virtue of training and licensure, an MHP is competent to testify as to the mental status of his or her patient. Going beyond that to a more specialized field may require a greater showing of competency.[5]

Generally, any medical practitioner can testify to the general medical standard of care, although there is a special statutory restriction on who may testify as to the standard of care for emergency room physicians.[6]

There are four requirements for the admission of expert testimony in California:

1. the subject matter of the testimony must be an area that is beyond the knowledge of the average juror or judge, and not an area that they can be educated on in the course of the trial through nonexpert testimony;

2. the field in which the expert has expertise must be sufficiently advanced that the testimony could be considered reliable (for example, an expert in the field of polygraphs would have trouble qualifying because of questions as to the reliability of polygraph exams);[7]

3. once the field has been determined to have sufficient development and reliability to warrant expert testimony, the individual expert must be established as having sufficient competency in that field to offer testimony; and

---

5. For example, in *Cooper v. Board of Medical Examiners,* 49 Cal.App.3d 931 (1975) an appellate court upheld an administrative law judge's decision that an MFCC could not testify to the standard of care for a psychologist. However, in *People v. Overly,* 171 Cal.App.3d 203 (1985), the court held that a trial court did *not* have to favor the testimony of a psychiatrist over that of a psychologist.
6. Health & Safety Code § 1799.110.
7. *Aengst v. Board of Medical Quality Assurance,* 110 Cal.App.3d 275 (1980); *People v. Jones,* 52 Cal.2d 636 (1959); *Witherspoon v. Superior Court,* 133 Cal.App.3d 24 (1982).

4. if the expert is relying on a specific technique or device to formulate his or her opinion, that device must also meet the standards of scientific accuracy and reliability before the testimony will be admitted.

Even if an expert is qualified to give testimony, the relevancy and probative value of the evidence must outweigh any prejudice or confusion created in jurors. Further, the court in its discretion may determine that particular expert testimony would be cumulative of testimony already given, and may exclude it on that basis.[8]

In determining whether particular expert testimony meets the standards of reliability and accuracy, the courts use what is referred to as the *Kelly–Frye* test.[9] This test is derived from two court cases and sets certain minimal standards that must be met before a technique or device can be considered sufficiently reliable to be introduced into evidence. Some of the areas that have met the Kelly–Frye test in recent years include Child Sexual Abuse Accommodation Syndrome[10] and the use of the Minnesota Multi-Phasic Personality Inventory.[11]

Some areas where the Kelly–Frye test has been held to bar testimony include use of hypnotically refreshed memory,[12] Rape Trauma Syndrome to show that a rape occurred,[13] and use of anatomically correct dolls.[14] Simply put, the Kelly–Frye criteria

---

8. Evid. Code § 723; *Horn v. General Motors Corp.*, 17 Cal.3d 359 (1976).
9. In *People v. Kelly*, 17 Cal.3d 24 (1976), the California Supreme Court held that the rationale of *Frye v. United States*, 293 Fed. 1013 (D.C. Cir 1923) applied to California cases. The U.S. Supreme Court in *Daubert v. Merrell Dow Pharmaceutical, Inc.*, 113 S.Ct. 2786 (1993) held that the Federal Rules of Evidence provided the standard for federal courts to use in determining the admissibility of scientific and expert evidence. The court concluded that the Federal Rules of Evidence superseded the *Frye* case. Thus, federal courts in California are now required to apply the Federal Rules of Evidence, not the *Frye* decision. However, the principles of the *Frye* case have been accepted by the California Supreme Court in *People v. Kelly, supra*, and made a part of state law. Thus, state courts can probably continue to use the Kelly–Frye criteria until the California Supreme Court indicates to the contrary.
10. This syndrome is used to explain a child witness's inconsistent behavior. *People v. Harlan*, 222 Cal.App.3d 439 (1990). However, there are two criteria that must be met for the admission of testimony: (1) the testimony must be directed to specific misconceptions jurors might have, and (2) the court must instruct the jury not to take the evidence as proof that the child was abused. *People v. Housley*, 6 Cal.App.4th 947 (1992); *People v. Bowker*, 203 Cal.App.3d 385 (1988); *In re Sarah M.*, 194 Cal.App.3d 585 (1987), Battered Child Syndrome is also recognized. *People v. Jackson*, 18 Cal.App.3d 504 (1971).
11. *People v. Stoll*, 49 Cal.3d 1136 (1989). But an expert could not use statements derived under sodium pentothal for the purpose of showing that the defendant was not a sexual psychopath. *People v. Jones*, 42 Cal.2d 219 (1954).
12. *People v. Shirley*, 31 Cal.3d 18 (1982), *People v. Guerra*, 37 Cal.3d 375 (1984).
13. *People v. Bledsoe*, 36 Cal.App.3d 236 (1984); *but see People v. Stanley*, 36 Cal.App.3d 253 (1984).
14. *In re Amber B.*, 191 Cal.App.3d 1682 (1987).

are that a particular technique or device must be recognized as authoritative by a significant minority (at a minimum) of the scientific community. The Kelly–Frye criteria can be met by establishing the general acceptance of the technique or device through expert testimony, by citation to authoritative scientific or legal journals that reflect the acceptance of the technique (assuming that the hearsay objection can be overcome), and by reference to any judicial opinions that have applied the Kelly–Frye test and accepted the technique or device as accurate. However, citation of cases in which a technique was accepted without discussion of the Kelly–Frye test or an opinion of a court from a state that does not follow the Kelly–Frye test may not be deemed sufficiently persuasive to cause a California court to accept it.

(B) When an Expert Witness May be Called to Testify

Generally, a court will not allow testimony by an expert as to matters of common knowledge: for example, whether a particular condition was obviously dangerous. The court will allow lay witnesses and jurors to conclude whether an individual's behavior was apparently irrational or reflected apparent intoxication.[15]

Some specific areas where MHPs have been found qualified to testify as experts include Rape Trauma Syndrome,[16] that a child has signs of being sexually abused, and that a person suffered emotional distress. MHPs, however, are not allowed to testify that because a defendant meets (or does not meet) a profile of child abusers or similar profiles that the person was likely (or not likely) to have committed a particular crime. This type of testimony is excluded for two reasons: profiles do not meet the Kelly–Frye test for reliability, and second, the fact that an individual does not meet a particular profile does not preclude the possibility that he or she engaged in a specific activity on a given

---

15. Expert testimony may be required to establish actual irrationality or actual intoxication, but the courts find that lay people can testify as to their perceptions of irrationality and intoxication, based on common experience and assuming there is no additional basis for excluding it.
16. Some other areas where MHPs may testify are the effects of divorce and separation on children for the purposes of child custody; professional standards of care (see, e.g., Cooper v. Board of Medical Examiners, 49 Cal.App.3d 931 (1975); the degree to which an individual is impaired so as not to be able to work; whether an individual suffers from any type of personality disorder; whether particular signs are crafted in a manner so as to adequately communicate messages to the average person; and an individual's ability to formulate the requisite intent to commit various criminal acts.

occasion.[17] Testimony as to the typical reactions of molested children is admissible.[18]

Expert witnesses may be hired by either side to render forensic services. Further, the court has the specific power to appoint an independent expert to advise the court in any area or matter in which the court feels the necessity for such assistance.[19] As noted above, such an expert may be called upon by the court where the records of an MHP are subpoenaed. As an independent expert for the court, an MHP may have judicial immunity, in addition to the quasi-judicial immunity discussed earlier.[20] Typically, the cases where a court appoints an MHP as an independent expert involve criminal law, family law, and estate proceedings. Most courts have a family law division with a specialized panel of MHPs who have expertise in custody evaluations. The court generally requires individuals who are in custody or divorce litigation to stipulate to a particular MHP, who will then be appointed by the court to conduct evaluations.[21] Somewhat rarer is the court's use of an independent expert to advise the court on professional standards of care.

(C) Form and Content of Testimony

Unlike lay witnesses, an expert may testify in the form of an opinion and on a hypothetical basis.[22] As a general proposition, witnesses are entitled to testify only to those matters of which they have personal knowledge.[23] However, experts are allowed to formulate their opinions differently, in part because of their specialized training, and in part because an expert could not have personal knowledge of all the requisite information to formulate the necessary opinion other than by reviewing documents provided. Further, an expert's opinion may be based on hearsay that would otherwise be inadmissable, such as the opinions of others, but only to the extent that an expert would typically rely on such opinions in formulating an opinion. For example, an MHP could testify as to diagnosis and conclusions based in part on review of

---

17. *People v. McAlpin*, 53 Cal.3d 1289 (1991) ; *People v. Ruiz*, 222 Cal.App.3d 1241 (1990).
18. *People v. Harlan*, 222 Cal.App.3d 439 (1990), upholding testimony of an LCSW who testified as an expert to reactions of a child molestation victim whom the LCSW had not actually examined.
19. Evid. Code § 730.
20. *Howard v. Drapkin*, 222 Cal.3d 843 (1990).
21. Los Angeles County Family Law Department, *Policy Manual* § XI. Note that panels of experts may be used by the administrative law judges of the Medical Quality Hearing Panel under Gov't Code § 11371(d).
22. *People v. Bassett*, 69 Cal.2d 122 (1968).
23. Evid. Code § 702.

medical records and testing performed by others who are not testifying at the trial.

Generally, experts must be disclosed 70 days before a civil trial and must be made available for deposition before taking the stand.[24] Even when an attorney makes a late disclosure, most trial courts will require that the expert submit to a deposition first, even if the deposition is on the eve of trial.[25] The expert is entitled to be paid his or her normal hourly fee for the time actually spent in deposition. A failure to tender the fee means that the expert does not have to appear for the deposition.[26]

The legislature recently expanded the category of individuals who are entitled to be paid a fee for their testimony to include percipient experts. Percipient experts are those individuals who have specialized training or experience but who are not retained for the purpose of litigation. For example, an MHP who was treating a plaintiff before a civil suit was filed and who is required to give a deposition would be entitled to be paid his or her normal hourly fee, but only for the time actually spent testifying in the deposition.[27] When an MHP is retained by the defense to conduct an independent psychiatric evaluation of the plaintiff, the expert's report must be given to the other side, regardless of how favorable the conclusions are. An expert's report is transmitted to the opposing side by the attorney for the side that retained the expert.[28] In an independent psychiatric evaluation, the party to be evaluated does not have a right to have an attorney present, but may tape the proceedings.[29]

At trial, an expert is asked questions initially by the side that retained him or her, which is referred to as direct examination. In cross-examination, the opposing side then gets a chance to ask questions to try to cause the expert to reassess his or her position, to question the expert's expertise or credibility, or both. When both sides are finished, the court may choose to ask its own questions of the expert. Generally, a deposition is conducted as cross-examination without any direct examination because the attorney who hired the expert knows what his or her opinion is. Typically, attorneys conducting cross-examinations at deposition and at trial attempt to impeach the expert by contrasting his or her

---

24. Civ. Proc. Code § 2037.
25. However, in such an instance the court generally will only do so if the party seeking to use the expert shows that the failure to list the expert was due to mistake, inadvertence, or excusable negligence. Civ. Proc. Code § 2037.6(a).
26. Civ. Proc. Code § 2034.
27. Id.
28. Civ. Proc. Code § 2032.
29. Civ. Proc. Code § 2032(g)(2); *Vinson v. Superior Court*, 43 Cal.3d 833 (1987). But under *Civ. Proc. Code*, § 2032(g)(1), a party does have a right to have an attorney or representative present at a physical examination.

testimony with articles written by him or her that appear to be inconsistent, with generally accepted treatises written by other experts in the field, or with prior inconsistent testimony.[30] However, an expert is not allowed to be cross-examined on a treatise or article on which he or she did not rely and which is not considered authoritative in the field. In other words, if the article or treatise is so obscure that it is not considered authoritative, it is not likely that the court will allow an expert to be questioned on it. Of course, an expert is always subject to questioning to establish bias, financial interest in the litigation, or any other basis for questioning the expert's impartiality.[31]

While witnesses are generally not allowed to intrude on the province of the trier of fact by testifying to what the ultimate facts are, an expert's opinion is not inadmissible if it touches on the ultimate legal issue.[32] For example, experts may testify as to whether a defendant acted within the standard of care, whether a defendant is competent to stand trial in a criminal proceeding, or whether a plaintiff was emotionally distressed. However, an expert cannot testify as to whether a defendant is guilty of a crime.[33]

Expert opinions that are based on mere possibility are generally excluded by a trial judge on the grounds that they are not probative in value, but there is no specific rule excluding expert testimony based on possibility. For an MHP's expert testimony to be accepted as probative, it must be based on reasonable medical certainty or reasonable medical probability.[34]

---

30. Attorneys usually check services such as *Jury Verdicts Weekly*, which compiles listings of when experts have testified in other cases. Further, private services available through plaintiff and defense attorney organizations also compile histories on expert witnesses, which are available at a slight fee.
31. In this regard, experts must be cautious not to allow fees for services to rise to the level where they would be seen as giving the expert a financial interest in the litigation. This not only constitutes a basis for impeachment, but would also probably be seen as an ethical problem by most professional organizations.
32. For example, in *in Re Cheryl H.*, 153 Cal.App.3d 1998 (1984), the court held that a psychiatrist could testify to her opinion that a child had been sexually abused but not to her opinion that the father was the abuser.
33. *Miller v. Los Angeles County Flood Control Dist.*, 8 Cal.3d 689 (1973).
34. *Jones v. Ortho Pharmaceutical Corp.*, 163 Cal.App.3d 396 (1985), 402-03 (1985); *Dumas v. Cooney*, 235 Cal.App.3d 1593, 1603 (1991).

Because of difficulties in the sequencing of witnesses and accommodating the schedules of judge, jury, counsel, and witnesses, it is often necessary to take the expert's testimony out of chronological order—i.e., before certain facts have been established. Therefore, hypothetical questions may be used that allow the expert to assume a specific set of facts and testify as to opinions based on those facts. However, if the expert testifies as to a hypothetical situation and the facts underlying the hypothetical opinion are not subsequently established, the expert's opinion may be disregarded as based on facts not in evidence. Typically, therefore, an opposing attorney on cross-examination will ask the expert which hypothetical facts are key to his or her opinion so that the attorney may determine which ones to attack. It is a rare case where an expert will be able to testify without some element of hypothetical questioning.

It should be clear that an expert is not to take the role of advocate. Instead, an expert is to provide the court with his or her assessment based on his or her professional opinion. Recent amendments to professional ethical standards have suggested that taking an advocate's role in a forensic matter can subject an expert to discipline by his or her professional associations, such as the American Psychological Association.[35]

---

35. Although no valid statistical data is available regarding the number of complaints made against MHPs for testimony they gave in court, the author's experience in the last several years has indicated a dramatic upswing in the number of civil suits, ethics complaints, and complaints made to California licensing agencies about MHPs, particularly because of testimony in custody proceedings. *See, e.g., Gootee v. Lightner*, 24 Cal.App.3d 274 (1990); *Howard v. Drapkin*, 222 Cal.App.3d 843 (1990); *Roe v. Superior Court*, 229 Cal.App.3d 832 (1991); *Silberg v. Anderson*, 50 Cal.3d 205 (1990). There is also a somewhat anomalous case where a party was allowed to sue his own expert for negligence because the result, based on the expert's testimony, was deemed inadequate. *Brousseau v. Jarrett*, 73 Cal.App.3d 864 (1977).

5C.3

Polygraph Evidence

Although California at one point had a statute licensing polygraph examiners, that statute expired with no equivalent legislation taking its place. Historically, California courts have found polygraph examinations to be inherently unreliable and have not allowed them to be used in evidence.

(A) Admissibility of Polygraph Examinations

The California Supreme Court has held that polygraph examinations do not meet the criteria of scientific admissibility set forth in the Kelly–Frye test. As such, the results of polygraph examinations have not been allowed into evidence in criminal proceedings[1] or administrative proceedings.

The Evidence Code provides that the results of a polygraph examination, the opinion of a polygraph examiner, or any reference to an offer to take, failure to take, or the taking of a polygraph exam shall not be admitted into evidence in any criminal proceeding, including pretrial and post-conviction motions and hearings, or in any trial or hearing of a juvenile for a criminal offense, whether heard in juvenile or adult court, unless all parties stipulate to the admission of such results.[2]

---

1. *People v. Morris*, 53 Cal.3d 152 (1991); *People v. Harris*, 47 Cal.3d 1047 (1989).
2. Evid. Code § 351.1.

In a recent case, the California Supreme Court held that it also was an unconstitutional invasion of the right of privacy to require certain categories of public employees to submit to polygraph examinations as a condition of employment.[3]

---

3. *Long Beach City Employees Ass'n v. City of Long Beach*, 41 Cal.3d 937 (1986).

5C.4

Competency to Testify

To testify as a witness in a civil or criminal trial, a person must possess the requisite mental capacity and the ability to express himself or herself clearly and adequately. Whenever there is a serious question about a potential witness's competency, the attorneys should raise the issue; in some cases, however, the court may raise the issue on its own motion. The issue of competency to testify often arises with child witnesses in the context of whether they understand their obligation to tell the truth and are sufficiently mature to be able to relate reliable information. When questions arise about an adult or child witness's competency, the opinions of MHPs may be sought.

(A) Legal Test of Competency to Testify

As a general proposition, every person, irrespective of age, is qualified to be a witness and no person is disqualified to testify in any matter unless based on a specific statutory provision.[1] The determination of whether a particular witness is competent to testify is entrusted to the sound discretion of the trial court.

There are a number of statutory grounds for disqualification. The major grounds for disqualification are

1. the individual's inability to express himself or herself (either directly or through an interpreter) with sufficient clarity; and

---

1. Evid. Code § 700 & *comments*.

2. the individual's inability to understand the duty of a witness to tell the truth.[2]

The legislature's comments to Section 700 indicate that a person's capacity to be a witness depends on his or her ability to understand the oath and to perceive, recollect, and communicate that which the witness offers to relate. However, the statute requires the court to determine only the prospective witness's capacity to communicate and understanding of the requirement to tell the truth. A witness's ability to perceive and recollect the matter that is the subject of the testimony is dealt with somewhat differently. It is axiomatic that an individual must have personal knowledge of the facts to which he or she testifies;[3] the capacity to perceive and recollect is a prerequisite to obtaining that personal knowledge. The term *perceive*, as defined by the Evidence Code, means to acquire knowledge through the senses.[4] Thus, a person's ability to perceive and recollect relates to the *admissibility* of the testimony regarding a particular matter, rather than the individual's *competency* as a witness.

The question of competency can become particularly difficult when the potential witness is a young child, especially in sexual molestation cases. The complexity of this question has been one of the factors that has led to greater liberality in the admission of statements by children.[5] For example, the law provides that a statement made by a child will not be deemed hearsay for the purposes of establishing a crime of sexual abuse, if the statement was included in a written report of a law enforcement official or an employee of the county welfare department and tends to prove that the child was the victim of sexual abuse. In addition, the statement must have been made before any confession by the defendant, and the court is instructed to view with caution the testimony of a person who is recounting hearsay where there is evidence of personal bias or prejudice. The court is also to consider whether there are any significant inconsistencies between the confession and the statement concerning the facts established by the minor child's statement that would render the statement unreliable. The court also has to determine whether the minor child is unavailable as defined by law and whether the defendant's confession was memorialized in a trustworthy fashion by law enforcement officers.

---

2. Evid. Code § 701.
3. Evid. Code § 702.
4. Evid. Code § 170.
5. Evid. Code § 1228.

(B) Determination of Witness Competency

The three most common grounds for determining a witness to be incompetent are that the witness suffers from mental illness, that the witness is a child who does not know the significance of telling the truth, and that the witness is an individual who suffers from statutory disqualification.[6] A history of drug or alcohol abuse does not by itself make a witness incompetent because it does not, without more information, establish a lack of capacity to observe, perceive, or recollect.

The California Supreme Court addressed the question of the competency of a witness suffering from mental illness in a case in 1957.[7] The court identified several criteria for making this determination:

1. whether the proposed witness's mental condition is such that he or she was deprived of the ability to perceive the event about which he or she is to testify, or deprived of the ability to recollect and communicate with reference thereto;

2. whether the witness did perceive accurately, does recollect, and is communicating accurately and truthfully are questions of credibility to be resolved by the trier of fact; and

3. the question of whether a witness is competent is left to the sound discretion of the trial court.

In that case, the court noted that great caution must be exercised in qualifying as competent a witness who has a history of insane delusions relating to the very subject of inquiry in a case in which the question is not simply whether or not an act was done, but the manner in which it was done. In such a situation, the testimony as to details may mean the difference between a criminal conviction and acquittal.

Although that decision was based on statutory language which has since been superseded by Evidence Code provisions,[8] these principles remain generally the same.

It is clear, however, that in determining whether a witness is competent a trial judge must ask more than whether the witness

---

6. Evid. Code § 703.5. For example, no judge or arbitrator can testify in any subsequent civil proceeding as to any statement or conduct, decision, or ruling at the prior proceeding, except to the extent that the statements could give rise to a charge of civil or criminal contempt, constitute a crime, be the subject of investigation by the agencies that investigate judges, or give rise to disqualification of a judge.

7. *People v. McCaughan,* 49 Cal.2d 409 (1957).

8. Evid. Code §§ 701, 702; *People v. St. Andrew,* 101 Cal.App.3d 450, 458 (1980).

understands the obligation to tell the truth. When a question is raised as to the mental competency of the witness, the court must satisfy itself that the witness is competent through questioning.[9]

In dealing with child witnesses, however, the mere fact that a child's testimony is inconsistent or exaggerated does not mean that the child is not a competent witness. As one court stated the test:

> the fact that a very young witness makes inconsistent or exaggerated statements does not indicate an inability to perceive, recollect, and communicate or an inability to understand the duty to tell the truth. The child's competency depends on these factors alone; questions about whether aspects of her testimony were believable are questions of credibility for the trier of fact. They are not relevant to the issue of her competency to testify.[10]

California courts have repeatedly rejected the argument that sexual abuse allegations involving children under the age of 14 be corroborated because to do so would allow a criminal defendant to be acquitted when the only witness was the victim.[11]

There is an important distinction between a witness' competency and a witness' reliability. Once the court determines that the witness is competent, the issue of reliability is left to the jury to determine.

(C) Competency of Rape Victims to Testify

Although some states may allow the testimony of rape victims to be challenged based on their sexual history, California takes the approach that sexual history is generally not relevant and is protected under the right of privacy. However, if the victim volunteers information of this nature, his or her sexual history may then be introduced. In a civil suit or criminal prosecution, a

---

9. In *People v. St. Andrew, supra* note 8, a criminal conviction was reversed in part because of a failure to adequately establish the level of competency of a witness, based on testimony by a psychiatrist that she was "grossly psychotic, with delusions, hallucinations, compulsive and violent behavior."

10. *Adamson v. Department of Social Services*, Cal.App.3d 14, 20 (1988). A four-year-old was testifying in a license revocation hearing before an administrative law judge to sexual molestation by a day-care center operator. The court noted that although the administrative law judge had stated that some of the child's statements were inherently incredible, the same judge concluded that the child was a credible witness.

11. *People v. Harlan*, 222 Cal.App.3d 439 (1990). (Four-year-old's testimony of sexual abuse does not require corroboration); *People v. Pilgrim*, 215 Cal.App.2d 374 (1963) (six-year-old's testimony as to sexual abuse does not require corroboration).

motion, supported by affidavits, must be made to the court before any such testimony can be introduced, unless the rape victim opens the door by alleging, for example, that the rape affected her sexual functioning (*see* chapter 5D.11).[12]

---

12. Evid. Code §§ 1103, 1106.

5C.5

Psychological Autopsy

Just as a general autopsy refers to an attempt by experts to draw conclusions about the physical aspects of someone who is dead, a psychological autopsy refers to an attempt by experts to draw conclusions about his or her psychological aspects.[1] The mental state of a person who is dead can be critically important, especially in murder trials or in other cases where intent is necessary to find guilt. A psychological autopsy could also be important in ascertaining whether a decedent committed suicide, was killed accidentally, or was murdered. For example, in the case of a person whose death was due to a single-car accident, the person's strong religious beliefs might counter an insurance carrier's claim that the death was a suicide (to avoid paying death benefits).

As of late 1994, however, no statute and no California appellate case has specifically approved the use of psychological autopsies. Thus, the presumption is that psychological autopsies are governed by the general standards on the admissibility of expert testimony, and specifically, that they must be shown to be sufficiently accepted in the mental health community to be deemed reliable. This determination would be made on a case-by-case basis.

The two arguments used against admission of psychological autopsies are that they are speculative and that they seek to

---

1. *See* Shaffer, *The Psychological Autopsy in Judicial Opinions Under Section 2035* 3 Loyola L. Rev. 1 (1970). Also see Robert Litman, *Psychological Autopsies in Court* 14 Suicide and Life Threatening Behavior 88 (1984).

introduce evidence of a decedent's character that would not be admissible if the person were alive.[2]

---

2. Sanborn & Sanborn, *The Psychological Autopsy as a Therapeutic Tool* 37 Diseases Nervous System 4 (1976); *State v. Montijo,* 160 Ariz. 576, 774 P.2d 1366 (1989).

Section 5D

Criminal Matters

5D.1

Screening of Police Officers

Police officers have unique powers over other citizens, including the right and means to use deadly force if necessary. Because police officers are given such power, it is particularly important that they be screened to eliminate applicants who might abuse the power entrusted to them.

MHPs may be involved in the process of screening police officers by evaluating applicants as to their emotional and mental condition, in counseling police officers, and/or rendering opinions about the emotional state of police officers who are the subject of administrative or civil actions based on their conduct while on duty. MHPs should also be aware that the evaluations they perform may be discoverable by criminal defendants or civil plaintiffs.

(A) Criteria for Peace Officers

In California, the criteria to become a peace officer are set by the Commission on Peace Officer Standards and Training, a division of the Department of Justice.[1] The commission establishes minimum standards relating to the physical, mental, and moral fitness that govern the recruitment of any city police officers, peace officers, members of the county sheriff's office, marshalls, district attorney investigators, etc.[2] The commission issues certificates for peace officers and for the California Highway Patrol, which are awarded based on a combination of training, education, experi-

---

1. Penal Code § 13500.
2. Penal Code § 13510.

ence, and other prerequisites determined by the commission. The commission can make such inquiries as are necessary to ensure that every city, county, and district receiving state aid pursuant to the Penal Code is complying with the standards for recruitment and training.[3]

The commission prepares guidelines for courses of instruction in various areas, including the use of tear gas,[4] how to investigate sexual assault cases,[5] how to investigate allegations of child abuse or neglect,[6] how to question child witnesses,[7] how to handle domestic violence complaints,[8] and racial and cultural diversity training.[9]

To be a peace officer, an individual must meet the following standards:

1. a citizen of the United States or a permanent resident alien who is eligible for and has applied for citizenship;[10]
2. at least 18 years of age;
3. fingerprinted for purposes of searching local, state, and national fingerprint files to disclose any criminal record;
4. of good moral character as determined by a thorough background investigation;
5. a high school graduate, passed the General Education Development Test indicating high school graduation level, or obtained a two-year or four-year degree from a college or university accredited by the Western Association of Colleges and Universities; and
6. found to be free of any physical, emotional, or mental condition that might adversely affect the exercise of the powers of a peace officer.

To determine item number 6, the applicant's physical condition is evaluated by a licensed physician. The applicant's emotional mental condition is evaluated by either a licensed physician or a licensed psychologist who has a doctoral degree in psychology and at least five years of postgraduate experience in the diagnosis and treatment of emotional and mental disorders.[11]

---

3. Penal Code § 13512.
4. Penal Code § 13514.
5. Penal Code § 13516.
6. Penal Code § 13517.
7. Penal Code § 13517.5.
8. Penal Code § 13519.
9. Penal Code § 13519.4.
10. The requirement that peace officers be citizens or permanent resident aliens has been upheld against constitutional challenge. *Cabell v. Chavez-Salido*, 454 U.S. 432 (1982).
11. Gov't Code § 1031.

Any permanent resident alien who is employed as a peace officer is required to diligently cooperate with the Immigration and Naturalization Service in the processing of an application for citizenship, and is disqualified from being a peace officer if three years after the filing of the application for employment he or she has not obtained citizenship because of failure to cooperate in the process. A permanent resident alien applying to be a peace officer is disqualified if his or her application for citizenship is denied.[12]

Additionally, individuals may be disqualified from serving as peace officers for the following reasons:

1. convicted of a felony in California, or a felony in another state that would have been a felony if committed in California;

2. charged with a felony and found by a superior court to be mentally incompetent;

3. found not guilty by reason of insanity of any felony;

4. determined to be a mentally disordered sex offender; or

5. adjudged addicted or in danger of being addicted to narcotics and convicted or committed to a state institution.[13]

(B) Discovery of Peace Officer Personnel and Psychological Records

A criminal defendant may seek discovery of a peace officer's personnel records by filing a written motion with the appropriate court or administrative body with notice to the governmental agency that has custody of the records. A motion must be supported by affidavits showing good cause and the relevancy of the records to the particular case.[14]

The defense in a criminal case may also seek access to records of citizen complaints that led to investigations or discipline of a peace officer.[15] A typical case where disclosure is sought by a criminal defendant of a peace officer's personnel records, includ-

---

12. Gov't Code § 1031.5.
13. Gov't Code § 1029.
14. Evid. Code § 1044; *People v. Memro*, 38 Cal.3d 658 (1985); *Pitchess v. Superior Court*, 11 Cal.3d 531 (1974); In *City of San Jose v. Superior Court*, 5 Cal.4th 47 (1993), the California Supreme Court held that the right to such discovery extended to juvenile proceedings.
15. Evid. Code § 1045.

ing psychological history, is where the defense is alleging excessive force by a peace officer in connection with an arrest.[16]

MHPs may become involved in the evaluation of peace officers and/or the interpretation of records produced pursuant to a successful motion.[17]

While criminal defendants may gain access to such records, it is less likely that plaintiffs in civil actions against the police can obtain such records unless the defendant police officer affirmatively waives his or her right of privacy.

(C) Peace Officers Bill of Rights

Peace officers are protected by the Public Safety Officers Procedural Bill of Rights, which ensures the following rights:

1. to engage in political activity when off duty and out of uniform;[18]

2. protection for officers during interrogations that could lead to disciplinary action;[19]

3. to review and respond in writing to adverse comments entered in an officer's personnel file;[20]

4. not to be compelled to submit to polygraph examinations;[21]

5. not to be subject to searches of lockers or personal storage spaces except under certain circumstances;[22] and

6. not to be required to disclose personal financial information except in certain circumstances;[23]

---

16. Evid. Code § 1046.
17. Peace officers' personnel records are required to be confidential under section 832.7 of the Penal Code except as required by § 1043 of the Evidence Code. As an example, where defendants tried to obtain psychological test results of peace officers to show excessive force or a bias against homosexuals, the court ruled the results were not properly discoverable because the defendants were charged with a civil disturbance and that the peace officer's rights to privacy outweighed the rights of the defendants. Penal Code § 832.8; *Arcelona v. Municipal Court of City & County of San Francisco*, 113 Cal.App.3d 523 (1980). In that instance, the civil disturbance followed the conviction of Dan White in the death of former San Francisco Mayor George Moscone and Supervisor Harvey Milk.
18. Gov't Code § 3302.
19. Gov't Code § 3303.
20. Gov't Code §§ 3305, 3306.
21. Gov't Code §§ 3307.
22. Gov't Code § 3309.
23. Gov't Code § 3308.

7. to administrative appeal for any disciplinary action taken against them, or for any promotion denied on any grounds other than as specified;[24] and

8. not to be subject to retaliation for exercising these rights.[25]

MHPs may be involved in administrative actions against police officers as witnesses for either the police department or the defense.

---

24. Gov't Code § 3304.
25. Gov't Code § 3308; *See generally Binkley v. City of Long Beach*, 16 Cal.App.4th 1795 (1993); *Baggett v. Gates*, 32 Cal.3d 128 (1982); *Burden v. Snowden*, 2 Cal.4th 556 (1992).

5D.2

Competency to Waive the Rights to Silence, Counsel, and a Jury

Americans have been made familiar, through television programs and movies, with the rights of an arrestee to silence, to counsel, and to a jury trial. These rights were first enunciated by the U.S. Supreme Court in 1966 in the landmark case of *Miranda v. Arizona*.[1] Under this decision, law enforcement officers have a duty to advise an accused of his or her rights, referred to as giving a *Miranda* warning. The rights to counsel, the right against self-incrimination, and the right to a jury trial are preserved in the constitutions of both the United States and California. However, these rights may be waived knowingly and intelligently. MHPs may be asked to render opinions as to whether someone was competent to waive those rights when he or she allegedly waived them.

(A) Right to Silence

The right to remain silent after arrest is derived from the constitutional protection against self-incrimination. The theory is that an accused, rather than aiding the government's case, may elect to say nothing. The trigger for invoking the right to silence is a custodial interrogation. Thus, if an individual is not taken into custody, the right arguably does not arise. If someone is taken into custody, however, that person must be immediately informed of the *Miranda* rights, which means reading a simple and easily understandable statement that the person has the right to remain silent, that any statements made can be used against him

---

1. 384 U.S. 436.

or her, that he or she has the right to legal counsel, and that if he or she cannot afford legal counsel, one will be appointed for them. The person arrested may waive any of these rights after being informed of them, but the waiver must not be as the result of any coercion on the part of the arresting officers. Generally, whenever a confession is given by an accused, the issue of the voluntariness of the waiver will arise. Statements given by a defendant who has not been advised of his or her *Miranda* rights are likely to be excluded at trial.

Once a defendant invokes the right to counsel, he or she cannot be interrogated further until counsel has been made available.[2] However, not all conversations between the police and a suspect constitute interrogation, and interrogation is what triggers the right to counsel.[3]

The voluntariness of a confession must be evaluated in light of any compelling influences or psychological ploys used by the police.[4] The waiver of the right must be a free and deliberate choice, not made under intimidation, deception, or coercion, and with full awareness of the value of the right being waived and the consequences of waiving it.[5] The waiver of constitutional rights is established by a preponderance of the evidence, not evidence that proves beyond a reasonable doubt.[6] An MHP may testify as to the voluntariness of the defendant's waiver.[7]

The involuntariness of a confession can be based on a failure to advise of a defendant's right to silence, psychological coercion, or physical abuse or any combination of these factors. However, police officers are not required to try to dissuade a defendant from confessing when he or she indicates a desire to do so. The key issue is whether the defendant's action was voluntary, and the court looks to a number of factors to determine that.[8]

(B) Right to Counsel

A criminal defendant has the right to be represented by legal counsel of his or her choice.[9] When a defendant is charged with the commission of a crime over which the Superior Court has jurisdiction and a written complaint has been filed with the court,

---

2. *Edwards v. Arizona*, 451 U.S. 477 (1981); *People v. Clark*, 5 Cal.4th 950 (1993).
3. *People v. Mickey*, 54 Cal.3d 612 (1991); *People v. Clark, supra* note 2.
4. *Arizona v. Mauro*, 481 U.S. 520 (1987).
5. *Moran v. Burbine*, 475 U.S. 412 (1986); *People v. Clark, supra* note 2.
6. *Colorado v. Connelly*, 476 U.S. 157 (1986); *People v. Clark, supra* note 2.
7. *People v. Clark, supra* note 2.
8. *People v. Mickey, supra* note 3.
9. U.S. Const. Amend. VI. *See also People v. Clark, supra* note 2.

the defendant must be taken before a magistrate of the court in which the complaint is on file. The magistrate delivers to the defendant a copy of the complaint, informs the defendant that he or she has the right to the assistance of counsel, and asks whether the defendant desires the assistance of counsel. If the defendant requests counsel, the court must allow the defendant reasonable time to obtain counsel. In a capital case (one punishable by death), the court must inform the defendant that he or she must be represented by counsel at all stages of the proceedings. Representation will be at the defendant's expense if the defendant is able to pay for counsel, or at public expense if he or she is not able to pay. Upon the request of a defendant, the magistrate may require a peace officer to take a message to any counsel whom the defendant may name in the judicial district in which the court is sitting. If the magistrate believes that the defendant is a minor, the magistrate must either notify the parent or guardian by telephone or messenger, or appoint counsel.[10]

The right to counsel generally attaches as soon as possible after a defendant has been taken into custody. Once an attorney has been requested or has been appointed, all communications between the police/prosecutors and the defendant must be made either through the attorney or in the attorney's presence. The question of whether a defendant has voluntarily waived a right to counsel is based on whether it is a voluntary, competent, and intelligent waiver. All the circumstances are considered. While defendants are allowed to represent themselves, the courts discourage it and will look very closely at any situation where a defendant elects to represent himself or herself instead of having legal counsel. A defendant does not have to have the same skill and knowledge as an attorney to represent himself or herself.

Both adults and juveniles may waive their *Miranda* rights to counsel, but any waiver by a minor will be more carefully scrutinized.[11]

(C) Right to Waive a Jury Trial

Both the California and U.S. constitutions guarantee defendants the right to a jury trial unless it is waived with the approval of the court. Given the requirement that criminal juries must return unanimous verdicts, the right to a jury would seem to be an advantage for a defendant. However, a defendant or his or her counsel may be concerned that a jury would be less sympathetic

---

10. Penal Code § 859.
11. *People v. Lara*, 67 Cal.2d 365 (1967); *In re Gault*, 387 U.S. 1 (1967).

than a judge and may elect to proceed with a trial by the judge alone. Further, whenever a defendant seeks to minimize his or her potential punishment by pleading guilty to a lesser charge, the court must establish the knowing and intelligent waiver of the right to a jury trial. However, the California Supreme Court has said that only the most compelling reasons can justify an interference with a defendant's prerogative to decide whether to stand trial or plead to a particular charge.[12] Thus if the court determines that the defendant has voluntarily waived the right of jury trial with the advice of counsel, and is not doing so for purposes of delay, the waiver will be upheld.

---

12. *People v. Hill*, 12 Cal.3d 731 (1974).

5D.3

Precharging and Pretrial Evaluations

A preliminary examination is a judicial proceeding to determine whether there is sufficient evidence to try a defendant on criminal charges. The preliminary examination is generally requested by the defense. The process of preliminary examination was originally intended to eliminate meritless complaints. Because a very small percentage of criminal cases actually go to trial instead of being resolved by a plea bargain or motion to dismiss, the California Supreme Court has indicated that preliminary examinations may be the only judicial proceeding of substantial importance that takes place in a criminal prosecution.[1] As part of the preliminary examination, an evaluation may be conducted of a defendant's mental condition.

California does have diversion programs allowing individuals who would otherwise be prosecuted for criminal offenses to receive treatment as an alternative to punishment. The determination as to whether a defendant is appropriate for diversion is generally made at the pretrial stage. For certain offenses the district attorney can screen cases for eligibility at the preliminary examination stage. However, the court may also allow diversion pursuant to a hearing.[2] MHPs may become involved in diversion through evaluation of possible candidates for the diversion program and may be involved in treatment programs that are part of the diversion program.

---

1. *San Jose Mercury-News v. Municipal Court*, 30 Cal.3d 498 (1982).
2. Penal Code § 1000 et seq.

(A) Rationale of Pretrial Diversion

Typically, pretrial diversion is used for individuals who have no prior substantial criminal record, who are charged with the type of crime that would tend to indicate a treatable problem such as use of drugs, child abuse, or domestic violence. A secondary reason for using diversion programs is overcrowding of jails and prisons and the fact that diversion offers a less costly alternative to incarceration. Generally, a request for diversion must be made before a defendant is convicted.[3]

(B) Criteria for Diversion

California has a number of diversion programs targeting different groups of potential defendants. These include persons accused of

1. possession of narcotic drugs, but only for personal use;[4]
2. engaging in domestic violence;[5]
3. abusing or neglecting a minor;[6]
4. misdemeanors;[7]
5. traffic violations;[8] and
6. writing bad checks;[9]

Until 1986, California had a diversion program for mentally retarded defendants, but that statute was subsequently repealed.[10]

The diversion programs involving misdemeanor offenders, traffic violators, and bad-check writers do not address the defendant's psychological condition. Therefore, this section will deal with only the criteria for diversion to other types of programs.

---

3. *People v. Alonzo*, 210 Cal.App.3d 466 (1989).
4. Penal Code § 1000.
5. Penal Code § 1000.8.
6. Penal Code §§ 1000.12, 1000.30, 1001.70.
7. Penal Code §§ 1001 to 1001.9, 1001.50.
8. Penal Code § 1001.40.
9. Penal Code § 1001.60.
10. Penal Code § 1001.35

(C) Narcotics Cases

An individual may be eligible for diversion in a case involving the possession of narcotics for personal use only. To qualify, a defendant must meet the following criteria:

1. the drugs in question could not have been held for sale, but were intended for personal use only;
2. the defendant has no prior conviction of any offense involving drugs;
3. the offense that was charged did not involve violence or threatened violence;
4. there is no evidence of any other offense relating to narcotics or dangerous drugs other than small amounts of various drugs such as marijuana, cocaine, and prescription drugs obtained through a fictitious prescription;
5. the defendant's record does not indicate that probation or parole has ever been revoked prior to completion;
6. the defendant's record does not indicate that he or she has been the subject of a diversion program for a period of five years prior to the commission of the acts in question; and
7. the defendant has no prior felony conviction within five years of when the acts were committed.[11]

The district attorney is directed to review the defendant's file to determine whether any of these conditions apply. If so, upon the agreement of the district attorney, the defense attorney, and the judge, an investigation is made as to whether the defendant is eligible for diversion. If the defendant is found eligible, the district attorney must file with the court a declaration in writing or state on the record the grounds upon which the determination is based and make the information available to the defendant and his or her attorney. The legislature intended that this procedure would allow the court to set the diversion hearing at the arraignment. If the defendant is found to be ineligible for diversion, the district attorney must file with the court a declaration in writing or state on the record the grounds upon which the decision is based. This information is made available to the defendant and his or her attorney.

Referrals to diversion programs granted on or after January 1, 1995, can be only to diversion programs that have been certified by the county drug program administrator, or to diversion programs that provide services at no cost to the participant and have

---

11. Penal Code § 1000.

been deemed to be credible and effective by the court and the county drug program administrator. Prior to January 1, 1995, this same principle applied, except only to the maximum extent possible.

The statute specifies what the district attorney's statement concerning the defendant's eligibility for diversion should include,[12] and provides that the probation department shall be directed by the court to make an investigation into a defendant's background, education, prior substance abuse, and other factors that would indicate that the defendant would benefit from education, treatment, or rehabilitation.[13] The results of any investigation by the probation department concerning eligibility for diversion cannot be admitted in any action or proceeding subsequent to the investigation, even if diversion is denied or is subsequently revoked once granted.[14]

The court holds a hearing and, after considering of any information relevant to its decision, determines if the defendant should be diverted and referred to education, treatment, or rehabilitation. If the defendant is referred to diversion, bail is exonerated. The diversion period can be no less than six months and no longer than two years, and progress reports are required to be filed during that time, as directed by the court.[15]

(D) Diversion in Domestic Violence Cases

A defendant may be eligible for diversion in a misdemeanor case of domestic violence or spousal abuse when the following three conditions apply:

1. the defendant has had no convictions for any offense involving violence within seven years prior to the acts in question;
2. the defendant's record does not indicate that probation or parole has ever been revoked without being completed; and
3. the defendant has not been diverted within five years prior to the acts in question.[16]

The prosecuting attorney must review his or her file to determine whether or not these conditions apply, but the defense

---

12. Penal Code § 1000.1.
13. *Id.*
14. *Id.*
15. Penal Code § 1000.2.
16. Penal Code § 1000.6.

attorney may also review the prosecutor's file to determine if the conditions apply. If the defendant is eligible, the prosecuting attorney must notify the court, the defendant, and the defense attorney of that fact, and the defendant may move for diversion. If the prosecutor finds that the defendant is ineligible for diversion, the prosecutor must file with the court a declaration in writing or state for the record the grounds upon which the decision is based.

For the purposes of this particular diversion program, domestic violence means intentionally or recklessly causing, or attempting to cause, bodily injury to a family or household member or placing them in reasonable fear of imminent serious bodily injury to themselves or another. However, a family or household member does not include a child.[17] As with the drug abuse diversion program, the statute specifies what the prosecuting attorney must put in his or her notice about the individual's eligibility for diversion. There is an additional requirement that the prosecuting attorney must state in the notice that, for the period of the diversion, the defendant may be ordered not to contact the victim and prohibited from annoying, molesting, attacking, striking, threatening, harassing, sexually assaulting, battering, or disturbing the peace of the victim.[18] The probation department is authorized to prepare an investigation taking into account the defendant's background and prior acts of violence.[19]

The court will set a hearing to determine if the defendant qualifies for the diversion program. At the hearing, the court must consider the nature and extent of the injury inflicted upon the victim, any prior incidents of domestic violence, and any factors that would adversely influence the likelihood of successful completion of the diversion program. If the court finds diversion is appropriate, it inquires into the financial condition of the defendant and if he or she is able to pay the expense of such counseling, as the court may order. If the defendant is directed to diversion and the bail is exonerated, the period for diversion shall be no less than six months and no longer than two years.[20]

(E) Child Abuse and Neglect Counseling

The legislature has enacted this diversion program with a specific statement that is not intended in any respect to deprive a prose-

---

17. Id.
18. Penal Code § 1000.7.
19. Id.
20. Penal Code § 1000.8.

cuting attorney of the ability to prosecute persons accused of child abuse and neglect to the fullest extent of the law if the prosecuting attorney so chooses. However, in lieu of prosecution, the prosecuting attorney may refer the defendant to the county department in charge of public social services for counseling or psychological treatment,[21] and such other services as the department deems necessary. In determining whether or not to make the referral the prosecuting attorney must seek the advice of the department.[22]

When the charge is sexual abuse of a minor, no person can be diverted for counseling in lieu of prosecution, except upon a written agreement between the prosecuting attorney and the defendant. In addition, all of the following conditions must apply:

1. the defendant is a family member of the victim: i.e., a parent, stepparent, sibling, aunt, uncle, cousin, grandparent, or member of the victim's household who had developed a family relationship with the victim;

2. the defendant's criminal record does not indicate that diversion has been terminated or probation or parole has been revoked within the previous ten years;

3. the defendant has not been referred for counseling or other services pursuant to the diversion program prior to the commission of the acts in question; and

4. the defendant has no prior conviction for any felony, sexual offense, or any offense in which a minor is a victim of sexual abuse, and has no conviction for any felony offense involving violence against another during the previous 10 years in which the defendant was free of prison custody.

In addition, the prosecuting attorney may impose additional relevant criteria for determining whether a defendant qualifies for the program.[23] If a defendant is diverted, then the county department responsible for public social services or the probation department must monitor his or her progress in the program and report to the prosecuting attorney at agreed-upon intervals.[24]

If a person suspected of sexually abusing a child fails to participate in or fails to successfully complete the counseling or

---

21. Penal Code § 1000.12. A prosecutor was not required to make a referral for counseling or consult the department of social services when a defendant inflicted a potentially life-threatening injury on his son. *People v. Glover*, 111 Cal.App.3d 914 (1980). The diversion program can be contrasted with the child abuse prosecution program setting up specially trained units to increase the likelihood of convictions. Penal Code § 999.9(q).
22. Penal Code § 1000.12.
23. Penal Code § 1000.13; *People v. Everett*, 186 Cal.App.3d 274 (1986).
24. Penal Code § 1000.14.

program, or is subsequently charged with any offense involving violence against another person or abuse or neglect of a child, that fact shall be reported to the prosecuting attorney by the department of social services or the probation department, and the prosecuting attorney must then determine whether or not to prosecute for the violation that gave rise to the referral.[25]

The counseling program shall not exceed five years from the time the person is referred for diversion.[26]

When an individual is referred for diversion pursuant to this particular program, he or she is responsible for paying the administrative costs of the referral and the cost of counseling or psychological treatment determined to be necessary.[27]

(F) Parental Diversion

When a parent has been accused of violating the Penal Code section against physical child abuse with respect to his or her children, diversion may be allowed if the defendant's record does not indicate that probation or parole has ever been revoked, and if no prior diversion has been used. No person can be diverted under this particular program without the approval of the local prosecutor. The probation department must conduct an investigation to determine whether education, treatment, or rehabilitation would benefit the defendant. The court may hold a hearing to determine if the defendant qualifies for parental diversion. If the court orders diversion, it may inquire into the financial condition of the defendant and impose an order requiring the defendant to pay for the reasonable costs of diversion.[28]

(G) Completion of Diversion

One of the benefits of diversion is that if the program is successfully completed, the arrest upon which the diversion was based is expunged from the record—as if it never occurred. The person who went through the diversion may indicate in response to any question concerning his or her prior criminal record that he or she was not arrested or diverted.

---

25. Penal Code § 1000.15.
26. Penal Code § 1000.18.
27. Penal Code § 1000.17.
28. Penal Code §§ 1000.72, 1000.73.

(H) Diversion Does Not Preclude Administrative Discipline

Successful completion of the diversion program cannot be used in any way, without the consent of the person who engaged in the diversion, to deny an application for any employment, benefit, license, or certificate.[29] However, the Board of Medical Quality Assurance was not prevented from using information in a physician's records of arrest for possession of cocaine, in disciplinary proceedings that began prior to the successful completion of the diversion.[30]

---

29. Penal Code §§1001.75, 1000.5.
30. *B.W. v. Board of Medical Quality Assurance*, 169 Cal.App.3d 219 (1985).

5D.4

Bail Determinations

Bail is an amount of money set by and posted with the court to ensure that a criminal defendant appears at subsequent proceedings. The absence of bail was one of the chief grievances against England when the American Revolution occurred. Therefore, the right to bail is a constitutional one—under the California Constitution, as well as the U.S. Constitution. Bail cannot be excessive for the acts charged.[1] If bail is not required, a defendant is released on his or her own recognizance.[2] Bail may be sought at different stages of the proceedings: after the initial arrest of the defendant but before conviction, after conviction but before sentencing, and after conviction pending appeal. MHPs may become involved in evaluating whether a particular defendant is a risk to the community or a risk to flee the jurisdiction. Such evaluations are not required, but may be submitted to by a defendant as part of his or her request to have bail set.

(A) Determining Whether Bail Is Appropriate

While bail is generally required for most crimes, it is not appropriate in certain cases. Typically, a defendant charged with an offense that is punishable by death cannot be given bail when the

---

1. *Cal. Const.* art. I, § 12.
2. Penal Code § 1270. A release on one's own recognizance in violent felony cases is governed by Penal Code § 1319, which provides that the release is to be denied when it appears by clear and convincing evidence that the defendant previously was accused of a felony and failed to appear.

proof of his or her guilt is evident or the presumption of such guilt is great.

In 1982 California enacted Proposition 4, which amended the California Constitution to provide that bail be allowed in all cases except for (a) capital crimes when the facts are evident or the presumption is great; (b) felony offenses involving acts of violence when the facts are evident or the presumption is great, and the court finds upon clear and convincing evidence that there is a substantial likelihood that the defendant's release would result in great bodily harm to others; or (c) felony offenses when the facts are evident or the presumption great, and the court finds upon clear and convincing evidence that the defendant has threatened another with great bodily harm and that there is a substantial likelihood that the defendant would carry out the threat if released.

The law requires that a schedule of bail be established on a countywide basis. This schedule then provides guidelines to the judge for the setting bail in any particular case.[3]

In offenses where large amounts of controlled substances or dangerous drugs are involved, the judge is required to set a higher bail.[4]

Generally, bail is set in a hearing following the arrest of the defendant as a precondition to the defendant being released, pending the trial. The amount of the bail can be posted either in cash or through a bond obtained from a bail bond company. Generally, a bail bond company requires the defendant to pay a percentage of the bail in cash and it posts the entire amount.[5] If the defendant fails to appear, the bond or bail that has been posted is forfeited to the court. While the courts and bond companies in the past have accepted for bail the pledge of real estate, the downturn in the California real estate market has made real property much less acceptable.

In general, the entitlement to bail before a conviction is a matter of right except in capital cases.[6] There is no absolute right to bail following conviction on appeal.[7]

After conviction of an offense that is not punishable by death, a defendant who has made application for probation or who has filed an appeal may be entitled to bail in the following cases:

1. as a matter of right before judgment is pronounced, pending an application for probation where the crime is a misde-

---

3. Penal Code § 1269b, c, & d.
4. Penal Code § 1269b.
5. Penal Code § 1269a; *Los Angeles County v. Surety Insurance Co.*, 165 Cal.App.3d 704 (1985).
6. Penal Code § 1271.
7. *In re Podesto*, 15 Cal.3d 921 (1976).

meanor, or where the appeal is from a judgment that imposes only a fine;

2. as a matter of right before judgment is pronounced, pending application for probation in cases of misdemeanors or when the appeal is from a judgment imposing imprisonment in a misdemeanor case; and

3. as a matter of the court's discretion in all other cases.[8]

The court may exercise its discretion to allow bail on appeal if it is established by clear and convincing evidence that the defendant is not likely to flee and does not pose a danger of safety to any other person in the community. Further, the appeal must not be for the purpose of delay, and must raise a substantial legal question, which, if decided in the defendant's favor, is likely to result in reversal.[9]

(B) Determining Amount and Conditions of Bail

In determining whether to grant bail after arrest and before conviction, the court is to take into account the protection of the public, the seriousness of the offense charged, the previous criminal record of the defendant, and the probability of his or her appearing at trial or a hearing in the case. The public safety is the primary consideration. Further, no bail can be accepted unless the judge or magistrate is convinced it was not criminally obtained.[10] In considering the seriousness of the offense charged, the judge or magistrate must consider the injuries to the victim, threats to the victim or a witness, the seriousness of the crime charged, use of a firearm or other deadly weapon, and the use or possession of controlled substances.[11]

A defendant may be released on bail by the posting of bail in the amount fixed by a judge in a hearing at the time of the defendant's initial appearance or, if the defendant has not made

---

8. Penal Code § 1272.1. In one case, a defendant, who was convicted of five felonies involving drugs, had resided in the city for 15 years, owned his own business, had no prior criminal history, and was earning a substantial annual income. A psychiatrist, a criminologist, and the probation officer concluded that the defendant was no threat to the community and no risk to flee. However, the trial judge disagreed and refused to set bail. The Supreme Court reversed, holding that even though there was no absolute right to bail the defendant had established an entitlement to it. *In re Pipinos*, 33 Cal.3d 189 (1982).
9. Penal Code § 1272.1.
10. Penal Code § 1275.
11. *Id.*

an initial appearance in court, bail shall be set in an amount fixed in a warrant of arrest. If no warrant of arrest has been issued, the bail shall be based on the amount in the uniform countywide schedule.[12]

Bail may be approved and accepted by the officer in charge of a jail where an arrested person is held in custody, an employee of a sheriff's department or police department who is assigned to accept bail, or the clerk of a justice or municipal court in which the offense was alleged to have been committed, or the clerk of the Superior Court in which the case against the defendant is pending.[13]

At the defendant's appearance to answer to the charges, the court may order a discharge on bail and set bail.[14]

The court has the discretion based on the various factors set forth above to set bail in those cases where bail may be granted. The bail may be posted in cash or surety bond executed by a certified admitted surety insurer.[15]

A judge may read the arrest report when setting bail.[16]

A defendant in custody has a right to automatic review of the bail amount set within five days of when it is set.[17]

---

12. Penal Code § 1269b.
13. Penal Code § 1268b.
14. Penal Code § 1269a.
15. Penal Code § 1269b.
16. Penal Code § 1204.5; *O'Neal v. Superior Court*, 185 Cal.App.3d 1086 (1986).
17. Penal Code § 1270.2.

5D.5

Competency to Stand Trial

Under both California and federal law, a criminal trial can proceed only if the defendant is competent to stand trial. Generally, where a criminal defendant is found to be not competent to stand trial, he or she is transferred to an appropriate mental health facility until such time as he or she is eligible to stand trial. MHPs may be requested to evaluate the competency of a criminal defendant, either at the request of the defense or by appointment of the court.

(A) Test of Competency

Under California law, no person can be tried or adjudged guilty if found mentally incompetent. The test is whether, as a result of a mental disorder or developmental disability, a defendant is unable to understand the nature of the criminal proceedings or to assist counsel in conducting the defense in a rational manner.[1] One statutory section applies to a persons who are incompetent as a result of a mental disorder and are charged with a felony.[2] Two other sections apply to persons charged with a misdemeanor whom the judge has reason to believe are mentally disordered and as such may be incompetent to stand trial.[3] A third section applies to defendants who are incompetent as a result of a devel-

---

1. Penal Code § 1367.
2. Penal Code § 1370.
3. Penal Code §§ 1367.1, 1370.01.

opmental disability or a developmental disability and a mental disorder.[4]

If, during the pendency of an action and prior to judgment, a doubt arises in the mind of the judge as to the mental competence of the defendant, the judge must state that doubt on the record and inquire of the attorney for the defendant whether in the attorney's opinion the defendant is mentally competent. If the defendant is not represented by counsel, the court must appoint counsel. At the request of the defendant or his counsel, or upon the court's own motion, the court must recess the proceedings for as long as may reasonably be necessary to permit the attorney to confer with the defendant and form an opinion as to the defendant's mental competence. If the attorney expresses the opinion that the defendant may be mentally incompetent, the court must order a hearing to determine the defendant's mental competence. Even if the attorney indicates that he or she believes that a defendant is mentally competent, the court may still order such a hearing, which will be held in Superior Court.

Once an order for a hearing on the mental competence of the defendant has been held, all proceedings in the criminal prosecution are suspended until the question of mental competence has been determined. If the defendant is declared mentally incompetent, any jury that has been impaneled will be dismissed. If the defendant is determined to be competent, the case will proceed to trial.[5] If the defendant presents substantial evidence of incompetency, due process requires that the court conduct a full competency hearing at any time prior to judgment.[6] The competency hearing is mandatory when there is substantial evidence of incompetency, even if the court does not entertain a doubt as to the defendant's mental state.[7] Absent substantial evidence of the defendant's incompetence, the decision of whether to order a competency hearing is left to the discretion of the trial court.

There is, however, no need to conduct a second competency hearing in a capital case, absent a change of circumstances from an unsuccessful initial attempt to raise competency to stand trial.[8]

---

4. Penal Code § 1370.
5. Penal Code § 1368.
6. *People v. Jones*, 53 Cal.3d 115 (1991). The report of a single qualified professional concluding that the defendant is incompetent is substantial evidence necessitating a competency hearing, even though contradicted by other reports in evidence. *People v. Leever*, 173 Cal.App.3d 853 (1985).
7. *People v. Jacobo*, 230 Cal.App.3d 1416 (1991). However, a defendant's conduct in attacking his own counsel in the courtroom and having a long history of drug abuse was not sufficient to mandate a competency hearing.
8. *People v. Kelly*, 1 Cal.4th 495 (1992). *People v. Jones, supra* note 6.

(B) Raising the Competency Issue

The court may raise the issue of the defendant's competency on its own motion, or the defense may raise the issue. Once the issue has been raised, the court appoints a psychiatrist or licensed psychologist, or any other expert the court deems appropriate, to examine the defendant. If the defendant or defendant's counsel indicates that the defendant is not seeking a finding of mental incompetence, the court must appoint two psychiatrists, licensed psychologists, or one of each—one named by the defense and one by the prosecution. If it is suspected that the defendant is developmentally disabled, the court appoints the director of the regional center for the developmentally disabled, or a designee of the director, to examine the defendant, and may order the defendant confined for examination in a residential facility or state hospital.[9]

(C) Competency Hearing

The issue proceeds to trial before a jury unless the defendant waives a jury. The defendant proceeds first, offering evidence in support of allegations of mental incompetence. If the defendant does not offer any evidence in support of the allegation of mental incompetence, the prosecution may elect to do so. Once the defense case is presented, the prosecution presents its case; both sides may have rebuttal testimony.

The defendant is presumed to be mentally competent unless a preponderance of the evidence proves that the defendant is mentally incompetent. If the jury is involved, the jury's verdict on this issue must be unanimous.[10]

(D) Competency Evaluation

As noted above, the court appoints either psychiatrists or licensed psychologists to conduct the evaluations of the defendant.

The testimony of examining MHPs is critical to the issue of competency, as is the testimony of any MHP who is critical of how the evaluations were conducted.[11]

---

9. Penal Code § 1369; *People v. Hale*, 44 Cal.3d 531 (1988) (failure to hold the competency hearing following evidence for psychiatrist's opinions that defendant needed some type of mental health care was an abuse of discretion and violated defendant's due process rights).
10. Penal Code § 1369; *People v. Campbell*, 63 Cal.App.3d 599 (1970); *People v. Superior Court*, 51 Cal.App.3d 459 (1975).
11. *People v. Prince*, 203 Cal.App.3d 848 (1988). The evidence of the experts is then presented to the judge or the jury.

(E) Confidentiality and Privileged Communication

Under the California Evidence Code, there is no confidentiality privilege in an action initiated at the request of a defendant to determine sanity.[12] In addition, the proceeding may trigger the patient–litigant exception under Penal Code section 1016. However, the statements made by the defendant in the examination by the court-appointed expert to determine competency to stand trial are subject to a claim of privilege at the time of trial.[13]

In addition, the reports of an expert who is retained prior to commencement of the criminal case, who evaluates the defendant, are privileged unless he or she testifies.[14]

At least one court has held that neither the statements of the defendant to psychiatrists appointed to determine his or her competence, nor the fruits of such statements, may be used in the guilt phase of the trial.[15]

The rule keeping out the testimony from a competency evaluation is to avoid a situation where a psychiatrist's assessment resulted in an accused's own statement assisting the prosecution and discouraging an accused from being candid in a psychiatric competency examination.[16] There is, however, a distinction when a defendant seeks to raise an issue through tendering his psychiatric condition at the criminal trial, such as by alleging that a confession was coerced based on his or her mental condition. In such an instance, the waiver of the privilege may arise to allow the testimony of a psychiatrist who had conducted the competency evaluation.[17] Further, when the competency evaluation is initiated by a defendant as opposed to the court, there is greater latitude in letting the information in.[18]

(F) Disposition if Defendant is Found Incompetent to Stand Trial

If a defendant is found incompetent to stand trial, judgment is suspended until the person does become mentally competent,

---

12. Evid. Code § 1023.
13. *People v. Arcega*, 32 Cal.3d 504 (1982).
14. *Roberts v. Superior Court*, 9 Cal.3d 330 (1973). *People v. Danis*, 31 Cal.App.3d 782 (1973).
15. *Tarentino v. Superior Court*, 48 Cal.App.3d 465 (1975); *People v. Rocha*, 6 Cal.App.4th 1533 (1993).
16. *People v. Arcega, supra* note 13; *People v. Rocha, supra* note 15.
17. *People v. Rocha, supra* note 15; *Buchanan v. Kentucky*, 43 U.S. 402 (1987).
18. *People v. Williams*, 44 Cal.3d 883 (1988).

and the defendant is delivered to a hospital for the care and treatment of the mentally disordered, or any other public or private treatment facility to promote the speedy restoration and mental competence. Prior to making an order directing that the defendant be confined in a state hospital or other treatment facility, the court orders a community program director or other designee to evaluate the defendant and submit a written recommendation as to whether the defendant should be required to undergo outpatient treatment or committed to a state hospital or treatment facility. No person can be admitted to a state hospital or other treatment facility or placed on outpatient status unless he or she has been evaluated by the community program director or a designee.

When the court directs that the defendant be confined in a state hospital, the court must provide a series of documents to the state hospital or the treatment facility, including a commitment order, and the maximum term of the commitment, based on the maximum sentence for the crime the defendant is charged with. A state summary of the defendant's criminal history, any arrest reports, any court-ordered psychiatric examinations or evaluations, and the community program director's placement recommendation report must also be provided.[19]

Within 90 days of the commitment, the medical director of the state hospital or other treatment facility in which the defendant is confined must make a written report to the court and the community program director concerning the defendant's progress towards recovery or mental competence. If the defendant is on an outpatient status, the outpatient treatment staff makes the report. In turn, the community program director reports to the court. If the defendant has not regained mental competence but there is a substantial likelihood that he or she will in the foreseeable future, then the defendant remains in the state hospital or other treatment facility on an outpatient status. Thereafter, at six-month intervals, or until the defendant becomes mentally competent, reports are made to the court with copies to the prosecutor and defense counsel. If the reports should indicate there is no substantial likelihood that the defendant will regain mental competence in the foreseeable future, the defendant is returned to the committing court to conduct an investigation and hearings on whether a conservator should be appointed for the defendant.

After three years from the date of commitment, or a period of commitment equal to the maximum term of imprisonment provided by law for the most serious offense that the defendant is charged with, if the defendant has not recovered mental compe-

---

19. Penal Code §1370.

tence, he or she is returned to the court for further determination. At that point, the court holds a hearing to determine if a conservator should be appointed for the defendant.[20]

When a defendant is found mentally incompetent due to a developmental disability, the procedure is similar except that the recommendation is made by the director of a regional center, or his or her designee, and the defendant is delivered to a state hospital for care and treatment of the developmentally disabled, as opposed to a hospital for the mentally disordered.

Under the statute, a developmental disability means a disability that originates before an individual attains age 18, continues or can be expected to continue indefinitely, and constitutes a substantial handicap. This includes mental retardation, cerebral palsy, epilepsy, and autism. This includes handicapping conditions found to be closely related to, or requiring similar treatment to, mental retardation, but does not include handicapping conditions that are solely physical.[21] For developmentally disabled patients, a report is made within 60 days of commitment by the medical director of the facility. If it appears the defendant will become mentally competent within 90 days, the court may order the defendant to remain in the facility for that period of time. Within 150 days of the commitment, if the defendant becomes mentally competent, the medical director reports to the court and the regional director on the defendant's progress. Any defendant who has been committed under this statute or on an outpatient status for six months and is still hospitalized must be returned to the committing court for a hearing.

If a defendant returns to mental competency, he or she must be returned to the court for a hearing. If the criminal action against the defendant is dismissed, the medical facilities holding him or her must be so advised. Defendants generally cannot be held past the maximum period of time allowed for proceedings against them, unless they are determined to be otherwise subject to involuntary hospitalization.

When a defendant has been adjudged mentally incompetent, the Superior Court may dismiss any misdemeanor charges upon 10 days' notice to the district attorney.[22]

---

20. *Id.*
21. Penal Code § 1370.1(a).
22. *Id.* § 1370.2.

5D.6

Provocation

Provocation is a defense in criminal cases when there is no dispute that a death or injury occurred and was caused by the defendant. Provocation means that the acts that the defendant is charged with were in response to acts or conduct of the alleged victim. MHPs frequently are called on to testify as to the emotional state of the defendant at the time of the injury in question.

(A) Definition of Provocation

Provocation is a common defense in a murder case because it can get the charge reduced to manslaughter. This defense asserts that the killing was done in the heat of passion in response to acts by the decedent that would cause an ordinary man or woman of average disposition to act irrationally or without due deliberation and reflection—with passion rather than with judgment.[1] It is possible, though rare, for the defense of provocation to be used in response to a charge of battery or aggravated assault to try to negate the element of intent.

(B) Availability of the Defense

The defense of provocation has the following components:

1. the acts asserted to be provocative must be of such a nature and extent that they would render an ordinary person of average disposition liable to act irrationally and without due

---

1. *People v. Wharton*, 53 Cal.3d 522 (1991); *People v. Rich*, 45 Cal.3d 1036 (1988).

deliberation and reflection, and from passion rather than from judgment;[2]

2. the period of time elapsing between the acts of provocation and the fatal blow must not be so long that a reasonable person would have cooled off and be able to act from judgment rather than passion;

. 3. the defendant must in fact have been driven to passion so that at the time of the act his or her reason was so disturbed or obscured, he or she could not reflect and therefore acted from passion; and

4. the defendant must not have actually cooled off.[3]

The questions of the reasonableness of the provocation and whether sufficient time elapsed between provocation and the fatal blow for passion to subside are questions for the jury to resolve.[4] However, provocation need not be instant, but may occur over a period of time so long that the cumulative effect is to impassion the defendant as required by law.[5] Mere words alone are not enough to constitute adequate provocation for murder.

Provocation and heat of passion are not deemed synonymous with diminished capacity for the purpose of reducing a murder charge to manslaughter. [6]

---

2. *People v. Rich, supra* note 1.
3. Penal Code § 195; *People v. Wharton, supra* note 1, at 569-72.
4. *People v. Wickersham,* 32 Cal.3d 307 (1982).
5. *People v. Berry,* 18 Cal.3d 509 (1976) (two-week period of taunts and insults could be adequate provocation); *People v. Wharton, supra* note 1, at 569-72.
6. *People v. Spurlin,* 156 Cal.App.3d 119, 128 (1984).

5D.7

Mens Rea

The term *mens rea* is often used to describe the mental state requisite to commit a particular crime that requires specific intent. The level of punishment for intentional crimes (i.e., those requiring specific intent) is higher than the level of punishment for other types of crimes. For example, the punishment for murder is often more severe than the punishment for manslaughter, which is defined as the unintentional killing of a human being. MHPs are often called to testify to whether a particular defendant had the capacity to formulate the requisite criminal intent. Lay witnesses may testify to their observations or beliefs regarding the mental state of a person whose mental state is at issue. For example, a lay person may testify as to whether a person appeared inebriated or angry.

(A) Culpable Mental States

The law uses various terms to identify specific states of mind that are part of the statutory criminal code.[1] These terms can be misleading because they have a very strict meaning in criminal law and a somewhat less strict meaning in civil cases. Under California law, there are four major states of mind, which are listed here in decreasing order of seriousness:

1. *Willfully* implies a purpose or willingness to the commission or omission of the act. It does not require any intent to violate the law, to injure another, or to acquire any advantage.

---

1. Evid. Code § 870.

2. *Knowingly* means only an awareness that facts exist that bring the act or omission within the provisions of the Penal Code. It does not require any knowledge of the unlawfulness of such acts or omissions. *Knowingly* does not require any knowledge of the unlawfulness of the act or omission. This requirement is satisfied when a defendant has knowledge of the facts, but not the law.[2]

3. *Malice* and *maliciously* mean a wish to vex, annoy, or injure another person, or an intent to do a wrongful act established either by proof or by presumption of law.

4. *Corruptly* means a wrongful design to acquire or cause some pecuniary or other advantage to the person guilty of the act or omission referred to or to some other person.

5. *Neglect, negligence, negligent,* and *negligently* mean a want of such attention to the nature of probable consequences of the act or omission that prudent individuals ordinarily use in acting in their own interests.[3]

When an intent to defraud is required to establish a crime, it is sufficient if the intent appears to defraud any person, association, corporation, or body politic.[4]

MHPs may be called as witnesses to explain whether a particular individual had the capacity to form one of these specific mental states. (For example, the person was unable to form the requisite intent due to substance abuse, medication, or impairment.) An individual can lack the capacity to form a specific mental state but still be mentally competent to stand trial.

---

2. *People v. Taylor*, 7 Cal.App.4th 677, 692 (1992).
3. Penal Code § 7. For cases defining "willfully," *see People v. McCaughey*, 67 Cal.App. 683 (1968) [261 A.C.A. 149]; *People v. Atkins*, 53 Cal.App.3d 348 (1975). For cases defining the term "corruptly," *see People v. Hess*, 107 Cal.App.2d 407 (1951). For cases defining the term "malice" in a criminal context, *see Messick v. Superior Court*, 57 Cal.App. 340 (1922); *People v. Andrews*, 234 Cal.App.2d 69 (1965); *People v. Silva*, 41 Cal.2d 778 (1953). For cases defining the term "knowingly," *see People v. Calban*, 65 Cal.App.3d 578 (1976); *People v. Garcia*, 250 Cal.App.2d 15, 21 (1967) (knowledge is not equal to intent; knowledge requires awareness of facts).
4. Penal Code § 8.

5D.8

Diminished Capacity

The defense of diminished capacity asserts that a person accused of a specific intent crime lacked the requisite intent due to intoxication, trauma, or some mental illness or defect. MHPs have been requested to testify as to various conditions that might lead to diminished capacity of a criminal defendant. This chapter discusses the current status of the diminished capacity defense, limitations on its use, and the origin of limitations on its use.

(A) A Volition of Diminished Capacity as Defense

California allowed diminished capacity as a defense until 1982, when a ballot initiative passed by the voters became state law. That law abolished diminished capacity defenses and provided that in any criminal or juvenile court proceeding, evidence concerning an accused person's intoxication, trauma, mental illness, disease, or defect is *not* admissible to show or negate the capacity to form the particular purpose, intent, motive, malice aforethought, knowledge, or other mental state required for the commission of the crime charged.[1]

---

1. Penal Code § 25(a).

(B) Diminished Capacity Penalty Stage

Evidence of diminished capacity or of a mental disorder may be considered as mitigating by the court only at the time of sentencing or other disposition or commitment.[2] In addition to limiting the use of the diminished capacity test, the ballot initiative, referred to as Proposition 8, provided that the criminal law provisions governing diminished capacity cannot be amended by the legislature except by a statute passed in each house by a roll-call vote of two-thirds of the membership, or by a statute that becomes effective only when approved by the electorate.[3]

(C) Background of Abolition of Diminished Capacity

Although it is often difficult to pinpoint the origins of a change in law, the abolition of the diminished capacity test was certainly hastened by two cases. The first was the criminal prosecution of former San Francisco supervisor, Dan White, for the murder of Mayor George Moscone and Supervisor Harvey Milk. In that case, Mr. White was convicted of a lesser charge based on psychiatric testimony regarding his diminished capacity due to consumption of junk food, including Hostess Twinkies.

The criminal case which led to the change in law was a California Supreme Court decision rejecting the then current formulation and adopting a formulation that a person is not responsible for criminal conduct if at the time of the conduct and as a result of mental disease or defect, he or she lacked substantial capacity to appreciate the criminality of his or her conduct or to conform his or her conduct to the requirements of law.[4] Thus, current California law severely limits the application of the diminished capacity test.

(D) Effect of the Change in Law

The effect of the change in criminal law is that in the guilt phase of a criminal trial, any expert testifying about a defendant's mental

---

2. Penal Code § 25(c).
3. Penal Code § 25(d).
4. *People v. Drew*, 22 Cal.3d 333 (1978).

illness, mental disorder, or mental defect cannot testify as to whether the defendant did or did not have the required mental state, and an expert is not allowed to testify to the ultimate fact of a defendant's mental state. Instead, the evidence is admissible only in addressing whether the accused actually formed the required specific intent, or premeditated, deliberated, or harbored malice aforethought when a specific crime was committed. However, this does not preclude the introduction of psychiatric or psychological evidence on whether the accused had a mental disease, mental defect, or mental disorder at the time of the alleged offense.[5] Therefore, when a general intent crime is charged, evidence of mental disease or defect is not allowed.[6]

(E) Intoxication and Diminished Capacity

At the same time that the diminished capacity test was abolished, the law was changed regarding voluntary intoxication. Now, no act committed by a person while in a state of voluntary intoxication is any less criminal by reason of that intoxication. Evidence of voluntary intoxication is admissible solely on the issue of whether or not the defendant actually formed the required specific intent, or premeditated, deliberated, or harbored malice aforethought when a specific intent crime has been charged. Evidence of voluntary intoxication cannot be admitted to show lack of the capacity to form a specific intent.

Voluntary intoxication includes the voluntary ingestion, injection, or taking by any other means, of any intoxicating liquor, drug, or other substance.[7]

---

5. *People v. Whitler*, 171 Cal.App.3d 337 (1985); *People v. Lynn*, 159 Cal.App.3d 715 (1984); *People v. Jackson*, 152 Cal.App.3d 961 (1984).
6. *People v. Velez*, 175 Cal.App.3d 785 (1985). Penal Code § 29.
7. Penal Code § 22. *People v. Visciotti*, 2 Cal.4th 1 (1992); *People v. Ramirez*, 50 Cal.3d 1158 (1990), *cert. denied*, sub nom *Ramirez v. California* 498, U.S. 1110 (1990); *People v. Williams*, 44 Cal.3d 1127 (1988), *cert. denied*, sub nom *Williams v. California* 488 U.S. 975 (1988).

5D.9

Criminal
Responsibility

Generally, the mental condition of a criminal defendant (and specifically, whether the defendant suffers from any form of mental illness) is not raised simply by the filing of a criminal prosecution. Instead, the defendant's mental illness, if any, must be tendered specifically by raising it as a defense. In civil cases, a defendant may have the opportunity to require a plaintiff to submit to a mental examination if a plaintiff's mental condition is tendered as an issue.[1] In criminal law, however, the prosecutor's right to an evaluation of the defendant's mental condition only arises once the defendant has tendered his or her mental condition. Unfortunately, such evaluations often lead to conflicting opinions by MHPs, resulting in public antipathy toward MHPs, which is reflected by the passage of Proposition 8 in 1982 limiting the use of the insanity defense and the defense of diminished capacity (*see* chapter 5D.8). However, there is still a place under the statutory scheme for evaluation of the defendant by an MHP to determine the individual's state of mind.

(A) Effect of Proposition 8 on Insanity Defense

The 1982 initiative also limited the insanity defense. The defense of not guilty by reason of insanity is available only when the accused proves by a preponderance of the evidence that he or she was incapable of knowing or understanding the nature and qual-

---

1. Civ. Proc. Code § 2032.

ity of his or her act and of distinguishing right from wrong at the time of the commission of the offense.[2]

(B) Legal Determination of Insanity

California originally adhered to the M'Naghten rule as the standard for determining whether a criminal defendant was legally insane.[3] In 1978, the California Supreme Court repudiated the M'Naghten rule and adopted instead an American Law Institute formulation that a person is not responsible for criminal conduct if at the time of the conduct, and as a result of mental disease or defect, he or she lacked substantial capacity either to appreciate the criminality of his or her conduct or to conform his or her conduct to the requirements of law.[4]

One of the express purposes of Proposition 8, however, was to reverse the Supreme Court's position on criminal insanity and reinstate the M'Naghten rule.[5]

The M'Naghten rule has two criteria that must be presented in the disjunctive rather than the conjunctive to the jury.[6] The test is whether, at the time of the offense, the mental disease or defect rendered the defendant incapable of either knowing or understanding the nature and quality of his or her act, or distinguishing right from wrong.[7]

An example of the knowing right from wrong criterion is a defendant's claim that he murdered his wife to gain a public forum to express his belief that there was a conspiracy not to draft professional athletes during the Vietnam war. It was the defendant's belief that no jury would convict him if they were aware of the facts that indicated that he did not see killing his wife as violating generally accepted moral standards.[8]

---

2. Penal Code § 25(b). This is referred to as the M'Naghten test for insanity. Proposition 8 was not intended to create a new test of insanity, but only intended to abrogate prior decisions and return to the M'Naghten test, which had been followed for many years. *People v. Horn*, 158 Cal.App.3d 1014 (1984).
3. The M'Naghten rule is derived from a British case, *M'Naghten's Case* (1843) 10 Clark & Fin. 200, 210, 8 Eng. Rep. 718, 722, and is widely followed in the United States.
4. *People v. Drew*, 22 Cal.3d 333 (1978); *People v. Martin*, 108 Cal.App.3d 1014 (1980).
5. *People v. Horn, supra* note 2.
6. *People v. McCaslin*, 178 Cal.App.3d 1 (1986).
7. The California Supreme Court has indicated that the "distinguishing right from wrong" criterion means whether a defendant was capable of realizing that his or her acts were morally wrong. *People v. Kelly*, 1 Cal.4th 495 (1992).
8. *People v. Stress*, 205 Cal.App.3d 1259 (1988).

(C) Burden of Proof

A plea of not guilty by reason of insanity can be found only if the accused person proves by a preponderance of the evidence that he or she met the M'Naghten standard.[9] In the absence of such proof, all persons are presumed capable of committing crimes except

1. children under the age of 14, in the absence of clear proof that at the time of committing the act charged against them, they knew of its wrongfulness;

2. idiots;

3. persons who were operating under an ignorance or mistake of fact that disproves any criminal intent;

4. persons who committed the act charged without being conscious thereof;

5. persons who committed the act in question through misfortune or by accident when it appears there was no evil design, intention, or culpable negligence;

6. persons who committed the act under threats or menace sufficient to show they had reasonable cause to believe their lives would be in danger if they refused (however, this will not justify a crime that is punishable by death).[10]

(D) Mental Examination

If a defendant asserts an insanity defense, to the extent it is currently allowed by law, the question most often becomes not who will be retained to perform the evaluation but who will pay for the evaluation. If the defendant is unable to afford an expert to conduct such an evaluation, he or she may be entitled to such an evaluation at public expense. The prosecution and defense in an appropriate case can agree upon an examiner, or each side can pick one evaluator.[11] If the defendant has sufficient monetary resources, he or she may obtain an examination and retain an expert of choice. If the defendant intends to offer evidence about his or her mental state, the prosecution also has the right to have the defendant undergo a psychological examination.

In 1990, the California electorate approved an initiative measure known as Proposition 115, which requires a criminal defen-

---

9. Penal Code § 25(b).
10. Penal Code § 26.
11. Penal Code § 1369.

dant and his or her attorney to share with the prosecuting attorney the names of all witnesses the defense intends to call at trial, together with any relevant written or recorded statements of those persons, or reports of the statements of those persons, including any reports or statements of experts made in connection with the case and specifically including the results of any physical or mental examinations, scientific tests, experiments, or comparisons that the defendant intends to offer in evidence at trial.[12] Thus, the report of an MHP retained by the defense to examine the defendant and provide testimony as to his or her mental condition is clearly subject to production to the prosecution. However, Proposition 115 contained an express provision that neither the defense nor the prosecution was required to disclose any materials that come within the attorney work-product privilege. This has been interpreted to mean that while a defense MHP's report is required to be produced, the defense may excerpt from it any communications that fall within the attorney–client or attorney work-product privilege. This may allow a deletion of the defendant's version of the disputed incident.[13]

The court may also determine that an individual should be evaluated as to competency to stand trial. In such an instance, the court appoints an MHP to evaluate the defendant. That evaluation and the statements made therein are not privileged. The U.S. Supreme Court has held that when a court orders a psychiatric evaluation that the defendant does not consent to, the defendant has the right to remain silent to avoid self-incrimination.[14]

It is clear from the passage of Proposition 8 that the California electorate intended to take the ultimate fact of whether a defendant was sane or not at the time of the commission of a particular act out of the hands of MHPs to be decided by a jury. Thus, the testimony given by MHPs in criminal matters is important but not conclusive. To the extent that the matter concerns intoxication or sobriety, non-expert witness opinions may be considered.[15]

---

12. This proposition language has been codified in *id.* § 1054.3.
13. *Rodriguez v. Superior Court*, 14 Cal.App.4th 1260 (1993).
14. Evid. Code § 1023; *Powell v. Texas*, 492 U.S. 680 (1989).
15. *People v. Spencer*, 60 Cal.2d 64 (1963), *cert. denied*, 377 U.S. 1007 (1964); *People v. Ruiz*, 265 Cal.App.2d 766 (1968).

(E) Confidentiality and Privileged Communications

As noted previously, the physician–patient privilege does not apply in criminal proceedings (*see* chapter 4.3).[16] While the psychotherapist–patient privilege (*see* chapter 4.3) does apply, it does not apply to a court-ordered evaluation for competency to stand trial, or where the defendant has raised an issue concerning his or her sanity.[17] It appears, however, that to the extent the evaluating MHP is retained by the defendant for the purpose of evaluating whether there are any mental competency defenses to be raised, some of the information may be within the attorney–client or attorney work-product privilege.[18] Admissions made by a defendant to an evaluating MHP that are not within the attorney–client privilege can be introduced in court.

(F) Commitment of Defendants Found Not Guilty by Reason of Insanity

When a defendant is found not guilty by reason of insanity, he or she is committed to the Department of Mental Health for a period not to exceed the maximum prison sentence for the offense he or she was charged with.[19] If sanity is restored sooner, he or she may petition for release.[20] At the conclusion of the maximum period for which the individual could have been sentenced for the offense, he or she must be released unless the district attorney petitions the court to extend the commitment for two years based on a substantial risk of harm to others due to mental disease, defect, or disorder.[21] The proceedings to terminate or extend commitments are civil in nature, and the person committed does not have the same rights as a criminal defendant does in a proceeding to determine competency to stand trial.[22]

---

16. Evid. Code § 998.
17. *Id.* § 1023.
18. *Rodriquez v. Superior Court, supra* note 20. However, if an evaluating expert testifies in court, the privilege is waived, *People v. Garauz*, 34 Cal.App.3d 611 (1973); *People v. Broderick*, 231 Cal.App.3d 584 (1991); *People v. Coleman*, 48 Cal.3d 112 (1989).
19. *People v. Angeletakis*, 5 Cal.App.4th 963 (1992); Penal Code § 1026.5.
20. Penal Code § 1026.2; *People v. Angeletakis, supra*, note 19.
21. *Juarez v. Superior Court*, 196 Cal.App.3d 928 (1987).
22. *People v. Angeletakis, supra*, note 19; *People v. Tilburg*, 54 Cal.3d 56 (1991); *Department of Developmental Services v. Ladd*, 224 Cal.App.3d 128 (1990).

5D.10

Battered Woman's Syndrome

In criminal cases, MHPs may be called upon to testify about the effects of battering on an individual, generally where the victim has attacked the alleged batterer.

The term *battered woman's syndrome* generally refers to a woman who has been physically abused over an extended period of time by a male, usually her husband or boyfriend. California is one of the states that recognizes battered woman's syndrome as a defense to criminal charges as a result of a violent act by the female victim against the male abuser.[1] California law specifically provides that either the prosecution or the defense in a criminal matter may introduce testimony regarding battered woman's syndrome, including testimony as to the physical, emotional, or mental effects upon the beliefs, perceptions, or behavior of victims of domestic violence, except when the evidence is offered against a criminal defendant to prove the occurrence of the act or acts of abuse that form the basis of the criminal charge. To introduce this testimony, the proponent of the evidence must establish its relevancy and introduce the testimony through a properly qualified expert witness. The statute expressly provides that the battered woman's syndrome shall not be considered a new scientific technique for the purposes of the *Kelly–Frye* test discussed in chapter 5C.2.[2]

---

1. For a definition and discussion of battered woman's syndrome, *see* L. E. A. Walker (1979). *The Battered Woman*. New York: Harper & Row; and L. E. A. Walker (1984). *The Battered Woman Syndrome*. New York: Springler.
2. Evid. Code § 1107; note that this section is only a rule as to the admissibility of evidence, not a substantive change in the criminal law regarding the availability of the defense.

Battered woman's syndrome may be considered by a jury in determining whether the defendant's acts were provoked (*see* chapter 5D.6) or as a mitigating factor. It could be argued that battered women's syndrome would negate the specific mental state necessary for murder (*see* chapter 5D.7) and reduce liability to manslaughter. In addition, after a person has been convicted and sentenced for a crime, the Board of Prison Terms may recommend that the Governor commute the sentence or pardon the person, based on battered woman's syndrome.[3]

---

3. Penal Code § 4801.

5D.11

Rape Trauma
Syndrome

Rape trauma syndrome describes a pattern of symptoms resulting from rape or sexual assault. MHPs may testify about rape trauma syndrome in civil or criminal litigation to explain subsequent conduct by or damage to a victim. In addition, such testimony may be needed to establish that a victim's behavior is consistent with having been raped. MHPs may testify about rape trauma syndrome either as experts in litigation or as treating therapists. It is important for MHPs in testifying and in treating rape victims to be aware of limitations on evidence of a victim's sexual conduct.

MHPs may testify as to the effects of a rape on a victim in either civil or criminal litigation, either as forensic experts or as treating therapists.

(A) Admissibility of Rape Trauma Syndrome

Rape trauma syndrome is a term that covers the various symptoms attributable to a rape or attempted rape.[1] Testimony regarding rape trauma syndrome is admissible to explain the victim's conduct or to indicate that the victim suffers from symptoms that are consistent with being raped,[2] but, the evidence is not admissible to show that a rape occurred or that a particular individual committed a rape. In discussing rape trauma syndrome, the

---

1. A. W. Burges, & L. I. Holmstrom, *Rape Trauma Syndrome,* 31 Am. J. of Psych. 981–86 (1974).
2. *Delia S. v. Torres,* 134 Cal.App.3d 471 (1982).

California Supreme Court described it as a therapeutic tool to help identify, predict, and treat emotional problems, not a device to determine the truth or falsity of a rape claim. The Court further noted that rape counselors generally try to avoid judging the credibility of their client and do not probe for inconsistencies or investigate their client's allegations.[3] When testimony is allowed by a court as to rape trauma syndrome, it is to prove that the victim did not consent to the sexual activity. The syndrome may also be admissible in cases involving child sexual abuse and in defense of a victim who retaliates against the rapist.

(B) Admissibility of Sexual Conduct of Victim

California also has enacted a rape shield law, which prevents defendants in criminal or civil cases from introducing the victim's prior sexual history unless the issue is expressly tendered.[4] The law expressly provides that when there is a prosecution of one of a series of specified sex crimes, except when the crime is alleged to have occurred in a local detention facility or a state prison, opinion evidence, reputation evidence, and evidence of specific instances of the victim's sexual conduct are not admissible by the criminal defendant to prove consent. However, if the prosecutor introduces evidence that relates to the victim's sexual conduct, the defendant may cross-examine the witness who gives the testimony and offer relevant evidence limited specifically to the rebuttal of the evidence introduced by the prosecutor.

Where testimony as to the sexual conduct of the victim is offered to attack her credibility, a written motion must be made by the defendant to the court and the prosecutor stating that the defense has an offer of proof of the relevancy of the evidence and the relevancy of attacking the witness's credibility. The motion must be accompanied by affidavits. If the court finds that the offer of proof is sufficient, it shall order a hearing out of the presence of the jury and allow the questioning of the victim regarding the area specified in the motion. At the conclusion of the hearing, if the court finds that the evidence that the defendant proposes to offer regarding the victim's sexual conduct is relevant and not

---

3. *People v. Bledsoe*, 36 Cal.3d 236 (1984). In *Carney v. Santa Cruz Women Against Rape*, 221 Cal.App.3d 1009 (1990), the Court of Appeals held that a trial court properly excluded testimony regarding rape trauma syndrome in a libel case because the alleged rape victim's behavior was not consistent with a rape; therefore, evidence on the syndrome was not appropriate.
4. Evid. Code §§ 1103, 1106.

inadmissible, the court can specify by order what evidence may be introduced by the defendant and the nature of questions to be asked before the jury.[5]

Recently, an appellate court upheld the introduction of plaintiff's sexual history as a prostitute and topless dancer in a civil suit alleging a sexual relationship between the plaintiff and her therapist.[6]

---

5. Evid. Code §§ 782, 783.
6. *Patricia C. v. Mark D.*, 12 Cal.App.4th 1211 (1993).

5D.12

Hypnosis of Witnesses

Hypnosis has been used both clinically and forensically to obtain details about alleged incidents and allow individuals to recall memories that are not readily accessible in conscious memory. The California Supreme Court rejected hypnotically refreshed memory as unreliable evidence because of the possibility of confabulation—i.e., the creation of false memories. The Court's decisions, however, have been modified by statute to allow hypnotically refreshed testimony in certain circumstances. Because of the potential impact on criminal prosecutions, MHPs who are performing hypnosis must be conscious of these limitations.[1]

(A) Hypnotically Induced Information in a Police Investigation

California does not have any laws specifically regulating the use of hypnosis in police investigation, so the police often use hypnosis to try to refresh a witness' memory of details. The problem arises when the information is sought to be introduced in court. Further, in police investigations the hypnosis is sometimes conducted by non-MHPs such as investigators and attorneys.

---

1. *People v. Shirley*, 31 Cal.3d 18 (1982); *People v. Guerra*, 37 Cal.3d 385 (1984); *People v. Johnson*, 47 Cal.3d 576 (1988); *People v. Miller*, 50 Cal.3d 954 (1990).

(B) Hypnotically Induced Testimony

As noted above, initially the California Supreme Court concluded that hypnotically refreshed memory was inherently unreliable and could not be used to support a criminal prosecution.[2]

The Court relied in large part on the testimony of psychiatrist Dr. Donald Schaeffer from the University of California at Irvine. Dr. Schaeffer's opinion was that the process of hypnosis caused the subject to want to please the examiner and if the subject could pick up on unconscious cues, the examiner could bias the answers.

The legislature responded by enacting a statute that provides that the testimony of a witness in a criminal proceeding is not inadmissible, even when the witness has previously undergone hypnosis for the purpose of recalling events, if all of the following requirements are met:

1. the testimony is limited to those matters that the witness recalled and related prior to undergoing hypnosis;

2. the substance of the pre-hypnotic memory was preserved in written, audiotape or videotape form prior to the hypnosis being conducted;

3. the hypnosis was conducted in accordance with all of the following procedures:

   (a) a written record was made prior to hypnosis documenting the witness's description of the event and the information that was provided to the hypnotist concerning the subject of the hypnosis;

   (b) the witness gave an informed consent to the hypnosis;

   (c) the hypnosis session, including the pre- and post-hypnosis interviews, was videotape-recorded for subsequent review; and

   (d) the hypnosis was performed by a licensed medical doctor, psychologist, or licensed clinical social worker experienced in the use of hypnosis, or a licensed MFCC certified in hypnosis by the Board of Behavioral Science Examiners and independent of and not in the presence of law enforcement officers, the prosecution, or the defense; and

4. prior to the admission of the testimony, the court holds a hearing at which the proponent of the evidence proves by clear and convincing evidence that the hypnosis did not so affect the witness as to render the witness's pre-hypnosis recollection

---

2. *People v. Shirley, supra* note 1.

unreliable or to substantially impair the ability to cross-examine the witness concerning his or her pre-hypnosis recollection. At such a hearing, each side has the right to present expert testimony and to cross-examine.[3]

In essence, the statute addresses many of the objections raised by the California Supreme Court in its prior decisions and provides a structure in which the proponent of hypnotically refreshed testimony can introduce such testimony. One of the key objections of the California Supreme Court that is reflected in the statute is that once an individual has undergone hypnosis, there tends to be a hardening of memory even as to false memories, which makes it difficult to effectively cross-examine the witness because the witness truly believes what he or she is saying, even though the testimony may be clearly untrue. When the statutory procedures have been followed and pre-hypnosis memory can be verified through audiotapes or similar corroboration, the Court has upheld the introduction of testimony from hypnotized witnesses about their pre-hypnosis recollections.[4]

Despite the seriousness of this issue for criminal prosecutions, there has been no equivalent case law or statutory provisions regarding admissibility of such testimony in civil cases.

---

3. Evid. Code § 795.
4. *People v. Alcala*, 4 Cal.4th 742 (1992); *People v. Hayes*, 49 Cal.3d 1260 (1989).

5D.13

Eyewitness Identification

Eyewitness identification can be particularly critical in a criminal trial in several different ways. Initially, the eyewitness's testimony identifying the defendant as the person who may have committed the crime may be an essential part of the prosecution's case. Because of the lapse in time between the identification and the trial, eyewitness's memory may fade. Therefore, the extent to which an eyewitness can identify someone or recall events at a trial months later is also critical. MHPs may testify as to published studies reporting mistakes made by eyewitnesses to attempt to raise a reasonable doubt as to the guilt of a defendant.

(A) Admissibility of Eyewitness Testimony

The testimony of one witness alone is sufficient to establish identity.[1] To a criminal defendant, raising questions regarding an eyewitness's identification can be crucial. In a 1984 case, the California Supreme Court decided that a psychologist's testimony about psychological factors affecting eyewitness testimony could properly be put before a jury. In that case, the trial court had not allowed the psychologist to testify, and the record reflected that the psychologist's testimony would have concerned the state of mind, expectations, focus of attention, suddenness, stress, differential race, and other factors that were said to affect an eyewitness's memory. The psychologist also intended to testify that

---

1. Evid. Code § 411.

memory was not a passive recorder of events, but was subject to both selective and constructive interpretation.

The trial court had concluded that the Kelly–Frye test (discussed in chapter 5C.2) mandated exclusion because the literature on factors affecting memory was not sufficiently well developed. The Supreme Court rejected this contention and held that the decision whether or not to allow expert testimony on those psychological factors that may affect eyewitness reliability is left to the discretion of the trial judge.[2]

---

2. *People v. McDonald*, 37 Cal.3d 351 (1984).

5D.14

Competency to Be Sentenced

California law provides that criminal defendants cannot be sentenced while they are mentally incompetent. However, the level of competency required for valid sentencing is not higher than the competency level to stand trial. If a prior determination has been made that a defendant is competent to stand trial, a second hearing on competency to be sentenced is ordinarily unnecessary, although such a hearing can be requested.[1] Therefore, the procedure and standard are the same as that set forth in chapter 5D.5. A defendant who is not competent to be sentenced is treated the same way as a defendant who is not competent to stand trial.

---

1. *People v. Wharton*, 53 Cal.3d 522 (1991).

5D.15

Sentencing

Once a defendant has been found guilty, the court may request an evaluation by MHPs before imposing a sentence. The court may consider the possibility of probation if the charge is one for which probation is allowed. Special provisions apply to cases involving the death penalty.

(A) Pre-Sentence Mental Health Examination

After a plea or a verdict of guilty, the court establishes a time within 20 judicial days for pronouncing sentence. During that time, the court refers the case to a probation officer for a report on whether the individual is eligible for probation. The court may extend the time to hear certain procedural motions and may further extend the time until the probation officer's report is received. If in the opinion of the court there is a reasonable ground to believe the defendant is insane, the court may extend the time for pronouncing sentence until the question of insanity has been heard and determined.[1]

The victim of any crime, or the parent or guardian of a minor victim, or the next of kin if the victim has died has the right to attend all sentencing proceedings and must be given adequate notice by the probation officer of all such proceedings. The victim, or the parent or guardian of a minor victim, or next of kin has a

---

1. Penal Code § 1191. The court also considers whether enhancements are warranted, Cal. Ct. R. 433.

right to appear personally or by counsel at the sentencing proceeding to express his or her views concerning the crime, the defendant, and the need for restitution. The court in imposing sentence is required to consider the statements of victims, parents or guardians, or next of kin and must state on the record its conclusion concerning whether the person would pose a threat to public safety if granted probation.[2]

If the defendant shows cause that he or she is insane and if, in the opinion of the court, there is a reasonable ground to believe the defendant is insane, the question of insanity shall be tried as specified in chapter 5D.5. If a jury finds that the defendant is sane, judgment shall be pronounced. If the jury finds the defendant to be insane, he or she shall be committed to a state hospital for the care and treatment of the insane until sanity is restored.[3]

In cases where a person is convicted of a felony and is eligible for probation, before judgment is pronounced the court refers the matter to the probation officer for investigation and a report to the court on the circumstances surrounding the crime, the prior history, and the record of the defendant, which may be considered either in aggravation or mitigation of the punishment.[4]

In cases where a person is convicted of a misdemeanor, the court may either refer the matter to a probation officer for investigation and a report, or summarily pronounce a conditional sentence. If the case is not referred to a probation officer, the court in sentencing may consider any information concerning the defendant that could have been included in the probation report.

In determining what sentence to impose and whether to grant probation, the court is to consider a series of factors in aggravation and mitigation. In convictions of child abuse or neglect, the investigation may include a psychological evaluation to determine the extent of counseling necessary for successful rehabilitation that may be mandated by the court during the term of probation. Such an evaluation may be performed by a psychiatrist, psychologist, or licensed clinical social worker, and must be included in the probation officer's report to the court.[5]

The general objectives in sentencing are

1. protecting society;
2. punishing the defendant;

---

2. Penal Code § 1191.1.
3. Penal Code § 1201.
4. Cal. Ct. R. 411.
5. Penal Code § 1203(h). If the required psychiatric examination is not provided, a sentence may be reversed and the case remanded for sentencing after such a report has been provided. *People v. Glover*, 111 Cal.App.3d 914 (1980).

3. encouraging the defendant to lead a law-abiding life in the future, and deterring him or her from future offenses;

4. deterring others from criminal conduct by demonstrating its consequences;

5. preventing the defendant from committing new crimes by isolating him or her for the period of incarceration;

6. securing restitution for the victims of crime; and

7. achieving uniformity in sentencing.[6]

To provide the court with adequate information, the probation officer's presentence investigation report must include information about the defendant's prior record of criminal conduct, including convictions as an adult and sustained petitions in juvenile delinquency proceedings, and any relevant facts concerning the defendant's social life and character, history, family environment, and social history, including medical/psychological information and record of substance abuse or lack thereof. The report also must contain a discussion of suitability and eligibility for probation, aggravating and mitigating factors, and restitution.[7]

When a sentence of imprisonment is imposed, the sentencing judge must select the upper, middle, or lower term on each count for which the defendant has been convicted. The middle term shall be selected unless imposition of the upper or lower term is justified by circumstances in aggravation or mitigation.[8]

Circumstances in aggravation or mitigation must be established by a preponderance of the evidence. Selection of the upper term is justified only if, after evaluation of all the relevant facts, the circumstances in aggravation outweigh the circumstances in mitigation. The relevant facts are included in the case record, the probation officer's report, and other statements regarding aggravation or mitigation that have been introduced. The selection of the lower term is justified only if, after considering the same facts, the circumstances in mitigation outweigh the circumstances in aggravation.[9] Circumstances in aggravation include the following:

1. whether the crime involved great violence or bodily harm, or threat of great bodily harm, or acts disclosing a high degree of cruelty, viciousness, or callousness;

2. whether the defendant was armed or used a weapon;

3. whether the victim was particularly vulnerable;

---

6. Cal. Ct. R. 410.
7. Cal. Ct. R. 411.5; Penal Code § 1203.10.
8. Cal. Ct. R. 420(a); Penal Code § 1170(b).
9. Cal. Ct. R. 420(b); Penal Code § 1170(b).

4. the defendant induced others to participate in the commission of a crime or occupied a position of leadership or dominance of other participants in the crime;

5. the defendant induced a minor to commit or assist in the commission of a crime;

6. the defendant threatened witnesses or prevented or dissuaded witnesses from testifying, suborned perjury, or in any other way illegally interfered with the judicial process;

7. the defendant was convicted of other crimes for which consecutive sentences could have been imposed, but for which concurrent sentences are being imposed;

8. the manner in which the crime was carried out indicates planning, sophistication, or professionalism;

9. the crime involved an attempted or actual taking or damage of great monetary value;

10. the crime involved a large quantity of contraband;

11. the defendant took advantage of a position of trust or confidence to commit the offense;

12. the defendant has engaged in violent conduct that indicates he or she is a serious danger to society;

13. the defendant's prior convictions as an adult, or sustained petitions in juvenile delinquency proceedings, are numerous or of an increasing seriousness;

14. the defendant has served a prior prison term;

15. the defendant was on probation or parole when the crime was committed;

16. the defendant's prior performance on probation or parole was unsatisfactory.[10]

Circumstances in mitigation include the following:

1. the defendant was a passive participant or played a minor role in the crime;

2. the victim was an initiator, willing participant, aggressor, or provoker of the incident;

3. the crime was committed because of an unusual circumstance, such as great provocation, which is unlikely to recur;

4. the defendant participated in the crime under circumstances of coercion or duress where the criminal conduct was partly excusable for some other reason, which did amount to a legal defense;

---

10. Cal. Ct. R. 421.

5. the defendant was induced by others to participate in the crime with no apparent predisposition to do so;

6. the defendant exercised caution to avoid harm to persons or property, or the amounts of money or property taken were deliberately small, or no harm was done or threatened against the victim;

7. the defendant believed that he or she had a claim or right to the property taken or for other reasons mistakenly believed that the conduct was legal;

8. the defendant was motivated by his or her desire to provide necessities for his or her family or self;

9. the defendant had no prior record or an insignificant record of criminal conduct, considering the recency and frequency of prior crimes;

10. the defendant was suffering from a mental or physical condition that significantly reduced culpability for the crime;

11. the defendant voluntarily acknowledged wrongdoing prior to arrest or at an early stage of the criminal process;

12. the defendant is ineligible for probation and but for that ineligibility would have been granted probation;

13. the defendant made restitution to the victim; and

14. the defendant's prior performance on probation or parole was satisfactory.[11]

(B) Sex Crimes Sentences

Every person who has been convicted of a violation of a sexual offense, including rape, unlawful intercourse with a female under age 18, rape of a spouse, sodomy, and oral copulation, is required to submit to a blood test for evidence of antibodies to the probable causative agent of acquired immune deficiency syndrome.[12]

A defendant who has pleaded not guilty by reason of insanity and the question of whether the defendant was sane or insane at the time the offense was committed must be tried. If a jury determines that the defendant was insane at the time the offense was committed, unless the defendant has recovered his or her sanity, the court shall direct that the defendant be confined in a state hospital for the care and treatment of the mental disorder or any other appropriate public or private treatment facility approved by the county mental health director. Alternatively, the

---

11. Cal. Ct. R. 423.
12. Penal Code § 1202.1.

court may order the defendant placed on outpatient status. This would specifically apply to mentally disordered sex offenders. Prior to making the order directing that the defendant be confined in a state hospital or other treatment facility, or placed on an outpatient basis, the court shall order the community program director or a designee to evaluate the defendant and submit to the court a written recommendation as to whether the defendant should be placed on outpatient status or confined in a state hospital. After considering the placement recommendation of the community program director, if the court orders that the defendant be confined in a state hospital or other public or private treatment facility, the court must provide the following documents, which are to be taken with the defendant to the state hospital or treatment facility:

1. a commitment order, including a specification of charges;
2. a statement setting the maximum term of commitment;
3. a statement setting forth the amount of credit for time served, if any, to be deducted from the maximum term of commitment;
4. the summary criminal history information regarding the defendant;
5. any arrest reports;
6. any court-ordered psychiatric examinations or evaluations; and
7. the community program director's placement recommendation report.[13]

Note, however, that for a person committed as a mentally disordered sex offender who is placed on outpatient status, the time spent on outpatient status except when in a locked facility does not count as actual custody and shall not be credited toward the maximum term of commitment.[14]

(C) Alternative Sentencing Program

California has a pilot project known as the California Alternative Sentencing Program.[15] The purpose of the program is to provide selected first-time offenders with discipline and rehabilitation in a structured environment for the purpose of changing deviant behavior through physical exercise, programs on substance abuse

---

13. Penal Code § 1026.
14. Penal Code § 1600.5.
15. Penal Code § 1173.

and the elimination of chemical and alcohol dependency, and other education, and to provide emotional stability to help develop moral and ethical thinking abilities and other skills.[16] To be eligible for the program, the following criteria must exist:

1. the offender must not have previously served a term of imprisonment in a state or federal prison;

2. the offender must not have served a term in the California Youth Authority for any one of the crimes listed below;

3. the offender must not have had a prior conviction as an adult for one of the crimes specified below; and

4. the offender must have been sentenced to the state prison for not less than 12 months and no more than 36 months and, after deducting preconfinement credit, have 24 months or less to serve of their term.

Defendants who are convicted of committing or attempting to commit any of the following offenses are not eligible for the program:

1. murder or involuntary manslaughter;

2. mayhem;

3. rape;

4. kidnapping;

5. sodomy by force, violence, duress, or menace;

6. oral copulation by force, violence, duress, or menace;

7. lewd acts on a child under 14;

8. any felony punishable by death or life imprisonment;

9. any felony in which the defendant inflicts great bodily harm on any person other than an accomplice, or any felony in which the defendant uses a firearm;

10. robbery;

11. any robbery that took place in an inhabited dwelling house or trailer coach, and where the defendant personally used a deadly or dangerous weapon;

12. arson;

13. penetration of another by a foreign object against the victim's will by force, violence, duress, or menace;

14. rape or penetration of genital or anal openings by a foreign object in concert;

15. continual sexual abuse of a child;

---

16. Penal Code § 1173.1.

16. attempted murder;

17. assault with intent to commit mayhem, rape, sodomy, oral copulation, rape in concert, lascivious acts upon a child, or penetration by a foreign object;

18. assault with a deadly weapon or with force likely to produce bodily injury;

19. burglary of the first degree; or

20. various other specified statutory grounds.[17]

As part of the alternative sentencing program, offenders are subject to physical and mental health screening. The mental health screening is to be conducted by a licensed psychologist or psychiatrist.[18]

(D) Death Sentence Evaluations

The death penalty has been amended by the California electorate to include additional special circumstances.[19]

The California Supreme Court has specifically upheld the constitutionality of the death penalty law.[20]

A case in which the death penalty may be imposed is tried in two separate phases. The guilt phase is determined first. If the trier of fact determines the defendant is guilty of first-degree murder, at that time the jury determines the truth of all special circumstances charged, except when a defendant was previously convicted of murder. If the defendant is found guilty of first-degree murder and was previously convicted of murder in the first or second degree, there is a further proceeding on the question of the truth of the prior murder as a special circumstance. If the defendant is found of guilty of first-degree murder and one or more of the special circumstances has been charged and found to be true, then his or her sanity on any plea of not guilty by reason of insanity is determined as provided in a special section of the Penal Code. If thereafter the defendant is found to be sane, further proceedings on the question of the penalty proceed under the death penalty special-circumstances statute.[21]

The penalty for a defendant found guilty of murder in the first degree is death or life imprisonment without the possibility

---

17. Penal Code § 1173.2.
18. Penal Code § 1173.3.
19. *Yoshisato v. Superior Court*, 2 Cal.4th 978 (1992).
20. *People v. Fierro*, 1 Cal.4th 173 (1991); *People v. Jones*, 53 Cal.3d 1115 (1991), *cert. denied*.
21. Penal Code § 190.1.

of parole if any one or more of the following special circumstances has been charged and specially proven to be true:

1. the murder was intentional and carried out for financial gain;

2. the defendant was previously convicted of murder in the first degree or second degree;

3. the defendant in this proceeding has been convicted of more than one murder in the first or second degree;

4. the murder was committed by means of a destructive device, bomb, or explosive planted, hidden, or concealed in any area or place where the defendant knew, or reasonably should have known, that the acts created a great risk of death to human beings;

5. the murder was committed for the purpose of avoiding or preventing unlawful arrest, or to perfect or attempt to perfect an escape from lawful custody;

6. the murder was committed by means of a destructive device, bomb, or explosive that was mailed, delivered, or attempted to be mailed or delivered, and the defendant knew, or reasonably should have known, that his act or acts would create a great risk of death;

7. the victim was a peace officer who was intentionally killed while in the course of performing his or her duties, and the defendant knew, or reasonably should have known, that the victim was a peace officer engaged in the performance of his or her duties, or the victim was a peace officer killed in retaliation for performance of his or her official duties;

8. the victim was a federal law enforcement officer who was intentionally killed while the defendant knew, or reasonably should have known, the victim was engaged in performance of his or her duties, or in retaliation for performance of his or her official duties;

9. the victim was a firefighter who was intentionally killed in the course of performing his or her duties and the defendant knew, or reasonably should have known, that the victim was a firefighter engaged in performing his or her duties;

10. the victim was a witness to crime who was intentionally killed for the purpose of preventing his or her testimony in any criminal proceeding, or in retaliation for his or her testimony in any criminal or juvenile proceeding;

11. the victim was a prosecutor, assistant prosecutor, or former prosecutor in a local, state or federal prosecutor's office, and the murder was intentionally carried out in retaliation for, or to prevent performance of, the victim's official duties;

12. the victim was a judge or former judge of any court of record in the local, state, or federal system in California or any other state, and the murder was intentionally carried out in retaliation for, or to prevent the performance of, the victim's official duties;

13. the victim was an elected or appointed official of the local, state, or federal government, and the murder was carried out in retaliation for, or to prevent the performance of, the victim's official duties;

14. the murder was especially heinous, atrocious, or cruel, manifesting exceptional depravity. The phrase *especially heinous, atrocious, or cruel manifesting exceptional depravity* means a conscious or pitiless crime that is unnecessarily torturous to the victim;

15. the defendant intentionally killed the victim while lying in wait;

16. the victim was intentionally killed because of his or her race, color, religion, nationality, or country of origin;

17. the murder was committed while the defendant was engaged in, was an accomplice in, or was attempting the commission of, or fleeing after committing or attempting to commit, any of the following specific felonies:

    (a) robbery;

    (b) kidnapping;

    (c) rape;

    (d) sodomy;

    (e) performing a lewd or lascivious act upon a child under the age of 14;

    (f) oral copulation;

    (g) burglary in the first or second degree;

    (h) arson;

    (i) train wrecking;

    (j) mayhem; or

    (k) rape by instrument.

18. the murder was intentional and involved the infliction of torture; or

19. the defendant intentionally killed the victim by administration of poison.[22]

---

22. Penal Code § 190.2.

The statute also provides that every person who is not the actual killer and who with the intent to kill aids, abets, counsels, commands, induces, solicits, requests, or assists the killer in the commission of the murder in the first degree also is subject to the death penalty or confinement for life in prison without possibility of parole in any case in which one or more of the special circumstances have been found to be true.[23]

When the special circumstances listed above are alleged and the trier of fact finds the defendant guilty of first-degree murder, there must also be special findings on the truth of each alleged special circumstance. In a case of a reasonable doubt as to whether a special circumstance is true, the defendant is entitled to a finding that it is not true. If the defendant was convicted of first-degree murder by the court sitting without a jury, the trier of fact on the special circumstances shall be a jury unless a jury is waived by the defendant and by the people. If the defendant has pleaded guilty instead of going to trial, the trier of fact on special circumstances shall be a jury unless the defendant and the people waive the jury.

There are various other technical requirements governing different situations that relate to the results of the initial hearing on the defendant's guilt and the findings as to special circumstances, but they are beyond the scope of this chapter. Perhaps the most significant issue for MHPs is that at the penalty phase of a death penalty case, evidence presented in the prior phase of the trial, including any proceeding based on a plea of not guilty by reason of insanity, is considered if the trier of fact is the same. If the trier of fact that convicted the defendant of a crime for which the death penalty attaches was a jury, that same jury must consider any plea of not guilty by reason of insanity and the truth of any special circumstances which may be alleged, unless for good cause the court discharges the jury and impanels a new one.

The law also lists a series of aggravating and mitigating circumstances to be taken in account in determining whether to impose the death penalty as opposed to life imprisonment:[24]

1. the circumstances of the crime of which the defendant was convicted and the existence of any special circumstances found to be true;

2. the presence or absence of criminal activity by the defendant that involved the use or attempted use of force or violence or threats of violence;

3. the presence or absence of any prior felony conviction;

---

23. Penal Code § 190.2(c)(d).
24. Penal Code § 190.3.

4. whether or not the offense was committed while the defendant was under the influence of an extreme mental or emotional disturbance;

5. whether or not the victim was a participant in the defendant's homicidal conduct or consented to the homicidal act;

6. whether or not the offense was committed under circumstances that the defendant reasonably believed to be a moral justification or extenuation;

7. whether or not the defendant acted under extreme duress or under substantial domination by another person;

8. whether or not at the time of the offense the capacity of the defendant to understand the criminality of his or her conduct, or to conform his or her conduct to the requirements of law, was impaired as a result of mental disease or defect or the effects of intoxication;

9. the age of the defendant at the time of the crime;

10. whether or not the defendant was an accomplice to the offense, and whether his or her participation in the commission of the offense was relatively minor; or

11. any other circumstance that extenuates the gravity of the crime even though it may not be a legal excuse for the crime.

After having heard and received all of the evidence and the arguments of counsel, the trier of fact considers and takes into account the aggravating and mitigating circumstances. If the aggravating circumstances outweigh the mitigating circumstances, the trier of fact must impose the death penalty. If the trier of fact determines that the mitigating circumstances outweigh the aggravating circumstances, the trier of fact must impose a sentence of life imprisonment without the possibility of parole.[25]

---

25. *Id.*

5D.16

Probation

Probation is a suspension of a sentence on a criminal defendant, subject to various terms and conditions, including psychotherapy. MHPs may provide testimony to help the court to determine if probation is appropriate.

(A) Definitions

Probation means the suspension of a sentence imposed by a court and an order of a conditional and revocable release to the community under the supervision of a probation officer. A *conditional sentence* means the suspension of a sentence and the order of revocable release in the community, subject to certain conditions established by the court, without the supervision of a probation officer. The California legislature has indicated its intent that both conditional sentences and probation are authorized whenever probation is authorized as a sentencing option for infractions (such as violations of minor traffic laws) or misdemeanors.[1]

(B) Probation Investigation

In every case in which a person is convicted of a felony and is eligible for probation, the court refers the matter to a probation officer to investigate the circumstances surrounding the crime and the prior history and record of the defendant that may be

---

1. Penal Code § 1203(a).

considered, either in aggravation or mitigation of the punishment. Information from MHPs may be contained in this report. The probation officer makes a written report containing these findings and recommendations, including recommendations as to any fines that the defendant is required to pay. The report is made available to the court and the prosecuting and defense attorneys before a sentencing hearing. At the hearing, the court shall consider the report of the probation officer and determine if there are any circumstances in mitigation. If the court determines that there are circumstances in mitigation, or that the ends of justice would be served by granting probation, it may place the defendant on probation. If probation is denied, the probation report is sent to the Department of Corrections at the institution to which the offender is sent.

(C) Probation Generally Not Allowed

Probation is not allowed, except in unusual cases, in any of the following situations:

1. the defendant has been convicted of arson, robbery, burglary, burglary with explosives, rape with force and violence, murder, attempt to commit murder, train wrecking, kidnapping, escape from state prison, or conspiracy to commit one or more of those crimes, and was armed with a weapon at those times, unless the person had a lawful right to carry a deadly weapon;

2. the defendant used or attempted to use a deadly weapon to perpetrate the crime for which he or she has been convicted;

3. the defendant willfully inflicted great bodily injury or torture in the perpetration of the crime;

4. the defendant has previously been convicted twice in California of a felony, or convicted in any other place of a public offense, which, if committed in California, would have been punishable as a felony;

5. unless the defendant has never previously been convicted in California of a felony (or in any other state of an offense, which, if committed in California, would have been a felony), he or she has been convicted of burglary with explosives, rape with force or violence, murder, attempt to commit murder, train wrecking, extortion, kidnapping, or escape from state prison, or conspiracy to commit one or more of those crimes;

6. the defendant has been previously convicted once in California of a felony (or in any other place of a public offense,

which, if committed in California, would have been punishable by a felony) if he or she committed any of the following acts:

(a) unless the defendant had a lawful right to carry a deadly weapon at the time of perpetration or when he or she was arrested for the previous crime, he or she was armed with a weapon at either of those times;

(b) the defendant used or attempted to use a deadly weapon while perpetrating the previous crime; or

(c) the defendant willfully inflicted great bodily injury or torture in perpetrating the previous crime;

7. the defendant is a public or peace officer of the state who, in the discharge of the duties of his or her public office, accepted, gave, or offered to accept any bribe, embezzled public money, or was guilty of extortion:

8. the defendant knowingly sold or gave away certain drugs;

9. the defendant intentionally inflicted great bodily injury in the commission of arson, or intentionally set fire to, burned, or caused the burning of an inhabited structure;

10. the defendant inflicted great bodily injury or caused the death of a human being in the commission of a felony by the discharge of a firearm from or at an occupied motor vehicle proceeding on a public street or highway; and

11. the defendant possesses a short-barrel rifle, short-barrel shotgun, a machine gun, or a silencer.[2]

(D) Electronic Monitoring

California also has a program that allows home detention and electric monitoring, which the County Board of Supervisors may authorize for minimum-security inmates and low-risk offenders who have been committed to a county jail. These programs are fairly recent innovations designed to help reduce overcrowding in the prison system.[3]

---

2. Penal Code § 1203. Note that a probation officer is given statutory immunity from suit for his or her duties in providing a presentencing report and that a defendant is not necessarily entitled to cross-examine the person who prepared the presentence report. *DeMoran v. Witt,* 781 F.2d 155 (9th Cir. 1986); *People v. Smith,* 38 Cal.3d 945 (1985).

3. Penal Code § 1203.016.

(E) Specific Crimes Where Probation is Not Allowed

In addition to the language set forth above regarding probation, several statutes prohibit probation for specific types of conduct. For example, the Economic Crime Act of 1992 applies to defendants convicted of felonies for thefts of amounts exceeding $50,000 in a single transaction or occurrence. Under that law, probation will not be granted to a defendant if he or she was previously convicted of an offense where circumstances allowing enhancement of the sentence were found to be true, even if the enhancement was not imposed by the sentencing court. In evaluating whether or not to order probation under these circumstances, the court is to take into account whether the defendant has attempted to pay restitution to the victim.

Further, the court will not allow probation to any person convicted of theft in an amount exceeding $100,000 in a single transaction or occurrence, except in unusual cases.[4] Probation will not be granted to any person convicted of using, soliciting, inducing, encouraging, or intimidating a minor to commit a felony except in unusual cases where the interest of justice would be served.[5] Where a defendant has attempted to engage in various crimes, including murder, rape, and battery against persons who are passengers, operators, drivers, or other occupants of any public transit vehicle, the court is required to impose some period of actual confinement.[6]

Probation will not be granted to any person who used a firearm during the commission or attempted commission of certain specified crimes, including murder, robbery, kidnapping, burglary, rape, or assault with intent to commit rape or sodomy or to escape. Probation also will not be granted to any person who was previously convicted of a felony for murder, robbery, kidnapping, burglary, rape, assault with intent to commit rape or sodomy, or to escape, or who is convicted of a subsequent felony and who is personally armed with a firearm.[7]

Probation will not be granted to a defendant convicted of violating specific statutes dealing with sexual abuse or sexual assault by force, violence, duress, menace, or fear of immediate and unlawful bodily injury, except in unusual cases where the interest of justice would best be served.[8]

---

4. Penal Code §§ 1203.044, 1203.045.
5. Penal Code § 653.
6. Penal Code § 1203.055.
7. Penal Code § 1203.06.
8. Penal Code § 1203.065. This does not apply to certain diversion proceedings.

(F) Probation in Child Abuse Cases

Probation also will not be granted to any defendant who engaged in lewd or lascivious acts with a child under the age of 14 where any of the following circumstances apply:

1. the defendant used violence, duress, menace, or fear of injury on the victim or another person;

2. bodily injury was caused to the child victim;

3. the defendant who engaged in the acts was a stranger to the child victim and made friends with the child victim for the purpose of committing the acts (unless the defendant honestly and reasonably believed the victim was 14 years or older);

4. the defendant used a weapon during the commission of the acts of molestation;

5. the defendant had a prior conviction for committing sodomy or oral copulation by force, violence, duress, menace, or fear of immediate unlawful bodily injury on the victim or another person;

6. the defendant was convicted of kidnapping a child victim for the purpose of committing a molestation;

7. the defendant was convicted of committing child molestation of more than one victim at the same time or in the same course of conduct:

8. the defendant engaged in sexual conduct with a victim under the age of 11;

9. the defendant occupied a special position of trust and commited an act of substantial sexual conduct. *A position of special trust* means a position occupied by a person in a position of authority who, by reason of that position, is able to exercise undue influence over the victim. This includes, but is not limited to, a natural parent, adopted parent, stepparent, foster parent, relative, household member or adult youth leader, recreational director, adult athletic manager, adult coach, teacher, counselor, religious leader, doctor or employer; and

10. the defendant used obscene matter depicting sexual contact.

Criteria 7 through 10 above do not apply if the court makes all of the following findings:

1. the defendant is the victim's natural parent, adopted parent, stepparent, or relative, or is a member of the victim's household;

2. a grant of probation to the defendant is in the best interest of the child;

3. rehabilitation of the defendant is feasible in a recognized treatment program designed to deal with child molestation, and if the defendant is to remain in the household, a program that is specifically designed to deal with molestation within the family; and

4. there is no threat of physical harm to the child victim if probation is granted.

The court shall order a psychiatrist or psychologist appointed, pursuant to the law on child molestation, to include a consideration of these factors in making his or her report to the court.[9] For example, an MHP may be called on to testify as to whether the defendant's rehabilitation is feasible in a program designed to deal with child molestation.

Various statutes also limit probation for crimes involving drug offenses, particularly where minors are used as agents[10] and where the crime inflicts great bodily harm.[11] Further, there is a special statute providing that probation shall not be granted to any person who commits or attempts to commit certain specified crimes against a person who is 60 years of age or older, a blind person, a paraplegic, a quadriplegic, or a person confined to a wheelchair, and such disability is known, or reasonably should be known, to the person committing the crime, and where great bodily injury is inflicted upon the victim. The crimes under this statute include murder, robbery, kidnapping, burglary of the first degree, rape by force or violence, and assault with intent to commit rape or sodomy.[12]

---

9. Penal Code § 388.1, 1203.066; *People v. Cicero,* 157 Cal.App.3d 465 (1984); *People v. McLaughlin,* 203 Cal.App.3d 1037 (1988).
10. Penal Code §§ 1203.07, 1203.073, 1203.076.
11. Penal Code § 1203.075.
12. Penal Code § 1203.09.

5D.17

Dangerous Offenders

California law seeks to identify and punish those individuals who are likely to be repeat violent offenders. MHPs may be involved in treating such individuals in penal facilities or state hospitals (*see* chapter 5D.21) and in assessing the dangerousness of such individuals.

It is clear from the various sentencing laws that have been passed that the California legislature and the people of the state are concerned about the use of weapons and acts of force and violence in the commission of crimes. Sentences may be enhanced for the use of weapons or violence (*see* chapter 5D.18), and probation may be denied or limited based on the use of violence or weapons (*see* chapter 5D.16). An individual who has been found incompetent, or convicted of, or found not guilty by reason of insanity (*see* chapter 5D.9) of murder, mayhem, infliction of great bodily injury, robbery with a deadly weapon in which the victim suffers great bodily injury, assault with intent to commit murder, or any felony involving death, great bodily injury or serious threat of bodily injury, and who has been transferred to a state facility for treatment may not be granted outpatient status until he or she has actually been confined in a state hospital or other facility for at least 90 days. The director of the state hospital or the treatment facility to which the person has been committed (*see* chapter 4D.21) must advise the committing court that the defendant is no longer likely to be a danger to the health and safety of others while on outpatient status, and that the defendant will benefit from such a status before a defendant may be placed on outpatient status. Information from MHPs involved in the treatment or assessment of such individuals may be used in the report to the court. The court must specifically approve the recommendation and plan for outpatient status before the individual can be so released.[1]

Generally, however, the statutes imposing enhancement of criminal sentences for violent acts do not take into account psychological harm to the victim, but rather focus on prior offenses, use of weapons, and if the victim is a member of a specially protected class, such as children, the elderly, or the disabled.

In 1994, two separate statutes were adopted increasing the sentences of criminals with two prior felony convictions who are convicted of felonies.[2] Although the two statutes define prior felony convictions similarly, the statutes use different language as to which prior convictions can be counted to reach qualifying as "strikes." Generally, prior felonies that are violent or serious qualify as "strikes." Where a person convicted of a felony has one qualifying prior felony conviction, he or she may be subjected to twice the prison term allowed by law for the offense then being prosecuted.[3] The statutes also limit the prosecution's ability to plea bargain.

Both statutes require the sentencing court to deny probation on the then-current offense. Furthermore, the court is precluded from suspending any prior sentence for prior offenses, and is precluded from taking into account the time between the convictions. Furthermore, the defendant must be sentenced to state prison and cannot be ordered to diversion or to the California Rehabilitation Center.[4]

As of the date this book went to press, the *California Bar Journal*, which is an official publication of the California Bar Association, asserted that over 100 appeals were pending regarding application of the "three strikes" statute.[5] It is thus possible that cases will be decided invalidating some or all of these statutes. MHPs who need to be certain of criminal sentencing possibilities must check the current status of these statutes.

---

1. Penal Code §§ 1600 to 1604.
2. Penal Code 667(b–i) (effective 3/17/94) and Penal Code 1170.12 added by Proposition 184 (effective 11/9/94).
3. Penal Code §§ 667(e)(1), 1170.12(b)(1).
4. Penal Code §§ 667(c), 1170.12(a).
5. McCarthy, N. (1995, March). A year later, "3 strikes" clogs jails, slows trials. *California Bar Journal*, p. 1.

5D.18

Habitual Offenders

State law requires state law enforcement agencies to cooperate with the Department of Justice to maintain files on sexual habitual offenders. Other types of habitual offenders are also identified by California agencies. Those who meet the criteria may receive longer sentences. MHPs may be involved in treating or assessing criminal defendants who may be habitual offenders.

(A) Legislative History

The question whether a disproportionate number of crimes are committed by repeat offenders has been raised on a number of occasions in California. In 1992, the California legislature determined that a substantial and disproportionate number of sexual offenses are committed by a relatively small number of multiple and repeat sex offenders.[1] The legislature therefore enacted the statewide sexual habitual offender program to identify, locate, apprehend, and prosecute sexual habitual offenders.

(B) Criteria for Sexual Habitual Offenders

As used in the statute, *sexual habitual offenders* means persons who

1. have been convicted of two or more violent offenses which include at least one sex offense; or

---

1. Penal Code § 13885.

2. have been convicted of an offense listed under a specific section of the Penal Code dealing with sexual offenses, and meet one of the following additional criteria:

    (a) three or more felony arrests for sex offenses on their record;

    (b) five or more felony arrests for any type of offense on their criminal records;

    (c) ten or more arrests, either felony or misdemeanor for any type of an offense on their record; or

    (d) five or more arrests, either felony or misdemeanor for any type of offense, including either

        (1) at least one conviction for multiple sex offenses; or

        (2) at least two arrests for a single sex offense.[2]

(C) Maintenance of Files by Law Enforcement

The State Department of Justice is required to establish and maintain comprehensive files on persons identified as sexual habitual offenders. The Department of Corrections, the Department of Motor Vehicles, and law enforcement agencies are required to cooperate with the Department of Justice. In addition, the department prepares a summary profile on each sexual habitual offender for distribution to law enforcement agencies.

(D) Non-Sexual Habitual Offenders

California also has a criminal apprehension program,[3] the goal of which is to identify career criminals. As in many other states, the sentences of habitual offenders can be enhanced for a variety of reasons, including an intention to inflict grave bodily harm, but only if infliction of grave bodily harm is not an element of the offense with which the defendant is charged.[4]

In addition, the California legislature as part of the Street Terrorism Enforcement and Prevention Act of 1988 requires that

---

2. Penal Code § 13885.4.
3. Penal Code § 13851.
4. Penal Code § 12022.7. While a battery is a general intent crime, to have enhancement of a sentence, a specific intent to inflict bodily harm is required. *In re Sergio R.*, 228 Cal.App.3d 588 (1991); *People v. Hawkins*, 15 Cal.App.4th 1373 (1993).

if any person is convicted of a felony committed for the benefit of, at the direction of, or in association with any criminal street gang, he or she shall be punished by an additional term of one to three years at the court's discretion. If the underlying felony is committed on the grounds of, or within a 1,000 feet of, a public or private school during the hours that minors are using the facility, for an additional term of two to four years may be imposed at the court's discretion.[5]

Under California's death penalty law a series of special circumstances may change the punishment for murder from imprisonment to the death penalty.[6]

---

5. Penal Code § 186.22.
6. Penal Code § 190.2.

5D.19

Competency to Serve a Sentence

The law is concerned with a criminal defendant's competency both before and after a trial. The standard for competency to stand trial is discussed in chapter 5D.5 and is the same as the competency to serve a sentence. However, the competency to be executed comes under a different procedure, discussed in chapter 5D.23.

Mental health treatment of prisoners is discussed in chapter 5D.20. When a prisoner becomes mentally disordered while serving a sentence, he or she can be transferred to a mental health facility as described in chapter 5D.21.

5D.20

Mental Health Services in Jails and Prisons

The provision of mental health services to inmates is particularly important given that some are suffering from emotional or mental disturbances that are not sufficient to constitute grounds for placement in a psychiatric hospital, and that California attempts to rehabilitate prisoners. In fact, prisoners may maintain actions for failure to provide certain minimal medical and mental health care on the ground that it constitutes a form of cruel and unusual punishment.[1] MHPs may be involved in providing these services to inmates.

(A) Mental Health Services in California Jails

Although the terms are often used interchangeably, there are technical differences between jails and prisons: Generally, jails are maintained by the counties, as opposed to the state, and are used for the following circumstances:

1. for the detention of persons committed in order to secure their attendance as witnesses in criminal cases;

2. for the detention of prisoners charged with crime and committed for trial;

3. for the confinement of persons committed for contempt or upon civil process by their authority at law;

---

1. *Ochoa v. Superior Court*, 39 Cal.3d 159 (1985); *Estelle v. Gamble*, 429 U.S. 97 (1976).

4. for the confinement of persons sentenced to imprisonment for the conviction of a crime.[2]

Generally, county sheriffs are keepers of the jails.

Screening is to be done on all prisoners at the time of intake, including evaluation of medical and mental health problems and developmental disabilities.[3]

Whenever a county prisoner requires medical treatment necessitating hospitalization that cannot be provided at the county jail or county hospital because of lack of adequate detention facilities, and when the prisoner also presents a serious custodial problem because of his or her past or present behavior, the prisoner may be transferred to the nearest state prison or correctional facility that would be able to provide the necessary treatment. The county sheriff can request a local superior court judge to order the transfer, with the consent of the Director of Corrections. The prisoner cannot be transferred if the physician responsible for the prisoner's health care determines that a medical emergency exists that requires the transfer of the prisoner to the state prison or correctional facility before the hearing. The court must have a hearing on this issue at which the prisoner has a right to be present.[4]

The county, city, and California Youth Authority are authorized to seek to recover their costs for providing medical care.[5] In any case where it appears that the person in custody in the jail or juvenile detention facility may be mentally disordered, the person in charge of the jail or juvenile detention facility or any judge of the court may cause the prisoner to be taken to a facility for 72-hour treatment and evaluation pursuant to the Welfare and Institutions Code section on involuntary commitment (see chapter 5E.4).[6] The person transferring the prisoner must inform the facility in writing of the reasons the person is being transferred. That statement is confidential. The local mental health director, or his or her designee, may examine the prisoner before transfer to the facility for treatment and evaluation. Once the prisoner has been transferred, the Welfare and Institutions Code sections governing voluntary hospitalization generally apply. Notice of the transfer is also given to the attorney for the prisoner and the prosecuting attorney in any criminal or juvenile proceedings. (Additional information about this process is discussed in chapter 5D.21.) The sheriff is not required to receive into the jail a person

---

2. Penal Code § 4000.
3. 15 CCR § 1207.
4. Penal Code § 4007.
5. Penal Code § 40011.1.
6. 15 CCR § 1209.

who is in need of immediate medical care until the person has been transported to a hospital or medical facility so that his or her medical needs can be addressed prior to booking them into the jail.[7] Wherever a jail averages more than 100 persons per day in confinement, there must be a duly licensed and practicing physician available at all times.[8] A prisoner may elect to decline treatment by the county or city jail physician and provide medical treatment at his or her own expense. In such a case, the sheriff or chief of police may have the prisoner removed from the jail to a privately owned and operated medical facility or hospital. The prisoner will be liable for the costs of treatment and the costs incurred by the county or city in providing the necessary custody and security only to the extent that such costs exceed the costs that would have been incurred if the county had provided treatment.[9]

Female prisoners are allowed family planning services 60 days prior to a scheduled release date, and pregnant prisoners are still entitled to be eligible for abortion to the extent allowed under the Therapeutic Abortion Act.[10]

The Board of Corrections has minimum standards for local detention facilities, including health and sanitary conditions that take into account input from experts in criminology and penology and psychiatrists.[11]

(B) Mental Health Services in California Prisons

Prisons generally involve longer-term incarceration and prisoners convicted of more serious crimes than do jails. *Prisons* generally refers to all the facilities, camps, hospitals, and institutions for the confinement, treatment, employment training, and discipline of persons who are in the legal custody of the Department of Corrections.[12]

The Department of Corrections has a medical facility, the primary purpose of which is the receiving, segregation, confinement, treatment, and care of males under the custody of the Department of Correction and the agency thereof who are

---

7. Penal Code § 4015. This statute reflects the legislature's intent that the cost associated with providing medical care to an arrested person be borne by the arrested person's private medical insurance or any other source of medical coverage for which the arrested person is eligible.
8. Penal Code § 4023.
9. *Id.*
10. Penal Code §§ 20423.5, 4023.6, 402a.
11. Penal Code § 6030.
12. Penal Code § 6082.

1. mentally disordered;
2. developmentally disabled;
3. addicted to the use of controlled substances; or
4. suffering from any other chronic disease or condition.[13]

The Department of Corrections and the Department of Youth Authority may employ MHPs such as psychologists who are not professionally licensed.[14] The medical facility, like a regular prison, has a warden who is appointed by the governor on the recommendation of the Director of Corrections.[15]

The supervision, management, and control of the medical facility, and the responsibility for the care, custody, treatment, training, discipline, and employment of persons confined therein are vested in the director of the Department of Corrections.[16] In addition, California has begun a program of trying to create substance abuse community correctional detention centers. The legislature in enacting this program noted that the percentage of state prisoners whose primary offense was a violation of the drug laws was 24%, and that over an eight-year period the number of parole violators returned to the prison for drug violations increased 2,200%. The legislature concluded that there was an undeniable relationship between public safety, recidivism, and substance abuse.[17] Thus, its intent is to provide a program that involves a rigorous program of substance abuse testing, a drug-free environment, substance abuse treatment, employment services, basic education services, mental health services, and family counselling.[18] MHPs may be involved in the provision of these services.

California has also established community correctional re-entry centers to provide services to individuals near the conclusion of their terms in prison so that they may be able to make a successful readjustment to society. These centers provide counseling in the areas of drug and alcohol abuse, stress, and employment skills, and victim awareness.[19]

Additionally, the Department of Corrections is required to examine and study each new prisoner. There must be an investigation of all the pertinent circumstances of the prisoner's life, such as the existence of any strong community and family ties, the

---

13. Penal Code § 6102. Note that formerly this statute used different terminology and included epileptics and "psychopaths and sex offenders".
14. 66 Op. Atty. Gen. 371 (1983).
15. Penal Code § 6105.
16. Penal Code § 6106.
17. Penal Code § 6240.
18. Penal Code § 6245.
19. Penal Code § 6258.

maintenance of which may aid in the prisoner's rehabilitation, and the circumstances preceding the violation of the law for which he or she was committed to prison. Based on this examination, the Director of Corrections classifies the prisoners and, when reasonable, attempts to assign the prisoner to an institution of appropriate security level and gender population near the prisoner's home. When a diagnostic study indicates it is appropriate, the director causes a psychiatric or psychological report to be prepared for the community release board before the release of an inmate. These reports are prepared by a psychiatrist or psychologist licensed to practice in California.

However, the requirement that a psychological report be prepared by a psychiatrist or psychologist who is licensed arises only when a diagnostic study so indicates. The diagnostic study itself does not have to be prepared by a licensed psychiatrist or psychologist, but may be prepared by a correctional counselor.[20] The statute requires mental health services in prison be provided by a licensed physician, psychologist, or other licensed health professional, except that psychologists working in the prison system before January 1, 1985, may continue to do so, as well as persons employed on January 1, 1989, to supervise or provide consultation on diagnostic or treatment services. Additionally, the license requirement may be waived in order for a person to gain qualifying experience to be licensed as a psychologist, but the waiver cannot exceed two years in length.[21]

The Department of Corrections has specific authority to hire MHPs, including psychiatrists and psychologists, to provide such services as necessary, including screening of mental disorders, determination of mental competency of inmates to participate in a classification hearing, evaluation of parolees during temporary detention, determining whether mental health treatment should be a condition of parole, and such other services as may be required that are consistent with their license.[22] The Department of Corrections is required to provide facilities and licensed professional personnel for its psychiatric and diagnostic clinics and as many branches as are required for the state prisons or institutions. All required mental health treatment or diagnostic services are to be provided under the supervision of a licensed psychiatrist or a licensed psychologist who holds a doctoral degree and has at least two years of experience in the diagnosis and treatment of emotional and mental disorders. All such clinics are under the direction of a psychiatrist or psychologist. However, a psychia-

20. *Wasko v. Department of Corrections*, 211 Cal.App.3d 996 (1989). Penal Code §§ 5068, 5068.5.
21. Penal Code § 5068.5; 66 Op. Atty. Gen. 37 (1983).
22. Penal Code § 5058.5.

trist is required to be available to assume responsibility for acts of diagnosis or treatment that may only be performed by a licensed physician.

The psychiatric and diagnostic clinic is to study each prisoner, his or her career and life history, the cause of his or her criminal acts, and recommendations for his or her care, training, and employment with a view to his or her reformation and protection of society. However, the recommendations are submitted to the Director of Corrections and are not effective until approved by the Director, who may modify or reject the recommendations as he or she sees fit.[23]

The Department of Corrections has a manual governing its operations, which addresses some of these issues as well.

(C) Inmate–Psychotherapist Confidentiality

As noted in chapters 4.2 and 4.3, the right of privacy and the psychotherapist–patient privilege are codified in California. Services provided by MHPs to prisoners are not exempted from the psychotherapist–patient privilege since there is no criminal-proceeding exception to the psychotherapist–patient privilege— only a specific statutory exception would allow the relationship to be treated as not confidential. Further, the regulations covering inmate mental health services expressly provides for confidentiality.[24] There is no psychotherapist–patient privilege if the psychotherapist is appointed by the Board of Prison Terms to examine a patient under a section of the Penal Code dealing with the disposition of mentally disordered prisoners upon discharge. That statute requires the Department of Corrections to evaluate each prisoner for severe mental disorders during the first year of the prisoner's sentence, and severely mentally disordered prisoners are required to be provided with an appropriate level of mental health treatment while incarcerated and after being returned to the community.[25]

Evaluations pursuant to this statutory section are not privileged, further, if a prisoner expressed a threat of violence to a

---

23. Penal Code § 5079.
24. 15 CCR § 1205.
25. Penal Code § 2960. Note that this has been subjected to constitutional attack, *People v. Gibson*, 204 Cal.App.3d 1425 (1988), on the grounds that it had an *ex post facto* effect on certain prisoners and denied equal protection by continuing confinement simply because their mental illness continued.

third party, is dangerous to himself or others,[26] or where a proceeding is brought to determine a defendant's sanity or competency.[27]

Thus MHPs should be clearly aware as to whether their services will be confidential or not, based on their status.

(D) Right to Refuse Treatment

Prisoners may be entitled to refuse to undergo treatment with psychotropic medications on an involuntary basis, although they can be required to take such medications during a 72-hour hold period.[28] California's Penal Code specifically provides that prisoners may not be deprived of their rights except as necessary to maintain reasonable security. A prisoner's refusal to take psychotropic medications did not threaten prison security where the prisoner was not a threat to self or others.[29] However, no organic therapy may be given without the prisoner's informed consent. Organic therapy is defined to mean psychosurgery, shock therapy, and the use of drugs, electric shock, electric stimulation, or infliction of physical pain as an aversive or reinforcing stimulus, in a program of aversive, classical, or operative conditioning. However, non-organic therapy such as psychotherapy, psychoanalysis, group therapy, milieu therapy, or other therapies or programs involving communications or interaction among physicians, patients, and others without the use of drugs, do not require the prisoner's informed consent under this statutory section.[30] If the proposed organic therapy is not agreed to, the warden may petition the court for permission to administer such therapy.[31]

---

26. Evid. Code § 1024.
27. Evid. Code §§ 1023, 1025.
28. 15 CCR § 1217; *People v. Thomas*, 217 Cal.App.3d 1034 (1990).
29. *Keyhea v. Rushen*, 178 Cal.App.3d 526 (1986).
30. Penal Code § 2670.5.
31. Penal Code §§ 2675, 2676.

5D.21

Transfer From Penal to Mental Health Facilities

Prisoners found to be mentally disordered may be transferred to mental health facilities. This chapter discusses the circumstances under which prisoners may be assessed as mentally disordered and transferred to facilities to receive treatment.

(A) Assessment of Mentally Disordered Prisoners

As discussed in chapter 5D.20, when a prisoner in a county jail may be mentally disordered, the prisoner can be taken to a facility for 72-hour treatment.[1] If the prisoner is retained or remanded to a facility, the facility must transmit a confidential report by the person in charge of the jail or juvenile detention facility to the judge who caused the prisoner to be taken there, describing the prisoner's condition. Such reports must be sent at the end of each period of confinement.

(B) Conversion to Voluntary In-Patient Status

A prisoner who has been transferred to an inpatient facility may convert to voluntary inpatient status without obtaining the consent of the court, the person in charge of the jail, or the local

---

1. 15 CCR § 1209.

mental health director. If there is such a conversion of voluntary status, the person in charge of the facility must transmit a report as described above.

(C) Transfer to State Hospital for Treatment

Similarly, when a prisoner is deemed mentally disordered by the Director of Corrections, he or she may be transferred to a state hospital for treatment and the time spent there is deducted from the prisoner's sentence.[2] If, in the opinion of the hospital superintendent the prisoner has been treated to the extent that he or she would not benefit from further treatment or care, the Director of Corrections is notified and the prisoner is re-transferred.[3]

(D) The Necessity for Adequate Mental Health Care

Both the California and U.S. Supreme Courts have indicated that under certain circumstances prisoners who receive medical care may be able to assert claims that the care was so substandard as to constitute a form of cruel and unusual punishment.[4] The question is whether the services were so woefully inadequate that they went beyond simple negligence. Generally, however, the state has immunity from ordinary negligence in the provision of medical services.[5]

---

2. Penal Code § 2684; *see generally In re Huffman*, 42 Cal.3d 552 (1986). Furthermore, in a jail setting, mentally disordered inmates are to be segregated. 15 CCR § 1052.
3. Penal Code § 2685.
4. *Ochoa v. Superior Court*, 39 Cal.3d 159 (1985); *Youngberg v. Romeo*, 457 U.S. 307 (1982) (involving involuntary commitment and rights of mentally retarded and persons); *Estelle v. Gamble*, 426 U.S. 97 (1976).
5. Gov't Code § 845.6.

5D.22

Parole

When a prisoner is paroled, he or she is allowed to be released before the expiration of the term of his or her sentence. The most important distinction between probation and parole is that, to be put on parole an individual must actually serve some time in prison. Further, while determinations regarding probation are made by the court at the time of sentencing, parole determinations are made by the Board of Prison Terms.[1] Eligibility for parole generally arises after the prisoner has served a portion of the sentence. MHPs may become involved by providing testimony as to whether a prisoner's mental illness or disease makes parole inadvisable. MHPs may also provide parolees with psychotherapy or counseling as a condition of parole.

(A) Definitions

The term *parole authority* means the Department of Corrections with regard to persons sentenced under the law before enactment of the determinate sentencing law, except for persons found to meet criteria for mental disorders. It means the Board of Prison Terms for persons sentenced to terms under the determinate sentencing law, except for persons meeting criteria for mental disorders.[2]

---

1. Penal Code § 5075.
2. Penal Code § 3000. *Determinate sentencing* means fixing the term or range of a term by statute instead of giving complete discretion in sentencing to the judge. *Id.* § 1170.

The term *severe mental disorder* as used here means an illness, disease, or condition that substantially impairs the person's thought, perception of reality, emotional process, or judgment; or that grossly impairs behavior; or that demonstrates evidence of an acute brain syndrome for which prompt remission, in the absence of treatment, is unlikely. The term does not include a personality or adjustment disorder, epilepsy, mental retardation, or other developmental disabilities, or addiction to or abuse of intoxicating substances.

The term *remission* means a finding that the overt signs and symptoms of the severe mental disorder are controlled, either by psychotropic medications or by psychosocial support.

(B) Parole Determination

In California, parole determinations are made based on information supplied by the Department of Corrections on how a prisoner has functioned and on other information that the prisoner seeks to have considered. In this regard, an MHP may testify. However, California also allows the individuals affected by the prisoner's crime to make statements in opposition to parole.

At the expiration of a term of imprisonment of one year and one day, or a term of imprisonment imposed, or where a term has been reduced pursuant to various credits based on the prisoner's performance, the prisoner may be released on parole unless the parole authority for good cause waives parole and discharges the inmate. The period of parole cannot exceed five years in the case of a person imprisoned for any offense other than first- and second-degree murder for which a life sentence is given, and cannot exceed three years in case of any other inmate unless the parole authority for good cause waives parole and discharges the inmate. The parole authority must consider the request of any inmate regarding the length of parole and the conditions thereof. After successful completion of parole or at the end of the maximum statutory period of parole, whichever is earlier, the prisoner must be discharged from custody.

The Department of Corrections must meet with each prisoner at least 30 days before his or her good-time release date and provide the conditions and length of parole up to the maximum period provided by law. The prisoner has a right to ask for reconsideration of the length and conditions of parole by the parole authority.

A person who has been convicted of first-degree murder and has been on parole continuously for seven years, or a person who has been convicted of second-degree murder and has been on parole for five years, must be discharged from parole, unless the Board of Prison Terms determines that he or she will be retained on parole.[3] Special provisions apply to patients who have severe mental disorders that are not in remission or cannot be kept in remission without treatment. A prisoner cannot be kept in remission without treatment if, during the year before the question arises before the Board of Prison Terms or a trial court, he or she has been in remission and he or she has

1. been physically violent (except in self defense);
2. made a serious threat of substantial physical to another person;
3. intentionally caused property damage; or
4. has not voluntarily followed a treatment plan that a reasonable person would follow.

An additional criterion is that the severe mental disorder was one of the causes of, or was an aggravating factor in, the commission of a crime for which the prisoner was convicted and sentenced.

(C) Psychological Evaluation Prior to Release on Parole

Before releasing a prisoner on parole, the person in charge of treating the prisoner and a practicing psychiatrist or psychologist from the State Department of Mental Health must evaluate the prisoner. In addition, the chief psychiatrist of the Department of Corrections must certify to the Board of Prison Terms all of the following facts:

1. the prisoner has a severe mental disorder, which is not in remission, or cannot be kept in remission, without treatment;
2. the severe mental disorder was one of the causes, or was an aggravating factor in, the prisoner's criminal behavior;
3. the prisoner has been in treatment for severe mental disorder for 90 days or more within the year before the parole release date;
4. that the prisoner used force or violence or caused serious bodily injury in committing the crime for which he or she was imprisoned; and

---

3. Penal Code § 3000.1. Note that because of the effect of the nature of the conviction on the entitlement to parole, the courts have required that a defendant be advised of parole consequences before his or her guilty plea is accepted. *In re People v. Moser*, 5 Cal.App. 591 (1992).

5. that by reason of his or her mental disorder, the prisoner represents a substantial danger of physical harm to others.

If the professionals performing the psychological evaluations disagree as to whether the prisoner has a severe mental disorder, or whether the disorder is in remission or can be kept in remission without treatment, or that the severe mental disorder was a cause of or aggravated the prisoner's criminal behavior, and a chief psychiatrist has certified the prisoner to the Board of Prison Terms as required, the Board of Prison Terms may order a further examination. The examination is to be by two independent psychiatrists or psychologists who must concur with the chief psychiatrist's certification for parole to be granted. With these various criteria, a prisoner may be granted parole on the condition of receiving treatment from the State Department of Mental Health.[4]

(D) Psychological Treatment Following Parole

A patient who meets the mental disorder criteria is to receive inpatient treatment unless the State Department of Mental Health certifies to the Board of Prison Terms that there is reasonable cause to believe that the parolee can safely and effectively be treated on an out-patient basis. The State Department of Mental Health places the parolee in the correct program.

(E) Hearings on the Prisoner's Mental Condition

The parolee has a right to a hearing before the Board of Prison Terms for the purpose of proving that he or she meets the criteria for a severe mental disorder. Before such a hearing, the board at the request of the prisoner shall appoint two independent professionals who are not state government employees and have at least five years of experience in the diagnosis and treatment of mental disorders. These individuals shall include psychiatrists and licensed psychologists who have a doctoral degree in psychology. The Department of Corrections and the State Department of Mental Health are required annually to submit to the Board of Prison Terms a list of 20 or more independent psychiatrists and psychol-

---

4. Penal Code § 2962.

ogists who meet the requisite criteria.[5] At the hearing on whether the prisoner has a severe mental disorder, the prisoner has a right to be represented by an attorney and the right to a jury trial. The hearing is a civil hearing. The standard of proof is *beyond a reasonable doubt*, and if the trial is by jury, the jury must be unanimous in its verdict.

If the court or jury finds that the prisoner has a severe mental disorder that is not in remission, or cannot be kept in remission without treatment, but that by reason of the severe mental disorder, the prisoner represents a substantial danger of physical harm to others, the prisoner shall be recommitted to the facility in which he or she was confined at the time the petition for hearing was filed. The prisoner may also be recommitted to any outpatient facility at which he or she was being treated, or committed to the State Department of Mental Health facility in which he or she was imprisoned. The commitment is for a period of one year from the date of termination of parole or previous commitment, or from the scheduled date of release from prison. If the court finds that there is reasonable cause to believe that the committed person can safely and effectively be treated on an outpatient basis, he or she shall be released to an outpatient status.

Not later than 180 days before the termination of parole or release from prison, if the prisoner has refused to accept treatment as a condition of parole, the state hospital treating the prisoner must submit to the district attorney of the county of commitment a written evaluation on remission. The district attorney then files a petition for continued involuntary treatment for one year.

The petition for recommitment can be filed to determine whether the severe mental disorder is not in remission and cannot be kept in remission without treatment, and whether by reason of the prisoner's severe mental disorder, he or she represents a substantial danger to the public.[6]

(F) Board of Prison Terms

The Board consists of nine members called *commissioners*, who are appointed by the governor, with the advice and consent of the Senate, and serve for terms of four years. Prisoners who are eligible for parole but denied parole may petition the board. At hearings before the board, prisoners are entitled to counsel. When a prisoner becomes eligible for parole, the Board of Prison Terms

---

5. Penal Code § 2978.
6. Penal Code § 2972.

is required to notify the sentencing judge of that fact. The prosecuting attorney is also informed, as are the victims and/or next-of-kin of victims.[7] Victims and next-of-kin of victims have a right to present evidence before the board to indicate that the crime was of an especially brutal nature and thus warrants denying parole.[8]

(G) Parole Conditions

In addition to the conditions related to mental health, prisoners who are on parole may be required to participate in community service.[9] A parolee may be required not to use any controlled substances or drugs,[10] may be required to pay attorney fees or fines previously imposed,[11] abstain from the use of intoxicating liquor,[12] participate in programs to clean up litter,[13] make restitution to their victims,[14] not possess any firearms,[15] and obtain counseling regarding battered children,[16] child molesting,[17] or spousal abuse.[18]

Additionally, with the parolee's consent, electronic monitoring devices may be used to allow home detention.[19]

(H) Immunity for Crimes by Parolees

Not surprisingly, a series of lawsuits have been filed over the decision to parole particular individuals who commit crimes while on parole. In a typical such case, the California Supreme Court held that the state was immune from suit for the release of a prisoner on parole based on statutory immunity. The facts in that case were particularly compelling because the prisoner had a history of violence and the prison officials had indicated that he would be a threat to others, particularly young children, if he were released. Nevertheless, he was released, and within 24

---

7. Penal Code § 5075.
8. As an example, Charles Manson, convicted in the Sharon Tate murders has been denied parole on a number of occasions in recent years.
9. Penal Code § 1203.04.
10. Penal Code § 1203.1.
11. Penal Code § 1214.2
12. Penal Code §§ 1203.02, 3053.5.
13. Penal Code § 374.3 et seq.
14. Penal Code §§ 1203.01, 3000, 5077.
15. Penal Code § 12025.
16. Penal Code § 273d.
17. Penal Code §§ 647.6, 1203.1.
18. Penal Code § 273.5.
19. Penal Code § 1203.016.

hours, he sexually assaulted and viciously murdered a young boy whose parents filed suit. Despite these compelling facts, the Supreme Court held that no claim against the state could be asserted.[20] Thus, MHPs involved in this decision to place an individual on parole should be immune from suit if the parolee commits a crime.

---

20. *Thompson v. County of Alameda*, 27 Cal.3d 741 (1980); Gov't Code § 845.8.

5D.23

Competency to Be Executed

Under California law, a person who is mentally incompetent cannot be executed. However, there is no special standard governing competency to be executed, and it is not higher than competency to stand trial.[1] MHPs may be called upon to evaluate or treat prisoners who have been sentenced to execution, but who either are not, or contend they are not, competent.

(A) Competency to be Executed

The California Supreme Court has expressly held that it is unconstitutional for the state to execute incompetent individuals.[2]

(B) Investigation of Competency of Persons Sentenced to Death

Whenever a defendant is sentenced to death, and a day is set for execution, the warden of the state facility to which the defendant has been delivered for execution must notify the director of Corrections. The director of Corrections is required to select and appoint three MHPs (referred to in the statute by the archaic term *alienists*), all of whom must be from the medical staff of the De-

---

1. *People v. Kelly*, 1 Cal.4th 495 (1992), *cert. denied*, 113 S.Ct 232 (1992). The law therefore provides for evaluation of prisoners who are sentenced to execution to determine whether they meet the Supreme Court's requirements.
2. *Id.*

partment of Corrections, to examine the defendant and investigate his or her competency. MHPs are required to examine the defendant, investigate his or her competency, and report their opinions and conclusions in writing to the governor and the warden of the facility at which the execution is to take place, at least 20 days prior to the scheduled date of execution.[3]

If the defendant has been delivered to the warden for execution and the warden has reason to believe that a defendant has become incompetent, the warden must call that fact to the attention of the district attorney of the county in which the prison facility is situated. It then becomes the duty of the district attorney to file in Superior Court a petition requesting a determination of the defendant's competency. The court must impanel a jury at once to determine whether the defendant is incompetent.[4]

A defendant who seeks to delay his or her execution on the ground of lack of competency bears the burden of proof.[5]

(C) Verdict of the Jury

If the jury determines that the defendant is incompetent, the court must make an order to that effect, and the order must direct that the defendant be taken to a medical facility of the Department of Corrections and kept in safe confinement until his or her reason is restored.[6] The warden must suspend the execution and transmit a certified copy of the court's order to the governor, and deliver the defendant with the certified copy of the order to the medical facility named in the order.[7]

If a jury finds that the defendant is sane, the warden must proceed with the judgment of execution.[8]

(D) Restoration of Competency

When a defendant recovers his or her competency, the superintendent of the medical facility he or she is in must certify the restoration of competency to the judge of the Superior Court who ordered the defendant committed as incompetent. The judge must then fix the date for execution, after a 10-day written notice to the defendant and the district attorney of the county in which

---

3. Penal Code § 3700.5
4. Penal Code § 3701.
5. *Williams v. Duffy*, 32 Cal.2d 578 (1948), *cert. denied*, 335 U.S. 840 (1948).
6. Penal Code § 3703.
7. Penal Code § 3704.
8. *Id.*

the defendant was originally sentenced and to the district attorney of the county in which the defendant was committed to a medical facility. A hearing is then held before the judge who issued the original order, without a jury, to determine whether or not the defendant has regained competency.

If the defendant does not have an attorney, the court must appoint an attorney to represent the defendant at that hearing. If the court determines that the defendant has recovered his or her competency, the judge must certify that fact to the governor, who must issue a warrant to the warden appointing a day for execution. The warden must then return the defendant to prison for execution of judgment.

If, however, following the hearing, the judge determines that the defendant still has not recovered his or her competency, the defendant is again remanded to the custody of the medical facility to be kept in safe confinement until competency is restored.[9]

Defendants under sentence of execution who were found not competent were once transferred to a state hospital, but since 1972, defendants are sent to a medical facility of the Department of Corrections.[10]

---

9. *Id.*
10. Penal Code § 3704.5.

5D.24

Pornography

Pornography is material deemed to be obscene. Issues involving pornography typically arise in cases seeking to convict individuals for obscenity. MHPs may become involved in such cases by testifying as to community standards and as to whether a particular work has any redeeming social value.

(A) Definitions

Under California law *obscene matter* means matter taken as a whole, which to the average person applying contemporary statewide standards, appeals to prurient interests, depicts or describes in a patently offensive way sexual conduct, and lacks serious literary, artistic, political, or scientific value.[1]

Matter is defined as any book, magazine, newspaper, or other printed or written material, or any picture, drawing, photograph, motion picture, or other pictorial representation, or any statue or figure, or any recording, transcription, or mechanical, chemical, or electrical reproduction of any other article, equipment, machine, or material. *Matter* includes live or recorded telephone messages when transmitted, disseminated, or distributed as part of a commercial transaction.

Obscenity can also include live conduct, which is defined as any physical activity, whether performed alone or engaged in with other persons, including but not limited to singing, speaking, dancing, acting, simulating, or pantomiming, where the pre-

---

1. Penal Code § 311.

dominant appeal to the average person, applying contemporary statewide standards is to prurient interest.

Prurient interest means a shameful or morbid interest in nudity, sex, or excretion and is conduct that goes substantially beyond customary limits of candor in description or representation of such matters. Furthermore, such conduct must lack significant literary, artistic, political, or scientific value. Whether the conduct appeals to prurient interest is judged with reference to average adults unless it appears the presentation is designed for clearly defined deviant sexual groups, in which case the appeal is judged with reference to that group.

(B) Laws Governing Obscenity and Pornography

California has enacted laws governing obscenity and pornography, which are subordinate to the constitutional rights and limitations articulated by the U.S. Supreme Court. The issues are complicated by the fact that while there is a right to possess obscene and pornographic materials in one's home, it is illegal to sell, transport, or give such material to others.[2]

California prohibits the sale, distribution, or exhibition of obscene matters and their possession, preparation, publication, or printing with intent to distribute or exhibit to others. Additionally, it is a felony to advertise for sale or distribution any obscene matter knowing that it depicts a person under the age of 18 years personally engaging in or simulating sexual conduct. [3] It is also a public offense for any person to knowingly possess or control any matter that depicts a person under the age of 14 years personally engaging in or simulating specified sexual conduct. However, it is not necessary to establish that this is obscene material to establish a violation of the law.[4]

There are also statutory provisions specially addressing computer and telephone access services that provide obscene material.[5] Further, developing, copying, or exchanging photographs of children engaged in sexual conduct is a crime.[6]

---

2. *Paris Adult Theater I v. Slaten*, 413 U.S. 49 (1973).
3. Penal Code § 311.10.
4. Penal Code § 311(11).
5. Penal Code § 311.8.
6. Penal Code § 311.3.

Some California municipalities have tried to address obscenity issues legislatively, by using zoning ordinances to prohibit nude entertainment.[7]

(C) The Role of MHPs in Pornography Cases

MHPs become involved in pornography issues to determine whether a particular work violates contemporary community standards regarding sexual mores, appeals to prurient interests, or violates customary limits of candor in the description or representation of nudity, sex, or excretion. Additionally, MHPs may be asked to testify to whether a particular work has any redeeming social value.[8] Appellate courts are not suited to establish what community standards are, and therefore it is critical that the record in an obscenity case contain proof of what the community standards are.

In an early obscenity case, the California Supreme Court held that expert opinion should be introduced in obscenity cases because an average jury is unlikely to represent the views of the entire community.[9] This decision was reversed by the passage of a statute providing that, in the prosecution of obscenity cases, any evidence that would tend to establish contemporary community standards is admissible but expert testimony is not required by either side.[10]

Whether any particular publication, broadcast, literature, or live performance is obscene depends on the specific content and the currently operative definition. Because of the overriding impact of the U.S. Supreme Court decisions and attempts by local municipalities to try to regulate such conduct, it is not unusual for several significant obscenity cases to be brought each year.

---

7. *See Startrack, Inc. v. County of Los Angeles*, 65 Cal.App.3d 451 (1976).
8. Penal Code § 311 to 312.1.
9. *In re Giannini*, 69 Cal.2d 563 (1968).
10. Penal Code § 312.1.

5D.25

Services for Sex Offenders

MHPs may be involved in the assessment or treatment of individuals who are sexual offenders. Athough California once treated all sex offenders as mentally disordered, now only those found to be mentally ill are subject to psychiatric care.

(A) History of the Mentally Disordered Sex Offenders Act

Until 1982, California had a program dealing with the treatment of mentally disordered sex offenders.[1] The legislature's repeal of the Mentally Disordered Sex Offenders Act was premised in part on a change in attitude in that the commission of sex offenses was no longer viewed as stemming from mental disease. In repealing the act, the legislature recognized and declared that the commission of sex offenses is not, in and of itself, the product of mental disease, and that henceforth someone who was believed to have a serious, treatable mental illness would be transferred to a state hospital for treatment in the same way as other mentally ill prisoners in need of acute psychiatric care.

The purpose of committing mentally disordered sex offenders was to provide adequate treatment and controls by isolating individuals from society, and to protect the public from the repeated commission of sex crimes.

Under the act, a mentally disordered sex offender was defined as any person who, by reason of mental defect, disease, or

---

1. Welf. & Inst. Code § 6300 et seq.

disorder, was predisposed to commit sexual offenses to such a degree that he or she was dangerous to the health and safety of others.[2] (California's law governing sex offenders prior to the Mentally Disordered Sex Offender Act, the Sexual Psychopaths Act, was also repealed.)[3]

(B) Procedure After Conviction of a Sex Offense

Generally, when a person was convicted of any sex offense, the trial judge could, if there was probable cause to believe that the defendant was a mentally disordered sex offender, adjourn the proceedings or suspend the sentence and certify the person for hearing and examination to determine whether he or she was a mentally disordered sex offender. A "sex offense" was defined as any offense for which registration as a sex offender was required by the Penal Code. The California Supreme Court has held that registration is constitutionally precluded if the facts and circumstances of a particular offense indicate that the registration requirement would be cruel and unusual punishment as to an individual defendant.[4]

(C) Evaluation by MHPs

The court was authorized to appoint either two or three certified clinical psychologists, each with a doctoral degree in psychology and at least five years of post-graduate experience in the diagnosis of mental disorder, or psychiatrists who had devoted their practice primarily to the diagnosis and treatment of mental and nervous disorders for not less than five years, to examine the allegedly mentally disordered sex offender to ascertain whether that person met the statutory criteria.[5] Each examiner was required to file with the court a separate written report.[6] The court

---

2. Welf. & Inst. Code § 6300.
3. *See People v. Barzee*, 213 Cal.App.2d 139 (1963), holding that procedures under the Sexual Psychopaths Act are essentially civil in nature; *People v. Hymes*, 161 Cal.App.2d 668 (1958); former Welf. & Inst. Code §§ 5500 to 5521.
4. Registration of sex offenders is required as defined in § 260 of the Penal Code. *See In re Reed*, 33 Cal.3d 914 (1983); *People v. King*, 16 Cal.App.4th 567 (1993).
5. Welf. & Inst. Code § 6307.
6. Welf. & Inst. Code §§ 6308, 6309.

could consider other expert evidence, as well.[7] If the person was found not to be a mentally disordered sex offender, he or she would be returned to the court for disposition as the court deemed proper.[8] If it was determined that the individual *was* a mentally disordered sex offender and could benefit by treatment in a state hospital or other treatment facility, the court had the discretion to order the person committed to a state hospital or to the county mental health director for confinement in an appropriate public treatment facility.[9] There were special provisions relating to how long the individual could be committed.[10]

(D) Current Law

Under current law, an individual would be evaluated for treatment either in conjunction with a competency hearing at the time of trial (*see* chapter 5A.17 as to juveniles, and chapter 5D.5 as to adults) or a special diversion program (*see* chapter 5D.3).

---

7. Welf. & Inst. Code § 6311, 6312.
8. Welf. & Inst. Code § 6315.
9. Welf. & Inst. Code § 6316.
10. Welf. & Inst. Code § 6316.2

5D.26

Services for Victims of Crimes

MHPs who treat victims of violent crimes may under certain circumstances, be compensated by the State of California, pursuant to a victims' compensation statute. MHPs may also be asked to evaluate applicants for victims' compensation. This chapter discusses the history of victims' compensation law, the procedure, and the criteria that must be met for an award.

(A) Background of Victims' Rights Legislation

In 1982, California amended its constitution to provide a comprehensive scheme for the rights of victims of crimes: the so-called victims' bill of rights.[1] California has been in the forefront of states providing restitution and services for victims, and it has taken a multifaceted approach. As explained below, part of the amendment's intent is to provide funds for victims to obtain therapy in the wake of traumatic crimes and to give victims a voice in the determination of whether to parole criminals. As defined in the victims' bill of rights, the rights of victims include not only restitution from the criminal for the financial losses suffered, but also a right to ensure that public safety is protected by subjecting the criminals to adequate punishment. The legislature has recognized that being a victim or witness in the criminal justice system can further traumatize people, and has attempted

---

1. Cal. Const. art. I, § 28.

to provide services for both victims of and witnesses to crime through local centers.[2]

(B) State Board of Control

The agency entrusted with carrying out the legislative and constitutional mandates regarding monetary compensation to victims or witnesses of crime is the State Board of Control. The board holds hearings to determine the extent to which the victims or witnesses of crime may be entitled to indemnification.

(C) Definitions

A *victim* is defined as a resident of California, including military personnel or families stationed in California. A *victim* cannot be a nonresident. This has been subject to constitutional attack as denial of equal protection, but the courts have upheld the limitation of the legislation to residents.[3] A *victim* must also meet one of the following criteria:

1. be a person who sustains injury or death as a result of a crime;
2. be a person who is legally dependent upon a person who suffers injury or death as the result of a crime;
3. be a family member of a victim, or a person in a close relationship with the victim, if they were present during the commission of the crime or if their presence is medically required for successful treatment of the victim of the crime; and
4. in the event the crime resulted in the death of the victim, any individual who legally assumes the obligation or who voluntarily pays the medical or burial expenses.[4]

An injury is defined to include physical or emotional injury or both. However, emotional injury is not compensable unless it is incurred by a victim who also sustains either physical injury or threat of physical injury. The statute provides that for a number of specific cirmes, including sexual assaults, an individual who sustains emotional injury is presumed to have sustained physical injury for the purpose of compensation.[5]

---

2. Penal Code § 13835.
3. *Ostrager v. State Board of Control*, 99 Cal.App.3d 1 (1979), appeal dismissed, 449 U.S. 807 (1980).
4. Gov't Code § 13960.
5. Gov't Code § 13960(b).

(D) Availability of Services to Nonresidents

Nonresidents may recover for pecuniary losses as a result of criminal acts occurring within California, but only where the Board determines that federal funds are available to pay the award.[6]

(E) Procedure for Asserting a Claim

Applications for assistance must be filed with the Board. The applications must be verified, contain information required by law, and filed within one year after the date of the crime.[7] In one case, the Board was deemed estopped to deny a claim when it was filed past the one-year period, but the police department investigating the crime had failed to provide the claims forms to the victims.[8]

It is axiomatic that the victim must cooperate with the Board staff in processing the application, and that the failure to cooperate may lead to a denial of the application.[9]

If the application is accepted, the claim must be processed within 90 days.[10]

(F) Test for Compensation

The Board must approve the application if the preponderance of the evidence establishes that the victim (1) incurred the injury as the result of a crime and (2) suffered a pecuniary loss.[11] *Pecuniary loss* is defined as the amount of expenses for which the victim will not be reimbursed from any other source, including medical treatment, mental health counseling, loss of income or support, and non-medical care and treatment rendered in a court with any recognized, religious method of healing.[12]

As noted above, California has a statute that generally requires hearings at public agencies to be open to the public (*see* chapter 4.5). However, until January 1, 1994, the Board is autho-

---

6. Gov't Code § 13960.5.
7. Gov't Code § 13961.
8. *Hartway v. State Board of Control*, 69 Cal.App.3d 502 (1976).
9. Gov't Code § 13962.
10. *Id.*
11. Gov't Code § 13964.
12. Gov't Code § 13960(d)(4).

rized to exclude from its hearings on applications for assistance anyone except the Board members; its staff; the victim; the victim's representatives, witnesses, parents, or guardians; and other individuals of the victim's choice.[13]

California has a Good Samaritan Act,[14] which provides for compensation of individuals injured in providing assistance to others. However, no one may recover under both the Good Samaritan Act and the Victims of Crime Act.[15]

(G) Evaluation by an MHP

The Board may obtain an independent evaluation by an MHP of the victim if the Board believes it is necessary.[16] Where the Board refers a crime victim to a private, nonprofit mental health agency for treatment, that agency is reimbursed for its services at the normal and customary fee charged by the nonprofit agency to clients with adequate means for payment of services—not to exceed the maximum reimbursement rate set by the Board.[17]

(H) Other Assistance for Victims of Crimes

The Board is required to maintain local assistance centers, to counsel victims of rape or other specified sex crimes.[18] Further, whenever a law enforcement officer is investigating a rape or specified sex crime, he or she is required to immediately provide the victim with a card identifying the names and locations of rape-victim counseling centers, together with his or her own phone number, a statement on the proper procedures for the victim to follow after the sexual assault, and a statement that the sexual assault by a person who is known to the victim, including a spouse, is still a crime.[19]

---

13. Gov't Code § 13963.1.
14. Gov't Code § 13970 et seq.
15. *Webster v. State Board of Control*, 197 Cal.App.3d 29 (1987).
16. Gov't Code § 13965.
17. *Id.*
18. Gov't Code §§ 13835.2, 13962.5.
19. Penal Code § 264.2.

Voluntary or Involuntary Receipt of State Services

5E.1

Medicaid/Medi-Cal

MHPs may treat patients whose treatment is paid for by a government-funded program called Medi-Cal. This chapter discusses the background of Medi-Cal and the criteria for medical payment or inpatient mental health services. In addition, this chapter discusses an actual case regarding the potential liability of MHPs treating Medi-Cal patients. The laws and regulations governing Medi-Cal are so extensive that this chapter can give only an overview.

(A) Medicaid/Medi-Cal Program, Generally

Medicaid is the federally supported program whereby the states provide direct payments to suppliers of medical care and services to individuals receiving cash payments in programs, such as Social Security Disability Insurance (SSDI), Aid to Families with Dependent Children (AFDC), and Supplemental Services Insurance (SSI) for the elderly, blind, and disabled. Medicaid is categorically linked to SSI and AFDC, which means an individual is automatically eligible for Medicaid if he or she is in one of these programs or is medically needy, and all costs are paid by the government. Individuals who are disabled and receiving SSDI are eligible for Medicaid, but they must pay a share of the costs. In California, Medicaid is referred to as Medi-Cal.

The Medicaid program was initiated in 1965 with the goal of ensuring access by the poor to mainstream medical care via public insurance. Each state is required to develop a state plan that includes mandatory services and optional services as determined by the state. The federal government pays 50 percent of the Medi-Cal payments. The program offers a generous benefit package covering most optional Medi-Cal services and most optional eligibility groups.

In California, the State Department of Health Services is the state agency approved by the Secretary of the U.S. Department of Health and Human Services to administer the Medi-Cal program.[1]

(B) Payment for Inpatient Treatment by Medi-Cal

Inpatient services in general hospitals are covered for all ages, but only when provided on the signed order of the physician responsible for the care of the patient.[2] Inpatient hospital services in an institution for mental diseases are also covered for persons of all ages, provided that the institution for mental diseases is certified as a psychiatric hospital under title XVIII of the Federal Social Security Act.[3] Inpatient hospital services, whether in an institution for mental illness or in the psychiatric unit of a general hospital, are covered only for persons 65 years or older or under 21. Someone receiving such services prior to his or her 21st birthday, who continues without interruption to require and receive such services, is covered to his or her 22nd birthday.[4]

Emergency hospital services do not require authorization prior to admission. However, all hospitalization resulting from emergency admissions require approval by the Medi-Cal consultant. Approval must be obtained by the hospital on the day of admission or, when the day of admission is not a state working day, the first date working day thereafter. Authorizations may be granted for up to a maximum of 30 days.[5] All other hospitalization is covered only if prior authorization is obtained from the Medi-Cal consultant before the hospital admission. Continued necessary hospitalization beyond the specified number of days is covered only after approval by the Medi-Cal consultant has been obtained by the hospital or on the last day of the previously approved period of hospitalization. If a request is approved, the number of days of hospitalization must be authorized as determined by the Medi-Cal consultant on the basis of medical information submitted. No request for authorization of extensions can

---

1. Welf. & Inst. Code § 10720 et seq.
2. 22 CCR § 51303.
3. Welf. & Inst. Code § 14021; 42 U.S.C.A. § 1395 et seq.
4. 22 CCR § 51327(a)(5).
5. 22 CCR § 51327(a)(2).

be approved for more than one year for acute care or one year for long-term care. Claims for non-emergency hospitalization are to be accompanied by an approved pre-admission authorization request and an approved extension of hospital stay if the stay extends beyond the period previously authorized. For long-term care, the attending physician must recertify, at 30, 60, and 90 days after initial certification and every 60 days thereafter, the patient's need for continued care in accordance with the procedures specified by the director.[6]

(C) Payment for Outpatient Services by Medi-Cal

Medi-Cal reimburses outpatient services for psychological treatment if those services are rendered in a hospital outpatient department or clinic.[7] However, coverage of psychological services is limited to a maximum of two services in any one calendar month.[8] *Services* includes all care, treatment, or procedures provided to a beneficiary by an individual practitioner on one occasion.[9]

Minors are entitled to additional psychological treatment if it is determined to be necessary.

(D) The Two Medi-Cal Systems of Payment

California currently has two systems of providing mental health services under Medi-Cal: the Fee for Service/Medi-Cal system and the Short–Doyle/Medi-Cal system. Under the Fee for Service/Medi-Cal system, the need for outpatient mental health services is determined by the individual practitioner providing the services. Under the Short–Doyle/Medi-Cal system, the determination is based on statewide standards. At the present time, the two systems are being integrated, with the goal of statewide implementation of a single managed mental health care plan in each county. Counties will be given the choice to serve as Local Mental Health Care Plans offering an array of mental health services, with standards set by the state in accordance with federal Medicaid requirements. All eligible Medi-Cal beneficiaries would receive their mental health services through the plan. The

6. 22 CCR § 51327(a) et seq.
7. 22 CCR § 51331.
8. 22 CCR § 51304.
9. *Id.*

determination of whether an individual would be eligible for these services would be based on statewide criteria. If a county elects not to serve as a Local Mental Health Care Plan, the state would select a plan for the county.

The implementation of the statewide managed health care plan is in three phases. Phase I involved changes in the Short–Doyle/Medi-Cal program to include increased financial accountability and cost containment, as discussed in chapter 5E.2. Phase II involves the consolidation of state funding for the Short–Doyle/Medi-Cal plan and the Fee for Service/Medi-Cal mental health services at a county level. Phase III is the implementation of capitated funding for mental health services through managed care contracts, as discussed more fully in chapter 5E.2. Implementation of Phase I was set for 1993, Phase II was set for October 1994, and Phase III was set for July of 1997, with full implementation targeted for July of 1998.[10]

(E) Potential Liability of MHPs Treating Medi-Cal Patients

In a key case, a Medi-Cal patient was discharged from a hospital after only four days, although her physician believed she should have been hospitalized for eight days. After the discharge, she experienced complications, which led to the amputation of her leg. The patient sued the state for refusing to authorize the additional four days of treatment, but the discharge decision was within the standard of care of the medical community. The court held that the patient could not assert a claim against the state and that her only recourse, if any, was against her physicians for not initiating a reconsideration procedure available under Medi-Cal. However, the court did conclude that a Medi-Cal recipient is entitled to medical care that meets the usual standards of medical practice, and that physicians are required to meet those standards in treating Medi-Cal patients.[11]

This case demonstrates that MHPs must be careful not to let the quality of services be impaired by the question of coverage.

---

10. California Dep't of Mental Health, *Medi-Cal Managed Health Care* (June 1, 1994).

11. *Wickline v. California*, 192 Cal.App.3d 1630 (1986). In a subsequent case, the same Court of Appeals commented that its statement in *Wickline* suggesting that civil liability for a discharge decision was solely the responsibility of a treating physician was *dicta* (i.e., unnecessary to the decision and therefore nonbinding). *Wilson v. Blue Cross*, 222 Cal.App.3d 660, 667 (1990).

5E.2

Health Care Cost-Containment Systems

California has always had the largest number of Medicaid recipients of any state in the United States.[1] In 1982, the California legislature, with support from industry and the executive branch, passed landmark health care cost-containment legislation that dramatically changed Medi-Cal. The legislative package changed the mix of Medi-Cal beneficiaries and the benefits offered to them.[2]

Under Medi-Cal, MHPs are affected by the cost-containment systems currently in effect and those to be in effect in the future. chapter 5E.1 discusses the Medicaid/Medi-Cal program in more detail.

(A) Medi-Cal Managed Care, Generally

The State Department of Health Services (in consultation with the State Department of Mental Health and the State Department of Alcohol and Drug Programs) establishes procedures for claims submission and rates for reimbursement of Short–Doyle mental health Medi-Cal services. These rates are effective from July 1 to June 30 of the fiscal year in which the rates are established.[3]

---

1. J. F. Holahan & J. W. Cohen, *Medicaid: The Trade-off Between Cost Containment and Access to Care* (1986).
2. B. Preston, M. Ruther, D. Baugh, & R. McDevitt, *Outcomes of California's Medicaid Cost Containment Policies, 1981–84.* 14 Health Care Financing Review (May 19, 1993).
3. Welf. & Inst. Code § 14021.5.

Contracts may be established on a bid or nonbid basis with any qualified individual, organization, or entity to provide services to, arrange for, or manage the care of Medi-Cal beneficiaries. At the director's discretion, contracts may be exclusive or nonexclusive and may provide for delivery of services consistent with managed-care principles, techniques, and practices directed at ensuring the most cost-effective and appropriate scope, duration, and level of care. The contracts may also provide for alternate methods of payment, including prospectively negotiated reimbursement rates, fee for service, retainers, capitation, shared savings, volume discounts, lowest bid price, negotiated price, rebates, or other basis, at the director's discretion. A goal of the system is to provide financial incentives for providers to participate in the Medi-Cal program in cost-efficient ways.

The director may require individual providers or groups of providers, as a condition of participation in the Medi-Cal program, to enter into capitated contracts in order to correct or prevent irregular or abusive practices. No provider can be reimbursed for services rendered to the Medi-Cal beneficiaries if he or she has not entered into a contract of the type described above.[4]

The renewal of a provider's contract is contingent on meeting the requirements of the law and regulations established by the Department of Mental Health. The renewal of the contract can be conditioned on the provider agreeing to a plan for correction of any deficiencies found by the department. The department may terminate or decline to renew any contract where the director determines the action is necessary to protect the health of patients or the Medi-Cal funds.[5]

---

4. Welf. & Inst. Code § 14087.3. Note that the director also has the discretion to enter into contracts with individuals or organizations to perform targeted case management of selected services or beneficiary populations, where it is expected that the case management will reduce the program expenditures.
5. Welf. & Inst. Code § 14087.4.

5E.3

Voluntary Civil Admission of Mentally Ill Adults

California law provides for the voluntary admission of mentally ill persons to state-operated or county-designated facilities. MHPs may be involved in treating such individuals either as outpatients or as inpatients. This chapter discusses the criteria for voluntary admission and discharge of mentally ill adults. The criteria for involuntary commitment of mentally ill adults are discussed in chapter 5E.4. The criteria for voluntary and involuntary commitment of adults who are alcoholics or drug addicts are discussed in chapters 5E.5 and 5E.6, respectively.

(A) Evaluation and Admission

An application to admit an adult into a mental-health facility shall be made voluntarily by the person, when he or she is competent to make such a decision.[1] The statute also provides that any person received in such a manner in a state hospital shall be deemed a voluntary patient.

(B) Discharge

If a voluntary adult patient requests discharge, he or she may leave the hospital or institution at any time by giving notice of his or her desire to leave to any member of the hospital staff and by following normal hospitalization discharge procedures.[2]

---

1. Welf. & Inst. Code § 6000.
2. *Id.*

5E.4

Involuntary Civil Commitment of Mentally Ill Adults

Some mentally ill persons may be subject to involuntary commitment to receive mental health services. MHPs may be involved in treating, assessing, or admitting mentally ill adults who are committed involuntarily to receive mental health services. This chapter discusses the statutory procedures and criteria for involuntary commitment, the criteria for release of involuntarily committed individuals, the immunity MHPs have for deciding to release the individuals, and the rights of the involuntarily committed individuals. The criteria for involuntary commitment of adults who are alcoholics or drug addicts are discussed in chapters 5E.5 and 5E.6, respectively.

(A) History of Involuntary Commitment

Involuntary commitment is governed by the Lanterman–Petris–Short Act (LPS).[1] LPS replaced a statutory scheme that allowed indeterminate commitment, and it removed legal disabilities imposed on the mentally ill. LPS provides for voluntary treatment with specified periods of involuntary observation, and crisis treatment for those individuals who are unable to care for themselves or who are a danger to themselves or others.[2] There are three key periods of time under LPS:

---

1. Welf. & Inst. Code § 5000 et seq.
2. *Thorn v. Superior Court*, 1 Cal.3d 666 (1970); *Reise v. St. Mary's Hospital & Medical Center*, 209 Cal.App.3d 1303 (1987), *appeal dismissed.*

1. an initial 72-hour hold period to allow for evaluation;
2. an additional 14-day period, following certification, to allow intensive treatment; and
3. a 180-day period after the 14-day period, when a person who demonstrates a danger to others may receive additional treatment. During or after the 14-day period of intensive treatment, a conservator may be appointed.[3]

(B) Involuntary Admission

When any person, as result of a mental disorder, is a danger to others or to himself or herself, or is gravely disabled (i.e., unable to provide food, clothing, or shelter), a peace officer or other professional person designated by the county, on probable cause, may take, or cause to be taken, the person into custody and place him or her in a facility designated by the county and approved by the State Department of Mental Health as a facility for 72-hour treatment and evaluation.[4]

The professional must make an application in writing, stating the circumstances under which the person's condition was called to the attention of the professional, and also stating that the professional has probable cause to believe that that person is, as a result of a mental disorder, a danger to himself or others.[5]

If the facility for 72-hour treatment and evaluation admits the person, it may detain him or her for evaluation and treatment for a period not to exceed 72 hours. Saturdays, Sundays, and holidays may be excluded from the 72-hour period if the Department of Mental Health certifies for each facility that evaluation and treatment services cannot reasonably be made available on those days.[6]

Before admitting a person to the facility for 72-hour treatment and evaluation, the professional person in charge of the facility or his designee shall assess the individual in person to determine the appropriateness of the involuntary detention. If in the judgment of the professional person in charge of the facility, or his or her designee, the person can be properly served without being detained, he or she shall be provided evaluation, crisis intervention, or other inpatient or outpatient services on a voluntary basis.[7]

---

3. *Reise v. St. Mary's Hospital & Medical Center, supra* note 2; Welf. & Inst. Code §§ 5300 to 5306.
4. Welf. & Inst. Code § 5150.
5. *Id.*
6. Welf. & Inst. Code § 5151.
7. *Id.*

(C) Psychological Evaluation

Any person admitted to a facility for 72-hour treatment and evaluation must receive an evaluation as soon after admission as possible, and must receive whatever treatment and care his or her condition requires for the full period that he or she is held. The person shall be released before 72 hours have elapsed only if the psychiatrist directly responsible for the person's treatment believes, as a result of his or her personal observations, that the person no longer requires evaluation or treatment. If any other professional who is authorized to release the person, believes the person should be released before 72 hours have elapsed, and the psychiatrist directly responsible for the person's treatment objects, the matter must be referred to the medical director of the facility for a final decision. If the medical director is not a psychiatrist, he or she must appoint a psychiatrist to make the decision. If the matter is referred, the person may be released before 72 hours have elapsed only if the psychiatrist making the final decision believes, as a result of his or her personal observations, that the person no longer requires evaluation or treatment.[8]

Persons who have been detained for evaluation and treatment and are receiving medications as a result of their mental illness, must be given written and oral information about the probable effects of the medication by a person designated by the mental health facility. The State Department of Mental Health is required to develop and promulgate written materials, for use by county mental health programs, addressing the effects of the medication. The following information must be given orally to the patient:

1. the nature of the mental illness, or behavior, for which the medication is being given or recommended;
2. the likelihood of improving or not improving without the medication;
3. reasonable alternative treatments available; and
4. the name, type, frequency, amount, and method of dispensing the medications, and the probable length of time that the medications should be taken.

The patient's chart must indicate whether this information has been given. If the information has not been given, the designated person must document in the patient's chart the reason. A failure to provide information about the probable effects and

---

8. Welf. & Inst. Code § 5152(a).

possible side effects of the medication does not constitute new grounds for release.[9]

If an involuntarily committed patient is judicially determined to have the capacity to give an informed consent to the use of antipsychotic drugs, and refuses to consent, the patient cannot be required to undergo the treatment. If the patient has been judicially determined to be incapable of giving informed consent, and is being held either for 72 hours or the 14-day extended period, the patient may be required to accept the medically prescribed drug treatment.[10]

(D) Release

Persons who have been detained for evaluation and treatment must be released, referred for further care and treatment on a voluntary basis, or certified for intensive treatment, or a conservator or temporary conservator can be appointed as required.[11]

(E) Certification for Extended Treatment

If a person under a 72-hour hold has been evaluated, he or she may be held for an additional 14 days of intensive treatment related to the mental disorder or impairment, or chronic alcoholism, under the following conditions:

1. the professional staff of the evaluating agency or facility has found that the person is a danger to self or others or is gravely disabled;

2. the facility providing intensive treatment is designated by the county to provide such treatment and agrees to admit the person; or

3. the person has been advised of the need for treatment but is unwilling or unable to accept it on a voluntary basis.[12]

For the purposes of certification, a person is not *gravely disabled* if he or she can survive safely with the help of family, friends, or others who are willing to help and indicate their

---

9. Welf. & Inst. Code § 5152(c).
10. *Reise v. St. Mary's Hospital & Medical Center*, 209 Cal.App.3d 1303 (1987), *appeal dismissed*.
11. Welf. & Inst. Code § 5152(b).
12. Welf. & Inst. Code § 5250; *Thorn v. Superior Court*, 1 Cal.3d 666 (1970).

willingness to help in writing.[13] The law specifies the form of certification to be used and the signatories.[14] A certification review hearing must be held within four days of the certification, if requested by the patient.[15] The hearing is to be conducted by a certification review hearing officer who is an administrative law judge or court-appointed commissioner, a medical doctor, a licensed clinical social worker, a marriage, family, and child counselor, a licensed psychologist, a registered nurse, a lawyer, or a certified law student. The review officers are selected from a panel approved by the local mental health director, county public defender, and county counsel or district attorney. An employee of the county mental health program or any facility designated by the county for 72-hour evaluation cannot be a certification review hearing officer.

The location of the hearing must be compatible with and least disruptive of treatment.[16]

At the hearing, the patient has the right to assistance by an attorney or advocate, the right to present evidence, the right to question persons presenting evidence in support of certification, and the right to be heard.[17]

If the person has received medication within 24 hours prior to the beginning of the hearing, the person conducting the hearing shall be informed of that fact and of the probable effects of the medication.[18]

Reasonable attempts must be made by the mental health facility to notify family members or any other person designated by the patient as to the time and place of the certification hearing unless the patient requests that this information not be provided.[19]

If the hearing officer finds probable cause to believe the patient is a danger to self or others or is gravely disabled, the certification is approved.[20]

---

13. Welf. & Inst. Code § 5250.1.
14. Welf. & Inst. Code § 5252.
15. Welf. & Inst. Code §§ 5254, 5256.
16. Welf. & Inst. Code § 5256.1.
17. Welf. & Inst. Code § 5256.4(a).
18. Id.
19. Welf. & Inst. Code § 5256.4(c).
20. Welf. & Inst. Code § 5256.6.

(F) Immunity from Liability of Treating MHPs

The professional person in charge of the facility providing 72-hour treatment and evaluation, the medical director of the facility, and the psychiatrist directly responsible for the patient's treatment are immune civilly and criminally for any action by a person released before the end of the 72 hours.[21]

(G) Rights of Those Committed

Persons who have been involuntarily detained for evaluation or treatment, as well as those who are voluntary patients, have the right to

1. wear their own clothes;
2. keep and use their own personal possessions, including toilet articles;
3. keep and be allowed to spend a reasonable sum of their own money for canteen expenses and small purchases;
4. have access to individual storage for private use;
5. see visitors each day;
6. have reasonable access to telephones, both to make and receive confidential calls;
7. have access to materials such as stamps for correspondence; and
8. refuse convulsive treatment, psychosurgery, or modification or control of thoughts or behavior, and other related treatment.[22]

(H) Judicial Remedy

An involuntary commitment can be challenged in court by a writ of *habeas corpus*.[23] This is a petition filed in Superior Court which asserts that an individual is wrongfully held and is directed against the persons and/or facilities holding the petitioner. This remedy is independent of the procedures discussed above.

---

21. Welf. & Inst. Code § 5154; *Michael E.L. v. San Diego County*, 228 Cal.Rptr. 139, 183 Cal.App.3d 515 (1986), *cert. denied*, 480 U.S. 946 (1987).
22. Welf. & Inst. Code § 5325; 22 CCR § 79313.
23. Welf. & Inst. Code § 5275; *Thorn v. Superior Court*, 1 Cal.3d 666 (1970).

5E.5

Voluntary Admission and Involuntary Commitment of Alcoholics

Alcoholics may seek voluntary admission to treatment, in the same way as any other adult (*see* chapter 5E.3). In addition, alcoholics who are a danger to themselves or others may be involuntarily admitted in the same way as mentally ill adults (*see* chapter 5E.4). MHPs may be involved in assessing or treating alcoholic patients, whether voluntarily or involuntarily hospitalized. This chapter discusses the general criteria for detention, evaluation, and treatment of alcoholics, as well as the immunity MHPs have for decisions regarding release. The criteria for voluntary and involuntary treatment of adults who are drug addicts are discussed in chapter 5E.6.

(A) Evaluation and Treatment

Although the statute specifically does reference chronic alcoholism as a grounds of being gravely disabled, an individual who is inebriated, but not an alcoholic, might qualify for a 72-hour evaluation.[1] Because this program is administered by the counties, it varies from county to county.

A person who is a danger to self or others may, upon reasonable cause, be taken into custody and placed in a facility designated by the county and approved by the State Department of Alcohol and Drug Abuse as a facility for 72-hour treatment and evaluation of inebriates.[2]

A 72-hour treatment and evaluation facility should include a screening, evaluation, and referral facility which may be a mobile

---

1. Welf. & Inst. Code § 5172.1.
2. Welf. & Inst. Code § 5170.

crisis unit, first-aid station, or ambulatory detoxification unit; a detoxification facility for alcoholic and acutely intoxicated persons; or an alcohol recovery house.[3]

The evaluation facility must make a report in writing, stating the circumstances under which the person's condition was discovered and the personal observations of the person who took the inebriate into custody.[4] If the facility admits the person, it may detain him or her for evaluation and detoxification up to 72 hours. The service to be provided consists of evaluation, detoxification, and referrals for further care and treatment. Social and rehabilitative services can also be provided during this period. An inebriated person must be examined for gross medical needs, and the results of the examination recorded in the file. If there are indications of any disorder requiring immediate medical or surgical attention, such services must be provided by the facility, or the inebriated person is to be referred and transported to an appropriate medical facility.[5]

A person admitted to a facility for 72-hour treatment and evaluation shall receive an evaluation as soon as he or she is admitted, or as soon as possible thereafter. The person shall be released before 72 hours have elapsed if, in the opinion of the professional person in charge of the facility, the person no longer requires evaluation or treatment.[6] However, the person may voluntarily remain in a facility for more than 72 hours if the professional in charge of the facility determines he or she is in need of and may benefit from further care and treatment.[7]

(B) Immunity From Liability for Release of Inebriates

If the above provisions for detention and evaluation of an inebriate have been met, neither the professional person in charge of the facility providing 72-hour treatment and evaluation, nor the medical director of the facility (or a designee), nor the psychiatrist directly responsible for the person's treatment can be held civilly or criminally liable for any action by a person released before the end of 72 hours.[8]

---

3. Welf. & Inst. Code § 5170.1.
4. Welf. & Inst. Code § 5170.3.
5. 9 CCR §§ 9446 to 9450.
6. Welf. & Inst. Code § 5172.
7. Id.
8. Welf. & Inst. Code § 5173.

5E.6

Voluntary Admission and Involuntary Commitment of Drug Addicts

MHPs may be involved in the assessment or treatment of adults who are drug addicts. This chapter discusses the criteria for admitting drug addicts to facilities for treatment, both voluntarily and involuntarily. The criteria for voluntary or involuntary hospitalization of mentally ill adults are discussed in chapters 5E.3 and 5E.4, respectively. The criteria for voluntary and involuntary commitment of adults who are alcoholics are discussed in chapter 5E.5.

(A) Admission for Treatment

Any person who believes himself or another to be addicted to the use of narcotics, or in imminent danger of becoming addicted to their use, may report such belief to the district attorney, under oath. When there is probable cause, the district attorney may petition the Superior Court for a commitment of the addicted person to the director of Corrections for confinement in the narcotic detention, treatment, and rehabilitation facility.[1]

A peace officer or health officer who has reasonable cause to believe that a person is addicted to the use of narcotics must file a written application, stating the circumstances under which the person's condition was called to the officer's attention, including facts upon which the officer has reasonable cause to believe that the person is addicted or is in imminent danger of becoming addicted to the use of narcotics.[2]

---

1. Welf. & Inst. Code § 3100.
2. Welf. & Inst. Code § 3100.6.

(B) Evaluation After Admission

Within 24 hours of admittance, a physician shall conduct an examination to determine whether the person is addicted to narcotics and may provide the person with medical aid as necessary to ease symptoms of withdrawal. If, after examination, the physician does not believe the person is addicted to the use of narcotics, the physician must immediately report his or her belief to the physician or superintendent in charge of the hospital or institution, who shall discharge the person immediately.[3] If, the person has been taken into custody, he or she must be informed of his or her right to be represented by counsel.[4]

---

3. *Id.*
4. Welf. & Inst. Code § 3104.

5E.7

Services for Developmentally Disabled Persons

Services for developmentally disabled persons are generally governed by the Lanterman Developmental Disabilities Services Act,[1] which is similar in some respects to the Lanterman–Petris–Short Act on the involuntary commitment of mentally ill adults (*see* chapter 5E.4). California law provides various residential and outreach services to developmentally disabled and retarded persons. Services are provided by the State Department of Developmental Services and regional centers throughout California.

(A) Definitions

Under the Welfare and Institutions Code, a *developmental disability* is a disability that originates before age 18; continues, or can be expected to continue, indefinitely; and constitutes a substantial disability for that individual. The term includes mental retardation, cerebral palsy, epilepsy, and autism, as well as disabling conditions found to be closely related to mental retardation or to require treatment similar to that required for mentally retarded individuals. It does not include other handicapping conditions that are solely physical in nature.[2]

Services and support for persons with developmental disabilities means specialized services and support or special adaptations directed toward the alleviation of a developmental disability; toward the social, personal, physical, or economic rehabilitation of an individual with a developmental disability; or toward the

---

1. Welf. & Inst. Code § 4500 et seq.
2. Welf. & Inst. Code § 4512(a).

achievement and maintenance of independent, productive, normal lives.

The determination of which services should be provided is made on an individual basis, considering the needs and preferences of the person and his or her family.[3] Services and support may include, but are not limited to, diagnosis, evaluation, treatment, personal care, living arrangements, speech therapy, mental health service, protective and other social services, daily living skills training, emergency and crisis intervention, homemaker services, and various other detailed services.[4]

(B) Entitlement to Services

An adult person may apply to be voluntarily admitted if he or she is in a state of mind rendering him or her competent to make such a decision.[5] In the case of a minor, the application shall be made by his or her parents, or by the parent or guardian with custody, and shall be made to a mental hospital designated by the director of mental health or the director of developmental services to admit minors on voluntary applications.[6]

A voluntary adult patient may leave the hospital or institution at any time by giving notice of his or her desire to leave to any member of the hospital staff and by completing normal hospitalization departure procedures. A minor person who is a voluntary patient may leave the hospital after completing normal hospitalization procedures after the parents—or the parent, guardian or other person with custody of the minor—give notice to the superintendent or other person in charge of the parents' desire to remove the minor from the hospital.[7]

If the treatment to be rendered is of an involuntary nature, the guidelines set forth in Welfare and Institutions Code § 5150, discussed in chapter 5E.4, apply equally to the treatment of developmentally disabled persons.

---

3. Welf. & Inst. Code § 4512(b).
4. Id.
5. Welf. & Inst. Code § 6000.
6. Id.
7. Id.

(C) Rights of Persons With Developmental Disabilities

Persons with developmental disabilities are guaranteed the same legal rights and responsibilities guaranteed to all other individuals.[8] Persons with developmental disabilities shall have rights including, but not limited to, the following:[9]

1. a right to treatment and rehabilitation services and support in the least restrictive environment and in an environment that fosters developmental potential, directed toward achievement of the most independent, productive, and normal life possible;
2. a right to dignity, privacy, and humane care;
3. a right to participate in publicly supported education, regardless of degree of disability;
4. a right to prompt medical care and treatment;
5. a right to religious freedom and practice;
6. a right to social interaction and participation in community activities;
7. a right to physical exercise and recreational opportunities;
8. a right to be free from harm, including unnecessary physical restraint, or isolation, excessive medication, abuse, or neglect;
9. a right to be free from hazardous procedures; and
10. a right to make choices in their own lives including, but not limited to, where and with whom they live, relationships with people in the community, and the way in which they spend their time, including education, employment, and leisure time.

A person with developmental disabilities who has been admitted or committed to a state hospital, community care facility, or health facility also has the following rights:[10]

1. to wear his or her own clothes and keep his or her own personal possessions, as well as keep and spend a reasonable amount of his or her own money for canteen expenses and small purchases;
2. to have access to individual storage space for private use;
3. to see visitors each day;

---

8. Welf. & Inst. Code § 4502; 17 CCR § 50510.
9. Welf. & Inst. Code § 4502(a)–(j).
10. Welf. & Inst. Code § 4503.

4. to have reasonable access to telephones, both to make and receive confidential calls;

5. to mail and receive unopened correspondence, and to have ready access to letter-writing materials, including stamps;

6. to refuse electroconvulsive therapy;

7. to refuse behavior modification techniques that cause pain or trauma;

8. to refuse psychosurgery, which includes operations such as a lobotomy, psychiatric surgery, and behavioral surgery; and

9. to make choices in areas including, but not limited to, his or her daily living routines, choice of companions, leisure and social activities, and program planning and implementation.[11]

In addition, a person with a developmental disability who resides in a state hospital and who is involuntarily detained has the right to have access to a current copy of the Welfare and Institutions Code and assistance from a client's rights advocate to read and understand the code.[12] Such persons also have the right to give or withhold consent for their treatment in the absence of a judicial order or provision of law that entrusts the treatment decision to another person.[13]

Persons with developmental disabilities are *not* to be placed in seclusion; they are only subject to a "time out" procedure in accordance with regulations and procedures consistent with the law.[14] Restraints are not to be used on persons with developmental disabilities unless certain extreme conditions exist.

Individual treatment programs are created for the developmentally disabled by interdisciplinary teams, and these programs govern the treatment process.[15]

---

11. 17 CCR § 50510(b).
12. 17 CCR § 50510(c)(1).
13. 17 CCR § 50510(c)(2).
14. 17 CCR § 50515(a).
15. 17 CCR § 50515(b).

5E.8

Hospice Care

MHPs may be involved in providing psychological services to individuals who are cared for in hospices. Hospices are alternatives to hospital care, designed to provide terminally ill individuals with care in a less institutional setting. California regulates hospices to assure the quality of services.

(A) Definitions

Hospice care is the provision of supportive services, including psychological services, offered to terminally ill individuals who have voluntarily elected to receive such care in lieu of curative treatment related to their terminal conditions.[1] A hospice is a public agency, private organization, or subdivision thereof, that is primarily engaged in providing items and services to terminally ill individuals, that makes such services available as needed on a 24-hour basis, and that provides bereavement counseling for the immediate family and significant others.[2] A terminally ill patient is defined as one "whose medical prognosis as certified by a physician is that his or her life expectancy is six months or less."[3]

Services that a hospice may provide include

1. nursing services;

2. physical, occupational, and speech-language pathology;

3. medical–social services under the direction of a physician;

---

1. 22 CCR § 51180.
2. 22 CCR § 51180.1.
3. 22 CCR § 51180.2.

4. home health aid and homemaker services;
5. medical supplies and appliances;
6. drugs and biologicals;
7. physician services;
8. short-term inpatient care; and
9. counseling.[4]

(B) MHP Services

In addition to providing traditional nursing services, MHPs may provide hospice patients with psychological services to manage pain or to deal emotionally with impending death. MHPs may also be involved in providing services to family members of terminally ill patients on how to deal with their own grief or how to interact with the patient.

---

4. 22 CCR § 51180.

Limitations On and Liability for Practice

6.1

Informed Consent for Services

Under California law an MHP is required to obtain the patient's consent before providing services (except for certain emergency services) and before entering a course of treatment. The patient's consent also must be obtained before disclosing confidential information to third parties. Treatment rendered without the patient's consent that involves some form of touching can constitute a *battery*, which is an intentional tort. In addition, if the patient's consent is not *informed*, and the treatment produces any adverse consequences, it may lead to a malpractice suit by the patient and disciplinary action by the licensing board.

(A) Definition of Informed Consent

The doctrine of informed consent was articulated first in cases involving physicians;[1] however, the requirement that a patient give informed consent to treatment is equally applied to licensed or certified MHPs.[2] The essence of informed consent is that the patient is given an adequate amount of information regarding the risks of a particular therapy or procedure to make a rational decision about whether the risks warrant undergoing the procedure. The patient must be advised of alternative forms of treatment and their likelihood of success, as well. Finally, the MHP

---

1. *Cobbs v. Grant,* 8 Cal.3d 229 (1972); *Truman v. Thomas,* 27 Cal.3d 285 (1980).
2. *Rains v. Superior Court,* 150 Cal.App.3d 933 (1984).

must advise the patient of the consequences of failing to undergo the recommended treatment.

The principle of informed consent is to shift to the patient the decision-making authority and to reverse the historical trend of treatment options being presented in an authoritarian manner. The patient, not the MHP, is the person who must make the ultimate decision. For the decision to be meaningful, it must be based on a sufficient amount of understandable information. It is the prerogative of the patient, not the mental health professional, to determine the direction under which health care should proceed after being advised of the various therapeutic alternatives.[3]

The MHP's duty to disclose involves two general categories of information: (1) the risks of death or serious harm known to be inherent in a procedure, explained in layman's terms, and (2) whatever other information is required in a particular case by the standard of practice.[4]

In 1992, the California Supreme Court addressed the question of the extent to which a medical professional has a duty to inform a patient of different schools of thought on a proposed procedure—in that case, a surgical procedure.[5] While this decision dealt specifically with physicians, it offers guidance on the limitations of the informed consent doctrine as applied to MHPs. The Court stated that as a general rule a difference of medical opinion concerning the desirability of one particular procedure over another does not establish that the determination to use a particular procedure was negligent. The Court noted that medicine is not a field of absolutes and that different doctors may disagree in good faith as to what would be a proper treatment or diagnosis. Instead, a professional must use his or her best judgment to pick the proper procedure.

Once a procedure has been selected by the professional, the fact that others would disagree or that there are other schools of thought on the correct treatment may be material information that should be disclosed to allow the patient to give an informed consent. However, the duty of disclosure does not necessarily include the existence of various schools of thought. In short, the existence of other schools of thought about a procedure need be disclosed only if it would be material to the patient's decision on whether to consent.

The disclosure rule applies whether the procedure involves treatment or a diagnostic test. The MHP must explain both the risks of the test treatment and the potential consequences of

---

3. *Cobbs v. Grant*, 8 Cal.3d 229, at 243 (1972).
4. *Arato v. Avedon*, 5 Cal.4th 1172 (1993).
5. *Mathis v. Morrissey*, 11 Cal.App.4th 332 (1992).

declining to follow the recommended course of action. Thus, the material risk of not undergoing the procedure must be disclosed, as well as the risks of the procedure.[6]

As for the amount of information disclosed, one court has stated that

> the patient's interest and information does not extend to a lengthy polysyllabic discourse on all possible complications. A mini-course in medical science is not required. A mental health professional who is seeking a patient's consent for a therapeutic procedure must, in order to satisfy the fiduciary duty to disclose and obtain informed consent, disclose all personal interests unrelated to the patient's health, which may affect his or her professional judgment. This includes economic and research interests.[7]

The informed consent procedure must also take into account the patient's ability to understand the information and tailor the consent disclosure to the patient's individual situation. For example, if the patient is a young child, developmentally disabled, or suffering from severe thought disorders, the information may be communicated in a different fashion.

(B) Consent Forms

The use of written consent forms is mandated by case law and, in certain situations involving hospitalization, by the Lanterman–Petris–Short Act,[8] as discussed in chapter 5E.4.

MHPs must guard against using forms that are so detailed or technical that they are difficult for patients to understand. The law looks to the method of communicating the information to ascertain also that it is substantive and not perfunctory. Even when forms are used, the professional must make sure that the patient has read and adequately understood the form and consented to the procedure, and should note this in the patient's chart.

At least one case has suggested that there are limits to what a patient can validly consent to. In that case, several adults were treated with a form of psychotherapy that involved physically beating them. The defendants argued they could not be sued

---

6. *Truman v. Thomas*, 27 Cal.3d 285 (1980).
7. *Moore v. Regents of the University of California*, 51 Cal.2d 120 (1990) quoting *Cobbs v. Grant, supra* note 3. However, MHPs are not required to disclose every contingency which might affect the patient's non-medical rights and interests. *Arato v. Avedon*, 5 Cal.4th 1172 (1993).
8. Welf. & Inst. Code § 5326.5 provides that *written informed consent* means that a person knowingly and intelligently, without duress or coercion, clearly and explicitly manifests consent.

because the plaintiffs had consented to the treatment; however, the Court of Appeals refused to accept the consents as a defense. This decision implies that a patient's consent will not be deemed valid if the acts consented to would otherwise be illegal or contrary to public policy (such as a sexual relationship between therapist and patient).[9] An earlier case held that whether touching is therapeutic or nontherapeutic in nature goes to the essence of the act and may vitiate a consent.[10]

---

9. *Rains v. Superior Court*, 150 Cal.App.3d 933 (1984).
10. *Inderbitzen v. Lane Hospital*, 124 Cal.App.2d 462 (1932).

Right to Refuse Treatment

Once a patient has been given the necessary information as to the risks of a potential procedure, the patient has the legal right to refuse voluntary treatment, assuming the patient has the mental capacity to make such a decision. MHPs should be aware of the patient's right to refuse treatment. The rights of involuntarily committed patients who refuse treatment has been the subject of some dispute in recent years, in California and elsewhere. This issue, as related to civilly committed individuals, and developmentally disabled individuals, is discussed in chapters 5E.4 and 5E.7.

(A) Right to Refuse Treatment

The California Supreme Court has supported the right of a patient to refuse medical treatment even if that means that the patient ultimately will not survive, but it has not extended this right to minors. The Court has declared that every adult of sound mind has the right to determine what to do with his or her body. Thus, a competent and informed adult has a fundamental right to refuse or demand withdrawal of medical treatment in any form.[1] A parent generally has the right to decide on whether treatment will be accorded to a minor child. However, the courts in most instances will not allow a parent to put a child in risk of serious injury or death due to a refusal of medical treatment."

---

1. *Truman v. Thomas*, 27 Cal.3d 285 (1980); *Thor v. Superior Court*, 5 Cal.4th 725 (1993).

Even though a patient may refuse to undergo a particular test or treatment, the patient must still be informed of the risks of the decision not to proceed. In fact, a failure to inform a patient of the risks of a decision not to proceed with a particular test or course of treatment has been held to be malpractice. When a patient refuses a recommended treatment, the MHP must consider whether to continue or terminate the patient relationship.

Regulation of Aversive and Avoidance Conditioning

California law does not generally regulate the use of aversive and avoidant conditioning. However, electrical convulsive therapy (ECT) and behavior modification techniques used on individuals with developmental disabilities in a state hospital, regional center, or health facility are subject to special procedural requirements. MHPs who want to utilize these techniques with patients must first obtain authorization.

(A) Requirements for Use of Behavior Modification

Behavior modification means subjecting a patient to stimuli, events, acts, activities, or responses that are intended to cause the patient to change, adapt, or alter the occurrence or performance of his or her behavior (except behavior otherwise privileged by law).[1]

Care providers are prohibited from using any form of behavior modification intervention that may cause pain or trauma to a patient, unless the technique has been developed into a program that is fully described in an interdisciplinary team treatment plan and endorsed by a qualified professional or a Behavior Modification Review Committee.[2] (See chapter 5E.7 for additional information.) Both California courts and the California legislature have recognized that ECT has acknowledged benefits in the treat-

---

1. 17 CCR § 5801.
2. 17 CCR § 5802.

ment of certain illnesses, primarily depression, but that it can also be intrusive and possibly hazardous.[3]

(B) Requirements for Use of ECT

The Legislature has enacted a series of requirements intended to safeguard patients, particularly involuntarily committed patients, in the use of ECT and psychosurgery. These include requiring obtaining a patient's voluntary written informed consent to the use of ECT or that of a responsible relative, guardian, or conservator when a patient does not have the capacity to give written, informed consent. When a physician or the patient's attorney believes that the patient does not have the capacity to give consent to ECT or psychosurgery, then a noticed evidentiary hearing in Superior Court is held to determine the patient's capacity.[4] These provisions are contained in part of a comprehensive law known as the Lanterman–Petris–Short Act, which was designed to protect the rights of mentally disabled persons.

At a hearing to determine capacity, the standard is clear and convincing evidence, which is a higher standard than the preponderance of evidence standard,[5] required for civil suits.

While ECT and psychosurgery are specifically regulated, a more general section of the law states that persons with mental illness have the right to treatment services that help the person to function independently, and that the treatment should be provided in ways that are least restrictive of personal liberty.[6] The use of aversive or avoidant conditioning could come within the scope of this statutory provision, although to date there are no cases applying this law to this type of therapy.

(C) Court Challenge to ECT

One appellate court interpreting the original statutory scheme for ECT found that the law unconstitutionally infringed on the right of voluntary patients who are competent to consent to ECT treatment that could help them. The court noted that a patient's inability to obtain appropriate mental health treatment, including

---

3. *Northern California Psychiatric Society v. City of Berkeley*, 178 Cal.App.3d 90 (1986); *Lillian F. v. Superior Court*, 160 Cal.App.3d 314 (1984); Welf. & Inst. Code § 5325.
4. Welf. & Inst. Code §§ 5326.5, 5326.7, 5327; *Northern California Psychiatric Society v. City of Berkeley, supra* note 3.
5. *Lillian F. v. Superior Court, supra* note 3.
6. Welf. & Inst. Code § 5325.1.

ECT, could ultimately lead to an impairment of the patient's thinking. Therefore a patient could be seriously harmed by a statute that proscribed ECT under all circumstances.[7] Subsequently, the legislature amended the law to specifically guarantee a mentally ill patient's right to treatment services.[8]

An interesting constitutional issue developed when the City of Berkeley in 1982 enacted a municipal ordinance absolutely prohibiting the administration of ECT and imposing criminal punishment. This ordinance was held to be unconstitutional in light of the comprehensive scheme enacted by the California legislature.[9]

7. *Aden v. Younger*, 57 Cal.App.3d 662 (1976).
8. Welf. & Inst. Code § 5325.1.
9. *Northern California Psychiatric Society v. City of Berkeley* 178 Cal.App.3d 90 (1986). In *St. Francis Memorial Hospital v. Superior Court*, 205 Cal.App.3d 438 (1988), a psychiatrist unsuccessfully sued a hospital for suspending ECT because a treatment in her practice depended on it. The hospital had stopped administering ECT pending new guidelines.

Quality Assurance for Hospital Care

MHPs who function in a hospital setting may find that their professional services are reviewed by hospital committees to monitor the quality of care rendered to patients. MHPs may also serve on Quality Review Committees, assessing the services or qualifications of other MHPs. This chapter discusses the establishment of Quality Assurance Programs and the confidentiality of such proceedings, as well as the denial or loss of hospital staff privileges.

(A) Statutory Basis for Quality Assurance

The Federal Health Care Quality Improvement Act and various federal programs such as MediCare require the governing body of every certified hospital to establish a Utilization Review Committee to review professional practices.[1] The purpose of the review is to reduce morbidity and mortality and improve patient care.

Hospitals are also required to maintain a quality assurance program to review psychiatric services in areas such as suicide, attempted suicide, patient attempts to escape the hospital, assaults on patients, slip and falls, patient abuse and neglect, use of seclusion and restraints. The use of restraints, discharge planning, and outcomes must be reviewed on an least an annual basis.

---

1. 42 *U.S.C.* 1111 et seq. Such standards are also reflected in the Joint Committee of Hospital Accreditation, *Accreditation Manual for Hospitals* (1988).

Members of utilization review and quality assurance committees are given statutory immunity from suit by any person whose actions are reviewed by the committee. However, the immunity is qualified in that the recommendations must be made without malice and in the reasonable belief that the action or recommendation is warranted based on the facts disclosed.[2]

(B) Confidentiality

To encourage candor, the committee proceedings are not only confidential but also are protected from disclosure in any subsequent civil proceeding, no matter how relevant they may be. The prohibition does not apply to a person who is a party to any action or proceeding, the subject matter of which was reviewed at a committee meeting. The prohibition also does not apply to any person requesting staff privileges or to any action against an insurance carrier action alleging bad-faith refusal to accept a settlement offer within policy limits.

The same protection against disclosure is given to members of ethics committees, professional societies, and psychological review committees of state or local psychological associations, but, similarly, it does not apply if the person whose conduct is being reviewed sits on the hospital committee, or if the membership of the professional society committee exceeds 10 percent of the membership of the society.[3]

(C) Denial or Loss of Staff Privileges

The denial of staff privileges and the loss of staff privileges has led to a fair amount of litigation. The California Supreme Court has held that hospital bylaws must provide due process and must be sufficiently clear as to minimize the risk that they can be used arbitrarily or discriminatorily.[4] Generally, neither a private nor a public hospital may unreasonably or arbitrarily exclude an otherwise qualified person from staff membership.[5]

The use of hospital facilities is considered a property interest directly related to a physician's livelihood.[6] However, there is a

---

2. Civ. Code § 47(c).
3. Evid. Code §§ 1157, 1157.5 to 1157.7.
4. *Miller v. Eisenhower Medical Center*, 27 Cal.3d 614 (1980), where the denial was based on an inability to work with others.
5. *Willis v. Santa Ana etc. Hospital Ass'n*, 58 Cal.2d 806 (1962), *Anton v. San Antonio Community Hospital*, 19 Cal.3d 802 (1977).
6. *Ezekial v. Winkley*, 20 Cal.3d 267 (1977).

distinction between denials of privileges directed specifically toward the exclusion of a particular individual or group, and denials that may result in exclusion of individual practitioners as a practical matter but are undertaken for less personally directed reasons. The first type of situation is legally actionable, but the second is not.[7]

Professional societies that are tinged with a public function, such as the state medical, psychological, and dental associations, also must provide due process in denying and expelling members.[8]

---

7. *Redding v. St. Francis Medical Center*, 208 Cal.App.3d 98, 104 (1989).
8. *Pinsker v. Pacific Coast Society of Orthodontists*, 1 Cal.3d 160 (1969).

6.5

Malpractice Liability

The number of malpractice lawsuits against MHPs in California has proliferated dramatically in recent years.[1] A malpractice action is a civil suit brought by a patient against an MHP where the issue is whether the MHP met or breached the standard of care applicable to similarly licensed and trained individuals in the locality in which the acts occurred. A malpractice suit may be brought for alleged errors in treatment and for omissions or failure to act. chapter 6.6 discusses other types of suits against MHPs for their professional acts, including sexual misconduct claims.

(A) Malpractice Law

Professional malpractice is not subject to any one specific statute; rather, various duties to patients, the breach of which may give rise to civil liability, are covered by several separate statutory provisions. As a general proposition, California requires that all individuals in the course of their actions refrain from harming others if possible.[2]

---

1. Pope, K. S., & Vasquez, M. J. T. (1991). *Ethics in psychotherapy and counseling: A practical guide for psychologists.* San Francisco: Jossey-Bass.
2. Civ. Code § 1708.

(B) Standard of Care

While the general principles relating to professional malpractice were primarily articulated in litigation involving physicians, they apply equally to MHPs. An MHP has the duty to exercise in the treatment of the patient the degree of care, knowledge, and skill ordinarily possessed and exercised in similar situations by the average professional in that field and in that geographic area. When an MHP does not apply that degree of care and skill, and injury results, he or she may be liable for negligence. Further, to the extent that the MHP is either a specialist, or holds himself or herself out as a specialist, he or she will be held to the degree of care, knowledge and skill ordinarily possessed and exercised by a specialist in that area.

The *standard of care* is the minimum standard below which a practitioner cannot fall. It is based on the average competent professional, not the best or the brightest. The standard of care takes cognizance of the fact that competent treatment can lead to unsuccessful results—the mere fact that the result was unsuccessful does not mean that the treatment was negligent. When an MHP has to make a judgment call and is proven to be wrong, the error in judgment is not necessarily malpractice. The law recognizes that MHPs cannot be held to a standard of perfection in decision-making. Instead, if the requisite degree of skill and care is used, a judgment call that proves wrong is not actionable.[3] As long as an MHP uses reasonable judgment and does not depart from the standards of the profession, the failure to make the correct decision will not be malpractice.

Where the mental health professional holds him or herself out as a specialist, the standard of care is the same degree of skill and care possessed by the average specialist in that particular area. If an MHP holds himself or herself out as a specialist without the necessary training or experience for that specialty, that in itself may be negligence. The MHP will still be held to the specialist's standards because he or she was holding himself or herself out as qualified to provide such services.

Generally, the standard of care is established in a civil suit by testimony of experts in the profession.[4] Certain statutes provide for specific causes of action that may be included in civil suits, such as claims of a sexual relationship with a patient.[5] By the same token, other statutes create specific immunities from suit for various therapeutic actions, such as warning that a patient is a

---

3. *Polikoff v. United States*, 776 F.Supp. 1417 (S.D. Cal. 1977).
4. *Sinz v. Owens*, 33 Cal.2d 749 (1949).
5. Civ. Code § 43.93.

risk to a third party[6] and determining that a patient requires involuntary hospitalization as a risk to others, themselves, or by being gravely disabled.[7] However, if the conduct complained of is a violation of any specific statute whose intent is to protect the public, the conduct is considered negligence *per se*, which means that no evidence of expert testimony on the standard of care is necessary. For example, if an MHP fails to make a statutorily required report of child abuse and either the patient is harmed again by the abuser or another child is harmed who alleges that the abuse would not have occurred if a report had been made, the professional may be liable for negligence *per se*.

Establishing the standard of care through expert testimony is required only where the MHP's conduct is beyond the knowledge or understanding of lay people or common experience. Where the conduct is so obviously devoid of reasonable skill that even a lay person would know the conduct is negligent, expert testimony is not required. Examples would be raping a patient, billing for services that are not actually provided, or a non-psychiatrist providing medication to a patient. The classic examples for medical malpractice cases are where a surgeon left a sponge in a patient's body and where the wrong limb was removed due to a misunderstanding.

(C) Proximate Cause

Finding that an MHP failed to comply with the requisite standard of care is only one part in the process of determining whether a patient can recover for alleged malpractice. Once it is established that a duty to the patient has been breached, the next question is whether there are any legally cognizable damages that can be awarded. It is possible to have a technical breach of a duty without any legally compensable injury, in which case the MHP might be held liable for negligence, but owes no damages. An example would be where an MHP breaches a patient's confidentiality by disclosing information to another therapist but because the information does not become publicly known, the patient does not experience any actual embarrassment or emotional distress from the disclosure.

Where injury is alleged to have occurred, the patient must also prove that the injury was caused by the MHP's failure to comply with the standard of care. The term used to indicate the requisite causal connection between the acts of the MHP and the

---

6. Civ. Code § 43.92.
7. Welf. & Inst. Code §§ 5150, 5151.

alleged injury is *proximate cause.* In 1991, the California Supreme Court rejected a definition of proximate cause that the court found to be unnecessarily confusing and adopted a definition believed to be more understandable to lay people: whether the conduct was a "substantial factor" in causing the injury.[8] MHPs may also be liable where there is a level of pre-existing damage and the conduct complained of exacerbates but does not cause the pre-existing condition.[9]

(D) Statute of Limitations

The statute of limitations is a cut-off for claims that are otherwise valid, based on the theory that it is unfair to the defendants to allow a plaintiff to sit on a claim and bring it after the memories of witnesses have faded. The rationale behind the statute of limitations is that it would be unfair to allow the passage of time to impair a defendant's ability to adequately present the defense. For a malpractice claim, the standard is one year from the date that the patient knew or should have known of the malpractice, or three years as an outside limit from the date the acts occurred.

In California, patients must give an MHP 90 days' notice of their intent to file a lawsuit.[10] This is to allow the MHP a 90-day period in which to explore whether the case can be settled without litigation. The Supreme Court has determined that if the statute of limitations is running out and the notice of intent to sue is sent within the last 90 days before the statute expires, it will extend the statute for 90 days. In short, under certain circumstances, a plaintiff may have one year and 90 days in which to file suit.[11] However, the statute of limitations may be suspended or tolled for any of several reasons, including that the patient was mentally incompetent, that the defendant was out of the jurisdiction, or that the patient was unable to discover the claim because of fraud on the part of the defendant.

---

8. *Woods v. Young,* 53 Cal.3d 315 (1991).
9. Where it is contended that the negligence has exacerbated a pre-existing condition, the jury must determine the level of pre-existing damage and the extent to which it was exacerbated. The MHP cannot be held responsible for the level of pre-existing damage—only for the exacerbation, which requires allocation of the damages.
10. Civ. Proc. Code § 364. Effective January 1, 1994, § 364.1 provides that no action based on the professional negligence of a physician may be commenced unless the 90-day notice is also sent to the Medical Board of California.
11. *Woods v. Young,* 53 Cal.3d 315 (1991).

The patient must realize that harm has occurred before the statute begins to run.[12] A patient bringing a malpractice claim may also plead different legal theories that are subject to different statutes of limitation, such as breach of oral contract (two-year statute of limitations), breach of written contract (four-year statute of limitations), and fraud (three-year statute of limitations).

The statute of limitations is extended for minors. Medical malpractice claims by a minor must be commenced within three years of the date of the alleged wrongful act, except that actions by a minor under the age of six must be commenced within three years or prior to the minor's eighth birthday, whichever provides a longer period of time.[13]

(E) Avoiding Malpractice

There is no way to avoid being sued for malpractice; however, MHPs can take steps to minimize being found liable for malpractice by becoming familiar with the rules and regulations promulgated by their licensing boards and professional associations.

Additionally, MHPs must realize that by being a member of professional associations, they are held to have knowledge of the contents of their publications, such as monthly journals. Thus, it is incumbent on each MHP who is a member of a professional association to read these journals. Since the question in malpractice often is what steps the MHP took that were within or contrary to the standard of care, consultation with experts in the profession is an important adjunct to knowledge of the professional standards. In short, when a situation arises where the MHP is not clear on how to act, or where a case is particularly troublesome, the fact that some type of consultation was obtained can be important evidence of an attempt to comply with the standard of care. By the same token, the absence of any consultation with another MHP relative to the standard of care can be pointed to as an indication of lack of awareness of the risks undertaken and/or professional arrogance.

In certain circumstances, referral to a specialist may be mandatory. If peer consultations are obtained, they should be documented in the file. By the same token, if for any reason the MHP does not decide to take the advice given by the peer consult, he or she must document the reasons why. If a consultation is obtained but ignored, that can give rise to intentional tort exposure.

---

12. *De Pottel v. Hansen*, 228 Cal.App.3d 537 (1991); *Marriage & Family Center v. Superior Court*, 228 Cal.App.3d 1647 (1991).
13. Civ. Proc. Code § 340.5; *Young v. Haines*, 41 Cal.3d 833 (1986).

(F) Malpractice Review Committees

While some states require submission of medical malpractice claims to a review committee, California does not have any such statute.

(G) Limitations on Damages

In 1975, California enacted a comprehensive statute governing medical malpractice actions, the Medical Injury Compensation Reform Act. Under MICRA, a patient cannot obtain more than $250,000 in noneconomic damages, such as for emotional distress or pain and suffering.[14] However, the Supreme Court has indicated that where a complaint contains both malpractice claims that come within MICRA and non-malpractice claims such as fraud, the MICRA dollar limitations apply only to the malpractice claims.[15]

Before a punitive damage claim can be asserted in any malpractice action, a motion must be made, supported by affidavits, to obtain the court's approval. This is because there used to be numerous frivolous punitive damage claims asserted as part of malpractice actions. Recently, the California Supreme Court held that the requirement that a motion be made before claiming punitive damages in a malpractice context applied even where non-malpractice claims are included, because to do otherwise would encourage artful pleading to get around the requirements of law.[16]

Other provisions of MICRA include the right of the defendant to pay a judgment in increments over time instead of in a lump sum, and the right of the defendant to introduce evidence of the extent to which damages were paid by insurance and to obtain an offset for those amounts.[17] (In non-malpractice cases, proof of payment of damages by insurance is not generally allowed.)

---

14. Civ. Code § 3333.1; *Yates v. Pollack*, 194 Cal.App.3d 195 (1987); *see also Atkins v. Strayhorn*, 223 Cal.App.3d 1830 (1990), which held that a second cap may apply to a claim by the patient's spouse.
15. *Waters v. Bourhis*, 40 Cal.3d 424 (1985). The court has noted that this may lead to creative pleading by plaintiffs' attorneys.
16. *Central Pathology Service Medical Clinic, Inc. v. Superior Court*, 3 Cal.4th 181 (1992).
17. Civ. Code §§ 667.7, 3333.2

6.6

Other Forms of Professional Liability

In addition to the traditional malpractice claims discussed in chapter 6.5, MHPs may be sued for their professional acts on other legal theories. In fact, plaintiffs have an incentive to allege other theories to get a more favorable statute of limitations, or to try to escape application of the limitations on damages discussed in chapter 6.5. The different theories that plaintiffs may try to assert against MHPs include intentional torts, defamation, invasion of privacy, sexual misconduct, breach of fiduciary duty, and breach of contract. Being aware of these legal grounds for suit can help MHPs to avoid litigation.

(A) Intentional Torts

An *intentional tort* is a legal wrong inflicted by the defendant on the plaintiff that connotes an element of deliberateness and/or knowledge of potential harm to the plaintiff. The *intent* required for an intentional tort is the desire to bring about the readily foreseeable results of the defendant's action. In short, if the defendant knew or should have known that such consequences were likely to flow from his or her acts, it is not necessary to show that he or she specifically intended to harm the plaintiff. Intent is not equivalent to hostility but is instead equivalent to deliberateness or consciousness.

(B) Criminally Related Actions

An MHP who is found guilty under a criminal law can be held liable for the same behavior as an intentional tort under civil law.

In fact, because the standard of proof is higher in a criminal case than in a civil case, if a defendant is found guilty of a crime, he or she may not be allowed to deny liability in a civil suit concerning the same acts, based on the doctrine of collateral estoppel. In essence, this doctrine provides that a defendant is not entitled to relitigate the issue of liability if he or she has already litigated the issue in one court and lost. For example, an MHP prosecuted for rape and found guilty, may be precluded from disputing in a civil suit by the victim that the rape occurred; the civil suit would concern itself with civil defenses such as statutes of limitation and the amount of damages. The criminal case decision would be found to have already established as a fact that the rape occurred.[1]

(C) Defamation of Character

Defamatory statements can be oral or written. Oral defamatory statements are referred to as slander while written defamatory statements are called libel.

Libel is defined as a false and unprivileged publication by writing, printing, picture, effigy, or other fixed representation that exposes any person to hatred, contempt, ridicule, or obloquy, or which causes him or her to be shunned or avoided, or which has a tendency to injure the person in his or her occupation.[2] A statement that is defamatory on its face and is of such a character as to be actionable without showing of special damages is libel *per se.* Defamatory statements not libelous on their face are not actionable unless the plaintiff proves that the statements proximately caused special damages.[3] (This type of libel is called libel *per quod.*) Special damages are defined as damages the plaintiff proves he or she has suffered in respect to his or her property, business, trade, profession, or occupation.[4]

Slander is a false and unprivileged publication that is orally uttered (including communications by radio or any other mechanical media) that

1. charges any person with a crime, or with having been indicted, convicted, or punished for a crime;
2. imputes to the person the presence or existence of an infectious, contagious, or loathsome disease;

---

1. *Imen v. Glassford,* 201 Cal.App.3d 898 (1988); *Bernhard v. Bank of America,* 19 Cal.2d 807 (1942); *People v. Sims,* 32 Cal.3d 468 (1982).
2. Civ. Code § 44.
3. Civ. Code § 45.
4. *Slaughter v. Friedman,* 32 Cal.3d 149 (1982).

3. tends directly to impugn the person in his or her office, profession, trade, or business by imputing to him or her a general disqualification, or something that has a natural tendency to lessen the business profits;

4. imputes to the person impotence or a want of chastity; or

5. by natural consequence causes actual damage.[5]

In a defamation action, the plaintiff must show that the offensive statement was made to a third person, that there was no privilege between the defendant and the person to whom the information was communicated, and that harm resulted. There are two major defenses to a claim of defamation: one, that the communication was true. It is axiomatic that truth is a defense to a defamation action. Defamation as a cause of action is intended to compensate a person for *untruthful* communications that put him or her in a bad light or damage his or her reputation.

The second major defense to a defamation action is that the defendant was privileged to make the communication. California provides that no claim can be brought against a person who is a witness or participant in a judicial, legislative, or administrative proceeding, regardless of whether malice was present. The express policy behind this is to preclude litigation over what witnesses say, which would have a chilling effect on the witness's honesty and willingness to participate in the process.[6]

For MHPs, defamation issues most commonly arise in situations where the MHP is rendering an opinion in a custody dispute or some other civil proceeding, and one of the parties disagrees with the testimony and files a suit.[7] The statutory protection extends to those acts that were necessary to prepare for court testimony or in anticipation of testimony, even if the acts occurred outside the courthouse and the actual testimony never takes place.[8] There is, however, a distinction between speech and conduct. The statute is not intended to protect conduct not related to speech, such as illegal wire-tapping.[9] To the extent that an MHP is acting as a witness or a mediator, particularly in custody proceedings, he or she may be entitled to immunity from suit based on the judicial nature of the functions under a doctrine called *quasi-judicial immunity*.[10] Under this doctrine, if the functions performed by the MHP are analogous to those of a judge or other

---

5. Civ. Code § 46.

6. Civ. Code § 47b; *Silberg v. Anderson*, 50 Cal.3d 205 (1990).

7. Civ. Code § 46.

8. Civ. Code § 45(a); *Gootee v. Lightner*, 224 Cal.App.3d 274 (1990); *Block v. Sacramento Clinical Labs*, 131 Cal.App.3d 386 (1982).

9. *Kimmel v. Goland*, 51 Cal.3d 202 (1990).

10. *Howard v. Drapkin*, 222 Cal.App.3d 843 (1990).

participants in the judicial process, the MHP may be accorded immunity from suit without regard to whether the actions were malicious.

A series of cases have held that the statutory privilege cannot provide immunity for conduct in violation of the California Constitution's right of privacy. These cases generally concern an unauthorized disclosure in litigation of medical or psychological information that violates the patient's right of privacy.[11]

In addition to the absolute privilege under the statute governing judicial proceedings, there is a qualified privilege where an individual who is entitled or privileged to communicate to a third party does so without malice and in the interests of the person to whom the communication is made.[12]

An additional defense to a defamation claim is that the person about whom the statements were made is a public figure or public official.[13]

State law protects peer review committee members from liability for acts performed in reviewing the quality of medical or dental services,[14] as well as private communications to a hospital, hospital medical staff, professional society, medical or dental school, professional licensing board, peer review committee or underwriting committee that evaluates health professionals. However, the law does not protect private persons' communications to patients regarding the quality of medical or dental care received.[15]

(D) Invasion of Privacy

The right of privacy is protected under Article I, Section 1 of the California Constitution. The California Supreme Court in 1994 held that for a plaintiff to assert a claim for invasion of privacy, he or she must establish

1. a legally protected privilege interest,
2. a reasonable expectation of privacy under the circumstances of the case; and

---

11. *Cutter v. Brownbridge*, 183 Cal.App.3d 836 (1986); *Estate of Urbaniak v. Newton*, 226 Cal.App.3d 1128 (1991).
12. Civ. Code § 47(c); *Slaughter v. Friedman*, 32 Cal.3d 149, 156–157 (1982).
13. *New York Times Co. v. Sullivan*, 376 U.S. 254 (1964); *Gertz v. Robert Welch Inc.*, 418 U.S. 323 (1974); *Mosesian v. McClatchy Newspapers*, 205 Cal.App.3d 597 (1988).
14. Civ. Code § 43.7. However this privilege is *not* recognized under federal law. *Pagano v. Oroville Hospital*, 145 F.R.D. 683 (E.D.Cal. 1993).
15. Civ. Code § 43.8.

3. conduct by the defendant that constitutes a serious invasion of privacy.[16]

When a psychotherapist reveals information about a patient in a court proceeding where there is no waiver of the psycho-therapist–patient privilege, no subpoena, and no consent by the patient, the litigation privilege discussed above does not apply and a cause of action for invasion of privacy exists.[17] However, in a 1994 case the California Supreme Court held that a patient could not sue her doctor and his insurance company for invasion of privacy where the doctor had allegedly disclosed medical information to a doctor she was suing for malpractice. The court's rationale was that the patient had no reasonable expectation of privacy because the information would have been disclosed in the discovery process anyway. Furthermore, the court did not consider the disclosure there to be a serious invasion of privacy.[18] A claim of invasion of privacy goes beyond disclosure of information to include putting someone in an unfavorable light. Invasion of privacy has been held to include statements to the press regarding a person evaluated by an MHP.[19] Any unauthorized taping or electronic eavesdropping will also give rise to a claim for invasion of privacy.[20]

(E) Sexual Misconduct

The issue of sexual misconduct is one that is extremely important because of the prevalence of such claims nationwide.[21] Some of the largest verdicts in cases alleging sexual misconduct by therapists have come from California juries.[22]

The first case that addressed the issue of sexual contact between a California MHP and a patient was a 1959 criminal case upholding the conviction of a psychiatrist who had had sexual relations with a minor female patient.[23] Ironically, the patient had been in therapy to deal with her sexual promiscuity problem. The

---

16. *Hill v. National Collegiate Athletic Assn.*, 7 Cal.4th 1 (1994).
17. *Cutter v. Brownbridge*, 183 Cal.App.3d 836 (1986).
18. *Heller v. Norcal Mutual Ins. Co.*, 8 Cal.4th 30 (1994).
19. *Susan A. v. County of Sonoma*, 2 Cal.App.4th 88 (1991).
20. *Friddle v. Epstein*, 16 Cal.App.4th 1649 (1993).
21. See Pope, K. S., Sonne, J. L., & Holroyd, J. (1993). *Sexual feelings in psychotherapy: Explorations for therapists and therapists-in-training.* Washington, DC: American Psychological Association; Pope, K. S. (1994). *Sexual involvement with therapists: Patient assessment, subsequent therapy, forensics.* Washington, DC: American Psychological Association.
22. *Rosenstein v. Barnes*, Los Angeles Sup. Ct. NWC78755 (Mar. 24, 1984) ($250,000); *Ertel v. Kirstenbrock*, San Diego Sup.Ct. Nos. 595257, 588117, (Mar. 16, 1990) ($1,538,000); *Walker v. Parzen*, San Diego Sup.Ct. Nos. 437-631 (July 7, 1982) ($4,780,000).
23. *People v. Bernstein*, 340 P.2d 299, 171 Cal.App.2d 279 (1959).

first reported decision imposing discipline on a California MHP for engaging in a sexual relationship with a patient occurred nearly 20 years later. That decision concluded that a sexual relationship between a therapist and a patient constituted a form of gross negligence, even though there was no law, rule, or regulation specifically prohibiting sexual contact between therapist and patient.[24]

In 1979, the legislature enacted the first law expressly prohibiting sexual contact between a therapist and a patient in California.[25] There have been numerous prosecutions of therapists at the administrative level under this statute, although few cases have been reported at the appellate level. However, one Court of Appeals held that where a patient was suing a non-psychotherapist for an alleged sexual relationship, the patient had a cause of action only if the physician had represented the sexual activity as a part of treatment.[26]

The statute left open a question as to relationships between therapist and patient following the termination of therapy, but this was clarified with the enactment of a civil statute, effective January 1, 1988,[27] which created a special cause of action for patients who wish to sue their therapists for alleged sexual relationships. Under that statute, a sexual relationship between therapist and a patient is expressly forbidden during the course of therapy and for a period of two years thereafter.

Effective January 1, 1994, several major changes were made by the Legislature in the statutes governing misconduct. The administrative regulations, however, have never been revised to specifically address post-termination relationships.

The passage of the civil statute allowing patients to sue their therapists was in response to a Senate Task Force Report, which had reviewed the state of the law in this area and concluded that a special statutory cause of action was necessary. However, certain of the task force recommendations, most notably, to extend the statute of limitations, were not adopted by the Legislature.

Because of some pre-existing marriages between therapists and ex-patients, no cause of action can be asserted under this

---

24. *Cooper v. Board of Medical Examiners*, 49 Cal.App.3d 93 (1975). *See also Dresser v. Board of Medical Quality Assurance*, 130 Cal.App.3d 50 (1982).
25. Bus. & Prof. Code § 726. One justice in *Gromis v. Medical Board*, 8 Cal.App.4th 589 (1992), suggested the law is unconstitutionally vague.
26. *Atienza v. Taub*, 194 Cal.App.3d 388 (1987).
27. Civ. Code § 43.93.

statute by one spouse against another.[28] There have been conflicting decisions on the right of a patient's spouse to sue an MHP for having a sexual relationship with a patient. In one case, an appellate court held that a husband of a patient who had engaged in sexual relations with her psychotherapist, had a cause of action against the psychotherapist for the damage done to their marriage.[29] In 1993, an appellate court held that when a wife was a patient and had a sexual relationship with her therapist, her husband could not sue the therapist unless he was also a patient.[30]

The issue was further complicated by a California Supreme Court decision that considered the question whether a patient's complaints of sexual misconduct against a therapist came within the scope of the Medical Injury Compensation Reform Act (MICRA) for the purpose of certain attorney fees limitations.[31] After reviewing a number of out-of-state cases, the California Supreme Court concluded that while the MICRA provisions did apply to the negligence portions of a malpractice claim, a patient could plead certain theories, such as fraud, which were outside the reach of MICRA and therefore not subject to the damage limitations of MICRA. This ruling added a layer of complexity to the prosecution and defense of such cases.

The U.S. Court of Appeals for the 9th Circuit, which has jurisdiction over California in a case arising out of Washington state, has held that patients who are treated by MHPs employed by the U.S. government can maintain negligence theories under the Federal Tort Claims Act for such sexual relationships.[32]

The California Supreme Court has held that when an MHP engages in sexual misconduct with patients who are children, both the abused children and their parents have causes of action against the MHP.[33] There is, however, an open question in California as to the extent to which the employers and the partners of a psychotherapist who engages in sexual misconduct are vicariously liable for that person's acts.[34]

---

28. Civ. Code § 43.93(c). The 1993 revisions to Bus. & Prof. Code § 726 state that the proscription against sexual contact does not apply to a physician or surgeon and his or her spouse, or persons in an equivalent domestic relationship, where medical treatment other than psychotherapy was provided by the physician or surgeon.
29. *Richard H. v. Larry D.*, 198 Cal.App.3d 591 (1988).
30. *Smith v. Pust*, 19 Cal.App.4th 263 (1993).
31. *Waters v. Bourhis*, 40 Cal.3d 424 (1985).
32. *Simmons v. United States*, 805 F.2d 363 (9th Cir. 1986).
33. *Marlene F. v. Affiliated Psychiatric Clinics*, 48 Cal.3d 583 (1989).
34. *Id.* In a footnote in *Marlene F., supra* note 31, the California Supreme Court suggested that, although the question is open, it may follow an out-of-state line of cases opposing vicarious liability in certain circumstances. *See generally Evan F. v. Hughson United Methodist Church*, 8 Cal.App.4th 828 (1992).

Sexual misconduct with a patient can also be the basis for criminal charges, with the severity of the charge depending on the number of patients involved. This type of criminal statute is colloquially referred to as a "wobbler" because whether the conduct proscribed is a misdemeanor or a felony, depends on the circumstances. The criminal penalties can be as high as 16 months to three years in jail and up to $10,000 in fines.[35]

When a patient advises a psychotherapist of a sexual relationship with a prior psychotherapist, the treating psychotherapist is required to provide the patient with a booklet entitled *Sexual Intimacy is Never Okay,* which discusses the illegality of such conduct and remedies the patient may pursue. The therapist also must discuss with the patient the option of reporting the conduct to the appropriate state license board. However, if the patient refuses to authorize such a disclosure, the therapist must keep the information confidential. Failure to comply with this statute can subject the treating therapist to discipline.[36]

Although the laws are clear as regards MHPs, the situation with regard to other professionals and even medical professionals is less clear. For example, in a 1992 case, the Court of Appeals held that before the Medical Board could discipline a non-MHP physician for a sexual relationship with a former patient, there must be some showing of connection between that conduct and the physician's fitness to practice.[37] Subsequently, the statute on sexual misconduct by psychotherapists was specifically amended to include physicians and surgeons.[38]

Against this background of legislation and case law, it is obviously contrary to the best interests of both patients and MHPs for such relationships to occur. However, the number of cases being filed civilly and the number of administrative cases seeking to discipline therapists for such relationships, do not appear to be decreasing.[39]

---

35. Bus. & Prof. Code § 729(b)(1) to (5).
36. Bus. & Prof. Code § 729. The 1993 amendments were effective January 1, 1994.
37. *Gromis v. Medical Board,* 8 Cal.App.4th 589 (1992). This is true even though in that case the patient was a minor and the physician was several decades older.
38. Bus. & Prof. Code § 729, effective January 1, 1994. *But see* note 25, *supra.*
39. See Pope, K. S. *Licensing disciplinary actions for psychologists who have been sexually involved with a client: Some information about offenders.* 24 Professional Psychology: Research and Practice 347–377 (1993); Pope, K. S., Sonne, J. L., & Holroyd, J. (1993). *Sexual feelings in psychotherapy: Explorations for therapists and therapists-in-training.* Washington, DC: American Psychological Association; Pope, K. S. (1994). *Sexual involvement with therapists: Patient assessment, subsequent therapy, forensics.* Washington, DC: American Psychological Association.

(F) Sexual Harassment of Patients

Effective January 1, 1995, a new law created a cause of action by patients against psychotherapists for sexual harassment.[40] The statute expressly applies to psychotherapists and specifically mentions MFCCs, licensed clinical social workers, physicians, individuals with a master of social work degree, and teachers. (Other professionals such as realtors and attorneys are also included.)

This statute is part of the Unruh Civil Rights Act and entitles plaintiffs to similar remedies as plaintiffs in employment harassment or discrimination cases (see chapter 5B.1E). These remedies include compensatory damages, punitive damages, attorneys fees, and injunctive relief.[41] These remedies are much broader than those available in malpractice actions alleging sexual misconduct. It appears that the Legislature intended this category of cases not to be subject to MICRA's $250,000 damage cap (see chapters 6.5 and 6.6). Although malpractice cases alleging sexual misconduct are generally covered by professional errors and omissions policies, sexual harassment claims may not be covered. Furthermore, the vagueness of the statute is such as to raise grave concerns about potential false and/or frivolous claims.

(G) Other Forms of Professional Liability

Malicious prosecution is a claim that prior civil or criminal litigation was instituted without any reasonable basis and for a malicious purpose. It is a type of litigation that is strongly disfavored in California because it leads to repetitive litigation. In essence, a malicious prosecution claim is a lawsuit based on another lawsuit. A malicious prosecution claim can be based on a cross-complaint asserting counter-claims as well as on a complaint that initiated a civil or criminal proceeding.[42]

Abuse of process is a legal theory related to malicious prosecution, but not identical. Abuse of process occurs where, in an otherwise legal and justified proceeding, an individual used the process of the court for an unauthorized purpose.[43] Malicious prosecution and abuse of process are the only two theories recognized by the Supreme Court as exceptions to the litigation privilege referred to above.

---

40. Civ. Code § 51.9.
41. Civ. Code § 51.9(b) and § 52.
42. *Bertero v. National General Corp.*, 13 Cal.3d 43 (1974).
43. *Barquist v. Merchants Collection Ass'n*, 7 Cal.3d 94 (1972).

False imprisonment is where an individual is physically detained without legal authority or permission. A false imprisonment claim can arise if a patient is restrained from leaving a session room because he or she is suicidal. Obviously, the commitment of a patient to some type of mental health facility can form a basis for an assertion that the commitment was wrongful, although as noted above, there is a statutory immunity to the extent the commitment is pursuant to the law authorizing 72-hour holds.[44]

(H) Other Types of Civil Liability

The relationship between an MHP and a patient may give rise to other types of litigation based on other legal theories. In fact, the nature and complexity of the relationship is so great as to preclude a definitive listing of the different types of theories that may be asserted. The law governing MHPs is evolving as the professional standards evolve to deal with perceived problems.

For example, although there are no statistics confirming it, anecdotal experience indicates a substantial increase in the number of cases where dual relationships are alleged to have existed. Thus, any situation where an MHP has a secondary relationship other than a therapeutic one may give rise to claims of negligence, breach of contract, fraud, negligent misrepresentation, or exercising undue influence. Examples of various dual relationships that have been the subject of civil suits at the trial-court level include situations where the therapist has hired the patients to do secretarial or office management work or to perform menial work, such as house painting or hair cutting; engaging in real estate transactions with the patient; setting up an Amway distributorship with a patient; and engaging in a social but nonsexual post-therapeutic relationship with a patient. Since the standards regarding dual relationships are still being defined, the propensity for further litigation of this type is quite high.

(I) Breach of Fiduciary Duty

A fiduciary duty is a special duty imposed by the law where one party is in a superior position to another party either because of the nature of their relationship or because one party has specialized training. However, not every relationship where there is disparate knowledge or bargaining position creates a fiduciary duty.

---

44. Welf. & Inst. Code §§ 5150, 5151.

Among the relationships that have been recognized to be fiduciary relationships are attorney–client and doctor–patient. The relationship between psychotherapist and patient has been expressly recognized to be a fiduciary one in California.[45] The fiduciary has a special duty of care that requires putting his or her own interest secondary to that of the other party in the relationship. A fiduciary relationship also precludes self-dealing. Thus, any financial transaction between a fiduciary and a person to whom the duty is owed is subject to special scrutiny to ensure that there is no undue influence or advantage taken by the fiduciary. This has special application for MHPs in instances where a patient seeks to make a bequest to an MHP in a will, where gifts of high dollar value are exchanged, where there are any types of loan transactions, or even in instances where the issue is whether the advice that was given was in the patient's best interest.

The fiduciary nature of the relationship between doctor and patient has been a key factor in upholding liability for sexual relationships between mental and medical health professionals, both to the patient and to the patient's spouse.[46]

A claim that a fiduciary duty was breached may give rise to punitive damage exposure where a claim of simple negligence would not. Further, the measure of damages where a breach of a fiduciary obligation is claimed may be different and broader than the measure of damages for nonfiduciary breaches of duties. The measure of damages where a fiduciary has engaged in some type of business transaction is that the other party is entitled to recover all damages that are readily foreseeable and flowed from the breach of the fiduciary duty. The other party is entitled to be put in the situation that he or she would have been in had the breach of fiduciary duty not occurred.[47]

This may lead to higher verdicts than a simple negligence case. An example would be a patient investing in a business owned by an MHP, where representations were made as to its profitability. If the investment does not produce the predicted income, the patient might be able to recover, whereas a person involved in an arms-length transaction would not.

A contract is an agreement to do or not do a particular thing.[48] Generally, contracts are either *express*, i.e., the terms are stated,[49] or *implied*, i.e., the existence of the contract and its terms are

---

45. *Waters v. Bourhis*, 40 Cal.3d 424 (1985).
46. *Richard H. v. Larry D.*, 198 Cal.App.3d 591 (1988); *Waters v. Bourhis*, 40 Cal.3d 424 (1985), *but see Smith v. Pust*, 19 Cal.App.4th 263 (1993).
47. Civ. Code § 3343.
48. Civ. Code § 1549.
49. Civ. Code §§ 1619, 1620.

manifested by conduct. The essential elements of a contract are the following:

1. the parties are capable of contracting;
2. the parties have consented;
3. a lawful object of the contract; and
4. a sufficient cause or consideration.[50]

Generally, all persons are capable of entering a contract, except minors, persons of unsound mind, and convicts.[51] Minors and persons of unsound mind have limited capacity to contract.[52]

Certain contracts are required by law to be in writing to be enforceable.[53] Contracts are generally implied where there is a course of dealing between the parties, and the parties' actions allow a court to reasonably deduce what the terms of an understanding was. It is extremely unusual to find any allegation of an implied contract in malpractice litigation; however, a common allegation is that the MHP's actions not only were negligent but also breached an oral or written contract. A patient may seek to allege breach of contract because if a written contract is breached and it contains an attorney-fees clause, the patient may be able to recover attorney fees, as well.[54]

Providers of services, including MHPs, are generally not subject to theories of breach of implied warranty or strict liability in tort. These two legal theories are generally reserved for the providers of products.[55] However, if the written agreement contains express representations as to the quality of services to be provided or the conditions under which services will be provided, a claim for breach of express warranty may be asserted. For example, if the MHP states in writing that he or she will provide the best services available, that may be deemed to be a warranty. Similarly, if an MHP were imprudent enough to guarantee some type of positive result in a set period of time, putting that provision in a written contract could be deemed to be a warranty.

The other area where oral and written contracts are important is payment of fees. Where an MHP does not put the agreement or fee in writing, the patient may contest the fee with the result that

---

50. Civ. Code § 1621.
51. Civ. Code § 1556.
52. Civ. Code § 1557. Therefore, an MHP must be careful to ascertain a patient's legal capacity to contract before entering such an agreement.
53. This law is referred to as the statute of frauds. Civ. Code § 1624.
54. Civ. Code § 1717.
55. *Gagne v. Bertran*, 43 Cal.2d 481 (1954).

the therapist may end up being entitled only to the reasonable value of the services provided, not the agreed-upon rate.[56]

Where a written contract exists and addresses the amount and conditions for payment of fees, both parties must comply. Thus, not paying the fees in the manner as specified is a breach by the patient. If the MHP is charging in a manner that is not consistent with the contract that may likewise be a breach.

Breaches of contract may also arise where services are provided pursuant to an HMO contract, such as Blue Cross/Blue Shield, wherein representations are made regarding the nature of services that will be provided by the professional provider. This is an area that is just starting to be defined. MHPs should be aware, however, that the terms in the contracts that they have with HMOs may create obligations to the patient that patients can enforce as third-party beneficiaries of the HMO contract. In other words, the services to be provided to a patient must be consistent both with the contract with the patient and the contract with the HMO.

---

56. Where a contract is not written or is found to be legally insufficient, a professional is entitled to the reasonable value of his or her services as judged by rates paid to equivalent professionals in the community. This doctrine is called *quantum meruit*. For example, if the contract provided for a rate of $100 an hour, but the market rate for such services was $60 an hour, in the absence of a written contract the professional would be entitled to only $60 an hour.

6.7

Criminal Liability

There is no uniform criminal law in California specifically directed at MHPs, but there are statutes under which criminal penalties apply, and which MHPs are subject to. For example, sexual relationships between a therapist and a patient may be a misdemeanor or a felony, depending on the circumstances.[1] A therapist may be prosecuted for failure to report child abuse,[2] and a therapist may be guilty of billing fraud on a state or federal program. In California, the Medicare program is called Medi-Cal and a false billing under that program will subject an MHP to criminal liability.[3] A violation of any of the sections of the Business and Professions Code that relate to licensure of MHPs is a misdemeanor, but is rarely prosecuted unless the individual was engaged in practicing without a license or beyond the scope of his or her license.[4]

Where a person holding a state license in a business or profession is a criminal defendant, the state agency that issued the license may voluntarily appear to furnish pertinent information, make recommendations regarding specific conditions of probation, or provide any other assistance necessary to promote the interests of justice and protect the interests of the public. A court can order the licensing agency to participate if the crime charged

---

1. Bus. & Prof. Code § 729.
2. Penal Code §§ 11666, 11166.5.
3. *Reynaud v. Superior Court*, 138 Cal.App.3d 1 (1982); Welf. & Inst. Code § 14107.
4. Bus. & Prof. Code § 2053; *People v. Burroughs*, 234 Cal.App.3d 245 (1991); *People v. Brown*, 234 Cal.App.3d 918 (1991) (unlawfully practicing medicine in conducting a sex-change operation).

is substantially related to the qualifications, functions, or duties of a licensee or a permit or certificate holder.

(A) Parental Liability

California allows the imposition of criminal liability on parents for the acts of their children. The duty of parents to supervise and control their children is well established.[5] However, as part of the Street Terrorism Enforcement and Prevention Act, parents may be held liable for acts that encourage or contribute to the delinquency of their children. The Supreme Court upheld this law in 1993.[6]

(B) Sexual Offenses

There are a variety of sexual acts that may lead to criminal charges if engaged in by an MHP and a patient, a former patient, or a minor. Additionally, although it will not be discussed at length here, California recognizes spousal rape as a crime.[7]

(C) Definitions

Unlawful sexual intercourse is where any person induces someone other than their spouse to engage in sexual intercourse, penetration of the genital or anal openings by a foreign object, oral copulation, or sodomy, when the consent of the other person is procured by false or fraudulent representations or pretense made with the intent to create fear, and which does induce fear. The situation must be such that the fear would cause a reasonable person in like circumstances to act contrary to that person's free will, and the victim, in fact, acts out sexually because of the fear. *Fear* is defined as fear of unlawful physical injury or death to the person or any relative of the person or member of the person's family.[8]

Sexual battery is a crime that occurs where a person acts with the intent to cause a harmful or offensive contact with an intimate part of another, and a sexually offensive contact with that person directly or indirectly results. A sexual battery may also be found

---

5. *Singer v. Marx,* 144 Cal.App.2d 631 (1956).
6. *Williams v. Garcetti,* 5 Cal.4th 561 (1993).
7. Penal Code § 262.
8. Penal Code § 266c.

when a person acts with the intent to cause a harmful or offensive contact with another by use of his or her own intimate body parts, and a sexually offensive contact directly or indirectly results. A sexual battery may also occur when a person acts to cause an imminent apprehension of some harmful or offensive contact with an intimate body part, and a sexually offensive contact directly or indirectly results. This act subjects the perpetrator to both civil and criminal penalties.

Intimate part as defined in this statute means the sexual organ, anus, groin or buttocks of any person, or the breast of a female.[9]

In California, *rape* is defined as an act of sexual intercourse accomplished through force, violence, duress, menace, or fear of immediate and unlawful bodily injury, or where a person is incapable because of mental disorder or developmental or physical disability of giving legal consent, and that is known, or reasonably should be known to the person committing the act.

When a person is prevented from resisting a sexual advance by an intoxicating or anesthetic substance or controlled substance, sexual activity may be rape. Rape may occur where a person is unconscious of the nature of the act at the time that it occurs, and that is known to the perpetrator. When the sexual acts occur against the victim's will as a result of a threat of retaliation in the future against the victim or any other person and there is a reasonable possibility that the perpetrator will execute the threat, the conduct may constitute rape.[10]

It is unlawful to have sexual intercourse with a female under age 18 who is not the wife of the perpetrator.[11]

It is unlawful to engage in any lewd or lascivious act upon or with the body, or any part or member thereof, of a child under the age of 14 with the intent of arousing, appealing to, or gratifying the lust or passions or sexual desires of that child or of the person committing the acts. It is also unlawful to engage in such acts with the child where violence, force, duress, menace, or fear of immediate and unlawful bodily injury on the victim or another person is used.[12]

---

9. Civ. Code § 1708.5.
10. Penal Code § 261. Rape can also be a basis for a civil suit for damages. *Delia S. v. Torres*, 134 Cal.App.3d 471 (1982).
11. Penal Code § 261.5. The first case discussing liability of an MHP for sexual interaction with a patient was *People v. Bernstein*, 171 Cal.App.2d 279 (1949), where a psychiatrist engaged in a sexual relationship with a minor female patient who was under his care to deal with, among other problems, promiscuity.
12. Penal Code § 288. Where an MHP molests a child in his or her care, the parents may also be able to sue civilly in addition to whatever criminal penalties are obtained. *Marlene F. v. Affiliated Psychiatric Clinic*, 48 Cal.3d 583 (1989).

(D) Assault

Although the terms *assault* and *battery* are used synonymously, the two have different legal criteria which have particular significance for MHPs.

(E) Definitions

A *battery* is offensive touching without consent, while *assault* is putting someone in fear or reasonable apprehension of battery. For the crime of battery to occur, there must be an actual touching—either directly by the person or by an object such as a thrown rock, a stick held by the person, and so forth. For the crime of assault to be proved, no element of touching need be shown, only the fear of touching—even where the victim has an apparently protective shield.[13] A *criminal assault,* on the other hand, is an unlawful attempt with a present ability to commit a violent injury on another, with an intent to commit such an action. While technical batteries are often charged in civil litigation involving MHPs, it is rare to have any type of criminal battery case brought against an MHP unless it is of a sexual nature. However, civil liability has been recognized for a unique type of therapy that involved beating the patient. Such conduct would also clearly constitute a basis for criminal charges.[14]

The circumstance where MHPs are most likely to be charged with some type of nonsexual assault or battery is attempting to restrain a violent or suicidal patient. This is more commonly an allegation in a civil suit rather than in a criminal action, but it is technically possible.

(F) Assisting Suicide

Under California law, neither suicide nor attempted suicide is a crime. However, anyone who deliberately aids, advises, or encourages another person to commit suicide is guilty of a felony.[15] This statute has been upheld despite contentions that it violates the constitutional rights of privacy and free expression.[16] In 1992, the California electorate was presented with a proposition called

---

13. *People v. Valdez,* 175 Cal.App.3d 103 (1985), where the defendant shot at a gas station attendant who was behind a bullet-proof shield.
14. *Rains v. Superior Court,* 150 Cal.App.3d 933 (1984). In this case, the Center for Feeling Therapy used a technique referred to as *sluggo* therapy, which involved beating the patient. The court held that no one could validly consent to such a treatment.
15. Penal Code § 401.
16. *Donaldson v. Van de Kamp,* 2 Cal.App.4th 1614 (1992).

the Death with Dignity Act, which would have allowed physician-assisted suicide by exempting such cases from this statute; however, the electorate rejected this proposition.[17]

Two cases have discussed liability for aiding a suicide. The first case involved two juveniles who entered a suicide pact. The juveniles drove over a cliff in a car and one died. The juvenile who survived was convicted of murder, but the California Supreme Court reversed the murder conviction and held the only offense the juvenile could be charged with was aiding a suicide.[18] The second case was a civil suit against rock musicians and their music company, alleging that their music caused a 19-year-old boy to kill himself. The parents of the boy claimed that the musicians had violated this statute, thereby subjecting themselves to civil and criminal liability. The Court of Appeals, however, held no such claim could be brought.[19]

(G) Billing Fraud

In California, billing fraud has lead to several instances of criminal charges against MHPs involved in publicly funded programs such as Medi-Cal.[20] Any instance of billing fraud not only constitutes a crime, but also can be grounds for loss of licensure.[21] The most common type of billing fraud under Medi-Cal programs is billing for sessions that did not occur, and billing for services rendered to one family member under the names of other family members because the entitlement of one family member has expired.

Billing fraud may also lead to criminal charges where false statements are made to insurance carriers in order to procure payments.

---

17. Proposition 161.
18. In re Joseph Co., 34 Cal.3d 429 (1983).
19. *McCollum v. CBS, Inc.*, 202 Cal.App.3d 1989 (1988). Of particular interest is note 4, listing suicide themes in literature and music from *Hamlet* to *M*A*S*H.*
20. *Reynaud v. Superior Court*, 138 Cal.App.3d 1 (1982); *See Jaffe v. Cranford*, 168 Cal.App.3d 930 (1985), where the court held that a child psychiatrist prosecuted for medical fraud could not force his malpractice insurance carrier to pay for his defense.
21. Bus. & Prof. Code § 810 provides that it is unprofessional conduct to knowingly present or cause to be presented any false or fraudulent claim for the payment of a loss under a contract of insurance. It is also unprofessional conduct to knowingly prepare, make, or subscribe any writing with the intent to present the same, or to allow it to be presented or used in support of such action. In one case, a psychiatrist was disciplined for allowing unathorized and nonprofessional staff members to bill Medi-Cal insurance for patients he did not see. He was disciplined even though the Board found that his reasons were altruistic and that he did not profit from the billing. *Fort v. Board of Medical Quality Assurance*, 136 Cal.App.3d 12 (1982).

6.8

Liability of Credentialing Boards

MHPs who are licensees, or unsuccessful license applicants, of licensing boards may wish to file suit over board actions they believe to be unfair. This chapter discusses the extent to which such litigation is allowed and the immunity from suit that licensing boards generally have. MHPs who are members of licensing boards have immunity from suit.

(A) Licensing Board Immunity in General

Unlike private citizens, state and federal governments cannot be sued unless the government has previously waived its traditional immunity. The immunity that the government has is referred to as *sovereign immunity* and unless there is an express waiver of the immunity, no suit can be maintained. California has enacted a comprehensive Tort Claims Act, which sets forth the types of theories and types of acts under which the government may be liable. The act contains a number of conditions that must complied with before a suit can be brought against a governmental agency. The most important of these is a notice to the government of the potential claim which allows the governmental agency a set period of time in which to investigate the claim and make a determination as to whether to resolve it.[1]

As a general matter, the government is immune from suit for discretionary acts. The Boards that license professionals are gen-

1. Gov't Code § 915.4 et seq.

erally immune from suit on any type of negligence theories. However, they are not immune to suits which allege a violation of federal civil rights statutes or federal constitutional provisions. In the past there have been successful suits brought against the state license boards alleging discrimination which is in violation of federal law.[2] However, those are not suits for negligence or general damages. The ability to file suit against the licensing board to contest a grant, denial, or revocation of licensure is limited to a type of declaratory or injunctive relief which does not entitle the licensee or prospective licensee to monetary damages, except, potentially, attorneys fees.[3]

The rationale is simply that if governmental agencies were subject to suit every time that they denied or revoked a license the agencies would be in constant litigation and also would be unwilling to make the difficult decisions relative to qualifications that are necessary. While a process does exist to challenge these types of decisions, damage awards generally are not available. However, if it could be shown that a particular individual was denied a license or a license was revoked for racial, sexual or other statutorily prohibited grounds, then a potential exists for a damage award, although it would still be difficult to obtain.

(B) Immunity for Libel, Slander, Misrepresentation, and Failure to Warn

Generally, no government agency is liable for libel, slander, or misrepresentations made by its employees.[4] Government employees are generally immune from misrepresentations made in the course of their employment unless they are guilty of "actual fraud, corruption, or actual malice."[5] However the Supreme Court limited these immunities to misrepresentations which cause business and financial injuries. The court has allowed suits over misrepresentations concerning social services, primarily the failure to disclose or warn of a foster child's dangerous nature or past history of violence.[6] Subsequent cases have refused to extend immunity to government misrepresentations regarding an

---

2. *D'Amico v. Board of Medical Examiners*, 11 Cal.3d 1 (1974).
3. Gov't Code §§ 818.4, 821.2; *Rosenthal v. Vogt*, 229 Cal.App. 69 (1991); Civ. Proc. Code § 1057.
4. Gov't Code § 818.8; *Universal Byproducts Inc. v. City of Modesto*, 43 Cal.App.3d 145 (1974).
5. Gov't Code § 822.2; *Tokeshi v. California*, 217 Cal.App.3d 999 (1990).
6. *Johnson v. California*, 69 Cal.2d 782 (1968).

adopted child's medical condition.[7] Thus, where the misrepresentations lead to commercial injury the government is immune, but it is not where personal injuries result.[8]

These cases are predicated on the special relationship between the state and foster/adoptive parents, which creates a duty of disclosure. However, cases brought on similar theories over injuries inflicted by parolees or released mental patients have been unsuccessful because the lack of a special relationship allows the state to claim immunity.[9]

(C) Immunity for Institution of Criminal or Administrative Proceedings

Government employees and agencies are immune from suits over the institution or prosecution of judicial or administrative proceedings.[10] They are also immune for statements made to the media covering the investigation.[11] However some cases suggest that government employees are not immune for acts which violate the Federal civil rights law[12] or acts which violate the state whistle blower statute (a law prohibiting retaliation against employees who report government misconduct).[13]

---

7. *Michael J. v. Los Angeles County Department of Adoptions,* 201 Cal.App.3d 859 (1988).
8. *Tokeshi v. California, supra* note 26.
9. *Thompson v. Alameda,* 27 Cal.3d 741 (1980); Gov't Code § 845.8.
10. *Cappuccio, Inc. v. Harmon,* 208 Cal.App.3d 946 (1989).
11. *Citizens Capital Corp. v. Spohn,* 133 Cal.App.3d 887 (1982).
12. *Guillory v. Orange County,* 731 F.2d 1379 (9th Cir. 1984).
13. *Shoemaker v. Myers,* 4 Cal.App.4th 1407 (1992).

Antitrust Limitations on Practice

Antitrust litigation generally does not involve testimony about the emotional condition of consumers, so MHPs are generally involved in antitrust cases only if they are partners to the litigation. As a general matter, MHPs typically encounter antitrust issues in the denial of staff privileges or where an unfair competitive practice is alleged to have occurred. Professional associations of MHPs may also face antitrust issues related to denial or revocation of membership, and/or price fixing. Because professionals and professional associations can be subject to damages for violation of antitrust laws, it is important for MHPs to have an understanding of their provisions.

(A) Federal Antitrust Laws

Antitrust laws were enacted to curtail the perceived abuses of large corporations affecting the market for their products through noncompetitive means, such as agreeing on prices, driving smaller competitors out of business, dividing up the market, boycotts, and tying arrangements.

(B) Definitions

A *boycott* is a situation where a group of competitors would agree not to do business with another entity to force compliance with a price-fixing or market-division scheme.

A *tying* arrangement is one where a company agrees to sell a certain product or service, but only if the purchaser would also buy another product or service. Often this took the form of selling the most desirable company product with the condition that a less desirable product or service also be purchased: for example, the sale of a computer system with the requirement to buy only that manufacturer's software.

Price fixing is where a group of potential competitors jointly agree to set the price for services or products, as opposed to letting demand dictate the price.

The practices that come within the scope of the antitrust laws are illegal because they restrain free trade and lead to artificial market conditions. The focus of antitrust laws is the effect that the business practices have on competition and on the consumer's ability to have multiple choices based on the merit of an individual company's product or service. Antitrust laws are enforced by the U.S. Department of Justice and the Federal Trade Commission.

The primary federal antitrust statute is the Sherman Act.[1] The U.S. Supreme Court identified a number of factors that are to be considered in determining whether a private plaintiff has the legal standing to sue under the federal antitrust laws. The most significant of these factors is the nature of the alleged injury and whether it is of the type that the antitrust statute was intended to foreclose. Generally an antitrust plaintiff must show that the alleged violations tends to reduce competition in some market and that the plaintiff's injury would result from a decrease in completion in the market.

Associations of professionals have been found to be in violation of the Federal antitrust laws for various acts such as price fixing.[2]

(C) California Antitrust Law

California also has an antitrust law called the Cartwright Act.[3] The California Supreme Court has determined that the Cartwright Act is broader in reach than the Sherman Act, and that it applies to the medical profession.[4] Antitrust issues were also

---

1. 15 U.S.C. § 1 et seq. and the Clayton Antitrust Act, 15 U.S.C. § 13 et seq.; *Associated General Contractors v. California State Counsel of Carpenters*, 459 U.S. 519 (1983).
2. *Goldfarb v. Virginia State Bar*, 421 U.S. 773 (1975); *Arizona v. Maricopa County Medical Ass'n*, 457 U.S. 332 (1982).
3. Bus. & Prof. Code § 16700 et seq.
4. *Cianci v. Superior Court*, 40 Cal.3d 903 (1985).

raised in a recent case involving regulations limiting the practice of psychologists in hospital settings.[5]

There are various immunities from antitrust liability, including exemptions for labor organizations, religious and charitable organizations, and so forth. Attempts have been made to use antitrust provisions to attack hospital staff decisions as affecting competition for services. Whereas, generally, attempts to attack decisions regarding staff membership and discipline have been unsuccessful, where it is clear that there is an agreement between a hospital and a particular medical or mental health provider group that restricts the availability of medical or mental health services to the community, there is a potential that such a claim will be upheld.

(D) Peer Review Immunity

Various lawsuits have been filed alleging federal antitrust law violations by hospital peer review committees. However, the courts have held that the Health Care Quality Improvement Act of 1986 provides qualified immunity for peer review as part of a plan to provide effective peer review and monitoring of incompetent practitioners. Immunity exists if four criteria are met:

1. the peer review action meets federal fairness standards contained in the act;
2. there is adequate notice and a hearing;
3. the action was reported to the state agency as required; and
4. the peer review action commenced after November 14, 1986.

The process is presumed to be fair, but that is a rebuttable presumption. The standard for establishing fairness is an objective, not a subjective, standard and bad faith is immaterial.[6]

Generally antitrust issues will not be a consideration for the individual practitioner except to the extent that he or she is unable to become a member of a particular provider group.

---

5. *CAPP v. Rank*, 51 Cal.3d 1 (1991).
6. *Austin v. McNamara*, 979 F.2d 728 (9th Cir. 1992); *Patrick v. Burget*, 486 U.S. 94 (1988).

Appendix

Table of Cases

Table of Statutes

Table of Attorney General Opinions

Table of Rules of Court

Table of Administrative Regulations

Table of References to Constitution

Table of Cases

References are to page numbers in this book

R

S

Sehlmeyer v. Dept. of General Services, 183, 187
Shea v. Board of Medical Examiners, 114
Shoemake v. Myers, 346
Shoemaker v. Myers, 359, 588
Shortridge v. Municipal Court, 291
Silberg v. Anderson, 183, 215, 406, 571
Silva v. Superior Court, 13
Simmons v. United States, 575
Sindell v. Abbott Labs, 380
Singer v. Marx, 583
Sinz v. Owens, 564
Slaughter v. Friedman, 570, 572
Smalley v. Baker, 365
Smith v. Board of Medical Quality Assurance, 341
Smith v. Commissioner, 154
Smith v. Dept. of Motor Vehicles, 376
Smith v. Pust, 575, 579
St. Francis Memorial Hospital v. Superior Court, 559
Stanley v. Illinois, 241
Startrack Inc. v. County of Los Angeles, 514
Starrett v. Commissioner, 155
State Farm Casualty Co. v. Estate of Jenner, 363
State Rubbish Ass'n v. Siliznoff, 359
State v. Montijo, 415
State v. Superior Court, 93
Stills v. Gratton, 327
Storch v. Silverman, 228
Susan A. v. County of Sonoma, 573
Swett v. Gribaldo Jones & Associates, 378

T

Tarentino v. Superior Court, 443
Taylor v. Superior Court, 362
Thibos v. Pacific Gas and Electric Co., 379
Thing v. LaChusa, 360
Thomas v. Chadwick, 228
Thompson v. County of Alameda, 508, 588
Thor v. Superior Court, 555

Thorn v. Superior Court, 532, 535, 537
Tokeshi v. California, 587, 588
Truman v. Thomas, 551, 553, 555

U

Universal Byproducts, Inc. v. City of Modesto, 587

V

Vinson v. Superior Court, 404
Voight v. Commissioner, 155, 156

W

Walker v. Parzen, 573
Wasko v. Dept. of Corrections, 497
Waters v. Bourhis, 568, 575, 579
Webster v. State Board of Control, 521
Weisman v. Blue Shield of California, 132, 150
West Covina Hospital v. Superior Court, 138
Wickline v. California, 528
Williams v. Beechnut Nutrition Corp., 381
Williams v. Duffy, 510
Williams v. Garcetti, 583
Williams v. Superior Court, 189, 190
Willis v. Santa Ana etc. Hospital Ass'n, 561
Wilson v. Blue Cross of South California, 151, 528
Witherspoon v. Superior Court, 400
Wood v. Superior Court, 178, 187
Woods v. Young, 566

Y

Yates v. Pollack, 568
Yoshisato v. Superior Court, 476
Young v. Haines, 567
Youngberg v. Romeo, 501

Table of Statutes

CALIFORNIA STATUTES
Business and Professional Code

Section	Page	Section	Page
28	54	2004	22
29	54	2005	22
101	5	2006	21, 22
110	121	2007	22
116	5	2008	22
119	7	2010	22
123	7	2013(c)	27
125.3	9	2015	22
125.6	8	2018	22, 30
130	5	2050	23
145	9	2051	23
146	9, 41	2052	23
200 to 210	121	2053	23, 582
207	121	2056	151
209	121	2058	24
211 to 213	121	2060	24
473	116	2062	24
473.4	116	2065	24
480	5, 6, 25, 37, 38, 42, 47	2068	24
		2072	24
480(a)	6	2073	24
480(b)	6	2076.5	24
490	6, 7, 25, 26, 33, 38	2082	23
		2084	23
499	7, 33	2085	23
651	26	2086	23
658	8	2088	23
720	109	2089	23
726	63, 109, 574, 575	2091.1	23
		2096	23
729	63, 109, 576, 582	2100 to 2122	23
		2103	23
729(b)(1–5)	576	2107	23
805	138	2135 to 2153	23
805(a)(6)	138	2170 to 2186	23
810	586	2220	22, 25
820	64, 339	2221	24
822	341	2221.1	26
823	341	2222	14
827	341	2225	181
828	341	2225(a) to (e)	11
2000 et seq	21	2227	27
2001	22	2228	27
2003	22	2233	15

602   APPENDIX

Civil Code

Code of Civil Procedure

Corporation Code

Education Code

Elections Code

Evidence Code

Family Code

Government Code

Health & Safety Code

Insurance Code

Labor Code

Penal Code

Probate Code

Vehicle Code

Welfare & Institutions Code

Table of Attorney General Opinions

References are to page numbers in this book

Table of Rules of Court

References are to page numbers in this book

California Rules of Court

Table of Administrative Regulations

California Code of Regulations

Treasury Rulings and Regulations

Table of References to Constitution

References are to page numbers in this book

Index

LICENSURE
Exceptions/requirements, see each
profession in Sect. 1

M

MALPRACTICE
Generally, 6.5
MARRIAGE AND FAMILY
THERAPISTS
Generally, 1.8
MEDICAID
Generally, 5E.1
MENS REA
Generally, 5D.7
MENTAL HEALTH BENEFITS
State insurance plans, 3.2
MENTAL STATUS
Of professionals, 5B.1

N

NARCOTIC ABUSE
Involuntary treatment of, 5E.6
NEGLECT
Of adults, 5A.7
Of children, 5A.8, 5A.9
NEGLIGENCE
Malpractice, 6.5
NURSING
Licensure, 1.2

P

PARENT
Child abuse by, 5A.8
Termination of rights, 5A.10
PAROLE
Determinations, 5D.22
PARTNERSHIPS
Generally, 2.3
PARTY
In a lawsuit, Editors' Preface
PHYSICIAN
Licensure/psychiatrist, 1.1
POLICE OFFICER
Commitment role, 5D.1
Screening, 5D.1
POLYGRAPH
Evidence, 5D.3
PORNOGRAPHY
Generally, 5D.24
PRECHARGING EVALUATIONS
Generally, 5D.3

PREFERRED PROVIDER
ORGANIZATIONS
Generally, 2.5
PREGNANCY
Competency to consent to abortion,
5A.22
PREMEDITATION
Murder, 5D.7
PRESENTENCE REPORTS
Generally, 5D.15
PRETRIAL EVALUATIONS
Generally, 5D.3
Pretrial Intervention Program, 5D.3
PRISON
Mental health programs, 5D.20
Transfer to mental health unit, 5D.21
PRIVACY
Patient/client, 4.2, 4.3
PRIVILEGED COMMUNICATIONS
Generally, 4.3
Competency to stand trial, 5D.5
Insanity examinations, 5D.9
PROBATION
Generally, 5D.16
PRODUCT LIABILITY
Generally, 5B.10
PROFESSIONAL CORPORATIONS
Generally, 2.2
PROVOCATION
Generally, 5D.6
PSYCHIATRIC NURSES
Generally, 1.2
PSYCHIATRISTS
Generally, 1.1
PSYCHOLOGICAL AUTOPSY
Generally, 5C.5
PSYCHOLOGISTS
Generally, 1.4
Subdoctoral and unlicensed, 1.5

R

RAPE TRAUMA SYNDROME
Testimony, 5D.11
RECORDS
Confidentiality, 4.2
Extensiveness, ownership,
maintenance, access, 4.1
Privileged communications, 4.3
Subpoena, 4.4
REGULATION of
Aversion conditioning 6.3
Hypnotists, 1.10
Marriage and family therapists, 1.9
Polygraph examiners, 1.11

V

VICTIMS OF CRIMES
  Services for, 5D.26
VIOLATIONS
  Of licensure/certification, see each
    profession in Sect. 1
  Of professional standards, 6.5
VOCATIONAL DISABILITY
  Generally, 5B.3
VOLITION
  Generally, 5D.7
VOLUNTARY ADMISSION
  Mental health treatment
    Of adults, 5E.3
    Of minors, 5A.19

W

WAIVING CONSTITUTIONAL RIGHTS
  Generally, 5D.2
WARD
  Conservatorship of adults, 5A.3
  Conservatorship of minors, 5A.12
  Guardianship of adults, 5A.2
  Guardianship of minors, 5A.11
WITNESS
  Competency to testify, 5C.4
  Expert, generally, 5C.2
  Eyewitness identification, 5D.13
WORKERS' COMPENSATION
  Generally, 5B.2

Z

ZONING
  Community homes, 2.8

About the Authors

O. Brandt Caudill, Jr., Esq. is a defense attorney specializing in the representation of psychologists and other mental health professionals. With extensive experience in both civil and administrative law, he has litigated such precedent-setting cases as *Krikorian v. Barry* (1987) and *Gootee v. Lightner* (1990), both in the California Fourth District Court of Appeal. Earning a BA in psychology with high honors as a Phi Beta Kappa at Michigan State University, he received his JD in 1976 from the Georgetown University Law Center. He is a member of the California and the District of Columbia state bars. On the federal level, he is admitted to practice before the U.S. Ninth Circuit Court of Appeals and all United States District Courts in California.

A consultant to mental health organizations as well as individual practitioners, he has authored a number of publications in such areas as record keeping, vicarious liability, therapist–patient sex, recovered memories of abuse, and administrative proceedings, and has made presentations to the American Psychological Association, the California Psychological Association, and other professional organizations and universities.

Mr. Caudill is a partner in the law firm of Callahan, McCune, & Willis, with offices in Tustin, Los Angeles, and San Diego. He resides in Lake Forest with his lovely wife Christine.

Kenneth S. Pope, PhD, received graduate degrees from Harvard and Yale, is a Diplomate in Clinical Psychology, and is a Fellow of the American Psychological Assoication (APA) and the American Psychological Society (APS). Having previously served as clinical director and psychology director in both private hospital and community mental health center settings, he is currently in independent practice. He taught courses in abnormal psychology, psychological and neuropsychological assessment, and related areas at the University of California, Los Angeles (UCLA), where he served as psychotherapy supervisor in the UCLA Psychology Clinic. A recipient of the Frances Mosseker Award for Fiction, the Belle Meyer Bromberg Award for Literature, the California Psychological Association's Silver Psi Award and Distinguished Professional Contributions to Psychology as a Profession Award, the APA Division of Clinical Psychology (12) Award for Distinguished Professional Contributions to Clinical Psychology, and the APA Award for Distinguished Contributions to Public Service, he served as chair of the Ethics Committees of the

APA and of the American Board of Professional Psychology. He has authored over 100 scientific and professional articles; his books include *Sexual Involvement with Therapists: Patient Assessment, Subsequent Therapy Forensics, Sexual Intimacies Between Therapists and Patients* (with J. C. Bouhoutsos), *Sexual Feelings in Psychotherapy: Explorations for Therapists and Therapists-in-Training* (with J. L. Sonne and J. Holroyd), *The MMPI, MMPI-2, and MMPI-A in Court: A Practical Guide for Expert Witnesses and Attorneys* (with J. N. Butcher and J. Seelen), *Ethics in Psychotherapy and Counseling* (with M. J. T. Vasquez), *On Love and Loving, The Stream of Consciousness: Scientific Investigations Into the Flow of Human Experience,* and *The Power of Human Imagination: New Methods of Psychotherapy* (the latter two with J. L. Singer).